Social Memory in Athenian Public Discourse

Social Memory in Athenian Public Discourse

Uses and Meanings of the Past

Bernd Steinbock

University of Michigan Press
Ann Arbor

First paperback edition 2020

Published in the United States of America by the
University of Michigan Press
Manufactured in the United States of America
Printed on acid-free paper

A CIP catalog record for this book is available from the British Library.

First published in paperback March 2020

Library of Congress Cataloging-in-Publication Data

Steinbock, Bernd.
Social memory in Athenian public discourse : uses and meanings of the past / Bernd Steinbock.
p. cm.
Includes bibliographical references and index.
ISBN 978-0-472-11832-8 (cloth : acid-free paper)—
ISBN 978-0-472-02841-2 (e-book)
1. Athens (Greece)—Relations—Greece—Thebes. 2. Thebes (Greece)—Relations—Greece—Athens. 3. Thebes (Greece)—Foreign public opinion. 4. Memory—Social aspects—Greece—Athens—History—To 1500. 5. Collective memory—Greece—Athens—History—To 1500. 6. Historiography—Social aspects—Greece—Athens—History—To 1500. 7. Discourse analysis—Greece—Athens—History—To 1500. 8. Athens (Greece)—Politics and government. 9. Athens (Greece)—Social life and customs. 10. Greece—History—To 146 B.C. I. Title.
DF285.S74 2012
303.48'23850384—dc23 2012033643

ISBN 978-0-472-03778-0 (pbk. : alk. paper)

For

Kathryn, Maximilian, Kunigunde, & Wenzel

Preface

Prompted by the abundant historical allusions in Athenian political and diplomatic discourse, this book analyzes the uses and meanings of the past in fourth-century Athens, using Thebes' role in Athenian memory as a case study. It explores how Athenians learned about their past and what this past meant to them. It examines how individual speakers operated within this complex memorial framework and to what extent these shared images of the past influenced the decision-making process in fourth-century Athens, where a free citizenry publically debated its foreign and domestic policies in the assembly, the law courts, and other democratic institutions. This study is based on the premise that Athenian social memory, that is, the shared and often idealized and distorted image of the past, should be viewed not as an unreliable counterpart of history but as an invaluable key to the Athenians' mentality. Against the tendency of viewing the orators' references to the past as empty rhetorical phrases or propagandistic cover-ups for *Realpolitik,* it argues that the past constituted important political capital in its own right. Integrating literary, epigraphic, and archaeological evidence with recent scholarship on memory, identity, rhetoric, and international relations, it contextualizes the orators' historical allusions within the complex net of remembrances and beliefs held by the audience and thus tries to gauge their ideological and emotive power.

The concept of social memory is a very useful analytical tool, since it allows viewing the manifestation and transmission of a shared image of the past as a dynamic process that leaves room for contestation, acknowledges the interdependence between ideology and social memory, and regards the past as a repository for future decision making. By examining various "carriers" of social memory, this study assesses how deeply a specific memory was rooted in Athenian historical consciousness and how persuasive it ultimately was. It explains common distortions in its transmission and determines the leeway orators had in departing from predominant versions. I approach these questions from two different angles. After establishing my methodological framework, I first explore thematically the different "carriers" of social memory available to the speakers and their audience and then turn to one exemplary case and examine the role of Thebes in Athenian social memory and public discourse. Historical references to Thebes cluster around four particular events: the mythical story of the burial of the fallen Argives, Thebes' collaboration with the Persians in 480, the Theban proposal to eradicate Athens in 404, and Theban aid to the Athenian democrats in 403. Since these collective memories were frequently evoked in debates about Athenian-Theban relations, this study will also help us to better comprehend some of the policy choices both *poleis* made during the fourth century BC.

Historical memory in ancient Greece continues to attract much scholarly attention. Since the completion of this manuscript, six important books have been published that share many of my concerns and engage with some of the same issues. In *The Greeks and Their Past* (Cambridge, 2010), Jonas Grethlein charts the field of literary memory in fifth-century Greece and, employing a phenomenological model that connects memory and temporality, examines the differences and communalities in the attitude toward the past in various poetic genres, oratory, and historiography. Peter Hunt's *War, Peace, and Alliance in Demosthenes' Athens* (Cambridge, 2010) uses the political speeches of the Attic orators to give us a more nuanced understanding of the complex factors that influenced Athenian foreign policy decisions. In *Polis and Revolution* (Cambridge, 2011), Julia Shear draws on theories of remembering and forgetting to elucidate the Athenians' responses to the oligarchic regimes of 411 and 404/3. *Die griechische Welt: Erinnerungsorte der Antike* (Munich, 2010) and *Griechische Heiligtümer als Erinnerungsorte* (Stuttgart, 2011), edited by Elke Stein-Hölkeskamp and Karl-Joachim Hölkeskamp and Matthias Haake and Michael Jung, respectively, explore the memorial functions of important physical and symbolic places in Greece as *lieux de mémoire*. Finally, *Intentional History: Spinning Time in Ancient Greece* (Stuttgart, 2010), a collection of essays edited by Lin Foxhall, Hans-Joachim Gehrke, and Nino Luraghi, studies Greek collective memory and features several papers on topics related to my monograph. Unfortunately, these studies appeared too late to be adequately taken into account in the present study.

In a book on memory, I ought not to forget to acknowledge the people who helped me along the way. This project originated during my time at the University of Michigan, where Ruth Scodel and David Potter provided the best guidance a young scholar could hope for. Ever since I met Ruth Scodel, I have profited from her farsighted advice, wide-ranging intellect, keen criticism, and readiness to offer help promptly whenever needed. David Potter deserves no less gratitude. From the very beginning, he has supported my work with relentless enthusiasm, astute criticism, and a formidable scholarly vision. He encouraged me to conceive of my project in much broader terms and to consider its larger implications. My work also benefited enormously from the expertise and advice provided by Susan Alcock, Ray Van Dam, and especially Sara Forsdyke, who has been an unfailing source of encouragement and support over the years. I am very grateful to the Department of Classical Studies at Michigan for providing such an intellectually stimulating environment. In particular, I would like to thank Richard Janko, Benjamin Acosta-Hughes, H. D. Cameron, Sabine MacCormack, Benjamin Fortson, Bruce Frier, Traianos Gagos, Vassilios Lambropoulos, Jim Porter, Jay Reed, Sara Ahbel-Rappe, David Phillips, Lauren Caldwell, Kendra Eshleman, Kris Fletcher, Robert Chenault, John Lobur, Jake MacPhail, Geoff Maturen, Mike Sampson, Adam Rabinowitz, Jeremy Hartnett, Patrick Hogan, Sanjaya Thakur, Nathan Bethell, Adam Kemezis, Kate Bosher, and Richard Persky.

I would also like to record my gratitude to the people who laid the philological and historical groundwork for this project: my professors at the Friedrich-Alexander-Universität Erlangen and at the Albert-Ludwigs-Universität Freiburg, Egert Pöhlmann, Severin Koster, Ulrich Schmitzer, Peter Högemann, Ulrich Eigler, Bernhard Zimmermann, Michael Reichel, Thomas Baier, Jochen Martin, Nino Luraghi, and Hans-Joachim Gehrke, who first introduced me to the concept of intentional history in one of his courses. Their seminars and lectures have influenced me more than they can imagine. Special thanks are due to Walter Kißel for supervising my *Staatsexamen* thesis and to Wolfgang Srb for helping me find my way in academia from the first day I entered the halls of the *Seminar für Klassische Philologie* in Erlangen. For inspiring conversations during those years, I am grateful to Kai Flosdorff, Heiko Niemeyer, Alexander Arenz, Oke Lafrenz, Evi Grillmeier, and Oliver Hellmann.

I owe special thanks to my colleagues in the Department of Classical Studies at the University of Western Ontario for the collegial and supportive environment they foster. In particular, I would like to thank Debra Nousek, Kelly Olson, David Wilson, Bonnie MacLachlan, Matt Carter, Kendall Sharp, Elizabeth Greene, Randall Pogorzelski, David Lamari, Alexander Meyer, and Leslie Murison. I am also grateful to our graduate students for the critical feedback they offered whenever I put my ideas to the test in lectures and seminars and to Aara Suksi, who, as department chair, has provided support in many important ways. I owe a special debt to Christopher G. Brown, who has been a caring mentor and an inspiring role model ever since I came to Western.

For much helpful discussion and advice, I thank the audiences of several papers I presented at the University of Western Ontario, at McMaster University, and at the annual meetings of the American Philological Association in Boston and Montreal, the Classical Association of the Middle West and South in Madison and Cincinnati, the Classical Association of Canada in Toronto, and the Greek History and Theory Group at Ohio State University and Northwestern University.

I am most grateful to the following scholars, who have all read drafts of individual chapters and offered invaluable suggestions and encouragement: David Potter, Ruth Scodel, Sara Forsdyke, Susan Alcock, Ray Van Dam, Robert Chenault, Christopher G. Brown, Charles Leslie Murison, and Aara Suksi. For their unfailing assistance in technical matters, I thank Simeon Ehrlich, Jonathan Vickers, and Cameron Kroetsch. I owe a particular debt to Ellen Bauerle and Mary Hashman for their editorial acumen and diligent work and to the two anonymous referees of the University of Michigan Press for their judicious criticism and many useful comments. All mistakes and misconceptions that remain are, of course, my own.

On a more personal level, I would like to thank my father, who, with countless stories, first kindled my interest in history when I was little; he made me cry for Icarus, fear for Siegfried, and relive the feud between the knights of the Neideck and the Streitburg. His passion was contagious, and *gewappnet mit Geduld,* he answered all the nagging questions a child can ask. I am equally grateful to my mother for her unconditional love and support, perhaps most of all in letting me follow the path I have chosen, which led me across the Atlantic. I also thank my in-laws and my friends in Germany, Canada, and the United States for their support and encouragement and, in particular, my siblings, Claudia, Petra, and Felix, for not letting me forget who I am.

My deepest gratitude goes to my wife, Kathryn, who, as mother, homemaker, and dissertator, carried the heaviest burden during the writing of this book. Without her selfless support and love, I could not have finished this project. I dedicate this book to her and to our three children, Maximilian, Kunigunde, and Wenzel, for all the joy they give me anew every day.

Contents

Abbreviations xi

Introduction: Objectives, Methods, Concepts 1
Objectives 2
What Is Social Memory? 7
Social Memory in Ancient Greece: From Mythical Times to the Recent Past 19
Social Memory in Athenian Public Discourse 29

1. Carriers of Athenian Social Memory 48
Festivals and Public Commemorations 49
Different Memory Communities 70
Monuments and Inscriptions 84
Rhetorical Education 94
Assembly and Law Courts 96

2. Athens' Counterimage: The Theban Medizers 100
Fourth-Century Allusions to Thebes' Medizing 101
Theban Conduct during the Persian War 103
Athenian Disposition toward Thebes in 479 105
Memorialization of Thebes' Treason 106
Remembering Theban Medism throughout the Fifth Century 113
Contexts for the Recollection of Theban Medism in the Fourth Century 118

3. Mythical Precedent: Athenian Intervention for the Fallen Argives 155
Oratorical Allusions to the Burial of the Seven 156
Constitutive Elements and Formative Influences 158
The Burial of the Seven in Diplomatic and Political Discourse 196

4. A Precarious Memory: Theban Help for the Athenian Democrats 211
Belated Praise for Theban Aid? 212
The Situation in Thebes in 404/3 215
Theban Support for Thrasybulus in Athenian Social Memory 232

5. Persistent Memories: The Proposed Eradication of Athens 280
The Debate about Athens' Fate in 405/4 281
Fourth-Century Allusions to the Proposed Destruction of Athens 285
Traumatic Fear of Annihilation 291
Semantic and Visual Conceptualizations: City Razing and Enslavement 301
Imagining the Unimaginable: The Eradication of Athens 309
Plataea, Melos, and Troy as *Aide Mémoire* 323
Contexts for the Recollection of the Theban Proposal 326

Conclusion 342

Bibliography 357

Index Locorum 377

General Index 393

Abbreviations

The abbreviations used herein for ancient authors' names and works follow those of the *Oxford Classical Dictionary (OCD)* and, when not available there, the *Greek-English Lexicon* of Liddell, Scott, and Jones (LSJ). In rendering Greek names and places, I have used Latinized forms, except where familiarity dictates otherwise. The translations of Greek and Latin into English are my own but sometimes draw freely on standard published translations. All dates are BC unless otherwise noted. Abbreviations of journal titles follow those used by *L'Année Philologique,* with a few slight and familiar variations. The following abbreviations are used for standard reference works:

ARV^2	J. D. Beazley. *Attic Red-Figure Vase-Painters.* 2nd ed. Oxford, 1963.
CAH^2 IV	*The Cambridge Ancient History.* Vol. 4, *Persia, Greece, and the Western Mediterranean, c. 525 to 479 B.C.* 2nd ed. Cambridge, 1988.
CAH^2 V	*The Cambridge Ancient History.* Vol. 5, *The Fifth Century B.C.* 2nd ed. Cambridge, 1992.
CAH^2 VI	*The Cambridge Ancient History.* Vol. 6, *The Fourth Century B.C.* 2nd ed. Cambridge, 1994.
DK	H. Diels and W. Kranz, eds. *Die Fragmente der Vorsokratiker.* 6th ed. Berlin, 1951–52.
FGrHist	F. Jacoby, ed. *Die Fragmente der griechischen Historiker.* Berlin and Leiden, 1923–58.
IG	*Inscriptiones Graecae.* Berlin, 1873–.
LIMC	*Lexicon Iconographicum Mythologiae Classicae.* Zurich, 1981–99.
LSJ	H. G. Liddell, R. Scott, and H. S. Jones, eds. *Greek-English Lexicon, with a Revised Supplement.* 9th ed. Oxford, 1996.
M&L	R. Meiggs and D. Lewis, eds. *A Selection of Greek Historical Inscriptions to the End of the Fifth Century B.C.* Rev. ed. Oxford, 1988.

Merkelbach & West	R. Merkelbach and M. L. West, eds. *Fragmenta Hesiodea.* Oxford, 1967.
OCD	S. Hornblower and A. Spawforth, eds. *The Oxford Classical Dictionary.* 3rd ed. Oxford, 1996.
PCG	R. Kassel and M. Austin, eds. *Poetae Comici Graeci.* Berlin, 1983–.
PMG	D. L. Page, ed. *Poetae Melici Graeci.* Oxford, 1962.
R&O	P. J. Rhodes and R. Osborne, eds. *Greek Historical Inscriptions, 404–323 BC.* Oxford, 2003.
RE	A. F. von Pauly, G. Wissowa, and W. Kroll, eds. *Real-Encyclopädie der classischen Altertumswissenschaft.* Munich, 1893–.
SEG	*Supplementum Epigraphicum Graecum.* Leiden, 1923–.
Syll.[3]	W. Dittenberger, ed. *Sylloge Inscriptionum Graecarum.* 4 vols. 3rd ed. Leipzig, 1915–24.
TrGF	B. Snell, R. Kannicht, and S. Radt, eds. *Tragicorum Graecorum Fragmenta.* 5 vols. Göttingen, 1971–2004.
Voigt	E.-M. Voigt, ed. *Sappho et Alcaeus: Fragmenta.* Amsterdam, 1971.
West[2]	M. L. West, ed. *Iambi et Elegi Graeci. Vols. 1–2.* 2nd ed. Oxford, 1989–92.

Introduction

Objectives, Methods, Concepts

"What you're doing in Iraq is as important and courageous and selfless as what American troops did in places like Normandy and Iwo Jima and Korea. Your generation is every bit as great as any that came before it. And the work you do every day will shape history for generations to come."[1]

(U.S. President George W. Bush addressing U.S. troops in Baghdad, Iraq, on December 14, 2008)

"Each American who has served in Iraq has their own story. Each of you has your own story. And that story is now a part of the history of the United States of America, a nation that exists only because free men and women have bled for it, from the beaches of Normandy to the deserts of Anbar, from the mountains of Korea to the streets of Kandahar. You teach us that the price of freedom is great."[2]

(U.S. President Barack Obama addressing U.S. troops in Camp Lejeune, North Carolina, on February 27, 2009)

"But it is not possible, it is not possible that you were wrong, Athenians, to take on the danger for the freedom and safety of all [the Greeks]—I swear by those of your forefathers who bore the brunt of battle at Marathon, by those who stood in the ranks at Plataea, by those who fought the sea battles at Salamis and Artemisium, and by the many other men who lie in the public tombs, brave men, all of whom the city buried, deeming them all equally worthy of the same honor, Aeschines, not just those among them who were successful or victorious." (Dem. 18.208)

(Demosthenes justifying Athens' stance at Chaeronea to an Athenian jury in 330 BC)

1. http://www.presidency.ucsb.edu/ws/index.php?pid=85287&st1=#axzz1ntHhsZm.
2. http://www.presidency.ucsb.edu/ws/index.php?pid=85807&st=&st1=#axzz1ntHhsZm.

Objectives

Though separated by more than twenty-three hundred years, these statements have a lot in common. All three speakers recall the past in order to persuade their audiences to adopt a particular view of the present. By equating the troops' service in Iraq to the achievements of the "Greatest Generation," President George W. Bush conveys a sense of the importance and greatness of the current mission. President Barack Obama firmly grounds the soldiers' present undertaking in Iraq and Afghanistan in the American tradition: they, like their predecessors at Normandy and Korea, preserve their country through their willingness to fight and die for the sake of freedom. Similarly, to justify, before an Athenian jury, Athens' decision to oppose Philip of Macedon, Demosthenes evokes their ancestors' accomplishments during the Persian Wars; they—so the implication goes—had fought for the freedom and safety of all the Greeks, just as his generation did at Chaeronea.

The speakers allude to these past events because they regard them as deeply meaningful for their respective communities. These allusions resonate with the audiences and thus function as powerful emotive arguments in public debate. It is precisely this use of the past that lies at the heart of my investigation. That we are thereby dealing with *social memory* and not history per se is my central premise. The D-day landing (June 1944), the battle of Iwo Jima (February 1945), the Korean War (1950–53), the land battles of Marathon (490 BC) and Plataea (479 BC), and the sea battles at Salamis and Artemisium (480 BC) are all historical events, yet they are not mentioned by the speakers for the sake of constituting and disseminating historical knowledge. We learn nothing about the historical circumstances, the enemy, the reasons for these wars, the course and outcome of the battles, the strategies and tactics employed, their repercussions and aftermath. On the contrary, common knowledge is taken for granted. These events have become an integral part of the social memory, that is, the collective historical consciousness of a community. The particular historical circumstances had faded over time, and these events had become symbols of national character.[3] Such shared images of the past, often idealized and distorted, have long been viewed as an unreliable counterpart of history.[4] To refute such "myths" and uncover the historical reality behind them has been one of the historian's most noble tasks. Yet, in recent decades, anthropologists,

3. A. Assmann (2001) 6824.

4. For this reason, such myths were deliberately abandoned by professional historians in the nineteenth century, who established critical historiography as an autonomous discursive discipline with its own standards of truth and authority, specific rules of verification, and intersubjective argument. Cf. A. Assmann (2001) 6824–25; Markovits & Reich (1997) 14–15.

sociologists, and historians have discovered social memory as a subject of study in its own right, as an invaluable key to a group's mentality, which can provide insights into the ideological forces that hold a society together.[5] By offering people a shared image of their past, social memory creates feelings of identity and belonging and provides them with a design for their future. Yet social memory is also—by its very nature—elusive and dynamic. Just as social groups change over time, so do their memories: the past—while not entirely at the disposal of the present—is nevertheless constantly "modeled, invented, reinvented, and reconstructed by the present."[6]

These are some general characteristics of social memory that can be observed across time and space, as comparative studies have shown. Yet it is important to emphasize that the formation, transmission, and contestation of social memory depends on each society's particular communicative framework. Classical Athens is an especially interesting case, since it exemplifies, as Rosalind Thomas has shown, a society in transition from orality to literacy, where oral modes of communication played a predominant role.[7] Following the rise of memory studies in other fields, classicists have begun to use social memory as an analytical tool to explore how the ancient Greeks remembered their past. By and large, these scholars focus on the ideological power and societal functions of collective memories and explore the transmission and changing meanings of various oral traditions.[8]

Despite these important inroads into Greek social memory, many significant aspects have not yet been sufficiently explored. In light of the striking similarities between the quotations cited above, three questions in particular are worth asking. First, how did fifth- and fourth-century Athenians learn about their past, and what did this past mean to them? Second, how did individual speakers make use of the past and operate within the complex Athenian memorial framework? Third, to what extent did these shared images of the past influence the decision-making process in a polis like fourth-century Athens, where a free citizenry publically debated its foreign and domestic policies in the assembly, the law courts, and other democratic institutions?

At first sight, it may seem impossible to recover the role that a people's

5. For a comprehensive introduction to social memory studies, see Fentress & Wickham (1992); Misztal (2003); Erll & Nünning (2008). For a discussion of important characteristics, see "What Is Social Memory?" below, 7–19.

6. J. Assmann (1997) 9.

7. R. Thomas (1989).

8. See, for instance, Loraux (1986), (2002); R. Thomas (1989); Higbie (1997); Forsdyke (1999), (2001), (2005), (2011); Gehrke (2001), (2003); Wolpert (2002); Alcock (2002); G. Anderson (2003); Jung (2006); Luraghi (2008); Foxhall, Gehrke, & Luraghi (2010); Shear (2011). For a decidedly nonfunctionalist approach, see Grethlein (2010). For Roman social memory, see Walter (2004); Gowing (2005); H. I. Flower (2006); Stein-Hölkeskamp & Hölkeskamp (2006); Dasen & Späth (2010).

memories played in their decision-making process more than twenty-three hundred years ago. Yet, in the case of fourth-century Athens, we are fortunate to have access to a type of evidence often misunderstood, the historical allusions in the surviving speeches of the Attic orators. These are, if not a verbatim record, at least a close reflection of arguments actually made in Athenian public discourse. This is, to some extent, also true for the speeches in Xenophon's *Hellenica:* Xenophon, as an Athenian and contemporary, was closely familiar with fourth-century Athenian historical consciousness.

By contextualizing the orators' allusions within the complex net of remembrances and beliefs held by their audiences, I seek to assess the ideological and emotive power of these shared memories, which I regard not as merely empty rhetorical phrases or propagandistic cover-ups for *Realpolitik* but as crucial factors in political decision making.[9] In so doing, I also try to explain common "distortions" in their transmission and to determine the leeway that orators had in departing from predominant versions.[10]

I approach these important questions from two different angles. First, in chapter 1, I *thematically* examine the different "carriers" of Athenian social memory available to the speakers and their audiences. Young Athenians learned about their past through polis-wide public commemorations and festivals, as well as through the process of socialization as members of smaller subgroups (e.g., families, sympotic groups, *demes,* and tribes), all of whom had their own memorial traditions. Contact with guest-friends could provide insight into the memorial repertoire of other Greek communities. Landmarks, monuments, and inscriptions, forming the Athenian *cadre matériel,* functioned as material reminders of crucial events, while assembly and law courts provided the venue for the orators' refreshing and reshaping of the past. Elite speakers could also draw from the works of the Greek historians, poets, and other orators.

Second, since the Athenians' shared image of the past originated, to a large extent, from their experience with other Greek and foreign communities, I focus, in chapters 2–5, on one exemplary case: the role of Thebes in Athenian social memory and discourse. From early on, the Athenian' relations with their northern neighbor Thebes were very complex, varying over time from military cooperation and peaceful coexistence to tense rivalry and outright war, thus providing both cities with a broad spectrum of experiences from which to draw

9. Cf. Markovits & Reich (1997) 9–20, who argue that "collective memory is a crucial ingredient in every country's policymaking and perhaps nowhere more important than in foreign policy" (18). See "Public Discourse and Decision Making," 30–36.

10. I use the term *distortion* in a neutral sense, without the connotation of willful manipulation, simply to denote the discrepancy between what we think actually happened and the way it was remembered. For this reason, Oswyn Murray (2001) 28 introduces the term *deformation* for this phenomenon.

(fig. 1). Whenever Athenian-Theban relations were discussed, participants in the debate called on earlier experiences to explain their analysis and propose their solution to others, as seen, for instance, in the negotiations leading to an Athenian-Theban alliance in 395. This study will thus help us to better comprehend some of the policy choices both *poleis* made during the fourth century BC.

Historical references to Thebes cluster around four particular events, each discussed in a separate chapter in this book: Thebes' medizing in 480–479 (chap. 2), the mythical story of the burial of the fallen Argives (chap. 3), Theban aid to the Athenian democrats in 403 (chap. 4), and the Theban proposal to eradicate Athens in 404 (chap. 5).[11] In each case, I explore how a particular event was perceived, how its recollection was subsequently transformed from "remembered" to "commemorated" history, and by which means it was transmitted to younger generations. By comparing these memories to the actual historical events (as far as we can reconstruct them) and by taking into account general characteristics of social memory, I explain various "distortions" in the process of their transmission.

My reading of the Attic orators from the perspective of social memory also has further merits. First, it contributes to the solution of an old problem, that is, how best to understand the orators' historical allusions.[12] Second, thanks to Herman Mogens Hansen and others, we have come to a much better understanding of the technical aspects of the Athenian assembly, the law courts, and other democratic institutions, but we still do not fully comprehend what it was to *be* an Athenian.[13] I hope this reconstruction of the Athenian memorial framework will complement the work of Josiah Ober, Greg Anderson, Sara Forsdyke, and others and enhance our understanding of the shared collective consciousness that bound the Athenians together within their institutions.[14] A further objective of this book is to engage in the debate about ways of doing history. Framing this historical investigation in terms of social memory has two particular virtues. First, it naturally integrates a variety of different source

11. It might seem odd that the chapter sequence does not follow the chronology of the events. I begin with Thebes' medizing (chap. 2), since I regard the Persian Wars (including Athens' experience of Thebes in it) as the most important moment for the formation of the Athenian self-image. It was this very self-image, I argue, that was projected back into the past and that shaped the collective memory of the mythical exploit on behalf of the fallen Argives (chap. 3). Similarly, I end this monograph with the chapter on the Theban proposal to eradicate Athens (chap. 5), since the annihilation of Thebes through Alexander in 335 brings together all of Thebes' sins and thus provides a suitable thematic and chronological capstone for this investigation.

12. See "Participant Evidence: The Attic Orators and Their Interpretation," 36–43.

13. Cf. Hansen (1991), which represents a comprehensive synthesis of his numerous individual studies of Athenian democratic institutions.

14. Ober (1989); G. Anderson (2003); Forsdyke (2005).

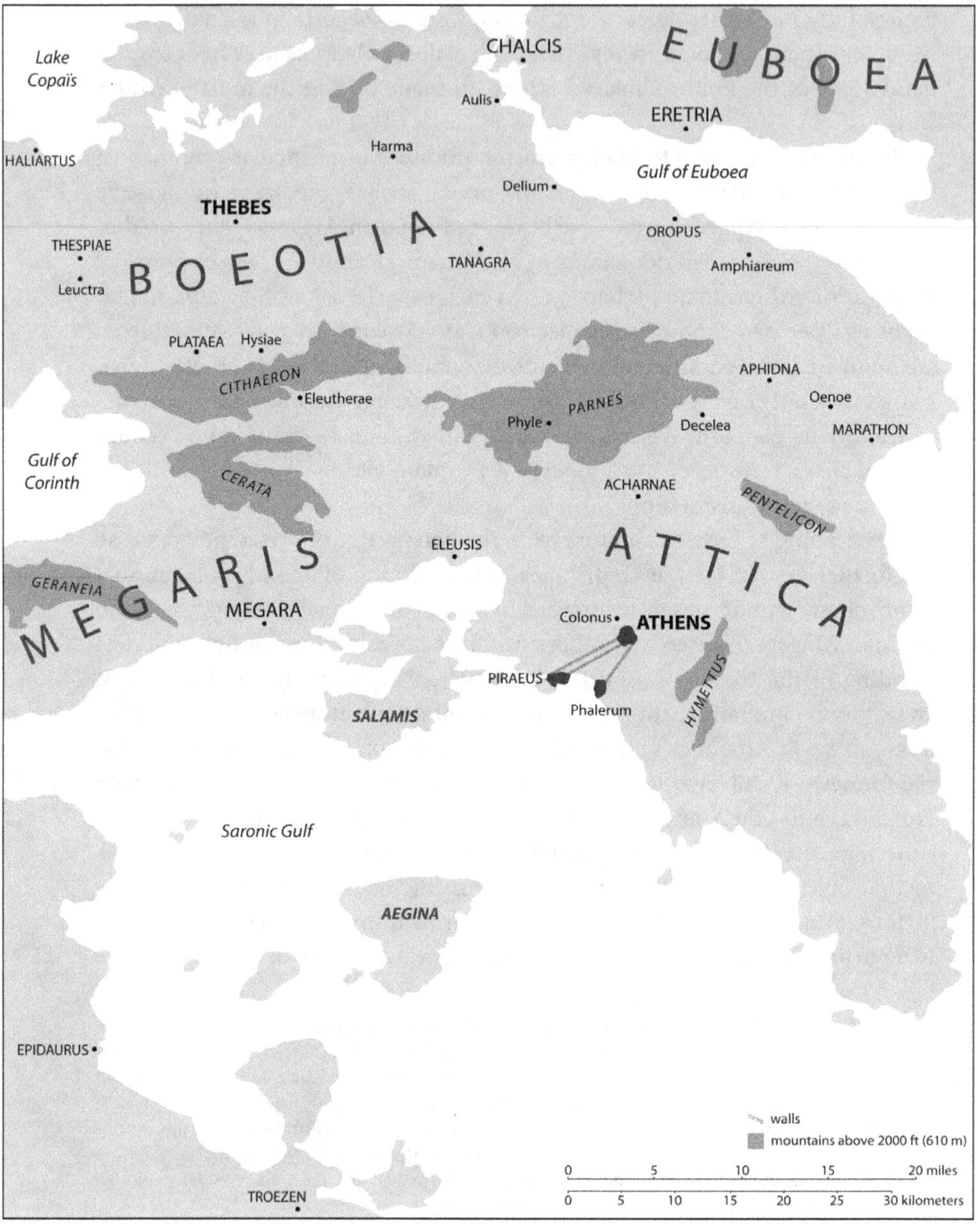

Fig. 1. Map of Attica and southern Boeotia

materials (literary texts of different genres, inscriptions, monuments, artifacts and other material remains, landscapes, geography, etc.) by tying them all together as elements of a community's memorial framework, elements that mutually influence and sustain each other. Second, when dealing with literary sources such as the Greek historians or the Attic orators, understanding the characteristics of social memory can help us to move beyond purely intertextual models of interpretation and develop a more nuanced appreciation of the conditions of origin and the ideological aspects of these works. Finally, this analysis of Athenian historical consciousness might serve as a model for other studies of historical social memory and discourse in the ancient world. I hope that this sociopolitical analysis of the orators' use of the past will be of interest to students of Athenian history, ideology, democratic discourse, and rhetoric.

This brief sketch of the central premises and the main objectives of this book is followed by a more detailed exposition of my methodology. This includes a discussion of some general characteristics of social memory, a delineation of my use of the concept, and an explication of my underlying assumptions concerning the nature of public discourse and decision making.

What Is Social Memory?

Social or collective memory—"the shared remembrances of group experience"[15]—is a powerful force in every community, since it creates collective identity by giving individuals a shared image of their past, providing them with an explanation of the present and a vision of the future.[16] Collective memory keeps alive the memory of crucial moments of the past, victories and defeats, inner conflicts and outside aggressions. These memories often cluster around foundational events of a heroic or traumatic nature and have a profound impact on the group's self-image and its sense of the world.[17] The exodus from Egypt, the Persian Wars, and the Revolutionary War of 1776 are examples of such "constellative myths" in Jewish, ancient Greek, and U.S. historical consciousness.[18] Collective memories generally do not stand up to the scrutiny of professional historians; they are often simplistic, contain fictitious elements,

15. Alcock (2002) i.

16. The body of scholarship on social memory is vast. For a concise introduction to the concept, see Markovits & Reich (1997) 14–20; Alcock (2002) 1–35. Fentress & Wickham (1992), Misztal (2003) and Erll & Nünning (2008) offer comprehensive treatments of the concept.

17. For this notion of shared historical experience as an imaginary bond that binds a group together, see Benedict Anderson's (1991) seminal work *Imagined Communities*.

18. For the exodus as constellative myth, see J. Assmann (1997) 7; for the Persian War, Alcock (2002) 74.

and show signs of distortions.[19] Yet they are real to the remembering community.[20] What people remember about the past shapes their collective identity and determines their friends and enemies.[21] Social memory can legitimize the status quo and serve as a repository for future decision making. For these reasons, it is also known as "myth," "meaningful history," "usable past," "imagined and remembered history," "cultural memory," "believed history," or "intentional history."[22]

Individual and Collective Memory

Social memory is a powerful force but is often hard to grasp; some critics even deny its existence. Their central objection is that remembering is an individual mental process and thus absolutely personal. "Just as a nation cannot eat or dance," argues one critic, "it cannot speak or remember."[23] This is a legitimate criticism, which seems to stem from the deep-rooted fear that social memory could become a new form of the old essentialist categories (collective, people, *Volk*) from which historians have only recently freed themselves.

Partially to disassociate themselves from such suspicions, most scholars in the field prefer the term *social memory* to Halbwachs' *collective memory.*[24] Maurice Halbwachs, a student of the French sociologist Émile Durkheim and the first to use the concept, deserves credit for establishing memory as a social category. Many of Halbwachs' tenets, such as the importance of collective memory for group identity as well as its presentist nature, are still the starting point for

19. Despite the current enthusiasm for memory studies, Gehrke (2001) 313 is right to remind us that where "history becomes myth, historical research must stand up and speak, urgently and emphatically."

20. Loraux (1986) 171; Fentress & Wickham (1992) 25–26. For the relationship between history and memory, cf. A. Assmann (2001).

21. For the link between collective memory and identity, see Prager (2001) 2223–24.

22. Cf. A. Assmann (2001) 6824. Fentress and Wickham (1992) 25 define social memory as an "expression of collective experience: social memory identifies a group, giving it a sense of its past and defining its aspiration for the future." Gehrke (2001) 286 introduces the term *intentional history* to denote "that which a society knows and holds for true about its past, [which] is of fundamental significance for the *imaginaire,* for the way a society interprets and understands itself, and therefore for its inner coherence and ultimately its collective identity." Misztal (2003) 158 defines collective or social memory as "a group's representation of its past, both the past that is commonly shared and the past that is collectively commemorated, that enacts and gives substance to that group's identity, its present conditions and its vision of the future." Closely related is Jan Assmann's *kulturelles Gedächtnis*; cf. J. Assman (1995) 132: "The concept of cultural memory comprises that body of reusable texts, images, and rituals specific to each society in each epoch, whose 'cultivation' serves to stabilize and convey that society's self-image. Upon such collective knowledge, for the most part (but not exclusively) of the past, each group bases its awareness of unity and particularity."

23. Funkenstein (1993) 4. For an excellent discussion of this problem, see Alcock (2002) 15–16.

24. Fentress & Wickham (1992) ix. While stressing the dynamic and communicative aspects of the concept, I will, for the sake of variation, use both terms interchangeably.

all research in the field.[25] Yet his view that all collective memory is "socially framed" and thus *entirely* dependent on the social group that determines what is "memorable" and how it will be remembered shows signs of social determinism and fails to acknowledge "the dialectical tensions between personal memory and the social construction of the past."[26] Scholars of social memory, therefore, have to conceive of a model that does justice to memory's collective aspects but "does not render the individual a sort of automaton, passively obeying the interiorized collective will."[27]

There are various ways to conceptualize collective memory without falling into the trap of reifying a monolithic group mind. Since social memory is based on the multitude of people who do the remembering, it is of paramount importance to consider the results of psychological research on individual memory.[28] Human memory is a highly complex system, and there is still much we do not know despite important advances in cognitive psychology and neuroscientific research.[29] This is not the place to attempt a systematic description of the various subsystems and conceptual subdivisions of memory.[30] Instead, I will focus on a few selected aspects that are relevant for my investigation of Athenian social memory.

It has been shown that we perceive the world that surrounds us with our

25. Halbwachs' seminal works consist of *Les cadres sociaux de la mémoire* (1925), *La topographie légendaire des évangiles en terre sainte: Ėtude de mémoire collective* (1941), and *La Mémoire collective* (1950), which was posthumously edited after Halbwachs' murder in Buchenwald in March 1945 and first translated into English in 1980. For recent critiques, see Misztal (2003) 50–56; Funkenstein (1993) 7–9; Connerton (1989) 36–40.

26. Misztal (2003) 54. Similarly, Fentress & Wickham (1992) ix.

27. Fentress & Wickham (1992) ix.

28. R. Thomas (1989) 11–13; Misztal (2003) 5; Erll (2008) 4–6; Manier & Hirst (2008) 254.

29. For a brief introduction to the psychology of individual memory, see Baddeley (1989); for a comprehensive discussion, Baddeley (1976). For its relevance for collective memory studies, see Fentress & Wickham (1992) 1–40; Misztal (2003) 9–12; Manier & Hirst (2008).

30. Baddeley (1989) 35 and Schacter (2001) 27–28 distinguish three interdependent subsystems: sensory memory (responsible for perception), working or short-term memory, and long-term memory. I am particularly concerned with the latter in this study. Another classification framework is based on the content of long-term memories: *episodic memories* refer to personally experienced events (i.e., we remember where and when we learned or experienced something), whereas *semantic memories* lack this temporal and spatial specificity (i.e., we remember a fact or thing but do not recall where we learned it): cf. Tulving (1983); Manier & Hirst (2008) 256. Yet Baddeley (1976) 317–18, (1989) 42–43, and Fentress & Wickham (1992) 20–21 call into question Tulving's strict dichotomy and rightly emphasize the interdependence between these two kinds of memories; semantic memory is continually underpinned and complemented by personal and sensory memory. Another useful way of subdividing long-term memories is to distinguish between *procedural memory* (i.e. knowing *how* to do something) and *declarative memory* (i.e. knowing *that* something occurred or is the case): cf. Manier & Hirst (2008) 256–57; Baddeley (1989) 43–45. In this study, I deal primarily with declarative memories, that is, with the deliberate and conscious act of recalling the past. Yet it is important to note that procedural memories also play an important role in preserving the past, which is embodied in nontextual performances and commemorative rituals, such as the Panathenaic procession. For this type of bodily social memory, see Connerton (1989).

senses (especially seeing and hearing) and make sense of new experiences with the help of the mental framework that we acquire in the process of our socialization.[31] We can only properly remember something if we first conceive of it in intelligible patterns. From the moment of perception, memories are, therefore, conceptualization and thus simplifications of a more complex reality.[32] In this process, language plays an important role, since it organizes the information in conceptual categories that are immediately available for articulation.[33] But memories are hardly ever purely semantic concepts. On the contrary, psychological experiments and everyday experience show that semantic and sensory (especially visual) memories tend to complement each other.[34] It is hard, for instance, to think of the battle of Marathon unaccompanied by any kind of visual images, be it Miltiades' leading the charge, Athenian hoplites running down the hill, or Persians fleeing to their ships. During this process of conceptualization, complex events become much more simplified and are associated with a few distinct visual images.[35]

Perceived information is held briefly in our working or short-term memory, where some of it is further encoded into long-term memory. The more we ponder or talk about an incident and the more we are emotionally involved, the more elaborative the encoding process becomes, and the more likely we are to retain the information in our long-term memory. We thus encode when and where an incident occurred, who was involved, what happened, and other distinguishing details of the event. These people, places, dates, and distinctive

31. Eber & Neil (2001) 3–6. Already Bartlett, one of the pioneers of cognitive psychology, pointed out that our knowledge of the world comprises a set of models or schemata derived from previous experience. When we learn something new, we base our learning on already existing schemata. Both the processes of learning and remembering thus involve an "effort after meaning." Cf. Bartlett (1932); Baddeley (1976) 9–15; Fentress & Wickham (1992) 32–36; Prager (2001) 2223.

32. Kertzer (2001) 13174: "The selective perception and radical simplification of potentially relevant stimuli are necessary if we are to make any sense at all out of the infinite number of potential observations that we could theoretically make." Cf. Fentress & Wickham (1992) 31–32. Gombrich (1972) 246–50 illustrates the process of visual conceptualization (and simplification) in an experiment involving children who were asked to copy a famous landscape painting. In the children's copy, the delicate meadow became a simple green patch, and the cloudy sky was turned into a uniform, light gray area. The children thus created a highly simplified representation of the original by translating the nuanced painting into a set of visual concepts.

33. Fentress & Wickham (1992) 28.

34. Cf. Bartlett (1932) 47–62; Fentress & Wickham (1992) 32–36. Participants were asked by Bartlett to remember postcards showing the faces of diverse military officers. Most of the participants came up with names and little stories as *aide-mémoire*. In this experiment, semantic and visual memories complemented and conformed to each other, even when both were wrong in the sense that the memories did not conform to the original picture.

35. In chapter 5, I will argue that the ritual city destruction of Crisa was "remembered" by fifth- and fourth-century Greeks as the first emblematic city destruction by a Greek alliance and that this social memory consisted of a few distinct visual and semantic conceptualizations, such as razing the walls and selling the inhabitants into slavery.

characteristics of the event can then serve as cues for later retrieval.[36] Such cues are of fundamental importance for my investigation of Athenian social memory. I will, for instance, make the case that Thrasybulus and the mountain fortress of Phyle could prompt the recollection of the return of the Athenian exiles in 403 BC. Also, striking similarities between current and past events (e.g., between the reigns of the Spartan-backed juntas in Thebes in 382–379 and in Athens in 404–403) can serve as cues for the recollection of the latter and thus revive a possibly latent memory.[37]

It is critical to stress that the act of remembering itself is a dynamic mental process that takes place in the present. When we remember, we consciously and deliberately recover the past.[38] Whatever memories route into consciousness, however, need to be "organized into patterns so that they make some kind of continuing sense in an ever-changing present."[39] This process is comparable to reconstructing isolated puzzle pieces into a coherent picture. The very process of recall thus involves a certain degree of "re-forming or re-structuring of the 'original' memory."[40] It also involves further elaboration: in retelling an event, we supply motives, thoughts, and details based on our current general understanding of the world.[41] Every recall functions as further encoding and thus increases the durability and stability of a particular memory; yet, at the same time, every recall is a new reconstruction and, therefore, subject to the distorting influences of our present predilections and concerns.[42] Memory is, therefore, always fluid and dynamic and never static.[43] Since a group's collective memory is based on the memory of its individual members, these characteristics of individual memory apply to the group's shared remembrances as well.

---

36. Schacter (2001) 26–33. Cf. R. Thomas (1989) 12.

37. Cf. chapter 4.

38. Memory has, therefore, been described as "dialogue with the past," as some kind of "active orientation towards the past" or as an "act of thinking of things in their absence." See Misztal (2003) 9.

39. Young (1988) 97–98, cited in Misztal (2003) 10. Schacter (2001) 146 speaks of "hindsight bias": "we reconstruct the past to make it consistent with what we know in the present." Cf. Bartlett's (1932) concept of the "effort after meaning." See also Middleton & Brown (2008) 242–43.

40. R. Thomas (1989) 12. One part of this structuring effort before sharing a memory involves organizing it into a story, which is subject to the rules and conventions of narrative. See also Prager (2001) 2224.

41. Cf. R. Thomas (1989) 12–13. Schacter (2001) 138–60 analyzes the different ways in which our current predispositions can distort our memories. He distinguishes between consistency and change biases, hindsight biases, and egocentric and stereotypical biases.

42. A good example is autobiographical memory. Since we experience the present as connected to and resultant of the past, the memories of our own past are always consistent with our current self-image. Cf. Misztal (2003) 10; Schacter (2001) 138–44.

43. Remembering is, therefore, fundamentally different from retrieving a written document from a storage archive. For a critique of the "textual model" of memory, which is widespread among oral historians and tends to reify memories, see Fentress & Wickham (1992) 1–8.

While it is the individual who does the remembering, social memory is nevertheless different from the sum total of individual thoughts about the past.[44] Social memory comes into existence when people *talk* about the memories that they consider important enough to share with others. Consequently, both *social relevance* and *communication* are indispensable elements of this concept. For a memory to be shared, it first has to be articulated and thus depends on the shared cultural forms and conventions of language.[45] For social memory to be a useful analytical tool, it needs to retain a sense of both its individual and collective dimensions. This "intersubjectivist" approach avoids both social determinism, which subordinates individuals entirely to a collective, and the individualistic bias of psychological theories, which often ignore the importance of communicative relations between people and their social embeddedness.[46] A good analogy for the relationship between collective and individual memory is the relation between language (*langue*) and speech (*parole*), as formulated by Saussure. Both language and collective memory are idealized systems that cannot exist without individual speech acts and memories, respectively. Barbara Misztal explains,

> Variations in individual memories, which can be compared to the scope of freedom with which we use language in particular speech, reflect the degree to which a given culture permits conscious changes and variation of the narrator in the contents, symbols and structures of collective memory.[47]

One of the objectives of this investigation is to assess the degree of freedom that individual Athenians had in departing from predominant social memories.

Another way of avoiding the impression of a unified and static collective consciousness is to emphasize the existence of numerous "memory communities" that are at work at any given time.[48] Every social group derives its group identity—at least partially—from its traditions and is thus able to foster its own social memory.[49] Since large communities, such as nations, consist of

44. Cf. E. Zerubavel (1997) 96.

45. Fentress & Wickham (1992) 47; Huyssen (1995) 3; A. Assmann (2001) 6822; Misztal (2003) 6, 11. Cf. Echterhoff (2008).

46. Misztal (2003) 5, 10. See also Funkenstein (1993); Schudson (1997); E. Zerubavel (1997); Prager (1998); Sherman (1999).

47. Misztal (2003) 11. Cf. Funkenstein (1993) 5–9.

48. For memory communities, see Burke (1989) 107; Alcock (2002) 15. Alternatively, some scholars use the term *mnemonic community*. Cf. E. Zerubavel (1996); Prager (2001) 2224; Misztal (2003) 15–19.

49. J. Assmann (1995) 127, 130. Cf. Wischermann (2002) 7, challenging scholars to divert attention from the "kulturellen Großgedächtnis" toward the multitude of competing visions of the past within any given society.

numerous subgroups—for example, regional and local communities, socioeconomic classes, ethnic and religious groups, the learned elite and the uneducated masses, the ruling class and the underrepresented—there are a variety of concurrent and possibly competing memories available to such a community at any given time.[50] In a free society, like classical Athens, a widely accepted image of the past needs to be negotiated, lest the social memories and group identities of its different subgroups function as centrifugal forces and endanger the cohesion of the polis as a whole.[51] A crucial arena for the contestation and negotiation of divergent memories in Athens is public discourse, manifest, for instance, in public commemorations, in the law courts, and in political debates.[52]

In conclusion, an emphasis on the communicative aspect of memory, on the interdependence between individual memory and its collective expression, and on the existence of and the individual's participation in different memory communities avoids the danger of reifying the monolithic group mind.

Ideology and Social Memory

As mentioned in the previous section, social memory is of critical importance for a group's identity and cohesion. Social groups change over time, and their memories change along with them. For this reason, it is imperative to look closely at the interdependence between a group's ideology and its collective memory.

Through cultural socialization, we acquire a particular mental framework, which aids us in making sense of the world.[53] Josiah Ober calls this mental framework "ideology" and describes it in the following way:

50. The American Civil War provides an excellent example of competing regional and ethnic memory communities. Cf. Horwitz (1998); Brundage (2000); Blight (2001), (2002).

51. For the importance of such a "Minimalkonsens in Sachen der eigenen Geschichte" for a democracy, cf. Winkler (2004). For competing memory communities in contemporary Germany, see Markovits & Reich (1997) 34–42. Through monuments, public commemorations, and official histories, oppressive regimes often try to establish their own version of the past as the dominant master narrative. They even go so far as to suppress and erase alternative memories that might undermine their legitimacy. But even there, it is possible for the oppressed groups to challenge the dominant versions of the ruling elite, for instance, by displaying publically the symbols of countermemories. The U.S. civil rights movement of the 1960s serves as an example of how a minority group successfully challenged the predominant master narrative: black countermemories of the Civil War era had been preserved within African American communities and became then—at least to some extent—part of the common U.S. historical consciousness. Cf. Kammen (1995) 334–35; Brundage (2000).

52. For an excellent discussion of the contestation and negotiation of the divisive memory of the Athenian civil war of 404/3 in fourth-century Athenian public discourse, cf. Wolpert (2002). See also Loraux (2002); Shear (2011) 286–312.

53. Eber & Neil (2001) 3–6; Brundage (2000) 4; Kertzer (2001) 13174.

> Each member of any given community makes assumptions about human nature and behavior, has opinions on morality and ethics, and holds some general political principles; those assumptions, opinions and principles which are common to the great majority of those members are best described as ideology.[54]

Ideology in this sense is not necessarily clearly articulated or logically consistent, but it comprises a set of "intellectual beliefs and emotional judgments"[55] sufficiently well organized to facilitate decisions and actions. Throughout this monograph, I follow Ober's use of the term *ideology* for this shared network of ideas, values, and beliefs within a particular community.

Ideology and social memory are intertwined in a complicated way. On the one hand, ideologies are, to a considerable extent, derived from social memory. A group's mental framework originates from its historical experience; especially heroic or traumatic experiences can fundamentally alter the image a group has of itself and of the world that surrounds it. Ideological frameworks, on the other hand, determine both the perception of the present and the recollection of the past. Consequently, changes in a community's ideological framework often lead to alterations in the social memory of earlier events.[56] This is because the natural tendency of social memory is "to suppress what is not meaningful . . . in the collective memories of the past, and interpolate or substitute what seems more appropriate or more in keeping with [a society's] particular conception of the world."[57] Often, the remembering community is not conscious of these changes.

The alteration of the Puritans' social memory during the course of the seventeenth century is a lucid example. Persecuted by King Charles I and the Church of England, they decided to emigrate to the New World to save their souls, until they would be recalled in glory to re-create their New Jerusalem at home. Yet, when Oliver Cromwell's Puritan Commonwealth offered such an opportunity only twenty years later, most Puritan immigrants did not return but declared that Christianizing heathen peoples in the New World was more imperative.

54. Ober (1989) 38. Cf. Finley (1982) 17, who speaks of a "matrix of attitudes and beliefs."

55. Hunt (1998) 20. This use of the term *ideology* is to be distinguished from its use in the narrower sense, which describes a fixed and contrived set of ideas, brought into a coherent system to promote a certain worldview, such as fascist or communist ideology.

56. Cf. Markovits & Reich (1997) 13–20. Forsdyke (2005) 259–67 offers a convincing analysis of the complex interaction between the actual historical experience of exile during the time of the Thirty and the ideological representation of exile in the Athenian democratic traditions. She demonstrates, among other things, that the recent experience of the Thirty also influenced the collective memory of exile under the Peisistratids.

57. Fentress & Wickham (1992) 58–59.

This required "that memories of their own rhetoric during the 1620s and 1630s be repressed or altered."[58]

One explanation for this phenomenon lies in the general nature of memory. Since we view the present as connected to and evolving from the past, we reconstruct our memories in accordance with the present situation; nevertheless, we regard our memories as constant and immutable.[59] A further explanation is the tendency of memory to efface previous memories in the case of habitual actions, as seen, for instance, at commemorative ceremonies. Especially in oral societies, which cannot easily refer to older versions, stories are successively altered in the process of transmission and adapted—consciously and unconsciously—to present needs.[60]

Gradual developments in a society's ideology might cause unnoticed changes and distortions in its collective memory. In comparison, extreme experiences, such as the overthrow of an older political system, a heroic victory, or a devastating defeat, often cause abrupt ideological shifts. These are frequently accompanied by the carrying out of active "memory politics" by those in charge: old traditions are suppressed or reinterpreted, and new myths, which are able to symbolize the new ideology, are created and transmitted through public commemoration, festivals, monuments, and so on.[61]

Since 1776, the new ideology of the United States of America has been deliberately promoted by annually celebrating Independence Day, with parades and public addresses that commemorate the declaration of independence from the British monarchy. The founding fathers were very conscious of the symbolic meaning of such a national holiday, as a letter written by John Adams to his wife on July 3, 1776, reveals.

> The Second Day of July 1776, will be the most memorable Epocha, in the History of America. I am apt to believe that it will be celebrated, by succeeding Generations, as the great anniversary Festival. It ought to be commemorated, as the Day of Deliverance by solemn Acts of Devotion to God Almighty. It ought to be solemnized with Pomp and Parade, with

---

58. Cf. Kammen (1995) 330–33, quotation at 331.

59. Schacter (2001) 138–60 calls the phenomena responsible for memory distortions of this kind "consistency bias" and "hindsight bias." Cf. Prager (2001) 2223–24.

60. This also happens in literate societies, if written records are not consulted. For the "blotting out" of previous memories through habitual actions, see Fentress & Wickham (1992) 39–40. For the crucial role of present needs, cf. Prager (2001) 2224.

61. For the formation and transmission of national memories in the modern period, see Fentress & Wickham (1992) 127–37; Hobsbawm & Ranger (1983). For changes in the commemoration of early American history after the Civil War, see Schwartz (1982).

> Shews, Games, Sports, Guns, Bells, Bonfires and Illuminations from one End of this Continent to the other from this Time forward forever more.[62]

In fifth- and fourth-century Athens, we also find major political and military upheavals—especially Cleisthenes' and Ephialtes' democratic reforms and the Persian War experience—that led to fundamental ideological shifts and changes in the Athenian master narrative and its commemoration.[63] Yet, for this period, it is much harder to identify the individuals behind particular memory politics and to pin down the date of new memorial practices, such as the public funeral for the Athenian war dead.[64] Moreover, given the multipolarity of social memory, it would be misguided to focus exclusively on the instigators and masterminds behind the official Athenian polis tradition and its manifold expressions in monuments, commemorative festivals, and other forms of public discourse. The processes in which heroic or traumatic experiences reshape a community's mental framework and become an essential part of its collective memory are extremely complex and cannot be characterized adequately by a theoretical model that views collective memory largely as the result of deliberate top-down memory politics.[65]

To get beyond the concept of political instrumentalization and fabrication, I will take the findings of other social memory studies into account in this one. It is especially useful to identify some general characteristics of how the memory of foundational events is shaped and transmitted and what kinds of distortions commonly occur.[66] In U.S. social memory, for instance, the War of Independence was memorialized in a variety of ways and has become paradigmatic, a symbol for the new nation and its ideology of freedom from tyrannical

62. A. Adams & J. Adams (1975) 142. July 2, 1776, was the day when the Continental Congress adopted a resolution severing ties with Great Britain. The formal Declaration of Independence was ratified on July 4.

63. For the "imagined political community" in Attica after Cleisthenes' reforms, see G. Anderson (2003). For the impact of the Persian War experience on the Athenian self-image, see Gehrke (2001), (2003); Jung (2006).

64. Greg Anderson (2003) makes a strong case for the role of Cleisthenes and his associates in deliberately using preexisting myths and cults (e.g., of the new eponymous tribal heroes) to foster a new communal identity and civic ideology. Their efforts were so successful particularly because they chose to emphasize the "reassuring continuities, real or imagined, with Athenian political tradition" (103). For the institutionalization of the Athenian public funeral, see Stupperich (1977) 200–239; Loraux (1986) 15–76.

65. For this "invention of tradition" approach, with its focus on the fabrication of collective memories by the ruling classes, see especially Hobsbawm & Ranger (1983). For a lucid critique of this approach, see Misztal (2003) 60–61.

66. Kammen (1995) 329–30 and Schudson (1995) 360, for instance, offer a broad array of reasons for memory distortions.

oppression. More particular reasons for the rebellion of the thirteen original British colonies—well researched by historians—have not penetrated the general historical consciousness. This is not surprising. If individual memories are visual and semantic conceptualizations, collective memories—to be shared by a large community—have to be conceptualized and simplified to an even higher degree.[67]

Distortions in collective memories abound. Often, they are self-serving to the remembering community. An event is remembered in accordance with the group's self-image; the memory of common achievements is embellished, and that of unflattering events is suppressed. The distortions in the case of the War of Independence can be ascribed to what Rosalind Thomas calls "the narrow needs of . . . patriotism."[68] Yet there are also other processes that lead to the simplification and deformation of collective memories. Events that are not actively commemorated may be forgotten when living memory fades. If those events are remembered, the process of "distanciation" often results in a loss of detail and emotional intensity. Another factor in the process of selection and simplification of shared memories is "narrativization."[69] Generally, the past is encapsulated into and transmitted through a narrative, a story. Consequently, the resultant memory is shaped by the characteristics of this narrative. A story usually has a clear structure (beginning, middle, and end), focuses on a few protagonists, uses causal links, and displays suspense and resolution.[70]

Distortions can also result from another peculiar feature of social memory: a community's charter myth can shape and assimilate the memory of both later and earlier historical events. The French Protestants' resistance against the revocation of the Edict of Nantes in the Camisard revolts of 1702–4, for instance, became a defining image for the inhabitants of the Cévennes mountains in southern France. Collective memories of any other local events of resistance against state authority—like the resistance against German occupation and the Vichy regime—contain the same images and stories and have thus become "camisardized." Other "important" events that do not fit this pattern—like Napoleon's reign and World War I—are disregarded in the historical consciousness of the people of the Cévennes.[71] Similarly, in the course of this

67. Cf. Fentress & Wickham (1992) 47–48.

68. R. Thomas (1989) 247.

69. For distanciation and narrativization, see Schudson (1995) 348–59.

70. The narrativization and commemoration of the Great Patriotic War in Russia is an illustrative example: the "story" begins with the German attack in June 1941, which enables Russians to remember their war dead but, at the same time, "conveniently helps them to overlook the 1939 Hitler-Stalin Non-Aggression Treaty that so significantly aided the build-up of the German military machine" (Schudson (1995) 355).

71. Joutard (1977); Fentress & Wickham (1992) 92–99; Alcock (2002) 6.

investigation, it will become apparent that after the Persian War, certain earlier and later events became "marathonized," since the Persian War experience in general and the battle of Marathon in particular had a tremendous effect on Athenian self-image.[72]

Most scholars engaged in memory studies recognize both the malleability of memory and its crucial role for a group's shared identity.[73] There is, however, disagreement about the nature of the relationship between past and present. Neo-Durkheimians, on the one hand, favor a sociological interpretation and emphasize the extraordinary role of the present in the construction of the past, which functions as a symbolic resource for the creation of a common identity. From this sociological perspective, social memory serves present-day needs and interests and generates an emotional bond of solidarity. Neo-Freudians, on the other hand, argue that the past intrudes on the present and that social memory expresses the legacy of traumatic pasts inscribed in the present. They insist that

> collective memory is a social process in response to social ruptures, or discontinuities, that have occurred in the past that, because not fully assimilated in conscious experience, subsequently interfere with the smooth functioning of collective life.[74]

This psychoanalytical approach has proven especially fruitful in studies of collective experiences of war or genocide, particularly the Holocaust.[75]

Although I am much indebted to neo-Durkheimians such as Halbwachs, Hobsbawm, Fentress, and Wickham, I regard the neo-Freudian approach as an important corrective to purely functionalist interpretations.[76] Two things in particular ought to be considered. First, extreme experiences are able to alter a community's ideological framework and thus considerably influence the perception and memory of later events. Second, the past is by no means entirely at the disposal of the present; memory cannot completely override history. Strong prior remembrances, especially of a heroic or traumatic nature, are part of an obdurate historical reality that cannot be ignored.[77]

72 For this effect of Marathon, see the section "Funeral Orations" in chapter 1, 49–58; Gehrke (2001) 302; Harding (1987) 35. For the Persian Wars as a paradigm, providing all the Greeks of the Roman imperial period with a "charter of identity," see Alcock (2002) 84.

73. Cf. Prager (2001).

74. Prager (2001) 2225. For a discussion of the neo-Freudian approach to social memory, see also Misztal (2003) 139–45.

75. For further bibliography, see Alcock (2002) 20. For studies of the memory of the Holocaust, see Friedlander (1991), (1992), (1993); LaCapra (1994); Novick (1999).

76. The traumatic aspect of a particular Athenian social memory is highlighted in "Traumatic Fear of Annihilation" in chapter 5, 291–300.

77. Cf. Schudson (1995) 351; Paez, Basabe, & Gonzales (1997). For history as a constraint, see Prager (2001) 2225; Appadurai (1981).

This complex interrelationship between past experiences and present needs has been described best by Jan Assmann: "The present is 'haunted' by the past and the past is modeled, invented, reinvented, and reconstructed by the present."[78]

Social Memory in Ancient Greece: From Mythical Times to the Recent Past

Since social memory is a wide-ranging concept, involving personal memories and communal commemoration, active memory politics and unintentional distortions, as well as a group's identity and ideology, it seems necessary to define how I shall use the term. I regard both the *communicative aspect* of sharing memories of the past and their *social relevance* for the members of a group as constitutive elements of the concept.[79] Consequently, my notion of social memory includes memories ranging from the mythical to the most recent past, memories cherished by the entire polis community as well as those shared primarily by the members of a small group.

Demarcating my use of the concept also allows me to situate my own approach within the context of other memory studies of the ancient world. It will become clear that my notion of social memory is rather broadly conceived to encompass aspects of Rosalind Thomas' oral tradition, Jan Assmann's communicative and cultural memory, Loraux' *Athènes imaginaire*, Gehrke's intentional history, Alcock's *cadre matériel*, Wolpert's civic memory, and Michael Jung's *lieux de mémoire*.[80] Exploring, in various ways, how the Greeks remembered their past and what this past meant to them, all of these scholars approach their subject from slightly different angles and thus reflect different strands of social memory studies.

Athenian Ideology and Collective Memory

In the last three decades, scholars have made great strides in disentangling the complex relationship between the Athenians' historical experience, ideology, and image of the past. In her seminal work on the Athenian funeral oration,

78. J. Assmann (1997) 9.

79. While people also share many other "memories," I will use the term exclusively to refer to the recollection of past events and experience (whether real or imaginary). Psychologists, in particular, call any recollection of previously learned information a memory. Cf. Fentress & Wickham (1992) xi; Manier & Hirst (2008) 253.

80. Cf. R. Thomas (1989), drawing on Vansina (1985); J. Assmann (1992), (1995), (1997); Loraux (1986); Gehrke (1994), (2001), (2003); Alcock (2002); Wolpert (2002); Jung (2006), drawing on Nora (1996).

Nicole Loraux brings to light the distorting influence that the Athenians' democratic and imperial ideology exerted on their version of the past: in this oratorical genre, a few selected historical and mythical events were celebrated as symbols of the never-changing noble Athenian character.[81] Similarly, Hans-Joachim Gehrke explores the interdependence between the Athenians' historical experience and their resultant self-image. After the Persian Wars, the Athenians came to see the victory at Marathon as the glorious manifestation of their role as protectors of the weak and as champions of Greek liberty.[82] Marathon was thus severed from its immediate historical context and became the quintessential event in the Athenians' "intentional history."[83] In his diachronic study of Marathon and Plataea as Greek *lieux de mémoire,* Michael Jung adds two further dimensions by focusing on the various "carriers" of these symbolic memories (rituals, monuments, literature) and by tracing their changing ideological implications and functions from the Persian Wars to Roman imperial times.[84] Finally, Susan Alcock reconstructs the *cadre matériel* of Roman Greece and makes a convincing case for the use of archaeology in ancient Greek memory studies.[85]

By examining the public commemoration and transmission of what we can call the "Athenian master narrative" (i.e., the prevalent version of the Athenian past), Loraux, Gehrke, and Jung have made significant contributions to our understanding of how the Athenians' shared image of the past is infused with democratic ideology and bound up with their self-image as hegemonic power.[86] Yet, by focusing primarily on the social significance and ideological function of outstanding events, these scholars pass over other important aspects of Athenian social memory, such as the different degrees of commemoration, the

81. See especially Loraux (1986) 132–71.

82. Gehrke (2003) 22.

83. Gehrke's "intentional history" coincides in many ways with my concept of social memory, as his definition reveals. Cf. Gehrke (2001) 298: "Intentional history would then be history in a group's own understanding, especially in so far as it is significant for the make-up and identity of the group."

84. Jung (2006) demonstrates that Pierre Nora's theoretical concept, which was developed for the analysis of contemporary French memorial practices, can successfully be applied to ancient memory studies. Following Nora (1996), Jung (2006) 15 considers *lieux de mémoire* as "literarische, symbolische, geographische oder personale Punkte, an denen sich ein kollektives Gedächtnis, die Erinnerung einer größeren sozialen Einheit konkretisieren und herausbilden kann."

85. Alcock (2002) 1–98.

86. For the term *master narrative,* see Forsdyke (2005) 242: "[T]hrough its multiple forums for collective deliberation and self-representation (the assembly, courts, theater, civic rituals and festivals) [the Athenian democracy] articulated a common version of the past that, at least in part, validated the principle of democratic rule. Democratic versions of the past, moreover—what Rosalind Thomas terms 'the official polis tradition'—formed the master narrative of Athenian history in the fifth and fourth centuries." The term *master narrative* is not meant to imply a fixed, official narrative. Rather, it denotes the sum of the converging versions of the Athenian past, which conveyed the Athenian self-image and were manifested and transmitted in the aforementioned ways. Cf. "Festivals and Public Commemorations" in chapter 1, 49–69.

interaction between different types of memories (e.g., those of the small group versus those of the polis), and the distorting influences in the actual transmission process of memories in a still widely oral society such as classical Athens.

Oral Tradition Studies

To address these aspects, I draw on the results of oral tradition research. This anthropological branch of memory studies was initially designed by ethnohistorians for the study of contemporary preliterate societies where collective memory provides the only access to these peoples' past.[87] In the last two decades, this methodology has been applied, with great success, to the study of Herodotus, whose work draws heavily on oral sources and still betrays many of the characteristics of oral communication.[88] Rosalind Thomas was the first classicist to use the concept of oral tradition for the systematic study of the interplay of various types of oral tradition in classical Athens.[89] Her findings are of paramount importance for my study, since oral traditions are the most prominent manifestations of Athenian social memory. Unlike other "carriers" of social memory, such as monuments and rituals, oral traditions preserve memories of the past in narrative form and are thus, if recorded, our best access to the Athenians' shared image of the past.

Thomas' analysis of the complex interrelation between oral traditions and the written word has led to a new understanding of the communicative conditions in fifth- and fourth-century Athens, which, despite the existence of writing, still showed many features of an oral society.[90] This is significant for two reasons. First, she demonstrates that this anthropological concept, which was first used for the study of contemporary preliterate societies, can also be applied

87. See Vansina (1965), (1985); Fentress & Wickham (1992) xi.

88. See, for instance, O. Murray (2001); Luraghi (2001); R. Thomas (1989) 4 note 4, for further literature. For exemplary studies of particular oral traditions in Herodotus, cf. R. Thomas (1989) 238–82; Forsdyke (1999). Since the 1930s, classicists have used theories of oral composition and performance for the study of the Homeric epics. For groundbreaking work, see Parry (1971); Lord (1960). For recent scholarship on Greek oral poetry, see Nagy (1996); Scodel (2002).

89. Rosalind Thomas (1989) draws particularly on the works of Vansina (1985), Finnegan (1977), and Henige (1974).

90. Rosalind Thomas (1989) 89 points out that in the law courts, for instance, fourth-century Athenians still placed more authority and trust in the testimony of witnesses than in written contracts. Thomas (1992) 15–28 argues convincingly against a strict dichotomy between oral and literate societies, as proposed by Goody & Watt (1963) or Havelock (1963). Consequently the arrival of literacy can no longer be seen as the sole cause of cultural developments, such as the rise of law and democracy or the discovery of logic. Following Thomas' lead, scholars of Greek culture now focus on the specific influence of writing on particular cultural practices like religion, law, medicine, science, philosophy, and history. Cf. Yunis (2003).

successfully to the study of an ancient, semiliterate society.[91] Writing does influence oral tradition, but "not simply by killing it."[92] By drawing on comparative anthropological studies, Thomas is able to explain many of the "distortions" in Greek oral traditions as typical results of the workings and processes of collective memory and thus provides a viable model for my case study of the memory of Thebes in Athenian historical consciousness.[93]

Second, while some aspects of social memory (especially its ideological implications and societal functions) are general characteristics observable across time and space, Thomas has made a strong case that the conditions and rules for its formation, negotiation, contestation, and transmission are specific to each culture and need to be studied within its particular context.[94] For this reason, chapter 1 of this book is devoted to the systematic study of the various ways in which fifth- and fourth-century Athenians learned about their past. Thomas' emphasis on the need to consider a society's particular communicative framework has further implications for this project. When analyzing and interpreting ancient Greek sources such as the Greek historians or the Attic orators, we have to give up the tacit presupposition that their attitudes toward oral communication, written documents, and the validation of information were the same as ours.[95] Our modern Western archive culture relies heavily on written preservation of knowledge and usually decides questions of historical authenticity by consulting documentary evidence.[96] Consequently, when politicians distort the past (whether deliberately or inadvertently), they can be called out by historians or journalists, as in the case of U.S. presidential candidate Barack Obama's erroneous claim, in a Memorial Day speech, that his uncle "was part of the first American troops to go into Auschwitz and liberate the concentration camps."[97] In classical Athens, however, people drew

91. The applicability of oral tradition research is not restricted to a semiliterate society. See O. Anderson (1990) 677. In his review of Rosalind Thomas' monograph, he criticizes her tendency to limit many features of the oral transmission of memory to the particular *transitional* situation of fourth-century Athens, asserting that even today, our social memory is constituted mainly through oral communication (through parental instruction, teaching in school, public commemorations, films). The only difference is that, thanks to our archive culture, we *can* know more, if we want to. See also Fentress & Wickham (1992) 46, 97.

92. R. Thomas (1989) 10.

93. Cf. R. Thomas (1989) 6–14.

94. While focusing on the processes of formation and transmission, Rosalind Thomas (1989) does not neglect the ideological implications and societal functions of oral traditions. Consequently, there is considerable overlap with the findings of Loraux (1986), Gehrke (1994), (2001), (2003), and Jung (2006).

95. See below for a more detailed discussion of previous studies of the orators' historical allusions.

96. For our modern archive culture, cf. Fentress & Wickham (1992) 78. Winkler (2004) stresses the importance of professional historians in modern democracies in checking and demythologizing grossly distorted versions of the past.

97. http://www.reuters.com/article/topNews/idUSN2740383620080527. On the following

their knowledge of the past almost strictly from oral sources and generally had no means (and little inclination) to fact-check. Accordingly, Athenian public speakers often took common knowledge for granted or referred to poets and the elders, who carried much more authoritative weight for contemporary Athenians than they do for us.[98]

Another merit of Thomas' work consists of her emphasis on the multipolarity of Athenian oral traditions. She demonstrates that in order to understand the complexity of the Athenian memorial framework, we have to look beyond the public funeral oration, which presents "a coherent vision"[99] of Athens' past and encapsulates only a few paradigmatic events. Apart from this "official polis tradition," she analyzes personal reminiscenses and correctly insists that "oral tradition and the stuff of oral history form a continuum."[100] Nevertheless, following Jan Vansina, Thomas defines oral traditions as "testimonies which have been transmitted over at least a generation."[101] In this respect, my concept of social memory differs from Thomas' oral tradition.[102] Since the same mental processes are at work in remembering a transmitted and an experienced incident, I also include allusions to recent events in my analysis of Athenian collective memory.

Remembered and Commemorated History

That the experiences and memories of the most recent past indeed form an important part of a community's social memory is evident from Andrew Wol-

day, May 27, 2008, the Obama campaign corrected the error after receiving much criticism: Obama had mistakenly referred to Auschwitz instead of Buchenwald. A quick check of the historical records revealed that his great-uncle Charlie Payne had served in the Eighty-Ninth Infantry Division, which liberated Ohrdruf, a subcamp of Buchenwald, on April 4, 1945. Of course, even in our archive culture, most oral references to the past are not subjected to this level of scrutiny.

98. R. Thomas (1989) 201. For the assumption of common knowledge, see Dem. 19.65 (discussed in chap. 5); Lys. 19.48; Dem. 20.73, 21.78; Aeschin. 3.186; Lycurg. 106. For the elders as a source for knowledge of the past, see Din. 1.25 (discussed in chap. 4); Dem. 20.52, 77; Isoc. 16.4. For decrees, see Din. 1.25. Rosalind Thomas (1989) 83–93 argues that throughout the fourth century, the Athenians became slowly more document-minded and also referred to inscribed decrees.

99. R. Thomas (1989) 196–98, quotation at 196.

100. R. Thomas (1989) 11. She correctly observes that family tradition, in particular, cuts across these two distinct categories and comprises both long-standing oral traditions about one's family and the personal memories of family members involved in recent events. Fentress & Wickham (1992) 98 similarly stress the structural communalities of personal memories and oral traditions.

101. R. Thomas (1989) 13. She does, however, acknowledge that there is no strict separation between personal reminiscences (which comprise oral history) and oral tradition. Vansina (1985) 27–28 strictly separates oral tradition from oral history. He defines oral traditions as "verbal messages which are reported statements from the past beyond the present generation" and insists that there must be "transmission by word of mouth over at least a generation."

102. Another difference is her concentration on "verbal testimonies," whereas I also treat "incorporated" and material media (rituals and public monuments, respectively) as important carriers of Athenian social memory, all of which influence and sustain one another.

pert's study of how the Athenians remembered the gruesome civil war of 404/3. Wolpert shows how, after the amnesty of 403, both factions engaged in strategies of selectively remembering *and* forgetting and thus constructed a precarious, carefully negotiated civic memory of this fateful event, which prevented renewed civil strife. Two aspects of his study are particularly relevant for my investigation. First, Wolpert demonstrates that memory is not entirely at the disposal of the present and that the long-lasting psychological effects of traumatic experiences can be observed in fourth-century Athens.[103] Second, Wolpert illustrates that remembering and forgetting play out on different, yet interconnected, levels of civic discourse. Public commemorations and monuments promoted the transformation of the exiles' victory into a victory of the entire *demos* over a handful of traitors (i.e., the Thirty) and thus allowed both former oligarchic supporters and complacent democrats to identify with the victorious *demos*.[104] Yet the courts, despite the constraints of the amnesty, also served individual Athenians as a forum for recrimination and thus perpetuated the renegotiation of the memory of this bloody conflict.

A practical way to conceptualize this relationship between personal reminiscences and the collective memories of the society at large is offered by Aleida Assmann, who discerns private from public memory, that is, "remembered from commemorated history."[105] "Remembered history" is history as experienced and remembered by the individual. It is the part of collective memory that is based on everyday communication and thus also falls into the field of oral history.[106] It is necessarily "partial, biased, subjective and, therefore, also highly variegated."[107] Nevertheless, it displays several social aspects that justify including it in this investigation. First, an individual's perception and experience of history is shaped and collectivized by the group's shared mental framework. Second, personal memories show many similarities resulting from similar biographical patterns; while an event is usually remembered differently by the old and the young, women and men, soldiers and civilians, people within these subgroups share similar experiences. Third, these private memories are

103. Wolpert (2002) draws successfully on trauma studies of the Holocaust and the German occupation of France during World War II. In chapter 5, I will argue that the horrors of the Peloponnesian War and the threat of total annihilation at its end were responsible for the persistence of the proposal to eradicate Athens in Athenian collective historical consciousness.

104. Cf. the situation in the aftermath of World War II in West Germany. A collective forgetting allowed former Nazi perpetrators and "Mitläufer" to become an active part of the new democratic state, while the responsibility for Nazi crimes was laid squarely on the shoulders of the few top Nazi officials tried at Nuremberg.

105. A. Assmann (2001). These concepts have been developed jointly by Aleida and Jan Assmann, who uses the terms *communicative memory* and *cultural memory* to denote these two phenomena. Cf. J. Assmann (1992), (1997), and especially (1995).

106. J. Assmann (1995) 126. For oral history, see Joutard (1983); Passerini (1988); Thompson (1988); Levine & Sebe Bom Meihyb (2001).

107. A. Assmann (2001) 6822.

embedded in familial and social communication and thus supported by the individual memories of others.

Aleida Assmann emphasizes that remembered history consists not only of immediate personal experiences but also of the shared memories of parents and grandparents: "Thus, an embodied and participatory historical memory of approximately 100 years, is built up by oral transmission."[108] This three-generational oral memory is transient, and the memories of the first generation fade and perish as the memories of the fourth generation are added. This continuous fading out of remembered history is a normal process. Older memories that do not have any relevance for the present are thereby forgotten,[109] unless there is a strong interest in the history of ancestors (e.g., in the case of aristocratic families who sustain their social status through pedigree) or when the remembered history has a heroic or traumatic character (e.g., in the case of Holocaust survivors). The concept of remembered history is of course not restricted to families but also applies to small local communities with similar communicative conditions.

To this rather informal and erratic remembered history, we can contrast "commemorated history," a second, more organized type of social memory.[110] Unlike remembering, commemorating refers to an "intentional, formalized, and collective action."[111] Consequently, commemorated history covers past events, the memory of which seems important enough to a community to be made permanent. In the transition from remembered to commemorated history, both material and performative media play an important role.[112] In classical Athens, material media included monuments, inscriptions, relics, and books.[113] Performative media are symbolic forms of action, including rites, festivals, and ceremonies. As in the case of ceremonial commemorations at a memorial site, material and performative media are often combined.

108. A. Assmann (2001) 6823. Cf. J. Assmann (1995) 127.

109. This continuous fading out of remembered history causes the so-called floating gap in nonliterate societies where the historical consciousness is divided between a three-generational recent past and a mythical past of heroic character. Cf. A. Assmann (2001) 6823.

110. See also Manier & Hirst (2008), who use the psychological concepts "collective episodic memory," "collective distant/lived semantic memory," and "collective procedural memory" to establish a taxonomy of Jan Assmann's (1995) communicative and cultural memory.

111. A. Assmann (2001) 6823. See also Schudson (1995) 348, who distinguishes between three realms of social memory, (1) socially mediated individual memories (Assmann's "remembered history"), (2) cultural forms of social mediation, and (3) individual memories constructed from the cultural forms (Assmann's "commemorated history").

112. A. Assmann (2001) 6823. This classification corresponds to Connerton's (1989) distinction between "inscribed" and "incorporated" memorial practices. According to Jan Assmann (1995) 129, "cultural memory" is maintained through "cultural formation (texts, rites, monuments) and institutional communication (recitation, practice, observance)."

113. For a useful definition of *monument*, cf. Alcock (2002) 28.

Public and private memory mutually influence and sustain each other.[114] For public memory to retain its social relevance, it needs to be underpinned by the private memory of individuals who engage in communal commemorative activities. Most of the participants in rites of remembrance bring with them memories of family members touched by these vast events. This is what enables later generations to commemorate wars or revolutions "as essential parts of their lives."[115] At the same time, commemorated history often exerts a distorting influence on private memory, as we can see in Barack Obama's reference to his uncle liberating Auschwitz or, to a much larger extent, in Andocides' recollection of his (aristocratic) ancestors' services to the Athenian democracy.[116] Sometimes, however, remembered history can also be used to challenge the predominant master narrative of the community.[117]

Collective Memories of the Mythical Past

In the previous section, I have made the case that historical allusions to recent events ought to be included in this study. It is necessary to also look at the other end of the spectrum and decide whether paradigms drawn from the mythical period should be considered in this study of the orators' use of the past.[118] There are various reasons for their inclusion.

First, fifth- and fourth-century Greeks regarded stories that we would classify as mythical (i.e., as unhistorical or fictitious) as accounts of their past; not even Thucydides, the father of critical historiography, casts any doubt on the historicity of the Trojan War or the reign of King Theseus.[119] Even though the Attic orators usually acknowledged the Herodotean division of the past into a mythical and historical period (Hdt. 1.5, 3.122) and distinguished between

114. Fentress & Wickham (1992) 100–101. The Rock War of Kalymnos provides an excellent example. This 1935 clash between Italian *carabinieri* and the women of this Greek island is remembered differently by participants, by men and women, and in its local and national context. For a detailed discussion, see Alcock (2002) 11–13; Sutton (1998) 79–98.

115. Winter (2001) 12522.

116. For Andocides, see R. Thomas (1989) 139–44. For Obama's erroneous historical reference, see note 97 above. The fact that the name *Auschwitz* has become a synonym for the Holocaust in U.S. collective memory (as well as the insufficient familiarity with European geography) might explain the substitution of Auschwitz for the widely unknown subcamp Ohrdruf in the family memory of the exploits of Obama's great-uncle Charlie Payne.

117. See R. Thomas (1989) 237. Aeschines, for instance, challenges the chauvinistic Athenian master narrative by pointing to the city's foolish mistakes during the Peloponnesian War. To corroborate his assertions, he names his father and uncle as authoritative sources for these memories (Aeschin. 2.74–78); cf. "Different Memory Communities" in chapter 1, 70–84.

118. For a concise discussion of the nature of Greek myth with further bibliography, see Bremmer (1987b).

119. Cf. Thuc. 1.9–12 (on the Trojan War), 2.15 (on Theseus' synoecism of Attica). See Grethlein (2007) 363.

examples from the distant and the recent pasts, this distinction is never clear-cut, and the border between myth and history is rather fluid.[120]

Second, these myths fulfill the same social function as collective memories of historical events. These myths were an integral element of the communal memory of the different social groups that populated Attica. They aided the Athenians in understanding "who they were, where they had come from, why they worshipped the gods they worshipped or had the institutions they had."[121] Aristocratic families increased their social status and prestige by claiming descent from famous Homeric heroes.[122] Local heroes functioned as eponyms for fictive kinship groups or local communities.[123] While some of these claims date far back into the archaic period, others, such as those involving the Cleisthenic tribal heroes, were rather recent and represent examples of "invented traditions."[124] All of these heroes had mythical stories attached to them that provided the members of the group with a shared image of their past and fostered group identity.[125] The social memory of these mythical heroes was manifested and transmitted by, among other things, religious cults and festivals, which deserve special attention when dealing with the orators' allusions to the mythical past.[126]

Third, in oratorical practice, there is no essential difference between paradigms drawn from the mythical period as opposed to the historical one. The paradigmatic function is the same: both feats, the repulse of the Amazons in the time of Theseus and the victory over the Persians at Marathon, were equally able to symbolize Athens' "timeless" character as champion of the Greeks; and indeed, both examples were used by Athenian speakers in diplomatic contexts.[127] This is evident, for instance, from the Athenians' argument for the priv-

---

120. Gotteland (2001) 94–102; Perlman (1961) 158–59; Loraux (1986) 136–37; Todd (2008) 212. On the "antiquity" of myth, see, for instance, Aeschin. 2.31; Isoc. 4.30, 68; Lycurg. 83. For "ancient" times contrasted to "what is more recent," see Thuc. 1.73.2; Dem. 23.65, 60.8–9; Isoc. 6.24, 42. Cf. Parker (1996) 227.

121. Harding (2008) 3. Cf. Gehrke (2001) 286, 297–306; Krummen (1993) 215.

122. Miltiades, for instance, traced back his ancestry to Ajax's son Philaeus. Before the use of writing, aristocratic families remembered only three or four recent generations (cf. Aleida Assmann's "remembered history") and the heroic ancestor. This "floating gap" was eventually closed through the construction of full genealogies that involved manipulation, adding new generations and incorporating ancestors who were remembered in a vacuum; cf. R. Thomas (1989) 155–73.

123. Melite, for instance, functioned as eponymous heroine for the Attic *deme* Melite (Philochorus *FGrHist* 328 F 27), and Munichus (*IG* II^2 4590) had his sanctuary in the harbor Munichia in the Piraeus. Both had their own mythology; cf. Kearns (1989) 184–87.

124. For a comprehensive discussion of Attic heroes, see Kearns (1989). For the Cleisthenic tribal heroes, see Kron (1976); Parker (1996) 102–21; G. Anderson (2003) 123–34.

125. For the social functions of tribal heroes, see Parker (1996) 120–21; Kearns (1989) 86–92. For an example of the interplay of cult and mythology, see Parker (2005) 446.

126. Cf. "Cults and Festivals" in chapter 1, 65–69.

127. Cf. Clarke (2008) 289–90.

ilege to command the left wing at Plataea (Hdt. 9.27).[128] There are many other instances where speakers indiscriminately use examples from both the mythical and historical pasts. Urging the Spartans to conclude peace, the Athenian ambassador Callias mentions the shared distress about the recent destruction of Plataea and Thespiae (allies of Athens and Sparta during the Persian Wars) and reminds them of the benefits Heracles received from the mythical king Triptolemus (Xen. *Hell.* 6.3.4–6). Similarly, in diplomatic negotiations with Philip of Macedon, Aeschines claims the city of Amphipolis for Athens by arguing that this area had first been acquired by Theseus' son Acamas and had recently been confirmed as Athenian possession by Philip's father and others at a congress in Athens (Aeschin. 2.31–33).[129] Aristotle's *Rhetoric* further confirms that mythical and historical examples were used side by side in oratorical practice.

> How could we praise [the Athenians], if we did not know of the naval engagement at Salamis or the battle of Marathon, or what was done on behalf of the Heraclidae, and other similar things?[130] (Arist. *Rh.* 1396a12–14)

This shows that in Athenian social memory, the aid to the children of Heracles was on par with the historic victories at Marathon and Salamis.

Constitutive Elements of Social Memory

To sum up, drawing on the work of Loraux, Gehrke, Jung, Alcock, Thomas, Wolpert, and Assmann, I will use the concept of social memory in its broadest sense for my investigation of the role of the past in Athenian public discourse. I regard both the *communicative aspect* of sharing memories of the past and their *social relevance* for the members of a group as constitutive elements of the concept. In view of this definition, this study will need to consider the collective memory of events ranging from the mythical to the most recent past. Moreover, both the memories cherished by the entire polis community and those shared by smaller subgroups are part of the Athenian memorial framework. Consequently, both "remembered" and "commemorated" history ought to be

128. Higbie (1997) discusses the Athenians' and Spartans' negotiation with Gelon (Hdt. 7.159, 7.161.3) and the Athenian-Tegean dispute at Plataea (Hdt. 9.26–27) and emphasizes the great authority attributed by the Greeks to arguments from the mythical past.

129. For the use of myth in classical Greek diplomatic and political discourse, see Markle (1976); J. K. Davies (1993) 162; Parker (1996) 226–27; C. P. Jones (1999) 6–35; Natoli (2004a) 66–73. For the Hellenistic period, Gehrke (2001) 295 argues that "[m]yth and history had the same status" in *poleis* diplomacy. For the Athenian claim to Amphipolis, see Rhodes (2010) 232–33.

130. Grimaldi (1988) 281; Allan (2001) 25–26 note 21.

taken into account.[131] Demosthenes' previously cited allusions to the Persian War battles (Dem. 18.208) obviously qualify, since he recalls to the jurors events that have been memorialized by a variety of means (monuments, public commemorations, rituals, etc.). These battles function as *lieux de mémoire* and are deeply meaningful for the Athenian self-image.[132] Yet, the personal recollection of one of Lysias' clients fulfills both criteria (social relevance and communicative aspect) as well (Lys. fr. 286 Carey). This Athenian recalls in court how he and other Athenian exiles found asylum and support in the house of the otherwise unknown Theban Cephisodotus during the tyranny of the Thirty. This memory is certainly meaningful to him and his fellow exiles, since their Theban host aided them in their struggle against the Thirty (Lys. fr. 286.2). It also lies at the heart of the guest-friendship relationship between his family and his benefactor's.[133] It was this very memory, he claims, that drove him to action when, after the Spartan capture of the Cadmea in 382, Cephisodotus' son Pherenicus sought refuge in Athens (Lys. fr. 286.3). This passage allows us to observe how the private memory cherished by a small group was shared with a wider Athenian audience in the law courts. By mentioning the time of exile, it prompted and thus reinforced the widely shared collective memory of the rise and fall of the Thirty. Yet, at the same time, it also functioned, to some extent, as a corrective to the patriotic master narrative that by and large ignored the aid of the Thebans and usually begins the story of the democrats' glorious return with Thrasybulus' capture of Phyle.[134]

Social Memory in Athenian Public Discourse

So far, I have discussed some general characteristics of social memory and delineated my use of the concept in relation to other studies of the Greeks' memorial framework. In this section, I turn to the role that social memory played in Athenian public discourse and decision making. After a short exposi-

131. See also Fentress & Wickham (1992) x, for a similarly broad definition of "commemoration" (i.e., the public and social side of memory) as "the *action* of speaking or writing about memories, as well as the formal re-enaction of the past that we usually mean when we use the word."

132. Jung (2006).

133. See "*Xenia* and *Proxenia*" in chapter 1, 80–84.

134. Cf. chapter 4. For a modern example of how the shared memory of a small group could be used to challenge the prevalent master narrative, see the 1997 debate of the German parliament concerning the controversial exhibition *War of Annihilation: Crimes of the Wehrmacht, 1941–44*. Challenging the exhibition's verdict of the Wehrmacht as a criminal institution, the conservative leader Theo Waigel drew on his childhood memories to argue that the majority of soldiers had been honorable men of integrity: he recalled how, at the end of the war, Oskar Blümm, a general of the Wehrmacht stationed near Waigel's hometown, courageously protected the remaining inmates of a hospital for the mentally ill from murderous SS units. Cf. Thiele (1997) 206; Nolan (2001).

tion of my notion of public discourse and decision making, I will introduce my main sources, the Attic orators and the speeches in Xenophon's *Hellenica,* and briefly discuss previous approaches to the orators' historical allusions, before I set out my own methodological principles.

Social memory in classical Athens was constituted and transmitted in a variety of ways. The polis as a whole represented an idealized version of the past to itself in various public forums, such as public festivals and commemorations, monuments, dramatic plays, and the assembly and law courts. At the same time, different subgroups cherished their own traditions, which might either concur or compete with one another or with the Athenian master narrative. To get a sense of this complex memorial framework, one ought to take each of these carriers of social memory into account. Yet, in order to observe the negotiation of different versions of the past and assess the role they played in actual policy decisions, we have to turn to one specific area of Athenian public discourse, that is, the *political* discourse of the assembly and the law courts.[135]

Public Discourse and Decision Making

In a study that involves such allusive subject matter as people's memories and motives for action, I intend to be explicit about my underlying assumptions concerning the nature of collective memories, political discourse, and decision making. My premise is that social memory serves a double function in political debates. It provides a pool of collective experience for the perception and analysis of present realities, but it also serves as a repository of symbols and metaphors for the communication and illustration of a given problem to others and for effectively persuading the citizenry to pursue a particular policy to solve it.

For my analysis, I build on Ober's semiotic model of political discourse. In his study of mass and elite communication in classical Athens, he describes the role of symbols and metaphors in public discourse in general.

> Communication between the members of a society, especially in the context of political decision making, will make use of symbols (metaphors, signs) which refer to and derive from ideology. . . . The theoretical basis for this statement ultimately derives from a semiotic model of cognitive psychology that assumes that the human mind works through the process of analogy by means of symbols or metaphors. Thought and perception, and therefore language, are symbolic and metaphoric; thus,

135. For "political discourse" as "public discourse" in the narrow sense, see C. Calhoun (2001) 12594.

> communication is based on complex and intertwined symbolic references and cross-references.[136]

Ober furthermore asserts that the recipients of these symbolic and metaphorical messages will judge the soundness of the argument and the trustworthiness of the speaker on the basis of their own set of values and beliefs: "An individual's decisions, actions, and judgment of his or her fellows will be based, at least in part, upon ideology and symbolic communication."[137]

Ober's assumptions concerning the role of symbols and metaphors in discourse in general can easily be applied to the specific symbols and metaphors derived from a community's collective memory. Apart from their importance for the perception and illustration of a current problem, a third function of these symbols (not mentioned by Ober) is worth emphasizing. Social memory creates feelings of identity and group solidarity. As a result, symbols derived from social memory carry "heavy emotional weight."[138]

Accordingly, social memory functions as "symbolic capital," which is used by political leaders to create representations of the world in the past and present that others are willing to follow.[139] As Geertz, Bourdieu, and other adherents of Durkheim have argued, determinants in politics include not only material forces and common interests but also symbols, which are used to imagine and represent political groups and institutions and are employed to both legitimate and undermine the political status quo.[140] But the exact meaning of these symbols and the collective memories from which they derive are never fixed and can be contested, modified, and reinterpreted at any time by political agents struggling for dominance in the realm of symbolic capital.[141]

People in leadership positions often utilize the symbolic capital derived from their community's collective memory to garner support for particular policies.[142] At times, however, politicians advocate policies that seem to be at odds with the values and beliefs of their political community. In these cases, we

136. Ober (1989) 40.

137. Ober (1989) 41.

138. Kertzer (2001) 13175.

139. For symbolic processes and capital, see Bourdieu (1991); S. Harrison (1995); Apter (2001). Apter analyses the role of symbolic capital within political discourse.

140. Cf. Fortes & Evans-Pritchard (1940); Geertz (1985); Bourdieu (1991); S. Harrison (1995); Kertzer (2001). The theory of the politics of memory that focuses on the cultivation and invention of public rituals and traditions as modes of social control has first been explored by Hobsbawm & Ranger (1983). For a critique of this presentist approach to social memory, see Misztal (2003) 56–61.

141. Fentress & Wickham (1992) 129 characterize social memory as the "substructure of national historical consciousness, a largely uncontrollable rhetorical field inside which all political actors themselves have to operate."

142. Cf. Demosthenes in his *Second Philippic* (Dem. 6.7–12). See "Treacherous by Nature" in chapter 2, 143–49.

can see how political speakers use elaborate arguments to challenge commonly held views and we can see how they try to redefine the lessons to be drawn from the group's shared historical experience.

A good example of such an attempt could be observed at the extraordinary convention of the German Green Party on May 13, 1999, when the Green foreign minister Joschka Fischer sought his party's approval for the German participation in NATO's military intervention in Kosovo.[143] The Green Party, founded in 1980 by environmental and pacifist movements, had a strong antimilitaristic ideology.[144] Fascism, World War II, and the Holocaust were remembered as abhorrent crimes leading to the conviction "War, never again! Auschwitz, never again! Genocide, never again! Fascism, never again!"[145] Fischer used his party's collective memory of the Nazi past and its symbolic meaning, but he redefined it to support his policy of military intervention.[146] Whereas the two maxims "War, never again!" and "Auschwitz, never again!" were originally understood almost as a tautology, indicating the two sides of one coin and expressing Green pacifism vigorously, Fischer separated these two lessons from the past and made the prevention of Auschwitz and genocide the main priority.[147] By using the loaded terms *ethnische Kriegsführung* and *völkische Politik*[148] for Milosevic's policies, Fischer equated the Yugoslav regime with German Nazism. In so doing, he employed the symbolic meaning his party attributed to Auschwitz to show the necessity of military intervention in Kosovo in order to stop another genocide. The pacifist component "War, never again!" was thereby separated and ranked as secondary. For his attempt to modify his party's memory of the Nazi era and its meaning for the present situation, Fischer could fall back on the collective memory of German conservatives. In their eyes, the lesson to be drawn from the experience of World War II is different and does not generally forbid German military interventions.[149]

My endeavor to assess the influence of arguments from social memory on

143. See Erp (2003) 169. For Fischer's speech, see online at http://www.mediaculture-online.de/fileadmin/bibliothek/fischerjoschka_kosovorede/fischer_kosovorede.pdf.

144. Cf. the *Grundsatzprogramm* from 1980 and the *Offenbacher Friedensmanifest* from 1981.

145. Cf. Fischer's pledge to the credo of the Green party: "Aber in mir—ich stehe auf zwei Grundsätzen: Nie wieder Krieg, nie wieder Auschwitz; nie wieder Völkermord, nie wieder Faschismus: beides gehört bei mir zusammen. Und deswegen bin ich in die Grüne Partei gegangen."

146. For Fischer's earlier attempts to reshape the Green Party's collective memory and ideology in light of the atrocities in Bosnia in 1995, see Erp (2003) 164.

147. For the role of collective memory in this German policy debate, see also Markovits & Reich (1997) 11.

148. Fischer's use of the term *völkische* is especially remarkable. Owing to its strong associations with Nazi ideology, it is no longer used in contemporary German discourse. By employing Nazi terminology to characterize Milosevic's policies, he implicitly equates Milosevic to Hitler.

149. In "Challenging the Master Narrative" in chapter 2, 149–54, I make the case that Demosthenes, similarly, challenged the Athenian master narrative of the Thebans as archetypical medizers.

actual policy decisions in fourth-century Athens presupposes that such arguments did in fact play a significant role, which is an assumption not all scholars share. Many ancient historians seem to adhere to a model of politics that considers the maximization of self-interest the primary, if not the only, factor in politics—a theory that, applied to the international arena, became famous under the name of Realism. Realism downplays international law, morality, domestic politics, and the possibility of interdependence and views states as the prime actors in a hostile anarchic environment, in which they incessantly pursue power and security according to rational criteria of self-interest.[150] Many historical studies of fourth-century Greece apply these principles of *Realpolitik* to explain the reasons for the various shifts in the diplomatic policies and military alliances that took place in this volatile century.[151]

Our sources leave no doubt that participants in the debates frequently used historical analogies, invoked the ancestors' heroic achievements, or pleaded to repay former benefactions. Such arguments are, nevertheless, not taken fully into consideration as historical factors.[152] They are often dismissed as merely "rhetorical," that is, as empty phrases that are used by the speakers to conceal self-serving interests and are irrelevant for the explanation of a chosen course of action.[153] The prevalence of this explanatory model is not surprising, given the powerful influence exerted by one of Realism's acclaimed founding fathers, Thucydides, who identified Sparta's fear of Athens' growing power as the "truest yet least talked about reason" for the Peloponnesian War (Thuc. 1.23.6). It would be a mistake, however, to reduce Thucydides' multifaceted historical account to a confirmation of Realist theory.[154] Thucydides' interest in power politics is undeniable. Yet, just because he viewed self-interest as an important political force does not mean that other factors did not play a role as well. His Mytilenaean debate is a case in point. Both of his set speeches are based on arguments of expediency. Yet he himself lets us know that the Athenians regarded the previous day's decision as "cruel and excessive" and that, in the

150. Cf. Morgenthau (1948); Waltz (1959); Markovits & Reich (1997) 8–10; Ober (2001) 274–75; Stein (2001); Kegley & Wittkopf (2004) 35–42.

151. Cf. Mosley (1971); Hamilton (1979); Cartledge (1987); Buckler (1980), (2003); Buck (1998); Buckler & Beck (2008). Badian's (1995) exploration of the impact of the memory of fifth-century imperialism on fourth-century Athenian foreign policy is a welcome exception.

152. Admittedly, some historians do mention such arguments, if they are reflected in our sources. But they usually do not ascribe much significance to them. Cf. Hamilton (1979) 150–51; Cartledge (1987) 283; Buck (1998) 68–70. See the discussion of Thebes' volte-face following the Peloponnesian War in "The Situation in Thebes in 404/3" in chapter 4, 215–32.

153. See, for instance, Hamilton (1979) 201–2, analyzing the speech the Theban ambassadors delivered in Athens in 395 BC (Xen. *Hell.* 3.5.8–15). Hamilton appreciates its Realist arguments but dismisses the rest as "rhetorical or tendentious."

154. Low (2007) 16–21; Ober (2001).

renewed debate, "different opinions were expressed on both sides of the issue" (Thuc. 3.36) before Cleon and Diodotus took the stage. Based on what we know of political speeches in the fifth and fourth centuries, those unnamed speakers very likely made conventional appeals to the Athenians' sense of pity and justice.[155]

Another reason why the Realist paradigm is so attractive to ancient historians might lie in the fact that its principles (maximization of self-interest, pursuit of power and security, alliances and balance of power) seem universally applicable and do not require us to consider more subjective factors, such as people's memories and beliefs. Granted, it is difficult to reconstruct the collective memory of people in the past, but this should not lead us "to erase the presence and power of the past from their lives."[156]

Undeniably, political decisions are largely based on considerations of self-interest, and fourth-century public speakers did make such arguments.[157] Yet individuals and collectives generally tend to consider other, not strictly utilitarian factors as well, such as issues of morality, self-image, and prestige.[158] Recent studies have shown, for instance, that in Greek culture, reciprocity is a normative principle that governs the relationships between individuals as well as states.[159] Consequently, when promoting an alliance, public speakers recall past benefactions that ought to be repaid.[160] In this form, arguments from social memory hold considerable argumentative and emotive force in political debates. Furthermore, it would be wrong to view considerations of self-interest

155. Hornblower (1991) 419; Pelling (2000) 119, 122. Several speeches in Thucydides also employ arguments from social memory to a large extent. See, for instance, the Plataeans' appeals to the Spartans in 429 and 427 (Thuc. 2.71 and 3.53–59, respectively). Cf. Hornblower (1991) 445.

156. Alcock (2002) 24.

157. To counter Aeschines' moralistic arguments, Demosthenes, for instance, declares that the Athenians saved the Spartans in the 360s not thanks to their virtue but because it was useful (συμφέρον) for Athens (Dem. 19.75). Similarly, Aeschines claims that the Athenian-Theban alliance of 339 should not be credited to Demosthenes; it resulted from the crisis, fear, and Thebes' need for an alliance (Aeschin. 3.237, 239). Isocrates declares expedience (τὸ ὠφέλιμον) to be the main criterion in foreign politics (Isoc. 5.42–45), but only in order to counter the anticipated objection that cities will never be able to overcome the collective memory of their long-standing hatred toward each other (5.39–41). Earlier in this address to Philip, Isocrates himself draws heavily on arguments from collective memory, demonstrating the good services rendered to Philip's ancestor Heracles by Argos, Thebes, Sparta, and Athens (5.32–34).

158. Sometimes they also give in to irrational impulses such as feelings of anger or elation, as Aristotle's excursus about the emotions in book 2 of his *Rhetoric* shows; cf. Kennedy (1991) 122–24. For Demosthenes' evocation of emotions and the importance of honor and prestige in Athenian foreign policy debates, see Montgomery (1983) 105–7. Yunis (2000) makes a convincing case that Demosthenes won the case against Aeschines in 330, precisely because he rejected a success-oriented model of politics and evoked a shared image of the past that resonated with the jurors on an emotional level.

159. Herman (1987) 130–42; Gehrke (2001) 291–92; Low (2007) 36–54.

160. See Xen. *Hell.* 6.3.13 and 6.5.33, 40, 44; Isoc. 14.1, 57.

and moral obligations as *generally* antithetical and incompatible, as Thucydides' Melian dialogue suggests.[161] More often, different kinds of arguments are used that can complement and reinforce each other in the decision-making process. In view of this, it is not surprising that Aristotle's *Rhetoric,* a handbook on the art of public speaking that reflects the fourth-century oratorical praxis, lists various means of persuasion (arguments based on *logos, ethos,* and *pathos*) and accommodates both arguments of expediency (τὸ συμφέρον) and evocations of mutual obligations and justice (τὸ δίκαιον).[162] For historians to focus exclusively on the principles of *Realpolitik* in reconstructing fourth-century foreign politics is, therefore, reductionistic.

Studies of present-day foreign relations confirm that collective memory is indeed a factor to be taken into account. The political scientists Markovits and Reich make a convincing case that contemporary German foreign politics cannot be explained within the realist paradigm. Germany's reticence to take on international responsibilities in accordance with its economic and military abilities is due largely to an ideology "shaped by the collective memory of Germany and its neighbors."[163] Similarly, the traumatic memory of German expansionism and occupation is still so deeply entrenched in the collective historical consciousness of many Europeans that it can cause them to make political decisions contrary to their objective self-interest. The Danes, for instance, voted initially against the ratification of the Maastricht Treaty in June 1992, even though they could expect large economic benefits from the creation of the European Union. Only on the second vote did they overcome their profound suspicion of Germany and vote "with their brains and not their hearts," as one Dane put it.[164]

Another aspect of Markovits and Reich's study is worth mentioning. Over time, neighboring states generally experience phases of intense rivalry and outright war as well as periods of peaceful coexistence and cooperation. As a result, their collective memory comprises both negative and positive views of their neighbors, which are available to buttress either antagonistic or cooperative policies.[165] Most of Germany's neighbors ultimately supported Germany's reunification, thanks particularly to their recent, positive experiences, despite the horrors they had suffered under Nazi occupation. In a similar vein, I will

161. Cf. Low (2007) 160–77.

162. On these three artistic means of persuasion, see Kennedy (1991) 14. Since arguments from social memory are often emotionally charged and thus can fall into the rubrics *ethos* and *pathos,* social memory fits well within Aristotle's framework for persuasion. For the view that justice and expediency are often interdependent and can coincide, see Arist. *Rh.* 1362a20, 1362b28; [Dem.] 7.46; Isoc. 15.79; [Arist.] *Rh. Al.* 1425a10–16. For a lucid discussion of this issue, see Low (2007) 166–73.

163. Markovits & Reich (1997) 4 (for their critique of realism, see 8–14).

164. Markovits & Reich (1997) 26, 96–99.

165. Markovits & Reich (1997) 28.

argue that even though the Thebans generally occupied an overwhelmingly negative place in Athenian historical consciousness due to their alliance with Xerxes (see chap. 2) and their proposal to eradicate Athens (see chap. 5), the Athenians, nevertheless, did not entirely forget Theban aid for the Athenian democrats in 404/3. I will make the case (see chap. 4), that this memory, while precarious, was from time to time revived in Athenian public discourse and helped move the Athenians to conclude the Athenian-Theban alliance of 395 and to offer asylum to Theban refugees after the Spartan seizure of the Cadmea in 382 and after Philip's and Alexander's victories over Thebes in 338 and 335. Considerations of *Realpolitik* surely played an important role in these decisions. I contend that the memory of Thebes' support for the Athenian *demos* in 404/3 was a significant factor in these debates, as it offered the Athenians another good reason to cooperate with their generally despised northern neighbors.[166]

Participant Evidence: The Attic Orators and Their Interpretation

For their study of present-day German and European foreign policy, Markovits and Reich were able to draw on a wealth of data. Comprehensive records of political debates, newspaper articles, and countless opinion polls allowed them to assess the attitudes of both leading politicians and the electorate at large and thus to gauge the influence of collective memory on particular policy decisions. It is much harder for students of ancient history to reconstruct the role the past played in a community's decision making.[167] Sometimes Greek and Roman historians briefly mention collective memories that were, in their view, decisive factors in a particular historical situation. In 371 BC, for instance, the Athenians, according to Xenophon, favored peace negotiations with Sparta because they had grown angry at their Theban ally for "annihilating cities [i.e., Plataea and Thespiae] that had been faithful in the war against the barbarian [i.e., the Persian War of 480–479] and were friendly to Athens" (Xen. *Hell.* 6.3.1). It is even more difficult, however, to observe how *individual* politicians operated within an ancient society's memorial framework and how competing social memories were negotiated and contested in political debates.

In the case of fourth-century Athens, we are extremely fortunate, since the corpus of the ten Attic orators contains the texts of about 140 speeches, most of

166. Given the confines of a monograph and the already existing thorough treatments of *Realpolitik* in the fourth century, I will limit my discussion to the role of social memory in these debates, which I regard as not a replacement of but a complement to, rational calculations of self-interest.

167. Often, those who study ancient history have to put bits and pieces of scarce evidence together just to get a glimpse of what people in the past might have thought about their past. Cf. Alcock (2002).

which were—if not verbatim, then at least in this approximate form—actually delivered in the Athenian assembly, in the law courts, or on public occasions.[168] They can therefore be regarded as "participant evidence" for fourth-century Athenian political discourse.[169] These speeches are full of references to the past and can thus be used for studying both the content of Athenian social memory and its use within the political arena.

For several reasons, I have decided to use speeches from Xenophon's *Hellenica,* even though they certainly do not represent the original speeches verbatim. Xenophon, however, was a contemporary of the events he reports and participated in Athenian memory communities of the fourth century. He was often in a position to witness the speeches he relates or to learn their content from trustworthy sources.[170] But even when he composed speeches himself, we can assume that he was guided by what the speaker in a particular situation would have been likely to say; Xenophon knew Athenian attitudes well enough to apply those arguments from the past that were usually made in the Athenian assembly and that appealed to an Athenian audience. Consequently, his speeches are an important source for reconstructing fourth-century Athenian social memory.[171]

Thanks to their timeless quality as rhetorical masterpieces and their priceless value as participant evidence for fourth-century history, the speeches of the Attic orators have long been a primary object of scholarly attention. Particu-

168. For a complete list of these speeches, see Ober (1989) 341–49. Following MacDowell (2000) 22-26 and Hunt (2010) 270-74, I generally view the extant texts as drafts of the actual speeches, which underwent only minor revisions before publication. For a more pessimistic view concerning the authenticity of the transmitted speeches of the Attic orators, see Worthington (1991b), (1992) 37. He suggests that speeches were heavily revised to impress an elite reading audience with literary sophistication. Wolpert (2002) 146, however, argues correctly that orators, if they revised their speeches before publication, "would not render the published version less persuasive." Instead, they would try to make their speeches more convincing by improving passages that had not pleased the original mass audiences. Consequently, the revised speeches are an even closer reflection of widely shared collective memories and beliefs. Cf. Hunt (2010) 273–74. Isocrates' speeches are a bit more problematic, since most of them were not written for delivery before an actual mass audience. It is evident, however, that his discourses are composed to closely resemble actual speeches; they are structured in the same way, contain the same types of arguments, and draw on the same collective memories as the speeches delivered by other Athenian orators. Cf. Naiden (2006) 182; Clarke (2008) 301. For this reason, it is justified to include them in this investigation.

169. Potter (1999) 22 notes, "Participant evidence is provided by texts purporting to report or influence a specific event, or closely linked series of events, by a person who was involved either as an actor or witness."

170. Cf. Buckler (1982); Dalfen (1976). For an approach to the speeches in Thucydides that is similar to my approach to Xenophon's speeches, see Ober (1989) 46–47; Pelling (2000) 112–22. See also Gotteland (2001) 12–14, who includes historiographical speeches in her analysis of the use of myth in political discourse.

171. Loraux (1986) 133 also noticed Xenophon's Athenocentrism concerning his use of historical examples in a speech delivered in Xen. *An.* 3.2.11–14.

larly, the orators' use of the past has already been studied extensively. Before I set forth the methodological principles of my own approach, a brief discussion of previous interpretations of the orators' historical allusions seems in order. A critical analysis of their underlying assumptions will show that yet another take on this well-known body of evidence is justified.

Three (overlapping) approaches can be discerned.[172] One group of scholars has analyzed historical allusions from the perspective of classical rhetoric, according to which well-known historical examples are to be employed as illustrations of current situations and thus as artful means of persuasion.[173] The examples were supposedly drawn from a more or less rigid set of historical *topoi*.[174] While it is certainly warranted to analyze historical paradigms as part of an orator's rhetorical technique and as formal elements within the overall rhetorical structure of a speech, this approach also has some shortcomings. It presupposes that the orators closely followed the prescriptions of rhetorical theory. Consequently, historical allusions are categorized in an attempt to reconstruct the underlying rhetorical doctrines.[175] These often overly schematic studies ignore that classical rhetoric, which stemmed from the analysis of oratorical praxis, ought to be regarded as a secondary phenomenon.[176] Indeed, it is hard to imagine that Demosthenes tried to fit his speeches into such a theoretical corset.[177] Moreover, there is no evidence for a written collection of historical *topoi* from which the orators would choose, and a rigid set of orally transmitted *topoi* cannot exist due to the fluid and dynamic nature of oral discourse.[178] In addition, by focusing almost exclusively on the speakers' rhetorical techniques, these studies underrate the sociopolitical aspect of the orators' allusions to the past. Due to their frequency, such allusions are often dismissed as empty rhetorical commonplaces. Such a stance, however, ignores that the memories of these events were deeply meaningful to the respective community.[179] A snide remark by the Greek intellectual Plutarch reveals the sustained effectiveness of allusions to the Persian Wars—*the* historical *topos* par excellence—more than

172. For discussion of these approaches, see Perlman (1961) 150–53, (1986) 359; Robertson (1984) 382–83.

173. That fourth-century rhetoricians indeed reflected on the systematic use of historical examples to further the orator's cause is evident from Isocrates (1.34, 2.35, 4.9) and Aristotle's *Rhetoric* (1368a29–30, 1393a26–b2).

174. Worthington (1992) 20.

175. See especially Jost (1935); Nouhaud (1982).

176. Perlman (1961) 150 calls it "a clear example of putting the cart before the horse."

177. Already Dionysius of Halicarnassus showed in his *First Letter to Ammaeus,* on the basis of chronology, that Demosthenes could not have used Aristotle's *Rhetoric.*

178. Perlman (1961) 150–51 convincingly refutes the existence of a rigid set of *topoi.*

179. Ober (1989) 44 notes, "Rhetorical topoi were repeated by different orators over time; they were therefore familiar but certainly not empty of content. Indeed, topoi were reiterated precisely because of their symbolic value and demonstrated power to influence an audience." Wolpert (2002) 139 argues similarly concerning the frequent allusions to the Thirty.

half a millennium after the actual events: public officials were still able to "stir up the multitudes" by recalling Marathon, the Eurymedon, and Plataea, which made "the masses swell and prance about in vain" (Plut. *Mor.* 814a–c).[180]

In a second line of approach, historians have tried to determine the mutual influence of the Greek historians and the Attic orators. Some scholars investigated the extent to which Isocrates' rhetorical theories influenced fourth-century historiography,[181] while others tried to detect the orators' historiographical sources by careful philological analysis. The results of the latter inquiry were rather disappointing, for the orators' version of historical events often diverged considerably from extant historiographical accounts. This has led to the verdict of the orators' "truly astonishing ignorance"[182] of the history of their city. Considering the fact that our main sources for the history of classical Greece consist of a small corpus of literary texts, it is not surprising that intertextual references are a primary object of historical and philological studies. Yet the basic underlying assumption of such an approach—namely, that fourth-century Athenians regarded the works of the historians as an important authority for historical knowledge (or at least should have done so)—has been shown untenable by Rosalind Thomas. She has demonstrated that classical Athens was still predominantly an oral society where the written word had much less authoritative weight than in our modern archive culture.[183] To expect fourth-century Athenian politicians to comply with historiographical standards established by nineteenth-century historians is not only anachronistic but disregards our own experience of the use of the past in contemporary political discourse.[184] Political debates, rather than historiographical works, are therefore the proper backdrop for analyzing and judging Athenian oratory.[185]

A third group of scholars, more sensitive to the political aspects of Athenian oratory, views the orators' historical allusions as a reflection of contemporary political attitudes. In a seminal article, Pearson proposed that the well-educated orators "were willing to respect the prejudices and the sensitiveness"[186] of their ignorant audience and were at pains to avoid giving the impression of lecturing them on history.[187] Other scholars have tried to detect signs of manipulation and propaganda used by the orators to further their immediate political

180. Alcock (2002) 84.

181. Cf. von Scala (1892) 102–21 on Isocrates; Barber (1935) 75–83 on Ephorus; G. Murray (1946) 150–53 on Theopompus.

182. Jacoby *FGrHist* 3b (Suppl.) i.95.

183. See R. Thomas (1989) and my discussion under "Oral Tradition Studies" above, 21–23.

184. Cf. Bach (1977) on historical allusion in contemporary German political discourse.

185. Harding (1987) 36, 38.

186. Pearson (1941) 229.

187. Pearson (1941) 213 ascribes, for instance, the orators' frequent references to family tradition and common knowledge to their anxiety not to display their superior knowledge and their bookish learning. Cf. Blass (1874) 7. Similarly, Ober (1989) 179.

goals.[188] I share with this group of scholars the objective of situating the orators' historical allusions within their own sociopolitical context, yet I disagree with some of their underlying assumptions. Most of these scholars assume that an accurate knowledge of history was available to the orators. History is often seen as "something ready-made, waiting to be 'used' by the orators."[189] Erroneous, inaccurate, and vague accounts are interpreted as either pretended ignorance before the uneducated masses or as conscious distortion and political propaganda. Certainly, Athenian politicians used the past to their own advantage; yet to regard every discrepancy as a willful manipulation, motivated by the orator's self-interest, ignores two crucial points.[190]

First, given the communicative conditions of fourth-century Athens, we cannot assume that the orators had a definite knowledge of what happened in the past, which they then deliberately distorted to manipulate their audiences. Social memories are fluid and dynamic. Memory studies show that, apart from deliberate falsification, there is a host of alternative and equally plausible explanations for the distortions in the orators' representations of the past.[191] Consequently, I shrink from using the term *propaganda* in this context, since it is so closely associated with the modern phenomenon of mass communication and manipulation.[192] There is no question that the Attic orators vigorously advocated and promoted their ideas and policies and tried to sway public opinion by any means possible; yet political propaganda and demagoguery are two phenomena that belong more to the history of totalitarian regimes in the twentieth century, with its archival and technical possibilities, than to fourth-century Athens.[193]

188. On the orators' manipulation and political propaganda, see especially Perlman (1961); Nouhaud (1982); Harding (1987); Worthington (1994a); Weißenberger (1996); Paulsen (1999). Similarly, Allroggen (1972) ascribes the orators' differing views of historical figures and events to their respective political affiliation. Adopting Pearson's (1941) approach, Milns (1995) surveys the historical paradigms in Demosthenes' public speeches.

189. Robertson (1984) 381, on Nouhaud (1982).

190. Worthington (1994a) 109 offers a verdict that is emblematic for this view: "That the accuracy of the historical information contained in speeches by the Greek orators is open to doubt is no small understatement. . . . [T]he orators lie, distort, deliberately deceive, suppress the truth, and prevaricated as a matter of course." Similarly, Harding (1987) 38 notes, "In short, they were liars and cheats and their words cannot be trusted on any topic, unless supported by independent evidence."

191. For a critique of such "cynical" interpretations of modern U.S. memory distortions, cf. Kammen (1995) 329–30. See also Schudson (1995) 360 and the section "Ideology and Social Memory" above, 13–19.

192. Similarly, R. Thomas (1989) 206 note 39: "The term 'propaganda' is misleading because it implies (i) systematic dissemination and (ii) that the disseminators know their propaganda to be untrue. In the context of oral transmission, both orators and audience had little means of distinguishing mere propaganda from Athenian history." Exploring the use of myth as propaganda, Bremmer (1997) draws on this modern concept but links it closely to the concept of social memory.

193. For the pejorative connotation of the term *propaganda,* see Chaffee (2001) 9326. As a

Second, most of these scholars focus on the role of the speaker. Yet we should keep in mind that it was the orator's objective to convince his listeners, who would base their decisions on his credibility.[194] Even if an orator was aware of diverging versions in Herodotus or Thucydides,[195] he was likely to follow a more widely shared version, since his recounting of a specific event was "checked" by the expectations and memory of his audience.[196] Moreover, I assert that the widespread assumption that the orators' historical allusions reveal a low level of historical knowledge among common Athenians is misconceived. The fact that regular Athenians had a less accurate view of Athenian history than Herodotus or Thucydides does not mean that they did not care about their past. Quite the opposite is the case, as this monograph seeks to demonstrate.

One concrete example should suffice to illustrate the difficulties in how best to approach the orators' historical allusions. In 343 BC, in his indictment of his fellow ambassador Aeschines, Demosthenes decried the pitiful fate of the Phocians, whose towns had been demolished at the end of the Third Sacred War (356–346 BC). He concluded his description of the Phocians' pathetic plight with the words

> And yet, that these men [i.e., the Phocians] once voted against the Thebans when they made a proposal for our enslavement, I hear from you all [ὑμῶν ἔγωγ' ἀκούω πάντων]. (Dem. 19.65)

When dealing with the orators' historical paradigms, the first (obvious) task is to determine which event an orator is alluding to. Here, Demosthenes is referring to an incident that happened sixty-one years earlier, at the end of the Peloponnesian War in 404 BC. Xenophon reports that the Spartans and

---

result of the rise of *Ideologiekritik* in Germany after the "1968 Revolution," German classicists are particularly fond of exposing the orators' manipulations. See, for instance, Paulsen (1999) 17, on the goals of his commentary on Dem. 19 and Aeschin. 2: "Und vielleicht das Wichtigste: Beide Reden sind exemplarisch für die Wirkungsweisen von politischer Propaganda und Demagogie, deren Mechanismen zu durchleuchten und Gefahren zu erkennen von überzeitlichem Interesse ist."

194. Ober (1989) 43–44 points to the orator's duty, as prescribed in Aristotle's *Rhetoric*, to "accommodate himself to the ethos—the ideology—of his audience." This also applies to social memory, which is closely linked and intertwined with ideology.

195. Rosalind Thomas (1989) 201–2 argues against the notion that the orators possessed superior knowledge and consciously "descended to an alien level of historical ignorance purely for the gratification of their audience."

196. R. Thomas (1989) 200; Clarke (2008) 300, 303.Wolpert (2002) xiii notes, "The stakes in deliberative and forensic oratory were too high for a speaker to risk professing values that the audience did not endorse." This also applies to attitudes concerning past events. Harding (1987) 37 emphasizes that most Athenians "were well informed about contemporary affairs" and that the orator, therefore, "had to show that he was conversant with the details, if he was to maintain his credibility as a political adviser."

their allies were discussing the terms of Athens' surrender at a conference in Sparta, when

> the Corinthians and Thebans in particular, but also many other Greeks, spoke against making a treaty with the Athenians and proposed to destroy their city. The Lacedaemonians, however, refused to enslave a Greek city that had done great service in the greatest dangers that had befallen Greece. (Xen. *Hell.* 2.2.19–20)

The proposed annihilation of Athens is frequently evoked in the extant speeches of the Attic orators, but Demosthenes' allusion is our earliest reference to the role of the Phocians. As a result, previous commentators find Demosthenes' assertion "I hear from you all" baffling, quickly dismissing it as "a simple phrase without any particular weight,"[197] as a rhetorical trick employed by a clever politician to make his innovation acceptable to his audience. Demosthenes' rhetorical strategy is clear enough. He masterfully contrasts the recent destruction of the Phocians with their (alleged) opposition to the proposed destruction of Athens; Athens' failure to reciprocate and do the same for the Phocians in 346 is squarely placed on Aeschines' shoulders (Dem. 19.64–66).[198]

Orators indeed frequently employ phrases like "as you all know" or "as you all remember" in their references to the past. In his *Rhetoric,* Aristotle comments on the suggestive power of this *topos:* even if the listener is not familiar with a particular fact, he will agree with the speaker out of embarrassment at his ignorance of what was supposedly common knowledge (Arist. *Rh.* 1408a32–36).[199] Consequently, commentators suspect conscious manipulation on the part of the orator whenever this phrase accompanies a new or (to us) unknown version of past events.[200] Yet, while the "you all know" *topos* could indeed have this effect, it does not follow that the audience is necessarily unfamiliar with the incident in question. This is evident from the fact that this very *topos* is also used for such notorious events as the Trojan War or the Persian Wars.[201]

197. Nouhaud (1982) 306 notes, "Il est plus curieux que le fait soit très connu au point que Démosthène puisse affirmer: ὑμῶν ἔγωγ' ἀκούω πάντων. Il s'agit sans doute encore d'une simple formule sans portée particulière." Nouhaud concedes, however, that the Phocians might have been among the unnamed majority of cities that ultimately followed the Spartans in their refusal to destroy Athens. Similarly, Weil (1883) 269; Paulsen (1999) 123.

198. In his rhetorical categorization of the orators' historical allusions, Nouhaud (1982) 78 note 218 lists this paradigm under the rubric "Confrontation de deux situations."

199. See Pearson (1941) 215–19; Ober (1989) 149–50, 180.

200. Cf. Pelling (2000) 28–29, who calls this the "truth universally acknowledged" ploy. For the "only a topos" fallacy, see Rhodes (1994) 157–58.

201. See, for instance, Lycurg. 62 (Troy), 75 (Persian Wars); Isoc. 6.99–100 (Thermopylae). Concerning Demosthenes' use of this topos, Pearson (1941) 219 admits that "the great majority of

Similarly, since speakers frequently point to the memory of older citizens when introducing historical paradigms, such prefatory remarks have been seen as the orator's way to avoid "giving the impression that he knew more about the past than the average citizen."[202] It is true that these remarks shift the corroborating authority away from the speaker and thus convey a measure of modesty. Yet we cannot invert the argument and conclude that since this *topos* is employed, the incident must have been unfamiliar to the audience. In Athens, the elders were indeed the most important and authoritative source for knowledge of the past.

For these reasons, we should not dismiss references to the elders or the "as you all know" *topos* a priori but should further investigate whether the orator's claim to recall a widely known collective memory might in fact be true. Concerning Demosthenes' Phocian paradigm, I will argue that it is indeed likely that Demosthenes had "heard it from them all" in 343.[203] The outcome of this investigation can shed new light on the effectiveness of this particular historical example. If we are able to determine how Demosthenes' contemporaries felt about the memory of their proposed annihilation and what they thought about the proponents and opponents of this plan, we are in a much better position to gauge how this argument might have resonated with his audience.

Procedure and Methodological Principles

As I mentioned earlier in this introduction, a survey of the corpus of the Attic orators and the speeches in Xenophon's *Hellenica* shows that fourth-century allusions to Thebes cluster around four particular events, each discussed in a separate chapter in this book: Thebes' medizing in 480–479 (chap. 2), the mythical story of the burial of the fallen Argives (chap. 3), Thebes' support for the Athenian democrats in 403 (chap. 4), and the Theban proposal to eradicate Athens in 404 (chap. 5). Each chapter begins with a brief discussion of the extant oratorical references to the event in question, which will reveal their most striking features. In each case, I explore how the event was perceived by contemporaries, why and how it was remembered, and how this memory was transmitted down to the time of the speakers.[204] It will become apparent that

his historical allusions are to famous events and characters in Athenian history, of which the patriotic Athenian certainly liked to be reminded."

202. Ober (1989) 181. Cf. Pearson (1941) 217–19.

203. For a full discussion of this particular allusion, see "The Role of the Phocians" in chapter 5, 331–36. I will make the case that, since listing former benefactions was a regular feature of Greek diplomatic discourse, references to the Phocians' vote against the Theban proposal to eradicate Athens were probably a regular part of the Phocians' lobbying for Athenian support during the Third Sacred War (356–346) and were therefore indeed as familiar to the Athenians by 343 as Demosthenes claims.

204. The mythical chapter 3 on the burial of the fallen Argives is the obvious exception, since

this process could vary considerably depending on the nature of the particular memory.

The memory of Thebes' medizing, examined in chapter 2, was so intrinsically linked to the Athenian self-image after the Persian Wars that a variety of means transformed it from "remembered" to "commemorated" history. Young Athenians learned about the Athenian and Theban roles in the Persian Wars as part of the official polis tradition in regular, polis-wide public commemorations and festivals, while landmarks, monuments, and inscriptions functioned as material reminders and constituted the Athenian *cadre matériel.*

In chapter 3, I examine the constitutive elements of the mythical story of the Athenian intervention on behalf of the Seven against Thebes and explore the reasons why—out of the enormous pool of Greek myths—this particular collective memory came to be one of the four paradigmatic myths celebrated in the Athenian master narrative of the funeral orations. A study of the various carriers of this collective memory, including local cults, the tragic stage, and pictorial representations, will show that it was seen as a prefiguration of the hegemonic Athenian self-image, derived from the Persian War experience. Its frequent use by fifth- and fourth-century speakers reveals the importance of collective memories from the mythical period in Greek inter*poleis* diplomacy. Owing to the enduring Athenian-Theban enmity throughout most of the classical period, the memories of Thebes' medism and its coercion by Athens to return the bodies of the fallen Argives remained socially relevant for the Athenians and ensured their transmission to younger generations.

The memory of Thebes' aid for the democratic exiles around Thrasybulus, discussed in chapter 4, was much more precarious. Due to the long-standing Athenian-Theban antagonism, we do not find any polis-wide efforts to commemorate this generous Theban act in Athens. Since memories fade without repeated retrieval, private memories and the assembly and law courts were of paramount importance for the preservation of this memory. Based on various clues, I argue that former democratic exiles (bound by the norms of guest-friendship) were able to reinstill this latent memory in Athenian public discourse on various occasions throughout the fourth century, when Athenian aid for Thebes was under discussion. This is to be expected in a society where repaying former benefactions is a normative principle in personal and inter-*poleis* relations.[205] Moreover, social memory studies show that similar political

it is not based on a historical event. But even in this case, we can examine partial shifts in emphasis and the various means of transmission of this collective memory.

205. Similarly, Rosalind Thomas (1989) 247 suggests that the Spartan request for Athenian aid during the Helot revolt of 462 might have been responsible for keeping the memory of their role in ousting the Peisistratids alive in fifth-century Athens.

constellations can refresh the memory of otherwise forgotten events. The arrival of Theban refugees in Athens after the capture of the Cadmea by a Spartan-backed junta could thus prompt the memory of Theban assistance to Athenian refugees in Thebes at the time of the Thirty. Drawing on these characteristics of social memory, I am able to explain how this precarious memory was transmitted from 404 down to 323, where it first appears in our extant texts.

In chapter 5, I make the case that the traumatic experience surrounding Athens' surrender was responsible for the unusual persistence of the memory of Athens' proposed eradication in 404. Furthermore, I will argue that the general Greek concept of a ritual city destruction by a Greek alliance, as it was remembered for the case of Crisa, played a role both in the actual discussion of Athens' fate and in the preservation of this memory beyond the boundaries of Athens. Consequently, Thebes' advocacy for the annihilation of Athens as well as its medism were common knowledge throughout the fourth century and, not surprisingly, were marshaled by Alexander the Great to justify his destruction of Thebes in 335.

In each chapter, I compare the extant historical allusions to one another but also to the actual historical events, as far as we can reconstruct them with the help of historiographical sources, material evidence, and analytical reasoning. This allows us to see distortions more clearly, but it is, admittedly, also a tricky endeavor. I do not want to fall back into the earlier scholarly paradigm that viewed the Greek historians as the guardians of an almost Rankean truth; after all, they operated within the same communicative framework as their contemporaries, the orators.[206] Yet there are distinct differences between the genres of historiography and oratory. The orators' goal was persuasion, and social memories were employed for the purpose of winning the argument. The Greek historians investigated the past and tried to promote what they regarded as the historical truth; often, they responded to and reacted against other historians.[207] This does not presume that they always provide a trustworthy and historically accurate account, but their report is usually much more detailed and "the one generally accepted by historians as most reliable."[208] Yet their versions should be accepted not at face value but only after a careful historical analysis that takes into account other testimonies and the historical context of the event in question. Such testimonies also include the much later reports of Diodorus Siculus and Plutarch in cases where their accounts are known to be derived

206. Marincola (2007) 105–6.

207. See, for instance, Thucydides' correction of two misapprehensions "of the other Greeks" concerning the votes of the Spartan kings and the Pitanate division (Thuc. 1.20.3), which is undoubtedly aimed at Herodotus. Cf. Hornblower (1991) 57–58.

208. R. Thomas (1989) 7.

from contemporary sources, such as the fourth-century Oxyrhynchus historian and Ephorus.[209] The juxtaposition of the orators' versions with ancient and modern reconstructions of the events can reveal certain distortions. By taking into account the workings and processes of social memory, I try to explain various deformations in the process of transmission.[210]

Naturally, not all of the orators' historical allusions were equally familiar to their audiences. I will use internal and external clues to assess how widely known a specific social memory was and how much argumentative and emotive force it possessed. The way in which an orator alluded to a particular event can thereby serve as an internal indicator of its familiarity. Persian War memories, for instance, were so prevalent that the names of the battlefields were sufficient to evoke the symbolic meaning of these quintessential events, as seen in Demosthenes' implicit comparison of his compatriots who fought at Chaeronea to the Athenian heroes of Marathon, Plataea, Salamis, and Artemisium (Dem. 18.208).[211] Since these paradigmatic memories lay at the heart of Athenian identity and were actively commemorated with monuments and festivals, the speaker was likely to strike an emotional chord and thus sway public opinion.

Sometimes, however, an orator analyzing a given situation might arrive at a solution for which the Athenian master narrative did not provide a suitable parallel. In this case, the orator could draw on alternative sources of knowledge of the past. Individual Athenians were not only exposed to the official polis tradition; they also fulfilled different social roles as companions and guest-friends and as members of their families, *demes,* and tribes, thus participating simultaneously in several subgroups that fostered their own collective memories. Consequently, individual orators were familiar with different versions of the past, from which they chose the most suitable for their purpose at hand. There are various clues that indicate when an orator relies on a less familiar historical example: he offers numerous cues (historical personage, places, dates) to aid his listeners in recollecting a particular event, makes a rather elaborate argument, or corroborates his assertion by pointing to the particular source of his paradigm.[212]

Apollodorus, for instance, deemed it necessary to remind his audience of

209. Diodorus Siculus, in particular, is known for following his sources generally very closely. Cf. Stylianou (1998) 132.

210. See the section "Ideology and Social Memory" above, 13–19.

211. Cited at the opening of this introduction.

212. Dinarchus, for instance, mentions both the dissolution of the democracy and Thrasybulus' mustering of the Athenian exiles in Thebes as cues for the memory of Theban aid (cf. Din. 1.25, discussed in chap. 4 of this book). For Demosthenes' elaborate reinterpretation of the lessons to be drawn from Thebes' medizing (Dem. 14.33–34), see "Challenging the Master Narrative" in chapter 2, 149–54.

the Marathon painting in the Stoa Poikile to offer proof for his claim that the Plataeans had indeed come to the aid of the Athenians ([Dem.] 59.94)—a fact that is often omitted in the official polis tradition of this quintessential Athenian victory.[213] Often, the orator does not reveal the source for his version, and we have to investigate on our own whence he might have acquired his knowledge of the specific historical incident. In this case, monuments, inscriptions, public commemorations, festivals, literary sources, and other carriers of social memory can serve as external indicators of how familiar this particular version was to the audience and how much argumentative and emotive force it possessed.

213. Cf. "Remembering the Plataeans" in chapter 2, 127–42.

CHAPTER 1

Carriers of Athenian Social Memory

In the introduction, I established a methodological framework that will allow me to study both how individual Athenians made use of the past within the complex Athenian memorial framework and to what extent these shared images of the past might have influenced the decision-making process in the Athenian assembly and the law courts. Following Rosalind Thomas, I have stressed that while many general characteristics of social memory can be observed across time and space, their manifestation, transmission, and negotiation depend on each society's particular communicative framework.

The following chapters focus on the collective memory of four particular events in the history of Athenian-Theban relations. In this chapter, I explore *thematically* the different ways in which social memory was manifested and transmitted in fifth- and fourth-century Athens. Both the orator and his listeners participated simultaneously in different memory communities and were exposed to a variety of different carriers of information about the past. First, I will focus on polis-wide festivals and public commemoration; they were of enormous importance for the Athenians' shared image of the past, since the entire polis community participated in them. Apart from these polis-wide commemorative activities, Athenians learned about their history in their *demes* and tribes, within their families, and within their groups of companions at the symposium. Personal relationships with outsiders as ξένοι or πρόξενοι gave insight into the memorial repertoire of other *poleis* and were therefore invaluable for the diplomatic relations between Greek states. Material records of the past, such as monuments and inscriptions, could either reinforce a dominant version of the past or serve as cues for events that might otherwise have faded from collective historical consciousness thanks to their growing irrelevance over time.

All surviving fourth-century speeches were written by highly trained orators. These orators were familiar with and had to pay attention to the knowledge and attitudes of their audiences, which were constituted by and large orally. Yet they also had access to written records of the past, such as the Greek historians, and to exemplary speeches of other orators, and they could draw on them if the situation required it. The assembly and the law courts themselves were central venues for the constitution and transmission of Athenian social memory. With different sources for knowledge of the past at his disposal, an orator could either reassert a widely known collective memory or modify and challenge it by falling back on alternative carriers of social memory. Changing political alignments and unexpected events played a crucial role, since they often provided the occasion for the orator to bring less familiar memories back into public discourse, thus reinforcing them and securing their transmission to younger generations. These different carriers of social memory mutually influenced and sustained each other. They created a complicated and dynamic system, in which the orator participated and operated.

Festivals and Public Commemorations

First, I will look at festivals and public commemorations, such as the Athenian funeral ceremony, dramatic performances, and religious festivals that were linked to key historical events. These polis-wide commemorative activities are of paramount importance for the Athenians' view of their past, since they provided a forum for the collective self-representation and articulation of a shared image of the past that validated the principle of democratic rule. These predominant versions of the past constituted the "master narrative of Athenian history"[1] in the fifth and fourth centuries, which Rosalind Thomas terms "the official polis tradition."[2]

Funeral Orations

The funeral oration (λόγος ἐπιτάφιος) was the culmination of the public funeral ceremony held for the Athenian war dead of each year. This custom replaced the elaborate aristocratic family burials of earlier times, and the funeral oration

1. Forsdyke (2005) 242. It is important to stress that the term *master narrative* does not denote a fixed, official narrative. Rather, it stands for the sum of the converging versions of the Athenian past, which conveyed the Athenian self-image and were manifested and transmitted in the aforementioned ways.

2. R. Thomas (1989) 208.

most likely originated soon after the Persian Wars.[3] Judging from the few funeral orations that have come down to us, these speeches were very conventional;[4] they had the same structure, expressed the same ideals, and extolled the same Athenian achievements.[5] They usually begin with a short *captatio benevolentiae* expressing the speaker's nearly impossible task to do justice to the deeds of the fallen.[6] The central part of the speech celebrates the manifestation of timeless Athenian ἀρετή from the origin of the city to the recent battles in which the heroes of the day have lost their lives. The topics in this *Tatenkatalog* typically include the autochthonous origin of the Athenian people, the repulsion of the invasions of the Amazons and Eumolpus' Thracians, Athens' aid in the restoration of the Heraclidae and the burial of the fallen Argives, and especially Athens' achievements during the Persian Wars.[7] The speech usually ends with a consolation of the relatives and an exhortation of the entire polis community.

The role of the funeral orations in shaping the Athenians' view of themselves and of their city's past cannot be overstated.[8] First, given the level of Athens' military activity in the classical period, this public funeral ceremony was often held every single year.[9] Second, unlike in the assembly and the law courts,

---

3. The precise time of origin is much debated and cannot be decided definitively. Stupperich (1977) 221–38 connects the custom to Cleisthenes' democratic reforms. Based on Dion. Hal. *Ant. Rom.* 5.17.4 (479 or 490 BC) and Diod. 11.33.3 (479 BC), Kierdorf (1966) 87–89 and Rosalind Thomas (1989) 207–8 date it to the aftermath of the Persian Wars. Von Wilamowitz-Moellendorff (1899) 193, Hauvette (1898), and Clairmont (1983) 13–14 connect it to Cimon's return of Theseus' bones in 475 BC, whereas Jacoby (1944) and Pritchett (1971–91) 4:106–24 date it to 465 BC, based on Paus. 1.29.4. Hornblower (1991) 292–93, Toher (1999), Flower & Marincola (2002) 152, and Jung (2006) 62 favor the mid-460s. Based on the *epitaphios*' democratic ideology, Loraux (1986) 64–69 dates it to the early 450s. Parker (1996) 133 favors the 470s or 460s.

4. Rosalind Thomas (1989) 200 explains, "Individual orators could select, omit, and add details to introduce a semblance of originality. But the underlying principles and ideals remained constant: the epitaphios forms a coherent expression of Athenian official 'ideology.'" Cf. Parker (1996) 137.

5. The extant funeral speeches include Thuc. 2.35–46 (Pericles for the dead of 431 BC), Lys. 2 (Corinthian War), Dem. 60 (Chaeronea, 338 BC), and Hyp. *Epit.* (Lamian War, 322 BC). For the reconstruction of the genre, we can also use fragments of an exemplary funeral speech written by Gorgias (DK 82 B5a, 5b, 6); Pl. *Menex.* 236d–249c, which is a parody of the genre; and Isoc. *Panegyricus,* which is a eulogy of Athens, using many of the themes of the funeral oration. The authorship of Lysias' and Demosthenes' funeral speeches has long been doubted on stylistic grounds, but they are now generally seen as genuine; cf. Todd (2008) 157–64 on Lys. 2. Herrman (2008) has demonstrated that Dem. 60 is most likely the very speech Demosthenes delivered in 338.

6. Lys. 2.1; Dem. 60.1; Thuc. 2.35.2.

7. Pericles' and Hyperides' funeral orations are exceptions. Both omit this traditional catalogue of deeds, the former with a short *praeteritio* (Thuc. 2.36.4) and the latter altogether.

8. There are now many excellent studies on the ideological implications of the Athenian funeral orations. See Kierdorff (1966) 83–110; Stupperich (1977); Walters (1980); Loraux (1986); R. Thomas (1989) 196–237; Tyrrell & Brown (1991) 189–215; Mills (1997) 58–78; Parker (1996) 131–41; Clarke (2008) 309–13.

9. Sage (1996) xi argues that, on average, Athens was at war at least two out of every three years down to 338. During the Peloponnesian (431–404), Corinthian (395–386), and Theban (378–371) wars, there must have been a public burial every year.

where Athenians would hear only scattered historical allusions, the funeral orations set out the city's past in narrative form and rough chronological order.[10] Third, the praise of past and recent Athenian achievements was not an end in itself but fulfilled a didactic function: the ἀρετή displayed by the fallen and their ancestors was normative, and all Athenians were encouraged to emulate their example.[11]

Finally, this shared image of the Athenian past was highly charged emotionally. This becomes clear when we consider this speech within its social context. The *epitaphios* was an integral element of the public funeral ceremony for those who had lost their lives fighting for the polis community. It was an activity of both religious and civic significance, which is clear from Thucydides' description (Thuc. 2.34).[12] The bones of the dead were laid out for two days, so that their relatives could bring their offerings. On the day of the funeral, the bones were put in coffins, tribe by tribe, and were carried in a solemn procession to the public cemetery in the Ceramicus. Citizens and noncitizens took part in this funeral procession, and female kin came and lamented at the tomb. After the bones had been laid into the earth, a man "chosen by the city, of proven intelligence and high esteem, ma[de] the appropriate speech of praise over them" (Thuc. 2.34). The fact that the delivery of this speech was reserved for Athens' leading citizen gave it additional weight. That this celebratory version of Athenian history indeed had a profound effect on the Athenian psyche is evident from Socrates' remarks in Plato's *Menexenus*.[13] Socrates claims that the *epitaphios* enchants his soul and makes him feel greater and nobler than before. This feeling of solemnity (σεμνότης) lasts for more than three days. Only then does Socrates realize that he does not live on the Islands of the Blessed (Pl. *Menex.* 234c–235c). In accordance with Plato's parodistic intentions, Socrates is of course ironic and exaggerates, but Plato's choice to parody this very aspect of the *epitaphios* suggests that it did, at least to some extent, have this stirring effect.

It is obvious that the self-congratulatory image of Athens presented in the chauvinistic funeral oration is full of exaggerations and gross historical distortions.[14] Yet it would be wrong simply to dismiss the *epitaphios* as propaganda. Rather, it provides a unique opportunity to study the processes of social memory and serves as an invaluable key to the Athenians' mentality, since, for most

10. R. Thomas (1989) 213; Clarke (2008) 312.

11. Loraux (1986) 144 calls the *epitaphios* the "the most official of lessons." Cf. Clarke (2008) 308.

12. Cf. Loraux (1986) 15–76; Stupperich (1977); Clairmont (1983). For the ritual aspect, see Walters (1980).

13. See Parker (1996) 137; R. Thomas (1989) 211.

14. See, for instance, Todd's (2008) commentary on Lys. 2.

of them, "Athens' past history was the past they heard about in the epitaphioi."[15] We find the same ideals, justifications, and examples elsewhere in Athenian public discourse, and there is every indication that most Athenians believed in them passionately.[16]

The Athenian funeral oration illustrates, in an exemplary way, the complex interdependence between a community's ideology and its image of the past. On the one hand, a group's ideology originates from its historical experience.[17] Consequently, the heroic victories over the Persians at Marathon and during Xerxes' invasion profoundly altered the Athenians' mental framework. In Athenian social memory, these events were much simplified and stripped of their immediate historical contexts; they became symbols of the national Athenian character. After the Persian Wars, the Athenians saw themselves as champions of the Greeks (προστάται τῶν Ἑλλήνων) against both barbarian invaders and Greek oppressors.[18]

Lysias' funeral oration best exemplifies the results of this process. Athens' support for the Ionian revolt and the burning of Sardis that prompted the Persian punitive expedition of 490 are forgotten.[19] Instead, the story begins with Persian ὕβρις and πλεονεξία: the king of Asia hubristically desires to add Europe to his dominion (Lys. 2.21). The Persians went straight to Attica, since they knew that the Athenians would help any other Greek city if they started elsewhere.[20] At Marathon, the Athenians fight "alone on behalf of all of Greece against many myriads of barbarians" (Lys. 2.20).[21] When Xerxes invaded, the Athenians embarked on their ships to protect the other Greeks and were victorious at Artemisium (Lys. 2.30–31).[22] They then selflessly abandoned their city and made the greatest contribution to the fight for the freedom of the Greeks at Salamis (Lys. 2.33–43). Whereas most of the Greeks abandoned their posts at Plataea, the Spartans and Tegeans routed the barbarians, and the Athenians and Plataeans defeated the Greek medizers (Lys. 2.46–47).

15. R. Thomas (1989) 213.

16. Strasburger (1958); R. Thomas (1989) 206.

17. See "Ideology and Social Memory" in the introduction, 13–19.

18. Walters (1980); Loraux (1986) 155–71; R. Thomas (1989) 196–237; Parker (1996) 131–41; Gehrke (2001) 301–4; Gehrke (2003) 22; Jung (2006) 128–65.

19. For this effect of "narrativization," see "Ideology and Social Memory" in the introduction, 17. Cf. also Todd (2008) 230.

20. That the sack of Eretria preceded the landing of Marathon (Hdt. 6.100–101) is forgotten. Only in Plato's pastiche are Athens and Eretria repeatedly coupled, no doubt in order to parody the commonplace of Athens' sole achievement at Marathon (Pl. *Menex.* 240a, c). Cf. R. Thomas (1989) 222–23.

21. The Plataeans are omitted. For a discussion of Athens' claim to have fought alone at Marathon, see "Remembering the Plataeans" in chapter 2, 127–42.

22. There is no mention of the rest of the Greek fleet. Moreover, according to Herodotus, the battle of Artemisium ended in a draw. Cf. Walters (1980) 5.

Lysias provides the most detailed treatment of the Persian War experience, but the same general tenor also pervades the other extant funeral orations.[23] It could even be more pronounced. In Demosthenes' *epitaphios,* the memory of the Persian Wars is completely stripped of its historical context (there is no mention of individual battles, Darius, Xerxes, or the Greek allies), and it is morphed into a symbol for Athens' role as undisputed champion of the Greeks.

> Those men single-handedly twice repulsed by land and sea [μόνοι δὶς ἠμύναντο καὶ κατὰ γῆν καὶ κατὰ θάλατταν] the army advancing from all of Asia, and at their personal risks established themselves as the authors of the common salvation for all the Greeks [κοινῆς σωτηρίας πᾶσι τοῖς Ἕλλησιν αἴτιοι κατέστησαν].[24] (Dem. 60.10)

We see here that the symbolic meaning of Marathon—the Athenians fighting *alone* on behalf of all the Greeks—was extended to Xerxes' invasion as well.[25] It is debated among scholars why Marathon, rather than Salamis (or Plataea), came to represent Athens' achievement in the Persian Wars.[26] Some have seen political motivation as the driving force behind the special emphasis put on Marathon, a favoring of the hoplite success over the naval victory at Salamis.[27] Rosalind Thomas, however, has convincingly rejected these political interpretations. The exceptional significance attributed to Marathon is best explained by the fact that Marathon was the first encounter with the Persians on Greek soil and the only solely Athenian victory, whereas both Salamis and Plataea were the victories of a broad alliance of Greek *poleis.* In a predominantly oral environment, Marathon could, therefore, epitomize the whole of the Persian Wars by telescoping the complementary events of 490 to 479 together.[28]

The Persian War experience fundamentally altered the image the Athenians had of themselves and of the world that surrounded them. It became a "cornerstone of their identity" and had "prescriptive force for future conduct."[29] In the eyes of the Athenians, Athens' hegemony was the natural and well-deserved result of the Persian Wars, as Lysias makes clear: thanks to their merits in

23. For a discussion of parallels in other funeral speeches, see Todd (2008) 210–73.

24. Similarly, Dem. 60.11.

25. Jung (2006) 130 note 11. Walters (1980) 8 argues convincingly that the Athenians turned the traumatic experience of abandonment by the Greeks—at Marathon and before and after Salamis—into a virtue and celebrated their μονομαχία against the Persians.

26. This emphasis on Marathon is particularly prevalent in Aristophanes' comedies: cf. *Ach.* 179–80, 692–99; *Nub.* 985; *Eq.* 781–83, 1334; *Vesp.* 682–84, 711. For oratorical references to Marathon, rather than Salamis, see "Remembering the Plataeans" in chapter 2, 127–42.

27. Cf. Loraux (1986) 161; Gehrke (2003) 23–24.

28. R. Thomas (1989) 224–26. Andoc. 1.107 provides an excellent example.

29. Gehrke (2001) 302.

defending the freedom of the Greeks, the Athenians "were considered worthy by all—both those who were sharing the risks with them and those against whom they were fighting—to become leaders [ἡγεμόνες] of Greece" (Lys. 2.47).[30]

A community's historical experience affects its ideology, but its ideology also, in turn, shapes its collective memory of earlier and later events, since communities tend to regard their characteristic traits as permanent and unchanging. Consequently, Athens' new hegemonic ideology was projected back into the distant past and led to the commemoration of a few selected mythical events that closely corresponded to the Athenians' self-image as defenders of Greek liberty against barbarian invaders and that could be seen as prefigurations of the Athenian victories over the Persians.[31] The repulsion of the invasions of the man-hating Amazons and of Eumolpus' Thracian hordes thus became an integral part of the patriotic Athenian master narrative of the *epitaphios.*[32]

In the eyes of the Athenians, Athens' role as champion of the Greeks (προστάτης τῶν Ἑλλήνων) involved not only the defense of Greece against barbarian invaders but also the protection of the weak against the unjust oppression of overbearing Greek powers. This latter aspect lies at the heart of the mythical stories of the burial of the fallen Argives and the return of the Heraclidae. In both cases, Athens protects the rights of suppliants (Adrastus and the Heraclidae) against hubristic Greek powers (the Thebans and Eurystheus).[33] That the protection of Greek liberty against both barbarian invaders and Greek oppressors are really two sides of the same coin is most evident in Lysias' résumé of the Athenians' achievements during their seventy-year-long naval supremacy.

> And neither did triremes sail out of Asia, nor did a tyrant established himself among the Greeks, nor was any Greek polis enslaved by the barbarians. This was the level of moderation and fear that their bravery [ἀρετή] inspired among all mankind. On account of these things, they alone [μόνους] ought to be the champions of the Greeks [προστάτας τῶν Ἑλλήνων] and the leaders of the *poleis* [ἡγεμόνας τῶν πόλεων]. (Lys. 2.57)

30. In Lysias' brief Persian War narrative (Lys. 2.20–47), Athens' merits for Greek liberty are mentioned seven times (Lys. 2.25, 26, 35, 41, 42, 44, 47). For Athens' hegemony as result of the Persian Wars, see also Isoc. 14.59.

31. Gehrke (2001) 302; Gotteland (2001) 129; Mills (1997) 58; R. Thomas (1989) 207–8; Castriota (1992); Harding (2008) 66.

32. On the Amazons, see Lys. 2.4–6; Pl. *Menex.* 239b; Isoc. 4.68–70; Dem. 60.8. On Eumolpus' Thracians, see Pl. *Menex.* 239b; Isoc. 4.68–70; Dem. 60.8.

33. For Athens' aid in the burial of the fallen Argives, see chapter 3.

The Athenians also believed that they alone possessed the moral qualities necessary for this position of leadership, first and foremost an innate sense of justice. This claim is linked to the autochthonous origin of the Athenian race: unlike the majority of peoples, the Athenians did not acquire their land through the unjust expulsion of an indigenous population but are sprung from the land itself (αὐτόχθονες, Lys. 2.17).[34] Consequently, the Athenians are the only people that cannot idly stand by when an act of injustice is being committed; they have to step in and protect the victims against their oppressors. This sense of justice and altruism pervades the mythical paradigms of the Athenians' aid for Adrastus and the Heraclidae,[35] but it is also an integral element of the Athenians' collective memory of Marathon. The Persians decided to attack Athens first, because they knew that "if they attacked any other polis, they would be fighting both with its inhabitants and with the Athenians, because the Athenians would eagerly come to the rescue of those who were being wronged [τοῖς ἀδικουμένοις]" (Lys. 2.22).[36]

So far, I have shown how the hegemonic ideology, derived from the Athenians' experience of the Persian Wars, determined which "events" of Athens' mythical past were commemorated. The Athenian master narrative focused on a few selected myths that closely corresponded to the Athenians' self-image as selfless defenders of Greek liberty against both barbarian invaders and Greek oppressors. This idealized memory of the Persian Wars, however, influenced not only the selection but also the very shape of those collective memories.[37]

Lysias' account of the Amazons' invasion, for instance, shows numerous parallels to the Athenians' memory of the Persian Wars. Like the Persian kings Darius and Xerxes,[38] the Amazons ruled over many races and had reduced all their neighbors to slavery (Lys. 2.5). Driven by the unjust desire for a land that was not theirs, they gathered the most warlike tribes and marched against Athens, where they all perished under the hands of the brave Athenians (Lys. 2.5–

34. See also Lys. 2.43; Pl. *Menex.* 237b–c, 238e–239a, 245c–d; Dem. 60.4; Hyp. *Epit.* 7. The autochthony myth could fulfill various functions. Following the aristocratic funeral practice to extol the noble birth (εὐγένεια) of the deceased, it was probably first introduced to ennoble the origin of the Athenian *demos* as a whole; cf. R. Thomas (1989) 217–19. The autochthony myth also supported Athens' claim to be the oldest Greek city: see Todd (2008) 227; Rosivach (1987) 302–4. The equality of all Athenians inherent in this shared origin could buttress the Athenian belief that their democracy originated already in mythical times (Lys. 2.18). Loraux (1986) 148–49 linked the origin of the autochthony claim to the chthonic birth of legendary Athenian kings such as Erechtheus and Erichthonius. For autochthony in fifth-century Athenian art, see Shapiro (1998).

35. See "*Prostates* of the Greeks" in chapter 3, 186–89.

36. Athens' selfless attitude also permeates the distorted memory of the Athenian rejection of Xerxes' offer. See "Treacherous by Nature" in chapter 2, 143–49.

37. For this phenomenon and the example of the Camisard revolts, see "Ideology and Social Memory" in the introduction, 13–19.

38. Cf. Lys. 2.21–47.

6).[39] We can grasp here a clear example of how earlier versions of this myth, according to which the Amazons' invasion was prompted either by Theseus' rape of Antiope (Plut. *Thes.* 26.1–27.2) or by her later abandonment in favor of Phaedra (Plut. *Thes.* 28.1), have become thoroughly "marathonized."[40] Similar tendencies can be found in the story of Eumolpus' invasion (Isoc. 4.66; Dem. 60.8; Pl. *Menex.* 239b): in the funeral orations, Eumolpus, once an Eleusinian prince and the *archegetes* of the priestly family of the Eumolpidae, became the leader of Thracian invaders.[41]

The Persian War experience and the resultant hegemonic ideology affected the Athenians' memory of not only earlier but also later events. This is evident, for instance, in Lysias' account of the Geraneia episode (ca. 459) during the First Peloponnesian War.[42] When the majority of the Athenian forces were conducting the siege of both Aegina and an Egyptian stronghold, Corinth seized the Geraneia in order to invade the Megarid and thus bring relief to their Aeginetan allies (fig. 1). Athens, however, did not lift the siege but responded by sending the young and old under Myronides. According to Thucydides, the Athenians first fought an indecisive and then a victorious battle, which led to the shameful stoning of a trapped body of Corinthian hoplites by Athenian light-armed troops (Thuc. 1.105–6). Lysias' epitaphic version, however, is heavily influenced by the Persian War paradigm: the Corinthians are invaders (Lys. 2.49, 50, 52), and their attempt on the Megarid is stylized as an invasion of Athenian territory (Lys. 2.52). Just as at Marathon, the Athenians face an overwhelming force: the Corinthians and their allies had taken the field in full force (πανδημεί, Lys. 2.49), while the Athenians mustered only the old and very young. But they, "trusting in their own spirit and holding the invaders in contempt, considered it right to face the danger *all alone* [αὐτοὶ μόνοι]" (Lys. 2.50). The two battles

39. Similarly, Isoc. 4.68–70; Pl. *Menex.* 239b; Dem. 60.8.

40. For the Amazons in the funeral orations, see Loraux (1986) 146–48; Castriota (1992) 43–49; Mills (1997) 58–59; Gotteland (2001) 131–61; Todd (2008) 216–17; Harding (2008) 64–67. Since, in Athenian social memory, Marathon came to epitomize the entire Persian War, I use the term *marathonize* to describe the formative influence of the Athenian Persian War experience on other Athenian collective memories. In a similar way, the social memory of the Camisard revolts "camisardized" the collective historical consciousness of the inhabitants of the Cévennes mountains. Cf. Fentress & Wickham (1992) 92-99; Alcock (2002) 6.

41. According to Euripides' *Erechtheus,* Eumolpus was the son of Poseidon and a Thracian princess and led an army of Thracians into Attica to support the Eleusinians in a war against Athens. Parker (1987) 202–4 argues convincingly that the Eleusinian priest Eumolpus (*Hom. Hymn. Dem.* 154) became first associated with Thrace thanks to the prestige of the Thracian Orpheus, another revelator of religious mysteries. Due to this association, the war of the Athenian king Erechtheus against Eumolpus was eventually remembered "as the prototype of the Persian wars, the first incursion of barbarian arms into Greece" (204). See also Buchner (1958) 71; Gotteland (2001) 161–67; Jung (2006) 150 note 78.

42. Rosalind Thomas (1989) 227–29 discusses in detail how Lysias' version of this account is shaped by the ideals of the *epitaphios*. Cf. also Todd (2008) 249–53.

are telescoped into one; there is no mention of a draw or of the brutal stoning of Corinthian hoplites. Instead, the Athenians set up a trophy for a deed, "most glorious for them, but most shameful for their enemies," and returned home "with the finest reputation" (Lys. 2.53). In the Athenian master narrative of the *epitaphios*, this episode thus fully conforms to the noble Athenian self-image derived from the Persian War experience.[43]

I have argued above that the *epitaphios* was probably the most important source for the Athenians' knowledge of their past. To us, this Athenian master narrative might seem trite, chauvinistic, and full of historical distortions. Yet we ought to keep in mind that this version of Athenian history was "*true for the Athenians*, in that it conform[ed] to the idea that they wish[ed] to have of themselves."[44] It is therefore not surprising that Athenian speakers in political or public discourse drew heavily on it, "wherever defence, praise or emulation of the ancestors was called for."[45] This is not the place to discuss the orators' use of the funeral orations comprehensively. A few examples should suffice.[46]

Herodotus reports about a quarrel between the Athenians and the Tegeans over the privilege to hold the left wing of the Greek army in the battle of Plataea in 479. The Athenians stake their claim on a list of past achievements that closely resembles the deeds celebrated in the funeral orations: aid for the Heraclidae, burial of the fallen Argives, the Amazonomachy, the Trojan War, and Marathon (Hdt. 9.27). It is generally agreed that this speech, as we have it, is anachronistic but closely reflects the kinds of arguments that Athenian speakers in Herodotus' own time (ca. 460–420) used to glorify their city.[47] The same applies to Herodotus' account of the Greek embassy to Gelon of Syracuse in 481. Herodotus' Athenians firmly reject Gelon's demand to obtain the naval command.

> For, we would then possess the greatest naval force in Greece in vain, if we, being Athenians [ἐόντες Ἀθηναῖοι], withdraw from the command in favor of the Syracusans—we who present ourselves as the oldest people

43. Like the Marathomachoi, Myronides was remembered as representative of the good old times. Cf. Ar. *Eccl.* 304; Nouhaud (1982) 224. On the "marathonization" of another more recent event, see "Athenian Contribution to the Theban Countercoup, 379/8" in chapter 4, 260–67.

44. Loraux (1986) 171. Cf. also Gehrke (2003) 22; R. Thomas (1989) 237. Thomas stresses that these "'distortions' would be encouraged or reinforced by certain ideals, and [that] again the line between deliberately misleading propaganda and wishful thinking might be blurred."

45. R. Thomas (1989) 211.

46. For a discussion of the Athenians' use of Marathon, see "Remembering the Plataeans" in chapter 2, 127–42.

47. Walters (1980) 22 note 26; Aélion (1983) 1:232; Loraux (1986) 65; R. Thomas (1989) 211; Hubbard (1992) 98; Flower & Marincola (2002) 152–53; Harding (2008) 66. Cf. "Precedent for the Battle of Plataea" in chapter 3, 196–98.

> [ἀρχαιότατον μὲν ἔθνος παρεχόμενοι] and who alone of the Greeks have never left their homeland [μοῦνοι δὲ ἐόντες οὐ μετανάσται Ἑλλήνων]. (Hdt. 7.161)

Both of these arguments are intrinsically connected to the Athenians' claim of autochthony, which was a central element of the Athenian funeral orations.[48]

In 330 BC, the Athenian statesman Lycurgus employed many arguments drawn from the funeral orations in his prosecution of the alleged deserter Leocrates. For instance, to emphasize the low point that Athens had reached in 338 after the defeat of Chaeronea, he contrasted Athens' proud claim to be free and autochthonous with the recent emergency measures of freeing slaves and conferring Athenian citizenship on resident aliens (Lycurg. 41).[49]

In a speech written by Isocrates for a lawsuit around 397, Alcibiades' son linked his ancestors' achievements firmly to the Athenian master narrative. According to his account, his forefathers established the democracy that trained the citizens so effectively in bravery that they "single-handedly [μόνοι] conquered in battle the barbarians who had attacked all of Greece [ἐπὶ πᾶσαν ἐλθόντας τὴν Ἑλλάδα]." For their justice, the Athenians won such a great reputation "that the Greeks voluntarily put in their hand the dominion of the sea" (Isoc. 16.27). Here, just as in the *epitaphios,* the two phases of the Persian Wars (i.e., the victory at Marathon and the repulsion of Xerxes' invasion) are telescoped into a single battle; Athens acted as champion of the Greeks and proved itself worthy of hegemony.

These are just a few examples that demonstrate that, whether on diplomatic mission, in the assembly, or in the law courts, Athenian speakers frequently evoked the past achievements and patriotic ideals familiar to them from the funeral orations.[50]

Dramatic Festivals

In the previous section, I have argued that the funeral oration was perhaps the most important carrier of Athenian social memory, since it regularly presented the Athenians with an idealized account of their city's achievements in

48. Thuc. 2.36; Lys. 2.17; Isoc. 4.24; Pl. *Menex.* 237b; Dem. 60.4; Hyp. *Epit.* 5. Cf. Parker (1996) 139; Gotteland (2001) 319–30. As further proof for their fitness to lead, the Athenians cite Homer's praise of the Athenian leader Menestheus, who was "the best man for ordering and marshaling the army" (Hdt. 7.161; cf. Hom. *Il.* 2.553–54).

49. Similarly, in his prosecution of Aeschines in 343, Demosthenes mentioned autochthony as a source of great pride and incentive to preserve one's liberty (Dem. 19.261).

50. For the use of the Athenian master narrative in an assembly speech, see Dem. 6.7–11, discussed further under "Treacherous by Nature" in chapter 2, 143–49.

rough chronological order, stretching from the mythical past to the present. In the Athenian *epitaphios,* we see the complex interdependence between a community's ideology (democratic and hegemonial) and the collective memory of its past ("marathonization" of earlier and later events). The *epitaphios* is, however, not the only manifestation of the Athenian master narrative. The same "beliefs, ideals, justifications and examples from Athenian history"[51] recur in other forms of Athenian public discourse, in the assembly and law courts and especially in the dramatic productions of dithyrambs, tragedies, and comedies, which were put on stage at the Great (or City) Dionysia and other Dionysian festivals. These civic festivals provided yet another opportunity for the entire polis community "to assert and renegotiate its collective history."[52]

Today, it is widely accepted that Athenian drama has to be understood within the political, social, and religious contexts of the Athenian polis.[53] The tragic stage, in particular, has received much scholarly attention as a forum for the self-representation of Athenian democracy, where current social, political, religious, and moral issues were dealt with in mythical guise. Athenian playwrights used both Panhellenic and Athenian myths for this purpose. While both types of myth could serve as vehicles of Athenian ideology and could be used for the expression of current issues and concerns,[54] I am here particularly interested in Athenian myths, since they provided the Athenians with a shared image of their city and its heroes in the mythical past. Athenian heroes and heroines appeared, for instance, in Aeschylus' *Eumenides* and *Eleusinians,* Sophocles' *Oedipus at Colonus* and *Triptolemus,* and Euripides' *Medea, Heraclidae, Hippolytus, Suppliants, Ion, Hercules Furens,* and *Erechtheus.* Thanks to the dramatists' continuous refreshing and reshaping, these ancient myths retained their relevance for fifth- and fourth-century Athenians.

If we want to grasp the role of drama in the formation of Athenian social memory, it is necessary to briefly consider the main festival at which dramas were performed. The festival of the Great (or City) Dionysia was held annually in late March and lasted for five days. The enormous political significance of this festival is evident from the fact that the entire polis participated in a solemn procession to the theater of Dionysus, where a bull was sacrificed, the annual tribute of the Athenian allies was displayed, special honors for citizens and foreigners were proclaimed, and the recent war orphans were symbolically adopt-

51. R. Thomas (1989) 200.

52. Clarke (2008) 300.

53. Such a "politicized" (as in "integral to the polis") understanding of (especially) tragedy was formulated as a corrective to the aestheticizing response to tragedy as timeless works of literature. For representatives of the new mainstream, see Goldhill (2000) 35 note 5.

54. Aeschylus' *Suppliants,* for instance, features the exemplary attitude toward suppliants, and Euripides' *Troades* and *Hecuba* reflect the experience of atrocities during the Peloponnesian War.

ed by the state.[55] The festival's four types of dramatic performances—dithyramb, comedy, tragedy, and satyr play—were organized as dramatic contests. Competing on the first day were ten dithyrambic choruses of men and ten of boys, representing the ten tribes of Attica. From extant fragments, we can infer that this genre largely drew on mythological themes. Two of Bacchylides' dithyrambs (Bacchyl. 17, 18), for instance, dramatized adventures of Theseus. These dithyrambic competitions greatly contributed to the formation of tribal identity. The honors went to the victorious tribe, not the poet. Practicing for this competition for several months must have strengthened the internal cohesion among the fifty men and fifty boys of each tribal chorus and increased their knowledge and attachment to the myths they performed.[56] The second day saw a contest of five comedies, which—at least during the fifth century—focused on current political events and public figures. For this reason, Aristophanes' plays are an immensely important source for popular attitudes and Athenian social memories.[57] By bringing these on stage, comedies did not merely reflect commonly held views but also helped to shape, reinforce and transmit them.

The tragic *agon* comprised three days, with three tragedies followed by a satyr play on each day. It has been noted that many of the exemplary mythic episodes known from the funeral orations were also the themes of tragedies.[58] Moreover, we also find tragedies that were not based on these mythical episodes but nevertheless expressed aspects of the noble Athenian character: in Sophocles' *Oedipus at Colonus* and in Euripides' *Medea,* for instance, Athenians graciously provide exile for suppliants. This should not surprise us. Since the Great Dionysia as a whole was an expression of Athenian civic identity, the tragic plays performed there were infused with Athenian ideology and helped to constitute the Athenian master narrative by choosing episodes from myth that exemplified the Athenian character.[59]

A few tragedies brought historical events to the stage. Phrynichus' *Phoenissae* and Aeschylus' *Persae* surely played a major role in processing the heroic experience of the Persian Wars. The very medium of tragedy and its traditional choice of mythical themes helped to memorialize the victory over the Persians and make it an essential part of Athenian patriotic mythology, thus endowing a historical event with mythic qualities.[60]

55. Cf. Pickard-Cambridge (1988) 58–63.

56. Cf. Zimmermann (1998) 20–21.

57. For the portrayal of the Marathomachoi in Aristophanes' comedies, for instance, see Ar *Ach.* 179–80, 692–99; *Nub.* 985; *Eq.* 781–83, 1,334; *Vesp.* 682–84, 711. For the proverbial memory of Thrasybulus' seizure of Phyle, see Ar. *Plut.* 1146. Cf. also "Athenian Memorialization of the Men from Phyle" in chapter 4, 235–45.

58. Cf. Aeschylus' *Eleusinians* and Euripides' *Erechtheus, Heraclidae,* and *Supplices.* Cf. Loraux (1986) 64–72; Parker (1996) 137–39. See chapter 3 in the present study.

59. For civic ideology at the Great Dionysia, see Goldhill (1990), (2000).

60. Gehrke (2003).

When considering the role of these dramatic performances for the orators' use of the past, we can distinguish between two phenomena. The first is that public speakers often evoked mythical characters and their stories in fairly general terms, without naming the particular source for their allusion. In a speech delivered in 352, for instance, Demosthenes argued that Aristocrates' proposal violated the prerogatives of the Areopagus court (Dem. 23.70). To emphasize the ancient origin and the revered status of this court, Demosthenes mentioned, among other things, the famous murder trial brought on by the Eumenides against Orestes (Dem. 23.66). Tragedies were not the only source for this collective memory but were certainly an important one: Orestes' trial stood in the center of Aeschylus' *Eumenides* and was mentioned in Euripides' *Electra* (1264–72), *Iphigenia in Tauris* (940–69, 1469–72), and *Orestes* (1648–52).[61] The tragic characters Orestes and Oedipus were also used by the Athenian orator Callistratus, at the time of Thebes' ascendency, in an attempt to convince the Arcadians not to conclude an alliance with Argos and Thebes, the very cities that had produced these depraved individuals (Nep. *Epam.* 6.1–3; Plut. *Mor.* 193c). Epaminondas' alleged reply is striking.

> We agree that a patricide was born among us and a matricide among the Argives; but after they had committed these crimes, we banished them, whereas the Athenians welcomed them. (Plut. *Mor.* 193d)

This anecdote shows how the same myth could have different meanings to two different memory communities. The Theban Epaminondas tried to disown Oedipus and link his crimes with Athens.[62] To the Athenians, the myth of Oedipus symbolized everything that was wrong with Thebes, as Zeitlin has argued convincingly in her seminal article on the depiction of Thebes as the "other" city (i.e., as an "anti-Athens") on the tragic stage.[63] At the same time, Oedipus' reception as suppliant by Theseus (as seen, e.g., in Sophocles' *Oedipus of Colonus*) fully conformed to the Athenian self-image of the altruistic hegemon.

In these two examples, speakers referred to characters known from tragedy without pointing to a particular source. We can identify a second phenomenon in the orators' use of drama, in a few cases where a speaker not only invoked a

61. The cult of the Eumenides and the Areopagus court itself also function as carriers of this collective memory. Demosthenes draws on a version (also found in Eur. *Or.* 1648–52 and Aristid. *Panath.* 172 Dindorf) that featured a jury of the Twelve Gods and not of Athenian citizens, as in Aesch. *Eum.* Cf. Wallace (1989) 88. We see here how different carriers of social memory could mutually influence and sustain each other.

62. Not surprisingly, it is not Oedipus who featured on Theban coins, but the Theban culture hero Heracles. Cf. "Appeals to the Theban Self-Image" in chapter 4, 223–32.

63. Zeitlin (1990).

tragic myth but incorporated a verbatim quotation from a particular tragedy. Lycurgus, for instance, contrasted Leocrates' desertion to the heroism displayed by King Erechtheus at the time of Eumolpus' invasion. After receiving an oracle that victory could only be assured by sacrificing his own daughter, King Erechtheus obeyed and was then able to drive the invaders out of the country (Lycurg. 98–99). The Athenian victory over the Thracian invaders was, of course, well familiar from the funeral orations, but Erechtheus' role was usually not mentioned in this democratic genre. Yet the self-sacrifice of the daughters of Erechtheus (the Hyacinthiae, as they are often called) was frequently evoked as a heroic paradigm in the assembly and the law courts.[64] It presumably played a major role within the institution of the *ephebeia* (Eur. *Erech.* fr. 370.87–89 Kannicht) and was important for the tribal identity of the members of the tribe Erechtheis (Dem. 60.27).[65] Despite the great familiarity of this myth, Lycurgus extended his example and cited fifty-five lines from Euripides' *Erechtheus,* in which Queen Praxithea wholeheartedly embraced the necessity of her daughter's sacrifice for the sake of the fatherland. The orator prefaced his quotation by claiming that Euripides chose this myth to provide his fellow citizens with a noble example to increase their patriotism (Lycurg. 100). He drives home his point with an *a fortiori* argument: if women, who are by nature fond of their children, bring such sacrifices, men must show even more devotion to their country and not shamefully desert it as Leocrates had done (Lycurg. 101). Poets always held a special place in Greek culture; by citing Praxithea's monologue verbatim, Lycurgus brought the full weight of Euripides' authority down on the defendant.[66] For the same reason, Demosthenes and Aeschines included verbatim quotations from tragedy in some of their speeches.[67]

We have seen that fourth-century orators evoked mythical characters and their stories and even quoted entire passages from Euripides' and Sophocles' plays to support their cases. This shows that, in the eyes of the orators, tragedies played a vital role in the constitution and transmission of a shared image of the past.[68] This is not surprising. The immediacy and excitement of watching these myths being acted out in full detail on the tragic stage must have left a deep impression on the audience.[69] If we want to assess the argumentative and

64. Lycurg. fr. X–XI 10 Conomis; Phocion in Diod. 17.15.2.

65. Cf. Kearns (1989) 59–63; Kron (1999) 77–82; Steinbock (2011) 299–303, 310.

66. For the orators' use of poetry in general, see Perlman (1964b); Clarke (2008) 288–89. For the role of poetry citations in Lycurgus' prosecution of Leocrates, see Allen (2000).

67. Aeschin. 1.128 (Eur. fr. 865 Kannicht, unknown tragedy); Aeschin. 1.151 (Eur. *Stheneboea* fr. 661.24–25 Kannicht); Aeschin. 1.152 (Eur. *Phoenix* fr. 812 Kannicht); Dem. 18.267 (Eur. *Hec.* 1); Dem. 19.245 (Eur. *Phoenix* fr. 812.7–9 Kannicht); Dem. 19.247 (Soph. *Ant.* 175–90).

68. Clarke (2008) 290.

69. For the emotional effect of Eur. *Supp.*, for instance, see A. M. Bowie (1997) 51–55.

emotive force of these allusions, we have to go a step further and explore how familiar these tragedies were to a fourth-century audience. Written copies of the works of the three great tragedians, even if they were available outside the poets' families and the guilds of tragic actors, were probably not the primary source for most people's familiarity with these tragedies.[70]

Classical Athens was a performance culture. To appreciate these dramatic performances as vital carriers of shared mythical stories, it is indispensable to look beyond the Great Dionysia and the few tragic texts that have come down to us. This festival was not the only venue for bringing myths onto the stage. It was preceded by a series of minor Dionysian festivals (the Rural Dionysia of the *demes,* the Lenaea, and the Anthesteria) extending from December to March.[71] All of these, with the possible exception of the Anthesteria, included agonistic performances of drama. Also, apart from Aeschylus, Sophocles, and Euripides, there were many more playwrights who composed tragedies on the same or similar topics, as the didascalic records reveal.[72]

Moreover, there is considerable evidence for the reproduction of the plays of Aristophanes and the three great tragedians. In the fifth century, unsuccessful plays could reenter the competition of the Great Dionysia in a revised form,[73] and reproductions may already have occurred at the Rural Dionysia.[74] Aeschylus held a particular position of honor: soon after this death in 456/5 BC, the Athenians passed a decree that "whoever wished to produce a work of Aeschylus should receive a chorus" (*Life of Aeschylus* 12); they thus provided for reproductions of his plays as part of the regular competition at the Great Dionysia.[75] In fourth-century Athens, there were various forms and opportunities for the reproduction of older plays. Inscriptional evidence shows more systematic productions of old plays, after one old tragedy and one old comedy was added (in 386 and 339, respectively) to the regular competition at the Great

70. The early transmission of the tragic texts is a vexed problem. Repeated reproductions of popular plays by actors played a decisive role; cf. Page (1934). But the importance of booksellers who provided texts for a selected group of readers should not be underestimated, as Mastronarde (1994) 39–41 points out. Clearly, Demosthenes, Aeschines, and Lycurgus, who included long verbatim quotations in their speeches, must have had an actual copy of the text.

71. Cf. Pickard-Cambridge (1988) 1–56; Wilson (2000) 21–22.

72. See Snell *TrGF* i.1–263. For lost tragedies featuring the burial of the fallen Argives and the likely reproduction of Eur. *Supp.*, see "Athens' Aid for Suppliants" in chapter 3, 174–86.

73. This is confirmed by the *argumenta* for Eur. *Hipp.*, Ar. *Nub.*, and Ar. *Pax.* Aristophanes' *Frogs* were reperformed in response to popular demand. Cf. Pickard-Cambridge (1988) 99–100.

74. Euripides produced a play at the Piraeus, and Sophocles and Aristophanes produced plays at Eleusis; cf. Pickard-Cambridge (1988) 52, 99.

75. Ar. *Ach.* 9–12; Ar. *Ran.* 866–69. Cf. Pickard-Cambridge (1988) 86; Wilson (2000) 22. Such reperformances would explain why Aeschylus' *Vita* says he won thirteen victories, while the *Suda* credits him with twenty-eight.

Dionysia.[76] It was usually professional actors who put fifth-century tragedies back on stage.

Epigraphic and literary sources confirm reproductions of Euripides' *Iphigenia in Aulis, Orestes, Cresphontes,* and *Hecuba;* Sophocles' *Antigone* and *Oenomaus;* and Aeschylus' *Propompoi.*[77] Not all of these plays were performed at the Great Dionysia, though.[78] At least from the early fourth century onward, the smaller festivals of the Rural Dionysia also offered an opportunity for the reperformance of old plays by troupes of professional actors who traveled from *deme* to *deme* with their repertoire of plays.[79] Every year in December, each *deme* organized its own festival of the Rural Dionysia, each held on a different day, so that people could go from one festival to another to gratify their desire for entertainment, as Plato tells us (Pl. *Resp.* 475d).

Furthermore, throughout the fifth and fourth centuries, large numbers of Athenians were not just passive viewers of drama but were actively involved in bringing these performances onto the stage. Every year, the Great Dionysia alone required 28 *choregoi* and featured 500 men and 500 ephebes in the dithyrambic choruses, 36 men in the tragic choruses, and 120 men in the comedic choruses.[80] Given the fact that written copies of tragedies were still rare, the high level of citizen involvement and the various types of reproductions can explain why fourth-century orators could presuppose their audiences' familiarity with fifth-century tragedies. Consequently, it is not surprising that when Isocrates mentioned, in his *Panathenaicus,* the primary source for everybody's knowledge of Adrastus' story, he referred not to written texts but to hearing the tragic poets at the Dionysia (τίς οὐκ ἀκήκοεν τῶν τραγῳδοδιδασκάλων Διονυσίοις, Isoc. 12.168–69).[81]

In sum, apart from the public funeral ceremony and the assembly and law courts, the dramatic festivals in Athens provided a vital forum for the self-representation of the Athenian demos, in which mythical (and historical) episodes were used to deal with current social, political, religious, and moral issues. Athenian playwrights fulfilled an important function in constituting and negotiating a shared image of the past that retained its relevance for the present. Orators, drawing on these stories and themes, could be confident that

76. Wilson (2000) 22–23.

77. Pickard-Cambridge (1988) 100.

78. Sophocles' *Oenomaus* was performed in the *deme* Collytus, according to Dem. 18.180. Cf. Radt *TrGF* iv.380–85; Yunis (2001) 211–12.

79. Pickard-Cambridge (1988) 42–43, 51–52. The activities of these guilds of actors were not restricted to Attica, however. Some actors, like Aristodemus and Neoptolemus, toured all over Greece, became famous, and were even, thanks to their good contacts, used as ambassadors. Cf. Dem. 19.12; Aeschin. 2.15; MacDowell (2000) 210.

80. Wilson (2000) 22.

81. Cf. "Sparing Thebes' Honor" in chapter 3, 201–10.

their paradigms would resonate well with an audience endowed with the experience of seeing them performed on stage.

Cults and Festivals

In addition to the public funeral ceremony and dramatic festivals, there were many other cults and festivals that greatly contributed to the formation of Athenian social memory.[82] In the eyes of the Greeks, human and divine spheres were closely intertwined.[83] Consequently, the Athenians believed that gods and heroes played a crucial and ongoing role in their city's history. Through cults and festivals, the Athenians honored their gods and heroes, thanking them for past benefactions and seeking to secure their protection and goodwill for the future.[84]

Given the complexity of Greek religion, it is impossible to do justice here to all aspects of this multifaceted phenomenon. Consequently, I will only touch on a few particular issues. The Athenians' knowledge of the past was not only transmitted visually and verbally through monuments, funeral orations, the tragic stage, and assembly and law court speeches; it was also "incorporated" in "performative ceremonies which generate[d] bodily sensory and emotional experiences, resulting in habitual memory being sedimented in the body."[85] Athenian cults and festivals were full of such ceremonial acts. Processions, libations, various types of sacrifices, communal meals, and musical and athletic competitions could all preserve "incorporated" memories connected to the gods' and heroes' actions in the city's past and could thus underlie and support other (visual and semantic) carriers of social memory.[86] It is impossible to measure the effect religion and ceremonial activities had on these collective memories. Yet, since the memories transmitted through cults and festivals were rooted in the realm of religion and constituted "episodic" memory, which is generally more intense than purely "semantic" memory, it is likely that these memories were highly emotionally charged and deeply engraved in Athenian collective consciousness.[87]

---

82. In this section, I focus primarily on polis-wide cults and festivals. For the significance of the innumerable tribal and local cults as focal points of tribal and local identities, see "Tribes and *Demes*" below, 71–73.

83. Bruit Zaidman & Schmitt Pantel (1992) 92.

84. Jung (2006) 68.

85. Hamilakis (1998) 117. Cf. Alcock (2002) 28 and the seminal work of Connerton (1989).

86. Cf. Gould (2001) 417–18.

87. A strict division between these different types of memory is impossible, since semantic memory is continually underpinned and complemented by personal and sensory memory. Cf. Manier & Hirst (2008) 256–57. See "Individual and Collective Memory" in the introduction to the present study, 8–13.

As a brief survey of cults and festivals will show, the Athenians' image of their past was closely bound up with the religious sphere, which resulted in a kind of "religious patriotism"[88] and manifested itself in various areas. *Poleis* competed with each other by attempting to promote local festivals to Panhellenic status or by instituting new cults and thus creating a "new" past for themselves.[89] This religious patriotism was most visible at the Panhellenic sanctuaries where Greek *poleis* commemorated their military triumphs through splendid votive offerings. As a result, the Sacred Way at Delphi became the site of regular "memory wars" between rival cities.[90] Religious patriotism was also an essential objective in the socialization of young citizens. In Athens, local heroes and heroines fulfilled a paradigmatic function in the ideological instruction of young recruits.[91] Cults and festivals played an essential role in their training as well, which is evident from the various ephebic processions and contests attested for many Athenian festivals.[92]

Cults and festivals not only fostered the Athenians' sense of community but also reminded them of their gods' and heroes' exploits. Worshipping the gods in cults and festivals inevitably invoked their mythology as well. The Panathenaea, for instance, culminated in the presentation of a woven garment (the *peplos*) to the olive wood statue of Athena Polias in her temple on the Acropolis.[93] This *peplos* traditionally depicted the Gigantomachy and thus prompted the memory of Athena's glorious role in the Olympians' battle against the forces of chaos.[94] Participants in this festival would also be reminded of the contest between Athena and Poseidon, which marked the beginning of Athena's patronage for the city. The Erechtheion (like its predecessor) contained the cults of Athena Polias and Poseidon as well as the most sacred spots on the Acropolis: the mark of Poseidon's trident, his saltwater spring, and the sacred olive tree, with which Athena had secured her victory (Hdt. 8.55; Paus. 1.26.5–27.2).[95] Moreover, the winners of the quadrennial Panathenaic games received prize amphorae. Filled with oil pressed from the sacred olive trees, which were supposedly descended from Athena's original gift, they served as reminders of the

88. Bruit Zaidman & Schmitt Pantel (1992) 96. Cf. Vielberg (1991) 66–67.

89. Cf. Forsdyke (2011).

90. See "Monuments and Inscriptions" below, 84–94.

91. See Steinbock (2011).

92. Cf. Persky (2009) 95–101.

93. For the details of this festival, see Deubner (1932) 22–35; Burkert (1985) 232–33; Parke (1977) 33–50; Parker (1996) 89–92; Shear (2001). For its sociopolitical implications, cf. Neils (1996); G. Anderson (2003) 158–77.

94. The Gigantomachy also featured on the east metopes of the Parthenon and on the inside of the shield of the Athena Parthenos statue; cf. Hurwit (2004) 17, 39–40. The patron goddess' battle against these forces of chaos served as a mythical analogue for the Athenians' fight against the barbarians; cf. Castriota (1992) 138–42.

95. Hurwit (2004) 42–45. The contest between Athena and Poseidon was also represented in the west pediment of the Parthenon.

beginning of Athena's patronage over the city.[96] Athena's victory over Poseidon was also commemorated with its own festival, the Niceteria.[97] Their quarrel is used in Plato's funeral orations to illustrate how dear Athens was to the gods (Pl. *Menex.* 237c).[98] The brevity of Plato's paradigm—Athena and Poseidon are not even mentioned by name—shows that, thanks to monuments, cults, and festivals, Athenians were expected to be very familiar with this crucial episode in their city's history. That rituals and cults served as important sources for knowledge of the past is evident from Isocrates' *Panegyricus.* In this speech, Isocrates points to the annual rites at Eleusis as proof of Athens' generosity in sharing Demeter's gifts with all humankind (Isoc. 4.29–31).[99]

Among the innumerable heroes and heroines who received cultic honors in classical Athens, Theseus was by far the most outstanding. His extraordinary rise to prominence as Athens' national hero started around 550 BC and reached its pinnacle in 476/5, when Cimon, instructed by an oracle, brought home the hero's bones, which were welcomed by the people with a splendid procession and laid to rest in the newly erected Theseion (Plut. *Thes.* 36.1–4; Plut. *Cim.* 8.5–7).[100] By the middle of the fifth century, many existing festivals had undergone an *interpretatio Theseana,* and "all became in some way commemorations of events" in the hero's career.[101] The Theseia, a sacrificial and athletic festival on a grand scale, was probably established on the occasion of the homecoming of the hero's bones (Ar. *Plut.* 627–28; Plut. *Thes.* 36.4).[102] With an annual procession to the Delphinium, the Athenians reenacted Theseus' visit to this shrine and his supplication of Apollo before his departure to Crete (Plut. *Thes.* 18.1). The Oschophoria were linked in myth with Theseus' return from this adventure (Demon *FGrHist* 327 F 6). The Hecalesia commemorated the hospitality Hecale gave Theseus before his fight with the Marathonian Bull (Philochorus *FGrHist* 328 F 109). On the Cybernesia, the Athenians honored Nausithous and Phaeax, Theseus' pilots on his voyage to Crete (Philochorus *FGrHist* 328 F 111). On the Synoecia, the Athenians commemorated the political unification of Attica by Theseus (Thuc. 2.15.2).[103] Consequently, when Apollodorus mentioned Theseus' synoecism of Attica in his speech *Against Neaera,* it was very familiar to his

96. Cf. Parke (1977) 34; Parker (1996) 90.

97. See Deubner (1932) 235 note 2; Parker (1996) 187 note 124.

98. Cf. Gotteland (2001) 326.

99. Clarke (2008) 290.

100. For Theseus' rise, see "Theseus—Another Heracles" in chapter 3, 169–74. For the return of his bones, cf. Parker (1996) 168.

101. Parker (1996) 169.

102. R. Osborne (2004) 208; Clarke (2008) 300 note 155.

103. See Kearns (1989) 168–69; Parker (1996) 169, 270; Deubner (1932) 201, 224–26; Harding (2008) 56–63. For the Synoecia, see G. Anderson (2003) 143–45. Unusual ritual practices, as in the case of the Oschophoria, were often explained through (new) aetiological myths connected to Theseus; cf. Parke (1977) 77–81.

audience ([Dem.] 59.75).[104] That these festivals indeed refreshed the memory of Theseus' exploits and thus transmitted them to younger generations can be inferred from Demon's account, which mentions that legends (presumably about Theseus) were told at the Oschophoria (Demon *FGrHist* 327 F 6).[105]

Cults, rituals, and festivals commemorated not only the legendary deeds of gods and heroes in the mythical past but also their divine intervention on behalf of the Athenians in more recent moments of crisis. Persian War victories in particular were ascribed to the gods to a considerable extent, as Herodotus' Themistocles makes clear (Hdt. 8.109.3).[106] As an expression of their gratitude, the Athenians newly instituted cults for gods and heroes and reinterpreted existing festivals in order to commemorate the divine contribution to their extraordinary achievements.[107]

The victory at Marathon was celebrated not on the actual anniversary but a few weeks later, on the sixth of Boedromion, at the Charisteria, a thanksgiving festival for Artemis Agrotera and Enyalius, the god of war (Plut. *Mor.* 349e). Before the battle, the Athenians had vowed to the gods to sacrifice one goat for every Persian slain. The number of Persians killed was so high, however, that the Athenians commuted the vow to an annual offering of five hundred goats (Xen. *An.* 3.2.12; Arist. *Ath. Pol.* 58.1). Escorted by the ephebes, the goats were led in a procession to the shrine of Artemis Agrotera on the Ilissus river (Plut. *Mor.* 862a; *IG* II^2 1028.8).[108] Before the battle, the Athenian army had encamped in the precinct of Heracles at Marathon (Hdt. 6.108). To celebrate the hero's aid, the Athenians converted the local Heracleia into a polis-wide festival with athletic games (*IG* I^3 3).[109] A cult of Zeus Tropaeus at the very site of the battle further helped to commemorate this great victory (*IG* I^3 255.11).[110] Upon learning of the Persians' arrival at Marathon, the Athenian generals had sent the runner Philippides as a messenger to Sparta. On this run, Philippides claimed to have seen the god Pan, who promised to help the Athenians. Consequently, after the battle, the Athenians established a shrine of Pan below the Acropolis and honored him with annual sacrifices and a torch race (Hdt. 6.105).[111] Similarly, for his help in destroying many Persian ships in a storm before the battle of Artemisium, the Athenians built a shrine for the wind god Boreas by the river

104. Cf. Gotteland (2001) 275.

105. Parke (1977) 78.

106. For the gods and heroes as Athens' allies in the fight against the Persians, see also Hdt. 8.143.

107. Parker (1996) 186–87; Jung (2006) 27.

108. Deubner (1932) 209; Parke (1977) 55; Simon (1983) 82; Barron (1988) 620; Parker (1996) 153; Jung (2006) 54–58.

109. Deubner (1932) 227; Parker (1996) 153; Jung (2006) 28–38.

110. Parker (1996) 153.

111. Simon (1983) 53; Parker (1996) 163–68; Jung (2006) 38–49.

Ilissus (Hdt. 7.189).[112] On the sixteenth of Munichion, the naval victory at Salamis was commemorated at the festival of Artemis Munichia in form of a regatta held by the ephebes (Plut. *Mor.* 349f).[113] Ajax of Salamis was invoked by the Greeks before the battle in the straits (Hdt. 8.64). After their victory, the Greeks dedicated a captured trireme to him (Hdt. 8.121), and the Athenians established a commemorative festival, the Aianteia, on the island of Salamis.[114] The victory of Plataea was commemorated in Athens in the form of a festival (Plut. *Mor.* 349f) and by erecting a monumental stoa in the Agora for Zeus Eleutherius, to whom the Greeks had made a famous sacrifice after the battle (Thuc. 2.71.2).[115]

All these new Athenian cults and festivals in commemoration of the Persian Wars "testify to the unique intensity with which the national crisis and triumph were experienced."[116] Yet Marathon, Artemisium, Salamis, and Plataea were not the only historical events commemorated in connection with particular religious festivals. According to Plutarch (Plut. *Mor.* 349f–350a), the Athenians also celebrated the exiles' return from Phyle (403 BC), Chabrias' victory over the Spartans at Naxos (376 BC), and the Athenian victory over their enemies at Mantinea (362 BC).[117] The Athenians are not exceptional in instituting rituals and festivals for the commemoration of significant historical events. The Thebans, for instance, used the spoils from the battle of Delium to establish the Delia, a regular festival for Apollo to commemorate their victory over the Athenians in 424 BC (Diod. 12.70.5).[118]

In conclusion, polis-wide cults and festivals (especially the public funeral ceremony and the dramatic festivals) greatly contributed to constituting common Athenian historical consciousness. Their religious and "bodily" aspect certainly helped to emotionally charge these social memories, which encouraged feelings of identity and belonging. If a speaker in the assembly or the law courts wanted to use the metaphors and symbols provided by these "official" polis traditions, it was sufficient to briefly allude to them, since they were deeply engraved in Athenian collective consciousness.[119]

112. Parker (1996) 156–57.

113. Deubner (1932) 204–7; Parke (1977) 137–39; Simon (1983) 81–82; Parker (1996) 155, 187 note 124.

114. Deubner (1932) 228; Parker (1996) 153–54.

115. The stoa dates to around 430 BC; cf. Parker (1996) 157, 239.

116. Parker (1996) 187.

117. Cf. Deubner (1932) 235; Parker (1996) 228–29, 238.

118. Cf. Schachter (1981–94) 1:47. For the importance of this victory for the Theban self-image, see Lewis (1992) 426. For commemorative festivals of other states, see Gauer (1968) 16.

119. See, e.g., Dem. 6.7–12, discussed further under "Treacherous by Nature" in chapter 2, 143–49.

Different Memory Communities

Individual Athenians participated not only in the polis as a whole but also in numerous subgroups: their family, *deme*, tribe, *genos*, phratry, age-set, upper-class club (ἑταιρεία), local and private religious associations, and so on.[120] These subgroups played a crucial role in every Athenian's life, and all of them fostered their own social memories, which promoted internal cohesion. That the bonds resulting from the shared experience in such subgroups were indeed very close is evident from the speech that Cleocritus, the herald of the initiates at Eleusis and one of the democratic exiles, reportedly delivered after the battle of Munichia in an attempt to reconcile the two civil war factions.

> Fellow citizens, why do you drive us out of the city? Why do you wish to kill us? For we never did you any harm, but we have shared with you [μετεσχήκαμεν δὲ ὑμῖν] in the most solemn rites and sacrifices and the most splendid festivals, we have been fellow members of a chorus [συγχορευταί] and schoolmates [συμφοιτηταί] and comrades in arms [συστρατιῶται], and we have braved many dangers with you both by land and by sea in defense of the common safety and freedom of us both. In the name of the gods of our fathers and mothers, in the name of our ties of kinship and marriage and comradeship—for all these many of us share with one another—cease . . . to sin against your fatherland. (Xen. *Hell.* 2.4.20–21)

The memories fostered by these subgroups could reinforce, supplement, and sustain each other, but they could also be in conflict.[121] The democrats' memories of the civil war certainly differed from those of the men of the city who had supported the Thirty.[122] If we want to grasp the contestation and negotiation of Athenian social memory in the law courts and the assembly, we have to take the memories of these different subgroups into account. In the following section, I will focus particularly on tribes and *demes*, families, sympotic companionships, and guest-friendships (ξενίαι and προξενίαι).

120. For *gene* and local and private religious associations, see Kearns (1989) 64–79; Parker (1996) 284–342. Each of these religious groups cherished the shared memory of its mythical *archegetes*. For *demes* and phratries, respectively, see Whitehead (1986); Lambert (1993). For age-sets in Athens, see Davidson (2006); Steinbock (2011) 290–92. For the role of all of these associations in maintaining the Athenian democracy, see C. P. Jones (1999).

121. See "Individual and Collective Memory" in the introduction, 8–13.

122. Cf. Wolpert (2002).

Tribes and Demes

The *demes* played a vital role in the political and social life of classical Athens.[123] These 139 local units were the political infrastructure of the Athenian polis. They were an important source of civic identity, as can be seen from the use of the *demotikon* instead of the *patronymikon* in public life and from the fact that citizenship was obtained through membership in a *deme*. The *demes* held assemblies and had their own officials, cults, and festivals.[124] Given the average size of these small towns, the *demes* were truly face-to-face societies. Even though they did not exist as administrative units before Cleisthenes' reforms, they continued "most of the practices and narratives of the old village[s]."[125] *Demes* had their own history and identity. The members of the *deme* Decelea, for instance, remembered the aid that Decelus, the *deme's* eponymous hero, allegedly provided to the Dioscuri when Theseus abducted Helen. Decelus was upset about Theseus' hubris (ἀχθόμενον τῇ Θησέος ὕβρι) and revealed to the Dioscuri their sister's whereabouts. As a result, the Spartans, out of gratitude, spared Decelea during their invasions of Attica in the Archidamian War (Hdt. 9.73).[126] This shows that a *deme* could have an identity distinct from (and, in this case, even somewhat in opposition to) the common polis identity and that these collective memories could become highly political relevant.

That individual *demes* had their own identities and political concerns is also evident in the case of Acharnae, Attica's largest *deme*.[127] Various sources attest that the Acharnians had a reputation for stern patriotism and belligerence (Pind. *Nem.* 2.16–17; Ar. *Ach.* 178–85, 204–36, 280–365, 665–75). According to Thucydides, the Acharnians played a special role at the time of the first Spartan invasion of Attica in 431. As the Spartan king Archidamus had anticipated (Thuc. 2.20.4), the Acharnians, faced with the destruction of their property, were the most outspoken critics of Pericles' strategy and lobbied vigorously for active resistance to the invaders (Thuc. 2.21.3). The Acharnians are here represented "as fully aware of their numerical and psychological influence in the polis."[128] It is not far-fetched to assume that this disaster became part of the Acharnians' shared history and identity and that the Acharnians remembered

123. Cf. Whitehead (1986).

124. Cf. Parker (1996) 114–16.

125. Kearns (1989) 92.

126. Titacus, presumably the eponymous hero of the *deme* Titacidae, also stood up to the Panathenian hero Theseus and betrayed the town Aphidna to the Dioscuri (Hdt. 9.73). See Flower & Marincola (2002) 236–39; Kearns (1989) 118, 154, 200.

127. For a comprehensive treatment of Acharnae, see Kellogg (2005).

128. Whitehead (1986) 399.

the destruction of their houses and fields more vividly and longer than other Athenians. This might be one of the reasons why, in his comedy, Aristophanes had the Acharnians express a deep longing for revenge and fierce opposition to making peace with the Spartans in 425 BC. That the Acharnians remained particularly patriotic and devoted to military service is evident from the fourth-century institution of the cult of Ares and Athena Areia in their *deme* (*SEG* 21.519), accompanied by the patriotic inscriptions of the Ephebic Oath and the Oath of Plataea (R&O 88).[129]

The *demes* were also the places where the memories of new citizens could be absorbed. We will see, in the case of the Plataeans and of Thrasybulus' foreign supporters, that new citizens were distributed among the *demes.*[130] These new citizens were able to share their previous experiences with their fellow demesmen. Through their mere presence, the new citizens thus served as reminders of the destruction of Plataea and the seizure of Phyle, respectively.

Unlike a *deme,* a tribe did not have a coherent territory but consisted of three geographically disconnected units—city, coastal, and inland *trittyes*—each comprising several *demes.* Despite their artificial composition and relatively recent origins in the reforms of Cleisthenes, the ten tribes were enormously important political and social units, on an intermediate level between *deme* and polis. Each tribe had its own eponymous hero and local cults, political meetings, and representatives in the council. The recruits were trained by tribe, the dithyrambic choruses at festivals were organized by tribe, and the war dead were listed and buried by tribe. All these activities ensured that the tribes were active political and social communities with their own sense of identity, history, and loyalty.[131]

The basis for this tribal loyalty and identity was laid during the *ephebeia,* the military training program for young men. We know, from the Aristotelian *Athenaion Politeia,* that before entering their first year of service, the recruits were taken on a tour of the shrines of the city (Arist. *Ath. Pol.* 42.3), where they probably learned about the paradigmatic deeds of their tribal and age-set heroes.[132] It is clear, from our sources, that the heroic example of the epony-

129. Rhodes & Osborne (2003) 442–43; Kellogg (2008).

130. See "Plataean-Theban Antagonism" in chapter 2, 120–27; "Athenian Memorialization of the Men from Phyle" in chapter 4, 235–45. Cf. Rhodes & Osborne (2003) 26.

131. For the eponymous heroes and the tribes' religious aspects, see Kron (1976); Kearns (1989) 80–92; Parker (1996) 103–4, 117–21.

132. For the tour of the shrines, see Mikalson (1998) 42; Rhodes (1981) 505; Parker (1996) 255. For the role of Attic heroes in the ideological instruction of Athenian ephebes, see Steinbock (2011) 297–306. The ephebate as we know it from the Aristotelian *Athenaion Politeia* (42) and from a whole series of ephebic inscriptions is, beyond doubt, a Lycurgan institution. It is generally accepted, however, that the *ephebeia* existed in some form before Epicrates' substantial reform of 335 BC. Cf. Reinmuth (1971) 23–38; Rhodes (1981) 493–95; Burckhardt (1996) 29–33; Gehrke (1997) 1072–74; Christ (2001) 416.

mous hero was essential for tribal identity. In the funeral speech for the fallen of Chaeronea, Demosthenes demonstrated how the members of each tribe had found inspiration in the example of their respective tribal hero (Dem. 60.27–31). Lycurgus cited the patriotic self-sacrifice of the daughter of Erechtheus in his prosecution of the deserter Leocrates (Lycurg. 98–101).[133] Similarly, when Alexander demanded the extradition of leading Athenian statesmen in 335, Phocion asked those men to imitate the daughters of Leos and of Erechtheus (the so-called Hyacinthiae) and to give their lives for their city (Diod. 17.15.2.).[134]

Moreover, we have some indication that historical events could be experienced and remembered differently by individual tribes. The fourth-century Atthidographer Cleidemus reports that all fifty-two Athenian casualties of the battle of Plataea belonged to the tribe Aiantis (*FGrHist* 323 F 22 = Plut. *Arist.* 19.6). It is reasonable to assume that this particular battle had, thanks to the high death toll, a special meaning for the Aiantidae. This tribe's sacrifice was also recognized by the polis at large: it was the privilege of men of the tribe Aiantis to perform the annual sacrifice to the Sphragithic Nymphs in commemoration of the Athenian victory at Plataea (*FGrHist* 323 F 22 = Plut. *Arist.* 19.6).[135]

It is evident that both *demes* and tribes were distinct communities in Athens, with their own historical experiences. Each Athenian citizen participated simultaneously in the memory community of his *deme*, tribe, and polis. Some of these subgroups were more invested than others in the recollection of particular events. These demotic and tribal memories could, however, be introduced into the polis-wide discourse of the assembly and law courts and thus played a vital role in the constitution and negotiation of Athenian social memory.

Family Traditions

Another important source for knowledge of the past in classical Athens was one's family.[136] Young Athenians learned their family history from older family members, as portrayed in Plato's *Laches* (179b–c).[137] Family history was embedded in wider Greek history, especially if one's ancestors had played an important part in it.[138]

133. This paradigm is also used in Lycurg. fr. X–XI 10 Conomis.

134. Cf. Kearns (1989) 59–63; Parker (1996) 251–52; Kron (1999) 77–82.

135. Cf. Plut. *Arist.* 11.3–4, *Mor.* 628e–f; Paus. 9.3.9; Jacoby *FGrHist* 3b (Suppl.) i.82–83; Schachter (1981–94) 2:185–86; Parker (1996) 103; Harding (2008) 105–6.

136. For a comprehensive treatment of family traditions, see R. Thomas (1989) 95–154.

137. See also Aeschin. 3.191.

138. Rosalind Thomas defines "family tradition" as "traditions about a family that are handed down within the family," but she acknowledges that these traditions are often bound up with traditions about wider Greek history passed down within the family. In both cases, the family is the source of knowledge of the past. Such traditions are to be distinguished from a third type, popular gossip and folktales *about* particular families. See Thomas (1989) 98.

In the assembly and law courts, Athenians frequently recalled their ancestors' involvement in glorious moments in the city's past in order to establish their own patriotic and democratic credentials.[139] In so doing, they refreshed their listeners' memory of these particular events. Aeschines, for instance, recalled to the jury that his father Atrometus "went into exile under the Thirty and later helped to restore the democracy [συγκατήγαγε δὲ τὸν δῆμον]" (Aeschin. 2.78).[140] Another speaker boasted that his grandfather Cleon "commanded as general your ancestors and captured alive a large number of Lacedaemonians in Pylos" ([Dem.] 40.25).[141]

Considering the unstable nature of "remembered" history, it is not surprising that family memories were particularly prone to the distortions exerted by the "official" polis tradition.[142] For example, both Andocides and the younger Alcibiades claimed (probably wrongly) that their ancestors had been generals in the demos' paradigmatic fight against the tyrants at the end of the sixth century (Andoc. 1.106; Isoc. 16.25–26).[143]

Yet some events that would otherwise have been forgotten were remembered (and, on occasion, brought into public discourse) thanks to family tradition. As we have seen, the Athenian master narrative preserved only the broadest outlines of the past, in a much simplified form. A family, however, had an interest in preserving in detail the glorious achievements of its members. The more prominent the ancestors were, the more a family could become an important source for polis history. Andocides, for instance, claimed that his maternal uncle Epilycus was on an embassy to arrange a truce with the Persian king, which the Athenians later abandoned to conclude an alliance with the rebel Amorges instead (Andoc. 3.29).[144] Neither Thucydides nor any other literary source makes mention of Epilycus' diplomatic mission, which has found support, however, in the form of an inscription (M&L 70) and can now be dated to 424/3.[145] Drawing on his own family tradition, Andocides thus reintroduced an obscure memory into Athenian public discourse.

Since family tradition focused on the activities of its members and preserved their unique perspective, it is not surprising that Andocides' version of Athenian history during the Pentecontaetia (Andoc. 3.3–8) seems utterly lop-

139. Rosalind Thomas terms this the family defense; see Thomas (1989) 108–12, 129–30.

140. For the special resonance of this phrase, see "Athenian Memorialization of the Men from Phyle" in chapter 4, 235–45.

141. R. Thomas (1989) 114, 116, 124. The Spartan shields were hung up in the Stoa Poikile and served as a material reminder of this important victory at Sphacteria in 425 BC (Paus. 1.15.5).

142. Cf. "Remembered and Commemorated History" in the introduction, 23–26.

143. R. Thomas (1989) 116–17.

144. Cf. R. Thomas (1989) 118–20.

145. Rhodes (2010) 119–21.

sided and full of distortions in comparison to Thucydides' account. Yet these distortions are probably not the product of willful manipulation but a result of the processes of memory in a predominantly oral society.[146]

Often, orators alluded to a family member or the elders in general to corroborate their historical paradigms.[147] In a culture in which oral communication played a vital role, such corroborations carried much more authoritative weight than they would in our own. As a result, an orator could even venture to challenge a prevalent social memory, manifested and transmitted through monuments and commemorative events, by pointing to his own family history as an equally authoritative source for knowledge of the past. Aeschines, for instance, pointed to the disastrous Sicilian expedition and the foolish rejection of a Spartan peace offer (events that he had learned of from his father and uncle) and thus countered his opponents' call to emulate (blindly) the ancestors' achievements at Salamis (Aeschin. 2.74–78).[148]

In sum, family traditions were embedded in and often conformed to the official polis tradition, but they also could preserve the memory of events that would otherwise have been forgotten. One's elders were regarded as an authoritative source for knowledge of the past and could even be used to challenge the predominant version of the Athenian master narrative.

The Symposium

The symposium, in its many manifestations, has been described as "a defining characteristic of Greek culture and society."[149] This archaic social institution of "drinking together" (συμπόσιον) is a form of Greek commensality, practiced by a small group of usually upper-class male companions (ca. fourteen to thirty) in the men's quarters (ἀνδρών) of a private home.[150] The participants wore garlands, and prayers and libations began and ended these ritualized drinking sessions.[151] The symposium provided a forum for the members of the group to celebrate and debate together, to express their group identity, and to enjoy various forms of entertainment, ranging from drinking games to artistic performances of poetry and music.[152] This aristocratic social institution, which was a key fac-

146. Cf. R. Thomas (1989) 119–21.

147. Cf. Din. 1.25, Dem. 18.50, 20.52, 20.77; Isoc. 16.4; R. Thomas (1989) 200–201.

148. Cf. R. Thomas (1989) 101, and Steinbock (forthcoming).

149. Murray (1983a) 258. Ever since scholars of lyric poetry have shifted their attention from the intensive study of texts and literary matters to aspects of performance, the symposium has become the prime object of inquiry from a variety of disciplinary angles. Cf. Murray (1990a); Murray & Tecuşan (1995).

150. Murray (1990b) 6–7.

151. For an ideal symposium, see Xenophanes' programmatic elegy (fr. B1 West^2).

152. The aristocratic symposium developed out of earlier forms of commensality, which we

tor in the sociopolitical and cultural history of the archaic period,[153] continued to be an important part of social life in the fifth and fourth centuries, even in democratic Athens.

The symposium played a vital role in the constitution and transmission of social memory, in Athens and beyond, for two reasons. First, it was essential for the composition and circulation of much of Greek poetry, since most iambic, elegiac, and monodic poetry was sung or recited in its intimate surroundings.[154] Despite their generic differences and their wide-ranging themes,[155] many poems dealt with historical events (of both private and public dimension) and thus functioned as important carriers of social memory, as we will see below.[156]

Second, symposia served as focal points for the formation of the identities of numerous small subgroups within the polis. In particular, the associations of young upper-class men (ἑταιρεῖαι) can be seen as separate memory communities, whose group identity could be distinct from the prevalent self-image of the democratic Athenian polis. This is not surprising, since the symposium was, from its inception and in many ways, "a place apart from the normal rules of society, with its own strict code of honour . . . and its own willingness to establish conventions fundamentally opposed to those within the *polis* as a whole."[157] The prevalent function of these ἑταιρεῖαι seems to have been of a social nature, that is, to come together at the symposium and enjoy its various forms of entertainment.[158] Yet, in accordance with their predominantly oligarchic sentiments, they could, at times become highly political, as shown by Thucydides' account of their role in the oligarchic coup of 411 BC (Thuc. 8.54, 65). It is important to stress, however, that not all groups who held symposia necessarily fostered

find in the Homeric epics, where leaders seek to attract support from outside the family through displays of generosity, particularly through the use of surplus agricultural produce for the entertainment and feasting of male companions. Cf. Murray (1983a) 259–62; Murray (1983b) 196–98.

153. For the early sixth century, the Lesbian poet Alcaeus provides the best example for the political significance of these aristocratic clubs (ἑταιρεῖαι), which forged their group identities in the symposium. Cf. Rösler (1980) 26–36; Murray (1983a) 266.

154. Gerber (1997b) 7; Rösler (1990) 230. For iambic and elegiac fragments, see West²; monodic fragments can be found in *PMG*.

155. This is not the place to engage in a detailed discussion of these poetic genres. For an excellent introduction to iambus, elegy, and personal and public poetry (replacing the older division between monodic and choral poetry), see Gerber (1997a).

156. Cf. the seminal article by Rösler (1990), who uses the Greek term μνημοσύνη to denote "the act of remembering the past" (230), which he views as an essential element of the symposium.

157. Murray (1990b) 7. Murray (1990c) makes a convincing case that the profanation of the religious mysteries and the mutilation of the herms in 415 BC were extreme examples of group bravado among aristocrats, revealing "an undemocratic contempt for the laws" of their native city (158).

158. This is indicated by the fact that many of the fragments of poetry recited or sung at the symposium are decidedly apolitical, featuring erotic themes or exhibiting general philosophical reflections. For the social aspects of these clubs, see G. M. Calhoun (1913) 26–29; C. P. Jones (1999) 224–26.

an antidemocratic self-image. While the symposium used to be the exclusive domain of the leisure class during the archaic period, there is evidence to suggest that it spread down the social ladder;[159] it seems that by the end of the fifth century, symposia were (in one form or another) practiced by a large number of Athenians, in accordance, of course, with their individual means.[160]

From early on, the symposium served as venue for the creation and expression of group identity among its members. Reminiscing about past events that were important to the particular group or the community at large was an essential element of this process. As Xenophanes, for instance, stated in his depiction of the ideal symposium, that man deserves praise "who after drinking proclaims noble things [ὅς ἐσθλὰ πιὼν ἀναφαίνει], so that there is a recollection of and striving for excellence [ὡς ᾖ μνημοσύνη καὶ τόνος ἀμφ' ἀρετῆς]" (fr. B1.19–20 West²). Rösler makes a strong case that the word ἐσθλὰ (noble things) denotes "examples of noble behaviour taken from the past,"[161] which Xenophanes then contrasted to the useless πλάσματα (invented stories) of their predecessors, such as the battles of the Titans, Giants, and Centaurs, and the memory of violent civil strife (fr. B1.21–23 West²).[162] Various types of poems that correspond to Xenophanes' ideal have come down to us. Some elegies mention particular events and commemorate exemplary bravery on the battlefield. Mimnermus, for instance, praised the strength and heroic spirit of a man "who routed the thick ranks of the Lydian cavalry on the plain of Hermus" (fr. 14 West²).[163] Closely related are elegies that feature glorifying accounts of the community's past. Mimnermus recalled events in the history of his native city Smyrna, including its foundation and the war against the Lydian king Gyges (fr. 9, 10, 13, 13a West²).[164] Similarly, Tyrtaeus reminded a Spartan audience of

159. Murray (1983a) 265 argues that already by the fifth century the symposium "was part of the social life of considerable sections of the hoplite class" in many Greek *poleis*.

160. For this downward spread in Athens, cf. Fisher (2000). See also Pownall (2008) on Critias' critique of the democratization of symposia (fr. 2 West² = DK 88 B2).

161. Rösler (1990) 230. For the paradigmatic use of the past in elegy, see now also Grethlein (2010) 54–68.

162. It is generally agreed that Xenophanes depicts an ideal symposium; consequently, his remarks should be understood as prescriptive. Civil strife was, in fact, a frequent theme at the symposium, as shown by several poems by Alcaeus (fr. 75, 129, 348 Voigt); cf. Rösler (1990) 231–32.

163. Mimnermus' source for this incident is not entirely clear. According to the manuscript tradition, Mimnermus learned it "from [his] elders who saw him" (τοῖον ἐμέο προτέρων πεύθομαι, οἵ μιν ἴδον, fr. 14.2 West²). Grethlein (2010) 64 emends the text and reads ὅς for οἵ, which makes Mimnermus the eyewitness of this man's bravery. According to the traditional reading, Mimnermus encourages his contemporaries to match the bravery of one of their ancestors: cf. West (1974) 74; Rösler (1990) 231; Gerber (1999) 97 note 1. In Grethlein's version, Mimnermus compares a more recent feat favorably to the ancestors' achievements. Regardless of which reading one prefers, Mimnermus presents the man's bravery as exemplary to his contemporary audience.

164. In a seminal article, Ewen Bowie (1986) argued for the existence of lengthy historical/narrative elegies, such as Tyrtaeus' *Eunomia* and Mimnermus' *Smyrneis*, written for performance at

their forefathers' war against the Messenians (fr. 5, 6, 7 West^2). In both cases, the "we" is projected back into the distant past; by identifying their contemporaries with their ancestors, both Mimnermus and Tyrtaeus emphasized the continuity between the past and the present and thus confirmed their respective communities' collective identities.[165] Moreover, through the use of various Homeric formulae, Tyrtaeus managed to heroize the First Messenian War and thus lent authority to the past, which made it suitable for his paraenetic purposes (fr. 5 West^2).[166] Another set of elegiac fragments, apparently closely related to these narrative/historical elegies, features martial exhortation (e.g., Tyrtaeus fr. 10, 11, 12 West^2; Callinus fr. 1 West^2).[167] It is likely that these elegies were not, as previously thought, recited in the field before an impending battle but instead belonged to the symposium as well, as Bowie has argued persuasively.[168]

None of the examples I have mentioned so far come from Athens, but the works of such famous poets as Simonides and Tyrtaeus were also recited at Athenian symposia and could even be quoted by Athenian orators to increase the patriotism of their Athenian audiences, as shown by Lycurgus' use of Tyrtaeus in his prosecution of the deserter Leocrates (Lycurg. 105–8; Tyrtaeus fr. 10 West^2). Tyrtaeus' case is indeed remarkable. Even though his poems were clearly addressed to Spartans, the Athenians firmly believed that he had been one of their own. According to a well-established Athenian tradition, the Spartans were instructed by the god in Delphi to request the help of the Athenian Tyrtaeus for the war against the Messenians.[169] The famous archaic poet Tyrtaeus had thus been fully incorporated into the Athenian memorial framework.

There is, of course, also evidence for sympotic poetry referring to events in the Athenian past, which shows that the symposium indeed played an impor-

public festivals. Grethlein (2010) 52, 69, 291–96 casts doubt on Bowie's hypothesis that these poems could fill a whole book in Hellenistic editions and were too long to be performed at the symposium; he comes to the conclusion that for historical elegies, "as for elegies in general, symposia were the prime place for their circulation" (69). Pointing to the *New Simonides* (especially fr. 11 Sider = fr. 11 West^2), he concedes, however, that some historical elegies may indeed have been written for and performed at public festivals. Later, of course, they could be recited at symposia as well. For the likely performance of the *New Simonides* at a commemorative festival at Plataea, see "Memorialization of Thebes' Treason" in chapter 2, 106–13.

165. Rösler (1990) 230–31; cf. Mimnermus fr. 9.6 West^2 ("by the will of the gods ***we*** took Aeolian Smyrna"; emphasis added); Tyrtaeus fr. 5.1–2 West^2 ("with ***our*** king, Theopompus dear to the gods, through whom ***we*** seized spacious Messene"; emphasis added). This projection of the "we" into the past is, of course, one of the main characteristics of the Athenian funeral orations. For persistent national characters, see also "Treacherous by Nature" in chapter 2, 143–49.

166. For a detailed discussion, see Grethlein (2010) 56–57.

167. It is particularly likely that Tyrtaeus used their forefathers' war against the Messenians (e.g., in fr. 5 West^2) to exhort contemporary Spartan soldiers. Similarly, Mimnermus probably recalled past events in Smyrna's history as a mirror to the fight against Gyges (cf. fr. 13, 13a West^2), as Grethlein (2010) 56–58 suggests.

168. E. L. Bowie (1990).

169. Cf. Pl. *Leg.* 629a; Lycurg. 105–6; Paus. 4.15.3; Diod. 8.27.1–2; Gerber (1999) 26–33.

tant role in the constitution and transmission of Athenian social memory. Solon's poems—in which he describes the Athenian social and political crisis of the early sixth century, defends his reforms, expresses his vision of a harmonious polis community, and warns the Athenians against Peisistratus—must have been widely circulating at Athenian symposia, given Solon's popularity in the fourth century.[170] In addition to their performance at the symposium, we know from Plato that Solon's poems were also sung by Athenian boys at the Apaturia festival (Pl. *Ti.* 21b).[171] Consequently, in his prosecution of Aeschines in 343 BC, Demosthenes could be confident that his citation of one of Solon's elegies would resonate with the Athenian jurors (Dem. 19.254–56 = Solon fr. 4 West^2).[172] Similarly, the feat of the tyrannicides Harmodius and Aristogeiton was commemorated not only through a public monument and the institution of a state cult but also in drinking songs, the so-called *scolia* (*PMG* 893–96).[173] That these songs were indeed incredibly popular in fifth-century Athens is evident from several allusions in Aristophanes' comedies.[174] The case of Harmodius and Aristogeiton illustrates, in an exemplary way, how different carriers of social memory mutually influenced and sustained one another.[175]

From its inception, the symposium was a place for the socialization and instruction of the young.[176] That the symposium remained an important vehicle for the transmission of Athenian social memory throughout the classical period is evident from a fragment by the comic playwright Antiphanes, which mentions the performance of old-fashioned songs such as the *Telamon, Paion,* or *Harmodius* (*PCG* Antiphanes fr. 85 Kassel-Austin). This proves that, well into the fourth century, boys at the Athenian symposium had to "glorify the heroic deeds of mythical and historical heroes, examples they should look up to in their own life."[177]

170. Cf. Solon fr. 4, 4a, 4c, 5, 6, 9, 10, 11 West^2. In her 2010 discussion of the transmission of Solon's poems, Noussia-Fantuzzi, while conceding the existence of a few written copies, nevertheless asserts that it is "not only possible but probable that Greek audience(s) in the archaic and classical period primarily encountered lyric, elegiac and iambic poetry through performance, and that the dissemination of small scale archaic poetry was predominantly if not exclusively oral" (52).

171. Cf. Noussia-Fantuzzi (2010) 54.

172. Some scholars doubt that Demosthenes indeed recited all thirty-nine lines of fr. 4 West^2; cf. MacDowell (2000) 312; Noussia-Fantuzzi (2010) 217. But we find two citations of Eur. *Erechtheus* and Tyrtaeus (of similar length) in Lycurgus' *Against Leocrates* (Lycurg. 100, 107). For the effectiveness of Demosthenes' quotation, see Rowe (1972). For its religious implications, cf. Martin (2009) 71–72.

173. For the statue group (which replaced the initial monument stolen by the Persians) and for the official cult of the tyrannicides, see Fabbro (1995) 137–44.

174. Cf. Ar. *Vesp.* 1225–26; Ar. *Ach.* 980, 1093.

175. Cf. R. Thomas (1989) 257–61.

176. Bremmer (1990) 137; Dover (1968) 251–52. Cf. the number of poems addressed to boys, such as Semonides fr. 1 West^2 and Alcaeus fr. 311 Voigt.

177. Bremmer (1990) 138. Cf. Ar. *Nub.* 1353–58, which refers to the recitation of one of Simonides' poems about a famous Greek wrestler.

Most of the sympotic allusions to the past that I have discussed so far, while recited by a small group at the symposium, seem relevant to the community at large (e.g., the deeds of Harmodius and Aristogeiton). But the symposiasts could also commemorate events that were primarily significant to the group itself. Alcaeus' poems, in which he reminds his fellow ἑταίροι of their common struggle against the tyrants in his native city Mytilene, are the best examples.[178] But sympotic expressions of the collective memory shared by the group of companions can also be found in Athens. Critias, for instance, after proposing the recall of Alcibiades in the Athenian assembly, composed the following elegy: "As for the proposal which led you back from exile, I proposed it among all the people, and by my motion I accomplished this deed" (Critias fr. 5 West^2 = DK 88 B5). Through this poem, Critias "reminded Alcibiades of his favor" (Plut. *Alc.* 33.1) and thus tried to oblige him for the future based on the principle of reciprocity. In Plato's *Republic,* Socrates quotes the opening line of an elegy composed by Glaucon's lover to celebrate the acts of bravery shown by Glaucon and his brothers in the battle at Megara (Pl. *Resp.* 368a = *adesp. el.* fr. 1 West^2).[179] This poem, once composed, was likely recited more than once and could thus keep the memory of Glaucon's feat alive among his companions.

In sum, the symposium played a vital role in the constitution and transmission of social memory in fifth- and fourth-century Athens. It was essential for the composition and circulation of much of Greek poetry, a significant part of which commemorated events that were meaningful to the symposiasts themselves or the larger community. The symposium itself functioned as a forum for the members of the group to celebrate and debate together and thus to forge and express their particular group identity.

Xenia *and* Proxenia

So far, I have only talked about different memory communities within Athens: each Athenian citizen was a member of the polis, his tribe, his *deme,* his family, his age-set, and numerous other religious, social, and political associations.[180] He was thus exposed to a variety of social memories that could sometimes be at odds but that usually complemented and sustained each other. Greek *poleis,* however, were not hermetically closed societies. The members of the upper classes, in particular, had various ties to other Greeks and to members of for-

178. Cf. Alcaeus fr. 75, 129, 348 Voigt; Rösler (1990) 232.

179. Cf. Rösler (1990) 233. This might be a reference to a battle against the Megarians in 409 BC, reported by Diod. 13.65, as Gerber (1999) 473 suggests. Glaucon was Plato's brother, and his lover might have been Critias.

180. Cf. the beginning of the section "Different Memory Communities" above, 70.

eign tribes and states, through which they were exposed to the shared memories of these communities. Two social institutions deserve mentioning in this context: *xenia* (ξενία) and *proxenia* (προξενία).

Xenia is best described as ritual friendship, a "bond of trust, imitating kinship and reinforced by rituals, generating affection and obligations between individuals belonging to separate social units."[181] From early on, it played a prominent role in Greek culture, as is evident from the Homeric epics. The guest-host relationship denoted as ξενία was reciprocal and inherited from father to son. It retained its powerful force in the classical polis. Consequently, individuals often found themselves in a conflict of loyalty when patriotism and guest-friendship appeared as antithetical principles. For instance, anticipating that his ξένος, the Spartan king Archidamus, might spare his own estates during the invasion of Attica, Pericles converted his private estates into public property to ensure his fellow Athenians of his loyalty and patriotism (Thuc. 2.13).[182]

The norms of ξενία demanded that an individual aided his ξένος in any way possible. We have seen, in the introduction to this book, how one of Lysias' clients took in Pherenicus, the son of his Theban ξένος Cephisodotus, when he fled to Athens after the capture of the Cadmea in 382 (Lys. fr. 286 Carey).[183] This unknown Athenian had found refuge in Cephisodotus' home in Thebes during the time of the Thirty and now felt the obligation to repay his debt. He even went to court on Pherenicus' behalf, as this fragment attests.

Lysias' client was not an exception. In chapter 4, I will make the case that other Thebans also received help from Athenian guest-friends when they were driven out of Thebes in 382. Cephalus and other Athenian democrats lobbied their fellow Athenians to grant these Thebans asylum, in gratitude for the aid they themselves had received when they sought refuge from the Thirty Tyrants in Thebes in 404/3.[184] It is evident that the bond of ξενία obliged these Athenians to support their former hosts. Plutarch calls them explicitly ἰδιόξενοι (in contrast to πρόξενοι), to stress the personal ties of friendship between them (Plut. *Mor.* 576a).[185]

Such ritualized friendships are an important source for knowledge of the past. During their stay in Thebes, the Athenian exiles certainly became familiar

181. *OCD* s.v. "friendship, ritualized." For a more detailed definition and a comprehensive discussion of ritualized friendship and related concepts, see Herman (1987); Gehrke (1985) 291–97; C. P. Jones (1999) 21; Low (2007) 36–54.

182. Herman (1987) 3.

183. See "Constitutive Elements of Social Memory" in the introduction, 28–29.

184. Cf. "Theban Exiles in Athens, 382–379" in chapter 4, 254–60.

185. See also the definition of ἰδιόξενοι and πρόξενοι in Ar. Byz. fr. 300P, 301P Slater; Herman (1987) 10 note 3.

with the Thebans' memorial framework, values, and beliefs. We can be reasonably sure that after the Spartan seizure of the Cadmea, the Theban exiles' Athenian ξένοι recalled to their fellow Athenians in the assembly the benefactions they themselves had received in 404, as well as any other positive experiences with the Thebans in the past. Cephalus and his friends were very successful in garnering Athenian support for their Theban friends. We know from an inscription found on the Acropolis (*IG* II^2 37; *SEG* 32.47) that these Thebans received formal recognition as exiles and were granted the status of *isoteleia*.

The ancient custom of *xenia* (ξενία), a bond of trust between two individuals, served as the model for the civic institution of *proxenia* (προξενία), "a bond of trust . . . between a *polis* and a prominent individual outside it."[186] A polis selected prominent citizens in other states as its "state-guest-friends" (πρόξενοι), who were expected to host its ambassadors, give hospitality to all its citizens, represent them in court, and protect its interests in general. In return, it would bestow special honors and privileges on these πρόξενοι.[187] Naturally, through intense personal contact, such πρόξενοι were particularly familiar with the mentality and traditions of the polis they represented.

This is evident in the case of Demosthenes, who was the πρόξενος of the Thebans in Athens. Plutarch reports that when Thebes was once slandered by a partisan of Alexander at Olympia, "Demosthenes came forward and recounted with historical proofs [διεξελθὼν μεθ' ἱστορίας καὶ ἀποδείξεως] all the benefits that the peoples of Thebes and Chalcidice had conferred upon Greece" (Plut. *Dem.* 9.1). Similarly, in Xenophon's *Symposion,* Socrates expresses the expectation that Callias, the son of Hipponicus, was in a position to know the Spartans' way of life intimately, thanks to his status as their πρόξενος and his frequent dealings with their prominent leaders (Xen. *Symp.* 8.39). Callias' intimate contact with his Spartan friends entailed a profound knowledge of their history and traditions, as is evident from his role as Athenian envoy to Sparta.

During the classical period, ξενία and προξενία were important factors in Greek diplomacy. For envoys, *poleis* often chose citizens who were ξένοι of the rulers or the πρόξενοι of the state to which the embassy was sent.[188] The *poleis* realized that, thanks to the special trust ξένοι and πρόξενοι enjoyed and due to their intimate knowledge of the traditions and mentalities of either polis, they were uniquely suited to sort out the differences and seek common ground between the two states.[189]

186. *OCD* s.v. "friendship, ritualized."

187. Cf. *OCD* s.v. *proxenos;* Adcock & Mosley (1975) 160–63. For a detailed discussion of προξενία and its origin in ξενία, see Herman (1987) 130–42; Gehrke (1985) 292–97; Perlman (1958).

188. Some of the ambassadors sent to Philip to negotiate the Peace of Philocrates were his personal ξένοι, particularly Aristodemus, Iatrocles, and Phrynon. See Paulsen (1999) 53 note 168.

189. Perlman (1958) 187; Adcock & Mosley (1975) 160–63. For the special trust that Athenians

The speech that the aforementioned Callias delivered as Athenian ambassador before the Spartan assembly in 371 provides an excellent example (Xen. *Hell.* 6.3.4–6).[190] It was Callias' goal to mend the fences between Sparta and Athens, by stressing their common views. According to Xenophon, he first established his credentials: his family had held the Spartan προξενία for several generations and was also highly esteemed in Athens for leadership in war and diplomacy. Knowing the Spartans, he used two paradigms that were likely to resonate with and illustrate the shared interest of both states. Both Athenians and Spartans were distressed about the recent destruction of Plataea and Thespiae (Xen. *Hell.* 6.3.5), presumably because they all had fought together against the Persian invaders in 480–79.[191] This was the prototypical example of a successful Athenian-Spartan cooperation.[192] Callias continued his speech by reaching back to the mythical beginnings of Athenian-Spartan cooperation. Athens and Sparta should never have gone to war in the first place, he argued, since

> the tradition is that the first strangers to whom Triptolemus, our ancestor revealed the mystic rites of Demeter and Core were Heracles, your founder [ἀρχηγέτης], and the Dioscuri, your citizens, and that it was upon the Peloponnese that he first bestowed the seed of Demeter's fruit. (Xen. *Hell.* 6.3.6)

Callias was aware of the high regard the Spartans had for their founding heroes, and as "torchbearer" (δᾳδοῦχος) of the Eleusinian mysteries, he knew the connection their Dorian ancestors had with Athenian heroes.[193] Moreover, since Sparta's Peloponnesian allies were present, he chose a mythical example that would appeal to them as well.

As ξένοι and πρόξενοι Athenians were able both to disseminate Athenian social memory and to gain access to the memorial repertoire of other Greek *poleis.* Social groups remember events that are relevant to them, and they do so in a way that complies with their own self-image. Through diplomatic contacts, unfamiliar versions or details of past events, cherished by memory communi-

who were Theban πρόξενοι enjoyed in Thebes, see Aeschin. 3.138–39; Trevett (1999) 197–98. For this reason, Demosthenes was sent as ambassador to Thebes after Philip's seizure of Elatea; cf. "Demosthenes and the Athenian-Theban Alliance of 339/8" in chapter 4, 268–71.

190. Cf. Gotteland (2001) 345–46; Dalfen (1976); Usher (2007) 226–27.

191. This is the reason Xenophon gives (*Hell.* 6.3.1) for the Athenian decision to seek peace with Sparta.

192. This cooperation was also highlighted by Spartan ambassadors to Athens in 369 (Xen. *Hell.* 6.5.34).

193. For this myth, see Parker (1996) 99–100. For Callias as torchbearer of the Eleusinian mysteries (and thus as a member of this illustrious memory community), see Parker (1996) 242, 302.

ties outside Athens, could be brought into Athenian public discourse and used to complement or challenge the prevalent Athenian master narrative.[194]

Monuments and Inscriptions

Monuments and inscriptions played a vital role in the Athenian memorial framework.[195] Following Alcock, I view monuments as "places, structures, or objects deliberately designed, or later agreed, to provoke memories."[196] Monuments are a special type of carrier of social memory, since they link past, present, and future through their very materiality. Together with landscapes, they constitute the physical setting, Halbwachs' *cadre matériel,* where memories can dwell.[197]

The Athenians (and the Greeks in general) were well aware of the crucial role of monuments for the creation and perpetuation of a shared image of their past. This is particularly evident from their extensive activities to memorialize military achievements. Immediately after a battle, the Greeks set up a trophy (τρόπαιον), usually consisting of a captured panoply, where the enemy army turned to flight.[198] In the case of the heroic victories over the Persians at Marathon and Salamis, the original trophies were replaced by more permanent stone monuments in the ensuing decades (Paus. 1.32.5, 36.1).[199] That τρόπαια were indeed regarded as palpable symbols for the community's accomplishments and as incentives for younger generations to emulate the ἀρετή of their forefathers is clear from an exhortation by Demosthenes in the assembly speech *On the Liberty of the Rhodians.*[200]

> I believe that . . . you ought to take actions worthy of the city [πράττειν ἄξια τῆς πόλεως], remembering that you enjoy listening when someone praises your ancestors, recounts their deeds, and mentions the trophies [τὰ τρόπαια]. Reflect, then, that your ancestors set up those trophies not

194. See "Challenging the Master Narrative" in chapter 2, 149–54, and "The Role of the Phocians" in chapter 5, 331–36.

195. Inscriptions are a special type of monument discussed at the end of this section.

196. Alcock (2002) 28.

197. The notion of the *cadre matériel* as a physical setting for collective memories, first proposed by Halbwachs (1925, 1941, 1980), was further developed by Nora (1996) into the concept of *lieux de mémoire,* which comprises both real and imagined places. Cf. Jung (2006) 15; Alcock (2002) 23–32. See "Athenian Ideology and Collective Memory" in the introduction to the present study, 19–21.

198. Pritchett (1971–91) 2:246–75; Jackson (1991).

199. Vanderpool (1966); Gauer (1968) 14; Hölscher (1998) 157–58; Jung (2006) 121–22.

200. Cf. R. Thomas (1989) 50–51; Clarke (2008) 285.

that you may gaze at them in wonder but that you may also imitate the virtues of those who set them up [ἵνα καὶ μιμῆσθε τὰς τῶν ἀναθέντων ἀρετάς]. (Dem. 15.35)

In a similar way as these trophies, funeral monuments erected on the battlefield or in the public cemetery in Athens served as material symbols for the city's achievements. After the Persian Wars, the Athenian war dead found their final resting place, after a splendid funeral ceremony, in the state burial ground, the *demosion sema,* which was "charged with heroic sacrality."[201] Their tombs, manifestations of the public honor granted to them, served as memorials of their heroism.[202] The fallen at Marathon were buried on the battlefield, in recognition of their extraordinary valor, as Thucydides remarks (Thuc. 2.34.5).[203] Their funeral mount was marked with stone stelae recording the names of the 192 dead for posterity (Paus. 1.32.3; Hdt. 6.117.1). There was also a separate grave for the fallen Plataeans and slaves.[204] Similarly, after the battle of Plataea, the Greeks buried their dead, city by city, on the battlefield (Hdt. 9.85);[205] some of these graves endured as memorials of this victory over more than six hundred years, well into Roman imperial times (Paus. 9.2.5).[206] The heroes of Thermopylae were buried where they had taken their last stand, and the spot was marked with a stone lion in memory of Leonidas (Hdt. 7.225.2); stelae set up on their graves by the Amphictyons bore the famous epigrams for the fallen Spartans, the seer Megistias, and the Peloponnesians, mentioned by Herodotus (Hdt. 7.228).[207] Isocrates remarks that this monument at Thermopylae was the object of affectionate regard and pilgrimage, even more than 130 years after the battle (Isoc. 5.148).[208]

When we consider the role of these monuments for Greek collective memory, we must not view them in isolation. They served as powerful symbols for the community primarily because they were invested with meaning through regular commemorative activities, often conducted at the monumental sites

201. Clairmont (1983) 45. Cf. Stupperich (1977); Travlos (1971) 300–303, 318. For the institution of the funeral ceremony, see "Funeral Orations" above, 49–58.

202. Cf. Lys. 2.66; Dem. 18.208.

203. That Thucydides considered the burial on the battlefield at Marathon an exception from the πάτριος νόμος of a public funeral in Athens (Thuc. 2.34.1) has given rise to much debate about the origin of this "ancestral custom." See Hornblower (1991) 292–93 for a brief discussion and further bibliography. Flower & Marincola (2002) 256 consider it an "invented" tradition and, following Jacoby (1944) 39–47 and Clairmont (1983) 7–15, date its origin to around 465 BC.

204. Both funeral mounts have been excavated; cf. Hammond (1992) 147–50 with further bibliography.

205. Cf. Flower & Marincola (2002) 254–56.

206. Cf. Jung (2006) 259–60.

207. Gauer (1968) 13, 118–20.

208. R. Thomas (1989) 51.

themselves. The Athenians annually participated in the public funeral ceremony and heard the praise of their ancestors' achievements amid their very tombs in the *demosion sema.* Similarly, regular offerings were provided at the graves of those buried on the Persian War battlefields.[209] The great emotional intensity associated with the collective memory of the Persian Wars resulted, at least in part, from those ritual activities—an example of Connerton's "incorporated" memorial practices—right at the monumental sites.[210]

Military achievements were memorialized not only through τρόπαια and funeral monuments but also through spoils dedicated as thank offerings to the gods in the city's shrines or at Panhellenic sanctuaries.[211] These spoils could serve as material reminders of battles or even particular episodes. The second-century AD traveler Pausanias still saw Mardonius' scimitar and the breast plate of the Persian cavalry commander Masistius in the temple of Athena Polias on the Acropolis (Paus. 1.27.1).[212] It is quite possible that the oral tradition of the Athenians' glorious fight against Masistius, which we find reflected in Herodotus' account (Hdt. 9.20–25), was attached to this famous artifact and told to Herodotus when he inquired about this trophy.[213] More than 120 years after their dedication, Demosthenes referred to Mardonius' scimitar and "the throne with silver feet" as the city's prizes (τἀριστεῖα τῆς πόλεως) for the victory over the barbarians (Dem. 24.129); from the lack of detailed descriptions, it is clear that Demosthenes expected his audience to be familiar with both of these votive offerings.[214]

Parts of the Persian War spoils were sold, and the money was used to erect monuments as thank offerings either in the city's shrines or at one of the Panhellenic sanctuaries.[215] From the booty at Plataea, the Greeks set up enormous bronze statues of Zeus and Poseidon at Olympia and the Isthmus, respectively, as well as the famous golden tripod on the Serpent Column in Delphi,

209. For regular offerings to the fallen at Plataea, see Thuc. 3.58.4; Kearns (1989) 55; Jung (2006) 262–64. Similar rituals can be assumed for the dead at Marathon; cf. Jung (2006) 65–66.

210. Battlefield memorials convey a particularly high emotional charge thanks to the sacredness derived from their very location; cf. Azaryahu (1993) 85. For the emotional intensity of Persian War memories, see, for instance, Dem. 18.202 (quoted in the introduction to the present study). For "incorporated" memories, which Hamilakis (1998) 117 says involve "performative ceremonies which generate bodily sensory and emotional experiences, resulting in habitual memory being sedimented in the body," see Connerton (1989); Alcock (2002) 28. See "Cults and Festivals," 65–69.

211. For a comprehensive discussion of Persian War dedications, see Gauer (1968).

212. Cf. Gauer (1968) 42–44; Castriota (1992) 135 with note 5.

213. For the strongly pro-Athenian coloring of this story, see Burn (1962) 517; Green (1996) 246. The family of the Athenian commander Olympiodorus (Hdt. 9.21.3) was probably also among the sources for this story, since both Herodotus and Lampon, the son of an Olympiodorus, were involved in the founding of Thurii. Cf. How & Wells (1923) 2.295; Lazenby (1993) 222.

214. For Xerxes' throne, cf. Harpocration s.v. ἀργυρόπους δίφρος.

215. See Gauer (1968).

which bore the names of all the Greek cities who "fought this war" (το[ίδε τὸν] πόλεμον [ἐ-]πολ[έ]μεον, M&L 27; Hdt. 9.81).[216] It is evident from Thucydides' Plataean debate that Greek *poleis* referred to these monuments in the diplomatic arena and thus tried to derive symbolic capital from their participation in the war against Xerxes (Thuc. 3.57.2).[217]

By dedicating spoils and monuments to the gods in Olympia and Delphi, Greek *poleis* advertised their military exploits to the wider Greek world and, in doing so, engaged in perpetual "memory wars" with each other. In Delphi, the Tegeans set up votive offerings from spoils taken from the Spartans (Paus. 10.9.5–6). The Spartan Lysander erected a monument after his victory over the Athenians at Aegospotami (Paus. 10.9.7–10), in close proximity to the Athenians' Marathon monument (Paus. 10.10.1–2).[218] The Argive-Athenian victory over the Spartans at Oenoe was memorialized with statues of the Seven against Thebes and the Epigoni (Paus. 10.10.3–4). The Thebans, in turn, built a treasury from the spoils of Leuctra, and the Athenians dedicated figureheads of ships and bronze shields taken from their enemies during the Peloponnesian War (Paus. 10.11.5–6).[219] These are just a few examples, but they illustrate how individual *poleis* used their votive offerings at Delphi to compete with each other for prestige in the Greek world.[220] This commemorative practice had further, far-reaching implications for the formation of Greek collective memory: thanks to these monuments, visitors to these Panhellenic shrines could become familiar with the memorial repertoire of other *poleis*.

With regard to these dedications at Delphi, it is worthwhile to stress another, obvious point: victory monuments simultaneously symbolize the victor's glory and the loser's disgrace. Not surprisingly, the latter often attempted to destroy such monuments in order to eclipse the memory of his own defeat.[221] According to Isocrates' Plataeans, the Thebans, who had collaborated with Xerxes, were demolishing (ἀφανίζουσιν) the trophies at Plataea, since they were memorials of their shame (Isoc. 14.59). Similarly, Aeschines reports that the Thebans wanted the shields removed, which the Athenians had recently rehung in the Apollo temple at Delphi, since they bore the inscription "The Athenians, from the Medes and Thebans, when they fought against the Greeks" (Ἀθηναῖοι ἀπὸ Μήδων καὶ Θηβαίων, ὅτε τἀναντία τοῖς Ἕλλησιν ἐμάχοντο,

216. Cf. "Memorialization of Thebes' Treason" in chapter 2, 106–13.

217. Cf. "Plataean-Theban Antagonism" in chapter 2, 120–27.

218. For this famous Cimonean monument, see Jung (2006) 96–108.

219. For an archaeological discussion of these and other votive monuments on the Sacred Way in Delphi, see Bommelaer (1991) 103–70.

220. Hölscher (1998) 164–65.

221. For the destruction of the monuments of the vanquished by imperial powers, see Alcock (2002) 26–27.

Aeschin. 3.116).[222] These emblems of their medism were surely an intolerable eyesore to the Thebans.

In Athens, the most impressive monuments were the temples and public buildings constructed after the Persian sack of the city in the high time of Athenian imperialism. It is clear from both the orators' allusions and the decorations of the buildings themselves that these structures were viewed as tangible manifestations of Athens' achievements (especially its victory over the Persians). Demosthenes refers to "the Propylaea, the Parthenon, the stoas and the docks" as results of the Athenian people's "love of honor" (φιλοτιμία) and as their "undying possessions" (κτήματα ἀθάνατα), set up in their honor, to complement the memory of their deeds (Dem. 22.76, 24.184).[223] The temples themselves were decorated with sculptures, reliefs, and paintings, which often depicted mythical analogies of Athens' triumph over the barbarians.[224] The Amazonomachy, for instance, was portrayed in the Stoa Poikile and on the Theseion, the pedestal of Olympian Zeus (Paus. 1.17.2), the shield of the chryselephantine statue of Athena, and the west metopes of the Parthenon.[225]

The Stoa Poikile deserves special attention. Probably commissioned by Cimon in the late 460s, it was located at the north side of the Agora, functioned as a public meeting place, and, according to Pausanias, contained the paintings of four paradigmatic events: the Amazonomachy, the sack of Troy, the battle of Marathon, and a battle at the Argive Oenoe (Paus. 1.15).[226] These monumental paintings provided its viewers with a sophisticated visual representation of these crucial historical and mythical events as Athenians in the 460s envisioned them. The Marathon painting, for instance, portrayed the entire course of the battle by focusing on its three distinct phases: the beginning, when Miltiades led the Athenian and Plataean forces against the Persians; the flight of the Persians into the swamp; and, finally, the fight at the Persian ships (Paus. 1.15.3). The inclusion of Athena, Heracles, and the Attic heroes Theseus, Marathon, and Echetlus shows that this event had taken on mythical qualities in Athenian historical consciousness by the 460s.[227] The prominence of the historical figures

222. Cf. "Memorialization of Thebes' Treason" in chapter 2, 106–13.

223. Cf. Dem. 22.13, 23.207; R. Thomas (1989) 50–51. For the Propylaea as testimony to Athens' glorious past, see also Aeschin. 2.74, 105.

224. Cf. Hölscher (1998) 167; Boedeker (1998) 189, 193.

225. Cf. Mills (1997) 32–33. For a comprehensive discussion of the use of mythic themes on public monuments as vehicles of Athenian ideology, see Castriota (1992).

226. The literature on the Stoa Poikile is vast. See E. B. Harrison (1972); Hölscher (1973) 50–84; Castriota (1992) 76–88. Pausanias' identification of the Oenoe painting is still heavily contested. Cf. Meiggs (1972) 469–72; Castriota (1992) 78 with note 91; Develin (1993). Francis & Vickers (1985) unconvincingly refer it to the Oenoe near Marathon; Jeffery's (1965) suggestion that the battle of Oenoe was shown in the mythic guise of the Seven against Thebes is too speculative.

227. Mills (1997) 40–42.

Miltiades and Callimachus suggests that their contribution to this success was deliberately commemorated.[228]

We can grasp here the mutual influence of two different carriers of social memory. The artist surely based his painting on the memories of contemporaries.[229] But once completed, the painting offered its onlookers a definite image of the event and thus, in turn, informed the memories of both participants and subsequent generations. Since the personal recollections of eyewitnesses are always variegated and particularly prone to the distorting effects of memory, this durable visual representation played an important role in the creation of a more stable and uniform version of the event, which underlies Herodotus' account of the battle (Hdt. 6.110–17). I do not suggest that Herodotus simply narrated the painting and did not follow his usual practice of consulting eyewitnesses and their descendants;[230] rather, by his time, private memories were sustained by and conformed to the main outline of the story as it was "told" by the Marathon painting.[231] Yet, as we can infer from a remark by Apollodorus, an orator active in the 340s, this painting, despite its prominence in the Agora, was not able to keep all aspects of the battle in the forefront of Athenian historical consciousness over time. Since Athenians were used to hearing, in funeral orations and assembly speeches, that they fought alone at Marathon, Apollodorus felt the need to point to "the ones with the Boeotian caps" in the Marathon painting to corroborate his assertion that the Plataeans had indeed participated in this battle ([Dem.] 59.94).[232] When trying to gauge the familiarity of a historical allusion, one should always weigh the relative impact of different carriers of social memory, such as the funeral orations and the Marathon painting in this case. This example illustrates how monuments could be used by knowledgeable individuals to revive obscure memories in Athenian public consciousness.

That the monuments set up on the Acropolis and in the Agora were an essential element in the Athenian memorial framework is evident from the orators' frequent use of them.[233] Aeschines called the statues and buildings in the Agora "memorials [ὑπομνήματα] of noble deeds" and pointed to the representation of Miltiades in the Marathon painting to prove his point that the Athe-

228. Jung (2006) 109–22.

229. E. B. Harrison (1972) 369–70.

230. For the painting as an important source for Herodotus, see Jeffery (1965) 44; E. B. Harrison (1972) 370; Francis & Vickers (1985) 109. For Herodotus scrutinizing eyewitnesses, see Hammond (1968) 14, 28, 47–57. In the case of Epizelus' story, Herodotus explicitly refers to oral tradition (Hdt. 6.117); cf. Hölscher (1973) 239 note 186.

231. For this phenomenon, see "Remembered and Commemorated History" in the introduction, 23–26.

232. See "Remembering the Plataeans" in chapter 2, 127–42.

233. See, for instance, the oratorical references to the Propylaea, the Parthenon, and the stoas cited earlier in this section.

nian demos had refrained from granting its leaders excessive honors in the past (Aeschin. 3.186). Lycurgus referred to the statues set up in the Agora in honor of victorious generals and the tyrannicides Harmodius and Aristogeiton (Lycurg. 51), whose monument was also mentioned by Demosthenes (Dem. 21.170).

By their very nature, monuments seem to be eminently stable things, ensuring commemorative continuity. Yet the interpretation placed on them can vary considerably over time, even as the monument itself remains relatively unchanged.[234] We can grasp a drastic form of this phenomenon during the archaic period, when Bronze Age tombs, whose original occupants had been entirely forgotten, came to be associated with the heroes of Greek epic and served as memorial sites for newly established hero cults.[235] But changes in the meaning placed on monuments can also occur in periods of cultural continuity. As part of Pericles' building program and paid for by the members of the Delian League, the Parthenon and the Propylaea were constructed in the 440s and 430s, *both* as victory monuments over the Persians *and* as visual manifestation of "the success and power of the Athenian state under Perikles' leadership."[236] Three generations later, Demosthenes ascribed the Propylaea, the Parthenon, and the other shrines "adorned with the spoils of the barbarians" not to Pericles but to the victors at Salamis (Dem. 22.13).[237] Over the course of a century, the Periclean context of the construction of these monuments had become secondary and thanks to their function as victory monuments over the Persians, they were associated with the Persian War generation itself.

It is important to keep in mind that the symbolic meaning of a monument is never fixed. Monuments, like other works of art, require an act of interpretation by the viewers, who each approach it with their own expectations, needs, and knowledge. Consequently, monuments have a horizon of meanings, in which "now one, now another meaning comes momentarily to the fore."[238] They resist uniform readings "even for a single point in time, let alone across the ages."[239]

The tomb of the Spartans in the Ceramicus provides a lucid example. In 403, Spartan and Peloponnesian troops under the command of King Pausanias arrived in Athens to support the oligarchs in the city, who had lost the battle

234. Alcock (2002) 28–29. Masada and Stonehenge are two famous examples of this phenomenon. For the changing meaning of Masada in Jewish collective memory from antiquity to the 1920s and to the present day, see Schwartz, Zerubavel, & Barnett (1986); Y. Zerubavel (1995); Wolpert (2002) 82–83. For Stonehenge, see Bender (1992).

235. Cf. the heroön of the Seven in Eleusis (Paus. 1.39.2). See "The End of the Seven and Local Cults" in chapter 3, 159–69.

236. Castriota (1992) 135. For further literature on these two monuments, see Castriota (1992) 279 note 4.

237. Castriota (1992) 135 with note 6.

238. Lefebvre (1991) 222.

239. Alcock (2002) 29–30.

of Munichia against the democrats. In the ensuing engagement in the Piraeus, Pausanias—after some initial difficulties—drove back the democrats and erected a trophy. After this victory, Pausanias initiated negotiations and arranged a peace between the two civil war factions: an amnesty was declared, and the Athenian democracy was restored.[240] The Spartans who had been killed in the final encounter received a funeral monument at the entrance to the *demosion sema*. This extraordinary honor was probably initially promised to Pausanias by the men in the city but then approved or at least tolerated by the democrats in recognition of Pausanias' role in ending the civil war. It was in the democrats' interest to bolster Pausanias' standing in Sparta vis-à-vis his rival Lysander, who had been the Athenian oligarchs' most fervent supporter.[241] This tomb was discovered in 1930. Thirteen skeletons were unearthed, as well as a marble block that preserves the general heading ΛΑ[KEDAIMONIOI] and the names of the two polemarchs Chaeron and Thibrachus (*IG* II^2 11678).[242]

What did this monument mean to its viewers, and which memories did it evoke? Pausanias and his Spartan soldiers must have been pleased. Their fallen comrades received their final resting ground at the *demosion sema*, the sacred state cemetery for prominent Athenian leaders and war heroes.[243] The inscribed tombstone identified the dead as Spartans, recorded the names of the two polemarchs, and could thus serve as a material reminder of the Spartan victory and of Pausanias' role in ending the civil war.[244] This is also how Xenophon, one of the men of the city and a notorious admirer of Sparta, viewed this monument. In his historiographical account of the Athenian civil war, he mentioned this tomb in the context of Pausanias' victory, and by reciting the names of the polemarchs Chaeron and Thibrachus and the Olympic victor Lacrates (Xen. *Hell.* 2.4.33), he memorialized their achievement for posterity.

In the thoroughly democratic genre of the funeral oration, however, Lysias presented a quite different interpretation of this monument. Those who were fighting for the democracy and had returned to the Piraeus (εἰς τὸν Πειραιᾶ κατῆλθον, Lys. 2.61)

> had as enemies both those who had previously fulfilled this role [i.e., the Spartans] and their own fellow citizens [i.e., the oligarchs from the city]. But nevertheless, having felt no fear of the multitude of their opponents and having risked danger in their own bodies, they set up a trophy

240. For these events, see Xen. *Hell.* 2.4.11–42; Krentz (1995) 143–54; Wolpert (2002) 26–28.
241. Cf. Tod (1933) 111; Clairmont (1983) 204.
242. Van Hook (1932); Willemsen (1977); Low (2006) 98 with note 38.
243. Krentz (1995) 151–52.
244. Todd (2008) 263.

> [τρόπαιον] over their enemies and produce as witnesses for their own valor [μάρτυρας δὲ τῆς αὑτῶν ἀρετῆς] the tombs of the Lacedaemonians [τοὺς Λακεδαιμονίων τάφους] that are near this monument. (Lys. 2.62–63)

In the patriotic Athenian master narrative of the funeral oration, the tombs of the Spartans had come to signify the superior valor of the Athenian democrats who killed them. The bloody conflict between two Athenian factions was hardly mentioned and was cast into the familiar mold of "few Athenians fighting against a multitude of enemies."[245] The two battles at Munichia and the Piraeus were conflated into one single victory ("they set up a trophy"), and the defeat to Pausanias' troops was forgotten.[246]

In this funeral oration, we can grasp how the Athenian demos, in the wake of the amnesty, reconstructed the past in civic memory in a highly selective way that both sides, the men in the Piraeus and the men in the city, could tolerate.[247] As a result of this process, the tomb of the Spartans could be viewed as yet another monument celebrating both the victorious return of the demos from exile and the fall of the Thirty and their foreign supporters.[248] The impact of this "official" version of the civil war on the Athenians' historical consciousness should not be underestimated, especially since Athenians were exposed to it regularly in funeral orations and assembly speeches. Granted, those who cared (like Xenophon) could refer to the funeral monument as evidence for Sparta's role in ending the civil war, but most Athenians probably preferred the idealized version, which allowed them to gloss over the painful aspects of this civil strife. Considering the relative impact of this funeral monument vis-à-vis the "official" polis tradition, it is surely wrong to point to the inscription on the tomb and claim that "the Athenians would have been reminded daily of the Spartan sacrifice and how the civil war had ended."[249] In light of these considerations, it is not surprising that Pausanias, writing in the second century AD, described the tomb of Thrasybulus, who "put down the tyranny of the so-called Thirty" (Paus. 1.29.3), but made no mention of the Spartan tomb. Later genera-

245. For this familiar *topos*, see "Funeral Orations" above, 49–58.

246. Wolpert (2002) 89; Todd (2008) 262–63.

247. Wolpert (2002) 75–99.

248. This Athenian master narrative obscured both the complicity of the men in the city in the crimes of the Thirty and the passivity of the majority of the demos. Other monuments commemorating the victorious return of the demos are the honorary decree for the men of Phyle (Raubitschek (1941) 288–89 = *SEG* 28.45; Aeschin. 3.187, 190), the decree recording the rewards for Thrasybulus' foreigner supporters (*IG* II^2 10), and the decree of Theozotides providing state support for the democrats' orphaned children (Stroud [1971]; *SEG* 28.46; Lys. fr. 128, 129 Carey). Cf. Wolpert (2002) 87. See "Athenian Memorialization of the Men from Phyle" in chapter 4, 235–45.

249. Tritle (2002) in his review of Wolpert (2002).

tions of Athenians probably saw no need to maintain this odd monument, and the memory attached to it faded into oblivion.[250]

A special type of monument were inscriptions, engraved in stone stelae, statue bases, and temple walls. These inscriptions, which could be found, for instance, on the Acropolis or in the Agora, fulfilled both a documentary and a monumental function.[251] In the course of the fourth century, Athenian orators wanting to corroborate their assertions about the past increasingly cited laws, decrees, and epigrams commemorating victories or honors voted to native or foreign benefactors.[252] Orators often referred to the stele on which a decree was inscribed and named its location instead of simply quoting a document found in the archive.[253] The reference to the location of a decree suggests that the orator expected his listeners to be familiar with these inscriptions and their placement and that they considered this information important. That there was a general expectation that people would read these decrees is also evident from the decrees themselves, especially when they contained lists of names of people who had received a special grant from the polis. Apollodorus, for instance, paraphrased a passage from the decree granting citizenship to the Plataeans, which indicates

> that the names of those who had been examined should be inscribed on a stone column, which should be placed on the Acropolis by the temple of the goddess, so that the grant might be preserved for their descendants and it might be possible for an individual to prove to which of them he is related. ([Dem.] 59.105)

This stone stele served not only as a record of the citizenship rights of individual Plataeans but also as a memorial of the Plataeans' loyalty toward Athens and of their undeserved fate, as Apollodorus' use of this stele demonstrates ([Dem.] 59.104).[254]

Beginning in the middle of the fourth century, orators frequently cited decrees related to Athens' greatest triumphs at the time of the Persian Wars. In his indictment of the alleged deserter Leocrates in 330, Lycurgus read out the Ephebic Oath and the Oath of Plataea in order to contrast the ancestors'

250. Todd (2008) 263 note 76.

251. For the monumental function of inscriptions, see R. Thomas (1992) 74–100.

252. Cf. R. Thomas (1989) 83–94, who makes the case that Athenians became more and more "document-minded." See also Clarke (2008) 291.

253. Cf. Aeschines' reference to the reward for the men of Phyle, inscribed on a stele in the Metroon (Aeschin. 3.187); cf. Sickinger (1999) 235.

254. See also "Plataean-Theban Antagonism" in chapter 2, 120–27.

heroism to Leocrates' cowardice (Lycurg. 76–78, 80–82).[255] In 348, Aeschines, according to Demosthenes (Dem. 19.303), made reference to a decree of Miltiades, urging the Athenians to march out to Marathon, and to a decree of Themistocles, ordering the evacuation of Athenians to Troezen in 480.[256] Inscriptions of the decree of Themistocles (M&L 23) and the Oath of Plataea (R&O 88) have been found, but since these inscribed versions date from the third quarter of the fourth century at the earliest, their authenticity has been much debated.[257] Scholars consider them to be copies of the original oath/decree; later reconstructions of the actual oath/decree, which was but imperfectly remembered; or conscious forgeries, invented wholesale in the fourth century.[258] Leaving the issue of authenticity aside, there is no doubt that the struggle against Philip, the new "barbarian" invader from the north, brought the Persian Wars increasingly into Athenian public discourse.[259] These inscribed decrees provided the orators with yet another powerful tool to corroborate their lessons from the past.

Rhetorical Education

Rosalind Thomas has shown that classical Athens was in transition from an oral to a literate culture. The increased use of writing is, therefore, an important factor for the constitution and transmission of Athenian social memory, at least among the educated elite. The search for the orators' written sources has dominated much of the scholarship on the orators' use of the past, but the results have been relatively meager.[260] For this reason, I decided to shift the perspective and to focus on the role of the audience. It is my central premise that the Athenian orator, whose goal was persuasion, had to take the attitudes of listeners into account. Consequently, I try to contextualize the orator's historical allusions within the complex Athenian memorial framework. Much of the research in this book is therefore guided by inquiring how a particular historical paradigm would have resonated with an Athenian audience.

---

255. Rhodes & Osborne (2003) 440–49.

256. See MacDowell (2000) 337–39. For the decree of Miltiades, see Arist. *Rh.* 1411a; Plut. *Mor.* 628e; Nep. *Milt.* 4.

257. Habicht (1961), in his seminal article, considers them falsifications. For the mentality behind this phenomenon, see R. Thomas (1989) 83–93. For the Ephebic Oath and the Oath of Plataea, inscribed on the Acharnae stele, see Rhodes & Osborne (2003) 440–49 (with further literature) and, most recently, Kellogg (2008). For a critical assessment of the Themistocles decree, see Jameson (1960); Meiggs & Lewis (1988) 48–52; Hammond (1988) 558–63.

258. Cf. Flower & Marincola (2002) 323–25.

259. Rhodes & Osborne (2003) 447.

260. For a sobering assessment of this approach, see Perlman (1961) 151–52. See "Participant Evidence: The Attic Orators and Their Interpretation" in the introduction, 36–43.

As I have argued above, the Athenian orator simultaneously participated in numerous memory communities and was exposed to a variety of different carriers of social memory (including books). Consequently, in crafting his historical paradigms, he would draw on those carriers of social memory that would (1) best suit his case and (2) be most familiar to his audience. Since the common historical consciousness of average Athenians was constituted predominantly orally, it seems highly improbable that the orator would, as a rule, draw his historical examples from books. I contend that this was, rather, the exception. That is not to say that the orator was not familiar with many written sources. Through his rhetorical training, he had access to the writings of Herodotus and Thucydides, to the tragedians, to exemplary speeches of other orators, and to the local histories of the Atthidographers.[261] But in his use of the past, he generally did not follow the historians, since other carriers of social memory carried more authoritative weight.[262]

Unsurprisingly, there are only a few cases where orators conspicuously copied their historical paradigms from other written sources. The most remarkable passages in this regard are Aeschines' use of Andocides' narrative of Athenian-Spartan relations during the fifth century (Andoc. 3.3–9; Aeschin. 2.172–76) and Apollodorus' use of Thucydides' Plataean episodes (Thuc. 2.71–78, 3.20–24; [Dem.] 59.98–103).[263] The latter case is particularly instructive. In his praise of the Plataeans' loyalty and devotion to Athens, Apollodorus dwelled on the siege and destruction of Plataea during the Peloponnesian War. This memory was deeply engraved in Athenian historical consciousness and would surely have resonated with his audience.[264] I suggest that, for the narration of this episode,

261. The works of the Atthidographers, which seem "to reflect very accurately the outlook of the speech-making classes (to which several in fact belonged)" (Parker (1996) 226), could certainly have served the orators as a useful source. The Atthidographers collected the local myths and aetiological stories of Attica and tried to bring them into a chronological order. Every Atthis begins in the mythical period and ends with the present. The history of the intervening centuries is recounted in ever-increasing detail. Cf. Jacoby (1949); Harding (1994), (2008); Clarke (2008).

262. Pearson's (1942) hypothesis that the orator respected the historical knowledge and attitudes of his audience is fundamentally correct (but we should discard the idea that the Athenians were utterly ignorant and the orators knew "how it actually was"). Rosalind Thomas (1989) 201–2 is too pessimistic about the orator's knowledge of the past. She radically dismisses the idea "that orators deliberately and consciously distanced themselves from the 'Thucydidean' version of their history, as it were, and descended to an alien level of historical ignorance purely for the gratification of their audience." In her view, the orator becomes the mouthpiece of one particular oral tradition. It seems more likely to me, however, that he was exposed to various carriers of social memory and could choose (and manipulate) the one most suitable for his rhetorical purposes.

263. R. Thomas (1989) 119, 202 note 19. For Aeschines' use of Andocides, see Paulsen (1999) 409–14. For Apollodorus' use of Thucydides, cf. Trevett (1990); Nouhaud (1982) 263–64; Pelling (2000) 61–65; and, in particular, Kapparis (1999) 379–86.

264. Pelling (2000) 61 calls it "a scar in the popular historical consciousness." Cf. "Plataean-Theban Antagonism" in chapter 2, 120–27.

Apollodorus found no better (i.e., more gripping) narrative than Thucydides' account. The orator, therefore, followed it closely but adapted it, where necessary, to suit his rhetorical needs.[265] This did result in historical "distortions," but I contend that these distortions were within the acceptable limits. In a culture where knowledge of the past was by and large transmitted orally, no two retellings of a particular event were exactly the same at any rate.[266] To expect the politician Apollodorus to comply with the truth standards of modern historiography is entirely unrealistic.

Undoubtedly, written sources could serve the orators as useful repositories of otherwise little-known events. In chapter 2, I argue that Xerxes' offer of peace to the Athenians in 480 was well remembered in fourth-century Athens. However, that it was Alexander of Macedon who delivered this message from the Persian king was not usually mentioned. Demosthenes added this detail in his *Second Philippic* to associate Philip—through his ancestry—with the barbarian invader (Dem. 6.11). It is quite likely that Demosthenes found this information in Herodotus' narrative and reintroduced it into Athenian public discourse. Thanks to its irrelevance, it had faded from common historical consciousness over the past century, but in the wake of Macedonian expansionism, it became relevant again.[267]

In conclusion, the orators rarely drew their historical allusions from written sources. They wanted to appeal to their audiences and therefore used, whenever possible, historical examples that were familiar to their listeners. At the same time, however, I suggest that through their elite rhetorical education, the orators were able to refresh little-known details or events in public discourse and thus to modify prevalent social memories if the situation required doing so.

Assembly and Law Courts

Thus far, I have tried to sketch an outline of the different sources available to the orator and the audience for knowledge of the past. The orator simultane-

265. Cf. the fitting verdict of Kapparis (1999) 385–86: "[T]he differences between the two accounts can be explained as a result of condensation, omission of details, lapse of memory, carelessness, expediency, or often a sense of different purpose compared with that of the historian." It is highly unlikely, therefore, that, for his Plataean paradigm, Apollodorus also used other passages from Thucydides, such as the latter's account of the fate of Scione (so Carey (1992) 138–39), or a second written source (Trevett (1990) 416 proposes Daemachus of Plataea *FGrHist* 65).

266. For this reason, it seems misleading to speak of "fabrication" and "falsifications," since doing so implies that the orator is aware of being lying. But in a sense, Apollodorus' version "*is* history: it tells us what the Athenians wanted to hear, or what Apollodorus hoped they wanted to hear, about their past," as Pelling (2000) 67 put it.

267. See "Treacherous by Nature" in chapter 2, 143–49.

ously participated in different memory communities, including his family, his group of companions at the symposium, his *deme,* his tribe, and the polis. Furthermore, the educated orator had access to written texts, such as exemplary speeches of other orators and writings of the tragedians, the historians, and the Atthidographers. Monuments and inscriptions could serve as cues for his own memory and to corroborate his assertions. Through his personal contacts as ξένος or πρόξενος to members of other *poleis,* he was also familiar with the shared memories of other Greek and foreign communities.

When he related the past to the present in the assembly and the law courts, the orator himself was a pivotal factor in the manifestation, negotiation, and transmission of Athenian social memory.[268] Drawing from all these different sources, the orator formulated a version of the past that "both accords with some kind of shared expectations on the part of the audience and offers its own nuances"[269] in order to influence particular political or judicial actions. For this purpose, the orator crafted the historical paradigm that best suited his argument. Naturally, not all of his historical examples were equally familiar to his audience, nor did they all bear the same emotional and argumentative weight. An orator was more likely to sway public opinion if he simply alluded to the lessons provided by the Athenian master narrative, since he could be sure to strike an emotional chord with his audience.[270] Yet, sometimes, in his analysis of a given situation, the orator would arrive at conclusions that called for a less familiar historical parallel. In that instance, he had to argue his case in more detail and provide an authoritative source for his assertion. Drawing on his family memory, Aeschines stressed his father's and uncle's credentials as patriotic democrats to confirm his narrative of the disastrous Sicilian expedition and the dire consequences of the defeat in 404 (Aeschin. 2.74–78).[271] Similarly, Dinarchus felt compelled to substantiate his assertions by referring to the elders and by quoting decrees: that the Theban archenemies had done something nice for the Athenians ran contrary to the general negative view the Athenians had of their northern neighbors and therefore needed corroboration (Din. 1.25).[272] Yet even when the orator evoked less familiar collective memories, he could be confident that at least some members of the audience would know of the event and be sympathetic to his conclusion, since they participated in the very memory community (*deme,* tribe, circle of friends, etc.) from which he drew his knowledge.

268. Cf. R. Thomas (1989) 198–99; Clarke (2008) 297–303.

269. Clarke (2008) 297.

270. Cf. "Treacherous by Nature" in chapter 2, 143–49.

271. See R. Thomas (1989) 101 and Steinbock (forthcoming). See also "Family Traditions" above, 73–75.

272. Cf. chapter 4.

Athenian social memory was incredibly dynamic, since knowledge of the past was primarily transmitted orally and within numerous different memory communities. Moreover, the law courts and the assembly were central venues for the continuous refreshing and reshaping of the past. Changing political alignments and unexpected events were of special importance, since they often provided the occasion for the orator to bring less familiar memories back into public discourse. In so doing, he reinforced them and secured their transmission to younger generations.

In his private prosecution of Athenogenes (ca. 330–324 BC), Hyperides' client reminded the jury that, when Troezenian refugees arrived in Athens in the 330s and requested asylum, the Athenians recalled the help (εὐεργεσία) they had received from the Troezenians against the barbarian, more than a hundred and fifty years ago (Hyp. *Ath.* 31).[273] It is generally agreed that this εὐεργεσία denotes the measures allegedly decreed by the Troezenians for the maintenance of the Athenian women and children after their evacuation from Athens in 480 (Plut. *Them.* 10.5).[274] The Athenians, acknowledging the debt they owed to the Troezenians, granted to the refugees both asylum and Athenian citizenship (Hyp. *Ath.* 31). This passage is incredibly important. It proves (1) that arguments from social memory were powerful factors in Athenian decision making, thanks to the Greek cultural norm of reciprocity, and (2) that the assembly and the law courts functioned as venues for the orators' perpetual refreshing and reshaping of the past. The Troezenian decree for the Athenian women and children was read out to the jurors in the courtroom in the private prosecution of Athenogenes (Hyp. *Ath.* 33), but it was also evoked (and probably even recited), a few years earlier, by the asylum-seeking Troezenians and their Athenian supporters in the assembly (Hyp. *Ath.* 31–33).[275] In both cases, the speakers tapped into one of the most deeply engrained Athenian social memories (the trauma of Athens' evacuation) and, at the same time, revitalized details (the Troezenian hospitality) that might otherwise have been forgotten.

The case of the exiled Rhodian democrats is similar. When they appealed for Athenian help in 351, Demosthenes tried to persuade the Athenian assembly not to abandon fellow democrats, by reminding them of the support the Athenian democrats had received from the Argives in the time of the Thirty (Dem. 15.21–23).[276] Demosthenes claimed that he had "heard often in this assembly" (ἀκούω δ᾽ ἐγὼ πολλάκις ἐνταυθί, Dem. 15.21) how speakers recalled the sup-

273. For the circumstances of these Troezenians' exile after the battle of Chaeronea and Hyperides' use of this episode in the prosecution of Athenogenes, see Whitehead (2000) 339–46.

274. Jameson (1960) 207; Frost (1961) 189–92; Whitehead (2000) 342.

275. Hyperides' client said explicitly that it was the Troezenians' decree, "on account of which [the Athenians] took them in and made them citizens" (Hyp. *Ath.* 33).

276. For the Argive support, see Wolpert (2002) 24.

port that other *poleis* had lent to the Athenian exiles at that time. This indicates that the orators' historical allusions in the assembly were indeed instrumental in ensuring the transmission of this particular memory down to Demosthenes' time.[277]

By resituating the orator's historical allusions within the sociopolitical realm, I argue that the orator is neither a mere mouthpiece of one particular tradition nor a propagandistic manipulator of the ignorant masses. Instead, it should become clear that he participated and operated within a complex net of remembrances and beliefs, comprising a variety of different memory communities and carriers of social memory. His historical allusions were therefore an integral part of the negotiation and manifestation of the Athenians' shared image of the past.

277. For a similar argument concerning the memory of Theban support for Thrasybulus, see chapter 4.

CHAPTER 2

Athens' Counterimage

The Theban Medizers

A survey of the Attic orators and the speeches in Xenophon's *Hellenica* shows that fourth-century allusions to events in the history of Athenian-Theban relations cluster around four particular episodes, each discussed in a separate chapter in this book: Thebes' collaboration with the Persians in 480–479 (this chapter), the mythical story of the burial of the Seven against Thebes (chap. 3), the Theban help for the Athenian democrats in 404/3 (chap. 4), and the Theban proposal to eradicate Athens at the end of the Peloponnesian War (chap. 5). I begin my discussion with the memory of Thebes' medism, since I regard the Persian Wars (including Athens' experience of Thebes in it) as critical for the formation of the Athenian self-image.[1] Since this very self-image was projected back into the mythical past and shaped the collective memory of the Athenian intervention on behalf of the fallen Argives, I will first turn to the Athenian memory of Thebes' collaboration with the Persians—often referred to in our sources as "medizing."

More than a century after the Persian Wars, Athenian speakers frequently referred to Thebes' medism during Xerxes' invasion. This raises a series of questions. Why was Thebes' collaboration with the Persians still relevant to Athenians in the fourth century? What did this collective memory mean to them? Why did they recall the Thebans' medism but not that of others? How would fourth-century Athenians have learned about Thebes' role in the Persian Wars; that is, how was this memory constituted and transmitted to younger genera-

1. Cf. "Funeral Orations" in chapter 1, 49–58.

tions, and on which occasions was it recalled? Can we detect any signs of distortions in this process?

Taking the unequivocal fourth-century portrayal of Thebes' medism as my starting point, I will examine Thebes' conduct during Xerxes' invasion as historical backdrop for my analysis of Thebes' role in Athenian social memory. This will reveal that the historical situation was much more complex than fourth-century Athenian allusions would have us believe. With this in mind, I will try to reconstruct the mental framework through which the Athenians perceived their neighbors' behavior in this crisis, as well as their attempts to memorialize their experience in the years following this heroic struggle. Concentrating on the development of Athenian-Theban relations during the Pentecontaetia and the Peloponnesian War, I will then explore why the Athenians considered the memory of Thebes' medizing important enough to transmit to younger generations and what sort of distortions surfaced in this process. The study of the manifestation and transmission of this particular memory can also shed new light on Herodotus' apparent anti-Theban bias.

After tracing the transmission of this Athenian memory through the fifth century, I will analyze the extant fourth-century allusions to Thebes' medizing in more detail. These can be attributed to two specific contexts: the Plataean-Theban conflict and potential barbarian invasions. The first of these naturally leads to another vexed problem, the Athenian memory of Plataea's role at Marathon, which is closely linked to the Plataean-Theban antagonism, as I will show. Demosthenes' use of Thebes' medism in the context of potential barbarian invasions indicates that an orator could either exploit a predominant social memory or venture to modify it by falling back on alternative sources for knowledge of the past. Yet, in that case too, he had to operate within the limits of his listeners' horizon of expectation.

Fourth-Century Allusions to Thebes' Medizing

That Thebes sided with Xerxes during his invasion was deeply rooted in Athenian historical consciousness. Even more than one hundred years after the Persian Wars, Athenian orators such as Isocrates, Demosthenes, and Apollodorus alluded to Theban medizing quite frequently.[2] In all of these fourth-century allusions, Thebes' medism is presented as an undisputed historical fact.

2. Cf. Dem. 14.33–34 (354 BC), 6.11–12 (344 BC); [Dem.] 59.95 (343–340 BC); Isoc. 14.30, 61 (ca. 373); Isoc. 12.93 (342–339 BC). [Dem.] 59 was most likely composed by Apollodorus and delivered in the late 340s: cf. Kapparis (1999) 48–52; Carey (1992) 3.

Shortly after Plataea's second destruction by the Thebans in 373, Isocrates' *Plataicus* contrasted Plataea's heroism with Thebes' medism during the Persian Wars. The Thebans are said to be guilty of "evil deeds, so willingly committed and so grave" (Isoc. 14.30) and are called "betrayers of all of Greece" (ἁπάσης τῆς Ἑλλάδος προδόται, Isoc. 14.30; οἱ τῶν Ἑλλήνων προδόται, Isoc. 14.62). The Athenian ancestors who fought in the battle of Plataea would consider it an abomination that

> those who considered it right to be the slaves of the barbarians [i.e., the Thebans] made themselves despots over the other Greeks, but that [the Plataeans] who had joined in the fight for freedom, alone of the Greeks, have been driven from [their] homes . . . and that the Thebans, who were drawn up in battle order with the enemy [Θηβαίους δὲ τοὺς τἀναντία παραταξαμένους], rule over this land. (Isoc. 14.61)

In his *Panathenaicus,* published in 339 BC, Isocrates criticized Sparta's treatment of Plataea by contrasting the role of the Plataeans and the other Boeotians—that is, first and foremost, the Thebans—during the Persian Wars.

> . . . and we [the Greek allies] accomplished this [the victory at Plataea] with the help of the Plataeans, who alone of the Boeotians [μόνους Βοιωτῶν] fought with us. And yet, after no great interval of time, the Lacedaemonians, to gratify the Thebans, reduced the Plataeans by siege and killed them all, with the exception of those who had been able to escape. (Isoc. 12.93)

In the late 340s, Apollodorus, the prosecutor in the case against Neaera, similarly stressed the contrast between the merits of the Plataeans and the role of the Thebans during the Persian Wars.

> And again, when Xerxes marched against Greece and the Thebans medized [Θηβαίων μηδισάντων], the Plataeans did not bring themselves to withdraw from their friendship with us, but alone of the other Boeotians [μόνοι τῶν ἄλλων Βοιωτῶν] [fought with us on the ships and in the field]. ([Dem.] 59.95)

In 344 BC, in the *Second Philippic,* Demosthenes explained Philip's preference for an alliance with the Thebans and Argives by pointing to Philip's knowledge of the Athenian ancestors' conduct during the Persian Wars. He sought the Thebans and Argives as allies, knowing "that the ancestors of the Thebans and Argives either fought on the side of the barbarian [συστρατεύσαντας τῷ βαρβάρῳ; i.e., the Thebans] or did not oppose him [i.e., the Argives]" (Dem. 6.11). Attempting to dispel Athenian fears of an imminent Persian attack supported by Thebes, Demosthenes asserted in the debate *On the Symmories* in 354 BC:

> I, for my part, believe that the Thebans are so far from joining the king in an attack against the Greeks that they would pay a lot of money, if they were able to give it, to get a chance of expiating their former sins [i.e., their medism] against the Greeks. (Dem. 14.33–34)

All of these fourth-century references to Thebes' conduct during the Persian Wars portray the Thebans as outright medizers. Even in the last example, where it is Demosthenes' objective to convince his listeners that the Thebans would never support the Persians again, their former allegiance to Xerxes is presented as an indisputable fact. There are, however, various clues in our sources that indicate that Thebes' relationship to the Persians was not as clear-cut as Athenian orators would have us believe. A brief review of Theban politics during Xerxes' invasion will help us to explain the reasons for this simplification in Athenian social memory.

Theban Conduct during the Persian War

There is no doubt that the Thebans sent, at some point, earth and water to Xerxes and fought alongside the Persians in the decisive battle of Plataea in 479, as Herodotus (7.132, 9.67–69) and many other authors corroborate. Yet a different source claims that, in the early stages of the invasion, five hundred Thebans led by Mnamias took part in the allied expedition to Tempe in Thessaly in order to establish a first defensive line against the advancing barbarian (Plut. *Mor.* 864e).[3] Furthermore, Herodotus reports that a contingent of four hundred Thebans fought under Leonidas' command at Thermopylae against the Persian army (7.205), staying with him even after the Persians had found the flanking route and after the greater part of the allied army had left (7.222). They finally surrendered to Xerxes and were branded as slaves (7.233).

This apparent inconsistency in the Thebans' behavior has troubled many historians. Some scholars follow Herodotus' account, which presupposes a per-

3. This information is probably derived from the fourth-century author Aristophanes of Boeotia. Cf. Graf (1979) 168; Demand (1982) 21.

sistent pro-Persian attitude on the part of the Thebans.[4] This unfavorable explanation has been called into doubt by scholars who are ready to accept a more complex historical reality. Buck, Graf, Demand, and Hammond, for instance, reconstruct a struggle between a pro- and anti-Persian faction in Thebes and thus argue that Thebes did not medize right from the outset.[5] This interpretation is supported by the historiographical tradition that Thebes participated in the expedition to Tempe and Thermopylae.[6] Furthermore, the existence of different Theban factions can also be seen in Herodotus' narrative of the battle at Plataea and of the allied siege of Thebes, following the Persian defeat. The phrase "those of the Thebans who medized" (οἱ μηδίζοντες τῶν Θηβαίων, Hdt. 9.67) is the strongest indicator in Herodotus that there was also a nonmedizing party in Thebes.[7] Besides, Buck stresses that the allies' defense of Thermopylae would not have made sense with the Thebans as wholehearted medizers in their rear; even if Herodotus' report of early Theban submission was correct, one should understand it as an insurance policy rather than as a sign of disloyalty to the Greek cause.[8] Hammond, however, accepts Herodotus' report of early Theban medizing but assumes that they reversed their policy—just as the Thessalians did (7.172.1)—due to pressure from the Greek alliance. They sent contingents to Tempe and to Thermopylae and fought well but then surrendered to the overwhelming Persian force; after the fall of Thermopylae, the "narrow pro-Persian group, headed by Attaginus and Timagenidas"[9] came into power, and Thebes became a firm Persian ally.

Even though we cannot fully recover the exact sequence of events concerning the Thebans' medizing—let alone their motives at the respective stages—the notion of an outright pro-Persian stance taken by *all* the Thebans from early on can be dismissed in favor of a more complex historical picture that allows for dispute among different Theban factions and for Theban wavering in the course of events. This raises several questions. Why did the Athenians in the

4. Cf. Hignett (1963) 100: "Thebes and the other pro-Persian states genuinely desired a Persian victory from the start, but were careful not to commit themselves to either side until they could make contact with the Persian land forces."

5. Buck (1979) 128–33; Graf (1979) 170–81; Demand (1982) 20–27; Hammond (1988) 544–45.

6. For the reliability of this tradition, see Demand (1982) 20–21.

7. For this interpretation of οἱ μηδίζοντες τῶν Θηβαίων, cf. Flower & Marincola (2002) 224. Diodorus, following the fourth-century historian Ephorus, explicitly mentions that "the inhabitants of Thebes were divided against each other with respect to the alliance with the Persians," in his report of the participation of "some four hundred Thebans of the other party" in Leonidas' campaign (Diod. 11.4.7). Ephorus probably reflects a Theban tradition. For Ephorus' sources, see also Stylianou (1998) 104–9.

8. Buck (1979) 131–32 notes a stylistic inconcinnity in Herodotus' list of early medizers (7.132.1) and considers the phrase "and the Thebans and the other Boeotians" a later addition by Herodotus, disregarding the actual course of events.

9. Hammond (1988) 544, 557 note 62, quote at 565.

fourth century indiscriminately regard the Thebans as medizers? Why did they particularly remember the Thebans' medism, rather than that of the Dolopes, Aenianes, Perrhaebi, Locrians, Magnetes, Malians, and Phthiotic Achaeans, who are also mentioned in Herodotus' list (7.132.1)? By what mechanism was this memory transmitted, and on which occasions was it recalled?

Athenian Disposition toward Thebes in 479

In this section, I will make the case that, based on their previous experience with Thebes, the Athenians perceived their northern neighbors as resolute medizers from the start, despite the Theban participation at Tempe and Thermopylae. It was this simplified version of outright medism that was publicly memorialized by various means and thus transformed from "remembered" into "commemorated" history.[10]

Both the perception of reality and the resultant shape of memories depend on a group's mental framework. The Athenians' general disposition toward the Thebans at the time of the Persian Wars is therefore decisive for the formation of the memory of Thebes' conduct in this conflict. The contemporary evidence for the decades preceding the Persian Wars is scarce. Our earliest literary source for Athenian-Theban relations during this period is Herodotus, who composed his account (which betrays knowledge of Athenian sources) in the second half of the fifth century as part of his narrative of archaic Athens. For this reason, we have to be aware of the fact that Herodotus' portrayal of Athenian-Theban relations at the end of the sixth century reflects how Athenians in the middle of the fifth century remembered their dealings with Thebes in the past. Despite these pitfalls, the events themselves give us at least a clue about the general Athenian mindset at the time of Xerxes' invasion.

Herodotus reports that by the end of the sixth century, Thebes had emerged as the leading power in Boeotia, pursuing a hegemonic policy that led to the formation of a federation in which Thebes was predominant.[11] The Boeotian city of Plataea, however, resisted the pressure to join the Boeotian League and, bordering Attica, sought protection for its independence (fig. 1).[12] The Athenians concluded an alliance with Plataea in 519 BC, which led to several military

10. Cf. "Remembered and Commemorated History" in the introduction, 23–26.

11. For the emergence of the Boeotian league and the Plataean-Athenian alliance of 519 BC, see Buck (1979) 107–17. According to Thuc. 3.68.5, the long-lasting Athenian-Plataean alliance was concluded in 519. Some scholars have suggested to amend Thucydides' text and to date this alliance down to 509 BC, but this has been refuted convincingly. Cf. Hornblower (1991) 464–66.

12. For the Plataeans' supplication of Athens, see also "Theseus—Another Heracles" and "Athens' Aid for Suppliants" in chapter 3, 169–86.

encounters between Athens and the Boeotian League (Hdt. 6.108, 5.77, 5.81).[13] According to Herodotus' investigations, in one of these battles, the Athenians utterly defeated both the Boeotian and Chalcidian armies and managed to take seven hundred Boeotian prisoners (Hdt. 5.77; M&L 15).

Since the overall situation between Athens and Thebes remained the same for the following two decades (Plataea still refused to join the Boeotian League and was a firm Athenian ally, as it proved in the battle of Marathon in 490), we can assume that Athenian attitudes toward Thebes were still characterized by suspicion and hostility. The memory of Thebes' repeated attempts to force Athens to give up its alliance with Plataea was certainly still powerful in 480–479. Many now middle-aged Athenians had taken part in these military campaigns themselves, and the glorious victory of 506 was memorialized on the Acropolis, the most prominent location in Athens. The Athenians set up a chariot with a tithe of the ransom money and hung up the prisoners' chains, thus perpetuating the memory of the Athenian triumph and their hostility toward the Boeotians (Hdt. 5.77; M&L 15). Furthermore, Herodotus attributed this decisive victory to the newly established form of government in Athens (5.78), a belief, undoubtedly shared by many Athenians in his own time, that may have originated as early as the victory itself and helped secure the memory of this battle. All this suggests that at the beginning of Xerxes' invasion, the Athenians were not particularly well disposed toward the Thebans, whom they considered the dominating force in the Boeotian League.

Another reason for the perception of Thebans as outright medizers was the experience of Athenian soldiers in the battle of Plataea itself. When the Greeks under Pausanias met the Persian forces and their Greek contingents, the Athenians held the left wing and directly faced the Thebans, who—according to Herodotus—fought zealously and lost three hundred of their πρῶτοι καὶ ἄριστοι (9.67). Thus, for the Athenians, this battle against the barbarians was actually a battle against the Thebans.

Memorialization of Thebes' Treason

Social memory and ideology are intertwined in a complicated way. Heroic and traumatic experiences can alter a society's mental framework, its very ideology. In the process of memorialization, such a defining event is taken out of its historical context, much simplified, and transformed into a symbol for the

13. From Herodotus' usage, it is evident that for the Athenians, the terms *Theban* and *Boeotian* were interchangeable, whenever activities of the Boeotian League at that time were meant. Cf. Buck (1979) 111; Demand (1982) 18. For the role of Plataea in Athenian social memory, see "Plataean Patriotism versus Theban Medism" below, 119–42.

character of the community. From these "founding myths," a group derives an awareness of its unity and peculiarity.[14]

Owing to the inevitable egoism of social memory, the enemy is often represented as the Other in a group's shared image of the past; social memory manifests itself "through a kind of identificatory determination in a positive ('We are this') or in a negative ('That's our opposite') sense."[15] As has long been noticed, the Athenians gained enormous self-confidence from their success in the Persian Wars and thought of themselves as the first city in Hellas, fighting as πρόμαχος for the freedom of the Greeks.[16] I argue that the Athenians' shared memory of the Persian Wars was determined not only by their own positive role as champions of Greek liberty but also by the negative roles of their enemies, first and foremost the Persians, but also the Thebans. The former were remembered as hubristic barbarian invaders and the latter as selfish traitors of Greece.[17] The Theban medizers thus became inextricably linked to the Persian invaders in Athenian social memory. This memory served as important "symbolic capital" within the Greek arena; it helped the Athenians to assert themselves as morally superior to their archrival in central Greece.[18] There are several clues indicating that soon after the Persian Wars, in the process of memorializing the victories over the barbarians, Theban medism was commemorated as well and became part of the Athenian master narrative.

Thebes' treason was nowhere more manifest than in the Plataea campaign. The Persians set up their camp in close proximity to Thebes. The Thebans supplied the Persian army (Hdt. 9.13–15) and contributed devoted troops to the Persian war effort (Hdt. 9.32, 67). For this reason, the memory of Theban medism was most closely associated with the battle of Plataea, which was commemorated as a victory of the Greek alliance both at Plataea and at Panhellenic sanctuaries. At the same time, each individual polis celebrated its own contribution to the allied war effort.[19] Athenians would thus be reminded of Thebes' medism through both Panhellenic and Athenian commemorative activities.

The victorious Greeks memorialized their victory in the form of spoils dedicated to the gods at Panhellenic sanctuaries.[20] They used a tenth (δηκάτη) of

14. Cf. "Ideology and Social Memory" in the introduction, 13–19.

15. J. Assmann (1995) 130. Cf. Mol (1976).

16. Cf. Miltiades' fictitious speech in Hdt. 6.109 (which reflects the fundamental principles of fifth-century Athenian ideology); Gehrke (2003) 22–23. For the Athenian "Könnens-Bewusstsein," see Meier (1993) 354–501. For the Athenians' self-image as champions of Greek liberty, cf. "Funeral Orations" in chapter 1, 49–58.

17. Cf. "Treacherous by Nature" below, 143–49.

18. For social memory as "symbolic capital," see "Public Discourse and Decision Making" in the introduction, 30–36.

19. For the memory of the battle of Plataea within both Panhellenic and particularistic memorial frameworks, see Jung (2006) 225–383.

20. For a comprehensive discussion of Persian War dedications, see Gauer (1968).

the booty of Plataea to set up monumental bronze statues of Zeus and Poseidon at Olympia and the Isthmus, respectively, as well as the famous golden tripod, resting on a bronze column in the form of three intertwined serpents at Delphi (Hdt. 9.81).[21] The Serpent Column, which stood at the end of the Sacred Way, facing the Apollo temple, bore the names of the thirty-one Greek cities that "fought this war" (το[ίδε τὸν] πόλεμον [ἐ]πολ[έ]μεον, M&L 27).[22] This monument, although erected from the spoils of Plataea, referred "to the whole of the Great Persian War"[23] and included also some island states that had fought at Salamis but took no part in the final battle. The list is headed by the Spartans, Athenians, and Corinthians, which is generally seen as a mark of recognition for the preeminent contribution these three *poleis* made to the allied war effort.[24] Probably the same list of states was inscribed on the Greek thank offering to Zeus at Olympia (Paus. 5.23).[25] The Thebans were not on these lists; their medism after Thermopylae surely far outweighed—in the eyes of the victorious Greeks—their participation in the allied expeditions at the beginning of Xerxes' invasion. There is no doubt that these memorials at Delphi and Olympia—Panhellenic sites of the greatest importance—helped to keep the memory of Thebes' medism alive. The absence of the Thebans, a major power in Greece, must have been apparent to every viewer. The later addition of the Tenians and the Siphnians to the list in Delphi proves that the Greeks did pay attention to who was inscribed on the Serpent Column and who was not.[26] That they cared is also evident in the "trial" of the Plataeans, who—after their surrender to the Spartans in 427—referred explicitly to the monument in Delphi as proof of their participation in the heroic defense of Greece (Thuc. 3.57.2).

The victory over the Persians was also commemorated at Plataea itself. The Greeks buried their fallen on the battlefield in separate tombs, city by city. Herodotus mentions the graves for the Spartans, Tegeans, Athenians, Megarians, and Phliasians and the cenotaph of the Aeginetans (Hdt. 9.85).[27] Given

21. For the commemorative significance of these Panhellenic dedications, see Jung (2006) 241–57. The Serpent Column itself (without the three heads) was later brought to Constantinople and survives to this day. For possible reconstructions and for pictures of the remains, see Gauer (1968) 81 fig. 4 and plates 1–3.

22. For the base and the column, see Bommelaer (1991) 165–67; Gauer (1968) 75–92. For Pausanias' initial dedicatory epigram and the circumstances of its removal, see Thuc. 1.132; [Dem.] 59.96–98; Hornblower (1991) 218; Trevett (1990) 409–11; Jung (2006) 246–48.

23. Meiggs & Lewis (1988) 59. Cf. Jung (2006) 254.

24. Jung (2006) 250. For explanations of the organization of the entire list, see Jung (2006) 251–54.

25. Paus. 5.23 mentions only twenty-seven names, but the four omissions may be due to the negligence of Pausanias or the bad shape of the monument, no trace of which survived; cf. Meiggs & Lewis (1988) 60.

26. Meiggs & Lewis (1988) 60.

27. For the significance of this and other cenotaphs in the inter*poleis* "memory wars," see Flow-

the importance of landscape and monuments—Halbwachs' *cadre matériel*—for the transmission of social memory,[28] these funeral memorials at the very site of the battle would have served Athenians as material reminders of this battle and their glorious victory over the Theban medizers, especially when we imagine Athenian veterans visiting Plataea to honor the fallen and recounting details of the battle to younger generations. That these monuments at Plataea were indeed able to perpetuate the memory of the victory not only over the Persians but also over the treacherous Thebans is suggested by Isocrates' Plataeans, who remark a century later that the Thebans were eager to destroy all these memorials, since "memorials of that time bring shame to them" (Isoc. 14.59).

The tombs of the fallen were only one aspect of the Greeks' commemorative activities at Plataea. According to Thucydides' Plataeans, Pausanias made a sacrifice to Zeus Eleutherius in the agora of Plataea after the battle and proposed to the allies to restore Plataea and to guarantee its independence (Thuc. 2.71.2).[29] Presumably in exchange for this guarantee of independence against Theban aggression, the Plataeans conducted annual rituals at the graves of all the fallen of the Greek alliance.[30] In their defense speech in 427, the Plataeans mention that every year, at public expense, they honor the Greek dead with traditional garments and food offerings (Thuc. 3.58.3–4).[31] From early on, these tombs thus served as a monumental site for regular commemorative activities.[32] According to Plutarch, upon the proposal of Aristides, the commander of the Athenian contingent, the Greeks also instituted an annual meeting of delegates from all the Greek states, a permanent cult for Zeus Eleutherius, and the Eleutheria, a quadrennial freedom festival in commemoration of the Greek victory (Plut. *Arist.* 21). Plutarch's testimony is late and probably reflects the commemorative practices of later centuries.[33] It is not inconceivable, however, that a precursor of this freedom festival was indeed celebrated in the early years after the battle, before the outbreak of Athenian-Spartan hostilities.[34] Several scholars have made the reasonable suggestion that the *New Simonides* (fr. 11

er & Marincola (2002) 254–56; Jung (2006) 259–60. Some of these tombs survived into Roman imperial times; cf. Paus. 9.2.5.

28. See "Monuments and Inscriptions" in chapter 1, 84–94.

29. Hammond (1992) 145.

30. Jung (2006) 264, 270. The Plataeans' annual funeral rites are described in more detail by Plutarch, writing in the second century AD (Plut. *Arist.* 21). Jung (2006) 263 suggests that they were probably essentially the same rites as the ones briefly mentioned by Thucydides.

31. Hornblower (1991) 453.

32. For the connection of monuments and "incorporated" memorial practices, see "Monuments and Inscriptions" in chapter 1, 85–86.

33. There is no clear evidence for the Eleutheria festival before the third century BC; cf. Étienne & Piérart (1975) 65–75, who suggest that it was probably instituted after the restoration of Plataea in 338.

34. Boedeker (2001) 152; Barron (1988) 610.

Sider = 11 West^2), an elegy praising this victory under Pausanias' generalship, had been composed for this very occasion in the years before Pausanias' fall from grace.[35] Simonides wrote poems on Plataea, Artemisium, Thermopylae, and Salamis, as fragments and testimonia show.[36] Such poems were the earliest historical narratives processing the experience of the Persian Wars and were therefore tremendously important for the memorialization of these events.[37] Since Simonides' Plataea elegy treated the battle itself as well (fr. 13–17 Sider = 13–17 West^2), it is quite possible that it also made mention of the Thebans fighting alongside the Persians; yet, due to the fragmentary state of the poem, this remains a speculation.

In the Athenians' collective memory, Plataea undoubtedly ranked behind their greatest achievements of Marathon and Salamis. This was partly due to the fact that Plataea was, to a considerable degree, a Spartan victory.[38] Nevertheless, both the Athenian traditions we can grasp behind Herodotus' account and various commemorative activities leave no doubt that the Athenians viewed the battle of Plataea also as a great Athenian triumph, the memory of which was to be made permanent.[39] As material manifestations of this victory, Mardonius' scimitar and the breastplate of the Persian cavalry commander Masistius were displayed in the temple of Athena Polias on the Athenian Acropolis; these thank offerings were well known over centuries, as references in Demosthenes and Pausanias show (Dem. 24.129; Paus. 1.27.1).[40]

This victory was also commemorated through regular ritual activities. In addition to Marathon and Salamis, the Athenians gave Plataea a permanent place in their sacred calendar (Plut. *Mor.* 349e–f).[41] Moreover, on behalf of all the Athenians and at public expense, the men from the tribe Aiantis regularly offered sacrifice to the Sphragithic Nymphs, at their cave on Mount Cithaeron, in recognition of their divine aid to the Athenian victory at Plataea (Cleidemus *FGrHist* 323 F 22 = Plut. *Arist.* 19.6).[42]

There is evidence suggesting that the Athenians commemorated Plataea not

35. Cf. Pavese (1995) 24; Rutherford (2001) 40; Aloni (2001) 101.

36. See the new edition of Simonides' fragments by Sider (2001).

37. Cf. Flower & Marincola (2002) 18.

38. Nouhaud (1982) 162; Flower & Marincola (2002) 28. In 472, the Athenian poet Aeschylus, while extolling Salamis as an Athenian triumph, credits the victory of Plataea to "the Doric spear" (Aesch. *Pers.* 815–20).

39. Examples of elaborated (possibly even invented) episodes are the Athenians' slaying of Masistius (Hdt. 9.20–24), their dispute with the Tegeans (Hdt. 9.26–28.1), and the Spartan request to change wings with them (Hdt. 9.46–47); cf. Flower & Marincola (2002) 29.

40. Cf. "Monuments and Inscriptions" in chapter 1, 84–94.

41. The festivals were probably instituted in the immediate aftermath of the Persian Wars. Cf. Deubner (1932) 235; Gauer (1968) 16; Parke (1977) 54–55; Barron (1988) 620.

42. See Plut. *Arist.* 11.3–4; Plut. *Mor.* 628e–f; Paus. 9.3.9; Jacoby *FGrHist* 3b (Suppl.) i.82–83; Schachter (1981–94) 2:185–86; Parker (1996) 103; Harding (2008) 105–6.

only as a victory over the Persians but even more as a triumph over Thebes.[43] This can be deduced, for instance, from the decoration of the temple of Athena Areia at Plataea. This shrine was built from the spoils of the battle of Plataea (Plut. *Arist.* 20.3) and contained two monumental paintings: one was a depiction by Polygnotus of Odysseus after having slain the suitors, while the other, by Onasias, showed "the former expedition of Adrastus and the Argives against Thebes" (Paus. 9.4.1–2).[44] These paintings, which were displayed in close proximity to the battlefield and probably commissioned under Athenian influence, were appropriate and highly dramatic mythic analogues for the struggle of the Athenians and the Plataeans (the only loyal Boeotioans) against the medizing Thebans at Plataea.[45] Polygnotus' slain suitors represent the Thebans: just as the suitors, motivated by ruthless self-interest, had betrayed their loyalty toward their king, Odysseus, the Thebans "betrayed their obligations to the common Hellenic defense in favor of their own perceived self-interest."[46] Onasias' painting most probably included the Athenian "sequel" to the myth of the Seven against Thebes, according to which the Athenians forced the hubristic Thebans to grant burial to the fallen Argives.[47]

In all likelihood the Athenians also dedicated spoils from the Plataea campaign at Delphi to commemorate their victory over the Persians and their Theban collaborators. For around 340 BC, the Athenians dedicated golden shields in the new temple of Apollo in Delphi (the old one was destroyed by a fire in 373) with "the appropriate inscription: The Athenians, from the Medes and Thebans, when they fought against the Greeks [Ἀθηναῖοι ἀπὸ Μήδων καὶ Θηβαίων, ὅτε τἀναντία τοῖς Ἕλλησιν ἐμάχοντο]" (Aeschin. 3.116). Even though these shields certainly reflect the bitter anti-Theban resentment felt in Athens in the years after Leuctra,[48] it is not unlikely that they were hung up to replace earlier votive offerings that were destroyed by the fire in 373.[49]

43. Flower & Marincola (2002) 28. Cf. Castriota (1992) 63–76.

44. According to Paus. 9.4.1, this shrine was built from the Plataeans' share of the spoils from the battle of Marathon (and not Plataea). Castriota (1992) 63–65 views the accounts of Plutarch and Pausanias as complementary and proposes that the shrine itself was built from the spoils of Plataea right after the battle, while the cult statue and the paintings were—with the help of Athenian funds—added during the 460s or 450s and reflect the Athenian influence. See also Gauer (1968) 31–32, 98–99.

45. Flower & Marincola (2002) 29.

46. Castriota (1992) 73. Similarly, the two loyal herdsmen who aid Odysseus serve as an analogue to the role of the Plataeans, who "alone of the Boeotians" were loyal to the Greek cause.

47. See E. Thomas (1976) 74; Castriota (1992) 67–70. See also "Athens' Aid for Suppliants" and "Punishment of Theban *Hybris*" in chapter 3 in the present study, 174–86 and 189–96.

48. Cf. Gauer (1968) 26; Flower & Marincola (2002) 30.

49. Adams (1919) 398–99. That golden shields with accompanying inscriptions were indeed dedicated as victory offerings at Panhellenic shrines is evident from the Spartan dedication at Olympia after the battle of Tanagra in 458. The inscription reads "from the Argives, Athenians, and Ionians" (M&L 36; Paus. 5.10.4).

That the Athenians at the beginning of the fourth century were aware that their ancestors at the battle of Plataea had actually fought not against the barbarians but against the medizing Greeks is evident from the account of the battle in Lysias' funeral oration.[50]

> The Lacedaemonians and the Tegeans routed the barbarians, while the Athenians and the Plataeans fought and conquered all the Greeks who had despaired of freedom and submitted to slavery. (Lys. 2.46)

That the Greek alliance, after the battle of Plataea, besieged the city of Thebes for twenty days to force the Thebans to hand over all those who had medized (αὐτῶν τοὺς μηδίσαντας, Hdt. 9.86) also helped to foster the memory of the Thebans as prototypical medizers. The members of the Greek alliance demanded the extradition of the chief collaborators in Thebes, presumably in order to fulfill, at least in some way, the oath they had sworn earlier "to 'tithe' to the god in Delphi [δεκατεῦσαι τῷ ἐν Δελφοῖσι θεῷ] those of the Greeks who had given themselves to the Persian without compulsion" (Hdt. 7.132).[51] Since δεκατεύειν actually means "to utterly destroy a city and to dedicate to the god a tenth of the spoils,"[52] it is not surprising to find that the prevalent opinion in fourth-century Athens held that Thebes had not been punished sufficiently for its medizing. This is evident from Xenophon's account, where the "old saying to have the Thebans tithed" (τὸ πάλαι λεγόμενον δεκατευθῆναι Θηβαίους) is twice used in the context of making war on Thebes (Xen. *Hell.* 6.3.20, 6.5.35). Since the term δεκατεύειν denoted the punishment planned for the medizers in 480, this saying functioned as yet another reminder of Thebes' collaboration with the Persian.[53]

In sum, by pointing to the Athenians' immediate experience of the Thebans before and during Xerxes' invasion and by furnishing some evidence for the memorialization of Thebes' medism after the battle of Plataea, I have shown why the Thebans were perceived and remembered as prototypical medizers by the Athenians after the war. However, it still needs to be explained why and how

50. For the role of the *epitaphios* in the formation of the patriotic Athenian master narrative, see "Funeral Orations" in chapter 1, 49–58.

51. For a discussion of this oath, the punishment of Thebes, and the concept of δεκατεύειν, see "Crisa as Model for the Theban Proposal in 405/4" in chapter 5, 310–19.

52. Flower & Marincola (2002) 257; How & Wells (1923) 2.177–78; Burn (1962) 345, 514; Siewert (1972) 66–69.

53. Unfortunately, we do not know how "old" this saying really was. It may have originated soon after the Persian Wars, but it is also conceivable that it was revived (if not coined) at the high time of anti-Theban feelings in the 370s and 360s.

the memory of Theban medism was transmitted over more than one hundred years and why it was still a powerful argument in political debates in fourth-century Athens. For this purpose, I will trace the transmission of this collective memory through the fifth and fourth century. In so doing, I will focus on specific occasions that had the capacity to invoke and thus reinforce the memory of Thebes' treason in Athenian public discourse.

Remembering Theban Medism throughout the Fifth Century

Spoils were dedicated, tombs were erected, and rituals were established to commemorate the victory over the Persian invaders and their medizing Greek allies. However, all these efforts do not automatically secure the transmission of the memory of Thebes' collaboration. The relevance of a particular social memory for subsequent generations is a crucial precondition for its transmission. There is a natural tendency "to suppress what is not meaningful . . . in the collective memories of the past, and interpolate or substitute what seems more appropriate or more in keeping with [a society's] particular conception of the world."[54] For the transmission of a certain memory, there have to be occasions that prompt the recollection of this previous event. This can explain why the medizing of the Dolopes, Aenianes, Perrhaebi, Locrians, Magnetes, Malians, and Phthiotic Achaeans (Hdt. 7.132.1) is never mentioned in any political debate. It was simply not relevant to the Athenians and thus faded from common historical consciousness. The case of Thebes was quite different, for Thebes and Athens remained bitter enemies throughout the fifth century. This atmosphere of enmity and antagonism provided a fertile breeding ground for anti-Theban sentiment in Athens and secured the memory of their respective allegiances in the Persian Wars.

Frequent military encounters throughout the fifth century offered plenty of occasions for the recollection of the victory over the Thebans at Plataea, as a brief historical sketch will show.[55] Boeotia, economically and politically weakened due to the Persian occupation and the outcome of the war, was contested between Athens and Sparta during the Pentecontaetia (fig. 1). By the 460s,

54. Fentress & Wickham (1992) 58–59; cf. "Ideology and Social Memory" in the introduction to the present study, 13–19. In Germany, for instance, the once much celebrated "Day of Sedan," commemorating the defeat of Napoleon III in the Franco-Prussian War of 1870/71, entirely vanished from collective historical consciousness.

55. Thucydides' account is the best source for the history of Athenian-Theban relations during this period. For modern reconstructions, see Buck (1979) 141–77, (1994) 9–24; Demand (1982) 27–45.

Boeotia was in στάσις, and Sparta intervened and established pro-Spartan oligarchies throughout Phocis, Locris, and Boeotia (Thuc. 1.107). The Athenians countered, in order to stop the growth of Spartan influence on their northern border. They were defeated by the Spartans and their allies at Tanagra in 458, but they prevailed over the Boeotians in a second battle at Oenophyta—after the Spartans had left—and brought all of Boeotia under their control (Thuc. 1.108). However, the period of Athenian domination was brief. In 447/6, Theban exiles seized Orchomenus, gathered support from other Boeotian cities, and annihilated an Athenian expeditionary force under Tolmides at Coronea (Thuc. 1.113). Thebes reestablished its hegemony in the Boeotian League and became a firm Spartan ally. During the Peloponnesian War, the Athenians and Boeotians fought each other constantly. The Thebans started the war by a night assault on the Athenian ally Plataea in 431 (Thuc. 2.2–6); in the same year, a cavalry skirmish took place at Phrygioi (Thuc. 2.22). In 427, after a long siege, the remaining Plataean defenders, together with an Athenian contingent, had to surrender to the Spartans and were executed, due to Theban pressure (Thuc. 3.52–68). In the following summer, the Athenians defeated a Boeotian army (Thuc. 3.91), but in 424/3, they themselves suffered a serious defeat at Delium (Thuc. 4.89–101).[56] In 421, Thebes rejected the Peace of Nicias (Thuc. 5.17, 22), and during the ensuing cold war, the Boeotians maintained only a series of ten-day truces (Thuc. 5.26). Throughout the Decelean War, the Boeotians took advantage of the Spartan occupation of Attica to ravage their Athenian neighbors and even seized the Attic border town Oropus (Thuc. 8.60.1).

As this brief sketch of Athenian-Theban relations during the rest of the fifth century reveals, there were plenty of occasions in which Athenian and Theban troops faced each other, just as at Plataea in 479. It is to be expected that Athenian politicians and generals used the emotionally charged memory of the victory over the medizing Thebans to rally the members of the assembly or the soldiers before battle in subsequent conflicts. Granted, we do not have direct evidence that Athenians evoked this particular memory, but we know from other cases that it was a common practice of Greek generals to bring to mind past victories to induce confidence in their soldiers.[57] The Theban *boeotarch* Pagondas, for instance, used the memory of the Theban victory at Coronea in 447/6 to encourage his troops before the battle against the Athenians at Delium in 424 (Thuc. 4.92).[58] On the other side, the Athenian *strategos* Hip-

56. For the repercussions of this battle on the Athenian view of the Thebans, see "Punishment of Theban *Hybris*" in chapter 3, 189–96.

57. Hornblower (1996) 81–86 convincingly refutes Hansen's (1993) skeptical view.

58. Just as the Athenians had done after Marathon, the Thebans memorialized their victory in this battle against the Athenians by instituting a regular festival at Delium, the Delia (Diod. 12.70.5).

pocrates reminded the Athenians of their success against the Thebans three decades earlier.

> Go forward, then, to meet them [i.e., the Thebans and other Boeotians], in a spirit worthy both of this polis, the foremost among the Greeks, which every one of you is proud to claim as his fatherland, and of the fathers who with Myronides conquered these men at Oenophyta and became at one time masters of Boeotia. (Thuc. 4.95.3)

This makes it plausible that Athenian generals, when fighting the Thebans during the Pentecontaetia, also drew on their victory over the medizing Thebans at Plataea to encourage their troops. Similarly, we can assume that veterans of the Persian Wars recalled their experience of the Thebans and gave advice to younger soldiers about to depart on campaign.[59] At least up to the beginning of the Peloponnesian War—about fifty years after the battle of Plataea—some Athenian veterans must still have been alive to convey their experience of this historic struggle to their sons and grandsons. It is likely that these situations served as cues and helped to keep alive the memory of Theban medizing and of the battle at Plataea in the decades immediately following the Persian Wars.

Herodotus' Thebans

At this point, I would like to turn to one particular stage in the process of transmission of the memory of Theban medism: Thebes' conduct during the Persian Wars as it was depicted by Herodotus, presumably during the 430s and 420s.[60] Many scholars have argued that Herodotus' unfavorable account of the Thebans is the result of the deep-rooted anti-Theban bias of his Athenian sources.[61] The concept of social memory enables us to identify some of the distorting forces behind this kind of bias. I will make the case that Herodotus' portrayal of the Thebans reflects the state of the collective memory of Thebes' medizing that one was likely to encounter in Athens during the third quarter of the fifth century. In the process of memorialization, the Athenians' persistently hostile disposition toward the Thebans and the frequent recollections of Theban medism

59. The Theban *boeotarch* Pagondas explicitly calls on the veterans of Coronea to remember their previous victory (Thuc. 4.92.7); their presence would have been an enormous psychological boost to the younger soldiers, as Hanson (1989) 93 argues. That young Athenians learned about their fathers' and grandfathers' military exploits is evident from Aeschin. 2.78 and Pl. *Lach.* 179c–d.

60. For Herodotus' use of oral traditions, see Luraghi (2001).

61. How & Wells (1923) 2.229; Hignett (1963) 147 note 3; Burn (1962) 417–19; Demand (1982) 26–27.

resulted in obliterating the more complex memories of contemporaries of the events, who knew of the Thebans' participation in the early allied war efforts at Tempe and Thermopylae and of the power struggle between pro- and anti-Persian factions in Thebes. Herodotus' characterization of Thebes' conduct during Xerxes' invasion shows that these memories were still alive but were becoming badly distorted in Athens.

Herodotus' account of the Theban conduct during Xerxes' invasion is contradictory at points.[62] On the one hand, there are many passages where Herodotus portrays the Thebans collectively as fervent medizers from early on.[63] On the other hand, his account of the battle of Plataea and the punishment of the medizing ringleaders also betrays the existence of pro- and anti-Persian factions in Thebes (Hdt. 9.67, 9.86.1).[64] His account of the Theban role at Thermopylae is particularly troubling and reveals the difficulties of squaring the memory of their participation with the image of the prototypical Theban medizer (Hdt. 7.205, 222, 233).[65] I suggest that four factors in particular were decisive for this specific portrayal of the Thebans: the memory of participants, the Athenian master narrative, the recent night assault on Plataea led by the Theban Eurymachus, and the so-called consistency bias.

When Herodotus questioned his various sources in the third quarter of the fifth century about the events of 480–479, the mere *presence* of a Theban contingent at Thermopylae was probably never disputed.[66] It is reasonable to assume that even Athenian veterans, when prompted, would still remember and could talk about this event. Yet, considering the workings of social memory, it is unlikely that they would have provided a historically accurate account; rather, by that time, their personal memory of the Theban participation at Thermopylae would have converged with the Athenian master narrative as commemorated by monuments, funeral orations, and battle harangues, which generally portrayed the Thebans as prototypical medizers. It is a well-known phenomenon in psychology that people have a natural tendency, when reminiscing about their past experience, to shape their memories in such a way as to make them consistent. While the memories of actions are less prone to such distortions, the opposite is true for the memory of past motives. Thus inaccurate or fictitious motives are often supplied to bring seemingly contradictory facts into a

62. See "Theban Conduct during the Persian War" above, 103–5.

63. Hdt. 7.205, 222, 233; 8.34; 9.2; 9.31.2; 9.40; 9.41.4; 9.87.2.

64. Cf. Flower & Marincola (2002) 224, 258.

65. Cf. Demand (1982) 21–22.

66. His sources included not only members of the Greek alliance but also people from the other camp. Hdt. 9.16, for instance, names Thersander from Orchomenus as a source for events in Thebes in 479.

coherent narrative.[67] I suggest that this "consistency bias" is responsible for the distorted picture of the Thebans' role in Leonidas' army as found in Herodotus. In the decades after the Persian Wars, Athenians who knew of the Theban contingent at Thermopylae had to come up with an explanation for this fact, which clearly contradicted not only their behavior during the rest of the war but also their portrayal in the Athenian master narrative according to which they fought fervently on Xerxes' side, as the Athenians themselves well knew.[68] To rescue an assumption underlying most prevalent social memories—namely, that historical actors have persistent characters—those Athenians would supply a suitable explanation to make the apparently inconsistent Theban behavior consistent with what all Athenians "knew": the prototypical Theban medizers fought with Leonidas only under compulsion (Hdt. 7.205), were retained as hostages in the final battle (Hdt. 7.222), and betrayed him as soon as they had a chance to do so (Hdt. 7.233). Herodotus' account indicates that in the 430s, the memory of Theban participation at Thermopylae was still a known fact in Athens, even though the circumstances and motives were badly distorted.

Herodotus' narrative suggests that one specific incident was responsible for bringing the latent memory of the Theban participation at Thermopylae back into Athenian public discourse. It seems that the Theban night assault on Plataea in 431 (Thuc. 2.2–6), planned by Eurymachus, the son of Leontiades who (according to Herodotus) had led the Theban contingent in 480,[69] provided the cue for recalling the Thebans' presence at Thermopylae in Athens after the night assault on Plataea in 431, when Herodotus had not yet completed his project.[70] Given the prominence of this Theban family and the importance of the patronymic in Greek culture, the son's action might well have been sufficient to prompt the memory of the father's role at Thermopylae.[71] That Herodotus digresses from his main narrative and mentions the Theban attack on Plataea in the very context of Leontiades' surrender supports this interpretation (Hdt. 7.233).[72]

67. For this "consistency bias," see Schacter (2001) 139–44.

68. Similarly, Hammond (1988) 557 note 62.

69. Contradicting Herodotus, Plutarch claims that the Theban contingent in 480 was led not by Leontiades but by Anaxandrus (Plut. *Mor.* 867a). Even if he was not the commander, Leontiades probably played a leading role in this Theban endeavor. Cf. Buck (1979) 129; Demand (1982) 22 with note 30.

70. It is interesting in this context that Herodotus never mentions the Theban contingent that took part in the Greek expedition to Tempe. The lack of an adequate cue in this case might explain the loss of this contradictory detail in Athenian social memory.

71. For the prominence of this family, see Demand (1982) 22. Some scholars go even further and argue that the surrender and branding of the Thebans at Thermopylae was a later Athenian invention to cast the sins of the son on his father. Cf. Graf (1979) 172.

72. Of course, it cannot be ruled out that Herodotus himself ascribed the motives to his Theban actors. Yet this assumption seems unnecessary in this particular case, since his portrayal of the

In fourth-century Athenian discourse, the Theban participation at Thermopylae is no longer mentioned, and one orator even claims that the Plataeans "alone of the other Boeotians" fought and died with Leonidas ([Dem.] 59.95).[73] I suggest that this memory faded in Athens as the postwar generation died, for it was not publicly commemorated and stood in contrast to the master narrative of outright Theban medizing.[74] Besides, there were no subsequent events, such as Eurymachus' attack on Plataea, which could have served as cues and would have prompted this particular memory, thus reinstilling it into Athenian public discourse.

In Thebes, however, the memory of internal strife between pro-Persian and pro-Greek factions was preserved, as Ephorus, Aristophanes of Boeotia, and Thucydides show. Diodorus, drawing on Ephorus, reports that "the inhabitants of Thebes were divided against each other with respect to the alliance with the Persians" (Diod. 11.4.7). In a passage in Plutarch, which is probably derived from the fourth-century historian Aristophanes of Boeotia, the Theban Mnamias is said to have participated with five hundred Thebans in the Greek expedition to Tempe (Plut. *Mor.* 864e),[75] and in Thucydides, the Thebans rebuke Plataean accusations concerning their medism by claiming that the δυναστεία of a few powerful pro-Persian Thebans had prevented the rest from siding with the Greeks (Thuc. 3.62). Thus, in Thebes, the memory of this intra-Theban conflict served an important function in the decades following the Persian Wars and was therefore preserved and transmitted: the Thebans could use it to exculpate themselves and counter charges made by other Greeks.[76]

Contexts for the Recollection of Theban Medism in the Fourth Century

I have thus far tried to explain how the "equivocal role"[77] the Thebans played during Xerxes' invasion could become the simplified memory of outright The-

---

Thebans fits so neatly into the memorial framework of his contemporary Athenians.

73. For an interpretation of [Dem.] 59.95, see "Remembering the Plataeans" below, 127–42.

74. There is no memorial at Thermopylae to serve as a reminder of the Thebans' participation. The funeral epigrams and the burial mound with the lion statue, symbolizing Leonidas, immortalized Peloponnesian valor only (Hdt. 7.228). For the legend of Leonidas' final stand, see Hignett (1963) 371–78; Burn (1962) 420–22; M. A. Flower (1998).

75. Graf (1979) 168. Cf. Aristophanes of Boeotia *FGrHist* 379. Jacoby *FGrHist* 3b (Komm.) i.160 gives 424 BC as *terminus post quem* and 362 BC as *terminus ante quem* for his work.

76. For further discussion of this Theban apology, see "Challenging the Master Narrative" below, 149–54.

77. Buck (1979) 175.

ban medism in Athenian social memory. Thanks to their hostile disposition toward their northern neighbor and their immediate experience in the battle of Plataea, the Athenians perceived the Thebans as traitors from the outset. Consequently, the battle of Plataea is remembered as a victory over both the Persian invaders and their Greek supporters. The persistent enmity between Athens and Thebes and frequent military encounters prompted and thus perpetuated this memory in the decades after the Persian Wars. However, the question arises why Theban medism was still a frequent topic in fourth-century Athenian discourse. Right after the battle of Plataea, it makes sense that the Athenians would boast of their victory over Mardonius and his Greek collaborators, especially when they came into conflict with Thebes again. But since Athens and Thebes were unremittingly hostile in the fifth century and fought numerous military engagements, it needs to be explained why the Athenians still evoked the particular fact of Theban medism, even though their subsequent history with Thebes provided them with abundant, more recent instances that could be used to rally anti-Theban sentiments. Fighting against Thebes per se did not necessarily prompt the memory of Theban medism in the fourth century.[78] Based on the references quoted at the beginning of this chapter, I will argue that there were two specific contexts that were likely to prompt the memory of Theban medism in Athenian discourse: the Plataean-Theban conflict and Thebes' conduct in the face of "barbarian" invasions. Both were recurrent themes in Athenian politics during the late fifth and fourth centuries.

Plataean Patriotism versus Theban Medism

The city of Plataea served as a special cue for the Athenian memory of Theban medism for two reasons. First, since the decisive battle against the Persians and their Greek allies (first and foremost the Thebans) took place on the very territory of the Plataeans, mentioning their city's name would inevitably remind the Athenians of this great victory. Second, Plataea (Athens' longstanding ally) and Thebes were deadly enemies throughout the fifth and fourth century. Since the Plataeans were—apart from the Thespians and Haliartans—the only Boeotians who were indisputably loyal members of the Greek alliance during Xerxes' invasion, it is no surprise that whenever the topic of Plataean-Theban antagonism came up in Athenian public discourse, the antithesis of Plataean patriotism versus Theban medism was ready to hand.

78. It seems that even when the Athenian commander Hippocrates was encouraging his troops before fighting the Boeotians at Delium in 424, he resorted not to the victorious battle of Plataea in 479 but to the more recent victory of Oenophyta in 458 (Thuc. 4.95).

Plataean-Theban Antagonism

In this section, I will make the case that the continuous Plataean-Theban conflict, which culminated in the destructions of Plataea in 427 and once again in 373, was a recurrent topic in Athenian public discourse. From the beginning of the Peloponnesian War, the antithesis of Plataean patriotism versus Theban medism functioned as a theme on which speakers on behalf of the Plataeans would rely throughout the rest of the fifth and the fourth centuries. The persistence of this conflict, made even more vivid through the presence of displaced Plataeans in Athens, could thus serve as a reminder of Thebes' medizing and ensure the transmission of this memory to younger generations.

This antagonism went back to the end of the sixth century, when Plataea refused to join the Theban-led Boeotian League and sought Athenian protection for its independence (Hdt. 6.108).[79] In 480, the Persians destroyed the cities of Plataea and Thespiae, when—according to Herodotus—they learned from the Thebans that both *poleis* refused to medize (Hdt. 8.50.2).[80] After the victory in 479, the Greek alliance passed a decree—in accordance with Pausanias proposal—to restore Plataea and to protect its independence (Thuc. 2.71.2).[81] In 431, a Theban column, aided by Plataeans in favor of the Boeotian League, made a night assault on Plataea to gain control of the city and incorporate it into the Boeotian League. However, the invaders were overcome, taken prisoner, and executed by the Plataeans. Expecting Theban retaliation, the Plataeans brought their older men, women, and children to Athens and fortified their city with an Athenian garrison (Thuc. 2.2–6). In the summer of 429, when the Plataeans refused to renounce their alliance with Athens, the Spartans and their allies (including the Thebans) began to besiege Plataea (Thuc. 2.71–78). In the winter of 428/7, half of the besieged managed to break out and flee to Athens (Thuc. 3.20–24). The rest, pressed by famine, finally surrendered in 427. Due to Theban pressure, they were all executed after a bogus trial, their city was eradicated, and their land was annexed by the Thebans (Thuc. 3.52–68).

What evidence do we have that the siege and destruction of Plataea did indeed evoke the antithesis of Plataean patriotism versus Theban medism, as I have claimed? Our most important source is the Plataeans' defense speech in Thucydides' Plataean debate (Thuc. 3.52–59).[82] This speech "circles endlessly

79. Cf. "Athenian Disposition toward Thebes in 479" above, 105–6.

80. Herodotus implies that it was the Thebans who prompted Plataea's destruction. This, too, might be an example of how all actions of the Thebans in Herodotus' account were informed by the Athenian master narrative of outright Theban medism.

81. For discussion of Pausanias' proposal, see Hammond (1992) 145; Hornblower (1991) 357–59.

82. For the Plataean debate, see Gomme (1956) 337–58; Macleod (1977); Hornblower (1991) 444–66; Pelling (2000) 72–81.

round the theme of the Plataians' stand on behalf of Greece at a time when Thebes medized," as Hornblower puts it.[83] The Plataeans sought clemency by reminding the Spartans of their merits in the Persian Wars and thereafter (54.1): they were the only Boeotians who rallied to defend the freedom of Greece, and even though they were an inland people, they took part in the sea fight at Artemisium. In the battle that was fought in their own land, they fought side by side with the Spartans and Pausanias (54.3–4). They also contrasted the advantage the Spartans now derived from their alliance with the Thebans to the far greater benefit they had received from the Plataeans and the rest of the Greeks at the time of Xerxes' invasion (56.4). In that crisis, "when the barbarian was threatening all with slavery, these men [the Thebans] were on his side" (56.4) and sought their own advantage, while the Plataeans were ready to hazard the noblest course despite the danger (56.4–5). Furthermore, the Plataeans pointed to the inscription on the tripod in Delphi as proof of their valor (57.2) and to their care and annual sacrifice for the Greeks (including the Spartans) who had died in the battle of Plataea and were buried in their land (58.4). Handing Plataean land over to the Thebans would mean that the Spartans would rest in enemy land among their murderers (i.e., the Thebans) who fought alongside the Persians (58.5).

Even though the speeches in the Plataean debate are surely not a verbatim record of this show trial, they at least convey the arguments that Thucydides thought "to be appropriate [τὰ δέοντα] and to reflect the general purport of what was actually said."[84] Moreover, Thucydides most likely had learned from those Plataeans who had managed to escape to Athens how the Plataeans in general felt about the fact that their city was being besieged by both the Spartans (their former brothers in arms) and their Theban archenemies.[85] Hornblower notes in his commentary that this speech is more traditional than other

83. Hornblower (1991) 445.

84. Hammond (1992) 146, citing Thuc. 1.22. For an excellent discussion of this difficult Thucydidean methodological statement, see Pelling (2000) 112–22, who argues that this "umbrella description . . . could cover a range of different procedures" (117). Given the fact that all the Plataeans present at the trial were executed, Pelling (72, 117) regards the historical substratum of this particular speech as rather low. Hornblower and Gomme are more optimistic. Pointing to the authenticity of the names of the Plataean speakers in Thuc. 3.52.5, Hornblower (1991) 443–44 considers this "additional evidence that a real speech was delivered by real people." Gomme (1956) 346 reasonably suggests that some honest Spartan or Theban might have been Thucydides' source, describing the Plataeans' speech with the words "the usual things—the Persian wars, the gods and the oaths, the special sanctity of Plataia, the honour of Sparta; but it was very honestly done."

85. Cf. Pelling (2000) 72. That the situation of 429–427 indeed evoked the memory of the Persian Wars is also evident from the Plataeans' initial negotiation with the Spartan king Archidamus, where they recall the oath, sworn by the Greek alliance, in accordance with Pausanias' proposal, to protect Plataea's independence due to their merits during Xerxes' invasion (Thuc. 2.71).

Thucydidean speeches in the "detailed way it dwells on the past."[86] I take this as further evidence in support of my thesis that arguments from social memory played an important role in public debate and decision making in the fifth and fourth centuries.[87]

Given the deep-rooted Athenian-Theban enmity, the Plataeans (and their Athenian friends) surely used the antithesis of Plataean patriotism versus Theban medism not only in negotiations with the Spartans but also when lobbying for support in Athens. There were several occasions that were likely to prompt this antithesis in public debates in the council and assembly: (1) when the Plataeans asked, in 431, for Athenian help after the Theban assault and the Athenians sent an army to replenish supplies, to evacuate the women and children, and to garrison the city (Thuc. 2.6); (2) when reports from Plataea and possible relief missions were discussed during the siege; (3) when 212 Plataeans made a sortie from the city and managed to get to Athens in the winter of 428/7 (Thuc. 3.24); and (4) when (according to Isocrates and Apollodorus) those Plataeans who escaped to Athens in 428/7 received Athenian citizenship through a block grant (Isoc. 12.93–94; [Dem.] 59.103–4).[88] The conferral of citizenship in the last instance could only be done by a decree of the demos. Since such a citizenship grant was viewed as a reward for received benefactions ([Dem.] 59.89), it is likely that the Plataeans' merits during the Persian Wars (and their enemies' medism) were brought up at this meeting of the assembly as well and were thus reinforced in Athenian historical consciousness.

At that time, the plight of the Plataeans was surely a hot topic not only in the debates in council and assembly but also in everyday conversation. Their mere presence must have served as a reminder. As a result of the Theban nighttime assault, many Plataeans—namely, the old men, women, and children—moved to Athens in 431 (Thuc. 2.6.4). Their number was further increased in 428/7, when 212 Plataean men managed to break through the siege (Thuc. 3.24.2). Even though these Plataeans were granted Athenian citizenship, they "formed a distinct, ethnic group."[89] They served together in the army as a separate unit

86. Hornblower (1991) 445. Apart from the Persian Wars, the Plataeans refer to their aid for the Spartans at Ithome (Thuc. 3.54.5) and to the beginnings of the Athenian-Plataean alliance in the sixth century (Thuc. 3.55.1).

87. See "Public Discourse and Decision Making" in the introduction, 30–36.

88. Thucydides does not mention this block grant, probably for artistic reasons, to highlight Athens' passivity during Plataea's plight; cf. Hornblower (1991) 465–66. Most scholars consider this decree genuine; see M. J. Osborne (1981) 28, (1982) 11–16; Gawantka (1975) 177–78 note 31; Hornblower (1991) 448–50; Trevett (1992) 190–91; Carey (1992) 139; Hammond (1992) 146–47; Kapparis (1995), (1999) 387–88; Pelling (2000) 65, 75–76. For a similar block grant for the heroes of Phyle, see *IG* II^2 10 and "Athenian Memorialization of the Men from Phyle" in chapter 4, 235–45.

89. M. J. Osborne (1982) 15 argues convincingly that these Plataeans had no intention of being properly integrated in the Athenian citizen body. They only accepted Athenian citizenship because

(Thuc. 4.67.2). One group of them took over the city of Scione when it was offered to them in 421 by the Athenians (Thuc. 5.32.1), and those remaining in Athens met once a month at the cheese market (Lys. 23.6), thus preserving their identity as Plataeans.[90] During and after the Peloponnesian War, their presence as a conspicuous group in Athens thus ensured the memory of their scandalous treatment by the Spartans and Thebans,[91] which could—by association—perpetuate the memory of Plataean patriotism and Theban medism.

These processes also work on the individual level. The 212 Plataeans who were made Athenian citizens were, according to the decree, "distributed among the *demes* and tribes" ([Dem.] 59.104) and could thus become the carrier and source of this memory in these local institutions. Apollodorus furthermore refers to a passage of this decree that indicates

> that the names of those who had been examined should be inscribed on a stone stele, which should be placed on the Acropolis by the temple of the goddess, so that the grant might be preserved for their descendants and it might be possible for an individual to prove to which of them he is related. ([Dem.] 59.105)

This stone stele itself could serve as a material reminder of the Plataeans' undeserved fate.

Neither the Peace of Nicias in 421 nor the peace concluding the Peloponnesian War in 404 led to the restoration of Plataea. During the Corinthian War (395–386), the Athenians and Thebans were close allies; Athenian support for the Plataean cause would surely have endangered this vital alliance with Thebes. Plataea was restored only in accordance with the Peace of Antalcidas—presumably with Spartan help after the seizure of the Cadmea in 382—and its former inhabitants returned from Athens (Paus. 9.1.4). After the democratic coup in Thebes in 379, Plataea served the Spartans as a base for their war against Thebes (Xen. *Hell.* 5.4.10, 14, 48). In 373, however, Plataea was seized and destroyed by the Thebans for the second time, and its inhabitants found asylum once again in Athens (Paus. 9.1.5–8; Diod. 15.46.6).

In 373, the Athenians were still allied with the Thebans, who were members of the Second Athenian Confederacy. However, there is plenty of evidence that this second destruction of Plataea by the Thebans greatly aggrieved the Athe-

they had no alternative at the time and waited for a chance to rebuild their native city.

90. It is not entirely clear (but inconsequential for my argument) whether this group consisted of the new Athenian citizens (M. J. Osborne (1982) 15) or of those who initially arrived in 431 and remained Plataean citizens (Hammond (1992) 146).

91. Pelling (2000) 61 calls the destruction of Plataea "a scar in the popular [Athenian] historical consciousness, a perpetual reproach to Thebes and Sparta and an emblem of the horrors of war."

nians. The fate of the Plataeans was again a theme in Athenian discourse and brought the old antithesis of Plataean patriotism versus Theban medism back into the forefront of Athenian consciousness, as the analysis of Isocrates' *Plataicus,* remarks in Xenophon, and public references to Plataea's fate throughout the next forty years will show.

Shortly after Plataea's destruction, Isocrates wrote the *Plataicus,* which purports to be an appeal of the Plataean refugees to the Athenian assembly.[92] We do not know how much the Plataeans' actual speech differed from the *Plataicus,* which might be either the speech that they commissioned, a revision of the speech that they delivered, or a pamphlet written by Isocrates to disseminate his political ideas. But as Naiden concludes convincingly, "it doubtless contained the arguments that Isocrates believed an Assembly listening to suppliants would expect."[93] Not surprisingly many of the arguments are drawn from Athenian and Plataean collective memory, and the antithesis of Plataean patriotism versus Theban medism is a crucial theme in this speech. Listing previous Theban crimes, the Plataeans also mention the Thebans' "evil deeds, so willingly committed and so grave" in times past—that is, their medism—and call them "betrayers of all of Greece" (Isoc. 14.30). In the last section, Isocrates refers to the tombs and trophies at Plataea that commemorate the victory of all Greece and bring shame to the Thebans (Isoc. 14.58–59). He has the Plataeans complain that those "who considered it right to be the slaves of the barbarians"—that is, the Thebans—have become despots over all the other Greeks and that the Plataeans who fought at Athens' side for freedom have been driven from their homes (Isoc. 14.61). It must not happen, they maintain, that the "Thebans, who were drawn up in battle order with the enemy" rule over this land (Isoc. 14.61). Already once before, the Plataeans, "the benefactors of Greece," had been destroyed by the Spartans to gratify the Thebans, "the betrayers of Greece" (Isoc. 14.62). This shows that even one hundred years later, the Plataean-Theban antagonism was able to evoke the memory of their respective conduct during Xerxes' invasion, which was presented in the starkest antithesis possible.

Xenophon confirms that in the late 370s, the Plataean-Theban conflict and, with it, the respective allegiance of the Plataeans and Thebans during the Persian Wars became important topics in Athenian political discourse once again. Xenophon attributes the Athenians' readiness to conclude peace with Sparta in 371 to their anger about recent Theban actions. They were angry at the Thebans,

92. For the destruction of Plataea in 373 BC, see Seager (1994) 177–78; Rhodes (2010) 271, 285.
93. Naiden (2006) 182. See also Jebb (1876) 2:176–78; Jaeger (1938) 199–201.

> seeing that the Plataeans, who were their friends, had fled from Boeotia to them for refuge, and that the Thespians were supplicating them not to allow them to be left without a city. . . . [The Athenians withdrew their support from the Thebans, who] were annihilating cities that had been faithful in the war against the barbarian and were friendly to Athens. (Xen. *Hell.* 6.3.1)[94]

According to Xenophon, Callias, one of the Athenian delegates at this peace conference, emphasized that the distress over the destruction of Plataea and Thespiae was felt by Athenians and Spartans alike (Xen. *Hell.* 6.3.5). When the Athenians saw that the Thebans were diplomatically isolated at this conference after their clash with Agesilaus over their claim to represent the entire Boeotian League, "they were of the opinion that now there was hope that the Thebans would be tithed [δεκατευθῆναι], according to the common saying" (Xen. *Hell.* 6.3.20)—indicating the type of punishment that had been planned for the medizers a century earlier.[95]

After the battle of Leuctra in 371, the Athenians sided with Sparta against Thebes. Even when the Theban hegemony collapsed after the battle of Mantinea in 362, leaving Greece in—according to Xenophon—an unprecedented state of chaos (Xen. *Hell.* 7.5.27), Athenian-Theban enmity remained a constant factor in Greek politics; in 357, they wrestled over Euboea, and during the Third Sacred War, the Athenians supported the Phocians against the Thebans.[96] In this hostile, anti-Theban climate, the restoration and independence of Plataea and other Boeotian towns was a recurrent theme in Athenian political discourse between 371 and 339, as several references show.

In 355, for instance, in his discourse *On the Peace,* Isocrates compared misguided Athenian imperial ambitions to the Thebans' seizure, contrary to their oaths, of Plataea, Thespiae, and other cities (Isoc. 8.17), and he likened Athenian practices to the Theban oppression of their neighbors (Isoc. 8.115). In 353, speaking about Athens' relations with Megalopolis, Demosthenes advised the assembly—in order to weaken Thebes—to restore Plataea and Thespiae by cooperating with their inhabitants and by appealing to the other states for support of this cause (Dem. 16.25). According to his testimony, this measure was frequently (πολλάκις) talked about in the assembly (Dem. 16.4). In 346, the

94. Often, orators assert that the Plataeans alone of the Boeotians fought for the Greek cause in the Persian Wars, while Thespiae's merits are ignored. For a discussion of this problem, see "Remembering the Plataeans" below, 127–42.

95. Cf. "Memorialization of Thebes' Treason" above, 106–13, and "Crisa as Model for the Theban Proposal in 405/4" in chapter 5, 310–19.

96. Cf. Sealey (1993) 102–3 (on Euboea), 108–9 (on the Athenian-Phocian alliance).

Athenian assembly voted to extend the Peace of Philocrates to Philip's descendants, after Aeschines' report of the second embassy gave rise to Athenian hopes that Philip would end the Theban dominance over Boeotia and restore the independence of Plataea and other Boeotian towns. In the fall of 346, in the speech *On the Peace,* Demosthenes referred to this unfortunate report of his fellow ambassadors, mentioning Plataea and Thespiae explicitly (Dem. 5.9–10).[97] In 343, pointing to this "false" report, he indicted Aeschines of willfully misleading the Athenian people, which again injected the topic of Theban oppression of Plataea and Thespiae into Athenian public discourse (Dem. 19.20–21, 42, 112, 325).[98]

These frequent references in the Attic orators show that the Theban-Plataean conflict remained an important issue from the 370s through the 330s. In an atmosphere of widespread anti-Theban sentiment, the persistent Plataean-Theban conflict and the presence of Plataean refugees in Athens functioned as an *aide-mémoire* for Athenian memory of their respective conduct during the Persian Wars and provided politicians with a powerful tool to activate and incite anti-Theban feelings.

So far, I have argued that it was the ongoing Theban-Plataean conflict that could prompt the memory of Thebes' and Plataea's respective alliances in the Persian Wars, as we have seen most clearly in Isocrates' *Plataicus.* Yet, since memory works by association, orators even used the antithesis of Plataean patriotism versus Theban medism in situations where this conflict was not the central issue. Unlike in Isocrates' *Plataicus,* in the pseudo-Demosthenic speech *Against Neaera,* the allusion to the Plataeans' role during the Persian Wars is not used as an argument against the Thebans in particular.

Apollodorus, who is most likely the author of this speech,[99] constructed a narrative of the Plataean merits toward the Athenians in order to demonstrate that the Athenians regarded their citizenship as such a valuable gift that they only awarded it for outstanding loyalty; he thus sharply contrasted the Plataeans' well-deserved citizenship to the shameless usurpation of Athenian citizenship by Neaera. Apollodorus deals with the Plataeans' virtues during the first and second Persian invasion, their indictment of Pausanias before the Amphictyons, the night assault on their city in 431, and their siege and escape,

97. In his fourth-century AD hypothesis, Libanius—pointing to a contradictory passage in *On the False Embassy* (Dem. 19.111–13)—suggests that Demosthenes wrote this speech but never delivered it. Sealey (1993) 157–58 and 170 argues convincingly for its delivery.

98. In 338, after the battle of Chaeronea, Plataea was finally restored by Philip II of Macedon: cf. Paus. 4.27.10, 9.1.8; Ellis (1976) 201; Rhodes (2010) 357. The Plataeans' hatred of their Theban oppressors was incessant, as their role in Thebes' destruction in 335 shows. Cf. "Alexander's Annihilation of Thebes" in chapter 5, 336–41.

99. Cf. Carey (1992) 3; Kapparis (1999) 48–52.

ending with the award of Athenian citizenship ([Dem.] 59.94–104).[100] To give this narrative its unity, Apollodorus tried to establish a causal chain between these separate episodes that finally led to Plataea's destruction by Sparta in 427. The Theban-Plataean antagonism is clearly not the central issue here, as Apollodorus' explanation for the Theban attack in 431 shows. To create a causal link between this assault and Pausanias' indictment by the Plataeans (more than forty years earlier), the orator downplays the role of the Thebans in 431, describing them as mere agents of Sparta ([Dem.] 59.98–99).

Although this narrative is not aimed specifically against Thebes, the Plataeans' role during Xerxes' invasion nevertheless prompts mention of Thebes' medizing, which is loosely attached in the form of a genitive absolute.

> And again, when Xerxes marched against Greece, with the Thebans medizing [Θηβαίων μηδισάντων], the Plataeans did not bring themselves to withdraw from their friendship with us, but alone of the other Boeotians [μόνοι τῶν ἄλλων Βοιωτῶν] [fought with us on the ships and in the field]. ([Dem.] 59.95)

The memories of the respective behavior of the two states in the Persian Wars was so closely linked in Athenian historical consciousness that talking about the one would almost inevitably lead to mentioning the other by association as well. This shows how deeply rooted the antithesis of Plataean patriotism versus Theban medism was in Athenian social memory.

Remembering the Plataeans

The aforementioned passage in *Against Neaera,* which contrasts Plataean patriotism and Theban medism, shows one peculiarity that is also to be found in other references to the Plataean and Theban allegiances during the Persian Wars. In Isocrates' *Plataicus,* the Plataeans argue that their ancestors "alone of those who lived outside of the Peloponnese" (μόνους τῶν ἔξω Πελοποννήσου) shared in their perils and thus helped the Athenians to save their city (Isoc. 14.57). Similarly, in the *Panathenaicus* (Isoc. 12.93) and in *Against Neaera* ([Dem.] 59.95), the Plataeans are said to have been "the only Boeotians" (μόνους Βοιωτῶν and μόνοι τῶν ἄλλων Βοιωτῶν, respectively) who fought with the Athenians against Xerxes. This claim is not historically accurate, since other

100. This historical narrative is "a unique case of identifiable reliance on an extant historical work in the Attic orators," as Kapparis (1999) 380 remarks; cf. R. Thomas (1989) 202 note 19. For a detailed analysis of Apollodorus' use of Thucydides for the description of the siege of Plataea in [Dem.] 59.98–104, see Nouhaud (1982) 263–64; Trevett (1990); Carey (1992); Kapparis (1999) 379–86; Pelling (2000) 61–65. Cf. "Rhetorical Education" in chapter 1, 94–96.

Boeotian towns—namely, Thespiae (Hdt. 8.50.2) and Haliartus (Paus. 9.32.4)—also refused to submit to the Persians. This distortion is often seen as mere rhetorical exaggeration on the part of the speaker,[101] but it is better explained if we take into account the collective memory of the Athenian audience:[102] through the persistent Plataean-Theban antagonism and the cruel destruction of Plataea in 427, the stark antithesis of Plataean patriotism versus Theban medism obscured the behavior of other Boeotian towns in this oversimplified scheme. This does not necessarily mean that the Thespians' anti-Persian stance was entirely forgotten—in fact, Xenophon refers to it after they had lost their town for the second time—but in this particular context of the Plataean-Theban conflict, it could simply be left out.[103] Unfortunately, we do not have sufficient data to reconstruct the Athenian memory of the Thespian and Haliartan role during the Persian Wars, which would allow us to explore in detail how their involvement was widely forgotten. There is, however, a suitable parallel: the Athenians' claim to have fought alone at Marathon, which meant the frequent suppression of Plataea's participation in this battle in Athenian public discourse. Fortunately, in this case, we know alternative carriers of social memory that can help us contextualize the orators' hyperbolic claims. An examination of this phenomenon can support my assertion that in particular contexts, details could be left out (unnoticed by the audience), but this does not necessarily mean that they were forgotten entirely. On the contrary, they could be retrieved, if suitable cues were offered.[104]

The apparent suppression of Plataea's help at Marathon has troubled many scholars. It has long been noticed that, especially in Athenian funeral orations, the Athenians are said to have fought alone against the Persians at Marathon, even though the Plataeans had come to their help πανδημεί (Hdt. 6.108.1). This peculiar phenomenon has been discussed most comprehensively by Walters,

101. Cf. Hornblower (1996) 131 and Pelling (2000) 77 on Thucydides' Plataeans in Thuc. 3.54.3.

102. In all three cases (Isoc. 12.93, 14.57; [Dem.] 59.95), this claim is expressed before an Athenian audience and meant to appeal to them. In Thucydides' Plataean debate, the Plataeans make the same claim before the Spartan judges (Thuc. 3.54.3). This exaggeration might be ascribed to the Plataeans' rhetorical strategy to highlight their merits vis-à-vis the other Boeotians who once medized but were now allied with Sparta. Alternatively, it might be seen as a reflection of the collective memory of the Plataeans or the Athenian Thucydides.

103. Describing the situation in Athens in 371, Xenophon names the destruction of both Plataea and Thespiae as the reason for Athens' growing annoyance with the Thebans, since they "were annihilating cities that had been faithful in the war against the barbarian and were friendly to Athens" (Xen. *Hell.* 6.3.1). It is very well possible that Thespian refugees, when pleading for help in the Athenian assembly, brought the merits they earned during the Persian Wars back into Athenian historical consciousness.

104. For these characteristics of memory, see "Individual and Collective Memory" in the introduction, 8–13.

who raises many valuable points.[105] Yet I believe that approaching this problem from the perspective of social memory can further enhance our understanding of this phenomenon. After a brief critique of Walters' analysis, I will focus on Athenian memorial practices and on hyperbolic assertions in patriotic contexts in general. A close interpretation of Athenian orators' allusions to Athens' feat at Marathon will show that, by and large, politicians and diplomats used arguments from the Athenian past, as that past was portrayed in the master narrative of the funeral orations. At times, however, Athenian speakers ventured to modify a dominant version by appealing to alternative carriers of social memory, as we will see in the case of Apollodorus. Such modifications were not unlimited; they were confined by the horizon of expectation of their audience.

Walters questions how the average hearer received "such falsifications" as the one about Marathon and whether the Athenians came "to believe the distortions they heard in the ἐπιτάφιοι."[106] There were several important reminders of the Plataean participation at Marathon. Prominent among them was the famous painting of the battle of Marathon in the Stoa Poikile. This showed the Plataean contingent, recognizable by their Boeotian helmets, rushing to the Athenians' help, as Neaera's prosecutor points out ([Dem.] 59.94). The traveler Pausanias, too, was able to identify this contingent as the Plataeans (Paus. 1.15.3). Pausanias further reports that there were two graves at Marathon, one for the Athenians and one for the Plataeans and slaves (Paus. 1.32.3); the latter was excavated not long ago.[107] Herodotus mentions that every four years since the battle of Marathon, when the Athenians offer sacrifice at the Great Panathenaea, "the herald prays for blessings both for the Athenians and the Plataeans" (Hdt. 6.111.2). Finally, Pausanias reports that, just like the Athenians, the Plataeans set up in their city a statue of Athena, made by Phidias from their share of the spoils at Marathon (Paus. 9.4.1). Concluding that it was "obvious to any Athenian, that the Plataians were at Marathon,"[108] Walters dismisses the view that such an oversimplification as the Athenian boast to have acted alone was normal and a "widely admitted and true fact,"[109] as de Romilly among others has claimed. He asserts instead that two distinct, official versions of the same event were equally well known and that both were in currency despite contradicting one another. Walters attributes this remarkable phenomenon to the cultural difference between the ancient Greeks and us with respect to viewing "what constituted a 'fact' of history." According to Walters, the Greek attitude

105. Walters (1981).
106. Walters (1981) 206–9, quote at 206.
107. Cf. Hammond (1992) 147–50 for a discussion and further bibliography.
108. Walters (1981) 208.
109. Walters (1981) 207, quoting de Romilly (1963) 245.

toward myths is responsible for the apparent acceptance of these two contradictory historical versions: "it was a typical ancient practice to give different, even conflicting accounts of important myths to promulgate opposing political messages."[110]

Walters is right to stress the material and ritual reminders of the Plataean role at Marathon and the great malleability of Greek myth, but I believe he is overstating his case in saying that both versions were equally well known and that it was "obvious to any Athenian that the Plataians were at Marathon."[111] An examination of both the particular contexts in which these versions appear and their interaction over time allows us to move beyond positing the paradoxical coexistence of two equally well-known official versions. Instead, this case gives us an insight into the relative weight of different carriers of social memory, the interaction between them, and their use in Athenian public discourse.

I agree with Walters that immediately after Marathon, both the Athenians and the Plataeans sought to commemorate Marathon as a common victory, as the tombs on the battlefield and the inclusion of the Plataeans in the prayer at the Great Panathenaea indicate. Even in the 460s, the participation of the Plataeans was publicly commemorated, when Cimon commissioned the Painted Stoa, depicting, among other things, the battle at Marathon. How and when, then, did the Athenian boast to have fought alone at Marathon come into being?

This claim first appears in Herodotus, in the context of a dispute between the Tegeans and the Athenians over the command of the left wing at Plataea in 479. According to his account, the Athenians claimed this honor by pointing to previous exploits, first and foremost to their fight at Marathon (μοῦνοι Ἑλλήνων δὴ μουνομαχήσαντες τῷ Πέρσῃ, Hdt. 9.27.5). This speech is to be regarded not as authentic but, rather, as a reflection of Athenian *topoi* of praise, with which Herodotus became familiar in Athens when he was composing his work. This and other praise *topoi* used in this speech are familiar from Athenian λόγοι ἐπιτάφιοι, which were instituted as part of the public funeral for the war dead of each year, probably shortly after the Persian Wars.[112]

In the course of the fifth century, as has been noticed widely and by Loraux, Thomas, Gehrke, and Jung recently, the events of the Persian Wars in general and of Marathon in particular were stripped of their historical context and transformed into symbols for the principal features of the Athenian character. The Athenians thought of themselves as champions of Greek liberty and as defenders of the weak, perceptions that were used to legitimize their claim to

110. Walters (1981) 211.
111. Walters (1981) 208.
112. See "Funeral Orations" in chapter 1, 49–58.

hegemony in Hellas. Even though the aforementioned scholars stress slightly different aspects of this process, all four agree that Marathon became the epitome of the Athenian achievement in the Persian Wars, that it was transformed into "paradigmatic history" (Loraux) or "intentionale Geschichte" (Gehrke), ranking among—or even surpassing—legendary mythological feats like the battle against the Amazons, the restoration of the Heraclidae, or the burial of the Seven against Thebes, as the list of exploits in the funeral orations and the battle depictions in the Painted Stoa show.[113]

Considering the characteristics of social memory, it is not surprising that in the process of memorialization, in which events are stripped of their historical context, much simplified, and turned into symbols of the character of the community, the participation of the Plataeans could become obliterated in general Athenian historical consciousness.[114] The funeral orations played the most important role in this process, since they provided the Athenians regularly with an idealized account of their city's past: at Marathon, the Athenians acted swiftly, trusted in their own valor, were badly outnumbered, and fought alone against myriads of barbarians for the freedom of the other Greeks (Lys. 2.20–26; Dem. 60.10). Thus, in this particularly patriotic context, Athenians were used to hearing of Marathon as a solely Athenian victory, *without* being aware of a "historical falsification,"[115] despite the existence of material evidence for the participation of the Plataeans. This does not necessarily mean that Plataean virtue was entirely forgotten; rather, it was suppressed as the occasion required it. I assert that such an omission in favor of patriotic hyperbole is a common phenomenon and not an idiosyncrasy of Greek culture.

Similar features of memorialization can be seen in contemporary commemorations of events of World War II in general and of the landing in Normandy in particular. During the dedication of the National World War II Memorial in Washington, D.C., on May 29, 2004, President Bush ascribed the victory in the Second World War to the character and ideals of America.

> [This memorial] is a fitting tribute—open and expansive, like America; grand and enduring, like the achievements we honor. The years of World War II were a hard, heroic and gallant time in the life of our country. When it mattered most, an entire generation of Americans showed

113. Loraux (1986) 155–71; R. Thomas (1989) 221–26; Gehrke (2003); Jung (2005) 126–65.

114. See "Ideology and Social Memory" in the introduction, 13–19, and "Funeral Orations" in chapter 1, 49–58. In this context, it would be interesting to investigate how deeply the memory of French support in the American Revolutionary War is rooted in U.S. historical consciousness.

115. Contra Walters (1981) 204.

> the finest qualities of our nation and of humanity. On this day, in their honor, we will raise the American flag over a monument that will stand as long as America itself.[116]

In President Bush's speech, the course of this war is summarized by the phrase "from Pearl Harbor to the coast of Normandy to the deck of the *Missouri*." These three events are able to symbolize this four-year-long existential struggle. In this particular American context, the allies were not mentioned at all, either by name or in general. Imagine readers in the distant future who do not know the history of World War II; if this speech is their only source for the event, they could get the impression that America fought alone against the "aggressive powers" of Germany and Japan "to oppose the ideologies of death." The participants in this ceremony knew, of course, that America did not fight alone, but in this particular patriotic context, the president was expected to talk about *American* sacrifice and achievement during World War II.[117]

Two years earlier, on May 27, 2002, President Bush celebrated Memorial Day at an American cemetery in Colleville-Sur-Mer, France, with the French president Jacques Chirac present. As one would expect in a Memorial Day address to the American people at home, the president devoted most of his speech to the heroism of U.S. soldiers. Yet, unlike the dedication in Washington, this ceremony did not take place in a solely American context. Therefore, it is not surprising that President Bush mentioned the American allies summarily and France even by name.

> On Memorial Day, America honors her own. Yet we also remember all the valiant young men and women from many allied nations, including France, who shared in the struggle here, and in the suffering. We remember the men and women who served and died alongside Americans in so many terrible battles on this continent, and beyond.[118]

On June 6, 2004, at a common celebration of the sixtieth anniversary of

116. For a transcript of this speech, see http://www.wwiimemorial.com/default.asp?page=dedication2.asp&subpage=speakers.

117. Cf. Wolcott (2004), especially 230: "Each year the D-day commemoration bolsters the impression that America alone conquered the Axis powers, the Brits pluckily hanging in there during the Blitz until we could get our show on the road and save civilization one mo' time. What the Russians, for example, achieved and endured is barely worth a mention." He continues, quoting Christopher Endy, "When it comes to World War II . . . , Americans have lost sight of the fact that even the World War II's 'greatest generation' could prevail only with substantial help from its allies, including the Soviets, British, Canadians, Chinese, and many others."

118. For President Bush's Memorial Day speech, see http://www.presidency.ucsb.edu/ws/index.php?pid=73018&st1=#axzz1nt2HhsZm.

the allied landing in Normandy, President Bush—as the occasion required—focused on the shared efforts to defeat Nazi Germany, acknowledging the contribution of France, "America's first friend in the world," but also of the Allied Expeditionary Force, "Britains, Canadians, Poles . . . , and brave citizens from other lands"[119] who helped liberate Europe from Nazi rule. Yet not even in this celebration of the "great alliance of freedom" were all allies mentioned by name. They, however, commemorated their role on D-day in their own national context, as shown, for instance, by the program *The Longest Day—A Look Back at the Heroic Czech Contribution to the D-day Landings,* broadcasted by Radio Prague.[120]

Of course, one has to acknowledge that the communicative conditions in ancient Greece were radically different from today. We acquire our historical knowledge through school education, books, the media, and so forth; public commemorations are less important in this process. Nevertheless, this example illustrates that the commemoration or recollection of a specific event depends on occasion and context.

If we compare the different sources for the transmission of the memory of Marathon—dedications, the annual thanksgiving festival for the special support of Artemis Agrotera (Arist. *Ath. Pol.* 58.1),[121] the mural in the Painted Stoa, participants in the events—the funeral orations for the war dead, which highlighted Marathon among a list of other heroic exploits, was certainly the most important one.[122] While material sources like dedications and paintings require a personal, interpretative act, based on the spectator's previous knowledge, funeral orations were regularly addressed to a mass audience and provided both a narrative and an interpretation of the event. Since the Athenians were used to hearing that they fought alone against the Persians in 490, Marathon could indeed become a solely Athenian victory in the common historical consciousness. Loraux emphasizes that the version of the past presented to the Athenians in the funeral orations is "*true for the Athenians,* in that it conforms to the idea that they wish to have of themselves."[123]

The public funeral ceremony was not the only occasion where Athenians would hear that they fought alone at Marathon. This claim was also frequently voiced by speakers in the assembly and on diplomatic missions. When people are faced with problems, they often look for similar experiences in the past. Social memories function as a repository of symbols and metaphors, which

119. For President Bush's D-day speech, see http://www.presidency.ucsb.edu/ws/index.php?pid=72648#axzz1nt2HhsZm.

120. For the script, see Czech Radio 7, Radio Prague, http://www.radio.cz/en/article/54667.

121. Cf. Simon (1983) 82.

122. Cf. "Funeral Orations" in chapter 1, 49–58.

123. Loraux (1986) 171. Cf. also Gehrke (2003) 22; R. Thomas (1989) 237.

enables political leaders to communicate to the public their analysis of the current situation and their proposed solution.[124] It is, therefore, not surprising that whenever Athenian speakers tried to advance their cause by praising Athens' merits in the Persian Wars or had to justify its leadership in Greece, they would fall back on the Athenian achievement at Marathon, an argument familiar to them from the master narrative so often repeated in the funeral orations.

An example of this can be seen in the dispute between the Athenians and the Tegeans over the command of the left wing at Plataea, as portrayed by Herodotus: the solely Athenian victory at Marathon outranks all other achievements (Hdt. 9.27).[125] Even though this Athenian speech is surely not authentic and reflects attitudes more likely to be found in the second half of the fifth century in Athens, it shows that in Herodotus' experience, Athenians did use such arguments to support their claim of leadership in the Panhellenic arena. Thucydides reports a similar occasion, when Athenian diplomats at Sparta in 432 deploy Athens' merits in the Persian Wars to justify rule over their former allies: "For we affirm that at Marathon we alone bore the first brunt of the barbarian's attack" (μόνοι προκινδυνεῦσαι τῷ βαρβάρῳ, Thuc. 1.73.4).[126] In 399, defending himself in the speech *On the Mysteries,* Andocides reminds his Athenian jury of the recall of exiles (at the dawn of Xerxes' invasion) and seeks to demonstrate the wisdom of this amnesty. In doing so he (erroneously) telescopes the events of 490 and 480–479 together and cites the victory at Marathon—the epitome of the Athenians' fight against the Persians—in terms well known from the funeral orations: regained unity enabled the Athenians to stand "as protectors of all the Greeks and to meet the barbarians at Marathon, in the opinion that their own valor [ἀρετή] was sufficient to face the barbarians' multitude; they fought and conquered, freed Greece, and saved their fatherland" (Andoc. 1.107). With the catch phrases προτάξαντες τῶν ῾Ελλήνων ἁπάντων and τήν τε ῾Ελλάδα ἠλευθέρωσαν, this passage is an excellent example of the results of memorialization, by which a historical event is stripped of its immediate historical context and transformed into a symbol for the character and beliefs of the community. In his *Panegyricus* (380 BC), a political speech advocating Athenian hegemony in Greece, Isocrates likewise resorted to Marathon, as it featured in Athenian ideology: the Athenians "did not wait for their allies, but making the common war their private cause, they met those who looked with

124. Cf. "Public Discourse and Decision Making" in the introduction, 30–36.

125. For the Athenians' reference to the burial of the fallen Argives in this speech, see "Precedent for the Battle of Plataea" in chapter 3, 196–98.

126. See also the speech of the Athenian envoy at Camarina (Thuc. 6.83.2). Even when referring to Marathon in their narratives, Thucydides (1.18.1) and sometimes Herodotus (6.116) reduce it to the Athenian-Persian antithesis. In Herodotus' fictitious account of Xerxes' war council, Artabanus tries to dissuade Xerxes from invading Greece by using this *topos* of Athenian glory (Hdt. 7.10.β.1).

contempt upon all of Greece with their own forces—few against many myriads" (Isoc. 4.86).[127]

In all these passages, Athenian speakers use Marathon as an argument to advance their cause, praising Athens' merits in the fight against the Persians and justifying its claim to leadership in Greece. These particular contexts, which require the praise of Athens, naturally led Athenian orators to use the collective memory of Marathon in the form familiar to them and their audiences from the patriotic funeral orations.[128] Yet one could object that these passages have little bearing on what the average Athenian knew about the role of the Plataeans, since the omission of the Plataeans' contribution in these particular patriotic contexts, requiring the praise of the Athenian achievements in the Persian Wars, was a common phenomenon, as we have seen. If we want to find out how the Plataean role in the Persian Wars was generally seen in Athenian historical consciousness, we have to turn to other contexts, where Athenian self-interest would be less likely to shape the orator's argument concerning the Plataeans' virtues during the Persian Wars.

Three occasions are attested in which the Plataean merits are enumerated for the sake of praising the Plataeans. These are (1) the Plataean defense before the Spartan judges in 427, as reported by Thucydides; (2) Isocrates' *Plataicus*, which purports to be a Plataean appeal to the Athenian assembly after the destruction of their city in 373; and (3) the prosecution speech *Against Neaera*, in which the author contrasts the virtuous Plataeans to the shameful Neaera. Nouhaud remarks that in all of these instances, one would expect the Plataeans to stress their role at Marathon among their achievements.[129] Yet this does not apply to Thucydides' Plataean debate. It is not surprising that the Plataeans did not mention their participation at Marathon in their defense speech before the Spartan judges in 427, if one takes the Spartan-Athenian antagonism into account (Thuc. 3.53–59). Their resistance to the Persians was a strong argument in their defense, but this could be made without mentioning Marathon. To allude to an event where the Plataeans alone of the Greeks aided the Athenians would have been problematic, since it could have been understood either as an implicit criticism of the late arrival of the Spartans at Marathon or as an early example of the Plataeans' "voluntary Atticism"[130] during the Pentecontae-

127. Similar tendencies can be observed in the memorial practices of the Peloponnesians, as the funeral epigram for the four thousand Peloponnesians who fought against three hundred myriads of Persians reveals (μυριάσιν ποτὲ τῇδε τριηκοσίαις ἐμάχοντο | ἐκ Πελοποννάσου χιλιάδες τέτορες, Hdt. 7.228). The role of the Boeotians, especially the Thespians who died with Leonidas, is forgotten.

128. See Lys. 2.20, 23; Dem. 60.10. See also "Funeral Orations" in chapter 1, 49–58.

129. Cf. Nouhaud (1982) 153.

130. The Thebans bring this charge (ἑκούσιον ἀττικισμόν) against the Plataeans in their reply (Thuc. 3.63–65).

tia and the current war. In this case, therefore, the omission of Marathon has to be attributed to the Plataeans' rhetorical sensitivity, since mentioning this feat could have been detrimental to their cause.

Isocrates' *Plataicus* presents a different situation. His Plataeans address not the Spartans but the Athenian assembly. Given our knowledge of the events at Marathon, we would expect the Plataeans to stress their ancestors' support for the Athenians in this battle. Yet Marathon is neither mentioned by name nor alluded to, as Nouhaud and others have claimed.[131] It is worthwhile to discuss Nouhaud's interpretation of this particular passage in the *Plataicus,* since it shows that when interpreting historical allusions in the Attic orators, we cannot rely on a priori assumptions but have to take other sources into account to be able to estimate the audience's familiarity with these events and to assess the argumentative weight of a particular historical paradigm. Isocrates' Plataeans make the following argument:

> Alone of the Greeks [μόνοι τῶν ῾Ελλήνων] you Athenians owe us this service in return, to come to our aid now that we have been driven from our homes. For our ancestors, they say, when in the Persian War your fathers had abandoned this land, alone of those who lived outside the Peloponnese [μόνους τῶν ἔξω Πελοποννήσου κοινωνοὺς] shared in their perils and thus helped them to recover their city. It is but just, therefore, that we should receive in return the same benefaction [τὴν αὐτὴν εὐεργεσίαν] that we first conferred upon you. (Isoc. 14.57)

Nouhaud tries to connect this passage to Marathon. The phrase "alone of the Greeks you Athenians owe us" is said to recall the Plataean contribution at Marathon, where the Plataeans "alone of the Greeks" helped the Athenians. However, the next sentence clearly refers to the events of 480–479, when the Athenians "had abandoned this land" and the Plataeans "alone of those who lived outside the Peloponnese shared in their perils." Nouhaud offers two explanations. Either this Plataean is thinking of Marathon but confuses it with events of the second Persian invasion, or he actually means the conflict of 480–479. Nouhaud rejects the second option, calling it "unthinkable" that a speaker who seeks to praise the Plataeans would not evoke Marathon. Then he proceeds to find an explanation for Isocrates' "imprecision": Isocrates did not want to contradict his *Panegyricus,* where he followed the tradition that the Athenians fought alone at Marathon.[132]

Nouhaud's explanation rests on two assumptions, which are both, in my

131. Cf. Mathieu & Brémond (1961) 87; Van Hook (1954) 134; Nouhaud (1982) 153.
132. Nouhaud (1982) 153–54.

view, incorrect. First, misled by our own historical knowledge, he presupposes that the memory of the Plataean aid at Marathon was deeply rooted in both Isocrates' and his audience's historical consciousness. However, the extant funeral speeches show that Marathon was commemorated as the battle of the Persian Wars that the Athenians had fought alone. We have to take into account that the members of the assembly were more likely to draw their knowledge of the Athenian past from public commemorations, such as the funeral speeches, than from Herodotus or Thucydides. I assert that Isocrates, an Athenian himself, made his Plataeans use historical arguments that he thought would resonate with an Athenian audience in this particular context, which is a debate in the assembly. Second, Nouhaud assumes that the phrase "you Athenians alone of the Greeks owe us" instantly evoked the memory of the Plataeans at Marathon, who likewise were remembered as the only Greeks to help the Athenians in 490. Given the importance of Herodotus for our own understanding of the Persian Wars, Nouhaud's instinctive reflex to connect this passage to Marathon is certainly understandable. However, we cannot simply assume that an Athenian audience would have had the same associations. Besides, he fails to notice that the text as it stands makes perfect sense in the context of other passages praising Plataean patriotism. The *tertium comparationis* in this historical paradigm is not the act of helping alone but the act of helping to recover one's lost city. It follows, then, that the Plataean speaker would refer to Xerxes' invasion, when the Plataeans alone of those outside the Peloponnese helped the Athenians "to recover their city" after they "had abandoned this land." It is but just, therefore, that now the Plataeans "should receive in return the same benefaction" as they first conferred on the Athenians. Marathon is not evoked in this passage, and the phrase "our ancestors alone of those who lived outside the Peloponnese" is substantially the same as the phrase "the Plataeans alone of the Boeotians," frequently used in the context of Xerxes' invasion (Isoc. 12.93; [Dem.] 59.95). Thus Isocrates' Plataeans indeed follow a common Athenian practice by focusing not on Marathon but on their merits during Xerxes' invasion whenever their contribution to the Persian War is under discussion.

The only instance where the Plataeans' role at Marathon is explicitly mentioned by an Athenian orator is the pseudo-Demosthenic speech *Against Neaera*. This passage is extraordinary insofar as it reveals how the author, Apollodorus, managed to reinstill a less familiar aspect of the Plataean role in the Persian Wars into public discourse, thus modifying Athenian social memory.

Apollodorus contrasted Neaera's shameless usurpation of citizenship to the well-deserved award of Athenian citizenship to the Plataeans, who benefited Athens consistently throughout the fifth century. This list of merits starts with the Plataeans' role at Marathon.

> The Plataeans, men of Athens, alone of the Greeks [μόνοι τῶν ῾Ελλήνων] came to your aid at Marathon, when Datis, the general of King Darius, on his return from Eretria after subjugating Euboea, disembarked in our land with a large force and pillaged it. ([Dem.] 59.94)

Yet the mere mention of the Plataeans' participation at Marathon did not seem sufficient to Apollodorus. He sought to provide a convincing corroboration for his assertion by pointing to a reliable source for this social memory.

> And even to this day the picture in the Painted Stoa displays a reminder of their courage; for each man is painted rushing to support as fast as he could, the ones with the Boeotian caps. ([Dem.] 59.94)

We can draw several conclusions from this validation: Apollodorus did not cite Herodotus or any other (lost) historian who reported the Plataeans' involvement in this famous battle; instead, he pointed to a painting displayed in a public building. This confirms the observation of many scholars that Athenian orators rarely drew their knowledge of history from the historians and never named their source when they did so.[133] Apollodorus' use of the short phrase <ἡ> ἐν τῇ ποικίλῃ στοᾷ γραφὴ without any further specification indicates that he expected everyone to be familiar with the Stoa Poikile, to know that one of the pictures depicted the battle of Marathon and also which of the four it was; otherwise, he would have had to identify it more precisely than "the picture in the Painted Stoa."[134] Yet it seemed necessary to him to mention a characteristic detail of the Plataeans' outfit, their Boeotian caps.[135] This indicates that he thought it possible that despite their familiarity with the painting, members of his audience might not be able to identify all the groups and characters displayed. This should not surprise us, since the patriotic master narrative did not mention the participation of the Plataeans. As a result, fourth-century Athenians looking at the painting could indeed have problems identifying this particular group of soldiers, since the social memory as expressed by the *epitaphios* and as depicted in the painting did not agree. However, those who had heard from Plataeans or their own elders that the Plataean army had in fact come to the aid of the Athenians at Marathon would recognize them in the painting by their characteristic caps.

Rosalind Thomas argues that societies with oral traditions—and to some

133. Cf. Pearson (1941).

134. For the Stoa Poikile, see "Monuments and Inscriptions" in chapter 1, 84–94.

135. For the artistic representation of the Plataeans in this painting, see E. B. Harrison (1972) 357.

extent, as I have shown above, even our modern society—can accommodate contradictory versions of past events without being aware of the discrepancy, if these versions are bound to separate contexts.[136] Apollodorus knew that in political speeches, the Athenians were used to hearing of Marathon as a solely Athenian victory. To modify this shared memory, he had to point them to a different source of knowledge of the Athenian past, a painting from more than a hundred years ago in the Stoa Poikile, providing them with a cue for this particular memory. By doing this, he reinstilled a latent memory into Athenian public discourse, thus bringing it into the forefront of Athenian collective consciousness.[137]

Another possibility would have been to point to yet another context and to refer to the inclusion of the Plataeans in the Athenian prayer at the Great Panathenaea, as reported by Herodotus (Hdt. 6.111.2). However, it would not be surprising if the original reason for this inclusion of the Plataeans was already forgotten by the middle of the fourth century. We have no indication that the battle of Marathon was explicitly mentioned in this prayer, and as we have seen, the Plataean merits were usually associated with Xerxes' invasion.

Unlike the Plataeans' participation at Marathon, their role in the war against Xerxes is a recurrent topic in Athenian political discourse (usually contrasting them to the medizing Thebans, as we have seen).[138] It is therefore not surprising that the mere assertion of their contribution without any validation seemed sufficient to Apollodorus in this case ([Dem.] 59.95). This passage is remarkable for another reason as well. The orator claimed that the Plataeans took part in every major battle of this war.

> And again when Xerxes marched against Greece, with the Thebans medizing [Θηβαίων μηδισάντων], the Plataeans did not bring themselves to abandon their friendship with us, but alone of the other Boeotians [μόνοι τῶν ἄλλων Βοιωτῶν], half of them faced the advancing barbarian with Leonidas and the Spartans at Thermopylae and perished with them, while the rest embarked on your triremes, since they did not have their own ships, and fought at sea alongside you at Artemisium and Salamis. And fighting the last battle at Plataea against Mardonius, the King's general, together with you and the fellow liberators of Greece,

136. R. Thomas (1989) 250.

137. For the modification of a prevalent social memory by falling back on alternative social memories, see the modern examples, drawn from the Green Party Convention in 1998 and the "Wehrmachtsdebatte," discussed in "Public Discourse and Decision Making," 30–36, and in the last note of "Constitutive Elements of Social Memory" in the introduction, 28–29.

138. Cf. Isoc. 12.93, 14.61; Xen. *Hell.* 6.3.1.

> they brought liberty as common gift to the other Greeks. ([Dem.] 59.95–96)

Apollodorus' account is historically inaccurate, as a comparison with Herodotus shows. It was not the Plataeans but the Thespians and the Thebans who fought at Thermopylae (Hdt. 7.202, 222). The Plataeans served on Athenian ships at Artemisium (Hdt. 8.1.1; Thuc. 3.54) but not at Salamis (Hdt. 8.44).

How can these distortions be explained? It cannot be ruled out that Apollodorus consciously invented the Plataean participation at Thermopylae and Salamis to exaggerate the praise of the Plataeans, as this suits his argument.[139] Yet I will make the case that, considering Plataea's role in Athenian social memory, it seems more likely that Apollodorus either entirely followed popular tradition or at least operated well within its boundaries.[140]

I have already established that it was a widely shared memory in Athens that while the Thebans were medizing, the Plataeans alone of the other Boeotians fought bravely against Xerxes' forces. That the Plataeans embarked on the Athenian ships was also a memorable fact and widely admired, especially given the fact that they did not have any naval experience whatsoever (Hdt. 8.1.1; Thuc. 3.54; Paus. 9.1.3). This emotive memory was certainly able to obliterate—over the course of more than 130 years—the detail that the Plataeans were unable to participate at Salamis despite their brave service at Artemisium (Hdt. 8.44). Even the claim that the Plataeans fought with Leonidas at Thermopylae would not have troubled the Athenian audience, since it conformed to what they were used to hearing in public speeches, that the Plataeans alone of the other Boeotians' fought against the Persians during Xerxes' invasion. This was one of the battles of this war, and Plataea was located right behind the Greek defensive line at Thermopylae; the Plataeans would thus have had a vested interest in stopping the Persian invasion there. That the Thespians and Thebans had fought alongside Leonidas at Thermopylae instead was also likely to have faded from Athenian historical consciousness by that time. The simplified commemorated version of outright Theban medism obscured the memory of the Thebans' participation at Thermopylae.[141] Similarly, the memory of the Thespians' role was easily eclipsed by the attractive legend of Leonidas' heroic sacrifice for the free-

139. Discussing Apollodorus' embellished account of the events of 431–427 ([Dem.] 59.98–103), Pelling (2000) 62–65 argues that Apollodorus introduced the falsifications himself, since it suited his rhetorical strategy to highlight Plataean pluckiness and Athens' exemplary response of granting them Athenian citizenship. Yet these are exactly the kind of distortions we would expect to find also in Athenian social memory of these events.

140. Cf. Trevett (1990) 408–9; Kapparis (1999) 376.

141. Cf. "Herodotus' Thebans" above, 115–18.

dom of Greece.[142] Operating thus within the horizon of expectations before an Athenian audience, Apollodorus did not upset or baffle his listeners with this exaggerated account of the Plataeans' achievements during the campaigns of 480–479.

This analysis has shown that even in situations requiring praise of the Plataeans, where a modern reader, knowing Herodotus, would expect the Plataean participation at Marathon to be mentioned, Athenian orators either refrained from doing so, as in the case of Isocrates' *Plataicus,* or thought it necessary, as in the case of *Against Neaera,* to use an elaborate accrediting strategy in order to provide the right cue for the Athenian audience to retrieve memories that were relatively unfamiliar within Athenian political discourse. Apart from the processes of memorializing the Athenian experience of Marathon into a patriotic master narrative, as seen in the *epitaphios,* a second factor can account for the obliteration of the Plataean participation in this battle. As I have argued earlier, the Plataean-Theban antagonism reinforced the memory of both Plataean patriotism and Theban medism. This antithesis also helped to link the Athenian memory of the Plataeans' merits in the Persian Wars specifically to Xerxes' invasion, thus eclipsing their role at Marathon, since it was in 480–479 that the Thebans were active medizers, whereas they stayed neutral in 490 and even became victims of a Persian raid at Delium (Hdt. 6.118).[143] Finally, the fact that the decisive battle of the second campaign was fought at Plataea also helped to reinforce the connection between Plataean patriotism and Xerxes' invasion. Lysias' funeral oration proves this point. While the Athenians are said to have fought alone at Marathon for all of Greece (Lys. 2.20), the mentioning of Plataea prompted the memory of the Plataean merits in this war, as well as of the specific disposition of forces in this battle.

> The Lacedaemonians and the Tegeans routed the barbarians, while the Athenians and the Plataeans fought and conquered all the Greeks who had despaired of freedom and submitted to slavery.[144] (Lys. 2.46)

Pointing to the specific patriotic context of the funeral oration and the cues that linked Plataea's merits to Xerxes' invasion, I have tried to show that the obscuring of the Plataean participation at Marathon is not the result of a willful

142. For this legend, see Hignett (1963) 371–78.

143. Cf. Buck (1979) 128.

144. That the Plataeans' merits were closely linked to the battle in their own land is also evident in a tradition (recorded in Plut. *Arist.* 20) according to which it was the Plataeans who were awarded the first prize of valor after the battle.

manipulation by a few Athenian propagandists but is explicable through the characteristics of Athenian social memory. By the second half of the fifth century, Athenians were used to hearing of Marathon as a solely Athenian victory, especially within the political discourse, while Plataean patriotism was associated with Xerxes' invasion.

Theban Conduct during Barbarian Invasions

In the introduction, I emphasized the critical role that collective memories play in public debate and decision making. When people are faced with problems, they generally look for similar experiences in the past. Thereby, social memories function as a repository of symbols and metaphors, which enable people in leadership positions to communicate their analysis of the current situation and their proposed solution to others.[145] It is therefore not surprising that whenever the Athenians were faced with the danger of a barbarian invasion, they fell back on their collective experience of the Persian Wars, drawing parallels and analogies in their discussions in order to find the proper response. Naturally, the prospective reaction of Athens' neighbors, first and foremost of Thebes, was an important issue in these debates. Consequently, Theban conduct during the Persian Wars again became a hot topic in Athenian public discourse in the context of potential Persian and Macedonian invasions in the fourth century.

In his extant speeches, Demosthenes alludes twice to Thebes' medizing. In the *Second Philippic,* he asserts that Philip sided with the Thebans and Argives, knowing that they would always betray Greece for their own benefit (Dem. 6.11–12). In *On the Symmories,* however, he draws the opposite lesson and claims that the Thebans are so ashamed of their collaboration with the Persians that they would do whatever it takes to redeem themselves (Dem. 14.33–34). In the first case, Demosthenes presents the Thebans as prototypical traitors of Greece, and in the second case, he asserts that they would never betray Greece again.

Previous scholars have used such passages to illustrate that the orators freely use historical examples, drawing those conclusions that best suit their purposes.[146] Such an approach, while focusing on the speaker's rhetorical techniques, by and large ignores the role of the audience. Yet the orators did not operate within a sociopolitical vacuum; it was the orator's objective to convince his listeners, who would base their decision on his credibility. His assertions were thus checked by the knowledge and expectations of his audience.[147]

By closely analyzing the two passages in which Demosthenes addresses

145. See "Public Discourse and Decision Making" in the introduction, 30–36.
146. Cf. Nouhaud (1982) 182–83.
147. Cf. "Participant Evidence: The Attic Orators and Their Interpretation," 36–43.

Theban medism, I will try to contextualize his assertions within the Athenian memorial framework. To properly assess Demosthenes' lessons from the past within their sociopolitical context, we have to ask the following questions: Are both of his inferences equally convincing to an Athenian audience? How could he arrive at such opposite conclusions, or, better, how could he expect to find any credibility for his claims within his audience? Which underlying assumptions does his argument betray? What sort of accrediting strategies did he use? In a close philological analysis, I will focus on Demosthenes' line of argument and his use of alternative carriers of social memory. The degree of sophistication in his argument will provide a clue to his audience's familiarity with his version of the past. In the first passage under discussion, mere allusions are sufficient, since he plunges right into the well-known master narrative of the funeral orations. In the case of the second passage, a more elaborate argument is needed for his attempt to challenge a dominant lesson of the past.

Treacherous by Nature

In his *Second Philippic,* delivered in 344 BC, Demosthenes sought to rouse his fellow citizens to resist Philip resolutely, arguing that, after concluding the Peace of Philocrates, all of the king's military and diplomatic endeavors were aimed against Athens.[148]

For this purpose, Demosthenes first described Philip's recent actions. He seized Thermopylae and Phocis and, having gained access to central Greece, arranged affairs in favor of Thebes, not Athens. Demosthenes then exposed Philip's motives. The Macedonian king is driven by πλεονεξία and the desire to subjugate the whole world, not by considerations of peace, tranquility, or justice (Dem. 6.7). This ὕβρις and πλεονεξία are exactly the same motives that the Athenians traditionally ascribed to the Persian king, as we can see in the funeral orations, Herodotus, and Aeschylus' *Persae.*[149] By introducing them, Demosthenes prepared his listeners for his attempt to assimilate Philip to Xerxes.

According to Demosthenes, Philip chose the Thebans, Messenians, and Argives as allies instead of the Athenians since, having recognized their respective characters, he knew that the Athenians would resist his attempt to subdue the other Greeks. The Athenians, Demosthenes explained, are "the only people who would never abandon the common rights [τὰ κοινὰ δίκαια] of the Greeks for any gain, nor trade their devotion [εὔνοια] toward the Greeks for any favor

148. For the historical context of this speech, see Sealey (1993) 170–74.

149. Cf. Lys. 2.21 (on Darius' πλεονεξία), 2.29 (on Xerxes' hubris); Hdt. 7.8 (Xerxes about Persia's imperial ambitions), 7.16 (Artabanus on Xerxes' hubris); Aesch. *Pers.* 807–8, 816–22 (Darius' ghost about Xerxes' hubris).

or any profit" (Dem. 6.9–10).[150] Demosthenes' description of Athens' ἦθος reflects the fundamental principles of Athenian ideology and self-image, which resulted to a large extent from the heroic experience of the Persian Wars as seen and perpetuated in the funeral speeches: ever since this great victory, the Athenians boasted of being the benefactors and champions of the Greeks, defending the wronged and checking arrogance and injustice.[151] Demosthenes could be sure that these core principles of Athenian ideology would resonate with his audience. Philip, he continued, knew that, "in return for benefits received," the Thebans "would, with respect to the rest, allow him to do whatever he wants and, so far from opposing or hindering him, would even join forces with him, if he ordered so." The same was true of the Messenians and Argives (Dem. 6.9).

Thus far, Demosthenes had not referred to the Persian Wars explicitly, even though the aggressor's πλεονεξία and desire to subjugate the whole world, as well as Athens' resolve to selflessly defend the Greeks, are inevitably linked to the memory of Xerxes' invasion. To drive home his point, Demosthenes now made explicit the analogy between the current situation and the campaign of 480: Philip naturally had to arrive at these conclusions about the Athenians and the Argives and Thebans, respectively, "looking not only to the present, but also taking into account the past" (Dem. 6.10). He had learned that the ancestors of the Athenians

> although it was possible for them to rule the other Greeks [ἐξὸν αὐτοῖς τῶν λοιπῶν ἄρχειν ῾Ελλήνων] at the price of obedience to the King, not only refused to entertain that proposal, when Alexander, their [i.e., the royal family's] ancestor [ὁ τούτων πρόγονος], came as messenger in this regard, but even chose to leave their land [τὴν χώραν ἐκλιπεῖν] and undertook to endure every hardship, and thereafter accomplished those deeds which all men are always eager to relate, though no one has ever been able to tell them worthily. (Dem. 6.11)

Judging by the frequency of its occurrence in Athenian public discourse, the rejection of the Persian offer was an essential part of the commemorated history of the Persian Wars and was thus quite familiar to Demosthenes' audience;[152] it is mentioned in Lysias' *epitaphios* (Lys. 2.33), in Isocrates' *Panegyricus* (Isoc. 4.94–96), in Demosthenes' *On the Crown* (Dem. 18.202–4), and in Lycurgus' *Against Leocrates* (Lycurg. 71).[153] All of these speakers (except for

150. The same sentiment is found in Dem. *Prooem.* 16.

151. Cf. Loraux (1986) 155–71; Gehrke (2003); R. Thomas (1989) 221–27. See "Funeral Orations" in chapter 1, 49–58.

152. For the transformation of "remembered" history into "commemorated" history, see "Remembered and Commemorated History" in the introduction, 23–26.

153. Cf. Nouhaud (1982) 190–93.

Lycurgus, who does not give a date at all) place this incident *before* the battle of Salamis and connect it to the Athenians' decision to abandon their city. This differs from Herodotus' account, which places Alexander's mission after the destruction of Athens and between the battles of Salamis and Plataea (Hdt. 8.136, 140–44).

This chronological confusion can best be explained as a result of the "distorting" effects in the manifestation and transmission of collective memories.[154] As is often the case, this particular distortion is self-serving to the remembering community. As Nouhaud notes, placing Xerxes' offer after Thermopylae and thus before the destruction of Athens makes it appear more attractive and simultaneously enhances the Athenian sacrifice to turn it down.[155] Yet this effect is not necessarily the result of a deliberate manipulation, as Nouhaud assumes, but can be attributed to other factors as well. Memories that are to be shared by a large community become much simplified; over time, the particular historical circumstances fade, and heroic or traumatic events become symbols for the remembering community. The details of Greek and Persian military strategy at the various stages of the campaign and the exact chronology of the Persian peace offer were thus largely forgotten. What counted was the Athenians' resolve not to succumb to the barbarian invader and their willingness to sacrifice their city for the sake of Greek liberty. For this core meaning, it mattered little whether Xerxes' offer was made before or after Salamis. Moreover, in the process of narrativization, events are usually organized in the form of a story structured by a causal chain of events.[156] Roughly knowing the course of events, it makes more sense to connect the Persian offer with their advance on Athens (after they passed Thermopylae) and with the moment in which the Athenians had to decide whether to stay or leave their city than with the aftermath of Salamis, when the decisive battle had already been won.

It is irrelevant for the symbolic meaning of this event—that is, to illustrate Athenian patriotism—that it was the Macedonian king Alexander who delivered the Persian offer; Lysias, Isocrates, and Demosthenes in *On the Crown* do not mention this detail. Yet it makes good sense for Demosthenes to name the messenger and to mention his ancestral connection to Philip in the context of the *Second Philippic;* by pointing out that Philip's forefather was closely associated with Xerxes, Demosthenes provided another suggestive argument for his analogy between the current situation and the past. Unfortunately, Demosthenes does not give us any hint concerning his source for this detail. It is pos-

154. See also Weißenberger (1996), who explores the "predating" of the Persian peace proposal from the traditional perspective of the orators' deliberate manipulation of history but comes to similar conclusions.

155. Nouhaud (1982) 191.

156. For these processes, see Fentress & Wickham (1992) 47–48; Schudson (1995) 348–59. See also "Ideology and Social Memory" in the introduction, 13–19.

sible that, despite our lack of evidence, the messenger's identity was from time to time mentioned in the Athenian master narrative of the funeral orations, but a different explanation is more plausible: through simplification and narrativization, the memory of the messenger's identity had faded from common historical consciousness in the course of a century. Demosthenes, however, as a member of the educated elite, who had enjoyed a thorough rhetorical training, was familiar with Herodotus and knew of the messenger's identity. When the political landscape in Greece changed with the rise of Philip, so that Athens was suddenly threatened by the possibility of a Macedonian invasion, this incidental detail gained a new relevance. It is likely that a politician of Demosthenes' stature and familiar with Herodotus' account would recognize the significance of Alexander's connection with Xerxes and reintroduce this latent memory into the public discourse.

There are at least some clues that support this hypothesis. First, Demosthenes scorned Philip by mentioning explicitly the fact that the Alexander who came on behalf of the Persian king was an ancestor of Philip's family (᾿Αλέξανδρος ὁ τούτων πρόγονος, Dem. 6.11). Second, the attempt to closely associate the Macedonian king with the Persian invader can already be found in the speech of a Spartan ambassador in Herodotus.

> But let not Alexander the Macedonian seduce you by his smoothing of Mardonius' proposal; he does only what one might expect of him; for, being a tyrant, he collaborates with a tyrant [τύραννος γὰρ ἐὼν τυράννῳ συγκατεργάζεται]. (Hdt. 8.142)

Third, the only other orator who names Alexander as Xerxes' messenger is Lycurgus, in the prosecution of Leocrates in 330 BC (Lycurg. 71), fourteen years after Demosthenes' speech. It is likely that by that time (after one and a half decades of Macedonian aggression), the memory of Alexander's collaboration with Xerxes was again well established in common Athenian historical consciousness, thanks to its new relevance. Given the tiny sample we have of all the speeches actually delivered in Athens, it is probable that Demosthenes' *Second Philippic* was not unusual in stressing the Alexander-Xerxes connection during the Macedonian ascendancy.

That Demosthenes is indeed borrowing from the master narrative of the Athenian funeral orations, of which Xerxes' offer was an integral part, is suggested by another clue: Demosthenes' use of the *epitaphios*' rhetorical *topos* of the inadequacy of any speaker to worthily praise the achievements of the Athenians.[157] Moreover, this *praeteritio* enables the members of the audience

157. Cf. Lys. 2.1; Dem. 60.1.

to think of the Athenians' heroic feats, as they themselves imagine them. Given that each Athenian is constantly exposed to various forms of memorialization of these events (monuments, rituals, festivals, public commemorations, etc.), this mere allusion, which leaves room for imagination, was probably more effective in exciting patriotic pride and stern resolve than any explicit narration of the ancestors' feats could ever be.

The organizing principle of this entire passage (Dem. 6.7–12)—the antithesis of the Athenians versus the Thebans and Argives—is reflected in the syntactic structure of Demosthenes' historical paradigm, which is set forth in a single sentence: Philip learned that the ancestors of the Athenians refused Xerxes' offer and abandoned their city but that "concerning the forefathers of the Thebans and Argives, the former fought on the side of the barbarian and the latter did not oppose him"[158] (Dem. 6.11). It was Demosthenes' objective in this speech to demonstrate that Philip's military and diplomatic measures were aimed against Athens. The analogy of circumstances—the occupation of Thermopylae and Phocis as well as the alliances with Thebes and Argos—enabled Demosthenes to draw the historical parallel to Xerxes' invasion of Greece. This correlation, however, only leads to the conclusion that an attack on Athens is impending and inevitable if one ascribes persistent and unchangeable national characters and motives to the political actors involved: the Athenians, the barbarian invader, and his allies.[159]

This is why Demosthenes chose to plunge right into the genre of the Athenian funeral oration, for it promoted this image of a timeless noble Athenian character, which he needed in order to make his analogy work.[160] In Athenian social memory, the events of Xerxes' invasion are memorialized as a symbol of the barbarian's ὕβρις and πλεονεξία, of the Athenians' selfless patriotism, and of the Thebans' selfish and treacherous nature. Having invoked these axioms of the Athenian master narrative, Demosthenes could draw the logical conclusion of his analysis. Hearing of the conduct of the Thebans and Argives during the campaigns of 480–479, Philip knows "that both of them will pursue their private interests, irrespective of the common benefit for the Greeks" (Dem. 6.12).[161] He believes that if he chose the Athenians,

158. Dem. 6.11: εὑρίσκει γάρ, οἶμαι, καὶ ἀκούει τοὺς μὲν ὑμετέρους προγόνους . . . , τοὺς δὲ Θηβαίων καὶ Ἀργείων προγόνους τοὺς μὲν συστρατεύσαντας τῷ βαρβάρῳ, τοὺς δ' οὐκ ἐναντιωθέντας.

159. For the orators' appeal to the unchanging national character of the Athenians, see Clarke (2008) 282–86.

160. Cf. R. Thomas (1989) 220–21.

161. Demosthenes takes up the theme of the selfish, treacherous Theban character again in 6.19: "That is why he [Philip] is wide awake and ready to strike, and why he is courting certain people to the detriment of our city—Thebans, I mean, and those Peloponnesians who share their views. He believes that due to their greed [διὰ μὲν πλεονεξίαν] they will welcome the present situ-

> he would choose friends for the pursuit of justice [ἐπὶ τοῖς δικαίοις], but if he attached himself to the others, he would find in them assistants of his own ambition [τῆς αὐτοῦ πλεονεξίας]. That is why, both now and then, he chooses them rather than [the Athenians] [ἐκείνους ἀνθ' ὑμῶν καὶ τότε καὶ νῦν αἱρεῖται]. (Dem. 6.12)

The grammatical subject of αἱρεῖται is not mentioned explicitly and needs to be inferred from the context. Since Demosthenes analyzes the recent political developments from Philip's perspective and seeks to illustrate his rationale (Dem. 6.6–12), Philip functions as the grammatical subject of all third-person singular verbs throughout the passage and thus also of αἱρεῖται.[162] However, since he is mentioned by name only once at the beginning of this passage (in Dem. 6.7), the phrase καὶ τότε καὶ νῦν αἱρεῖται, summing up Demosthenes' analogy of the past and present situation, becomes ambivalent, and it is not entirely clear who the governing subject is. I suggest that Demosthenes fashioned this ambiguity consciously in order to fuse Philip and Xerxes—two incarnations of the eternal greedy barbarian invader.[163] In the conclusion of his historical paradigm, Demosthenes affirmed the validity of his historical analysis, with its stress on unchanging national character, by dismissing other potential motives for Philip's choice, including a calculation of the resources gained by an alliance. Since Athens has the largest fleet and since it is Philip's objective to control the Aegean Sea, he would have chosen Athens, instead of Thebes, if he did not know about their respective characters (Dem. 6.12).

To sum up, in the *Second Philippic,* Demosthenes used—and thus perpetuated—the master narrative of the respective conduct of the Athenians and the Thebans during the Persian Wars, as it was promoted in the funeral orations. He thus evoked social memories that lay at the heart of Athenian ideology and symbolized "eternal" Athenian principles and character traits. Since these memories create feelings of identity and belonging, Demosthenes' analysis was likely to strike an emotional chord within his audience, infuriating them against Philip, the second Xerxes. The assumption, underlying the commemorated history of the Persian Wars, that historical actors possessed

ation, but due to the dullness of their character [διὰ δὲ σκαιότητα τρόπων] they will not foresee anything that may follow."

162. Cf. Dem. 6.7–12: ὁ Φίλιππος . . . κατέστη; . . . ἐχρήσατο; . . . προείλετο. . . . εἶδε . . . ἡγεῖτο . . . εὖ ποιεῖ. . . . ὑπείληφε . . . εὑρίσκει . . . ἀκούει . . . οἶδεν οὖν . . . ἡγεῖτ' οὖν . . . αἱρεῖται.

163. If one wants to argue for Philip as the exclusive subject of this sentence, one has to identify τότε αἱρεῖται with one of Philip's earlier actions—for example, the preferred treatment of Thebes right after the surrender of the Phocians, three years earlier. However, since the context immediately preceding dealt with the Persian War, the suggested fusion of Xerxes and Philip seems more plausible.

timeless national characters made the contemporary Athenians into defenders of Greek liberty, Philip a greedy barbarian, and the Thebans traitors by nature.

Challenging the Master Narrative

Demosthenes' use of symbols and metaphors for the analysis of a current problem and for the promotion of a particular response is a common phenomenon.[164] These symbols and metaphors, provided by the commemorated history of the community, were calculated to appeal—on both a rational and emotional level—to an audience invested with values and beliefs derived from this very past experience. Sometimes, however, politicians arrive at a solution that seems to contradict the shared experience of their audience. In his speech *On the Symmories,* Demosthenes was faced with precisely this problem.

In 354/3 BC, the Athenians were alarmed by rumors that the Persian king Artaxerxes III was mobilizing forces in preparation for an invasion of Greece.[165] It was Demosthenes' objective in his assembly speech to dissuade his fellow citizens from rushing to war with Persia without proper preparation and definite knowledge of the king's intent. His opponents, on the contrary, proposed an immediate declaration of war against Persia, invoking the memory of the Persian Wars and their ancestors' achievements (just as Demosthenes did ten years later in the *Second Philippic,* as we have seen). This can be inferred from Demosthenes' rebukes in his reply (Dem. 14.1, 8, 41).

To achieve his objective, Demosthenes had to demonstrate that the current political situation differed from that of 480 and that Xerxes' invasion was not a sound historical analogy, as implied by preceding speakers. Demosthenes did not deny that the king was the common enemy of all the Greeks—a concession to Athenian ideology, with its emphasis on unchanging national characters (Dem. 14.3). But he denied that the other Greeks would join an Athenian declaration of war, as long as Artaxerxes' hostile intent was not unmistakably clear (Dem. 14.3–5). He warned his fellow Athenians that in case of war, the king would successfully court other Greeks to turn against Athens. This was likely, he said, since the Athenians' attitude toward the king differed from that of the other Greeks.

> For many of them, it seems to me to be possible to neglect the other Greeks while pursuing their private interests, but for [the Athenians],

164. For a modern-day example, cf. the Bush administration's use of symbols and metaphors ("opposing dictators" and "fighting for freedom and democracy"), derived from the U.S. experience of World War II, in the run-up to Operation Iraqi Freedom in 2003. See Dower (2010) 10–11.

165. For the historical context of this speech, see Sealey (1993) 128–29.

> even when wronged by them, it is not honorable to exact such a penalty from the wrongdoers as to let any of them come under the sway of the barbarian. (Dem. 14.6)

By echoing the core values of Athenian ideology, Athens' high regard for justice, and its role as protector and πρόμαχος of all the Greeks, Demosthenes ensured the goodwill of his audience and demonstrated that his policy concurred with Athenian tradition. To gain the support of the other Greeks, Demosthenes proposed to marshal and equip the Athenian forces but also, following the principles of justice, not to instigate an unprovoked war (Dem. 14.7). Thus the large middle part of his speech contains his plan for the reorganization of the navy boards to assure the readiness of the Athenian fleet in case of a military conflict with the Persians in the future (Dem. 14.14–28).

At the end of his proposal, he returned to the problem at hand, trying to dispel the Athenian fear of an impending Persian invasion. He based his first argument on the deterrent of a newly organized Athenian fleet.

> And these naval reforms should occasion no small fear for the king; for he knows that with two hundred triremes [διακοσίαις τριήρεσιν], of which we provided one hundred, our ancestors destroyed a thousand of his ships [τοὺς προγόνους αὐτοῦ χιλίας ἀπολέσαντας ναῦς],[166] and he will hear that you yourselves have now three hundred triremes ready for sea, so that even if he were entirely mad, he would scarcely think it a light thing to make our city his enemy. (Dem. 14.28–29)

This historical paradigm is an innovative use of Athenian social memory in public discourse. Demosthenes did not invoke the memory of Salamis in order to incite his fellow citizens to emulate their forefathers in fighting against the barbarian. Instead, he claimed that, knowing the *outcome* of the battle of Salamis, king Artaxerxes had learned his lesson from history. He would be extremely reluctant to engage in a naval battle with the Athenians, knowing that their number of ships is even greater now than in 480 BC. By using αὐτοῦ in the phrase "our ancestors destroyed a thousand of *his* ships" (τοὺς προγόνους αὐτοῦ χιλίας ἀπολέσαντας ναῦς, Dem. 14.29), Demosthenes fused Xerxes and

166. It would be grammatically possible to connect αὐτοῦ to τοὺς προγόνους, meaning "Xerxes' ancestors," and to take ἀπώλεσαν in its weak meaning ("they lost"). However, the emphasis on the Athenians' achievement and the instrumental dative διακοσίαις τριήρεσιν strongly suggest that we should identify τοὺς προγόνους with the Athenians and should understand ἀπώλεσαν in its strong meaning ("they destroyed"). For this reading, see also Vince (1930) 399.

Artaxerxes, suggesting that this memory is as vivid for Artaxerxes as if he had experienced this loss of one thousand ships himself.[167]

Rejecting the notion that Artaxerxes' resources were unlimited, Demosthenes then emphasized the Athenians' resolve to defend their most important resource, their own country. Thereby, he suggested once more that Artaxerxes had learned his lesson (that the invasion of Greece brings disaster to Persia) from those of *his* ancestors who fought at Marathon (Dem. 14.30).

His next argument, addressing Thebes' medism, is of paramount interest to this investigation. The opening phrase "if now anybody should think that the Thebans will be on his side" (εἰ τοίνυν τις οἴεται Θηβαίους ἔσεσθαι μετ' ἐκείνου, Dem. 14.33) proves that Demosthenes expected his political opponents to point to the Thebans' earlier medism and—presupposing persistent character traits—to assert that they would readily medize again. This expectation was certainly widespread in Athens at that time. In 367, Pelopidas had conducted an embassy to Susa to gain Persian support for Thebes. According to Xenophon, he successfully marshaled the memory of Thebes' medism at the battle of Plataea as an argument to assure the king's goodwill (Xen. *Hell.* 7.1.34–35).[168] Even though it happened far away in Susa, this event was a live issue in Athenian public discourse, since Timagoras, one of the two ambassadors who represented the Athenians at the king's court on this occasion, had supported Pelopidas (Xen. *Hell.* 7.1.35). After his return to Athens, he was indicted by his fellow ambassador Leon and sentenced to death by the Athenian assembly (Xen. *Hell.* 7.1.38). As a result, the Theban attempt to reach out to the king by employing the memory of their previous cooperation refreshed the memory of Theban medism in Athens and stirred up anti-Theban sentiments anew.

Demosthenes acknowledged the difficulty of arguing against this widely shared anti-Theban stereotype, which portrays the Theban character as treacherous by nature: "Due to your hatred toward the Thebans you would not care to hear anything good about them, even if it were true" (Dem. 14.33).[169] While exposing his listeners' negative predisposition, Demosthenes implied that the positive things he had to say about the Thebans were indeed true. Then

167. For a discussion of Demosthenes' manipulation of the number of ships involved, see Nouhaud (1982) 189–90.

168. Buckler (1982) 200–201 makes a strong case for the credibility of Xenophon's report of Pelopidas' speech at Susa: "This speech does not look like a free composition which has little connection with what Pelopidas said at Susa. It apparently restricts itself to the essentials (τὰ δέοντα) either of what Pelopidas said or what the situation demanded."

169. In his speech *Against Leptines,* Demosthenes himself employed negative stereotypes and contrasted the Thebans' brutality and depravity to the Athenians' φιλανθρωπία and desire for justice (Dem. 20.109).

he launched a general attack against the validity of stereotypes derived from social memory, deprecating them as unsubstantial pretext (πρόφασις) and contrasting them to beneficial rational considerations (συμφέροντα λογισμὸν, Dem. 14.33). Yet Demosthenes did not follow up on this maxim. He did not, for instance, present a cost-benefit analysis that could illustrate the negative consequences of renewed medizing for the Thebans and thus make this seem an unlikely policy. Instead, he chose to challenge the prevalent stereotype that the Thebans *are* prototypical medizers, by setting forth his own version of the impact on the Thebans of their collaboration with the Persians.

> I, for my part, believe that the Thebans are so far from joining the king in an attack against the Greeks that they would pay a lot of money, if they were able to give it, to get a chance of expiating their former sins against the Greeks. (Dem. 14.33–34)

How can Demosthenes know this, or, rather, how can he expect to find any credibility for this claim within his audience? Numerous clues indicate that the Thebans felt the need to excuse their pro-Persian stance during Xerxes' invasion and tried to obliterate the memory of their medism. Thucydides reports that at the trial of the Plataeans in 427, the Thebans blamed their medism on the violent rule of a dynastic clique (δυναστεία ὀλίγων ἀνδρῶν), who joined Xerxes to enhance their own power and oppressed the people of Thebes (κατέχοντες ἰσχύι τὸ πλῆθος, Thuc. 3.62). By calling their collaboration "involuntary medism" (ἀκούσιον μηδισμὸν), they tried to exculpate themselves (Thuc. 3.64.5). The Plataean speaker in Isocrates' *Plataicus* stated indignantly that the Thebans, who have been guilty of betraying Greece as a whole, have seen fit to demand for themselves forgiveness (συγγνώμης τυχεῖν ἠξιώθησαν) for their evil deeds so willingly committed and so grave (Isoc. 14.30). Furthermore, they destroyed Plataea in 373 in order to wipe out the memorials of their shame (Isoc. 14.59). That the Thebans were indeed bothered by being reminded of their medism is confirmed by Aeschines' assertion that the Amphissians—in order to please the Thebans—indicted the Athenians before the Amphictyonic council for rededicating shields with the inscription "The Athenians, from the Medes and Thebans, when they fought against the Greeks" (Ἀθηναῖοι ἀπὸ Μήδων καὶ Θηβαίων, ὅτε τἀναντία τοῖς Ἕλλησιν ἐμάχοντο, Aeschin. 3.116). This shows that among the other Greeks, the Thebans were indeed anxious to eradicate the memory of their conduct during the Persian war.[170]

170. However, as Pelopidas' speech at Susa shows, when the situation demanded it, the The-

Besides these extant records of Theban remorse, we can assume that Athenians who had personal contact with Thebans were in a position to observe signs of shame and remorse in conversations. This was certainly true of Demosthenes himself, who was the πρόξενος for the Thebans in Athens.[171] But other Athenians as well had a chance to hear Thebans regretting their ancestors' choice, not only in the time between 382 and 378 BC, when three hundred Theban democrats found refuge in Athens,[172] but also in the years of Theban-Athenian cooperation during the Corinthian (395–386 BC) and Theban wars (378–371 BC).

Yet Demosthenes was well aware that his attempt to present the Thebans as utterly remorseful about their former medism might not fully resonate with his Athenian audience. He therefore anticipated the potential objection that it was in the Thebans' nature to medize again.

> If, however, one is utterly convinced that the Thebans are ill-fated by nature [φύσει δυστυχεῖς εἶναι], at any rate you all know this, that if the Thebans stand by the king, their enemies stand necessarily by the Greeks. (Dem. 14.34)

Demosthenes used the euphemism of being "ill-fated by nature"—that is, choosing the losing side of the barbarian—to describe Thebes' treacherous conduct toward the Greeks. He thus implies that Greeks would always conquer the Persians and their allies. The claim that at least all enemies of Thebes would firmly be on Athens' side in case of renewed Theban support for the king is Demosthenes' fallback argument for those Athenians who are firmly convinced that the Thebans will always medize as they medized at the time of Xerxes' invasion.

Demosthenes' use of the social memory of the Persian Wars in *On the Symmories* is remarkable. Other orators (and Demosthenes himself in the *Second Philippic*) employ this historical paradigm as simple analogy in the case of impending barbarian invasions. Based on the assumption of unchanging character traits, an assumption that underlies the master narrative of the funeral orations, the barbarian driven by greed is determined to invade Greece, the

---

bans did not hesitate to marshal the memory of their medism as an argument in their favor (Xen. *Hell.* 7.1.34–35). This incident, too, illustrates the importance of the performative context.

171. Cf. Aeschin. 2.141, 143. For Demosthenes' attitude toward Thebes, see Trevett (1999).

172. Cf. Xen. *Hell.* 5.2.31; Buck (1994) 71–72. See "Athenian Help for the Theban Democrats, 382–378" in chapter 4, 253–67.

Theban is treacherous by nature and will always support him, and the Athenian, as the champion of Greek liberty and justice, will resist against all odds.

Demosthenes did acknowledge the indisputable facts that the Persians, driven by greed and insanity, had invaded Greece and suffered catastrophic defeats at Marathon and Salamis and that the Thebans had collaborated with them. Yet in this speech, he dismissed the principle of persistent national characters and ventured to convince his audience, first, that the Persian king had indeed learned his lesson from history and would refrain from attacking Athens again and, second, that the Thebans, far from being treacherous by nature, deeply regretted their former medism. Using elaborate arguments, Demosthenes attempted to promote his own understanding of the Persian Wars and the lessons to be learned from them, thus challenging the dominant interpretation of this collective experience. Yet in this case as well, he had to operate within the limits of his audience's horizon of expectation.

CHAPTER 3

Mythical Precedent

Athenian Intervention for the Fallen Argives

In chapter 2, we saw how the Athenians, as a result of their experience of the Persian Wars, came to see themselves as champions of Greek liberty and to see their Theban neighbors as archetypical traitors who eagerly collaborated with the Persians. Athenians referred to Thebes' medizing in two particular contexts. The ongoing Theban-Plataean antagonism frequently prompted the antithesis of Theban medism versus Plataean patriotism. Similarly, the prospect of further barbarian invasions, be it by the Persians or by the equally hated Macedonians, could serve as a cue for the recollection of Thebes' treason.

In the eyes of fifth- and fourth-century Athenians, Thebes' crimes did not begin with its support for the Persians, however, but reached far back into the mythical past, when the Thebans refused to grant burial to the fallen Argives who had marched against Thebes under Adrastus' command to topple Oedipus' son Eteocles and win the throne for his brother Polynices. Adrastus, the sole survivor of the Seven against Thebes, fled to Athens and supplicated the Athenians to aid him in recovering the bodies of his dead comrades. Selflessly, the Athenians intervened and secured their proper burial in Eleusis.

This myth has already received a great deal of scholarly attention, but there remain further aspects worth exploring here.[1] This collective memory offers

1. For the development of this myth in tragedy and the funeral orations, see Bethe (1891) 93–99; Hauvette (1898); von Wilamowitz-Moellendorff (1899) 188–206, (1914) 241; Schroeder (1914) 40–43; Jacoby *FGrHist* 3b (Suppl.) i.442–48, ii.349–60; Zuntz (1955) 22–24; Mette (1963) 38–43; Kierdorf (1966) 89–97; Herter (1973) 1208–9; Collard (1975) 1:3–8; Stupperich (1977) 47–48, 228–34; Walters (1980) 10–14; Loraux (1986) 64–72; Aélion (1983) 1:231–43; Kearns (1989) 130–31; R. Thomas (1989) 207–8, 227, 233–34; Castriota (1992) 65–73; Hubbard (1992) 92–100; Parker (1996) 137–39; Mills (1997) 229–34; A. M. Bowie (1997) 45–56; Grethlein (2003) 109–99; Morwood (2007) 1–31;

a unique opportunity to examine how recent experiences, particularly during the Persian Wars and the period of Athenian hegemony, affected the image the Athenians had of their city's relationship with Thebes in the mythical past, a period that constituted an important part of Athenian historical consciousness. It also allows us to study the complex relationships between different carriers of social memory and the various ways in which this collective memory was transmitted to younger generations; local myths and cults, the tragic stage, the Athenian funeral orations, monuments and artifacts, and speeches held in the assembly mutually influenced and sustained each other.[2]

A brief survey of fifth- and fourth-century oratorical allusions will show that this myth could convey a whole range of interrelated meanings.[3] By focusing on individual aspects of this myth, I will then explore the origins and formative influences on this myth during the archaic and classical periods. In the final part of this chapter, I will examine how this paradigm was put to use in Athenian political discourse by Herodotus' Athenians, Xenophon's Procles of Phlius, and Isocrates' Plataeans, as well as in Isocrates' *Panathenaicus*. By resituating their allusions within the complex net of remembrances and beliefs held by their audiences, we will be in a better position to assess the emotive force and the persuasiveness of their arguments.

Oratorical Allusions to the Burial of the Seven

The mythical paradigm of Athens' intervention on behalf of the fallen Argives is frequently used in Athenian public discourse. The earliest extant oratorical reference to this myth is found in Herodotus' account of the quarrel between the Athenians and the Tegeans over the privilege to hold the left wing of the Greek army in the battle of Plataea in 479 BC. Listing their past achievements, including their aid to the Heraclidae, the repulsion of the Amazons, their participation in the Trojan War, and the glorious victory at Marathon, the Athenians also mention the following feat:

> Furthermore, we affirm that when the Argives who had marched with Polynices against Thebes had ended their lives and lay unburied, we

Harding (2008) 71; Lamari (2009); Krauskopf *LIMC* s.v. Adrastos i.232–33; Radt *TrGF* iii.175–76. For the orators' use of this episode, see, most comprehensively, Gotteland (2001) 198–213, and see Schmitz-Kahlmann (1939) 71–73; Buchner (1958) 67–71; Perlman (1961) 160–61; Nouhaud (1982) 18–19; Gray (1994b); Roth (2003) 196–201; Todd (2008) 218–21.

2. Cf. R. Thomas (1989) 198. See "Collective Memories of the Mythical Past" in the introduction, 26–28.

3. Following Parker (1987) 188, I use the phrase "meanings of this myth" as a "shorthand way of referring to the sum of qualities that cause people to listen to it with interest and remember it."

took the field against the Cadmeans, thus recovered the bodies, and buried them in our own land in Eleusis. (Hdt. 9.27.3)

This speech is surely anachronistic, but it closely reflects the kinds of argument used by Athenians of Herodotus' own time to glorify their city. The achievements mentioned by Herodotus were an integral part of the patriotic Athenian master narrative as we can grasp it in the Athenian funeral orations.[4] While it is impossible to determine with certainty at which point this catalogue of deeds found its final form (suggested dates range from the 470s to the 450s), most of the extant fourth-century funeral orations and other encomiastic speeches contain the same list of achievements already found in Herodotus.

The burial of the Seven is mentioned in Lysias' funeral speech (Lys. 2.7–10), written for Athenians who died during the Corinthian War (ca. 392–391); in Isocrates' *Panegyricus* (Isoc. 4.54–55, 58), an encomium of Athens that draws heavily on the praise *topoi* found in the funeral orations (ca. 380); in Plato's *Menexenus* (239b), which features a parody of the *epitaphios* (ca. 386); and in Demosthenes' funeral oration for the fallen of Chaeronea in 338 (Dem. 60.8).[5] Similarly, in his epideictic show piece *Encomium on Helen* (Isoc. 10.31) Isocrates mentions this episode to illustrate the piety of the Athenian king Theseus (ca. 370).[6] This mythical paradigm was not only used to glorify Athens but also functioned as a powerful argument in diplomatic contexts. In Isocrates' *Plataicus,* a speech written after the second destruction of Plataea by the Thebans in 373, the Plataeans argue that the memory of the noble deed of the Athenians' ancestors on behalf of the Argive suppliants ought to compel the Athenians to act now on behalf of Plataea (Isoc. 14.53–55). Similarly, Xenophon reports that in 370/69, after the Spartan defeat at Leuctra, the Peloponnesian ambassador Procles of Phlius urged the Athenians to rescue the Spartans from the Thebans, just as their ancestors had rescued the fallen Argives (Xen. *Hell.* 6.5.47).

In all of these allusions, the Athenians secure the burial of the Seven by defeating the Thebans in battle. This is stated explicitly in Herodotus, Lysias, Isocrates' *Panegyricus,* and Plato's *Menexenus* and clearly implied in Xenophon, Isocrates' *Plataicus* and *Helen,* and Demosthenes' funeral oration.[7] It is strik-

4. See "Funeral Orations" in chapter 1, 49–58.

5. For the date of Lysias' funeral oration, see Todd (2008) 157–64. Usher (1999) 19 dates Isocrates' *Panegyricus* to around 380.

6. Most scholars date this encomium to about 370 BC; cf. Mirhady & Too (2000) 15 note 1, 31–33. Zajonz (2002) 58–59 proposes an earlier date (ca. 393–380).

7. Hdt. 9.27.3: στρατευσάμενοι ἐπὶ τοὺς Καδμείους; Lys. 2.8–10: ἐστράτευσαν ἐπ' αὐτούς . . . ἐνίκων μαχόμενοι; Isoc. 4.58: ἀνελόμενοι γὰρ πόλεμον . . . τοὺς μὲν ἐπιστρατεύσαντες ἠνάγκασαν ἀποδοῦναι θάψαι τοὺς νεκροὺς; Pl. *Menex.* 239b: ὑπὲρ τῆς ἐλευθερίας καὶ Ἕλλησιν ὑπὲρ Ἑλλήνων μάχεσθαι . . . ἤμυναν Ἀργείοις πρὸς Καδμείους; Xen. *Hell.* 6.5.47: οὐκ εἴασαν ἀτάφους γενέσθαι; Isoc. 14.53: Θηβαίους ἀναγκάσαντες βουλεύσασθαι νομιμώτερον; Isoc. 10.31: βίᾳ Θηβαίων θάψαι παρέδωκεν; Dem. 60.8: τὰ τῶν κατοιχομένων νόμιμ' οὐ περιεῖδον ὑβριζόμενα.

ing, therefore, that we read of a peaceful resolution in Isocrates' *Panathenaicus* (Isoc. 12.170–73), his last discourse, completed in 339 BC. This passage is truly exceptional. Isocrates explicitly acknowledges that he is saying the opposite of what he has written about the same events in his *Panegyricus*. In his defense, he declares that this change is due to his prudence. This is the only passage in the corpus of the Attic orators where an orator admits that his current presentation of a mythical paradigm is at odds with his treatment of the same episode in an earlier speech.

This unusual passage has been exploited by scholars to draw conclusions about the orators' general practices. Nouhaud, for instance, uses Isocrates' confession to bolster his case that the Attic orators manipulated the past without limitations, according to the maxims "Each speech has its own truth" and "The end justifies the means."[8] Yet such a view by and large ignores the role of the audience. Since it was the speaker's objective to persuade his listeners, he had to take their knowledge and attitudes into account. For this reason, his version of the past had to be plausible and could not flatly contradict what his audience knew about a certain event. Orators certainly had more leeway in dealing with paradigms from the mythical vis-à-vis the historical period;[9] yet, even when using mythical episodes, public speakers usually did not create details ex nihilo but drew on familiar alternative versions. This is even true in the case of Isocrates' *Panathenaicus*. At the beginning of this paradigm, Isocrates explicitly mentioned the tragic poets at the Dionysia as a source for this story (Isoc. 12.168). We know from Philochorus that (unlike Euripides' *Suppliants*) Aeschylus' lost *Eleusinians* also featured a peaceful, diplomatic resolution (*FGrHist* 328 F 112 = Plut. *Thes.* 29.4–5). To be able to assess properly how public speakers operated within this complex Athenian memorial framework, it is necessary to reconstruct what fifth- and fourth-century Athenians "knew" about this mythical event and what it meant to them. For this purpose, it is indispensable to take all available carriers of this social memory into account.

Constitutive Elements and Formative Influences

The stories about mythical heroes were an essential part of a Greek community's shared image of its past. Consequently, they fulfilled important social functions and showed many of the general characteristics of social memory. These collective memories usually stayed in tune with present attitudes and concerns of the community that cherished them. Consequently, certain elements of the

8. Nouhaud (1982) 18–19; in his view, this applies to examples drawn from both the mythical and the historical periods. Gotteland (2001) 112–13 is more nuanced in her discussion of this passage.

9. Gotteland (2001) 113.

story could be changed, added, emphasized, downplayed, or suppressed.[10] In the case of the myth of the burial of the Seven, we find clues for continuous reshaping and reworking during the archaic and classical periods, which led to a variety of different versions inside and outside of Attica and to a conglomerate of interrelated layers of meaning in the Athenian master narrative of the funeral orations.[11]

For the sake of analysis, each of the following sections focuses on one particular aspect of this myth: the end of the Seven and local cults, Theseus' role as Attic culture hero, Athens' exemplary aid for the Argive suppliants, Athens' hegemonic role as champion of Greek liberty, and Athens' just punishment of Theban *hybris*. By scrutinizing these constitutive elements, I will explore the origins, formative influences, and different carriers of this collective memory from the Geometric period down to the fourth century.

The End of the Seven and Local Cults

I first turn to one of the most vital carriers of social memory when dealing with collective memories of the mythical past, that is, ancient Greek hero cult. This phenomenon has received a fair share of scholarly attention, and even though the origins and exact sociopolitical significance of individual hero cults are still debated, there is general agreement about the importance of hero cults as focal points of group identity.[12] The development of myth and saga, of narrative traditions concerning the hero, is intimately related to this function and often leads to the "convergence of the hero of cult with the hero of epic," as Emily Kearns points out.[13] I will make the case that various local communities in Attica and Boeotia sought a connection to the epic stories of the fateful end of the Seven against Thebes in order to position themselves competitively in the Panhellenic cultural landscape. The resultant local cults and stories are of great importance for our understanding of the role of this myth in Athenian public discourse.

That the Seven were buried in Eleusis was an integral part of the myth of the Athenian intervention for the fallen Argives in the fifth century. This is

10. See "Ideology and Social Memory" in the introduction, 13–19; Forsdyke (2005) 242.

11. In the past, scholars were particularly interested in reconstructing the chronological development of this myth. Von Wilamowitz-Moellendorff (1899) 196 and Hauvette (1898), for instance, viewed Aeschylus' *Eleusinians*, which featured a peaceful resolution, as the *terminus post quem* for the introduction of the bellicose variant, which first appears in Hdt. 9.27.3. Scholars nowadays are more cautious, arguing that the development of a myth is not a linear process and that in a predominantly oral society like fifth-century Athens, different, even contradictory versions could be circulating at the same time, especially if they belong to different contexts. Cf. R. Thomas (1989) 250; Stupperich (1977) 48; Walters (1980) 12–13 with note 26.

12. Cf. Kearns (1989) 103–37; Boedeker (1993); Hall (1999) 49–52; Boehringer (2001); Currie (2005) 47–59; Bremmer (2006); Forsdyke (2011).

13. Kearns (1989) 103.

evident from Aeschylus' *Eleusinians* (ca. 475–467), our earliest testimony for this story. This tragedy is—apart from two short fragments—lost, but its plot is known from Plutarch, who mentions that "the graves of the many are shown in Eleutherae, but those of the leaders near Eleusis, and this was a favor that Theseus granted Adrastus" (Plut. *Thes.* 29.4–5).[14] That the Seven were buried in Eleusis is also mentioned explicitly by Herodotus' Athenians (Hdt. 9.27.3) and in Lysias' funeral oration (Lys. 2.10). Their graves were still shown in Roman imperial times on the road from Eleusis to Megara, as the traveler Pausanias confirms (Paus. 1.39.2).[15]

This tradition almost certainly predates Aeschylus' tragedy, as the archaeological evidence suggests. In the area described by Pausanias, Mylonas has excavated a group of nine Middle Helladic tombs, three of which contained evidence of Late Geometric cult activity. They were surrounded by a *peribolos* wall, which also dates to the end of the eighth century. This indicates that from that time on, these graves were seen as belonging together and were venerated as a heroön. Six of these nine cist graves lay higher than the other three, which makes it likely that only the former were visible in the post-Mycenaean era. Mylonas, therefore, suggests that these are the graves that were identified as those of the fallen leaders of the Seven.[16]

It is impossible to determine with certainty at which point this identification with the Seven occurred. In mainland Greece, hero cults were proliferating especially in the eighth and sixth centuries. The first wave is connected to the mutual influence of cult and epic. People of the Geometric period looked at the larger and more magnificent Mycenaean tombs with awe and veneration and, stimulated by the spread of epic, thought of their inhabitants as heroes from another age. As a result, local tombs (and other places of worship) could be identified with a figure celebrated in the great epic cycles, which in turn could stimulate the development of further local myths.[17] The sixth-century increase in hero cults reflects the need of newly formed and rapidly developing *poleis* to root themselves in the mythological past, forge a common civic identity, and use these heroes as "cultural capital" in inter*poleis* competition.[18]

---

14. For a discussion of this testimonium and the two fragments, see Radt *TrGF* iii.175–76. For the date of the *Eleusinians*, see "Athens' Aid for Suppliants" below, 174–86.

15. For the location in the west cemetery at Eleusis, see Mylonas (1969) fig. 32.

16. Mylonas (1975) 2:153–54, 262–64, fig. 145; Kearns (1989) 130–31; Parker (1996) 35–6; Krauskopf *LIMC* s.v. Adrastos i.232. It is not entirely clear how many of the Seven were supposedly buried there. Adrastus surely survived, and Amphiaraus was normally thought to have been swallowed up by the earth in Boeotia (cf. Braswell (1998) 27–29, 35), but Kearns (1989) 130 is right to suggest that the numbers probably coincided.

17. Kearns (1989) 104–6, 129–31. Cf. Farnell (1921) 284, 340–42; Coldstream (1976); Burkert (1985) 204; Currie (2005) 47–59.

18. Boedeker (1993); Hall (1999); Forsdyke (2011) 151–57. Cf. Bremmer (2006) 15–20 who dates the origin of religious hero cults to the late sixth century.

Mylonas, Coldstream, Burkert, and Janko argue that this heroön was already dedicated to the Seven in Late Geometric times, when the *peribolos* enclosure was built.[19] The myth of the Seven against Thebes was already part of the epic tradition by the time of Homer[20] and was treated in detail in the seventh-century cyclical epic *Thebaid*.[21] In these works, there is no trace of any Athenian involvement, but the story of Adrastus' near escape from the battlefield is already attested for this early period. According to Pausanias (8.25.8), it was mentioned "in the *Thebaid* that Adrastus fled from Thebes [ἔφευγεν ἐκ Θηβῶν], 'his cloths in sorry state, with dark-maned Arion' [εἵματα λυγρὰ φέρων σὺν Ἀρείονι κυανοχαίτῃ]" (*Thebaid* fr. 6a Davies). Adrastus' divine horse Arion was already familiar to Homer (*Il.* 23.346), and a scholiast remarks about Arion that "thanks to him Adrastus alone was saved from the Theban war, whereas all the others perished. The story is in the cyclic poets [παρὰ τοῖς κυκλικοῖς]" (Schol. Hom. *Il.* 23.346a Erbse = *Thebaid* fr. 6c Davies).

Since Adrastus' escape as sole survivor was already part of the epic tradition in the seventh century BC, it is not hard to imagine how the awe-inspiring Bronze Age tombs in Eleusis might have become identified as the tombs of the other leaders of the Seven.[22] On his way back to Argos, it might be supposed, Adrastus naturally came by Eleusis. He might have brought the bodies of his fallen comrades with him, or, more likely, a local hero might have aided him in recovering the bodies and buried them in Eleusis, which was from now on under the buried heroes' protection.[23] Considering that Theseus was a minor figure in epic poetry and not native to Eleusis, it is doubtful, however, that he was, at this early stage, already associated with the burial of the Seven.[24]

It cannot be ruled out, however, that the tombs enclosed by the *peribolos* wall initially belonged to local Eleusinian heroes before they became associated with the Seven.[25] We know, from archaeological and epigraphical evidence, that a heroön for the Seven was set up in Argos in the middle of the sixth century, presumably to bolster Argos' claim to leadership in the Peloponnese, by

---

19. Mylonas (1975) 2:262–64; Coldstream (1977) 351; Burkert (1985) 203; Janko (1992) 163. Already before Mylonas' discovery, Jacoby *FGrHist* 3b (Suppl.) i.445 suggested that by the late sixth century, "the Eleusinian tombs may have had their name for a long time."

20. Hom. *Il.* 4.376–98, 5.801–8, 6.222–23, 14.113–21, 23.346–47; *Od.* 11.326–27, 15.247. Homer even knew of the more successful campaign of the Epigoni (Hom. *Il.* 4.399–403). See Janko (1992) 163.

21. Based on Paus. 9.9.5 = Callinus fr. 6 West^2, the *Thebaid* has been dated to the middle of the seventh century. Cf. M. Davies (1989) 22–23; Huxley (1969) 41–49.

22. Huxley (1969) 113–14 argues that Athenian and particularly Eleusinian interest in epic poetry began already at the end of the eighth century BC.

23. Jacoby *FGrHist* 3b (Suppl.) i.444.

24. See "Theseus—Another Heracles" below, 169–74.

25. Cf. Snodgrass (1980) 39; Kearns (1989) 130; Hubbard (1992) 97 note 53; Parker (1996) 35. Boehringer (2001) 63–64 and Bremmer (2006) 15–20 are even more skeptical about any cult activities at this site.

emphasizing its role in leading a Panhellenic group of heroes against Thebes in the mythical past.[26] It is quite possible, therefore, that the Eleusinian graves were identified as the tombs of the Seven in the context of inter*poleis* rivalry in the second half of the sixth century. Whenever this identification occurred, there must have been a story attached to the heroön, explaining how the Seven came to be buried in Eleusis. It was probably Adrastus' escape from the battlefield that provided the "hook" for the Eleusinians to "write" themselves into the story.[27]

This is not the only instance where we can see how the inglorious end of the Seven known from the epic tradition stimulated the development of diverse local myths and cults in the area. Eleutherae, a town situated on the pass over Mount Cithaeron on the road from Thebes to Eleusis and Argos (fig. 1), also displayed heroic tombs that, by the end of the fifth century, were identified as the graves of the common soldiers of the seven contingents.[28] The first-century BC geographer Strabo mentions that a village in the Boeotian district of Tanagra near the Attic border was called Harma (Chariot), either after the chariot of Amphiaraus, the seer of the Seven, or after that of Adrastus (Strab. 9.2.11).[29] Strabo further reports that another Harma, a (chariot-shaped) mountaintop, was located across the border in the vicinity of the Attic *deme* of Phyle (Strab. 9.2.11). Furthermore, a hill located two kilometers north of Athens on the road to Thebes was called Colonus Hippius (Horse Hill).[30] There was "an altar to Poseidon Hippius and Athena Hippia and a heroön to Peirithous and Theseus, Oedipus, and Adrastus" (Paus. 1.30.4). This is the place where, according to Athenian tradition, Adrastus had stopped on his flight from Thebes (*Etym. Magn.* s.v. Ἱππία).[31]

We cannot determine when each of these local traditions originated. Some might be as old as the initial Eleusinian story of the burial of the Seven. Others might have developed during the fifth century, as a result of the polis-wide popularity of Athens' intervention for the fallen Argives. It seems certain, how-

26. For the heroön of the Seven, see Pariente (1992). For the sociopolitical implications of the creation of this cult, see Hall (1999) 52–55; Forsdyke (2011) 151–54.

27. Cf. Jacoby *FGrHist* 3b (Suppl.) ii.349 note 6.

28. Cf. Plut. *Thes.* 29.4; Eur. *Supp.* 754–59. This distinction between the graves of the Seven and of the common soldiers is also found in Schol. Pind. *Ol.* 6.23d Drachmann.

29. The Boeotian town Harma was already mentioned in the catalogue of ships in Hom. *Il.* 2.499. That it was named after Amphiaraus' chariot is also mentioned by Paus. 9.19.4.

30. This is the place where Oedipus sought refuge in Attica. Cf. Paus. 1.10.4; Soph. *OC* 53–65. For the location, see Travlos (1971) 45 fig. 53, 164 fig. 213.

31. Schol. Soph. *OC* 712 de Marco also links Adrastus to this hill: ὁ γὰρ Κολωνὸς Ἱππεὺς [Ιππιος Jacoby] ὠνομάσθη πὰρ᾽ ἃς ἐξεθέμην αἰτίας διὰ τὸν Ἄδραστον. Unfortunately, it is unclear what these αἰτίας were. Cf. Jacoby *FGrHist* 3b (Suppl.) ii.350 note 10.

ever, that most of them were well familiar by the end of the fifth century.[32] For several reasons, these local myths and cults are of great importance for our understanding of the role of social memory in Athenian public discourse.

First, they illustrate how intensely different local communities tried to connect themselves to the Panhellenic world of epic and how this gave rise to various cults and diverse and competing local traditions.[33] The tombs in Eleutherae were probably originally thought to belong to the seven leaders and thus constituted a true rival claim to Eleusis.[34] Inhabitants of the Boeotian Harma believed that after the crash of his chariot in their hometown, Adrastus "saved himself on Arion" (Strab. 9.2.11), just as in the cyclic epic *Thebaid* (fr. 6a Davies). The people living near the Attic Harma also sought a connection to Adrastus' chariot, but it seems that, in their version, Arion did not play a role: "Adrastus was saved by the villagers"[35] (Philochorus *FGrHist* 328 F 113) and was perhaps escorted by them to their king, as Jacoby suggests.[36] The aetiological myth of Colonus Hippius, however, presupposes that Adrastus was still in possession of his chariot, drawn by at least two horses, which he halted at Colonus and "addressed as Poseidon and Athena" (*Etym. Magn.* s.v. Ἱππία).[37]

Second, these local myths and cults, which were an integral part of the collective memory of these local communities, helped foster a sense of local identity and social cohesion and constituted important "cultural capital."[38] This is evident, for instance, in the case of the villagers of the Attic Harma, whose alleged aid to Adrastus was, at least by Philochorus' time, formally recognized by Argos in the form of a grant of equal rights of citizenship (ἰσοπολιτεία, Philochorus *FGrHist* 328 F 113).[39]

---

32. Euripides' *Suppliants,* which dates to the late 420s (cf. Collard (1975) 1:8–14), mentions the burial of the common soldiers in Eleutherae (Eur. *Supp.* 754–59), and Jacoby *FGrHist* 3b (Suppl.) ii.350 note 23 suspects that Eur. *Supp.* 1200 contains an allusion to the ritual practice of the Pythaists, which was connected to the Attic Harma. Mills (1997) 163 suggests that Adrastus' association with Colonus Hippius dates back to the sixth century. See also Grethlein (2003) 256 note 2.

33. Cf. Harding (2008) 71.

34. von Wilamowitz-Moellendorff (1899) 190; Jacoby *FGrHist* 3b (Suppl.) i.443; Mills (1997) 231.

35. In Strabo's text, the citation from Philochorus follows immediately after the two alternative explanations for the name of the Boeotian Harma (i.e., named after either Adrastus' or Amphiaraus' Chariot). Yet Jacoby *FGrHist* 3b (Suppl.) i.442–43 and ii.349–50 makes a convincing case that Philochorus' quote must refer to the Attic Harma. Similarly, Harding (2008) 71.

36. Jacoby *FGrHist* 3b (Suppl.) i.443.

37. Addressing Arion as Poseidon makes particular sense in light of the tradition of Poseidon's parenthood to this divine horse. For Arion's pedigree, see Paus. 8.25.5–10; Matthews (1996) 142–44. That Adrastus drove a two-horse chariot during this campaign is also mentioned by Antimachus of Colophon, a contemporary of Plato, in his epic poem *Thebaid* (fr. 31 Matthews). In this poem the horses' names are Καιρός and Ἀρίον.

38. See "Tribes and *Demes*" in chapter 1, 71–73.

39. Gawantka (1975) 93–94 note 7, 220.

Third, these local traditions were the underpinnings of the versions familiar to us from the Athenian polis tradition of the *epitaphios* and the tragic stage. The graves at Eleusis and the various places connected to Adrastus' flight show that the tragedians and the Attic orators drew on local traditions familiar to them. This is most obvious in the case of the Eleusinian poet Aeschylus, who construed the plot of his tragedy about the Athenian intervention for the fallen Argives around the heroön of the Seven in his own hometown, Eleusis.[40] We do not know how familiar Athenians were with this Eleusinian tradition before Aeschylus brought it on the tragic stage, but it seems certain that the *Eleusinians* contributed to spreading a local tradition to the entire polis community.

Moreover, the tragedians and the Attic orators did not operate within a vacuum, even when they innovated. In Euripides' *Suppliants*, the Seven were not buried in Eleusinian soil; their ashes were returned to Argos (Eur. *Supp.* 1185–88). Euripides' innovation must have seemed plausible to his audience, since he carefully anchored it within well-established traditions: the Seven were cremated in Eleusis (1207). The place of their funeral pyres, "right by the turning to the Isthmus" (παρ᾽ αὐτὴν τρίοδον Ἰσθμίας ὁδοῦ, 1211–12), was turned into a sacred precinct in accordance with the orders of Euripides' Athena.[41] This τρίοδος was located in close proximity to the prehistoric heroön, identified as the tombs of the Seven by Mylonas.[42] Euripides thus operated well within the limits given by tradition: the heroön of the Seven—now marking the place not of their inhumation but of their cremation—was still where Euripides' audience would expect it.[43]

Fourth, polis-wide and local carriers of this myth mutually influenced and sustained each other.[44] The references to Eleusis in Herodotus (9.27.3) and Lysias (2.10) prove that the "official" version of this myth drew heavily on preexisting local traditions. Yet this master narrative could, in turn, also affect and change local traditions. As mentioned above, it is extremely likely that the tombs at Eleutherae were initially connected to the Seven themselves. Once this former Boeotian border town had been fully integrated into Attica and once the Eleusinian version of the myth had become the predominant one thanks to Aeschylus' *Eleusinians* and the Athenian funeral orations, the two competing versions were harmonized by identifying the tombs at Eleutherae no longer with the Seven leaders but, instead, with the common soldiers of the seven contingents.[45]

40. This was already emphasized by von Wilamowitz-Moellendorff (1899) 199.

41. For the corrupt phrase at the end of Eur. *Supp.* 1212, I follow Collard (1975) in reading Ἰσθμίας ὁδοῦ. Cf. Collard (1975) 2:417–18.

42. For a map of Eleusis, see Mylonas (1969) fig. 32.

43. Euripides' version probably found additional credence with those Athenians who knew the heroön of the Seven in Argos. Cf. Pariente (1992).

44. Cf. R. Thomas (1989) 198.

45. Cf. Philochorus *FGrHist* 328 F 112; Eur. *Supp.* 754–59. For Eleutherae's incorporation into

Finally, when judging the emotive force of this mythical paradigm in Athenian political and diplomatic discourse, we ought to take these local cults and traditions into account as well. They helped anchor the polis-wide version in the everyday experience of individual Athenians. The mentioning of Adrastus' arrival in Athens and the burials in Eleusis and Eleutherae must have resonated particularly with those Athenians who cherished the stories connected to Eleusis, Eleutherae, Harma, and Colonus Hippius within their own local community. Moreover, some of these sites (e.g., Eleusis and Colonus Hippius) featured hero cults for the Seven, Theseus, or Adrastus. It is likely that regular ritual activities at these shrines resulted in what Connerton termed "incorporated" memories of great emotional intensity.[46] Moreover, the sites themselves functioned as permanent material reminders and thus helped ensure the transmission of these local memories to younger generations.

Communities in Attica were not alone in connecting local topography with the epic stories surrounding the fate of the Seven. The same phenomenon can be observed around Thebes. We have already seen that the Boeotian town Harma derived its name either from Adrastus' or Amphiaraus' chariot (Strab. 9.2.11). In his survey of Thebes, Pausanias mentioned not only the graves of the Theban defenders Melanippus and Eteocles (Paus. 9.18.1, 3) but also a sanctuary for the Argive seer Amphiaraus, at the spot where he was swallowed up by the earth (Paus. 9.8.3),[47] and the tombs of the attackers Polynices and Tydeus (Paus. 9.18.1–3), whose burial in Thebes was already mentioned by Homer (Hom. *Il.* 14.144).[48] This Theban tradition knows nothing of an Athenian intervention and is at odds with the Eleusinian legend, according to which the Seven (including Tydeus) were buried in Eleusis.

That the dead Argives were buried at Thebes is also twice stated emphatically by Pindar. In *Nemean* 9, composed around 474 BC, Pindar writes,

the Athenian state at the end of the sixth century, see Paus. 1.38.8; G. Anderson (2003) 180–81. The local histories written by fourth- and third-century Atthidographers are an invaluable source for these local traditions that might otherwise have been forgotten over the centuries. They chronicled Athenian history from mythical times down to the present and were particularly interested in bringing order into local cults and myths by organizing them into a coherent historical narrative. Jacoby *FGrHist* 3b (Suppl.) i.443 makes the case that Philochorus integrated many local legends pertaining to Adrastus' flight and Theseus' intervention into his narrative of Theseus' deeds. For Atthidography in general, see Jacoby (1949); Harding (1994), (2008); Clarke (2008).

46. For "incorporated" memories, see Connerton (1989); Alcock (2002) 28. See also "Cults and Festivals" in chapter 1, 65–69.

47. This is a tradition rivaling the claims of both Oropus, where Amphiaraus was allegedly swallowed up by the earth during his flight from Thebes (Paus. 1.34.2), and the Boeotian Harma, which was named after his chariot (Strab. 9.2.11; Paus. 9.19.4).

48. Cf. Schachter (1981–94) 2:192. For the location of these sites in Thebes, see Symeonoglou (1985) 175 fig. 5.1, 177, 193–94.

> and on the banks of the Ismenus [Ἰσμηνοῦ δ' ἐπ' ὄχθαισι] they planted their sweet homecoming and fattened the white-waxing smoke with their bodies.[49] For seven pyres feasted on the young-limbed men [ἑπτὰ γὰρ δαίσαντο πυραὶ νεογυίους φῶτας]. (Pind. *Nem.* 9.22–24)

In *Olympian* 6, written in 468 BC, Pindar describes how Adrastus praised the dead Amphiaraus in Thebes.

> Afterward, when the corpses of the seven pyres had been completed [ἑπτὰ δ' ἔπειτα πυρᾶν νεκρῶν τελεσθέντων],[50] Talaus' son spoke, in Thebes [ἐν Θήβαισι], a word such as this: "I yearn for the eye of my army, good both as a seer and at fighting with the spear." (Pind. *Ol.* 6.15–17)

In these passages, Pindar states explicitly that seven pyres for the fallen Argives had been erected *in Thebes* (Pind. *Ol.* 6.16), at the banks of the Ismenus (Pind. *Nem.* 9.22), and that Adrastus (Talaus' son) appears to give a eulogy in Thebes for his dead seer Amphiaraus (Pind. *Ol.* 6.16).[51] There is no mention of withheld funeral rites, let alone an Athenian intervention on behalf of the fallen Argives. It is most likely that Pindar, in defense of the honor of his native city, took a stance against the Athenian version of this myth that, around this time, became a prominent part of the Athenian master narrative as we can grasp it in Aeschylus' *Eleusinians* and in the Athenian funeral oration.[52] This interpretation is further supported by Hubbard's observation that the reference to the seven pyres is necessary neither to the narrative of *Olympian* 6 nor to the one in *Nemean* 9.[53]

The origin of Pindar's version of a burial in Thebes in the immediate aftermath of the battle has been debated since antiquity. Some argue that the burial of the Seven in Thebes had always been an integral part of the epic story of the

49. For lucid discussions of this unusual image, see Hubbard (1992) 92–93; Braswell (1998) 88–91.

50. Based on the gloss ἐπισωρευθέντων, "heaped up" (Schol. Pind. *Ol.* 6.23b Drachmann), Braswell (1998) 91 rightly takes τελεσθέντων with νεκρῶν in the sense "when the corpses of the seven pyres had been completed, i.e. arranged for cremation." Hutchinson (2001) 382–83 regards the transmitted text as corrupt.

51. In antiquity, it was debated for which Argives these seven pyres had been built. Scholiasts noted that there should only be four pyres, not seven, since Amphiaraus disappeared, Adrastus survived, and Polynices remained unburied. To solve this apparent problem, they suggested that these pyres must belong to the common soldiers of the seven contingents that attacked the seven gates of Thebes (Schol. Pind. *Ol.* 6.23d Drachmann).

52. Bethe (1891) 98–99; Jacoby *FGrHist* 3b (Suppl.) i.445; Mills (1997) 233; Hubbard (1992) 97–100.

53. Hubbard (1992) 94.

Seven and was featured already in the cyclical epic *Thebaid*.[54] In their view, the seven pyres belonged to the legend as much as did the seven leaders with their seven units attacking the seven gates of Thebes.[55] This hypothesis has recently been strengthened by the discovery of the sixth-century heroön for the Seven in Argos. There, the inscription ερο̄ον | το̄ν εν Θε]βαις implies that the graves of the Seven were believed to be in Thebes.[56] At the other end of the spectrum, scholars like Hubbard suggest that this tradition might be "no more than an *ad hoc* product of Pindar's own era, devised as a cultic response to Athenian charges that the Thebans had not allowed funeral rites for the Argive dead."[57] It is, of course, also conceivable that it originated at some point during the archaic period, when emerging *poleis* were vying for status by rooting themselves in the Panhellenic world of epic. The discovery of ancient tombs in Thebes (just as in Eleusis and Eleutherae) might have led to their identification with the funeral pyres of the Seven.

While the date of origin of this tradition cannot be determined, it is clear from a fragment of Armenidas' *Thebaica* that there was an actual place in fifth-century Thebes that was called "Seven Pyres [Επτὰ Πυραί], either after the Seven against Thebes or after the seven children of Niobe who had been burned there" (Armenidas *FGrHist* 378 F 6 = Schol. Pind. *Ol.* 6.23a Drachmann). The Kastéllia, two hills that contained Bronze Age tombs and could easily be held for mass burial mounds, are located exactly where Pindar placed the Seven Pyres, east of the Cadmea, "on the banks of the Ismenus" (Pind. *Nem.* 9.22).[58]

54. von Wilamowitz-Moellendorff (1899) 189, (1922) 310 note 3; Walters (1980) 11; Aélion (1983) 1:234; Castriota (1992) 70; Hutchinson (2001) 381–82; more cautiously, Janko (1992) 163. This view is based on Hom. *Il.* 14.114, which placed Tydeus' tumulus (χυτὴ γαῖα) in Thebes, and on Schol. Pind. *Ol.* 6.26 Drachmann (= *Thebaid* fr. 7 Davies), which states in reference to Adrastus' eulogy of Amphiaraus, "Asclepiades says that this [ταῦτα] has been taken out of the cyclic *Thebaid*." Both of these testimonies are not unproblematic, however. First, it is unclear whether ταῦτα refers to the entire funeral scene in Thebes or, as is more likely, merely to Adrastus' particular words of praise for Amphiaraus, which could have been spoken at the moment of the latter's disappearance. Cf. Bethe (1891) 94–96; Jacoby *FGrHist* 3b (Suppl.) ii.351–52 note 24; Hubbard (1992) 96–97 note 51. Second, Schol. Hom. *Il.* 14.114a Erbse remarks about Homer's reference to Tydeus' tumulus in Thebes that "Zenodotus athetized [this line]; it was not in Aristophanes[' text of Homer]." Cf. Janko (1992) 163. The scholiast's testimony is, of course, not conclusive, given the predominant influence of the tragic poets (Aesch. *Eleus.* and Eur. *Supp.*) on Hellenistic literary critics.

55. See particularly, Braswell (1998) 92; Lefkowitz (1985) 276–77.

56. Pariente (1992) 201–2, 215; Hall (1999) 54.

57. Hubbard (1992) 97. Bethe (1891) 95–97 and Jacoby *FGrHist* 3b (Suppl.) ii.353 suggest that in the original, epic versions, the bodies of the fallen Argives were simply left on the battlefield as prey for dogs and birds (cf. Hom. *Il.* 1.4–5). The strongest argument for Pindar's invention of the seven pyres at Thebes is provided by Schol. Pind. *Ol.* 6.23a Drachmann, which named Pindar as the sole source for this episode: ὁ μὲν οὖν Ἀρίσταρχός φησιν ὅτι ἰδιάζει καὶ ἐν τούτοις ὁ Πίνδαρος ὡς καὶ ἐν ἄλλοις. Cf. Jacoby *FGrHist* 3b (Suppl.) ii.352; Hubbard (1992) 94.

58. Schachter (1981–94) 3:22–24. For the location of the Kastéllia hills, see Symeonoglou (1985) map A (J–K, 9–11). Cf. also Hubbard (1992) 94–96.

Yet the association of the Seven Pyres with the fallen Argives was not even undisputed in fifth-century Thebes, as Armenidas' alternative identification with the Niobids shows.[59] Consequently, it seems likely that Pindar, in his desire to take a stance against the Athenians' anti-Theban version, placed the burial of the Seven firmly in Thebes by connecting it to this local landmark. To what degree he thereby reaffirmed a known local tradition or invented a new one is impossible to determine.

If the interpretation is correct that fifth-century Athenians and Thebans fought fiercely over the correct version of the burial of the Seven, a passage in Euripides' *Phoenician Women* (ca. 410–409) might be another Athenian strike against Thebes in this memory war, in which both sides used local cults and traditions to support their claims. Euripides' Antigone asks a servant to identify the leaders of the attackers. In his description of the Seven, the servant mentions various Theban landmarks, the river Dirce (Eur. *Phoen.* 131), the tomb of Zethus (145), and the "tomb of Niobe's seven daughters" (159–60). This order suggests that the servant's description runs from west to north to east of the Cadmea.[60] Euripides thus identified the Seven Pyres (the Kastéllia hills) with the Niobids and, in doing so, implicitly contradicted Pindar's (and other Thebans') identification of this landmark with the graves of the fallen Argives.[61] Similarly, the assertion made by the second-century Theban historian Aristodemus "that there is nowhere in Thebes a tomb of the Niobids" (*FGrHist* 383 F 3 = Schol. Eur. *Phoen.* 159 Schwartz) could be read as a reaffirmation of the view found in Pindar that the landmark of the Seven Pyres marked (and thus proved) the burial of the fallen Argives in Thebes.[62] If we take Pausanias as an indicator, it seems that the Thebans eventually lost this memory war against Athens. Pausanias apparently knows nothing of an Argive burial in Thebes and identifies this landmark unequivocally with the children of Niobe (Paus. 9.16.7, 17.2).[63] Moreover, in his description of the tombs of the Seven in Eleusis, Pausanias remarks that "the Thebans say that they conceded the recovery of the bodies voluntarily and deny that a battle took place" (Paus. 1.39.2). This shows that in the end, even the Thebans acknowledged an Athenian intervention and the

59. Jacoby *FGrHist* 3b (Komm.) i.158 dates Armenidas to the last decades of the fifth century. Pottery finds at the Kastéllia hills suggest that some of the tombs may have been used for cultic purposes during the archaic and later periods, but apparently this was not done on a grand scale; cf. Schachter (1981–94) 3:24.

60. Mastronarde (1994) 647–49; Schachter (1981–94) 3:23 note 3.

61. Keramopoullos (1917) 376; Hubbard (1992) 95 note 45.

62. Hubbard (1992) 95 note 45. Aristodemus is also cited in Schol. Pind. *Ol.* 6.23a Drachmann, probably in support of Pindar's identification of the Seven Pyres, but a lacuna makes it impossible to know what exactly he said.

63. Schachter (1981–94) 3:24 argues convincingly that all of these sources are dealing with the same monuments, "whether they associate them with the Seven against Thebes or the Niobids."

burial of the Seven in Athenian soil. By that time, the only disputed question was whether the recovery had been achieved by means of war or persuasion.[64]

Theseus—Another Heracles

In the previous section, I have argued that the epic story of Adrastus' flight from the battlefield and the discovery of Bronze Age tombs in Eleusis probably led to the establishment of a heroön for the Seven and gave rise to a local Eleusinian myth concerning their burial. Similar phenomena can be found elsewhere in Attica and Boeotia, where local communities tried to "write" themselves into the story of the Seven by connecting local landmarks or cults to the world of these epic heroes. These local myths and cults are not only important for understanding the origins and the development of this mythical episode; they also give us a sense of how local and polis-wide memories mutually influenced and sustained each other during the classical period. In this section, I explore when and why Theseus became associated with the myth of the Seven.[65] I will make the case that the basic outline of the myth of the Athenian intervention on behalf of the fallen Argives, as we know it, probably took form in the last decade of the sixth century, when Theseus eclipsed Heracles as the great culture hero in Athenian mythology.

As mentioned above, it is impossible to know the earliest stories attached to the heroön of the Seven in Eleusis, but Theseus' minor status in both epic and local Attic mythology in the seventh century makes it seem unlikely that he was already a part of this story at that time. While Aeschylus' *Eleusinians* (ca. 475–467 BC) serves as the undisputable *terminus ante quem* for his appearance in this myth (Plut. *Thes.* 29.4–5), there are some clues that point toward a somewhat earlier date. By the middle of the fifth century, Theseus had emerged as the most prominent Athenian hero and as "embodiment of the best qualities of the nation in its own eyes."[66] His glorious deeds were celebrated in funeral orations and at religious festivals, in dithyrambs and on the tragic stage, and were

64. Pausanias' Θηβαῖοι could be either his contemporaries or, as Jacoby *FGrHist* 3b (Suppl.) i.445 and ii.353 note 32 suggests, writers of *Thebaica*, which would bring the Theban concession up to the third or fourth century BC.

65. All of the sources that make mention of the Athenian leader ascribe this feat to Theseus. This is not the case with regard to the other famous patriotic supplication myth, Athens' aid for the Heraclidae. We find two variants there. In the presumably older version, Theseus is in power. Euripides, however, ascribes this deed (probably for dramaturgical reasons) to his son Demophon (Eur. *Heracl.* 114–19). Cf. Allan (2001) 31–32; Grethlein (2003) 382–33.

66. Mills (1997) 25. Recent studies on Theseus abound: see Huxley (1969) 113–22; Herter (1973); Brommer (1982); Kearns (1989) 117–23; Calame (1990); Tyrrell & Brown (1991); Walker (1995); Mills (1997); G. Anderson (2003) 134–46.

displayed on countless vases and major public monuments.[67] Yet it is widely acknowledged that his rise to prominence as the quintessential Athenian hero was a relatively late development.[68]

During the early archaic period, Theseus falls short of Heracles, his later rival, in every respect. Judging from the few incidental references in early epic, Theseus was known only as a minor character.[69] He did not appear on Attic pottery before 570 BC, and with only one sanctuary within the city of Athens, there is no evidence for any significant role he might have played in Athenian cult at that time.[70] In this early period, Theseus was known as the slayer of the Minotaur and as a companion of the Thessalian king Peirithous, with whom he abducted Helen, battled the Centaurs, and descended into Hades.

Things changed drastically during the period 550–510 BC. Under the Peisistratids, Theseus emerged as, by far, the most prominent Athenian hero. In this period, his depiction on Attic pottery multiplies, and in addition to his well-known deeds, a number of new achievements appear, notably the struggles with the Marathonian Bull and the Crommyonian Sow, as well as the rape of the Amazon Antiope. These new episodes were clearly inspired by and modeled on the labors of Heracles, who fought with the Cretan Bull, the Erymanthian Boar, and the Amazon queen Hippolyte.[71] Given the Peisistratids' ambitious foreign policies, it is not surprising that they were interested in an Athenian version of Heracles, who "might develop into a lucrative source of Panhellenic prestige both for themselves and for their city."[72] Allegations that the Peisistratids manipulated the texts of Homer and Hesiod to brighten the hero's image before a Panhellenic audience (Plut. *Thes.* 20.1–2) further support this view.

67. See "Cults and Festivals" in chapter 1, 65–69.

68. G. Anderson (2003) 136. See also Tyrrell & Brown (1991) 168–88.

69. Centauromachy: Hom. *Il.* 1.265; Hes. *Scutum* 182. Aethra, Theseus' mother, with Helen in Troy: Hom. *Il.* 3.144. Ariadne: Hom. *Od.* 11.321–25; Hes. fr. 298 Merkelbach & West with Plut. *Thes.* 20.1–2. Theseus and Peirithous: Hom. *Od.* 11.631. Descent to Hades: Hes. fr. 280 Merkelbach & West with Paus. 10.28.2. For Theseus in early Greek poetry, see Huxley (1969) 117–22; Mills (1997) 6–18; G. Anderson (2003) 253 note 27. Some of Theseus' appearances in Homer have been suspected to be interpolations since antiquity; cf. Hereas *FGrHist* 486 F 1; Walker (1995) 35–37. For Theseus' non-Athenian associations, see Herter (1939) 258–62.

70. G. Anderson (2003) 137. Initially, Theseus seems to have had only one sanctuary in Athens; later, he had four or possibly six in all of Attica. He thus still ranged far behind Heracles even in the classical period. Cf. Kearns (1989) 166, 168–69.

71. There is some evidence suggesting that Theseus' role changed over time from Heracles' assistant—for example, on his expedition against the Amazons (Plut. *Thes.* 26.1) and in capturing the Ceryneian Hind (*Theseid* fr. 2 Davies)—to being his equal; cf. Huxley (1968) 116–17. The modeling of these new deeds on Heracles' labors has, on occasion, led to confusion in art and literature; cf. G. Anderson (2003) 255 note 35.

72. G. Anderson (2003) 138. Earlier interpretations suggesting that Peisistratus promoted Theseus to encourage Athenians "to identify his own actions and accomplishments with Theseus' deeds" (Tyrrell & Brown (1991) 161) are too narrow. The attempt by Walker (1995) 35–81 to completely disassociate Theseus' rise from the Peisistratids is not convincing.

After the expulsion of the Peisistratids in 511/0, Theseus' star rose even higher. This manifests itself in two ways. First, Theseus finally stepped out of the long shadow of Heracles. In Athens after 510, a whole series of new mythical episodes appeared in which the young hero, on his way from Troezen to Athens, rid the area of brutal outlaws (Sinis, Sciron, Cercyron, and Procrustes). Comprising the old and new episodes, a "cycle" of his illustrious deeds became a popular theme on Attic vases, and for the first time, Theseus was depicted more often than Heracles on Attic pottery.[73] The earliest extant literary narrative of the cycle is Bacchylides 18, a dithyramb, probably performed in the early 450s.[74] Yet it seems certain that Theseus' rising popularity in art was accompanied by other media, such as cult and poetry. For this reason, the earliest *Theseid,* an epic poem featuring Theseus' deeds, is generally dated to the last decades of the sixth century.[75] Theseus' new primacy over Heracles and his adoption as a national symbol is nowhere more manifest than on the Athenian treasury of Delphi, which was erected around 500 BC.[76] While the metopes display the deeds of both Heracles and Theseus, the latter's preeminence is ensured by featuring him on the more prominent southern side of the building and by showing him, instead of Heracles, in company of the goddess Athena.[77]

Second, after 510, Theseus' persona also acquired an entirely new dimension. While he was initially known primarily as the slayer of monsters and abductor of women, the new episodes depict him as a civilizing force and as the true benefactor of Attica, whose territorial integrity he ensures and defends. At that time, he also took on the qualities of a state-building king. The myth of Theseus' synoecism of Attica (Thuc. 2.15.1–2; Plut. *Thes.* 24) most likely originated in the context of Cleisthenes' tribal reforms.[78]

How exactly did these new episodes come into being? This is a very difficult question to answer. Greg Anderson envisions a top-down process, an act of deliberate creation, by Cleisthenes and his associates, of stories suitable to legitimate the new order through mythical precedents.[79] Anderson is certainly

73. Cf. Boardman (1975) 3–4. For the cyclic vases, see *LIMC* s.v. Theseus vii.32–53.

74. Barron (1980); Maehler (2004) 189–91.

75. Jacoby *FGrHist* 3b (Suppl.) i.445; Huxley (1968) 116–22; Herter (1973) 1046; Bernabé (1987) 136; Tyrrell & Brown (1991) 161; Mills (1997) 19–25; West (2003) 24–25. Walker (1995) 38–39 is more skeptical.

76. Pausanias (10.11.4) reports that the Athenians' treasury was built from the spoils of Marathon, but many date the structure's art and architecture to around 500 BC. Cf. Rausch (1999) 129–30; G. Anderson (2003) 140.

77. Boardman (1982) 4; Calame (1990) 404; Walker (1995) 52–53; Mills (1997) 29; G. Anderson (2003) 140.

78. G. Anderson (2003) 141–46. Cf. Kearns (1989) 117–19.

79. The explanation of Greg Anderson (2003) 142–45 is a classical case of the "invention of tradition" approach, pioneered by Hobsbawm & Ranger (1983). See also Parker (1987) 187–90. For a critique of this approach, see Misztal (2003) 56–61.

right, but this is only one part of the story. As I have argued above, polis-wide and local collective memories could mutually influence and sustain each other. We have seen how local communities, in Eleusis, Eleutherae, Harma, and Colonus, tried to find a connection to famous Panhellenic or polis-wide myths as well. Such bottom-up processes in the creation of new mythical episodes should not be ignored.[80] Moreover, this kind of active memory politics envisioned by the "invention of tradition" approach only worked if the newly invented stories seemed plausible to the populace. For this reason, new episodes usually drew on and expanded already familiar material and were thus anchored in the community's existing memorial framework.[81]

Where does the intervention on behalf of the fallen Argives fit into this development of the Theseus figure from 550 to 500 BC? Several clues suggest that Theseus became associated with the burial of the Seven in Eleusis in the last decade of the sixth century, when Theseus stepped out of the shadow of Heracles and emerged as a true Athenian culture hero. First, Theseus' recovery of the fallen Argives could be used to challenge the primacy of Heracles as the inventor of the Greek custom to recover the dead under a truce.[82]

> Theseus also aided Adrastus in the recovery of those who fell beneath the Cadmea, not as Euripides has portrayed it in his tragedy by conquering the Thebans in battle, but by persuading them and making a truce [πείσας καὶ σπεισάμενος]; for so most writers say; and Philochorus says also that this was the first truce ever made for the recovery of corpses [σπονδὰς περὶ νεκρῶν ἀναιρέσεως γενέσθαι πρώτας ἐκείνας]. But that Heracles was the first to give back corpses to his enemies [Ἡρακλῆς πρῶτος ἀπέδωκε νεκροὺς τοῖς πολεμίοις] has been written in the accounts about Heracles. . . . And Euripides' *Suppliants* is disproved by Aeschylus' *Eleusinians*. . . .[83] (Plut. *Thes.* 29.4–5 = Philochorus *FGrHist* 328 F 112)

80. The social memory of the inhabitants of Phyle who allegedly saved Adrastus and probably escorted him to King Theseus after his chariot crashed at Harma (Philochorus *FGrHist* 328 F 113) appears to be a good example of such a bottom-up development. Such local memories could be brought into the polis-wide discourse by the tragic poets (the episode might have been mentioned in Aeschylus' *Eleusinians*) or by speakers in the assembly. That this village received ἰσοπολιτεία from the Argives suggests that this social memory became politically relevant at some point before Philochorus' time. Cf. Gawantka (1975) 93–94 note 7, 220.

81. See the earlier discussion of Euripides' innovation concerning the ashes of the Argives (Eur. *Supp.* 1185–88).

82. This myth happens to be the first of Theseus' deeds mentioned by Plutarch to support his characterization of Theseus as "another Heracles" (Plut. *Thes.* 29.3).

83. We do not know which of Heracles' deeds serves as a basis of his claim. Nor is it entirely clear whether the acts ascribed to Theseus (σπονδαί) and Heracles (ἀπέδωκε νεκρούς) are seen merely as very similar or as identical, as Mills (1997) 232 and Jacoby *FGrHist* 3b (Suppl.) i.442 sug-

This passage shows Theseus as πρῶτος εὑρητής of σπονδαί and explicitly links his act as *Kulturstifter* (even linguistically) to the peaceful resolution of the conflict (πείσας καὶ σπεισάμενος) that featured in Aeschylus' *Eleusinians*, our earliest testimony of this myth.[84] These connections do not prove that the peaceful version of Theseus' intervention originated ca. 510–500 BC, but they make it seem more likely.

Second, in the myth of the burial of the Seven, just as in the new episodes of the cycle, Theseus emerges not only as a civilizing force but also as a unifier of Attica.[85] The association of Theseus with the old Eleusinian tradition makes it unmistakably clear that Eleusis was under the Athenian king's jurisdiction and thus an integral part of the Athenian state.[86]

Third, another aspect of this myth seems to be a reflection of the political constellation during the last decade of the sixth century. Many of our sources, including Aeschylus' *Eleusinians*, lay much emphasis on Adrastus' status as suppliant.[87] In 519, the Athenians accepted the supplication of the Plataeans and agreed to offer them protection against the overbearing Thebans (Hdt. 6.108). It is quite likely, therefore, that the form and appeal of this mythical episode, which we can first grasp in Aeschylus' tragedy, was also influenced by this recent historical experience.

How do we have to imagine the process whereby Theseus became associated with the tombs in Eleusis? It is conceivable that Theseus' new feat first emerged in poetry and found its way into the *Theseid* in the late sixth century.[88] Alternatively, the Eleusinians might have introduced Theseus into their traditional story due to his rising popularity.

If we compare the prominent role Theseus played in this myth to the extant references in the funeral orations and assembly speeches, it is truly striking that Theseus himself is never mentioned.[89] This does not mean, however, that fourth-century Athenians had forgotten about Theseus' role in this endeavor.

---

gest. *P Oxy.* 1241 col. iii.12–28 similarly connects both Theseus and Heracles with the Greek custom of recovering the fallen after battle. This papyrus seems to refer to the bellicose version, though. Cf. Jacoby *FGrHist* 3b (Suppl.) ii.349.

84. It cannot be ruled out that the identification of Theseus as πρῶτος εὑρητής of σπονδαί was made later by the Sophists (cf. Jacoby *FGrHist* 3b (Suppl.) i.442) or the Atthidographers. It is sufficient for my argument, however, that Theseus' act of recovering the dead under a truce could be seen as on a par with a comparable feat of Heracles.

85. Cf. G. Anderson (2003) 141.

86. The emphatic claim of Herodotus' Athenians that the Seven were buried "in our own land in Eleusis" (τῆς ἡμετέρης ἐν'Ελευσῖνι, Hdt. 9.27.3) might be a late reflection of the original emphasis on this fact.

87. See the following section.

88. Mills (1997) 232; Jacoby *FGrHist* 3b (Suppl.) i.444.

89. Cf. the oratorical references in the funeral orations (Lys. 2.7–10; Pl. *Menex.* 239b; Dem. 60.8) and in diplomatic contexts (Isoc. 14.53–55; Xen. *Hell.* 6.5.47).

Nor did they deliberately try to suppress it.[90] Just as in the case of the Athenian memory of the Plataean merits during the Persian Wars, it is a matter of context and occasion.[91] It was a democratic convention of the funeral oration to ascribe the ancestors' noble deeds to the Athenian demos as a whole and not to individual leaders.[92] Consequently, it is not surprising that speakers in the assembly followed this democratic practice and alluded to this mythical paradigm in the form most familiar to their audience. In other contexts, however, Theseus is well given his due, as is evident from Euripidês' *Suppliants,* one of Isocrates' display speeches (Isoc. 10.31), and Xenophon's *Memorablia,* where Socrates mentions, among other ancestral achievements found in the funeral orations, "all the wars waged in the days of Theseus" (Xen. *Mem.* 3.5.10), which is undoubtedly a reference to the Amazonomachy and the burial of the Seven.[93] Artistic representations, monuments, cults, the tragic performances, and local traditions thus complemented the "official" polis tradition perpetuated by the funeral oration and played an important role in transmitting the memory of Theseus' noble deed to younger generations of Athenians.[94]

Athens' Aid for Suppliants

In the previous section, I explored Theseus' role in the Eleusinian tradition of the burial of the Seven and argued that his association with this mythical episode probably dates to the last decade of the sixth century and is best understood in the context of his emergence as the Athenian version of the great Greek culture hero Heracles: Theseus rivals Heracles as πρῶτος εὑρητής of σπονδαί. He buries the Seven in Eleusis, which, after Cleisthenes' tribal reform, was seen as an integral part of Attica. Theseus' aid for Adrastus, the helpless suppliant, also recalls the Athenians' experience with the Plataeans who (in 519 BC) sought protection against the overbearing Thebans. It is this latter aspect of this episode that I will discuss next. I will make the case that Adrastus' act of supplication was a vital part of this myth and reflects both the Athenians' historical experience of suppliants (e.g., the Plataeans) and their role in Athenian hegemonic ideology and imagination. If we want to assess properly the emotive

90. Loraux (1986) 65–66 claims unconvincingly that the Athenian democracy tried to suppress the memory of Theseus' role in the paradigmatic myths of the funeral orations. Innumerous artistic representations of Theseus' deeds on fifth-century public monuments and Attic pottery demonstrate Theseus' continued popularity; cf. Castriota (1992). His appearances on the tragic stage show how easily he could be integrated into democratic ideology. See, in particular, Eur. *Supp.* 114, 293, 349–57, 404–8, 429–55; Mills (1997) 97–128.

91. See "Remembering the Plataeans" in chapter 2, 127–42.

92. Loraux (1986) 52; R. Thomas (1989) 213–16; Todd (2008) 213.

93. R. Thomas (1989) 212.

94. On the representation of this myth in the visual arts, see the following section.

power of this mythical paradigm when used in diplomatic discourse, we have to look beyond the brief accounts of this episode in the funeral orations and take other carriers of this collective memory into account as well. The ritual act of Adrastus' supplication of Theseus was displayed in detail on the tragic stage in Aeschylus' *Eleusinians* and Euripides' *Suppliants* and provided the focal point for numerous artistic representations of this myth.

Various scholars have connected this mythical episode to the Athenian-Plataean alliance of 519.[95] Both cases show obvious parallels concerning the triangular relationship between the overbearing Thebans, their victims (Adrastus and the Plataeans, respectively), and the sympathetic Athenians. However, the similarities do not end there. According to Herodotus (6.108), the Plataeans, "being hard pressed by the Thebans" (πιεζεύμενοι ὑπὸ Θηβαίων, Hdt. 6.108.2), eventually went to Athens, and "while the Athenians were offering sacrifice to the Twelve Gods, the Plataeans sat down at the altar as suppliants [ἱκέται ἱζόμενοι ἐπὶ τὸν βωμόν] and gave themselves over to the Athenians [ἐδίδοσαν σφέας αὐτούς]"(Hdt. 6.108.4).[96]

What is remarkable about this scene is that, according to Herodotus, the alliance resulted not from a normal diplomatic request addressed to the Athenian government or assembly but from the religious act of supplication.[97] Supplications (ἱκετεῖαι) occurred in many forms in Greek culture and are already attested in Homer.[98] Naiden describes this ritual as a four-step process.[99] First, the suppliant (ἱκέτης) approaches the person or altar they are supplicating. Second, they use a distinctive gesture—such as clasping knees, hands, or chin; falling low; or displaying a suppliant's bough (ἱκετηρία)—to identify themselves as suppliants. Third, they make their request, which can involve sparing their lives, protection against a pursuer, acceptance into the community, or aid in

95. Cf. Stupperich (1977) 231–32; Castriota (1992) 71; Mills (1997) 232; Grethlein (2003) 110. Hennig's (1992) attempt to characterize Herodotus' account of the Plataeans' supplication as a wholesale Athenian invention is not convincing. While it is true that recent experiences often revive and inform the memory of earlier events, there are no grounds to question the historicity of the Plataean supplication, let alone the Plataean-Athenian alliance in the late sixth century.

96. Gould (1973) 95 sees an act of ritual submission in the phrase ἐδίδοσαν σφέας αὐτούς. This phrase has led to vigorous debate about the nature of the Athenian-Plataean relations. Hammond (1992) 143–45 made a convincing case that Herodotus describes the conclusion of an alliance and not the forfeiting of Plataea's independence to Athens, as others have claimed.

97. See Aristagoras' attempt to win Spartan support for the Ionian revolt (Hdt. 5.49–51). Aristagoras supplicated King Cleomenes only after regular diplomacy failed.

98. See the comprehensive study of ancient supplication by Naiden (2006) and the seminal article by Gould (1973). Grethlein (2003) 7–15 offers a succinct survey of current religious, sociological, dramaturgical approaches to supplication in Greek history and literature. Gottesman (2006) explores the performance aspect and the symbolic capital involved in supplication.

99. Naiden (2006) 1–170.

obtaining their rights.[100] The final step consists of the response of the person being supplicated. While previous scholars have held the view that supplications were invariably successful (provided that the requirements of the ritual were met), Naiden convincingly argues that acceptance was not automatic; after evaluating the merits of the suppliant's case, the supplicandus could give a positive or negative response.[101] Nevertheless, despite the possibility of rejection, we should not underestimate the enormous pressure that the suppliant's association with the gods exerted on the supplicandus to grant the request.[102]

The similarities between the Plataeans' supplication in Herodotus and Adrastus' plea for help in Apollodorus' mythographical account are particularly striking.[103] Apollodorus reports,

> Adrastus alone was saved by his horse Arion. . . . Having arrived in Athens, he took refuge at the Altar of Pity [ἐπὶ τὸν Ἐλέου βωμὸν κατέφυγε], and placing the suppliant's bough [ἱκετηρίαν θείς], prayed that they bury the dead.[104] (Apollod. *Bibl.* 3.77–79)

Just as the Plataeans did, Adrastus approached the Athenians as suppliant (ἱκετηρίαν θείς) and sat down at the altar in the Athenian agora.[105] One might object that Apollodorus' *Bibliotheca* dates to the Roman imperial period and that Adrastus' association with the altar of Eleos/the Twelve Gods might therefore be a later invention. This is possible, but it seems more likely that Apollodorus drew on a fifth- or fourth-century tradition according to which the supplication took place in the Athenian agora.[106] This was, after all, the place where many suppliants (including the Plataeans) sought refuge in Athens from the late sixth to the fourth centuries.[107] Moreover, since the Athenian king

---

100. In fourth-century Athens, one assembly meeting per year was designated for supplications. In it "anyone who wishes, after placing a suppliant's branch [θεὶς ὁ βουλόμενος ἱκετηρίαν], may speak to the demos about any matter he may wish, whether public or private" (Arist. *Ath. Pol.* 43.6).

101. For a critique of earlier views, see Naiden (2006) 8–18.

102. Cf. Parker (1983) 185.

103. The altar of the Twelve Gods was regarded as the geographical center of Athens, it was located in the middle of the Agora and had been erected under the archonship of Hippias' son Peisistratus in 522/1 (Thuc. 6.54.6). Camp (1992) 40–42 with figs. 23–24.

104. "Placing the suppliant's branch" (ἱκετηρίαν θεῖναι) symbolizes the formal act of supplication of the Athenian demos. Cf. Arist. *Ath. Pol.* 43.6 (see note 100 above); Rhodes (1981) 527–28.

105. Apollodorus' altar of Ἔλεος has been identified with the altar of the Twelve Gods in the Athenian agora. It probably received the name "Altar of Pity" only later (possibly not before the second century BC), because of its function as a place of supplication and sanctuary. Cf. Travlos (1971) 458; Thompson & Wycherley (1972) 135; Stafford (2000) 199–225; Clark (2007) 32 note 7.

106. Aélion (1983) 1:233.

107. For historical supplications at altars in the Athenian agora, see Hdt. 6.108.4; Plut. *Per.* 31.2; Aeschin. 1.61; Lycurg. 93. Cf. Naiden (2006) 174.

resided in the city of Athens, it is plausible that some versions of this story located Adrastus' supplication of Theseus here.[108] The tradition that Adrastus' halted his horses at Colonus Hippius (*Etym. Magn.* s.v. Ἱππία), for instance, fits much better to a supplication in Athens than to one in Eleusis. While traditions might have varied concerning the precise place and circumstances of Adrastus' supplication, Adrastus' status as suppliant is securely attested in many fifth-century sources. The historical experience of the Plataeans' supplication against Theban aggression and the use of Theseus' oldest sanctuary in Athens as a place of asylum for slaves and for those "who were suppliants in any form" (Philochorus *FGrHist* 328 F 177) make it seem likely that Adrastus' supplication of Theseus was already an integral part of this myth at the end of the sixth century.[109]

To appreciate fully what Adrastus' supplication of Theseus meant to the Athenians, we have to turn to its treatment on the tragic stage, where it played a crucial role both in Euripides' *Suppliants* and, in all likelihood, already in Aeschylus' *Eleusinians.*[110] Aeschylus' tragedy was part of a trilogy about the Argive expedition against Thebes. The *Eleusinians,* which dealt with the recovery of the fallen Argives, was presumably preceded by the *Argive Women* (Ἀργεῖαι), in which the mothers of the Seven received the news of the death of their sons.[111] The third play of this trilogy might have been the *Nemea* (in the first position) or the *Epigoni* (in the third position).[112] Unfortunately, the date of this trilogy is not attested, but based on dramaturgical arguments, it seems clear that it was composed before Aeschylus' *Seven against Thebes,* which was performed in 467.[113] The *terminus post quem* for the production of the *Eleusinians*

108. Aélion (1983) 1:233.

109. The town Theseion, which existed already at the time of Peisistratus (Arist. *Ath. Pol.* 15.4) and which later—under Cimon—received the hero's bones (Plut. *Thes.* 36.4), was located near the Agora. Cf. Herter (1939) 289; Kearns (1989) 168–69; Harding (2008) 187. For the likely location, see Travlos (1971) 576–79 with fig. 722.

110. Many of the extant fifth-century tragedies either were structured around supplications (Aesch. *Supp.*; Eur. *Supp., Heracl.*) or contained supplication scenes (Aesch. *Eum;* Eur. *Med., HF, Andr., Hel.*; Soph. *OC*). For supplication in Greek tragedy, see Grethlein (2003).

111. The title Ἀργεῖαι, recorded by Harpocration s.v. χλῆδος and Hesychius s.v. ἀπόσκημμα, is favored by Mette (1963) 39–40, Gantz (1980) 158–59, and Lamari (2009) 415. Radt *TrGF* iii.133–34 and von Wilamowitz-Moellendorff (1899) 191 opt for the title Ἀργεῖοι (*Argive Men*), which is attested by the catalogue of Aeschylus' plays (Aeschylus T 78 Radt) and by *Etym. magn.* s.v. Ἐνηλύσια.

112. The *Nemea* probably featured an aetiological account of the foundation of the Nemean games by Adrastus, and the *Epigoni* probably featured the more successful campaign of the sons of the Seven. The order *Nemea, Argive Women/Men,* and *Eleusinians* is favored by von Wilamowitz-Moellendorff (1899) 191 and Mette (1963) 38–41. For the order *Argive Women/Men, Eleusinians,* and *Epigoni,* see Gantz (1980) 158–59; Aélion (1983) 1:233.

113. Aesch. *Sept.* contains a lengthy description of the individual Argive and Theban leaders but surprisingly does not feature the actual battle. This makes sense, if we suppose that an account of this battle was already included in the *Argive Women* or the *Eleusinians* and that Aeschylus refrained from repeating it. Moreover, Eur. *Supp.* 846–55 contains a general critique of such a battle

is even more speculative. It seems to fit best to an increased interest in Theseus after the ceremonial return of his bones from Scyros to Athens by Cimon in 475 BC.[114]

It is notoriously difficult to reconstruct a lost play based on its title and a few fragments. Yet, in the case of Aeschylus' *Eleusinians,* we are in a fairly good position to determine at least the basic outline of this tragedy. In his account of Theseus' aid for Adrastus, Plutarch explicitly juxtaposes Aeschylus' *Eleusinians* and Euripides' *Suppliants* (Plut. *Thes.* 29.4–5). In his eyes, the main difference between the two tragedies lies in the means with which Theseus accomplishes the recovery of the bodies. Euripides has Theseus conquer the Thebans in battle. In the *Eleusinans,* however, Theseus recovers the dead by persuasion and by concluding a truce (πείσας καὶ σπεισάμενος). Plutarch adds, presumably still referring to Aeschylus' tragedy, that the leaders of the Argives were buried in Eleusis and that this was a favor that Theseus granted Adrastus.[115] We thus have Theseus and Adrastus as the main characters in this play. The title Ἐλευσίνιοι suggests that the chorus consisted of Eleusinian men and that the *dramatis locus* was Eleusis.[116] Based on the available evidence, the outline of Aeschylus' *Eleusinians* can be tentatively reconstructed as follows: In the opening scene, Adrastus, accompanied by Argive suppliants, encounters the chorus of Eleusinian men, who send for their king, Theseus.[117] Adrastus reports about the fate of the Seven and implores the Eleusinians and Theseus to aid him in the recovery of the fallen.[118] The second part of the play probably contained a messenger report about Theseus' successful negotiations with Thebes and featured the extant line about the progressed putrefaction of the bodies beneath the Cadmea (Aesch. *Eleus.* fr. 53a Radt).[119] The third part doubtlessly featured

description and is probably an allusion to Aeschylus' description. Cf. von Wilamowitz-Moellendorff (1899) 192; Radt *TrGF* iii.175; Aélion (1983) 1:233; Hubbard (1992) 99 note 59. Lamari (2009) adds further (narratological) arguments for the hypothesis that the *Eleusinians* preceded Aesch. *Sept.*

114. Plut. *Thes.* 36; Walker (1995) 55–61. For this dating of the *Eleusinians,* see Hauvette (1898) 170–73; Aélion (1983) 1:233–34; Hubbard (1992) 99; Lamari (2009) 407. Karusu (1972) also favors a date in the late 470s, based on a vase (Athens N.M. 18606) datable just after 470 and illustrating three pairs of suppliant men on altars.

115. Zuntz (1955) 24 note 1; Mette (1963) 40–41.

116. Zuntz (1955) 24 note 1; Mills (1997) 231; Grethlein (2003) 111. That this tragedy was set in Eleusis is further suggested by the existence of the heroön of the Seven and by the fact that Euripides, despite some dramaturgical difficulties, followed Aeschylus in this choice of location. Cf. von Wilamowitz-Moellendorff (1899) 191–92.

117. For a discussion of Adrastus' companions, see below.

118. von Wilamowitz-Moellendorff (1899) 191; Jacoby *FGrHist* 3b (Suppl.) i.448; Mette (1963) 41.

119. This report could have been given by a messenger (Jacoby *FGrHist* 3b (Suppl.) ii.355 note 46) or by Theseus himself after his return (Mette (1963) 40).

the burial of the Seven in Eleusis, probably in the form of a joint lament of the chorus and an actor, as in Aeschylus' *Persians*.[120]

This discussion of the outline of Aeschylus' play enables us to address the long-standing problem of why Aeschylus featured a diplomatic resolution of this conflict, whereas the release of the bodies is enforced in battle in most of our extant sources. Most scholars assume that Aeschylus either inherited the peaceful version altogether or gave it its final form and that the bellicose version was introduced in the early 450s by the author of a funeral speech as the result of the Athenian-Argive alliance and renewed Athenian-Theban hostilities.[121] Considering the multipolarity and dynamic nature of Athenian social memory, manifested, in this case, in the existence of various divergent local myths and cults, which could coexist side by side, it is impossible to pin down the date of origin of either version.[122] In the previous section, I have cautiously suggested that the peaceful version, presenting Theseus as πρῶτος εὑρητής of σπονδαί, might have originated already at the end of the sixth century. Yet, given the Athenians' experience with Thebes before and during Xerxes' invasion, it seems likely that the bellicose version already existed by the time Aeschylus was writing the *Eleusinians*.[123] This raises the question, why did Aeschylus opt for the diplomatic solution? In light of the political circumstances, it was probably not his intention to spare Thebes' honor or to promote an Athenian-Theban rapprochement.[124] There are better explanations for Aeschylus' choice. First, if his trilogy already contained a detailed account of the Argive attack on Thebes, Aeschylus might have preferred to avoid yet another battle description, for

120. Jacoby *FGrHist* 3b (Suppl.) i.448. Based on a reference to funeral speeches in Athenian tragedies (Dion. Hal. *Ant. Rom.* 5.17.4), some scholars have argued that the *Eleusinians* already featured a long funeral speech by Adrastus (like Eur. *Supp.* 857–917). Cf. Hauvette (1898) 167–68; Zuntz (1955) 24 note 1; Aélion (1983) 1:234–35.

121. Von Wilamowitz-Moellendorff (1899) 196; Schroeder (1914) 42–43; Jacoby *FGrHist* 3b (Suppl.) i.446; Walters (1980) 12. Yet Herter (1973) 1209 and Roth (2003) 198 regard the bellicose version as the older one.

122. Cf. R. Thomas (1989) 250; Stupperich (1977) 48; Walters (1980) 13, 22 note 26.

123. In the following sections, I will examine in more detail to what extent the Persian War experience colored the Athenians' collective memory of this mythical episode.

124. Cf. Aélion (1983) 1:233–34; Roth (2003) 198 note 465. Similarly, Herter (1973) 1209, who suggests unconvincingly that Aeschylus altered the older, bellicose version to achieve an "ethisch vertiefte Umgestaltung einer roheren Überlieferung." Mills (1997) 230–1 note 28 is right to point out that even if the Thebans' submission mitigates to some extent their previous outrage, they are still the moral inferiors to Theseus. Aélion (1983) 1:232 tries to extract Aeschylus' presentation of the Thebans from Isoc. 12.168–72. Yet it is problematic to assume that Isocrates blindly followed the *Eleusinians*. It makes more sense to read Isocrates' historical paradigm within his own sociopolitical context, which was quite different from Aeschylus'. Moreover, it is not even clear that the diplomatic solution is flattering to Thebes. Hubbard (1992) 97 note 52, for instance, suggests that Aeschylus perhaps wished "to emphasize Theban cowardice in the wake of Thebes' recent Medism."

dramaturgical reasons.[125] Second, as a native of Eleusis, he probably followed the local tradition attached to the tombs of the Seven. Third, it is possible that Aeschylus (just as in his *Suppliants*) wanted to focus particularly on the plight of suppliants and Athens' selfless attitude toward them; Athenian-Theban relations played thereby only a subordinate role.

The supplication aspect of this myth was nowhere more palpable than on the tragic stage. This is evident from Euripides' *Suppliants,* which was performed between 424 and 420 BC,[126] but it can also be assumed for Aeschylus' *Eleusinians,* if my reconstruction of the outline of the play is correct and if Aeschylus' *Suppliants,* his surviving supplication drama about the Danaids, is any indication.[127] In the *Eleusinians,* Theseus is supplicated by Adrastus, who was probably accompanied by a delegation of Argive men who were either silent suppliants or constituted a secondary chorus.[128]

In comparison to Aeschylus, Euripides further increased the pathos of this story by introducing the grieving mothers of the Seven as the primary chorus. They have accompanied Adrastus to the temple of Demeter and Core in Eleusis in order to supplicate the Athenians. The ritual act of supplication develops in a highly dramatic way before the eyes of the audience and occupies the first quarter of the play. In the opening scene, we see Theseus' mother, Aethra, surrounded by the chorus at the stage altar (32–34, 102–3), and Adrastus is lying at the temple doors, surrounded by a secondary chorus, consisting of the sons of the Seven (21–22, 106–7). Aethra describes how the Argive women, with suppliant branches (ἱκετῆρι θαλλῷ) in their hands, kneel before her and touch her knees (10). Adrastus, in tears and lying prostrate on the ground, urges her to

125. An account of the Argive attack was given either in the preceding *Argive Women,* in Adrastus' supplication of Theseus, or in his funeral speech for the Seven. This battle description (alluded to by Eur. *Supp.* 846–55) can also explain the lack of it in Aesch. *Sept.* Cf. von Wilamowitz-Moellendorff (1899) 192; Radt *TrGF* iii.175; Aélion (1983) 1:233; Hubbard (1992) 99 note 59.

126. Both metrical analysis and considerations of the political background (especially the battle of Delium in 424 BC) point toward this time period. Cf. Collard (1975) 1:8–14; Morwood (2007) 26–30. The former favors 423 BC and the latter 420 BC.

127. The supplication scene in Aesch. *Supp.* occupies more than half of the entire play. See especially Aesch. *Supp.* 347–53, 418–37. Cf. Grethlein (2003) 48.

128. Mette (1963) 41 suggests that Adrastus was the leader of an Argive delegation who had no speaking parts. This seems likely for a number of reasons. Being dressed up in mourning garb and holding suppliant branches, they would have increased the pathos of the scene through their mere presence. Moreover, this dramaturgical device is also known from Aesch. *Eum.* 566–73, where the members of the newly constituted Areopagus council also appear as silent characters. Karusu (1972) 199 goes even further and suggests that the chorus itself consisted of Argive suppliants, six of whom (constituting one half-chorus) were displayed sitting in pairs on three altars on a vase (Athens N.M. 18606). This seems implausible given the title of this play. It might be possible, however, that these Argive suppliants constituted a secondary chorus, attested, for instance, in Aesch. *Eum.* 1032–47 in the form of Athenian women accompanying the departing Eumenides; cf. Pickard-Cambridge (1988) 236–37 for further examples.

entreat her son to recover the dead (24–25). After Aethra's exposition, the women formally supplicate her in the form of a choral song (ἱκετεύω σε, γεραιά, 42; ἱκετεύω σὸν παῖδα, 67). Upon his arrival, his mother informs Theseus about the identity of the suppliants. Adrastus approaches him and claims the status of ἱκέτης of both Theseus and his city (114). After admitting his mistakes in leading the ill-fated expedition against Thebes, he engages in the typical gestures of "total self-abasement"[129]: he falls upon the ground, clasps Theseus' knees, and begs him to take pity on him and on these grieving mothers and bring the bodies back for proper burial (168–75). When Theseus refuses to help, on the grounds that Adrastus has transgressed the will of the gods (229–31), Adrastus already shows signs of resignation (256–62), but the mothers of the Seven make one final plea. They move across the stage, leaving their suppliant branches around Aethra at the altar, cast their hands on Theseus' knees, and touch his chin, entreating him (in dactylic hexameters) to take pity on them and to bring about the burial of their sons (271–85).[130] After seeing his own mother, Aethra, moved to tears and after hearing her arguments for taking on this noble task, Theseus finally rules in favor of the suppliants and promises to advocate their cause in the assembly (346–55).[131]

Watching this dramatic supplication scene, with all its details, unfold on stage, Athenians would have left the theater with a lasting impression of their ancestors' exemplary attitude toward suppliants in the mythical past.[132] Consequently, when individuals or representatives of other *poleis* evoked the example of those Argive suppliants, it is reasonable to assume that their pleas would have had a special resonance with Athenians who had seen tragic performances of this myth. This line of argument presupposes that this myth was produced more than once or twice on stage. There is some evidence to support this view. Theseus' aid for the fallen Argives was probably treated by other playwrights as well. Achaeus, a younger contemporary of Sophocles, produced an *Adrastus* and a *Theseus* (*TrGF* 20 Achaeus T 1, F 1, 18, 18a Snell). Ion, who performed his first tragedy between 451 and 448, wrote the *Argives* (*TrGF* 19 Ion T 1, F 8a, 9, 9a Snell), and a *Suppliants* is attested for Apollodorus, who won his first victory around 380 BC (*TrGF* 64 Apollodorus T 1, 2 Snell).[133] Moreover, Euripides' *Sup-*

129. Gould (1973) 94.

130. According to Naiden (2006) 41, Euripides has considerably elaborated the traditional supplication scene by featuring two supplicandi, a queen and a king, and two subsequent supplications: the women initially supplicate both Aethra and the altar and then Theseus.

131. The current democratic practice of dual evaluation by council and assembly has thus been retrojected by Euripides into the mythical past; cf. Naiden (2006) 176.

132. Cf. A. M. Bowie (1997) 51, who describes the extraordinary effect of the funeral scene in Euripides' play on Athenian spectators.

133. Cf. Grethlein (2003) 109–10.

pliants and Aeschylus' *Eleusinians* were perhaps among the tragedies that were reproduced by actors in the fourth century, either as old tragedies at the City Dionysia or in local reproductions at the Rural Dionysia.[134] Two clues in particular support this hypothesis. First, in his *Panathenaicus*, Isocrates refers to hearing the tragic poets at the Dionysia as the primary source for everybody's knowledge of Adrastus' story (τίς οὐκ ἀκήκοεν τῶν τραγῳδοδιδασκάλων Διονυσίοις, Isoc. 12.168–69).[135] Second, according to Diodorus, the Athenian general Thrasyllus saw a vision in the night before the battle of Arginusae in 406 BC. He dreamed that he and the six other generals were acting Euripides' *Phoenician Women* in the crowded theater of Dionysus in Athens, while their competitors were performing the *Suppliants*. He dreamed that this resulted in a "Cadmean victory" for them and that they all died in imitation of those who made the expedition against Thebes (Diod. 13.97.6). This story is clearly a *vaticinatio ex eventu* that "predicts" the Athenian victory at Arginusae and the subsequent execution of six of the victorious generals for their failure to recover the dead.[136] It most likely reflects a fourth-century tradition that Diodorus found in his source Ephorus. If this is correct, we can view this story as a reflection of the fourth-century practice of actors to reproduce famous fifth-century plays. Given Euripides' popularity, the *Suppliants* might well have been included in the repertoire of troupes of professional actors, as were the actors' plays *Orestes, Phoenician Women,* and *Iphigenia at Aulis.*[137]

The collective memory of Athens' exemplary attitude toward the Argive suppliants was perpetuated not only through tragic performances but also through representations in the visual arts. The three known vase paintings that have been connected to this myth all show a supplication scene. First, a black-figure lekythos (Athens N.M. 18606) features three pairs of men sitting on three altars with suppliant branches in their hands. This vase has been linked by Karusu to Aeschylus' *Eleusinians* and dated to around 470 BC.[138] Second, a cup by the Codrus Painter (Basel Antikenmuseum, Inv. BS 432) shows two figures whose names can be restored as Θ[Η]ΣΕΥΣ and Α[ΡΓ]ΕΙΑ, who might be Polynices' wife, Argeia, daughter of Adrastus, or Argeia as a "representative" Argive suppliant (ca. 430 BC).[139] Third, the Attic red-figure Spina volute krater by the

134. For these two types of reperformances, see "Dramatic Festivals" in chapter 1, 58–65.

135. Since Isoc. 12.168–70 features the peaceful, diplomatic resolution, Isocrates might indeed have had Aeschylus' *Eleusinians* in mind.

136. M. A. Flower (2008) 167–69.

137. Cf. Collard (1975) 1:44 note 177.

138. Karusu (1972). Cf. Hammond & Moon (1978) 378–80 with fig. 11; Mills (1997) 233 note 38; Lamari (2009) 407 note 24. This image could also represent the supplication of the Heraclidae, though.

139. Berger (1968); Beazley (1971) 472; Collard (1975) 1:7.

Painter of Bologna 279 (Spina Ferrara T 579 = ARV^2 i.612) depicts two scenes that continuously merge into one another and belong closely together. The first scene (easily identifiable by Amphiaraus' chariot sinking into the ground) illustrates the Seven against Thebes locked in deadly combat with their Theban counterparts (fig. 2).[140] The second illustration features the sequel of this myth in Athens, as Simon and Castriota have demonstrated (fig. 3).[141] On the extreme right, Adrastus, leaning on a staff, is supplicating Theseus, who stands battle-ready, easily recognizable by the display of the Amazonomachy on his shield.[142] The upper level depicts Athena in the center, favorably contemplating a suppliant branch and flanked by the spirits of the Seven. On the lower level, we see the young Epigoni, like their heroic fathers, holding suppliant branches.

The complex treatment of space on the Spina volute krater shows many features of the pictorial advances attributed to large-scale paintings of the second quarter of the fifth century and strongly suggests that it depends on a monumental prototype. For this reason, many scholars have connected the duel scene on this vase to Onasias' panel painting in the temple of Athena Areia at Plataea.[143] This shrine was built from the spoils of the battle of Plataea (Plut. *Arist.* 20.3) and contained a colossal cult image of Athena by Phidias and two monumental paintings by Polygnotus and Onasias, which were placed on the walls of the pronaos (Paus. 9.4.1–2).[144] According to Pausanias, Onasias' painting depicted "the former expedition of Adrastus and the Argives against Thebes" (Paus. 9.4.2). Castriota has made a convincing case that Onasias' painting featured not only the battle between the Seven and their Theban opponents but also Adrastus' supplication of Theseus and that both scenes served as models for the painter of the Spina volute krater.[145]

In sum, the Athenian aid for the Argive suppliants was a vital element of this myth and served as a focal point for artistic representation on the tragic stage and in the visual arts. Consequently, when judging the emotive force of

140. The preeminent pair in the upper center probably represents Eteocles and Polynices. Cf. Castriota (1992) 69; Tiverios (1981) 153–54.

141. Simon (1963) 54–57; Castriota (1992) 67–70. Krauskopf *LIMC* s.v. Adrastos i.239 dates this volute krater to 475–450 BC; Mills (1997) 233 note 38, to 450–440 BC; and Gauer (1968) 99, to ca. 440 BC.

142. Castriota (1992) 68. Alternatively, Adrastus might be the figure to the right of Athena, as Simon (1963) 54 suggests.

143. Simon (1963) 56; Gauer (1968) 99; E. Thomas (1976) 73; Tiverios (1981) 153; Castriota (1992) 67; Krauskopf *LIMC* s.v. Amphiaraos i.699, 709.

144. For this shrine, see "Memorialization of Thebes' Treason" in chapter 2, 106–13.

145. Castriota (1992) 67–70. Simon (1963) 56–57 argues for a Polygnotan prototype of the supplication scene on the Spina volute crater and locates it in the shrine of Theseus, Peirithous, Oedipus, and Adrastus at Colonus Hippius (Paus. 1.30.4). Yet, given the unity of theme on the Spina volute crater, Castriota's hypothesis seems more convincing. For the significance of this painting as a victory monument over the medizing Thebans, see "Punishment of Theban *Hybris*," 189–96.

Fig. 2. Duels of the Seven before Thebes on the Spina volute krater by the Painter of Bologna 279. (National Archaeological Museum of Ferrara: Spina Ferrara T 579 = ARV^2 i.612. Reproduced by permission of the Italian *Ministero per i Beni e le Attività Culturali.*)

Fig. 3. Adrastus' supplication of Theseus on the Spina volute krater by the Painter of Bologna 279. (National Archaeological Museum of Ferrara: Spina Ferrara T 579 = ARV^2 i.612. Reproduced by permission of the Italian *Ministero per i Beni e le Attività Culturali.*)

appeals to Athens' exemplary attitude toward suppliants, these carriers of social memory ought to be taken into account.

Prostates *of the Greeks*

I have made the case that, by the end of the sixth century, Theseus had become associated with the local myth of the burial of the Seven in Eleusis and that the Athenians' historical experience of accepting the Plataeans as suppliants informed this myth as well. But it was undoubtedly the experience of the Persian Wars and the resultant hegemonic ideology that further shaped this myth and elevated it to one of the four emblematic mythical paradigms in the "official polis tradition"[146] of the funeral oration.

The heroic victories over the Persians at Marathon and during Xerxes' invasion profoundly altered the Athenians' self-image. In Athenian collective memory, these events were much simplified and stripped of their immediate historical contexts; they became symbols of the Athenian character. Marathon, where the Athenians single-handedly repelled the Persian invaders in defense of all the other Greeks, came to epitomize the entirety of the Persian Wars. As a result, the Athenians saw themselves as champions of the Greeks (προστάται τῶν Ἑλλήνων, Lys. 2.57) and believed Athens' hegemony was the natural and well-deserved result of the Persian Wars (Lys. 2.47). Since communities tend to regard their characteristic traits as permanent and unchanging, Athens' new hegemonic ideology also colored the Athenians' view of their distant past and led to the promotion of two selected myths that were seen as mythical prefigurations of Athens' defense of Greece against the barbarian invader.[147] The "marathonized" versions of the battles against the Amazons and Eumolpus' Thracian hordes thus became integral elements of the patriotic Athenian master narrative, as we can grasp it in the public funeral orations.[148]

In the eyes of fifth- and fourth-century Athenians, Athens' role as *prostates* of the Greeks involved the defense of Greek liberty not only against barbarian invaders but also against other Greeks. This is most clearly expressed in Plato's *Menexenus,* where Athens' four paradigmatic mythical exploits (Eumolpus, Amazons, help for Argives and Heraclidae) are introduced with the phrase "the Athenians believed they should fight for freedom both against Greeks on behalf of Greeks and against barbarians on behalf of all the Greeks" (Pl. *Menex.* 239b). That the protection of Greek liberty against both barbarian invaders and Greek

146. R. Thomas (1989) 208.

147. Gehrke (2001) 302; Gotteland (2001) 129; Mills (1997) 58; R. Thomas (1989) 207–8; Castriota (1992); Harding (2008) 66.

148. For a more detailed discussion, see "Funeral Orations" in chapter 1, 49–58.

oppressors are really two sides of the same coin is also evident from Lysias' characterization of the period of Athens' undisputed hegemony: no triremes sailed out of Asia, no tyrant established himself in Greece, and no Greek polis was enslaved by the barbarians (Lys. 2.57).

Athens' role as protector against Greek oppressors is nowhere more manifest than in the myths of Athens' aid for suppliants. It is not surprising, therefore, that after the Persian Wars, the stories of the Athenian aid for the Heraclidae and Theseus' intervention for the fallen Argives became emblematic for the Athenian character and were celebrated as mythical prefigurations of this aspect of Athens' self-image as *prostates* of the Greeks.[149] In Isocrates' *Panegyricus,* both of these myths are explicitly narrated under the category ἱκετεῖαι (Isoc. 4.54).

The basic outline of the myth of Theseus' aid for Adrastus probably existed already at the end of the sixth century.[150] Yet, if the "marathonization" of earlier versions of Theseus' Amazonomachy is any indication,[151] it is very likely that this collective memory was also considerably reshaped under the influence of Athens' new hegemonic ideology. Judging from the extant funeral orations and other patriotic genres, this myth came to embody many aspects of the hegemonic Athenian self-image known from the idealized Persian War narrative: Athens' unique sense of justice and altruism, its defense of the Greek *nomos,* and its military power.

According to their own beliefs, the Athenians exercised their hegemony in an entirely selfless manner, driven by an innate sense of justice.[152] This idea of Athenian justice and altruism permeates the idealized Persian War narrative,[153] but it also informed the collective memory of Athens' burial of the Seven. Isocrates prefaced this mythical paradigm by proclaiming that the Athenians have "at all times, without ceasing, offered their city as a common refuge and as a champion to those of the Greeks who were being wronged [τοῖς ἀδικουμένοις]" (Isoc. 4.52) and "come to the aid of the weaker even contrary

149. Cf. Kierdorf (1966) 90–93; Stupperich (1977) 47, 229; Loraux (1986) 67–68; R. Thomas (1989) 298.

150. There is some indication that the myth of the Athenian aid to the Heraclidae was also not a wholesale invention of the postwar area. Even though the first reference to the children of Heracles in Attica is found in Pherecydes (*FGrHist* 3 F 84), their persecution by Eurystheus was already known to Hecataeus (*FGrHist* 1 F 30). Moreover, competing local traditions seemed to have played an important part in the development of this polis-wide myth as well; cf. Allan (2001) 24–27.

151. See "Funeral Orations" in chapter 1, 54–56.

152. Walters (1980) 5. This claim is linked to the autochthonous origin of the Athenian race; cf. Lys. 2.17.

153. Cf. Lysias' account of Marathon: the Persians deliberately attacked Athens first, because they knew that "if they attacked any other polis, they would be fighting both with its inhabitants and with the Athenians, because the Athenians would eagerly come to the rescue of those who were being wronged [τοῖς ἀδικουμένοις]" (Lys. 2.22).

to [their] own self-interest [παρὰ τὸ συμφέρον] rather than join the stronger in oppressing others for [their] own advantage" (Isoc. 4.53). In a similar vein, Lysias emphasized that Athens' war against Thebes' for the recovery of the fallen Argives was entirely justified. The Athenians first sent heralds to secure the burial by diplomatic means (Lys. 2.7).[154] Only after the repeated Theban refusal did they march against Thebes, even though they had no previous quarrel with the Cadmeans and were not driven by any desire to gratify the Argives (2.8). Justice (τὸ δίκαιον) was their ally, and even in victory, they showed restraint (2.10).[155]

In their own eyes, the Athenians were the protectors not only of Greek liberty but of all aspects of the Greek *nomos*.[156] Consequently, according to the Athenian master narrative, the Athenians intervened on behalf of the dead Argives in order to enforce the Greek cultural norm of providing proper burial for fallen soldiers. This norm is referred to by Lysias as τὰ νομιζόμενα (Lys. 2.8), πάτριος τιμή, Ἑλληνικὸς νόμος, and κοινὴ ἐλπίς (Lys. 2.9);[157] by Isocrates as παλαιὸν ἔθος and πάτριος νόμος (Isoc. 4.55); by Demosthenes as τὰ τῶν κατοιχομένων νόμιμα (Dem. 60.8); and by Euripides as νόμιμά τε πάσης Ἑλλάδος (Eur. *Supp.* 311), πάσης Ἑλλάδος κοινὸν τόδε (*Supp.* 538), and τὸν Πανελλήνων νόμον (*Supp.* 526, 671).

The Athenians viewed their victories over the numerically superior Persians first and foremost as a manifestation of their military prowess. It is not surprising, therefore, that the Athenians' military ἀρετή is the central element of the chauvinistic master narrative of the funeral oration and is used, like a red thread, to connect the individual Athenian exploits. Its praise is also particularly fitting for the occasion, a state funeral for the recently fallen.[158] Consequently, in the *epitaphios*' version, the Athenians recover the bodies of the Seven by defeating the Thebans in battle (Lys. 2.10; Pl. *Menex.* 239b; Dem. 60.8).[159] This myth thus has become yet another paradigm for Athens' military superiority.[160] According to Isocrates, the two supplication myths illustrate both Athens' noble character

154. The same course of action is found in Eur. *Supp.* 346–48, 382–94.

155. Similarly, in Eur. *Supp.* 328, Aethra calls Theseus' intervention on behalf of the fallen Argives a just endeavor (σὺν δίκῃ σ' ὁρμώμενον), and Eur. *Supp.* 723–25 emphasizes Theseus' restraint after the victorious battle.

156. See, for instance, the Athenians' programmatic statements about the fight against the Persians in Hdt. 8.143–44. Cf. Walters (1980) 10–12; Loraux (1986) 67.

157. In light of Isocrates' πάτριος νόμος (Isoc. 4.55), I take πάτριος τιμή (Lys. 2.9) as "ancestral honor." Todd's rendering of the phrase as "the honour due to their fathers" (Todd (2008) 171) is unwarranted, since the children of the Seven are not explicitly mentioned in Lysias' *epitaphios*.

158. Loraux (1986) 68.

159. In Lys. 2.10, we find another clue for the "marathonization" of this myth, that is, an echo of the "few against many" *topos:* "acquiring many enemies [πολλοὺς μὲν πολεμίους κτώμενοι], but with justice as their ally, they conquered in battle."

160. Cf. Loraux (1986) 69; Walters (1980) 12.

and its power (ῥώμη, Isoc. 4.54). The latter manifests itself not only in its victory over the Thebans but also in the very fact that Adrastus chose to approach Athens: since, as Isocrates claims, suppliants always seek help from those whom they consider the most powerful, it follows that at that time, Athens was already seen as ἡγεμών and προστάτης of the Greeks (Isoc. 4.57).[161]

Punishment of Theban Hybris

As we have seen, after the Persian Wars, the mythical story of the Athenian burial of the Seven came to symbolize many aspects of Athens' hegemonial self-image: Athens' unique sense of justice and altruism, its concern for the Greek *nomos,* and its military ἀρετή. Yet these traits could be expressed by other Athenian myths as well.[162] There is one particular reason why this collective memory became one of the four emblematic myths of the Athenian master narrative: it was the city of Thebes, the anti-Athens, which committed this outrage against the dead and received its just punishment from the hands of the Athenians.

We have seen, in chapter 2, that in Athenian historical consciousness, Thebes became Athens' counterimage as a result of the Persian War experience. While the Athenians rejected Xerxes' offer, abandoned their city, and fought selflessly as champions of Greek liberty, the Thebans, motivated by ruthless self-interest, collaborated with the Persians and betrayed their obligations to the common Greek cause.[163] When one bears in mind that the cause of defeating and punishing the Persians for their desecration of Greek temples was touted as a sacred obligation,[164] then it is evident that Thebes' medism had a religious dimension as well: it was a transgression against the gods and the Greek *nomos.*[165] In light of these considerations, the story of the Athenian burial of the fallen Argives was ideally suited to serve as a mythical analogue for the Athenians' victory over the medizing Thebans in the battle of Plataea. In both cases, the Thebans committed an act of *hybris* and were punished by the Athenians.

It is not surprising, therefore, that the funeral orations heavily emphasized Thebes' transgression. Lysias and Demosthenes characterized the Theban refusal to grant burial to the Seven as offense against the dead (Lys. 2.7; Dem. 60.8), as ὕβρις (Lys. 2.9; Dem. 60.8), and as ἀσέβεια against the gods (Lys. 2.7, 10). Similarly, in Euripides' *Suppliants,* Thebes' behavior is repeatedly characterized as ὕβρις by the Argive chorus (*Supp.* 463–64, 511–12, 631–33), The-

161. See also Eur. *Supp.* 184–89.
162. Cf. Athens' exemplary treatment of the Danaids in Aesch. *Supp.*
163. See, in particular, "Treacherous by Nature" in chapter 2, 143–49.
164. See, for instance, the Athenian response to Mardonius' peace offer (Hdt. 8.143–44).
165. Castriota (1992) 67.

seus (*Supp.* 575), the messenger (Eur. *Supp.* 726–30) and finally by Adrastus, who gives the following verdict about the Thebans: "the malevolent people of Cadmus committed *hybris* upon *hybris,* and perished in turn" (*Supp.* 743–44). Unlike their Theban counterimage, the Athenians display extraordinary piety in this episode.[166] They have no ulterior motives. Seeing "that the gods below were not receiving their dues, and that an act of impiety was being committed against the gods above because sacred rites were being polluted" (Lys. 2.7), the Athenians intervene to provide a burial for the fallen and to thus uphold the Greek *nomos.*[167]

In all extant funeral orations, the Athenians recover the dead not through persuasion but after defeating the hubristic Thebans in battle. This makes sense if one thinks of this myth as a mythical analogue for the Athenian victory over the Theban medizers in the battle of Plataea. There is further evidence for this particular connection: probably in the late 460s or 450s, the temple of Athena Areia at Plataea, which was erected as a memorial of this very battle, received a monumental painting depicting the Seven against Thebes and most likely also Theseus' supplication by Adrastus and the Epigoni, which probably served as model for the Spina volute krater (figs. 2 and 3).[168]

I have used the terms *Athenian master narrative* and *official polis tradition* to describe those collective memories that were shared by the entire polis community and propagated in the public funeral orations, on the tragic stage, or by other polis-wide carriers of social memory.[169] Yet it is important to keep in mind that even the collective memories that became a part of the official polis tradition were not static. As I have tried to show throughout this chapter, in the case of the myth of the burial of the Seven, we find clues for continuous reshaping and reworking during the archaic and classical periods, which led to a variety of different versions inside and outside of Attica and to a conglomerate of interrelated layers of meaning in the Athenian master narrative of the funeral orations. While the basic outline of this myth—Theseus, supplicated by Adrastus, somehow recovers the fallen Argives and buries them in Eleusis—probably existed by the end of the sixth century, it was the Persian War experience and

166. Flower & Marincola (2002) 155.

167. For the religious implications of the withheld burial, see Parker (1983) 145; Todd (2008) 219.

168. Castriota (1992) 63–73. Cf. Flower & Marincola (2002) 28–29, and see "Athens' Aid for Suppliants" above, 182–86. A second painting by Polygnotus featured Odysseus having slain the suitors and thus also presented the punishment of the Theban medizers in mythical guise; cf. Castriota (1992) 73–76, and see "Memorialization of Thebes' Treason" in chapter 2, 106–13.

169. For the terms, see, respectively, Forsdyke (2005) 242; R. Thomas (1989) 208. Cf. "Festivals and Public Commemorations" in chapter 1, 49–69.

the resultant hegemonic ideology that made this particular myth resonate with the Athenians and turned it into one of the four myths celebrated in the *epitaphios* as emblematic for the Athenian character. As a synchronic survey of the funeral orations, Isocrates' *Panegyricus*, Euripides' *Suppliants*, and material carriers of this social memory has shown, this myth could express Athens' exemplary attitude toward suppliants, its unique sense of justice and altruism, its military power, its piety and concern for the Greek *nomos*, and its just punishment of Theban *hybris*. It could be viewed as a mythic prefiguration of the Plataeans' supplication and the victory over the medizing Thebans in the battle of Plataea.

Yet even though the catalogue of deeds in the *epitaphios* was conventional, there was enough leeway for the authors of each funeral oration to add, elaborate, downplay, or omit certain elements of this collective memory, depending on present attitudes and concerns. Lysias, for instance, places heavy emphasis on the religious obligation to bury the fallen, while the supplication aspect is rather underdeveloped.[170] In Plato's *Menexenus*, this myth is summed up by the claim that the Athenians "defended the Argives against the Cadmeans" (Pl. *Menex.* 239b), whereas Demosthenes focuses on the enforcing of the customary burial rites and does not mention the Argives at all (Dem. 60.8).

While this myth could convey all these interrelated layers of meaning, there were various events during the Pentecontaetia and the Peloponnesian War that brought individual aspects of this myth into the forefront of Athenian public discourse. Around 460 BC, Athens concluded an alliance with Argos (Thuc. 1.102.4), and the Athenians were supported by the Argives in their adventurist campaigns in Boeotia, where they faced the Thebans twice in battle, at Tanagra and Oenophyta, around 458 (Thuc. 1.107–8). The Argives who fell at Tanagra received the unusual honor of a monumental tomb in the *demosion sema* in Athens (M&L 35; Paus. 1.29.8).[171] The parallels between the historical situation of 458 and the story of the Athenian burial of the fallen Argives are so obvious (especially the diplomatic constellation: Athens and Argos against Thebes) that scholars have suggested that the bellicose version of this myth was developed and found its way into the *epitaphios* around this time.[172] Undoubtedly, in the aftermath of Tanagra and Oenophyta, the anti-Theban elements of this myth must have been particularly welcome to the listeners of the funeral orations.

170. The presence of Argive suppliants is only mentioned once in passing in Lys. 2.9.

171. Cf. Clairmont (1983) 136–38. Walters (1980) 12 with note 29 suggests that these Argives shared in the encomium as well; cf. Walters (1978).

172. Walters (1980) 12–13; Loraux (1986) 67–69 uses these parallels to date the institution of the *epitaphios* itself to the early 450s. For other dates, see "Funeral Orations" in chapter 1, 50. That the "pacifist" version of this myth existed before 460 BC is proven by Aeschylus' *Eleusinians*, which can be dated to 475–467; cf. "Athens' Aid for Suppliants" above, 177–78.

But there is no cogent reason to connect the origin of the bellicose version to the events of 460–458, since there were plenty of earlier occasions to increase the anti-Theban tendencies of this myth. Herodotus reports that the Athenians came frequently into conflict with Thebes after accepting the Plataeans' supplication (Hdt. 6.108). In 506 BC, the Athenians achieved a glorious victory over the Boeotians and Chalcidians, which they memorialized by dedicating a chariot on the Acropolis; the inscribed monument was destroyed by the Persians but later restored and known to Herodotus (M&L 15; Hdt. 5.77). Moreover, as I have argued above, the Athenians' experience with the Thebans during Xerxes' invasion was suitable to transform this myth into a mythical prefiguration of the victory over the hubristic Thebans in the battle of Plataea. For these reasons, Castriota seems correct in asserting that by the 450s, this myth "would have addressed a complex range of actualities"[173] resulting from the long-standing Athenian-Theban antagonism.

The issue of ensuring a proper burial for the fallen Argives (whether by force or persuasion) was certainly an essential part of this myth from early on. It is the very reason for Adrastus' supplication of Theseus. It featured in Aeschylus' *Eleusinians* (ca. 475–467 BC) and is mentioned by Herodotus' Athenians (Hdt. 9.27.3).[174] Thebes' refusal to grant burial to the Seven was probably already emphasized after the Persian War to highlight Thebes' *hybris* and its just punishment. But it seems clear that this aspect of the myth received yet another boost in 424, when the Theban-led Boeotians did not allow the Athenians to recover their fallen after the battle of Delium (Thuc. 4.97–101).[175] This is evident from Euripides' treatment of this myth, which, as most scholars agree, was prompted by the Theban action at Delium.[176] Euripides' *Suppliants* not only criticizes the Thebans for their refusal to release the bodies of the Seven but, in addition, increases the anti-Theban aspects of this myth in various ways.[177] The Thebans are shown as proactive in their wickedness. They send a herald to order the Athenians not to admit Adrastus into their country and, if he is already there, to "break the sacred spell of suppliant boughs and drive him from

173. See Castriota (1992) 65–73 on Onasias' painting of the Seven and Adrastus' supplication of Theseus in the temple of Athena Areia at Plataea. Quotation at 71.

174. The putrefaction of the bodies beneath the Cadmea is even mentioned in one of the fragments of this play (Aesch. *Eleus.* fr. 53a Radt).

175. The Boeotians accused the Athenians of having violated the temple at Delium and made the Athenian withdrawal from Delium a precondition for the release of the Athenian bodies. For a discussion of the Athenian-Theban exchange in Thuc. 4.97–99, see Hornblower (1996) 308–17 with further literature.

176. Collard (1975) 1:10; Hornblower (1996) 309. For an in-depth treatment of the similarities and differences between the events at Delium and the plot of the play, see A. M. Bowie (1997).

177. For the repeated characterization of Thebes' behavior as ὕβρις (Eur. *Supp.* 463–64, 511–12, 575, 631–33, 726–30, 743–44), see the discussion above.

[this] land" (Eur. *Supp.* 467–71). In his insolence, this herald asks to speak to the tyrant of this land (*Supp.* 399), characterizes the Athenian form of government as the rule of a mob (ὄχλος, *Supp.* 411), and then delivers a praise of tyranny. In the ensuing *agon,* Theseus and the Theban herald propound the respective merits of democracy and tyranny. In this dispute, just as in all other respects of this play, Thebes emerges as a true anti-Athens on the tragic stage (*Supp.* 399–464).[178] In the decisive battle, Theseus emerges as the superior general, and the Thebans are resoundingly beaten (*Supp.* 650–720). Unlike the Thebans after defeating the Seven, Theseus shows restraint in victory; recovering the bodies of the fallen Argives is his only concern (*Supp.* 720–30). Not surprisingly, the play also ends on a decidedly anti-Theban note. Athena predicts to the sons of the Seven that they will sack the city of Thebes and exact vengeance for the blood of their fathers (*Supp.* 1213–26). This reminder of Thebes' destruction by the Epigoni must have been pleasing to the Athenian audience, who had just suffered a crushing defeat from the hands of their Theban archrivals. Collard's characterization of this tragedy is right to the point.

> [Euripides] wrote his play in a deliberately patriotic gesture; by emphasising the mythical Theban crime he obscured any memory of Athens' recent sacrilege, and in Theseus' glorious victory the bitterness of the historical defeat.[179]

The Athenians' bitter experience with the Thebans at Delium affected the treatment of this myth not only on the tragic stage but also in the visual arts. In all likelihood, this myth was displayed on the west frieze of the famous temple of Athena Nike, situated beside the entrance to the Acropolis. The frieze can be dated to the late 420s on stylistic grounds.[180] The principal theme of this temple was victory. The roof contained ten Nike figures, one for each Athenian tribe.[181] The east pediment featured the gods' victory over the Giants, and the west pediment featured the Amazonomachy. The east frieze showed an assembly of gods,

178. Cf. Zeitlin (1990).

179. Collard (1975) 1:10 note 32. Similarly, Angus Bowie (1997) 51 views the dramatic "replay" of Delium as a "mythical/theatrical 'rectification' of recent events." In this play, Euripides' exploitation and further development of another aspect of this myth indicates his concern for the present. At the end of the play, Athena makes the Argives take an oath (in return for Athens' labor) to never invade Attica and to prevent other armies from doing so (Eur. *Supp.* 1185–95). In this way, Euripides may have been suggesting wishfully an Athenian-Argive alliance, which indeed (though on different terms) materialized in 420 BC. See Zuntz (1955) 75; Collard (1975) 1:10–11.

180. E. B. Harrison (1997) 109. The temple itself probably belonged to the Periclean building program, but work was stopped in 432, before its completion; cf. Hurwit (2004) 182–83.

181. Hurwit (2004) 184.

and the south frieze showed the battle of Marathon.[182] Even though most of the fragments are badly damaged, making exact identifications difficult, it is generally agreed that the north and west friezes depicted Athenians fighting other Greeks.[183]

Based on a thorough stylistic analysis of the fragments, Evelyn Harrison has recently offered a convincing reading of the frieze's overall program.[184] The divine assembly on the east frieze consists of the gods and goddesses named as guarantors of the Ephebic Oath, while the other three sides illustrate the ancestors' paradigmatic achievements to be emulated by Athenian soldiers.[185] The south frieze depicts the battle of Marathon, and the north frieze almost certainly depicts the pursuit and capture of Eurystheus during the battle for the Heraclidae, as portrayed in Euripides' tragedy (Eur. *Heracl.* 843–63).[186] The west frieze features Greek warriors attempting to lift up naked dead bodies while being attacked by other Greeks (fig. 4). Considering the overall program of the frieze, Harrison's identification of this scene as the battle between the Athenians and the Thebans over the bodies of the fallen Argives must, therefore, be correct.[187] The action reads from left to right and illustrates, in successive scenes, the act of rescuing the dead against enemy opposition. On the far left, on slab h, an Athenian tries to lift one of the dead Argives while a Theban tries to prevent him. In the second scene, also on slab h, he lets go of the body and fights the Theban on equal terms. On slab i, the Athenian (perhaps Theseus) then overpowers his Theban opponent in front of the trophy that the Thebans had erected earlier, after defeating the Seven. The rest of slab i shows the pursuit of an enemy. On the next marble slab, slab k, we see the successful recovery of the fallen. In the final scene, also on slab k, two Athenians defeat a pair of Thebans, and at the corner (l), a third Athenian blocks the approach of another Theban who advances to their aid.

If Harrison's persuasive reading is correct, then Thebes' hubristic refusal to release the fallen Argives and its just punishment from the hands of the Athenians was now literally etched in stone. Onasias' panel painting in the temple of Athena Areia and the Spina volute krater had highlighted Athens' exemplary

182. For the Marathonomachy, see E. B. Harrison (1972).

183. Hurwit (2004) 185–86.

184. Evelyn Harrison's (1997) readings have been favorably received by Pollitt (1999) 118 with note 1, Hurwit (2004) 185–87, and Schultz (2009).

185. The Amazonomachy in the west pediment also fits to this program. For the paradigmatic role of Athenian heroes in the ideological instruction of fourth-century Ephebes, see Steinbock (2011).

186. For the north frieze, see also Schultz (2009).

187. E. B. Harrison (1997) 120–22. Felten's (1984) attempt to identify this scene as a battle of the Trojan War is less convincing.

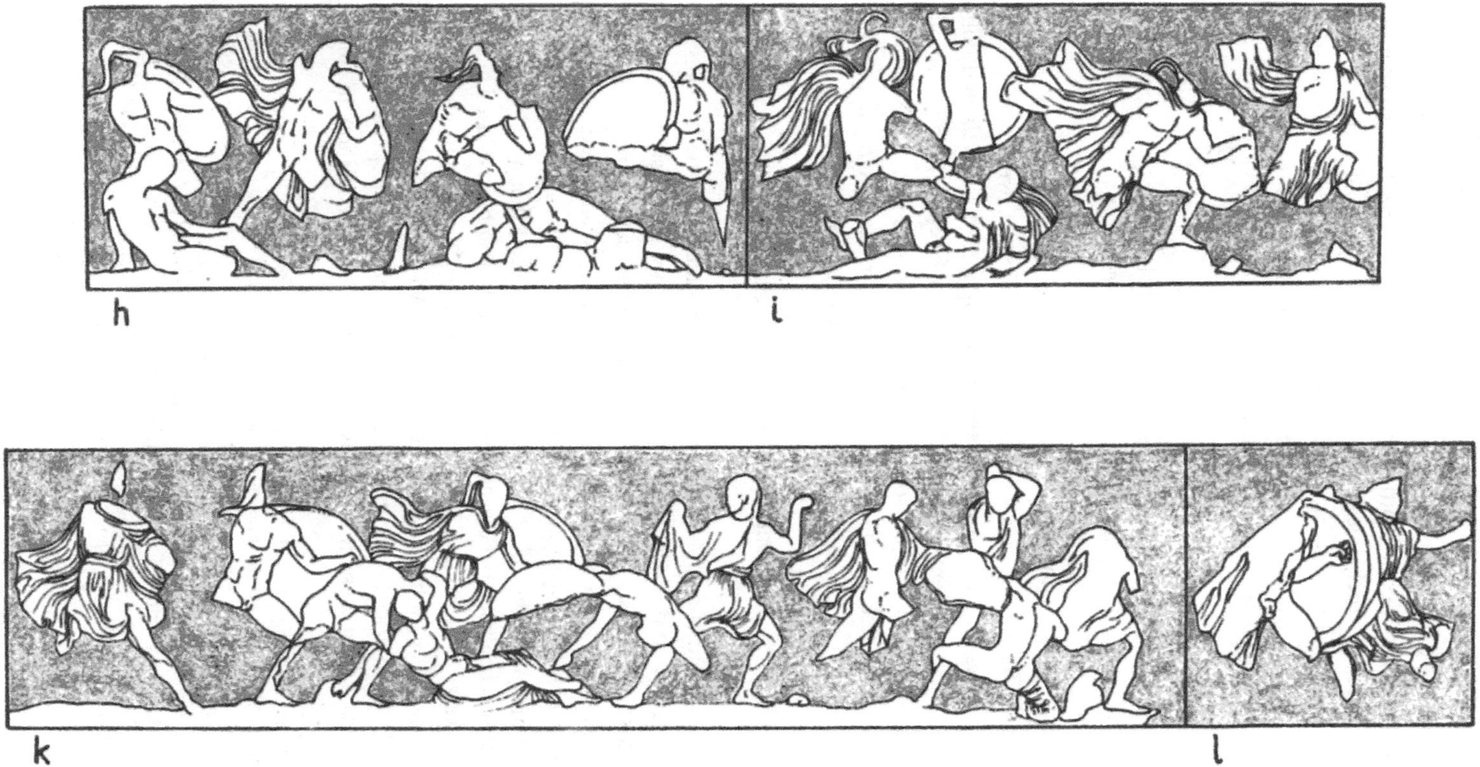

Fig. 4. Recovery of the fallen Argives (?) on the west frieze of the Nike temple. (After Boardman (1985) fig. 127.4; drawing by Marion Cox. Reproduced by courtesy of the author and Thames and Hudson, Ltd, London.)

attitude toward the Argive suppliants, whereas the recovery of the bodies was only alluded to by Theseus' battle-ready posture (fig. 3).[188] After the experience of Delium, the anti-Theban aspects of this myth clearly took center stage. From this time on, the prominent west frieze of the Nike temple served as a permanent reminder of Thebes' *hybris* and defeat for generations to come and thus reinforced the bellicose version of the funeral orations.

The Burial of the Seven in Diplomatic and Political Discourse

After the preceding exploration of the constitutive elements, formative influences, and different carriers of this collective memory, we are in a better position to assess the use of this mythical paradigm in diplomatic and political discourse. In the remainder of this chapter, I will examine how Herodotus' Athenians (Hdt. 9.27.3), Isocrates' Plataeans (Isoc. 14.53–55), Xenophon's Procles of Phlius (Xen. *Hell.* 6.5.47), and Isocrates in his *Panathenaicus* (Isoc. 12.168–72) exploited this mythical paradigm in particular historical situations.

Precedent for the Battle of Plataea

Herodotus recounts a quarrel between the Athenians and the Tegeans over the privilege to hold the left wing of the Greek army in the battle of Plataea. Herodotus' Athenians stake their claim on a list of past achievements, including their aid to the Heraclidae, the burial of the fallen Argives, the fight against the Amazons, their participation in the Trojan War, and, first and foremost, their *monomachy* at Marathon. It is generally agreed that the Athenian speech, as we have it, is anachronistic but closely reflects the kinds of argument used by Athenian speakers of Herodotus' own time (i.e., ca. 460–420 BC) to glorify their city.[189] Since the event itself (the dispute between Athens and Tegea) might well be historical and since the kinds of argument presented in the speech—namely, that present honor depends on past excellence—were common in ancient

188. It made sense for Onasias to focus on the supplication scene, since his painting could thus evoke both the Plataeans' supplication of the Athenians in 519 and the Athenian-Plataean victory over the medizing Thebans; the memory of the latter was ensured through the very location of the dedication in the temple of Athena Areia near the battlefield at Plataea.

189. The canonical catalogue of deeds was almost certainly developed within the genre of the *epitaphios*, which was instituted *after* the Persian Wars. Moreover, it is hard to imagine that the hegemonic ideology underlying these paradigmatic examples predated the repulse of Xerxes' invasion. Cf. "Funeral Orations" in chapter 1, 49–58.

Greece,[190] we can infer from this passage how Herodotus' Athenian contemporaries would argue in a similar diplomatic situation.

After mentioning their aid to the Heraclidae, the Athenians give an account of their second feat.

> Furthermore, we affirm that when the Argives who had marched with Polynices against Thebes had ended their lives and lay unburied, we took the field against the Cadmeans, thus recovered the bodies and buried them in our own land in Eleusis.[191] (Hdt. 9.27.3)

A brief analysis shows that Herodotus' Athenians make excellent use of this mythical paradigm by adapting it perfectly to the situation at hand. It is the Athenians' objective to convince the Spartans that they are most deserving and the ideal candidate to hold the left wing in the upcoming battle against the Greek medizers who hold the right wing of the Persian army.[192] This example serves, therefore, principally as proof of Athens' military excellence. The Athenians stress that they recovered the bodies after "taking the field against the Cadmeans" (στρατευσάμενοι ἐπὶ τοὺς Καδμείους). By calling the Thebans Cadmeans, the Athenians allude to Thebes' Phoenician founder Cadmus and thus drive home the point that they will beat the current medizers in the upcoming battle, just as they defeated the barbarian-born Thebans once before.[193] Moreover, by mentioning the burial of those "lying unburied," the Athenians present themselves as defenders of divine rites and of the νόμος Ἑλληνικός, which is reminiscent of an earlier exchange between the Spartans and the Athenians where the Athenians touted the fight against the barbarians as a religious obligation (Hdt. 8.143–44).[194]

The emphatic claim "we affirm [φαμεν] . . . that we buried them in our own

---

190. Flower & Marincola (2002) 147.

191. Hdt. 9.27.3: Τοῦτο δὲ Ἀργείους τοὺς μετὰ Πολυνείκεος ἐπὶ Θήβας ἐλάσαντας, τελευτήσαντας τὸν αἰῶνα καὶ ἀτάφους κειμένους, στρατευσάμενοι ἐπὶ τοὺς Καδμείους ἀνελέσθαι τε τοὺς νεκρούς φαμεν καὶ θάψαι τῆς ἡμετέρης ἐν Ἐλευσῖνι.

192. Castriota (1992) 71; Hubbard (1992) 98. That the Spartans are the primary audience is evident from the fact that the decision in this "big tussle of words" (Hdt. 9.26.1) was made by the Spartan army by acclamation (Hdt. 9.28.1).

193. Hubbard (1992) 97–98 note 54 points out that, in the wake of the battle of Plataea, Cadmus' identity as a Phoenician (and thus a barbarian) was variously exploited to hint at Thebes medizing. Cf. Bacchylides' dithyramb for Athens (Bacchyl. 19.46–48); Eur. *Phoen.* 638–39; Eur. *Bacch.* 1333–36. Calling the Thebans Cadmeans seems to have become a generic convention of the funeral orations, as Todd (2008) 219 argues. See also Lys. 2.7; Pl. *Menex.* 239b. Flower & Marincola (2002) 155 notice that this legendary victory over Thebes also prefigures the attack on Thebes after the battle of Plataea (Hdt. 9.86).

194. Cf. Castriota (1992) 67. See "Punishment of Theban *Hybris*" above, 189–96.

land in Eleusis [θάψαι τῆς ἡμετέρης ἐν Ἐλευσῖνι]" could fulfill several functions. Herodotus' Athenians seem to be aware of the possibility that others might challenge their version of the story. This was not unwarranted, considering the Theban counterclaims about the burial of the Seven in Thebes found in Pindar (*Nem.* 9.22–24; *Ol.* 6.15–17).[195] The mentioning of Eleusis makes sense for another reason. Since Athens' intervention on behalf of the fallen Argives is an Athenian social memory, the Spartans might not be familiar with it, but they might have noticed the Eleusinian heroön of the Seven on their march across the Isthmus. By pointing to the burial in their own land in Eleusis, the Athenians thus effectively corroborate their story.

Notably, there is no trace of the supplication by Adrastus or other Argives in this speech. This is not surprising. It would be counterproductive for the Athenians to emphasize the favor done to the Argives, who were Sparta's archenemies and suspect of being pro-Persian.[196] Moreover, the supplication aspect of this myth was entirely irrelevant in this context, since it was the Athenians' objective to present themselves as suitable opponents of the Theban medizers in the upcoming battle of Plataea. In sum, drawing on the chauvinistic Athenian master narrative, Herodotus' Athenians masterfully exploit this myth as a suitable paradigm for this particular historical situation.

Aiding Suppliants

This myth was used not only by Athenians in political and diplomatic discourse but also by people from other *poleis* who addressed the Athenian assembly. In 373, after the second destruction of their city by the Thebans, the Plataeans fled to Athens and appealed for Athenian help (Paus. 9.1.5–8; Diod. 15.46.6). Isocrates' *Plataicus* purports to be the very speech of the Plataeans at that time. We do not know how much the Plataeans' actual speech differed from the *Plataicus,* which might be either the speech that they commissioned, a revision of the speech that they delivered, or a pamphlet written by Isocrates to disseminate his political ideas. But it doubtless contained the arguments that Isocrates believed would be most appropriate for the Plataeans to make before an Athenian audience.[197]

---

195. Cf. "The End of the Seven and Local Cults" above. This emphatic avowal should therefore be taken not as an indication of recent "innovation in the tradition" (Flower & Marincola (2002) 155) but merely as an admission of existing counterclaims irrespective of the date of origin.

196. For Argos' stance during Xerxes' invasion, see Hdt. 7.148–52, 8.73; Hammond (1988) 544, 569.

197. Naiden (2006) 182; Seager (1994) 178. See also Jebb (1876) 2:176–78; Jaeger (1938) 199–201; and "Plataean-Theban Antagonism" in chapter 2, 120–27. That the Plataeans' case was indeed brought before the Athenian assembly is further supported by Diod. 15.46.6, who mentions that

In this speech, the Plataeans approach the Athenians as suppliants (ἥκομεν ἱκετεύσοντες, Isoc. 14.1), beseeching them to stand up to Thebes (currently an Athenian ally) and to restore Plataea to its rightful owners. Not surprisingly, the Plataean suppliants draw heavily on Athens' self-image as champion of the weak against unjust oppression (Isoc. 14.1). Toward the end of the speech, they develop a series of *a fortiori* arguments around this theme. It is not fitting, they argue, that every individual who suffers an injustice receives pity in Athens while the plea of a whole city so lawlessly destroyed should go unheard, especially considering the Athenian renown for helping suppliants in the past (Isoc. 14.52). In this context, the Plataeans recount the Athenian intervention on behalf of the fallen Argives, exploiting it as a mythical analogue for their own situation. The Athenian ancestors' exemplary attitude toward suppliants stands in the center of this analogy. When the Argives asked the Athenians to recover those who had died at the foot of the Cadmea, the Athenians "were persuaded by them and forced [ἀναγκάσαντες][198] the Thebans to adopt a resolution more in accordance with the *nomos* [βουλεύσασθαι νομιμώτερον]" (Isoc. 14.53). This reference to the νόμος Ἑλληνικός, a core value of Athens' hegemonic ideology, is likely to resonate with the Athenian audience. Pointing to the everlasting glory that this intervention on behalf of suppliants brought to those Athenians and their city, the Plataeans exploit the normative power of the ancestors' example to incite their descendants to live up to the standards set by their forefathers (Isoc. 14.53–54).

The Plataeans are not content to present this mythical paradigm as a one-to-one analogy to their own situation. With two further *a fortiori* arguments, they seek to prove that they are even more deserving of the Athenians' support than the Argives had been in the mythical past. First, the Argives had come as invaders of an alien land, whereas the Plataeans have lost their own. Second, it is worse that the living are deprived of their fatherland than the dead of their burial rites, since the former brings shame to the survivors, while the latter only brings shame to those who withhold the bodies (Isoc. 14.54–55).[199]

By highlighting Athens' exemplary attitude toward suppliants and by comparing their own situation to that of the Argives, Isocrates' Plataeans masterful-

---

these Plataeans, as a result, received a share in Athenian citizenship (ἰσοπολιτεία); cf. Gawantka (1975) 178 note 31a.

198. While ἀναγκάσαντες clearly implies the Athenian use of force, the Plataeans do not explicitly mention that the burial was achieved through a battle, perhaps in order to adapt this mythical paradigm even further to their particular situation. The Plataeans expected the Athenians not to declare an outright war against the Thebans but to exert primarily diplomatic pressure on their current Theban ally to restore the city of Plataea. That some Athenians supported Thebes in this matter is mentioned explicitly by the Plataeans (Isoc. 14.3).

199. Gotteland (2001) 202.

ly adapt this mythical paradigm to their case at hand. Since supplication scenes were frequently reenacted on the tragic stage, the evocation of the Argives' plea for help was highly emotionally charged.[200] Even though the Plataeans' appeal was not successful, it surely increased the Athenians' anger toward their current Theban ally and is named by Xenophon as the leading cause for the Athenians to seek a rapprochement with Sparta in 371 (Xen. *Hell.* 6.3.1, 5).[201]

After the battle of Leuctra in 371 BC, the Thebans attempted to destroy the Spartan alliance system by lending aid to Sparta's discontented allies in the Peloponnese. In 370/69, when Laconia itself was under attack, Sparta and its remaining allies asked the Athenian demos for military assistance.[202] According to Xenophon's account, their speeches contained various types of argument, including reminders of Athens' treaty obligations, appeals to Athens' self-interest, and evocations of former benefactions and joint accomplishments, particularly during the time of the Persian Wars (Xen. *Hell.* 6.5.33–48).[203]

In the last and decisive speech, Procles of Phlius used the Athenian intervention for the fallen Argives as a mythical analogue for the Spartans' current situation. Just like Isocrates' Plataeans, Procles first invoked, in general terms, Athens' self-image as protector of all those wronged and in fear. For Procles, the Athenian practice of providing succor to all in need is an object of jealous praise (ἐζήλουν, Xen. *Hell.* 6.5.45). Yet what he has heard (perhaps from Xenophon himself)[204] is being surpassed by the reality before his own eyes: the most famous Spartans and their most loyal friends have come to Athens to ask for help (Xen. *Hell.* 6.5.45). Procles thus implicitly presents the request itself as a testimony to Athens' hegemonial status, which presumably will resonate well with his Athenian listeners. Before introducing the Athenian intervention for the fallen Argives as a suitable analogue for the present political constellation, Procles prepares his audience by reminding them of another precedent involving Athenian-Spartan cooperation against Thebes, where their roles, however,

200. Cf. "Athens' Aid for Suppliants" above, 174–82.

201. Cf. "Plataean-Theban Antagonism" in chapter 2, 120–27.

202. Cf. Buckler (2003) 310.

203. The historical accuracy of Xenophon's (like Thucydides') speeches is a vexed problem (cf. Dalfen (1976); Buckler (1982) 192–96). Even though they certainly do not represent the original speeches verbatim, they are modeled on actual speeches and are thus an important source for the use of social memory in Athenian public discourse. Moreover, Xenophon was an Athenian, a contemporary of the events he reports, and acquainted with the political actors involved; cf. "Participant Evidence: The Attic Orators and Their Interpretation" in the introduction, 36–43. For the speeches in Xen. *Hell.* 6.5.33–48, see Usher (2007) 227–28 and "Sparta's Cry for Help" in chapter 5 of the present study, 328–31.

204. Both Procles of Phlius and Xenophon were guest-friends (ξένοι) of the Spartan king Agesilaus and thus surely knew each other well from Xenophon's time in Sparta. Cf. Cawkwell (1979) 24, 43; Buckler (1982) 191 note 16; Cartledge (1987) 264.

were reversed. In 404, the Thebans proposed to enslave Athens, but the Spartans saved Athens through their refusal; now Theban ambassadors request that the Athenians stand aloof and let the Spartans perish (Xen. *Hell.* 6.5.46).[205] Procles then mentions the noble deed (καλόν) performed by the Athenian ancestors "when they did not let the Argives who had died [τοὺς Ἀργείων τελευτήσαντας] at the Cadmea go unburied [οὐκ εἴασαν ἀτάφους γενέσθαι]" (Xen. *Hell.* 6.5.46). Like Isocrates' Plataeans, Procles engages in a series of *a fortiori* arguments. The Athenians now have an opportunity to even surpass their ancestors and perform a far nobler deed (πολὺ κάλλιον), if they do not "let the Lacedaemonians who still live [τοὺς ἔτι ζῶντας Λακεδαιμονίων] either suffer *hybris* or perish [μήτε ὑβρισθῆναι μήτε ἀπολέσθαι]" (Xen. *Hell.* 6.5.46). Both aiding suppliants and standing up to Thebes' *hybris* thus function as the *tertium comparationis* in this analogy.[206]

By falling back on mythical paradigms celebrated in the funeral orations as emblems of the Athenian character, Procles could be sure to strike an emotional chord with his audience. Indeed, this appeal was successful. The Athenians "voted to go to the aid of the Spartans in full force [βοηθεῖν πανδημεί] and chose Iphicrates as general" (Xen. *Hell.* 6.5.48).

Sparing Thebes' Honor

At last, I turn to Isocrates' *Panathenaicus,* which purports to be an address to a gathering at the Panathenaic festival in Athens.[207] Isocrates began work on

205. See chapter 5.

206. Procles also mentions the other paradigmatic supplication myth, that of Athens' aid for the Heraclidae (Xen. *Hell.* 6.5.47). In this case, too, checking *hybris* (i.e., that of Eurystheus) functions as the *tertium comparationis.* Procles also employs further *a fortiori* arguments. Saving the whole polis is nobler (κάλλιον) than saving merely the founders (i.e., the Heraclidae).

207. This discourse is unique since, apart from the encomium on Athens, it also contains a fair amount of biographical material, a polemic against Sparta, and a dialogue scene at the end featuring a reassessment of the speech by Isocrates and one of his students. As a result, Isocrates' objectives in writing this discourse are much debated. This speech has been viewed as a political pamphlet, as a defense of his educational views, as a showpiece to be used for rhetorical instruction, or as a response to Plato's critique of writing; cf. the useful summary in Roth (2003) 11–16. See also Norlin (1929) 368–71; Usher (1999) 318–21; Gray (1994a); Roth (2003); Natoli (2004b); Papillon (2004) 167–68. Signes Codoñer's (1998) recent interpretation seems most convincing to me: Isocrates' aim was to defend his record as statesman and his own idea of education in order to reject his adversaries' attacks. Praising archaic Athens allowed him to vindicate his patriotism and, at the same time, still be critical of Athenian politics during the fifth and fourth centuries. Even though this speech was not actually delivered but written for publication, there are various arguments for including Isocrates' treatment of the Adrastus' story in this study of the use of this myth in Athenian public discourse. First, this speech purports to be an address at the Panathenaic festival; in order to be convincing, it had to generally follow the generic conventions of such a speech before an Athenian mass audience. Second, since it was Isocrates' objective to convince his fellow citizens of his patriotism (as Signes Codoñer (1998) shows), he had to operate within the

this epideictic speech just before the celebration of the Great Panathenaia in 342 BC (Isoc. 12.17), but he was prevented by a severe illness from completing it for this occasion. After a three-year-long break, Isocrates returned to this discourse and finished it in 339 BC, at the age of ninety-seven (Isoc. 12.268–70), one year before the battle of Chaeronea and his own death. The avowed goal of this epideictic speech was to praise "the achievements of Athens and the ἀρετή of the ancestors" (Isoc. 12.5). Consequently, we find in it numerous historical paradigms drawn from the Athenian master narrative.

As part of his comparison of the military achievements of Athens and Sparta (Isoc. 12.151–98), Isocrates introduced the story of the Athenian burial of the Seven as an example of Athens' excellence in war (ἡ περὶ τὸν πόλεμον ἐπιμέλεια, Isoc. 12.168, 173). Yet, instead of falling back on the familiar version of the funeral orations or his *Panegyricus,* in which the Athenians enforced the burial of the Seven by crushing the hubristic Thebans in battle, he featured a diplomatic resolution (Isoc. 12.168–71). In a highly unusual authorial comment, Isocrates acknowledged the discrepancy between this and the earlier treatment of this myth in his *Panegyricus.*

> And nobody should suppose that I fail to realize that I happen to say the opposite [τἀναντία] of what I might be found to have written [φανείην ἂν γεγραφώς] about the same events in my *Panegyricus.* But I do not think that anyone of those who can comprehend these things [ταῦτα συνιδεῖν] is so full of ignorance and envy that he would not commend me and consider me prudent [σωφρονεῖν] for speaking about them in that way then and in this way now. I know that I have written about them in a noble and useful way [καλῶς γέγραφα καὶ συμφερόντως]. (Isoc. 12.172–73)

Unfortunately, Isocrates only hints at his reasons for treating this myth differently in this speech. The key to understanding this passage lies in the phrases ταῦτα συνιδεῖν, σωφρονεῖν and καλῶς καὶ συμφερόντως.[208] Some scholars view Isocrates' comment as a defense of his literary artistry and as an allusion to his readers' literary sensibilities.[209] It seems more convincing, however, to fol-

Athenian memorial framework. For Isocrates' speeches as reflection of Athenian oral discourse, see also Clarke (2008) 301–3.

208. Consequently, translations for these terms vary greatly. The expression οἱ ταῦτα συνιδεῖν δυνηθέντες, for instance, is rendered by Norlin (1929) 481 as "those who can grasp the meaning of these events." Roth (2003) takes this phrase as a reference to the astute reader's ability to detect the discrepancy in both speeches ("die das bemerken könnten"). I follow Papillon (2004) 208, who understands this phrase as a reference to Isocrates' prudent modification of the myth ("anyone who can understand these things").

209. Von Arnim (1917) 32–33 suggests that Isocrates viewed both treatments as "nice and useful" and proposed to freely manipulate myths in accordance with artistic requirements. Gray

low the *communis opinio* and take these words as a reference to his political σωφροσύνη, that is, his political tact and prudence. In the summer of 339, when Isocrates resumed work on the *Panathenaicus,* the political situation in central Greece was changing. With the Fourth Sacred War against Amphissa on the horizon, Thebes became wary of Philip's designs and seized the strategically important fortress Nicaea from the Macedonians (Philochorus *FGrHist* 328 F 56b). Demosthenes' vision of a rapprochement between Athens and Thebes seemed possible now. Indeed, when Philip occupied the Phocian town of Elatea in the fall of 339 (Dem. 18.169–87), the Athenians, in response to this immediate threat, put their long-standing resentments aside and opened negotiations with Thebes about an alliance.[210] Isocrates, fully aware of current political developments, did not want to appear as sabotaging the Athenians' diplomatic efforts. For this reason, we read in his *Panathenaicus* that the Thebans had returned the bodies of the fallen Argives voluntarily, which was more acceptable to contemporary Thebans.[211] Moreover, Signes Codoñer has made a convincing case that this was one of the passages that Isocrates revised in 339 (ἐπηνώρθουν, Isoc. 12.200). This hypothesis accounts for the oddity that Isocrates presents Thebes' voluntary release of the dead as an example for Athens' excellence in war (Isoc. 12.168, 173). In his initial draft, Isocrates had the Athenians recover the bodies of the fallen Argives after defeating the Thebans in battle. In 339, Isocrates kept the Adrastus' myth as an example of Athens' military excellence but heavily revised it due to the changed political situation.[212] This also explains why Isocrates felt the need to justify his new treatment of the Adrastus' myth in the *Panathenaicus.*[213]

Isocrates' authorial comment is truly exceptional. This is the only instance in the corpus of the Attic orators where an orator admits that his current presentation of a mythical paradigm is at odds with his treatment of the same epi-

(1994b) 97 contends that the pacifist version is, paradoxically, the more effective praise of Athens. Roth (2003) 200 argues that Isocrates chose the pacifist version due to the requirements of the particular rhetorical context: in contrast to Sparta, Athenians did not wage war against other Greeks. Yet in these readings, the oddity that Isocrates chose the pacifist version to illustrate Athens' excellence in war (Isoc. 12.168, 173) still demands a satisfying explanation.

210. Cf. Ellis (1994) 778–81; Buckler (2003) 493–99. For Demosthenes' embassy to Thebes, see "Demosthenes and the Athenian-Theban Alliance of 339/8" in chapter 4, 268–71.

211. Schmitz-Kahlmann (1939) 72–73; Perlman (1961) 160–61; Nouhaud (1982) 18; Signes Codoñer (1998) 72–73; Gotteland (2001) 208–9. Isocrates' congratulatory letter to Philip (Isoc. *Ep.* 3), which has generally been dated to the aftermath of Chaeronea, seemed to contradict this interpretation of Isocrates' anti-Macedonian stance in 339. Signes Codoñer (2001) 30–53 has removed this obstacle by dating this letter conclusively to the Peace of Philocrates in 346. Isocrates, who had earlier praised Philip as a worthy leader of a Panhellenic campaign against the Persians, never thought of addressing a second speech to him after 342, when Athens was clearly against Philip.

212. Isocrates was well aware that the peaceful version was less suitable to illustrate Athens' superiority in war than the bellicose one. For this reason, he stated the purpose of this paradigm both at the beginning and at the end (Isoc. 12.168, 173).

213. Signes Codoñer (1998) 72–74.

sode in one of his earlier speeches. Isocrates' epideictic speeches are, however, a special case, since they were written for dissemination as political pamphlets and as illustrative examples of the rhetorical education offered by his school. These discourses purport to be real speeches and consequently resemble real speeches in many ways. At the same time, they exhibit some features characteristic of written texts. In this authorial comment, Isocrates momentarily breaks the illusion of an oral discourse: he refers to both this and his previous discourse, the *Panegyricus,* as written texts by twice using the verb γράφω (Isoc. 12.172–73). What is more, his comment presupposes that he expects people to notice the difference he mentions, possibly by consulting their copy of the *Panegyricus.* Isocrates' comment is thus the result of a change of medium. It is extremely unlikely, however, that speakers in a predominantly oral environment, such as the assembly and the law courts, would admit (if, indeed, they noticed) that they had used a different version on an earlier occasion.[214] This assertion is supported by the lack of such authorial comments in the extant political and judicial speeches of Lysias, Demosthenes, and Aeschines. Nevertheless, Isocrates' remark has been used by scholars to draw conclusions about the orators' general practices. Nouhaud, for instance, exploits Isocrates' confession to bolster his case that the Attic orators manipulated the past without limitations according to the maxims "Each speech has its own truth" and "The end justifies the means."[215] Yet such a view by and large ignores the role of the audience. Since it was the speaker's objective to persuade his listeners, he had to take their knowledge and attitudes into account. For this reason, his version of the past had to be plausible and could not flatly contradict what his audience knew about a certain event.[216] Given the existence of numerous divergent local myths and cults, orators certainly had more leeway in dealing with paradigms from the mythical period vis-à-vis the historical one.[217] Nevertheless, even when dealing with mythical episodes, public speakers usually did not invent wholesale but drew on familiar alternative versions. This passage provides a unique insight into the challenges an orator faced when diverging from the predominant patriotic master narrative. I contend that Isocrates employed various techniques to make his version acceptable to his audience.

---

214. Rosalind Thomas (1989) 250 demonstrates that oral traditions can accommodate "different tales or versions with contradictory implications. They can be remembered or told in isolation from each other and so that the inherent contradictions are not striking."

215. Nouhaud (1982) 18–19: "Ce n'est pas seulement 'à chacun sa vérité' mais 'à chaque discours sa vérité'. . . . dans l'éloquence politique, la fin justifie les moyens." In Nouhaud's view, this applies to examples drawn from both the mythical and the historical periods. Gotteland (2001) 112–13 is more nuanced in her discussion of this passage.

216. See "Participant Evidence: The Attic Orators and Their Interpretation" in the introduction, 36–43.

217. Cf. Gotteland (2001) 113.

We have seen, in chapter 2, that if an orator drew on the lessons provided by the Athenian master narrative, brief allusions were sufficient to harness the emotive power of these collective memories.[218] On the other hand, if an orator wanted, for any reason, to challenge the predominant version of a past event, he had to argue his case in more detail or corroborate his assertions by pointing to alternative carriers of social memory.[219] Thanks to the Athenians' experience with the Thebans in the battle of Plataea and during the Pentacontaetia and the Peloponnesian War, the just punishment of Thebes' *hybris* on the battlefield had become an integral element of the collective memory of Athens' intervention for the fallen Argives as it was presented in the funeral orations, on the tragic stage (Eur. *Supp.*), and probably also on the west frieze of the Nike temple. Consequently, it was not an easy task for Isocrates to convince his listeners that the Thebans agreed to release the dead voluntarily.

Isocrates immediately directs the attention of his audience toward alternative carriers of this collective memory by naming the tragic poets at the Dionysia as sources for this story (Isoc. 12.168). As we know from Plutarch (Plut. *Thes.* 29.4–5), Aeschylus' *Eleusinians* did indeed feature a diplomatic resolution.[220] Yet, given the great number of dramatic performances in Athens, we cannot know whether Isocrates had this particular tragedy in mind.[221] This myth may have been the subject of other tragedies, such as Achaeus' *Adrastus* and *Theseus,* Ion's *Argives,* and Apollodorus' *Suppliants.* These are the titles attested in the historical record.[222] Perhaps some of these plays followed Aeschylus' *Eleusinians* and had Theseus recover the dead by persuasion. Another point is worth emphasizing: Isocrates does not refer to tragic *texts* but envisions his audience listening to (and watching) tragic performances at the Dionysia (τίς οὐκ ἀκήκοεν τῶν τραγῳδοδιδασκάλων Διονυσίοις, Isoc. 12.168). It is quite possible that Isocrates' contemporaries had indeed seen a performance of a pacifist version on stage. There were a few occasions in the history of Athenian-Theban relations in the fourth century that might have warranted a more moderate treatment of the Thebans. After the Spartan capture of the Cadmea in 382, the Athenians provided asylum to three hundred Theban refugees and supported the successful Theban countercoup. As a result, Athens and Thebes were allies until 371. Later, in 338, Athens and Thebes fought together against Philip at

218. Cf. "Treacherous by Nature" in chapter 2, 143–49.

219. See "Challenging the Master Narrative" and "Remembering the Plataeans" in chapter 2, 153–54 and 137–39, respectively. In the first instance, Demosthenes tried, with elaborate arguments, to present the Thebans as born-again Greek patriots. In the second case, Apollodorus pointed to the Marathon painting to prove that the Plataeans fought at Marathon.

220. See "Theseus—Another Heracles" and "Athens' Aid for Suppliants" above, 169–86.

221. Roth (2003) 199.

222. For fragments and dates, see "Athens' Aid for Suppliants" above, 181.

Chaeronea, and Athens provided a safe haven for Theban refugees after Alexander's destruction of Thebes in 335.[223] Perhaps Apollodorus' *Suppliants* was performed or Aeschylus' *Eleusinians* was reproduced during the earlier period of Athenian-Theban cooperation.[224]

I will now look at Isocrates' account of this story more closely. Unlike the extant funeral orations that usually plunge right into Athens' reaction to the withheld funeral rites,[225] Isocrates dwells on the figure of Adrastus and crafts a narrative that features an exposition of this myth that is reminiscent of the tragic stage: Adrastus wanted to restore the son of Oedipus, his own son-in-law; lost the entire army of Argos; saw the captains (λοχαγούς) perish; saved himself shamefully (αὐτὸς δ' ἐπονειδίστως σωθείς); and since he was unable to achieve a truce (σπονδαί) for the recovery of the dead, became a supplicant of the city (ἱκέτης γενόμενος τῆς πόλεως) at a time when Theseus was still in charge (ἔτι Θησέως αὐτὴν διοικοῦντος, Isoc. 12.169).

The term λοχαγοί is primarily used in tragedy to denote the leaders of the Argive expedition.[226] Adrastus' role as suppliant and the explicit mentioning of Theseus as the chief administrator (not king) of Athens also recall the treatment of this myth on the tragic stage.[227] Both in Aeschylus' *Eleusinians* and in Euripides' *Suppliants*, Adrastus and Theseus feature as the main characters, and Adrastus' supplication of Theseus takes up a significant portion of these plays.[228] Moreover, the mentioning of Adrastus' status as sole survivor could remind Isocrates' audience of the various local myths that were spun out of Adrastus' flight from the battlefield and focused on his arrival in Athens (e.g., myths connected to the Attic Harma and to Colonus Hippius).[229] Similarly, Adrastus' inability to achieve σπονδαί could serve as a cue to recall versions of this myth according to which Theseus, as a true culture hero, became the πρῶτος εὑρητής of σπονδαί by persuading the Thebans to release the bodies of the Seven voluntarily; this is the version that Aeschylus probably followed in

223. For a more detailed discussion of these events, see chapter 4.

224. Athens' generous aid to Theban refugees might have brought suppliant myths back onto the tragic stage. We know that Apollodorus won his first victory around 380 BC (*TrGF* 64 Apollodorus T 1, 2 Snell) and that old tragedies were reproduced in the fourth century; cf. "Athens' Aid for Suppliants" above, 182 and "Dramatic Festivals" in chapter 1, 63–64.

225. Lys. 2.7 introduces this myth by mentioning Adrastus and Polynices in a brief genitive absolute. Dem. 60.8 and Pl. *Menex.* 239b make no mention of Adrastus.

226. See Eur. *Supp.* 598; Soph. *Ant.* 141. Aesch. *Sept.* 42 has λοχαγέται, and Eur. *Supp.* 636 has ἑπτὰ δεσπόται λόχων; cf. Roth (2003) 199 note 466.

227. Cf. Eur. *Supp.* 349–57. The mention of Theseus is particularly striking since the funeral orations and assembly speeches ascribe this achievement conventionally to the demos as a whole and do not name the leader Theseus.

228. Cf. "Athens' Aid for Suppliants" above, 174–82.

229. Cf. "The End of the Seven and Local Cults" above, 159–69.

his *Eleusinians* and that was preserved by, among others, the Atthidographer Philochorus (Philochorus *FGrHist* 328 F 112 = Plut. *Thes.* 29.4–5).[230]

By mentioning the tragic poets at the Dionysia and by employing specific cues that point toward alternative sources for this myth, Isocrates reminds his audience of less familiar pacifist versions of this story, which are less offensive to contemporary Thebans.[231] Yet, in all other respects, Isocrates presents this paradigm in the familiar vein of the funeral orations to make sure that it would resonate with his Athenian audience. Not Theseus but the Athenian demos makes the decision about Adrastus' request and immediately sends an embassy to Thebes (ὁ δῆμος ἔπεμψεν, Isoc. 12.170).[232] The Athenians are driven to action by their concern for the divine law and the νόμος Ἑλληνικός (Isoc. 12.169–70).[233] Just as in the funeral orations, the whole example is set forth as a proof of Athens' military superiority.[234]

It is instructive to analyze in detail how Isocrates managed to downplay Thebes' *hybris.* (Isoc. 12.170–71). Athenian ambassadors are sent to the Thebans not to issue an ultimatum or to threaten the use of force openly (as in Eur. *Supp.* 389–94) but

> to counsel them [συμβουλεύσοντας] to deliberate in a more pious way [ὁσιώτερον βουλεύσασθαι] about the recovery of the dead and to give a

230. See "Theseus—Another Heracles" above, 172. Plutarch claims that most writers say (οἱ πλεῖστοι λέγουσι) that Theseus recovered the fallen Argives by persuading the Thebans and making a truce (πείσας καὶ σπεισάμενος, Plut. *Thes.* 29.4). Given the prominence of the bellicose version in the funeral orations and diplomatic speeches, this assertion seems baffling. It is certainly conceivable that the Boeotian Plutarch, out of patriotic bias, exaggerates the number of defendants of Thebes' honor (cf. Roth (2003) 198). It seems more likely to me, however, that Plutarch means "most of the Atthidographers," who are, after all (judging by the high number of citations), the main sources for his *Life of Theseus.* His assertion then makes sense, since the Atthidographers, who were particularly interested in recording and organizing the local legends of Attica, did not slavishly follow the polis-wide master narrative (cf. Harding (2008) 71) and since many of these local legends (e.g., those connected to Harma, near Phyle, and to Colonus Hippius) might indeed have featured a peaceful resolution.

231. That fifth- and fourth-century Thebans indeed contested the chauvinistic Athenian version is evident from Pindar (*Nem.* 9.22–24; *Ol.* 6.15–17) and Pausanias, who reports that "the Thebans say that they conceded the recovery of the bodies voluntarily and deny that a battle took place" (Paus. 1.39.2). Pausanias' Θηβαῖοι are probably the fourth- and third-century writers of *Thebaica,* as Jacoby *FGrHist* 3b (Suppl.) ii.353 note 32 suggests.

232. The swiftness of Athens' response (ὧν ἀκούσας οὐδένα χρόνον ἐπισχὼν ὁ δῆμος, Isoc. 12.170) is also a typical feature of the funeral orations. Cf. Lys. 2.26; Loraux (1986) 158–59.

233. Isocrates calls the burial of the fallen an "ancient custom [παλαιὸν ἔθος] and an ancestral *nomos* [πάτριον νόμον] that all men use continuously, not because it was established by human nature, but because it was decreed by divine authority (Isoc. 12.169)," as well as "the *nomos* common to all Greeks" (τὸν νόμον τὸν κοινὸν ἁπάντων τῶν Ἑλλήνων, Isoc. 12.170).

234. As discussed above, however, the bellicose version in Isocrates' initial draft was more suitable for this purpose.

> response that is more in accordance with the *nomos* [νομιμωτέραν] than the one they gave earlier. (Isoc. 12.170)

The ambassadors are supposed to merely "insinuate [ὑποδείξοντας] that the city of Athens would not allow them to transgress the law that is common to all Greeks" (Isoc. 12.171). According to Isocrates, the Thebans responded in the following way:

> Upon hearing this message, those who were then in charge at Thebes [οἱ κύριοι τότ' ὄντες Θηβῶν] made a decision that conformed neither to the opinions that some people have about them [ἔχουσίν τινες περὶ αὐτῶν] nor to their previous resolution; on the contrary, after both stating the case for themselves in reasonable terms [μετρίως περὶ αὑτῶν τε διαλεχθέντες] and denouncing those who had marched against them, they granted to our city the recovery of the dead. (Isoc. 12.171)

With this elaborate argument, Isocrates tries to make his account of Thebes' voluntary release of the bodies of the Seven seem plausible to his audience. The Thebans had a right to be angry about the unprovoked Argive attack. It is, therefore, excusable that they overreacted at first. What matters is that, in the end, they came to their senses and handed over the dead for burial. By anticipating disbelief among members of his audience, Isocrates (like Demosthenes in *On the Symmories*) explicitly acknowledged how difficult it was to go against the long-standing anti-Theban stereotypes.[235]

In this passage, we also find the strongest piece of evidence that Isocrates' reason for featuring a pacifist version was not literary but political—namely, to spare Thebes' honor lest he should sabotage the nascent Athenian-Theban rapprochement. This hypothesis alone can explain why Isocrates employed the lengthy phrase "those who were then in charge at Thebes" (οἱ κύριοι τότ' ὄντες Θηβῶν) instead of simply saying "the Thebans" (Isoc. 12.171).[236] In so doing, he managed to dissociate contemporary Thebans from their ancestors in the mythical past and to exculpate regular Thebans by laying the blame for the initial refusal exclusively on their rulers.[237] Isocrates was not alone in showing this

235. Cf. Dem. 14.33–34. See "Challenging the Master Narrative" in chapter 2, 151–54.

236. According to Gray (1994b) 97, the pacifist version is, paradoxically, the more effective praise of Athens. Roth (2003) 200 suggests that Isocrates chose the pacifist version to demonstrate that archaic Athens, in contrast to Sparta, did not wage wars against other Greeks. Neither of these literary interpretations can account for this particular oddity, though.

237. This very strategy was also employed by the Thebans to defend themselves and their fathers against the charges of medism. Cf. Thuc. 3.62, 3.64.5, and see "Challenging the Master Narrative" in chapter 2 of the present study, 149–54. The same rhetorical strategy can also be found in

kind of consideration for the Theban neighbors around this time. In his funeral oration for the fallen at Chaeronea, Demosthenes followed the conventions of the genre and mentioned the Athenian intervention for the fallen Argives, but like Isocrates, he exculpated Thebes as a whole by shifting the blame for this crime onto King Creon alone (Dem. 60.8).[238]

We have seen, both in Demosthenes' *Second Philippic* and in the historical paradigms used by Procles of Phlius and Isocrates' Plataeans, how important the notion of unchanging national characters was for the Athenians' view of themselves and the world around them.[239] Yet public speakers could give up this notion and, with rhetorical finesse, dissociate the current members of a group from their culpable ancestors, if the current political situation required it.[240] This rhetorical strategy is, of course, a phenomenon that can be observed across time and space. It is remarkable, for instance, how often U.S. public discourse attributes the crimes of World War II not simply to "the Germans" but to Nazi Germany—no doubt out of consideration for a fellow Western democracy and good NATO ally.

The analysis of the use of this mythical paradigm in particular historical situations has shown that certain aspects of this myth could be emphasized, downplayed, or omitted depending on the speaker's rhetorical requirements. Drawing on the bellicose version of the funeral orations and alluding to Thebes' Phoenician founder Cadmus, Herodotus' Athenians convince the Spartans that they have defeated the barbarian-born Thebans once before and will beat these medizers in the upcoming battle of Plataea (Hdt. 9.27.3). Isocrates' Plataeans (Isoc. 14.53–54) and Procles of Philus (Xen. *Hell.* 6.5.45–46) used the Argives as a mythical analogue to take advantage of Athens' self-image as champion of

---

Soph. *OT* 711–12, where Iocaste attributes the oracle that pronounced Laos' doom not to Apollo himself but merely to his servants.

238. Dem. 60.8: τὰ τῶν κατοιχομένων νόμιμ' οὐ περιεῖδον ὑβριζόμενα, ὅτε τοὺς ἕπτ' ἐπὶ Θήβας θάπτειν ἐκώλυεν Κρέων. See Perlman (1961) 160–61. Demosthenes does not feature a peaceful resolution, but he avoids an explicit reference to the enforcement of the burial in battle (as Lys. 2.10 has it) by choosing the rather vague expression "they did not allow [οὐ περιεῖδον] the lawful rites of the departed to be violated." In another section of this speech, Demosthenes even went as far as to claim that the fallen members of the Attic tribe Oeneis remembered that Thebes' founder Cadmus was the great-grandfather of their eponymous hero Oeneus and therefore fought fiercely not only for the sake of their own city but also for Thebes (Dem. 60.30). This is unusual, since on other occasions, Athenians would stress Cadmus' Phoenician origins to allude to Thebes' medizing; cf. "Precedent for the Battle of Plataea" above, 196–98.

239. Cf. "Treacherous by Nature" in chapter 2, 143–49, and "Aiding Suppliants" above, 198–201.

240. Since the example of the ancestors was so normative in Athens, we almost never find public speakers criticizing the Athenians of the past (Aeschin. 2.75–77 is the exception). Instead, the ancestors are frequently used to encourage contemporary Athenians to live up to their potential. For the notion of unchanging national characters in oratory, see also Clarke (2008) 285.

the weak against unjust oppression. For this reason, they heavily dwelled on the supplication aspect of this story. Yet there were indeed constraints on what an orator could and would say, imposed by the general historical consciousness of his audience. In his *Panathenaicus,* Isocrates diverged from the predominant Athenian master narrative to spare Thebes' honor. To make his account of Thebes' voluntary release of the bodies of the Seven seem plausible to his audience, Isocrates made an elaborate argument and drew on alternative carriers of this social memory. Nevertheless, Isocrates, like Demosthenes in *On the Symmories,* had to acknowledge how difficult it was to go against long-standing anti-Theban stereotypes.

CHAPTER 4

A Precarious Memory

Theban Help for the Athenian Democrats

Throughout the fifth and fourth centuries, Athenian-Theban relations were mostly hostile. Athens fought against the Theban-led Boeotian League at the end of the sixth century to protect Plataea's independence. During Xerxes' invasion (480–479), the Pentecontaetia (479–431), and the Peloponnesian War (431–404), Thebes was a staunch ally of Athens' enemies, first of the Persians and then of the Spartans. After its triumph over the Spartans at Leuctra (371), Thebes strove for hegemony in mainland Greece, and after the stalemate at Mantinea (362), it was allied with Philip II of Macedon in the Third Sacred War (356–346) against Phocis and Athens.

The conditions were nearly ideal for keeping the memory of Thebes' ultimate crime, its betrayal of Greece in 480–479, alive in Athenian collective consciousness. This continuous hostility rendered the memory of Thebes' treason significant enough for the Athenians to memorialize, transforming it from "remembered" to "commemorated" history. Thus it became an integral part of the Athenians' master narrative of their own role in the Persian Wars. While the Athenians saw themselves as champions of Greek liberty and protectors of the weak, the Theban archenemy came to epitomize the traitors of Greece. As we have seen in chapter 3, this noble Athenian self-image was also projected back into the mythical past: from time immemorial, the Athenians had repelled barbarian invaders (the Amazons and Eumolpus' Thracian hordes) and stood up to the arrogant and powerful on behalf of defenseless suppliants (the Heraclidae and Adrastus). Given the Athenians' experience with the Thebans during the Persian War, it is not surprising that Thebes was seen as anti-Athens in mythical times as well.[1] Moreover, there were plenty of occasions in the late fifth and fourth centuries to keep the memory of Thebes' treason in the forefront of Athenian public discourse. By and large, these occasions had to do with the continuous Theban-Plataean conflict and with Thebes' role in the case of potential barbarian invasions.[2]

Yet these long periods of utter hostility, which provided ideal conditions for the perpetuation of the stereotype of the eternal Theban traitor, were just one aspect in the history of Athenian-Theban relations. We find also periods of more or less peaceful coexistence and even of cooperation against Sparta and Philip II of Macedon (the Corinthian War in 395–386, the Theban War in 378–371, the battle of Chaeronea in 338). Given the hostile Athenian disposition toward the Thebans, discussed in chapters 2 and 3, one has to wonder, how could the Athenians ever conclude an alliance with these "prototypical traitors"? Was the Athenian decision to ally with the Thebans in 395 and 378 merely governed by considerations of *Realpolitik,* which led the Athenians to cast their resentments overboard? Or did proponents of this alliance also have any positive experiences with the Thebans, which they could use, in addition to utilitarian arguments, to promote this rapprochement? Again, how were these periods of Athenian-Theban cooperation remembered? Did any positive experiences result from them that Athenian orators could use later on? If so, how were these positive memories regarding the Thebans manifested and transmitted? This question is all the more important since the Athenian master narrative, as we have seen, largely promoted a negative view of the Thebans.

Belated Praise for Theban Aid?

A search for positive allusions to Theban benefactions vis-à-vis Athens does not yield many results. One instance, however, is outstanding. In his indictment of Demosthenes in 323, Dinarchus contrasted Demosthenes' alleged betrayal of Thebes in 335, when it was destroyed by Alexander the Great, to the Thebans' support for the Athenian demos in 404/3.[3]

> And these men [i.e., the Thebans], as our elders say [ὡς οἱ πρεσβύτεροι λέγουσι]—when the democracy in our city had been dissolved and Thra-

1. For Thebes as the antithesis of Athens in fifth-century Athenian drama, see Zeitlin (1990).
2. Cf. chapter 2.
3. For Dinarchus' life and works, see Worthington (1992) 3–12. Born in Corinth around 361/0, Dinarchus moved to Athens in his early twenties. He fought for Athens as a metic in the battle of Chaeronea in 338 and then became a speech writer. During the Harpalus affair in 323, he wrote one of the prosecution speeches against Demosthenes. Having lived in Athens for almost two decades, he is an invaluable source for Athenian social memory of the 320s.

> sybulus was gathering together the exiles in Thebes for the seizure of Phyle—despite the strength of the Spartans and their prohibition to harbor or let depart any Athenian, nevertheless aided the demos in returning and passed the decree, so often read out before you [τὸ πολλάκις ἀνεγνωσμένον παρ' ὑμῖν ἐψηφίσαντο ψήφισμα], that they would ignore any Athenian bearing arms passing through their territory.[4] (Din. 1.25)

This passage is most unusual. Dinarchus refers to an event that happened eighty years earlier, well before his lifetime. This naturally raises the question, how could the orator and members of his audience know about this incident? Dinarchus himself names two sources for this memory, the elders (ὡς οἱ πρεσβύτεροι λέγουσι) and the Theban decree "so often read out before [the Athenians]."

I contend that scholars have not paid enough attention to passages such as this one; references to the elders have often been dismissed as empty rhetorical *topoi,* simply inserted by the orators to lend credence to their allusions, the assumption being that the orators themselves had either freely invented or gained their superior knowledge about a specific historical incident from other written speeches or from the historians.[5] Rosalind Thomas rightly emphasizes the oral aspect of communicative conditions in fifth- and fourth-century Athens, arguing that the orators' allusions to the past were not derived from the historians but reflect oral traditions familiar to both the orators and their audiences.[6] If we seek to contextualize Dinarchus' historical allusion within the complex net of remembrances and beliefs held by his audience, we have to take his mention of the elders and the oft-cited Theban decree seriously. This is not to say that phrases like "as the elders say" are not widely used by the orators and do not constitute a commonplace or rhetorical *topos.* Yet we should not dismiss them a priori as a rhetorical cover-up for an orator's invention or superior knowledge. After all, the elders were indeed an invaluable source of social memory in fifth- and fourth-century Athens. Besides, even if the reference to the elders were a meaningless rhetorical phrase, it is very unlikely that an ora-

4. Din. 1.25: κἀκεῖνοι <μέν>, ὡς οἱ πρεσβύτεροι λέγουσι, καταλελυμένης τῆς δημοκρατίας τῆς παρ' ἡμῖν καὶ συνάγοντος ἐν Θήβαις Θρασυβούλου τοὺς φυγάδας ἐπὶ τὴν Φυλῆς κατάληψιν, καὶ Λακεδαιμονίων ἰσχ<υ>όντων καὶ ἀπαγορευόντων μηδέν' Ἀθηναίων ὑποδέχεσθαι μηδ' ἐκπέμπειν, ὅμως συνέπραττον τῷ δήμῳ τὴν κάθοδον καὶ τὸ πολλάκις ἀνεγνωσμένον παρ' ὑμῖν ἐψηφίσαντο ψήφισμα, † μὴ περιορᾶν ἐάν τις ὅπλα διὰ τῆς χώρας τῆς Ἀθηναίων † ἔχων πορεύηται· The passage is corrupt and has led to several proposed restorations; see the *apparatus criticus* of Conomis' 1975 edition. Thanks to Plut. *Lys.* 27.3 and Plut. *Pelop.* 6.5, there can be no doubt about the content of this Theban decree, though; cf. Conomis (1975) ad locum: "locus corruptus v. Saup. Epist. crit. 132–34 qui bene ad sensum scripsit: μηδέν' ὁρᾶν, ἐάν τις Ἀθηναίων ὅπλα ἔχων διὰ τῆς χώρας πορεύηται."

5. See my critique of these approaches and their underlying assumptions in "Participant Evidence: The Attic Orators and Their Interpretation" in the introduction, 36–43.

6. Cf. "Oral Tradition Studies" in the introduction, 21–23; R. Thomas (1989) 201–2.

tor would claim that a specific decree had often been read before the Athenians if it were not true. Otherwise he would lose all credibility; after all, he did not operate within a sociopolitical vacuum, and his assertions would be checked by the knowledge and expectations of his audience.[7]

This raises several questions. Who are the elders who talk about events from 404/3? Since this incident happened eighty years earlier, Dinarchus' phrase could not refer to eyewitnesses but must stand for at least their immediate descendants. In this case, we have to ask how and why this memory was transmitted to younger generations. Moreover, Dinarchus claimed that the Theban decree, passed in support of the Athenian democrats in 404/3, was "read often before the Athenians." Especially in light of the widespread anti-Theban sentiment in Athens (see chaps. 2 and 3), who would read a *Theban* decree to the Athenians, when, and why? To tackle these problems connected with the manifestation and transmission of this particular memory, I will first try to shed light on the historical situation in 404/3. This will serve as a foil for Dinarchus' account and enable us to detect potential distortions.

The main part of this chapter will trace the process of transmission of this memory in Athenian public discourse down to Dinarchus' time. Situations in Athenian-Theban history in which Thebes' help to the Athenian democrats could reappear in Athenian public discourse will thereby be of special importance. First, I will gather evidence for efforts to memorialize the democrats' successful return from Phyle, which could function as a cue for the recall of the Theban support as well. In Thebes, this "selfless" aid to the Athenians was memorialized more actively. Then I will analyze Xenophon's account of the Theban ambassadors who used this episode to forge a Theban-Athenian alliance against Sparta in 395. In 382, a small pro-Spartan faction took over the government in Thebes and expelled its political opponents, who found refuge in Athens. In 379/8, the Athenians supported these exiles in their effort to overturn the junta in Thebes. This event practically mirrored the situation of 404/3 when the Thebans aided the Athenian exiles to oust the regime of the Thirty. Naturally, this act of "selfless" Athenian help was remembered in Athens and featured prominently in the following decades. It thus served indirectly as a further cue for the memory of Thebes' support for Thrasybulus in 404.

After a long period of outright hostility (371–339 BC), these precedents of mutual Athenian-Theban benefactions again became relevant in their joint fight against the Macedonians. Demosthenes probably used these historical paradigms in forging the Athenian-Theban alliance of 339. Philip's retribution

7. See "Participant Evidence: The Attic Orators and Their Interpretation" in the introduction, 41–43; Harding (1987) 37.

against Thebes, the unsuccessful revolt initiated by Theban exiles with Athenian help, and Alexander's punishment of Thebes were further occasions at which the historical precedents of 404/3 and 379/8 would have figured in Athenian public discourse. Having thus traced recollections of Thebes' support for Thrasybulus through the fourth century, I will return to Dinarchus' use of this historical paradigm in his case against Demosthenes.

The Situation in Thebes in 404/3

Athens' surrender in the spring of 404 was bitter. Not only did it mean that the Athenians had to give up their empire, demobilize their fleet, demolish their long walls, restore their pro-Spartan oligarchic exiles, and submit to Sparta's foreign policy; coaxed by the Spartan general Lysander, the Athenian assembly also had to agree to dissolve their beloved democracy by appointing a committee of thirty men to reestablish the "ancestral" constitution, a code name for an oligarchic form of government. The Thirty were supported by a handpicked council and three thousand oligarchic-minded Athenians and militarily backed by a Spartan garrison. Their rule became increasingly more oppressive. First, they tried and executed well-known sycophants, but they soon turned on democratic opponents, wealthy citizens, and metics of good standing, whose property they confiscated to solidify their power. To escape persecution and extrajudicial execution, many leading democrats and wealthy metics fled the city and sought refuge in Thebes and other cities. Thrasybulus, the leader of the democratic exiles, set out from Thebes with a small band of citizens and noncitizen supporters and managed to occupy the Attic mountain fortress of Phyle, from which he launched guerilla attacks on the regime of the Thirty (fig. 1). Thrasybulus withstood several attempts of the Thirty to dislodge him from Phyle, and his band grew steadily from the initial seventy to several hundreds. Emboldened by their success, the exiles occupied the Piraeus, where they were joined by a multitude of democratic supporters whom the Thirty had banned from the city proper. In a full-scale hoplite battle at Munychia in the Piraeus, the exiles squarely defeated the troops of the Thirty and killed their leader Critias in the process. The Three Thousand in the city decided to replace the Thirty with a board of ten men and appealed once more for Sparta's intervention against the rebels in the Piraeus. After a victory in battle, the Spartan king Pausanias finally managed to broker a peace and an amnesty between the oligarchs in the city and the democrats in the Piraeus. Both sides agreed to restore the democracy and swear an oath "not to remember past wrongs." This amnesty included all Athenians except for the Thirty and their immediate henchmen, who found a temporary refuge at Eleusis. These are—in broad strokes—the major events leading from Athens' surrender in 404 to the restoration of the democracy in 403.[8]

To evaluate Dinarchus' allusion to the Theban aid for the Athenian democrats properly, we have to reconstruct in more detail the historical circumstances surrounding Thrasybulus' march on Athens and the return of the demos. Any support offered by individual Thebans or the Theban polis as a whole is thereby of particular interest. I have made the case in the introduction that after Rosalind Thomas' study of oral traditions in classical Athens, the Greek historians can no longer be seen as guardians of an almost "Rankean" truth; instead, they have to be regarded as participants within the same communicative framework as their contemporaries, the orators.[9] Consequently, when reconstructing the history of Athens in 404/3, we have to be aware that our sources are not simply a true historical record of the rule of the Thirty but have themselves been shaped by the workings of social memory and thus reflect how people remembered the civil war, rather than what actually happened.[10] Caution is especially warranted when dealing with later accounts that are not contemporary with the events they describe.

Our only contemporary historiographical account of the tyranny of the Thirty comes from Xenophon, an Athenian aristocrat with strong pro-Spartan sympathies and a well-known dislike for Thebes.[11] Unfortunately, Xenophon tells us very little about Thebes' contribution in ousting the Thirty. He reports that after Critias executed his more moderate rival Theramenes, the tyrannical reign of the Thirty intensified the persecution of its enemies, banned them from Attica, and caused many to flee to Megara and Thebes (Xen. *Hell.* 2.4.1). Xenophon continues his narrative with Thrasybulus' seizure of Phyle, a stronghold that served the democrats as a base for their ultimately successful opera-

8. For historiographical accounts of the tyranny of the Thirty, see Xen. *Hell.* 2.3–4; Arist. *Ath. Pol.* 34–41.1; Diod. 14.3–6, 32–33; Justin 5.8–10. For excellent recent treatments, cf. Rhodes (1981) 415–82; Krentz (1982); Buck (1998) 60–83; Wolpert (2002) 15–28; Forsdyke (2005) 196–204.

9. Cf. "Oral Tradition Studies" in the introduction, 21–23; R. Thomas (1989).

10. Wolpert (2002) and Forsdyke (2005) 196–204 offer two exemplary studies of this period and display great sensitivity to these historiographical issues. Wolpert makes the case that both the exiled democrats and the oligarchic supporters of the Thirty had to come up with a version of these events that was acceptable to both sides *because of its distortions*. Forsdyke explores how previous experiences of tyrannical oppression and exile under the Peisistratids shaped the perception and memory of the exile of the *demos* during the time of the Thirty.

11. For Xenophon's pro-Spartan and anti-Theban bias, see Cawkwell (1979) 7–46; Buck (1994) 74, (1998) 13. Recently, several scholars have challenged this orthodoxy and explained omissions and unevenness of treatment in the *Hellenica* by emphasizing Xenophon's artistic and moralistic objectives: see Gray (1989); Tuplin (1993); Dillery (1995); Pownall (2004) 65–112. Even if we can no longer simply point to Xenophon's biases as the sole explanation for historical inadequacies in his text, that Xenophon was an admirer of Sparta and showed much dislike for Thebes is still an undisputed fact and has considerable explanatory force, since these predispositions influenced Xenophon's perception and memory of contemporary events.

tions against the Thirty. Apart from Xenophon's remark that Thrasybulus "set out from Thebes" (Xen. *Hell.* 2.4.2) and that the Thebans refused to join the Spartan king Pausanias in attacking the exiles in the Piraeus (Xen. *Hell.* 2.4.30), we learn nothing of the Theban involvement in the ousting of the Thirty.

Yet Dinarchus is not the only author to emphasize Thebes' support for the democratic exiles. Three late authors, Diodorus, Plutarch, and Justin, also mention the fortunes of the democratic exiles and the aid they received from Thebes. All three report that the Spartans, in support of the Thirty, passed a decree that commanded the return of the exiles to Athens from wherever they might be in Greece (Diod. 14.6.1; Plut. *Lys.* 27.2; Justin 5.9.4). Argos and Thebes, however, ignored the Spartan order and harbored the Athenian refugees (Diod. 14.6.2–3; Justin 5.9.4). Moreover, according to Diodorus and Plutarch, the Thebans issued counterdecrees in support of the exiles (Diod. 14.6.3; Plut. *Lys.* 27.3; Plut. *Pelop.* 6.5).

Pointing to Xenophon's silence, some scholars have questioned the reliability of Diodorus' and Plutarch's reports, arguing that they are late and cannot have firsthand information. These objections, however, can confidently be dismissed.[12] It has been demonstrated that both Diodorus and Plutarch derive their information, through Ephorus, from the Oxyrhynchus historian,[13] who composed his history in the first half of the fourth century, covering events from at least 411 to 395.[14] There is no reason, therefore, to dismiss their testimony a priori. Xenophon's silence can be explained by his bias. Due to his

12. Hamilton (1979) 149–50.

13. For Ephorus as the intermediary source between the Oxyrhynchus historian and the epitomator Diodorus, see Stylianou (1998) 49–50, 89 with further literature; Bruce (1967) 24. Plutarch cites Ephorus explicitly as a source for his *Life of Lysander* (Plut. *Lys.* 17, 20, 25, 30). Consequently, when Diodorus and Plutarch agree on events in Thebes in 404/3, they most probably go back, via Ephorus, to the *Hellenica Oxyrhynchia.*

14. For authorship and date of composition of the *Hellenica Oxyrhynchia,* see Bruce (1967) 22–27; McKechnie & Kern (1988) 7–16; Meister (1990) 65–68; Shrimpton (1991) 182–95; Chambers (1993) xviii–xxv. The extant fragments describe events between 410 and 395. It is clear that the author intended to write a continuation of Thucydides' history and that his narrative thus began with events in 411. Given the level of detail in the extant passages, it seems likely that this history ended either with the battle of Cnidus in 394 or with the King's Peace of 387/6. Internal evidence indicates that the text was composed between 387/6 and 346 (cf. Bruce (1967) 4–5). The question of authorship is still heavily contested. Initially, many favored the historian Theopompus, who is known to have composed a continuation of Thucydides' history up to the battle of Cnidus in 394. The arguments against his authorship are strong, notwithstanding Bleckmann (2006). Theopompus was born around 377/6, and it seems improbable that he could have obtained the level of historical detail that the *Hell. Oxy.* features, while writing in 356 at the earliest. Moreover, Theopompus' known rhetorical style has nothing in common with the style of the *Hell. Oxy.* Some scholars have suggested an otherwise unknown author; it is hard to imagine, however, that the author of a work that was still widely circulating during the imperial period would not have been mentioned in any ancient source at all. With Bruce (1967) 27, Shrimpton (1991) 195, Chambers (1993) xxv, and Meister (1990) 65–68, I consider the Athenian Cratippus as the likeliest candidate. since he is known to have been a contemporary of Thucydides and to have written a continuation of his work.

pro-Spartan sympathies, he might have wanted to spare the Spartans from the blame of actively supporting the brutal persecution practices of the Thirty. Similarly, his well-known dislike for Thebes might have led him to suppress their contribution to toppling the terror regime of the Thirty.[15]

The Spartan extradition order also makes good sense given the historical circumstances. We can infer from our sources that most of the Athenian exiles fled on their own accord when it became clear to them that the Thirty had begun to target citizens of good standing, wealthy metics, and democratic leaders.[16] These citizens and metics found temporary refuge in Thebes, Megara, Argos, and Corinth.[17] It could not have been in the Thirty's interest, however, to create a large number of democratic opponents beyond the borders of Attica, where they were able to prepare a counterstrike in relative safety. For this reason, it makes sense that the Spartans—probably on the Thirty's request—issued the extradition order to their allied states.[18]

Another clue for the historicity of the Spartan order can be deduced from the wording of the Spartan decree, transmitted by these late authors. Diodorus writes,

> The Spartans issued a decree [ἐψηφίσαντο] that the Athenian fugitives [τοὺς Ἀθηναίων φυγάδας] were to be led [ἀγωγίμους εἶναι] to the Thirty from all over Greece and that anyone who prevented this should be liable to a fine of five talents. (Diod. 14.6.1)

The similarity in Plutarch's report indicates that he is indeed using the same source as Diodorus (doubtless the Oxyrhynchus historian via Ephorus).

> The Spartans . . . issued a decree [ἐψηφίσαντο] that the fugitives from Athens [τοὺς φεύγοντας ἐξ Ἀθηνῶν] were to be led back [ἀγωγίμους

15. For Xenophon's anti-Theban bias, cf. Cawkwell (1979) 7–46; Buck (1994) 74, (1998) 13.

16. Xen. *Hell.* 2.3.14, 38–40; Arist. *Ath. Pol.* 35.4. Cf. Forsdyke (2005) 197.

17. Thebes: Xen. *Hell.* 2.4.1; Lys. fr. 286 Carey; Diod. 14.6.3; Plut. *Lys.* 27.4–5; Justin 5.9.4. Megara: Xen. *Hell.* 2.4.1; Lys. 12.17. Argos: Dem. 15.22; Diod. 14.6.2; Justin 5.9.4. Corinth: Aeschin. 2.147–48. Cf. Krentz (1982) 69; Forsdyke (2005) 199.

18. This interpretation seems to be contradicted by Xenophon's testimony. He claims that the Thirty expelled everyone apart from their oligarchic supporters, first from the city and then from all of Attica, in order to seize their estates (Xen. *Hell.* 2.4.1). Forsdyke (2005) 198–200 argues convincingly that Xenophon's account is shaped by the democratic image of tyrannical rule and that this ban concerned only the city proper and was intended to exclude these people from the political process. Cf. also Krentz (1982) 64–66, (1995) 139–40. Similarly, Theramenes' statement that he was against "banishing [φυγαδεύειν] either Thrasybulus or Anytus" (Xen. *Hell.* 2.3.42) is reasonably explained by Buck (1998) 64 to mean that a "decree of exile and confiscation of real property *ex post facto* was promulgated soon after he [i.e., Thrasybulus] was gone."

> εἶναι] from everywhere and that all who impeded those who led them back would be in violation of the treaty. (Plut. *Lys.* 27.2)

The phrase ἀγώγιμος εἶναι is a juridical terminus technicus meaning "liable to seizure."[19] It is therefore quite likely that the references in Diodorus and Plutarch preserve an element of the original Spartan decree. Yet the two accounts differ slightly concerning the consequences of disobeying the Spartan order. While Plutarch merely states more generally that the delinquent will be in violation of the treaty between Sparta and its allies (ἐκσπόνδους εἶναι), Diodorus reports the specific detail of a fine of five talents. That this piece of information is correct is suggested by both Plutarch's and Diodorus' account of the Theban counterdecree, for both mention that the Thebans also proposed a fine (πρόστιμον; ζημίαν ὀφείλειν τάλαντον) against those who would not intervene to help an Athenian exile being led away (Diod. 14.6.3; Plut. *Lys.* 27.3).

In sum, Xenophon's silence can be attributed to his bias. Diodorus and Plutarch are known to have used the early fourth-century *Hellenica Oxyrhynchia* via Ephorus. The Spartan extradition order makes sense historically, and the terminus technicus ἀγώγιμος εἶναι and the details of the fines proposed in the Spartan and Theban decrees are therefore strong arguments for their historicity.[20]

Thus far, I have only discussed one element of the Theban decree: the fine for failing to provide help to an Athenian refugee being led away by Sparta's agents. I argued that this is a direct response to the fine threatened by the Spartans for aiding the fugitives. While Diodorus relates only this component of the Theban decree, Plutarch mentions further measures taken by the Thebans in support of the Athenian democrats. The Thebans also passed decrees

> that any house and city in Boeotia should be open to Athenians in need . . . and that if anyone should carry arms through Boeotia to Athens against the tyrants, no Theban should either see him or hear him. (Plut. *Lys.* 27.3)

The latter element is also mentioned in Plutarch's *Life of Pelopidas* (Plut. *Pelop.* 6.5). It is impossible to know for certain whether these anti-Spartan actions were issued in one and the same decree or in several, as Plutarch's text suggests (ἀντεψηφίσαντο Θηβαῖοι ψηφίσματα, Plut. *Lys.* 27.3). It is not difficult, however, to accept the historicity of these two further elements (taking in Athenian

19. Cf. LSJ s.v. ἀγώγιμος A.II.

20. Hamilton (1979) 149–50, Cartledge (1987) 283, Gehrke (1985) 174, Buck (1998) 65, and Wolpert (2002) 24 accept the historicity of these decrees.

refugees and turning a blind eye to their activities against the Thirty), once we have accepted that the Thebans even imposed a tremendous fine for not coming to the aid of a refugee in the moment of his arrest.

A further clue for the historicity of these Theban decrees is provided in a fragment written by Lysias around 380 BC for an unknown Athenian pleading in an inheritance case on behalf of his Theban guest-friend Pherenicus. This Athenian told the jurors that he and "any other Athenian who wanted" were received by Pherenicus' father Cephisodotus as guest-friends when they were in exile and that they returned to their country "having received many great benefactions both privately and publically [καὶ ἰδίᾳ καὶ δημοσίᾳ] from him" (Lys. fr. 286 Carey). Since we do not know of any other acts of official Theban support for the Athenian exiles, the speaker's mention of Cephisodotus' "public" benefactions might very well be an allusion to his involvement in passing one of the aforementioned pro-Athenian Theban decrees.

If we accept the historicity of the Theban decrees in support of the Athenian democrats in 404/3, we have to explain a very abrupt volte-face. Just half a year earlier, the Thebans proposed to the Spartan allies the complete annihilation of Athens (Xen. *Hell.* 2.2.19), but now they issued decrees in support of the Athenian refugees against Sparta's explicit order.[21] How can this reversal of Theban foreign policy be explained?

Luckily, our sources betray some reasons for this volte-face. We are particularly fortunate to possess a long fragment of the *Hellenica Oxyrhynchia*—the ultimate source for Diodorus and Plutarch, via Ephorus—that reports in great detail about the internal power struggle of two opposing factions within both Thebes and the other cities of the Boeotian League at the dawn of the Corinthian War in 395.

> In Thebes, the best and most notable of the citizens [οἱ βέλτιστοι καὶ γνω|ριμώτατοι τῶν πολιτῶν], as I have already said, happened to be in *stasis* with one another. Ismenias, Antitheus, and Androcleidas led one faction, and Leontiades, Asias, and Coeratadas the other. Those of the citizens around Leontiades supported the Spartans; those around Ismenias were accused of supporting the Athenians [[ο]ἱ δὲ περὶ τὸν Ἰσμηνίαν | αἰτίαν μὲν εἶχον ἀττικίζειν], arising from their support for the demos when it was in exile [ἐξ ὧν πρόθυμοι πρὸς | τὸν δῆμον ἐγένοντο ὡς ἔφυγεν]. However, they were not concerned for the Athenians [οὐ μὴν ἐφρόν||[τιζον] τῶ[ν Ἀ]θηναίων] but . . . when . . . they . . . chose rather . . . being ready to do evil. Since this was the situation in Thebes

21. For a detailed discussion, see chapter 5.

and both *hetaeriae* were influential, many came forward from the cities in Boeotia and joined one or other of the *hetaeriae.* At that time [i.e., in 395] and even a little earlier, those around Ismenias and Androcleidas were dominant [ἐδύναντο δὲ τ[ότε μὲν καὶ ἔτι | μικ]ρῷ πρότερον οἱ πε[ρ]ὶ τὸν Ἰσμη[νίαν καὶ τὸ]ν | [Ἀνδ]ροκλείδαν] among the Thebans themselves and in the council of the Boeotians, but previously those around Asias and Leontiades held sway over the city through persuasion [τὴν πόλιν διὰ π̣[ειθοῦς εἶ]χον] for some length of time.[22] (*Hell. Oxy.* 20.1–2 Chambers = 17(12).1–2 Bartoletti)[23]

We can infer from this account and the ensuing passage (*Hell. Oxy.* 20.3–5 Chambers) that, during the Peloponnesian War, the pro-Spartan faction led by Leontiades determined Theban foreign policy.[24] We also learn that in 395 "and even a little earlier," Ismenias and his followers became preeminent both in Theban politics and in the federal council of the Boeotian League.[25] There has been much discussion as to the exact date of Ismenias' ascendancy, since the phrase καὶ ἔτι μικρῷ πρότερον itself is unspecific enough to indicate a time period ranging from a few weeks to a decade.[26] If we accept the historicity of the Theban decrees in support of the Athenian exiles, however, it follows invariably that Ismenias' faction must have been determining Boeotian foreign policy in the summer and fall of 404, since they were the ones supporting the Athenian "demos when it was in exile" and since their pro-Athenian proposals had to be officially ratified by the Boeotian federal council.

Thanks to the *Hellenica Oxyrhynchia,* we are able to explain the radical

22. I follow Bruce (1967) 113 and Chambers in reading π̣[ειθοῦς instead of Bartoletti's κ[ρατοῦς, for the following chapter strongly suggests that Leontiades' cooperation with the Spartans brought many economic benefits, which makes it seem unlikely that Leontiades' faction had to resort to force to stay in power during the Peloponnesian War.

23. In this book, I number the chapters of the *Hell. Oxy.* as in the most recent edition by Chambers (1993). Bartoletti (1959) and McKechnie & Kern (1988) do not contain the most recent Cairo fragment. Consequently Chambers' chapter 20 is their chapter 17. Bruce (1967), in his commentary, follows the numbering of the *editio princeps* of the London papyrus; Chambers' chapter 20 is his chapter 12.

24. For an excellent discussion of the nature of political factions in ancient Greece, see Strauss (1986) 1–3, 11–36. Strauss examines the sociopolitical situation in Athens between 404 and 386, but his model of politics also applies to the situation in Thebes, as we can glean from the Oxyrhynchus historian.

25. For the constitutional structure of the Theban-dominated Boeotian League, cf. *Hell. Oxy.* 19 Chambers; Bruce (1967) 102–9, 157–64; Gehrke (1985) 168–72; Cartledge (1987) 277–79.

26. Cf. Hamilton (1979) 148; Buck (1998) 67. For the purpose of my argument, it is inconsequential whether members of Ismenias' faction actually managed to get elected into the office of *boeotarch* at this time. What matters is the fact that Ismenias and his faction managed to sway the federal councilors to adopt a pro-Athenian stance during the summer of 404 and thus determined Theban foreign policy toward Athens. Cf. Buck (1998) 70.

volte-face in Thebes in 404 as the result of a new faction ascending to power: Leontiades' pro-Spartan group lost its dominant position to Ismenias' *hetaeria.* Yet how did this change come about? We do not have any indication that Ismenias took over the government by force. This means he must have convinced the majority of the 660 members of the Boeotian federal *boule,* the body responsible for foreign policy decisions in the Boeotian League.[27] Also, from where did Ismenias' desire to support the Athenian exiles stem? And what are the arguments and motives that could have reversed the pro-Spartan course in Theban and Boeotian foreign policy?

The question about Ismenias' motives is hard to answer definitively. It has been suggested that Ismenias' faction was democratic and therefore pro-Athenian, while Leontiades' was oligarchic and thus pro-Spartan.[28] This is unconvincing. The Oxyrhynchus historian calls the leaders of both factions οἱ βέλτιστοι καὶ γνωριμώτατοι (*Hell. Oxy.* 20.1 Chambers), and once in power, Ismenias' faction did not show any signs of making the Boeotian constitution more democratic.[29]

In his explanation of the outbreak of the Corinthian War in 395, the Oxyrhynchus historian is combating the seemingly widespread notion that Timocrates' Persian bribes were responsible. Instead, he points to the internal power struggles between pro-Spartan factions and their anti-Spartan opponents in Boeotia and Argos as the decisive factor.

> But they [who hold the bribes responsible] do not know that all had long been ill-disposed toward the Spartans, looking out for a way that they might make their *poleis* adopt a war policy. For the Argives and the Boeotians [ἐμίσουν γὰρ οἱ μὲν Ἀργεῖοι καὶ Βοιωτ[οὶ . . . .]τωτạι][30] hated the Spartans because they treated as friends their enemies among the citizens. (*Hell. Oxy.* 10.2 Chambers)

This long-standing anti-Spartan attitude of Ismenias and his partisans is expressed even more clearly in another passage dealing with the outbreak of the Corinthian War.

---

27. For the role of the federal council, cf. Bruce (1967) 160; Buck (1998) 70. For the need to persuade the majority of uncommitted council members, see Cook (1988) 80.

28. Larsen (1955) 40.

29. Hamilton (1979) 145–46; Gehrke (1985) 174 note 61; Buckler (1980) 36–37.

30. It would be attractive to read Βοιωτ[ῶν προσ]τ<ά>ται with Gigante and Castiglioni and see in this phrase a clear reference to the ascendency of Ismenias' faction. This reading is difficult for two reasons, however. First, the ω in τωται is clear in the papyrus, so one would have to regard it as the scribe's error. Second, one would expect Βοιωτοὶ after Ἀργεῖοι for stylistic reasons. Cf. Bruce (1967) 60.

> Those around Androcleidas and Ismenias were eager to involve the Boeotians in a war with the Lacedaemonians, because firstly they wished to overthrow their supremacy, lest they would be destroyed by the Lacedaemonians on account of the pro-Spartan faction. (*Hell. Oxy.* 21.1 Chambers)

Moreover, in the long section quoted above, our historian emphasizes that Ismenias' motivation was not primarily concern for the Athenians (οὐ μὴν ἐφρόν||[τιζον] τῶ[ν Ἀ]θηναίων; *Hell. Oxy.* 20.2 Chambers). Unfortunately, the text breaks off here, and we do not hear more about Ismenias' true motivation. In conclusion, according to the *Hellenica Oxyrhynchia,* Ismenias' and his partisans' support for the Athenian exiles stemmed not primarily from sympathy for the Athenian democracy but, rather, from the intra-Theban power struggle with the Spartan-backed faction led by Leontiades, which was seen as a potentially fatal threat.[31]

Another source, however, suggests that personal relations between members of Ismenias' faction and individual Athenian refugees did help to bring about the Theban volte-face. The aforementioned client of Lysias claimed that he and other Athenian refugees were received by the Theban Cephisodotus as guest-friends and received many great benefactions both privately and publically from their ξένος (Lys. fr. 286.2 Carey). Despite years of enmity between Athens and Thebes, it is not unlikely that the traditional guest-friendship relations between aristocratic elites continued to exist between citizens of both *poleis.* The obligations arising from this ritual bond of ξενία would at least encourage private aid for the Athenian refugees, if it did not translate into public promotion of the Athenians' case.[32]

Appeals to the Theban Self-Image

It still needs to be explained how Ismenias managed to convince the majority of the citizens in the Theban *boulae* and especially in the federal council to support the Athenian democrats against Sparta's explicit prohibition. Hamilton, Cartledge, and Buck have identified some reasons for the Theban volte-

31. That this fear was not unwarranted is shown by the events of 382. See "Theban Exiles in Athens, 382–379" below, 254–60.

32. Buck (1998) 66 supposes that there might have been connections of consanguinity or guest-friendship between Ismenias and Thrasybulus as well. That ξενία did indeed play an important role in 404 is suggested by the Athenian support on behalf of their Theban guest-friends after the Spartan coup d'état in 382. See "Theban Exiles in Athens, 382–379" below, 254–60.

face.[33] While all of them offer a net of interlocking motives, it is clear that, in their view, the predominant factor was a calculation of *Realpolitik*:[34] the establishment of Lysander's pro-Spartan puppet regime in Athens to guard against Boeotian expansionism (Polyaen. 1.45.5; Xen. *Hell.* 2.4.30) as well as a Spartan intervention in Thessaly were perceived as threats to Thebes' security.[35] Further motives adduced were economic and psychological in nature. The end of the Decelean War meant a cessation of booty coming in from Attica; Leontiades thus lost a powerful argument for a staunch pro-Spartan stance (*Hell. Oxy.* 20.3–5 Chambers). Furthermore, Sparta's arrogant treatment of its major allies at the conclusion of the war increased anti-Spartan resentments in Thebes. The Spartans, for instance, refused to share the spoils of war equitably (Xen. *Hell.* 3.5.5; Plut. *Lys.* 27) and rebuffed the Theban proposal to annihilate Athens, with a remark about Athens' heroic role in the Persian Wars, thus implicitly slandering Thebes for its medism (Xen. *Hell.* 2.2.19–20).[36] In passing, Hamilton also mentions a "widespread feeling of revulsion at the excesses of the Thirty" and concedes that "purely humanitarian motives"[37] could have played their part in turning the Thebans against Sparta and their puppet regime in Athens. Yet in the historical reconstructions of Hamilton, Cartledge, and Buck, much less weight is given to such considerations than to the dictates of *Realpolitik*. All three historians seem to adhere to the principles of Realism: states are rational actors and always strive for power and security; consequently, it is by and large such factors that determine a country's foreign policy.[38]

Based on various explicit references in the later historiographical tradition, combined with contemporary numismatic and archaeological evidence, I shall make the case that, in addition to Realist arguments, ideological factors, such as the Theban self-image as the city of the great Greek culture hero Heracles, played a vital role in swaying public opinion in Thebes toward supporting the Athenian exiles in 404. Focusing on the emotional reaction in Thebes to the Athenian terror regime of the Thirty, Diodorus describes the Theban aid given to the exiled democrats as an immediate reaction to the banishing and killing (τοὺς

33. Hamilton (1979) 150–51; Cartledge (1987) 283; Buck (1998) 68–70.

34. For a critique of the theory of Realism and the importance of nonrational factors in foreign policy decisions, see "Public Discourse and Decision Making" in the introduction, 30–36.

35. For Sparta's intervention in Thessaly against Archelaus of Macedon in the summer of 404, see Cartledge (1987) 283 with further literature.

36. Cf. Cartledge (1987) 280. For a detailed discussion of the reasons to preserve Athens, see "Imagining the Unimaginable: The Eradication of Athens" in chapter 5, 309–23.

37. Hamilton (1979) 150.

38. Cf. Buck (1998) 70: "The Boeotian assistance to Thrasybulus, though it was at least in part the product of factional politics as well as of guest-friendship, followed a familiar Boeotian pattern: help for Athenian opponents of any regime in power at Athens. . . . Anything that would distract and weaken their Athenian neighbour was good to do." Similarly, Gehrke (1985) 174.

μὲν φυγαδεύοντες, τοὺς δὲ ἀναιροῦντες): the Thebans were "vexed about what was taking place" (τῶν δὲ Θηβαίων ἀγανακτούντων ἐπὶ τοῖς γινομένοις, Diod. 14.32.1).[39] Plutarch, in his *Life of Lysander*, characterizes the Theban decrees as "fitting and akin to the deeds of Heracles and Dionysus" (πρέποντα καὶ ἀδελφὰ ταῖς Ἡρακλέους καὶ Διονύσου πράξεσιν) and as "Hellenic and humane" (Ἑλληνικὰ καὶ φιλάνθρωπα, Plut. *Lys.* 27.3–4). It can, of course, not be ruled out that this merely reflects later self-serving Theban traditions or Diodorus' and Plutarch's own comments, but considering the contemporary Athenian practice, Thebes' self-image, and Diodorus' and Plutarch's likely sources (the *Hell. Oxy.* via Ephorus), it is entirely possible that we can grasp here a trace of the debate in 404.

Given what we know about the use of Athens' self-image in Athenian public discourse, it is quite likely that Ismenias evoked the Theban memory of their own culture heroes in order to incite his fellow citizens to oppose the evils of the Thirty Tyrants. For, as we have seen in chapter 2, fifth-century Athenians saw themselves as champions of Greek liberty and as protectors of the weak, checking arrogance and injustice. This "timeless" Athenian character was projected back into the past and manifested itself in numerous mythical feats, including the support for Adrastus' efforts to recover and bury the fallen Argives and for the return of the Heraclidae. These symbols of Athenian ἀρετή were propagated in, among other things, the Athenian funeral orations and were used as arguments in political and diplomatic discourse.[40]

Similarly, the Theban-born hero Heracles and the god Dionysus were important elements for the fifth-century Theban self-image.[41] The strongest evidence for this assertion can be found in the coinage of the Boeotian League, which—due to Thebes' ascendancy after the battle of Coronea in 447/6—was issued in the name of Thebes alone, as seen in the coin inscriptions ΘΕΒΑΙΟΣ (nom. sing.) or ΘΕΒΑΙΟΝ (gen. plur.).[42] From this time on, images of Heracles and Dionysus came to dominate the reverse, while the obverse continued to display the Boeotian shield, the long-standing symbol of the Boeotian League.[43] We thus find depictions of Heracles—advancing into battle (351), kneeling or standing to string a bow (352), carrying off the Delphic tripod (353), or, as a child, strangling serpents (354)—as well as facing or profile heads of Heracles

39. ἀγανακτέω originally denotes a physical reaction of the body to cold. The Thebans were, so to speak, "chilled" by what happened in Athens. Cf. LSJ s.v. ἀγανακτέω.

40. Cf. the Athenians' argument for primacy over the Tegeans before the battle at Plataea in Hdt. 9.27. See "Funeral Orations" in chapter 1 of the present study, 49–58.

41. Demand (1982) 49 even speaks of Heracles as the "alter ego" of the city of Thebes in the fifth century.

42. Kraay (1976) 111. Another inscription reads ΗΕΒΑ ΘΕΒΑΙΟΣ, which might be an engraver's blunder for ΗΕΡΑ(κλης) ΘΕΒΑΙΟΣ, as suggested by Kraay (1976) 111 note 1.

43. Both Kraay (1976) 111 and Demand (1982) 2–3 understand this imagery as an expression of the Theban self-image. For the chronology of the Boeotian coinage, see Head (1881).

(356–57) and Dionysus (358).[44] Images of Heracles and Dionysus or of their attributes (club, bow, amphora, ivy, grapes) continue to feature prominently on Thebes' coinage during the following decades as well.[45]

The Thebans' choice is not surprising, since, in Greek mythology, both Heracles and Dionysus are closely connected with their city. Heracles was born and grew up in Thebes, where his mother, Alcmene, and her husband, Amphitryon, lived in exile at Creon's court. Megara, Creon's daughter, became Heracles' first wife.[46] The Olympian god Dionysus sprang from the union between Zeus and Semele, the daughter of Thebes' founding father Cadmus. She gave birth prematurely to Dionysus, when she was consumed by Zeus' lightning bolt. Later, on his triumphant return from the East, Dionysus came back to Thebes to introduce his cult and punish those who had slandered his mother and opposed him.[47] Thebes even had the reputation to be the earliest home of Dionysus and his orgiastic worship in Greece.[48]

That the Thebans showed special reverence to these two gods is not only indicated by the aforementioned coinage but also confirmed by the prominence of their cults in Thebes. Heracles possessed a well-known sanctuary right outside the city (Paus. 9.11.4–6), as well as a number of holy places associated with his life and activities.[49] The cult of Dionysus was, along with that of Apollo Ismenius, one of the two chief cults in Thebes.[50] He had a shrine as Dionysus Cadmeus in the house of Cadmus on the Theban acropolis (Paus. 9.12.3–4) and another shrine as Dionysus Lysius near the Proitidian gate (Paus. 9.16.6–7). Heracles' special importance for Thebes is also corroborated by the Athenian orator Isocrates, who wrote in his *Philip* that the Thebans honor Heracles "both by processionals and by sacrifices more than the other gods" (Isoc. 5.32).

That the Thebans did evoke Heracles in diplomatic contexts is suggested by the historiographical tradition found in Justin's account of the destruction of Thebes by Alexander in 335. The Theban elder Cleades implored Alexander to spare the city that had "given birth not only to men but also to gods," thus alluding to Heracles and Dionysus. Moreover, he "worked upon the king, too, from his private superstitious regard for Hercules, who had been born at Thebes, and from whom the family of the Aeacidae [i.e., the Macedonian royal house, among others] was descended" (Justin 11.4.4–6).

44. Kraay (1976) 111, images of coins on plates 19–20.

45. Cf. Kraay (1976) 112–14 and [361–72] on plate 20.

46. For Heracles' birth in Thebes, see Hom. *Il.* 19.99; Pind. *Nem.* 1.33–72. For his marriage with Megara, cf. Eur. *HF* 9–12.

47. For Dionysus' birth and his return to Thebes, cf. Eur. *Bacch.* 1–55.

48. Demand (1982) 55, 69.

49. For a complete list of holy places in Thebes associated with Heracles, see Demand (1982) 49–52.

50. Demand (1982) 54–55.

That both Heracles and Dionysus had a special meaning for the Thebans is thus clear from their prominence in Thebes' cults and mythology. Yet it is much harder to define exactly what these two gods symbolized in the eyes of their Theban worshipers. Their role as culture heroes who bestowed on humans the advantages of civilization (e.g., wine, the Bacchic rites, and freedom from lawless monsters) was certainly one important facet.[51] This civilizing aspect in general and Heracles' fight against chaotic monsters in particular is clearly the *tertium comparationis* in the aforementioned passage in Plutarch's *Life of Lysander*, where the Theban counterdecrees in defiance of the Thirty Tyrants are called "fitting and akin to the deeds of Heracles and Dionysus" (πρέποντα καὶ ἀδελφὰ ταῖς Ἡρακλέους καὶ Διονύσου πράξεσιν), "Hellenic" (i.e., civilized) and "humane" (Ἑλληνικὰ καὶ φιλάνθρωπα, Plut. *Lys.* 27.3–4). Moreover, it is evident from a passage in Isocrates that Hercules' characterization as the epitome of φιλανθρωπία stems from the classical period and is not a later invention by Diodorus or Plutarch (Isoc. 5.114).[52] Considering Heracles' and Dionysus' role for the Theban self-image, it is likely that they were indeed invoked by Ismenias in the debate in 404 as paradigms for proper conduct toward the Athenian exiles.

Apart from serving as a general paradigm for Hellenic and human behavior, there might be another reason why Ismenias' would have wanted to draw on Heracles in this debate, as I will argue: throughout his life, Heracles frequently received help from Athena, the patron goddess of the Athenians. Heracles fought together with the Athenian king Theseus against the Amazons and rescued him from the underworld.[53] Moreover, according to the Athenian master narrative, it was the Athenians who restored Heracles' descendants to their rightful kingship over the Peloponnese. The figure of Heracles could thus personify the successful cooperation between Athens and Thebes. Since, during the fifth century, the Athenian-Theban relationship was characterized by utter hostility, it makes sense that a Theban speaker who wanted to encourage his fellow citizens to repay a former benefit and to support Athenian exiles would have to fall back on mythical examples of close cooperation between the two cities.

A prime example for this use of Heracles in diplomatic discourse is provided by the Athenian orator Isocrates. In his address to Philip II of Macedon, writ-

51. Demand (1982) 2–3 emphasizes the analogy between Heracles' labors and the Thebans' situation after the Persian Wars, when they had to struggle with the material and political consequences of their medizing.

52. The term φιλανθρωπία is indeed frequently used in fourth-century public discourse to denote the attitude of one polis toward another; cf. Dem. *Prooem.* 16. In 346 BC, Isocrates encouraged Philip II of Macedon to imitate his ancestor's (i.e., Heracles') φιλανθρωπία in his dealings with the other Greek states (Isoc. 5.114–16).

53. For Heracles' benefactions to Theseus, see Diod. 4.16.4, 4.26.1.

ten in 346, Isocrates promotes the idea of a Panhellenic campaign against Asia under Philip's leadership. Yet Philip, according to Isocrates, would first have to reconcile the four leading *poleis* in Greece: Argos, Sparta, Thebes, and Athens (Isoc. 5.30–31). He ought to show proper respect for these cities on account of their friendly conduct toward Heracles and his descendants, the ancestors of the Macedonian dynasty: "For you will find that each one of them is to be credited with great friendship toward your family and with great benefactions" (Isoc. 5.32).

Isocrates claims that Athens is particularly deserving of Philip's gratitude for two reasons.

> As far as our city is concerned, those whom we trust in matters of ancient history say that she helped Heracles toward immortality [συναιτίαν γενέσθαι τῆς ἀθανασίας] (in what way it is easy for you to learn at another time and not the right moment for me to tell you now) and his children towards salvation [τῆς σωτηρίας]. (Isoc. 5.33)

The latter achievement is an integral element of the Athenian master narrative, as it was promulgated, for instance, on stage and in the patriotic funeral orations:[54] the Athenians single-handedly saved his descendants from Eurystheus' power and put an end to his hubris. Yet the first example, concerning Heracles' immortality, is rather vague. Norlin, referring to a passage in Diodorus, takes it as an allusion to the Athenians being the first to offer sacrifices to Heracles as a god and not just as a hero.[55] It is not impossible that Isocrates had this story in mind when he claimed that Athens had "helped Heracles toward immortality" (συναιτίαν γενέσθαι τῆς ἀθανασίας). Yet one could argue that Heracles' immortality was first and foremost the reward granted to him by Zeus for the successful execution of his labors. Consequently, it would make more sense to see in this phrase an allusion to any help provided by Athens in completing these labors leading to immortality.

Granted, in the mythical tradition there is no mention of any aid provided by the city of Athens itself; but if we allow the patron deity Athena to stand in for her city, we find numerous cases where Athena assisted Heracles in his

54. Lys. 2.11–16; Isoc. 4.33–34; Eur. *Heracl.* Cf. chapter 1 in the present study. See also Loraux (1986) 67–69; Castriota (1992) 43–49; Parker (1996) 138–39; Forsdyke (2005) 234–37.

55. See Norlin (1928) 265. Natoli (2004a) 158 accepts this explanation. Quite possibly, Diodorus followed an Athenian tradition, which aimed to boost Athens' prestige vis-à-vis their northern rival Thebes: "Much the same thing was likewise done by the Thebans [i.e., to honor Heracles like a hero], but the Athenians were the first of all men to honor Heracles with sacrifices like a god, and by holding up their own piety toward this god as an example, they propelled first the other Greeks and then all men throughout the inhabited world to honor Heracles as a god" (Diod. 4.39.1).

labors. This is nowhere more palpable than at the temple of Zeus in Olympia, one of the most prominent Panhellenic sanctuaries. The metopes of this fifth-century masterpiece display the twelve labors of Heracles, and the goddess Athena is shown four times as his assistant (fig. 5).[56] Athena comforts young Heracles as he rests after killing the Nemean lion (first labor). Heracles gives the dead Stymphalian birds to Athena, who had provided him with bronze clappers (third labor); Boardman suggests that one should view the rock on which Athena is sitting as an allusion to the Athenian acropolis. With Athena's help, Heracles carries Atlas' load as he brings him the apples of the Hesperides (tenth labor). Finally, Athena, in full armor, indicates to Heracles the place at which to breach the walls of the stables of Augeas, to let in the river and cleanse them (twelfth labor). Even if Isocrates was referring to the Athenians' veneration of Heracles as a god and not to Athena's aid, the mentioning of both Athens and Heracles' immortality was likely to evoke also Athena's role in Heracles' labors, especially since this was well known in the fifth century, as the Olympian metopes prove.

Considering that Isocrates and Thrasybulus were both Athenians and contemporaries, it is not farfetched to assume that the latter might have drawn on the same paradigms in his plea for help and reminded the Theban federal council of the benefits bestowed on Heracles and his descendants by his mother city and her patron deity. It is equally plausible, of course, that it was Ismenias who, drawing on the collective memory of his Athenian guest-friend, introduced Athens' mythical benefactions into the current debate. Moreover, Ismenias could be confident that his argument based on Athena's aid for Heracles would resonate with his Theban audience. For, according to their local traditions, it was Athena who—by the blow of a stone—prevented Heracles, in his madness, from killing his foster father Amphitryon (Paus. 9.11.2).[57] This rock, called σωφρονιστήρ (restorer of reason), lay in Heracles' Theban sanctuary and thus served as a material reminder of Athena's benefaction.

Of course, it cannot be proved that Plutarch's comparison of the Theban decrees to Heracles' and Dionysus' φιλανθρωπία ultimately derives from the *Hellenica Oxyrhynchia*. Their author, especially if it is Cratippus, might not have incorporated set speeches into his work to dramatize political struggles like the conflict between Ismenias' and Leontiades' faction over the fate of the Athenian exiles in 404.[58] Yet it is quite possible that he stated the argu-

56. Boardmann (1985) 38, 47, fig. 22.

57. Cf. Demand (1982) 51.

58. Granted, apart from one short exhortation (*Hell. Oxy.* 18.2 Chambers), we do not have any indication that the Oxyrhynchus historian incorporated speeches into his work, and Dionysius of Halicarnassus states that Cratippus rejected Thucydides' method of including set speeches (Dion. Hal. *Thuc.* 16); cf. Shrimpton (1991) 184, 189. Bruce (1967) 6 is skeptical. Chambers (1993) xvii,

Fig. 5. Twelve labors of Heracles on the metopes of the temple of Zeus in Olympia, in which he is assisted by Athena in labors 1, 3, 10, and 12. (After Boardman (1985) fig. 22; drawing by Marion Cox. Reproduced by courtesy of the author and Thames and Hudson, Ltd, London.)

ments used by the former to secure the passing of the pro-Athenian decrees, which were mentioned in Plutarch's and Diodorus' common source, as we have shown. Moreover, as Bruce and others stress, judging from the extant fragments, it is clear that the Oxyrhynchus historian was very well informed about the internal power struggles in Athens and in Thebes.[59] The level of detail and the keen understanding of factional politics that are found in the discussion of the so-called Demaenetus affair in Athens (*Hell. Oxy.* 9–10 Chambers) and the struggle between the two Boeotian *hetaeriae* at the dawn of the Corinthian War make it seem likely indeed that our historian mentioned the arguments used by Ismenias in 404 as well. Moreover, his reference to the factional strife "mentioned earlier" (ὥσπερ καὶ πρότερον εἴρηκα, *Hell. Oxy.* 20.1 Chambers) could very well be an allusion to the heated debate in the summer of 404 in which Ismenias supposedly drew on Heracles' example to promote the idea of Theban help for the exiled Athenians against Leontiades' opposition.[60] Even though this reconstruction of the debate in Thebes in 404 rests primarily on references in the later historiographical tradition, combined with contemporary clues about the fifth-century Theban self-image and Hercules as epitome of φιλανθρωπία, one piece of evidence strongly supports my argument that the mythological connection between Heracles and Athens played a major role in Theban discourse in 404. After the overthrow of the Thirty in 403, Thrasybulus and other members of the exiled democrats expressed their thanks to the Thebans by setting up two colossal statues in the sanctuary of Heracles in Thebes—one of Athena, the other of Heracles (Paus. 9.11.6)—thus celebrating their close mythological ties.

Despite their growing anger at Sparta's imperialistic conduct and notwithstanding Ismenias' evocation of the ancient friendship between Thebes and Athens and Theban φιλανθρωπία, most Thebans were not ready to break openly with Sparta. The Thebans passed their counterdecrees, but they did not want to provide official military aid for the Athenian democrats.[61] This is clear

however, strongly believes that, just as Thucydides' and Xenophon's histories, the *Hell. Oxy.* contained speeches (in direct or indirect discourse). He makes the sensible suggestion to consider the Theramenes Papyrus (*P Mich.* 5982), which features fragments of a speech, as part of the *Hell. Oxy.*

59. Cf. Bruce (1967) 8: "[T]he passages which discuss the rivalries and policies of the leading factions in both Athens and Thebes can only have been derived from information provided by someone who had been in these cities at the time and had taken a keen interest in politics." See also Shrimpton (1991) 195; Schepens (2001) 223–24.

60. Bruce (1967) 110 assumes that ὥσπερ καὶ πρότερον εἴρηκα (*Hell. Oxy.* 20.1 Chambers) refers back to "οὐ γὰρ πολλοῖς [ἔ]τεσιν πρότερον ἔτυξον εἰς στασιασμὸν οἱ Βοιωτοὶ προελθόντες" (*Hell. Oxy.* 19.1 Chambers), that is, to the beginning of this episode dealing with Thebes' role in the outbreak of the Corinthian War in 395. Yet Bruce agrees that the beginning of this στασιασμός dates back to 404. The phrase "as I have said earlier" in reference to the Boeotian civil strife could, therefore, refer back to an account of the debate over the Athenian exiles in 404 as well.

61. Cloché (1918) 333 and Hamilton (1979) 148 reasonably suggest that between the two fac-

from our sources, which stress Ismenias' secrecy and private initiative in lending military support to Thrasybulus (Diod. 14.32.1; Plut. *Lys.* 27.4; Justin 5.9.8). The Thebans were firm, however, in their refusal to assist the Thirty and the Spartans to overcome the Athenian democrats, and they therefore ignored Pausanias' call for military aid (Xen. *Hell.* 2.4.30).

Theban Support for Thrasybulus in Athenian Social Memory

In the previous section, I tried to reconstruct the situation in Thebes in 404/3. Based on Xenophon and the *Hellenica Oxyrhynchia* (and later sources derived from it), I argued for the historicity of the Theban counterdecree(s) in support of the exiled Athenian democrats. Furthermore, we found some clues in Pausanias, Plutarch, and the Oxyrhynchus historian that gave us a glimpse of the sort of arguments probably used by Ismenias in the political debate in Thebes in 404.

With this in mind, we can return to our initial questions. Why was this precarious memory preserved in Athenian historical consciousness, and how was it transmitted down to Dinarchus' generation? Dinarchus himself mentions two carriers of this social memory: the elders and the Theban decree that was often read before the Athenians (Din. 1.25). Now we have to ask, at which occasions would a Theban decree be read out before the Athenians, and why would the participants in the event in 404 hand this information down to their descendants?

There are at least two means of approaching this question. First, I will explore whether there were any material commemorations of this event that could preserve this memory for future generations. Then, bearing in mind the characteristics of social memory in public discourse, we have to ask in which historical situations this event might have been mentioned and thus revived in Athenian public discourse during the course of the fourth century.[62]

Memorialization of the Theban Support in Thebes

In this section, I explore whether and, if so, by what means Thebes' help to the Athenian democrats was commemorated in Thebes. That the memory of this

tions, there was a floating mass of citizens who mostly supported Leontiades until 404 and then favored Ismenias' anti-Spartan policies. See also Cook (1988) 67.

62. For an excellent study of a specific social memory in public discourse in the course of changing historical circumstances, see Novick's (1999) study of the memory of the Holocaust in American life.

generous support was preserved by the Thebans is not surprising, since this action was consistent with the Theban self-image: following the tradition of their culture heroes Heracles and Dionysus, the Thebans crushed the savage forces of chaos (the Thirty Tyrants) and replaced them with order and civilization. This attitude is evident from the aforementioned characterization of the Theban decrees in Plutarch's *Life of Lysander.*

> In reply to [the Spartan command], the Thebans issued counterdecrees, fitting and akin to the deeds of Heracles and Dionysus [πρέποντα καὶ ἀδελφὰ ταῖς Ἡρακλέους καὶ Διονύσου πράξεσιν]. . . . And they did not merely vote such Hellenic and humane decrees [Ἑλληνικὰ καὶ φιλάνθρωπα], while failing to provide deeds corresponding to their words; no, Thrasybulus and those who with him seized Phyle set out from Thebes, while Thebans provided them with arms and money, with secrecy and a base for operations. (Plut. *Lys.* 27.3–4)

In the previous section, I argued that this analogy with the deeds of Heracles and Dionysus stems from a contemporary historiographical account of the power struggle in Thebes between Ismenias' and Leontiades' factions. Yet even if this analogy was not drawn in the debate of 404, the connection in Plutarch proves that at least at some point after the event, people associated Thebes' generous support for the Athenian exiles with the Theban culture heroes Heracles and Dionysus.[63] Even if it were Plutarch's own comment, we can trace it back to Theban memory communities; as a leading citizen of Chaeronea, a neighboring Boeotian town, Plutarch—even five hundred years after the events—was certainly familiar with Thebes' self-image as a benefactor of humanity, acting in the tradition of its two prominent gods. That the memory of past events conforms to the community's self-characterization is an important feature of social memory, as we have seen in the case of the Athenians, who saw themselves as πρόμαχοι of all the Greeks ever since their victory over the Persians at Marathon.[64]

There are some clues, however, suggesting that the association of Thebes' help with the deeds of Heracles originated in the debate of 404 itself or at least shortly thereafter. The most important indicator is the thank offering dedicated by the victorious Athenian exiles and set up in Thebes.

63. There is a possibility that the comparison with the deeds of Heracles and Dionysus goes back to the fourth-century historian Ephorus, who used the *Hellenica Oxyrhynchia* for this part of his history. In this case, Ephorus would provide us with an insight into how his contemporaries viewed the events in Thebes in 404.

64. Cf. "Ideology and Social Memory" in the introduction, 13–19, and "Funeral Orations" in chapter 1, 49–58.

> Thrasybulus, son of Lycus, and the Athenians who with him put down the tyranny of the Thirty—because their return from exile began from Thebes—dedicated in the sanctuary of Heracles colossal figures of Athena and Heracles, carved by Alcamenes in relief out of Pentelic marble. (Paus. 9.11.6)

These dedications fulfilled several functions. First, since these colossal statues were set up in the sanctuary of Heracles, a much-frequented site, Thebans were thus often exposed to this monument of their generous support and of the Athenians' gratitude. Second, even though Pausanias does not mention it explicitly, we can assume that the base of these figures bore a votive inscription disclosing the identity of the dedicator, since this was the common practice and since such an inscription was presumably the source of information for Pausanias. Theban visitors to the sanctuary were thus permanently encouraged to link the two statues to Thebes' aid for the Athenian exiles.

Third, the juxtaposition of these two respective polis deities, Athena and Heracles, symbolized the cooperation between Thebes and Athens in mythical times as well as in the present. That the images of patron deities were indeed used in diplomatic contexts to indicate the close relationship between their respective cities is evident from other contemporary monuments. Perhaps the best example for this phenomenon is the Athenian relief crowning the famous honorary inscription for the Samians of 405/4 (*IG* I^3 127 = *IG* II^2 1).[65] In this relief, Samos and Athens are represented by Hera and Athena clasping right hands, a gesture interpreted by Lawton to symbolize the particular agreement and, more generally, "unity and accord" between the two cities.[66] Alcamenes' relief of Heracles and Athena fulfilled a similar function.

The location of these colossal statues also underscored the close connection between Heracles and Athena, Thebes and Athens, since the sanctuary of Heracles was located right outside Thebes on the main road leading to Athens.[67] Moreover, Pausanias reports that the carvings on the pediments of the temple were the work of Praxiteles and displayed most of the twelve labors of Heracles, except for the slaughter of the Stymphalian birds and the cleansing of Elis (Paus. 9.11.6).[68] Judging from the iconography of Heracles' labors elsewhere, it is quite

65. The stele contains three decrees honoring the loyal Samians (M&L 94 and R&O 2) and was set up in 403/2, when the last decree was passed. The initial inscription was probably destroyed by the Thirty and therefore reinscribed in 403/2. Cf. Rhodes & Osborne (2003) 15, with an image of the entire stele on plate 1.

66. Lawton (1995) 30, 36. Cf. Forsdyke (2005) 221.

67. Cf. Frazer (1965) 5:47.

68. The famous Athenian sculptor Praxiteles is usually dated to the fourth century (Pliny *NH* 35.49 gives him a *floruit* of 364–361); the pediment with Heracles' labors must thus have been added

likely that, just as in the metopes of the temple of Zeus at Olympia, Athena was shown assisting Heracles in his endeavors.[69] The σωφρονιστὴρ λίθος, thrown by Athena to prevent the raging Heracles from killing his foster father Amphitryon and now displayed in Heracles' precinct, served as another reminder of Athena's benefactions (Paus. 9.11.2).[70] The collaboration between Athena and Heracles is thus emphasized in several ways.

Apart from these votive statues, another kind of monument was possibly used to memorialize this event: the Theban counterdecree(s) might have been inscribed on a stone stele and set up in a public place such as the agora or the Cadmea. This is just a hypothesis, of course, but it is not unlikely, since other decrees were inscribed as well and since, as we shall see later, Theban politicians, in all likelihood, used this decree in diplomatic missions to Athens throughout the fourth century.[71]

Athenian Memorialization of the Men from Phyle

Since the Theban support for the persecuted Athenian exiles is consistent with the Theban self-image, its memorialization in Thebes is to be expected. In Athens, the situation was different. Thanks to Athens' long-standing enmity toward Thebes, the conditions for memorializing this Theban benefaction were far from ideal, especially since the Athenian master narrative portrayed the Thebans as prototypical traitors, as we have seen in chapter 2. How was it possible, then, that the memory of this uncharacteristic Theban behavior was passed on for two generations, down to Dinarchus' time? I contend that the active memorialization of the return of the exiled democrats functioned as a fixed point to which the precarious memory of Theban aid could at times be attached.

If the Athenian democrats had not been triumphant against the Thirty, Thebes' support would most certainly have been completely forgotten. But as it turned out, the successful reestablishment of democracy was a pivotal event for the Athenians and was therefore memorialized by a variety of means.[72] Events that are frequently recalled by a large community become much simplified and

to the temple complex a few decades later than the two colossal statues. Nevertheless, from then on, the pediment would have been able to reinforce the theme of the collaboration between the two deities. For the attractive hypothesis of an earlier Praxiteles, see Frazer (1965) 5:48.

69. Cf. fig. 5 above.

70. This incident was also known to Athenians, as Eur. *HF* 1001–8 proves.

71. See, for instance, *IG* VII 2407 (= R&O 43) and *IG* VII 2408, two honorary decrees, dating from the 360s to the 350s.

72. Thrasybulus' splendid tomb in the *demosion sema,* for instance, commemorated the victory over the oligarchs as a victory for Athens (Paus. 1.29.3); cf. Wolpert (2002) 89. For a detailed analysis of the negotiation of the memory of the civil war and reconciliation in Athenian public discourse, see Wolpert (2002); Loraux (2002).

are cast into the form of a story, with beginning, middle, and end.[73] Through this process of narrativization, the different stations along the way from exile to victory—Phyle, Munichia, the Piraeus—became deeply rooted in Athenian historical consciousness. It is crucial to note that in the Athenian master narrative, the democratic success story begins not with Thrasybulus' departure from Thebes but with the seizure of the Attic fortress Phyle. The overthrow of the Thirty was by and large remembered as a solely Athenian achievement. There are several reasons, however, why the Theban contribution to the democrats' success was not entirely forgotten. First, memory works by association; the mentioning of the seizure of Phyle, which was located on the road from Thebes to Athens, could prompt the memory of the exiles' mustering in Thebes as well.[74] Second, individual Athenian exiles would remember the help they received from Theban guest-friends (ξένοι).[75] Third, the Athenian demos commemorated the triumph of the democratic exiles through monumental inscriptions. Some of Thrasybulus' initial supporters were foreigners (Thebans and Boeotians undoubtedly among them), who were honored by grants of citizenship or *isoteleia*. These foreign honorands and the inscribed decrees could serve as living and material reminders of the Theban contribution to the ousting of the Thirty.

The Attic fort Phyle, which is located on the Athenian side of the Parnassus pass on the road leading from Thebes to Athens, marks the beginning of the success story of the return of the demos (fig. 1).[76] Thrasybulus and his followers managed to seize this fort, rebuff the first attack by the Thirty and their troops, and then defeat a large number of Athenian and Spartan contingents by means of a surprise attack in the vicinity of Phyle (Xen. *Hell.* 2.4.2–7). The special significance of this first achievement is evident from innumerable references in the Attic orators. Very often, Thrasybulus and his fellow exiles are simply referred to as οἱ ἀπὸ Φυλῆς.[77] Similarly, in its shortest version, the overthrow of the Thirty is often summarily described as "returning from Phyle" (ἀπὸ Φυλῆς κατελθεῖν)[78] or as "leading the demos back from Phyle" (οἱ ἀπὸ Φυλῆς τὸν δῆμον καταγαγόντες),[79] as we can see in Lysias, Andocides, Aeschines, and Demosthenes. As is evident from Aeschines, the "men from Phyle" are considered the equals of Themistocles and Miltiades, and their achievement

73. For this phenomenon of narrativization, see "Ideology and Social Memory" in the introduction, 17, and Schudson (1995) 355.

74. Cf. "Individual and Collective Memory" in the introduction, 8–13.

75. See the detailed discussion in the following sections.

76. For the location of Phyle, cf. Strab. 9.2.11; *RE* s.v. Phyle, col. 1011.

77. Cf. Lys. 16.4, 31.8–9; Aeschin. 3.187; Dem. 24.134.

78. Lys. 28.12; Aeschin. 2.176, 3.195.

79. Aeschin. 3.181, 187, 190, 208; Dem. 19.280. Cf. Andoc. 1.80; Dem. 24.135; Philostr. *VS* 1.16.

is ranked as highly in Athenian social memory as Salamis and Marathon (Aeschin. 3.181).

Apart from the omnipresence of this memory in Athenian public discourse, as seen in the orators' allusions, the return of the demos was also commemorated through monumental inscriptions that could serve as material reminders for later generations.[80] Aeschines mentions an honorary decree and an epigram celebrating the courage of the men who took Phyle, proposed by one of the leading democrats, Archinus of Coele. This decree was inscribed on a stone stele and set up in the Metroon (Aeschin. 3.187–90).[81] Aeschines' account suggests that both decree and epigram appeared on a single document, and enough fragments of it have been excavated to allow a reconstruction (fig. 6).[82]

This stele contained a heading, the list of names of the heroes of Phyle, the epigram quoted by Aeschines, and the honorary decree proposed by Archinus of Coele in 403/02 (*SEG* 28.45).[83] Only two big letters (–HN) of the two-line heading that preceded the list of names survived. Based on the available space and well-known phrases in the historians and the orators, it has been restored as follows:

> [Ο Ι Δ Ε Κ Α Τ Α Λ Α Β Ο Ν Τ Ε Σ Φ Υ Λ] Η Ν
> [Τ Ο Ν Δ Η Μ Ο Ν Κ Α Τ Η Γ Α Γ Α Γ Ο Ν]
> [Οἵδε καταλαβόντες Φυλ]ὴν
> [τὸν δῆμον κατήγαγον][84]
>
> *[The following men, having taken Phyle, led the demos back]*

In this case, a well-known idiom from oratory was used to reconstruct this badly damaged heading. It would be a circular argument to assert that this

80. The tombs of Thrasybulus (Paus. 1.29.3) and of the fallen Spartans (Xen. *Hell.* 2.4.33) in the *demosion sema* also functioned as memorials of the victory of the demos. For the negotiation and commemoration of the troubling civil war memories, see Wolpert (2002) 75–99.

81. Sickinger (1999) 235 note 14 argues convincingly that Aeschines refers not to an archive copy stored in the Metroon but to an inscribed stele.

82. Cf. Raubitschek (1941), 288–89 = *SEG* 28.45. For the most recent discussions of this inscription, see Taylor (2002) and Shear (2011) 232–34. The identification of these fragments as part of the honorary decree for Thrasybulus and his fellow exiles who took Phyle is based on the congruence of the beginnings of the two elegiac couplets (lines 73–76) with the epigram quoted at Aeschin. 3.190; cf. Taylor (2002) 378. Additional proof is provided by the fact that at least five of the men who are honored are from the small *deme* of Phyle (lines 43–47), which suggests that the event being commemorated took place in or near Phyle; cf. Raubitschek (1941) 287, followed by Taylor (2002) 386. See the cover of this monograph for an image of no. 78, fragment c of this honorary inscription (Raubitschek (1941) 292. Reproduced by courtesy of the Trustees of the American School of Classical Studies at Athens).

83. Cf. Raubitschek (1941) 289; Taylor (2002) 381.

84. Raubitschek (1941) 288–89 = *SEG* 28.45.

Fig. 6. Reconstruction of the honorary inscription for the heroes at Phyle. (*SEG* 28.45 = Raubitschek (1941) 289 fig. 1. Reproduced by courtesy of the Trustees of the American School of Classical Studies at Athens.)

inscriptional phrase was able to shape the memory of this event and its verbal expression. Yet another decree (*IG* II^2 10 = R&O 4), which I shall discuss below, supports this very assertion.

We do know with certainty that the seizure of Phyle marks, in Athenian social memory, the beginning of the triumphant return of the democratic exiles and that this beginning was memorialized through monumental inscriptions such as this honorary decree. Using the phrase πρῶτοι καταπαύειν ἦρξαν, the honorary epigram explicitly calls the action at Phyle the beginning of the end of the terror regime of the Thirty.[85]

85. Wolpert (2002) 88 also emphasizes the stele's memorial and ideological function as a "visual reminder for all that the demos had returned and the democracy had been restored."

Τού[σδ' ἀρετῆς ἕνεκα στεφάνοις ἐγέραιρε παλαίχθων]
δῆμ[ος Ἀθηναίων, οἵ ποτε τὸς ἀδίκοις]
θε[σμοῖς ἄρξαντας πόλεως πρῶτοι καταπαύειν]
ἦρ[ξαν, κίνδυνον σώμασιν ἀράμενοι.][86]

[The ancient demos of the Athenians honored those men
for their virtue with crowns, who first began to check
those who ruled the city with unjust decrees,
accepting mortal danger.]

There has been much discussion as to which group of democrats was honored on this stele. Recently, Taylor, confirming Raubitschek's original interpretation, has argued persuasively that this decree honored both the Athenian exiles and their foreign supporters (ξένοι) who occupied Phyle and rebuffed the first attack of the Thirty.[87] There was also confusion about the size of Thrasybulus' initial group. Xenophon reports that Thrasybulus brought seventy followers from Thebes (Xen. *Hell.* 2.4.2). Pausanias, who might have seen the monument, speaks of sixty followers (Paus. 1.29.3). Aeschines states that one thousand drachmae were awarded, so that each man got less than ten, which brings the total number in the group up to one hundred (Aeschin. 3.187). Reconciling these different numbers, Raubitschek asserted that Thrasybulus came with seventy followers from Thebes and was joined immediately by thirty Athenian citizens from nearby *demes,* especially from Phyle itself. The first list contained the names of at least fifty-six Athenian citizens, organized by tribes, followed by the epigram and the decree (fig. 6). To bring the number up to the more than one hundred honorands mentioned by Aeschines, there must have been a second list below where the text has been lost, which contained the names of the over forty foreigners (metics and maybe slaves) who were part of Thrasybulus' original group. That Thrasybulus had non-Athenian supporters is evident from another inscription, the citizenship grant for the ξένοι of Phyle (*IG* II^2 10 = R&O 4). Since having fought in the democratic resistance was such a badge of honor, it is not farfetched to assume that the men whose names were listed on this honorary stele would, after their return, have happily shared their experience in Thebes and Phyle with their fellow citizens at home in their *demes* and tribes. They thus functioned themselves as carriers of the memory of Theban support.

86. Cf. Raubitschek (1941) 288–89 = *SEG* 28.45. The extant beginnings of the two elegiac couplets are identical with the epigram quoted in Aeschin. 3.190.

87. See Raubitschek (1941) 294 and Taylor (2002). Krentz (1982) 83–90 interprets this inscription as a decree honoring only the Athenian citizens among the seven hundred democratic fighters who defeated the troops of the Thirty in their *second* engagement in the vicinity of Phyle. In his view, Thrasybulus' troops consisted mainly of foreigners.

That the seizure of Phyle as the pivotal step toward liberation also became proverbial is evident from a line in Aristophanes' *Plutus,* produced in 388 BC.

> Μὴ μνησικακήσῃς, εἰ σὺ Φυλὴν κατέλαβες.
>
> *[Well, don't bear malice, if you took Phyle.]* (Ar. *Plut.* 1146)

This line is used by Hermes to indicate that Cario should not hold a grudge but should let him participate in his new riches. The scholia explain this verse as an allusion to Thrasybulus' magnificent coup to seize Phyle and to the amnesty the victorious democrats granted to the people in the city who had supported the Thirty. The exceptional significance of the capture of Phyle is stressed by the scholiasts:[88] "if you took Phyle" (εἰ σὺ Φυλὴν κατέλαβες) is said to be equivalent to "if you became rich" (εἰ καὶ ἐπλούτησας) or "if you became great" (εἰ μέγας γέγονας), like Thrasybulus, "who, having taken Phyle and having grown strong, was able to oust the tyrants and was deemed worthy of honor by the Athenians."[89] This very brief allusion in Aristophanes' comedy shows that the seizure of Phyle had become shorthand for the beginning of the deposition of the Thirty and was deeply rooted in Athenian collective consciousness by 388 BC. It could even be used as an analogy in different contexts.

The preservation of the memory of Thebes' support did not depend only on the Athenian exiles themselves, who showed their gratitude through the aforementioned dedications in Thebes and who were likely to share their exile experience with their fellow citizens after their victory; the exiled Athenians around Thrasybulus were supported by numerous non-Athenians, that is, metics and probably even slaves who contributed to Thrasybulus' success. The role of these ξένοι was not forgotten in the hour of victory but was officially acknowledged by the Athenian demos. At least some of these ξένοι were from Boeotia/Thebes and thus served as reminders of the Theban support for the Athenian democrats. Xenophon reports that after the battle of Munichia, Thrasybulus promised *isoteleia,* a prestigious legal status short of citizenship, to any ξένοι who would join them in their struggle (Xen. *Hell.* 2.4.25). Thrasybulus' overly generous grant of Athenian tax privileges for these ξένοι was successfully attacked by Archinus in a *graphe paranomon* (Arist. *Ath. Pol.* 40.2; Aeschin. 3.195), but the contribution of those ξένοι was officially recognized in other ways. According to Lysias' funeral speech, those ξένοι who died fighting against the Thirty at the Piraeus

88. Cf. Schol. Vet. Ar. *Plut.* 1146g, 1146h, α, 1146h β Chantry.

89. Schol. Vet. Ar. *Plut.*, 1146h β Chantry: εἰ μέγας γέγονας", ὥσπερ ὁ Θρασύβουλος, καταλαβὼν Φυλὴν καὶ ἰσχύσας, ἐδυνήθη καταλῦσαι τοὺς τυράννους, καὶ παρ' Ἀθηναίοις τιμῆς ἠξιώθη.

were given a public funeral and the same honors as the citizens (Lys. 2.66). Given the chauvinistic nature of the *epitaphios*, it is hard to imagine that Thrasybulus' foreign supporters featured regularly in the Athenian funeral speeches, but their funeral monument could certainly serve as a material reminder of their important contribution.[90] Moreover, fragments of an inscription found on the Acropolis show that by 401/0, the Athenians had changed their minds again and had indeed granted citizenship and *isoteleia* to those ξένοι who had been crucial for Thrasybulus' success (*IG* II^2 10 = R&O 4).[91] This decree appears to be a compromise between Thrasybulus' earlier proposal to grant *isoteleia* to any ξένοι who joined in the return from the Piraeus and Archinus' objections in 403.[92]

This decree is remarkable for several reasons. First, it divides Thrasybulus' foreign supporters into three categories on the basis of the stages of the struggle against the Thirty. The special significance of the seizure of Phyle is again underscored by the details of the decree. Only the first group, the nucleus who seized Phyle (ὅσοι συνκατῆλθον ἀπὸ Φυλῆς) together with those who assisted them toward the return to the Piraeus,[93] were granted full citizenship; the other two groups—those who fought at Munichia and those who remained in the Piraeus and supported the democrats afterward—received *isoteleia*, "equality of obligations" with the citizens in terms of taxation and military service.[94]

> [Λυσιάδες ἐγ]γραμμάτευε·
> [Ξεναίνετ]ος ἦρχε.
> [ἔδοξεν τῆι βολῆι καὶ τῶι δήμωι. Ἱπποθωντὶς ἐπρυτάν]ευε· Λυσιάδης
> ἐγραμμάτευε· Δημόφιλος ἐπ[εστάτε. Θρασύβ]-
> [ολος εἶπε· ὅπως ἂν ἀξίας χάριτας κομίσωνται οἱ ξέν]ο̣ι̣ ὅσοι
> συνκατῆλθον

90. Lysias, the author of this *epitaphios*, was a metic himself, was persecuted by the Thirty, and contributed considerably to Thrasybulus' campaign (cf. [Plut.] *X Or.* 835f–836a).

91. For a detailed discussion of this decree and its relationship to the literary testimonia of the debate concerning this citizenship grant, see Rhodes & Osborne (2003) 20–27. It is not absolutely sure that the first group received citizenship. I follow M. J. Osborne (1981) 37–41 and (1982) 26–43, who strongly argues for a citizenship grant for the first group and for *isoteleia* for the second and third groups. Krentz (1980) proposed that all three groups received merely *ateleia* (freedom from obligation), whereas Whitehead (1984) suggested that all three received citizenship.

92. Cartledge (1987) 286–97.

93. Taylor (2002) 385 argues convincingly that the second part of group one (ἢ τοῖς κατελ[θõσι συνελάβ]||[οντο ἐς τὴν κάθοδον τὴν εἰς Περαιᾶ, R&O 4.4–5) included not only the foreigners who joined Thrasybulus between the time after the Thirty's first attack and his march to the Piraeus, when his forces numbered at least one thousand, but also rich metics, like Lysias, who aided Thrasybulus with money and supplies.

94. M. J. Osborne (1982) 35–40 estimates from the dimensions of the stele that there were three tribally organized lists, with around 70–90 names in the first list, around 290 in the second, and around 560–80 in the third. Cf. Rhodes & Osborne (2003) 25.

ἀπὸ Φυλῆς ἢ τοῖς κατελ[θõσι συνελάβ]-
[οντο ἐς τὴν κάθοδον τὴν εἰς Περαιᾶ, περὶ μὲν τούτων] ἐψηφίσθαι
Ἀθηναίοις ἔναι αὐτοῖς καὶ ἐκγόν[οις πολιτεί]-
[αν· καὶ νε͂μαι αὐτὸς αὐτίκα μάλα ἐς τὰς φυλὰς δέκαχα]· νόμοις δὲ τοῖς
αὐτοῖς περὶ αὐτῶν τὰς ἀρχὰς χρ[ῆσθαι οἷς κ]-
[αὶ περὶ τῶν ἄλλων Ἀθηναίων. ὅσοι δὲ ἦλθον ὕστερον], συνεμάχησαν
δὲ τὴμ μάχην τὴμ Μονιχίασιν, τὸν δὲ [Περαιᾶ δ]-
[ιέσωισαν, ὅσοι δὲ παρέμενον τῶι ἐμ Περαιεῖ δήμωι ὅ]τε αἱ διαλλαγαὶ
ἐγένοντο, καὶ ἐποιõν τὰ προστατ[τόμενα, τ]-
[ότοις ἔναι ἰσοτέλειαν οἰκõσι Ἀθήνησιν κατὰ τὴν δοθεῖσαν ἐ]γγύησιν
καθάπε[ρ Ἀ]θηναίοις. τὸς δὲ [--------]

[Lysiades was secretary; Xenaenetus was archon [401/0].

3 Resolved by the council and the people. Hippothontis was the prytany; Lysiades was secretary; Demophilus was chairman. Thrasybulus proposed:

4 So that worthy gratitude may be obtained by the foreigners who joined in returning from Phyle or who gave assistance toward the return to the Piraeus to those who returned: concerning these, be it decreed by the Athenians that there shall be citizenship for them and their descendants; and distribute them immediately into the tribes tenfold; and the officials shall use the same laws concerning them as concerning the other Athenians.

7 Those who came later, joined in fighting the battle at Munichia, and made the Piraeus safe, who remained with the People in Piraeus when the reconciliation took place, and were doing what they were instructed: for these there shall be isoteleia *if they live in Athens, in accordance with the pledge given [?], as for the Athenians. The — — —]* (R&O 4)

Second, this decree prescribes that the ξένοι from Phyle were to be distributed among the ten tribes.[95] The Athenians generally celebrated the toppling of the Thirty as an exclusively Athenian achievement, but below this polis-wide level of commemoration, these new Athenian citizens would have served as living reminders of the foreign support through their very presence in demotic and tribal assemblies.[96] They and their children would have proudly imparted

95. If they did indeed receive full citizenship, they would also have to be assigned to a particular *deme;* unfortunately, we do not have any traces of this first list. The ξένοι of the two remaining groups, who received merely *isoteleia,* were—for military purposes—simply assigned to the ten tribes, as the extant lists indicate. Cf. Rhodes & Osborne (2003) 26–27.

96. Similarly, Pausanias' and the Spartans' role in ending the civil war did not enter the Athenian collective historical consciousness. In Lys. 2.63, for instance, the battle at Munichia (a democratic victory) and the final battle of the civil war (a defeat) are conflated into one victorious battle,

to their fellow demesmen and tribesmen their experiences of the time of exile and the struggle in Phyle. They thus formed memory communities that were able to preserve the precarious memory of Theban support at the early stages of the democratic resistance against the Thirty, especially since, with all likelihood, some of these new citizens were Boeotians or even Thebans. That individual Thebans had joined in Thrasybulus' campaign is known from historiographical (Plut. *Lys.* 27.4; Diod. 14.32.1; Justin 5.9.8) and epigraphical evidence. An honorary decree (*IG* II^2 2) praising an individual Boeotian as πρόξενος and εὐεργέτης can be dated to 403/2, the same year and prytany as Archinus' honorary decree for the heroes of Phyle (*SEG* 28.45), and is probably a reward for his active support of Thrasybulus.[97]

Third, there is strong evidence that people paid attention to and read both of these honorary inscriptions for the men of Phyle. Archinus' proposal ordered that the awarding of the crowns should not be done casually but "after careful inquiry by the *boule* to establish all those who were under siege at Phyle when the Spartans and the Thirty attacked the forces that had seized Phyle" (Aeschin. 3.187), and Sickinger ascribes the setting up of this monumental inscription in the Metroon (which was, after all, the *bouleuterion* in 403) to this very purpose.[98] The inscription granting citizenship and *isoteleia,* accompanied by a list of all the beneficiaries by name (*IG* II^2 10 = R&O 4), was even more important: in case someone challenged their legal status, these beneficiaries and their descendants could simply point to this monumental stele.

Another indicator for the role of these monumental inscriptions in the formation of social memory is provided by the expressions found in the orators. As noted earlier in the context of the reconstruction of the heading of Archinus' honorary decree, the phrases and terms used by the orators closely resemble the wording of the inscriptions.[99] Phrases commonly used to refer to the reestablishment of the democracy are "to return from Phyle" (ἀπὸ Φυλῆς κατελθεῖν) or "to lead the demos back from Phyle" (τὸν δῆμον κατάγειν).[100] Whereas the heading of Archinus' honorary inscription was restored by using the orators and therefore could not serve as proof of the congruence of the two media, the inscription granting citizenship and *isoteleia* (*IG* II^2 10 = R&O 4) can indeed

with the tombs of the fallen Spartans as monuments for the democrats' bravery; cf. Todd (2008) 262–63.

97. Raubitschek (1941) 287. For the honorary decree, see *IG* II^2 2, the *addenda et corrigenda* p. 655; *SEG* 32.38; "Theban Exiles in Athens, 382–379" below, 254–60. Cartledge (1987) 291 dates this inscription epigraphically to the year 398/7. In this case, too, the reasons for honoring this Boeotian are most likely connected with the aid provided in 404.

98. Cf. Sickinger (1999) 235 note 14.

99. *SEG* 28.45.1–2: [Οἵδε καταλαβόντες Φυλ]ὴν | [τὸν δῆμον κατήγαγον].

100. See the references in the orators cited above.

prove my assertion. On this stele, the earliest democratic resistance fighters are referred to as "those who joined in returning from Phyle" (ὅσοι συνκατῆλθον ἀπὸ Φυλῆς, R&O 4.4). This is exactly the same phrase Aeschines used to refer to Thrasybulus (ἕνα τῶν ἀπὸ Φυλῆς αὐτῷ συγκατελθόντων, Aeschin. 3.195). The closely related phrase "to return from Phyle" (ἀπὸ Φυλῆς κατελθεῖν) can be found in Lysias and Aeschines.[101] Even more remarkable is a passage in Lysias in which a speaker in 399 BC anticipates his opponent's line of defense.

> I hear that he [i.e., Agoratus] is concocting for his defense the plea that he went off to Phyle and joined in returning from Phyle [συγκατῆλθεν ἀπὸ Φυλῆς], and that this is the strongest point of his case. (Lys. 13.77)

Clearly, Lysias is here alluding to the inscription granting citizenship to Thrasybulus' foreign supporters at Phyle (*IG* II² 10.4 = R&O 4.4), which Agoratus was going to evoke to assert his status as an Athenian citizen.[102] This proves that such monumental inscriptions were indeed read in fourth-century Athens. Their wording circulated in public discourse and thus helped in shaping the social memory of these events.

With respect to the initial question concerning the commemoration of Thebes' support in Athens, we can conclude that the capture of Phyle is commemorated as the first decisive act in overthrowing the Thirty. Phyle, as the border town between Athenian and Boeotian/Theban territory, was thus able to serve as a topographical and narratological fixed point to which the more precarious memory of Theban support for the Athenian democrats could be attached, as we can see in Dinarchus' allusion to this episode.

> And these men [i.e., the Thebans], as our elders say—when the democracy in our city had been dissolved [καταλελυμένης τῆς δημοκρατίας τῆς παρ' ἡμῖν] and Thrasybulus was gathering together the exiles in Thebes for the seizure of Phyle [συνάγοντος ἐν Θήβαις Θρασυβούλου τοὺς φυγάδας ἐπὶ τὴν Φυλῆς κατάληψιν]— . . . aided the demos in returning [συνέπραττον τῷ δήμῳ τὴν κάθοδον] and passed the decree. . . . (Din. 1.25)

Similarly, in Plutarch's reference to the Theban aid, Phyle is mentioned to locate this episode in time and space.

---

101. Lys. 28.12; Aeschin. 2.176.
102. M. J. Osborne (1982) 32.

> And they [i.e., the Thebans] did not merely vote such Hellenic and humane decrees, while failing to provide deeds corresponding to their words; no, Thrasybulus and those who with him seized Phyle [οἱ σὺν αὐτῷ Φυλὴν καταλαβόντες] set out from Thebes, while Thebans provided them with arms and money, with secrecy and a base for operations. (Plut. *Lys.* 27.4)

In both cases, Phyle was used to prompt the recollection of Thebes' support for Thrasybulus and his fellow exiles. Through its very location on the road from Thebes to Athens, Phyle had the potential to remind the Athenians—with every mention of "the men from Phyle"—that the exiles had set out from Thebes.

To sum up, in Thebes, this event was remembered as a manifestation of the Theban character in the tradition of the Theban culture heroes Heracles and Dionysus (Plut. *Lys.* 27.4) and memorialized in the form of two colossal statues of Athena and Heracles, dedicated by the grateful Thrasybulus and the other exiles (Paus. 9.11.6). Moreover, it is quite possible that the Theban counterdecrees were inscribed in stone and set up in the agora or at the Cadmea. In Athens, the restoration of the democracy was considered a pivotal event in the city's history and therefore commemorated by a variety of means. In Athenian collective memory, the seizure of Phyle (not the departure from Thebes) marked the beginning of Thrasybulus' triumphant struggle. The nucleus of his followers who seized this fort on the Theban-Athenian border was memorialized through an honorary inscription (*SEG* 28.45), proposed by Archinus and set up in the *bouleuterion*. Even the contribution of Thrasybulus' foreign supporters—Thebans and Boeotians doubtless among them—was not forgotten but was rewarded by the grant of Athenian citizenship (*IG* II^2 10 = R&O 4). Both this monumental inscription and the new Athenian citizens themselves, distributed among the ten Athenian tribes, could serve as reminders of the foreign support for the Athenian exiles. These monumental inscriptions were read by Athenians, and their wording circulated in public discourse, thus shaping the memory of these events. Through its geographical location and its significance in the story of the return of Athenian democrats, Phyle could serve as a cue for the precarious memory of Thebes' support.

The Athenian-Theban Alliance in 395

The Thebans memorialized their support for the Athenians, and the much commemorated seizure of Phyle served the Athenians as a reminder of the

Theban contribution. But the transmission of this memory down to Dinarchus' generation (323 BC) was by no means secured, since, for the most part, Thebes played a negative role in the Athenian historical consciousness: the Thebans were remembered as prototypical medizers, and their proposal to eradicate Athens in 404 left a deep mark on Athenian collective consciousness.[103] Without analogous situations in the course of Theban-Athenian relations in the fourth century, such as could provide cues for the recollection of Thebes' aid for the exiled democrats and bring this event back into the forefront of Athenian public discourse, this memory would probably have faded from Athenian historical consciousness.

The first instance in which this event was recalled and played a major role in Athenian public discourse occurred at the dawn of the Corinthian War, in July 395.[104] The Thebans, threatened by the invasion of a Spartan army, sent an embassy to Athens to request a military alliance. In their speech before the Athenian assembly, the Theban ambassadors, as reported by Xenophon, mentioned, among other things, their role in the overthrow of the Spartan-backed Thirty and asked the Athenians now to repay this favor (Xen. *Hell.* 3.5.8).

My objective in this section is twofold. First, in discussing the Theban ambassadors' allusion to this past event, I argue that this diplomatic tactic helped preserve the memory of Thebes' benefactions in Athens. Second, using this speech in Xenophon for the reconstruction of the public debate in Athens in 395, I make a case for the relevance of arguments from social memory in decision making in classical Athens—a factor too often neglected by previous scholars.

Thanks to omissions and serious discrepancies between the historical accounts of Xenophon and the *Hellenica Oxyrhynchia,* the origins of the Corinthian War are "one of the most important and yet one of the most obscure problems in the history of Classical Greece."[105] The problems of chronology and the motives of all Greek communities involved are too complex to be discussed here and have little bearing on the question at hand. Instead, I focus my attention on the political debate in Athens that led to the conclusion of the Athenian-Theban alliance in 395.

In spring 395, the Boeotians had refused to submit to arbitration a dispute between their allies in Locris and the Spartan allies in Phocis and made a raid into Phocian territory (Xen. *Hell.* 3.5.3–7; *Hell. Oxy.* 21.3–5 Chambers). Annoyed about similar recalcitrant Theban acts in the recent past, the Spartans seized

103. For the Thebans as prototypical medizers, see chapter 2; Isoc. 14.30, 61; Dem. 14.33–34, 6.11; [Dem.] 59.95; Isoc. 12.93. For the Theban proposal to eradicate Athens, see chapter 5; Andoc. 3.21; Isoc. 14.31–32, 7.6, 15.319; Dem. 19.65–66.

104. For the date, see Hamilton (1979) 201.

105. Cartledge (1987) 289–93, 356–59, quote at 289. See also Perlman (1964a); Hamilton (1979) 182–208; Strauss (1987) 106–13.

on this opportunity and decided to launch "a two-pronged pre-emptive strike" against Boeotia.[106] Lysander and Pausanias were appointed to a joint command; the latter led the troops from the Peloponnese into Boeotia, the former gathered the Spartan allies in Phocis and was on the march to the rendezvous point at Haliartus, when the Theban embassy arrived in Athens.

The Athenians passed a decree to conclude a perpetual defensive alliance with the Theban-led Boeotian League ([συμ]μαχία Βοιω[τῶν καὶ Ἀ]θηναί[ων ἐς τὸ]|[ν ἀεὶ] χρόνον), a copy of which has been found on a stone stele on the Acropolis (*IG* II^2 14 = R&O 6).[107] Athens' "definite and deliberate acceptance of war against Sparta"[108]—for Lysander was already ravaging Boeotia at that time—has baffled many historians, especially since the Athenians had, only one year earlier, disavowed any responsibility for an episode known as the Demaenetus affair, for fear they might provoke the Spartans (*Hell. Oxy.* 9.1–3 Chambers).[109]

A brief sketch of Athenian-Spartan relations between 404 and 395 will help to bring light into the situation in 395. After the reestablishment of the democracy with King Pausanias' help, the Athenians at first resigned themselves to their role as Spartan allies. They erected a massive burial monument for the Spartans who had fallen in the fight against the democrats in the Piraeus (Xen. *Hell.* 2.4.33). In 400 BC, the Athenians sent three hundred cavalrymen for the Spartan expedition in Asia (Xen. *Hell.* 3.1.4), and in 399, they joined the Spartans in the campaign against Elis (Xen. *Hell.* 3.2.25). Around 398, however, the Athenian Conon was appointed (as a mercenary) to the command of the Persian fleet, and from this point forward, we find a strand of Athenian opinion that favored active cooperation with Persia against Sparta. Consequently, early in 396, Athens refused to contribute troops for Agesilaus' expedition against Persia (Paus. 3.9.2).[110] According to the Oxyrhynchus historian, Athenians around Epicrates and Cephalus secretly sent weapons and crews to Conon and were keen to involve the city in a war with Sparta (*Hell. Oxy.* 10.1–2 Chambers). Two Athenian envoys to the Persian king had already been arrested and executed by the Spartans, when a certain Demaenetus, without the knowledge of the Athenian people but with the secret approval of the council, put a trireme to sea on his way to Conon (*Hell. Oxy.* 9.1 Chambers). When this became known, there was a great outcry among the well-born and cultivated (γνώριμοι και χαρίεντες) Athenians, who were opposed to a war with Sparta.

106. Cartledge (1987) 358.

107. Cf. Rhodes & Osborne (2003) 38–41. Unfortunately, only the heading, which I have cited, and parts of the text of the treaty have survived; the decree itself, which might have betrayed the motives for the Athenian decision, is lost.

108. Hamilton (1979) 206. See also Cartledge (1987) 292.

109. Cf. Hamilton (1979) 177–208; Cartledge (1987) 289–93; Strauss (1987) 106–13.

110. Cf. Hamilton (1979) 174–75; Cartledge (1987) 287–89; Strauss (1987) 104–7.

In the assembly, the supporters of Thrasybulus denounced Demaenetus' action as risky and dangerous and asked the demos to publicly disavow responsibility for it (*Hell. Oxy.* 9.2 Chambers). The masses (οἱ πολλοὶ καὶ δημοτικοὶ) became frightened and followed Thrasybulus' advice (*Hell. Oxy.* 9.3 Chambers). Based on this passage in the *Hellenica Oxyrhynchia,* we can identify three political groups in Athens in 396:[111] (1) a minority group of wealthy, relatively conservative Athenians that was content with the status quo and did not want to endanger its possessions;[112] (2) a large faction of poor people, led by Cephalus and Epicrates, that became increasingly interested in involving Athens in a war to regain parts of its empire; and (3) a moderate democratic faction around Thrasybulus that would only embark on an imperialist adventure if the chances of success were high.[113]

Considering this clear decision *against* war with Sparta in the Demaenetus affair of 396, how was it possible that the Athenians embarked on a war with Sparta just one year later? Even more astonishing, what caused Thrasybulus, who had vehemently opposed provoking the Spartans in 396, to approve of going to war with them in 395? That Thrasybulus stood behind this policy can be inferred from Xenophon's remark that Thrasybulus was the one to formally announce the Athenian decree to the Theban ambassadors (Xen. *Hell.* 3.5.16).[114]

Unfortunately, the Oxyrhynchus historian's account of the Theban embassy and its reception in Athens is lost. Xenophon only reports that many Athenians spoke in favor of the ambassadors' request and that the Athenians voted unanimously for this alliance (Xen. *Hell.* 3.5.16). The ambassadors' speech is therefore the only source from which we can deduce the arguments and motives of the Athenians for concluding this alliance that amounted to war with Sparta.

There are nine main arguments of the Thebans (Xen. *Hell.* 3.5.8–15). First, the Athenians should not hold a grudge against the Thebans for proposing the destruction of Athens in 405/4 (3.5.8). Second, they should instead remember the Theban refusal to support the Spartans and the Thirty against the democrats in the Piraeus and repay this favor now (3.5.8). Third, especially the people in the city who had supported the oligarchy should take the field against the Spartans and punish them for their betrayal (3.5.9). Fourth, everyone knows that the Athenians want to recover their former empire, and this can be

111. Bruce (1963) 289–90.

112. Bruce (1967) 52–53 rightly remarks that the positive terms γνώριμοι και χαρίεντες, used by the Oxyrhynchus historian to denote the wealthy landholders, betray his sympathies for this group.

113. Cf. Bruce (1967) 51–57; Hamilton (1979) 180; Strauss (1986) 106–10.

114. Strauss (1987) 107–9 explains Thrasybulus' initial opposition to a war with Sparta as the result of his personal hatred for his rival Conon, the commander of the Persian fleet. This might be the case, but it seems unlikely that Thrasybulus used this argument in public debate to rally his supporters.

achieved by helping those who are now wronged by the Spartans. These discontented subjects are ready to revolt against the Spartans if someone offers them protection, just as the Athenian subjects did during the Peloponnesian War (3.5.10). Fifth, seeing the powerful Athenian-Boeotian alliance, other Spartan allies, such as the Argives, Eleans, Corinthians, Arcadians, and Achaeans, will join them, thanks to the ungrateful and arrogant conduct toward them by the Spartans after the war (3.5.11–12). Sixth, the Spartans promised freedom to the Greeks who revolted from Athens, but they instead gave them a double dose of slavery in the form of harmosts and decarchies. If the Athenians are willing to champion all those so plainly wronged, they will become the greatest leaders ever, not just of the islands, but also of the mainland and the Peloponnese (3.5.13–14). Seventh, the Boeotians, fighting for their own wronged selves, will be even more useful allies to the Athenians than they were to the Spartans before (3.5.14). Eighth, the Spartans' land rule can be broken more easily than the Athenians' naval empire could, since Sparta's subjects are numerous and equally armed (3.5.15). Ninth, the benefits of this alliance would thus be even greater for the Athenians than for the Thebans (3.5.15). As is evident from this brief sketch, Xenophon's Thebans employ a great variety of arguments, ranging from the obligation to repay past benefactions to the Athenians' prospect of recovering their lost empire. They stress the strength of this Athenian-Boeotian alliance and its effect on other discontented Spartan subjects and appeal to the Athenians to live up to their reputation as leaders of the wronged.

Despite the wide range of arguments brought forth by the Theban ambassadors, most scholars tend to focus on one particular kind of argument. As I have pointed out earlier, many modern historians of antiquity are apparently influenced by the political theory of Realism and regard the rational self-interest of states as the prime, if not the only, factor of international politics.[115] Hamilton's analysis of the Theban speech and the situation in Athens is a telling example and worth quoting in full.

> Although several scholars have found reason to criticize the speech as reported by Xenophon, there is sufficient evidence from the general context to permit us to accept at least the chief arguments adduced. The Thebans stress the generally recognized desire of Athens to regain her former hegemony, and they argue that this can be achieved only by waging a war against Sparta. The Boeotian alliance would benefit both states in such a war and therefore ought to be accepted. They also assert the willingness of Argos, Elis, Corinth, and various other states to challenge

115. Cf. "Public Discourse and Decision Making" in the introduction, 30–36.

> Sparta's position, and this point is valid enough. Their attempts to disclaim responsibility for having proposed the destruction of Athens in 404, and also the suggestion that Athens' leadership will be welcome to many states which are at that time suffering under the harsh rule of harmosts and decarchies imposed upon them by the Spartans, are *rhetorical or tendentious arguments* [my emphasis] rather than precise reflections of the facts, but do not detract from the value of the speech.[116]

Following the principles of Realism, Hamilton proceeds to give his explanation for the Athenians' sudden willingness to go to war with Sparta: a combination of "economic motives, patriotism, and fear of Spartan intentions."[117] The situation in 395 was "both more threatening and more promising for Athens"[118] than at the time of the Demaenetus affair one year earlier—more threatening thanks to Agesilaus' success in Asia and the Spartans' willingness to intervene in its allies' internal affairs; more promising thanks to the powerful partnership with Boeotia, the Persian funds promised by Timocrates, and the probability of winning over more discontented Spartan allies and thus recovering the old empire.[119]

I fully agree that rational calculation of economic benefits and security are crucial factors in decision making. Yet, as I have pointed out in the introduction to this book, I contend that other, nonrational factors are at least as important and that ignoring them in our sources means to deny the ancients the same complexity of life familiar from our own experience. Xenophon's Thebans use three arguments from social memory, which Hamilton has characterized as merely "rhetorical and tendentious," even though they are emotionally charged and thus carry much argumentative weight. First, the ambassadors devote their very first argument to the Theban proposal to destroy Athens at the end of the Peloponnesian War (Xen. *Hell.* 3.5.8). This shows that they considered this traumatic Athenian memory a major obstacle to an Athenian-Boeotian alliance.[120]

Second, Hamilton and Cartledge are right to identify the prospect of recov-

116. Hamilton (1979) 201–2.

117. Hamilton (1979) 202.

118. Hamilton (1979) 205.

119. Similarly, Cartledge (1987) 289–93, who sees the Athenians' desire to recover their empire as the prime reason for going to war with Sparta, since the empire promised posts and lucrative opportunities for the elite, land and grain supply for the poor, and had a "more genuinely panhellenist element than the Spartans could muster in favour of their empire" (293). See also Tuplin (1993) 63: "Similarly the Athenians act because Spartan *adikia* enhances their opportunity of recovering power, not because it offends their moral sense nor yet because their magnanimous tendencies make them respond to a less than deserving cry for help."

120. Cf. chapter 5, especially "Thebans Accused and Excused," 326–28.

ering the lost empire as the central element of the speech (Xen. *Hell.* 3.5.10–15), but in their analysis, they single out the empire's economic importance for the Athenians, which is not the main focus of the Theban ambassadors. Rather, they emphasize the ideological aspects of Athenian leadership. Three times they refer to Sparta's subjects as ἀδικούμενοι who are in dire need of renewed Athenian support (βοηθεῖν) and protection (προστῆναι).[121] The Spartans are characterized as τύραννοι and δεσπόται, who promised freedom (ἐλευθερία) but brought nothing but slavery (δουλεία).[122] It is obvious that Xenophon's Thebans echo core values of Athenian identity and self-image, known from the master narrative of the Athenian funeral orations and frequently employed by the Athenians themselves in the fifth century to justify their leadership in Greece:[123] after their heroic victory over the Persians at Marathon and Salamis, the Athenians saw themselves as champions of the Greeks (προστάται τῶν Ἑλλήνων), as defenders of Greek liberty (ἐλευθερία) against τύραννοι and δεσπόται, and as protectors of those being wronged (ἀδικούμενοι). Drawing on symbols and metaphors provided by Athenian social memory, the Theban ambassadors attempted to strike an emotional chord with their Athenian audience. The prospect of going to war as the defender of Greek liberty in accordance with the Athenian self-image, by lending support to Boeotia, which had been invaded by Spartan forces, was probably a crucial factor in the Athenian decision in 395. This was likely one reason why the Athenians did not want to provoke a war with the Spartans in the Demaenetus affair of 396; open cooperation with Conon's Persian fleet against the Greek heroes of Thermopylae and Plataea would have been awkward to reconcile with the Athenian self-image as champions of Greek liberty.[124]

The third argument from social memory employed by the ambassadors in Xenophon stems from Thebes' support for the Athenian democrats in 404/3.[125]

121. Cf. Xen. *Hell.* 3.5.10: τοῦτο δὲ πῶς μᾶλλον εἰκὸς γενέσθαι ἢ εἰ αὐτοὶ τοῖς ὑπ' ἐκείνων ἀδικουμένοις βοηθοῖτε; Xen. *Hell.* 3.5.14: πῶς οὖν οὐκ εἰκός, ἐὰν ὑμεῖς αὖ προστῆτε τῶν οὕτω φανερῶς ἀδικουμένων, νῦν ὑμᾶς πολὺ ἤδη μεγίστους τῶν πώποτε γενέσθαι; Xen. *Hell.* 3.5.10 (about the Thebans who will be their helpers): . . . ἀλλ' ὑπὲρ ἡμῶν αὐτῶν ἀδικουμένων βοηθήσομεν.

122. Xen. *Hell.* 3.5.12: ἀλλὰ τοὺς μὲν εἵλωτας ἁρμοστὰς ἀξιοῦσι καθιστάναι, τῶν δὲ συμμάχων ἐλευθέρων ὄντων, ἐπεὶ ηὐτύχησαν, δεσπόται ἀναπεφήνασιν; Xen. *Hell.* 3.5.13: ἀντὶ γὰρ ἐλευθερίας διπλῆν αὐτοῖς δουλείαν παρεσχήκασιν· ὑπό τε γὰρ τῶν ἁρμοστῶν τυραννοῦνται καὶ ὑπὸ δέκα ἀνδρῶν, οὓς Λύσανδρος κατέστησεν ἐν ἑκάστῃ πόλει.

123. Cf. "Funeral Orations" in chapter 1, 49–58.

124. Strauss (1987) 112 acknowledges the appeal of such arguments but considers them mostly as "propaganda," deliberately employed by the leaders to persuade the masses. He does not, however, address the Theban speech itself. Instead, he refers to a passage in Plato's *Menexenus* 244e and the inscription honoring Euagoras of 393 (*IG* II^2 20.17 = R&O 11.17), which show that Athens went to war in 395 "to stop Sparta from enslaving the Hellenes" and to fight "for Hellas." Hamilton (1979) does not address this fundamental difference from the situation of 396.

125. It is interesting to notice that neither the Thebans nor the Athenians mentioned the con-

> But when the Lacedaemonians summoned us to the expedition against the Piraeus, then the whole polis voted against joining them in the campaign. Since the Lacedaemonians are angry with us mainly because of you, therefore, we consider it just that you should come to the aid of our city. (Xen. *Hell.* 3.5.8)

It is worth pointing out that Xenophon's ambassadors only talk about the Theban refusal to heed Pausanias' call for support against the democrats in the Piraeus; they fail to mention the much more important Theban counterdecrees and the aid secretly provided for the seizure of Phyle by Ismenias and other Boeotians. This can easily be explained by Xenophon's intention in composing the Thebans' speech. This is also a convenient moment to address the problem of the authenticity of this speech in Xenophon's *Hellenica.*

Seager vigorously defends its authenticity: of course, it is not a verbatim record of what the Thebans actually said but "Xenophon's opinion of what they should have said,"[126] and it is thus a valuable guide to the public opinion in Athens at this time. Xenophon, as a contemporary and a member of Athenian memory communities, was certainly in a position to know which arguments and motives governed his fellow citizens at the time. Indeed, none of the arguments put into the mouth of the Thebans seems out of place, considering what we know from other sources of the political circumstances during these years.

At the same time, speeches in Greek historiography are also used to characterize the speaker, and this aspect must not be overlooked in assessing the ambassadors' appeal. Vivienne Gray sets forth a convincing interpretation of Xenophon's intention in composing this speech.[127] His anti-Theban bias is well attested generally and also shines through in his account of the Theban request for an alliance.[128] Gray argues that Thrasybulus' reply provides the key to how Xenophon wants us to read this speech.

> Thrasybulus, after replying to the ambassadors with the decree, also pointed out that although the Piraeus was without walls, they would nevertheless take the risk to repay a favor to them greater than the one they received. "For you," he said, "did not join the expedition against us, while we will fight on your side against them, if they march against you." (Xen. *Hell.* 3.5.16)

---

tested border town Oropus, which had been seized by Thebes in 402 (Diod. 14.17.3). One could make the case that both the Theban proposal to eradicate Athens and Thebes' help for Thrasybulus were so central to the Athenian collective consciousness that they needed to be addressed by the Theban ambassadors. In comparison, the case of Oropus was a matter of secondary importance.

126. Seager (1967) 97.

127. Cf. Gray (1989) 107–12.

128. For Xenophon's anti-Theban bias, see Cawkwell (1979) 7–46; Buck (1994) 74.

In accordance with his moralizing intentions, Xenophon emphasizes the high-mindedness of the Athenians, who are willing to repay favors with interest. The Thebans are characterized as mean-spirited people, who expect others to conform to the highest moral standards but themselves fall far short of them and act only from motives of self-interest. To bring out this difference between the Theban and the Athenian national characters, Xenophon allows his Thebans to mention only their refusal to follow the Spartan command. Their active help for the Athenian democrats (i.e., passing the counterdecrees and providing money and arms) is (probably consciously) omitted by Xenophon from their speech and his narrative for the sake of this broader point.

The fact that Xenophon, despite his dislike for the Thebans, mentions at least this minor aspect of Thebes' role in overturning the Thirty suggests that Thebes' support for Thrasybulus was indeed an important argument in the debate of 395 and was probably exploited by the Theban ambassadors to a greater extent than Xenophon reports. That Thrasybulus, in his reply, chose to comment solely on this one aspect of all the arguments in the Thebans' speech underscores my point. Thrasybulus was not alone in feeling gratitude toward the Thebans for their support in 404.[129] Considering the commemorative activities in Athens surrounding Thrasybulus' seizure of Phyle, which served as a cue for the recollection of the Theban contributions, we can be sure that these arguments from social memory would have resonated with much of the Athenian audience. At the same time, this Theban embassy and the unfolding public debate about a potential alliance also helped to invigorate further the memory of Thebes' support for Thrasybulus in Athenian historical consciousness. Moreover, the Theban speech in Xenophon proves that it was a common diplomatic practice in interstate relations to recount past favors and to ask for these benefactions to be repaid.[130] It is certainly reasonable to assume that in this situation, the Theban ambassadors would have read out the decrees the Thebans had passed in support of the Athenian exiles in 404, as Dinarchus' comment about the much-cited Theban decree suggests (Din. 1.25).

Athenian Help for the Theban Democrats, 382–378

In their request for an alliance in 395, the Theban ambassadors drew heavily on the support Thebes had provided to the democratic exiles in 404/3 and thus brought this memory back into the forefront of Athenian collective conscious-

129. Cartledge (1987) 291 and Strauss (1987) 107 and 111 regard Thebes' help in 404 as an important factor in Thrasybulus' newfound support of a war with Sparta; they do not discuss, however, the potential appeal of such an argument to the Athenian assembly.

130. Cf. Thuc. 2.71, 3.53–59; Xen. *Hell.* 6.5.40, 44; Isoc. 14.1, 57. See "Public Discourse and Decision Making" in the introduction to the present study, 30–36.

ness. Yet the time span of about seventy years between this embassy in 395 and Dinarchus' indictment of Demosthenes in 323 is simply too long to justify Dinarchus' assertion that the Theban counterdecrees were well known from the elders and frequent citations before the Athenians. Without further occasions for reviving this memory in Athenian public discourse, it would probably not have been transmitted down to Dinarchus' generation, especially considering the widespread hostile sentiment toward Athens' northern rival. In 382, however, events occurred in Thebes that resembled the situation of 404 in Athens so closely that the memory of the Thirty and their ousting became instantly a "hot topic" in Athenian discourse again.[131]

Theban Exiles in Athens, 382–379

After the conclusion of the King's Peace in 387/6, the Spartans enjoyed, as they had at the end of the Peloponnesian War, a period of uncontested supremacy in Greece. Using the autonomy clause as an instrument of their rule, they forced the Thebans to dissolve the Boeotian League (Xen. *Hell.* 4.1.31–36), which naturally increased the tension between the anti- and pro-Spartan factions in Thebes (Xen. *Hell.* 5.2.25). In 382, when the Spartan commander Phoebidas, on his way to Olynthus, encamped his troops outside the city of Thebes, the pro-Spartan leader Leontiades grasped the opportunity and persuaded Phoebidas to seize and garrison the Cadmea, the Theban acropolis (Xen. *Hell.* 5.2.25–32). This coup d'état, sanctioned by the Spartan state post eventum, brought to power a small Spartan-backed junta led by Leontiades, who arrested and tried his anti-Spartan rival Ismenias and those of his followers who did not manage to escape from Thebes (Xen. *Hell.* 5.2.33–36).[132]

The historical parallels to Athens in 404 are indeed astonishing. In each case, the Spartans intervened in the internal affairs of another polis, suspended the traditional constitution, and brought to power a pro-Spartan junta (Xen. *Hell.* 5.4.1), which persecuted its political enemies, driving them into exile. Just as in 404, the Spartans demanded that foreign cities "expel the exiles as men

131. That close similarities between current and past events are indeed able to refresh distant memories in public discourse could be observed in the United States in the days following September 11, 2001: the surprise attack on Washington and New York instantly prompted the memory of the Japanese attack on Pearl Harbor in December 1941 among older Americans, and both the media and the general public drew parallels and argued about the proper response; cf. Dower (2010) 4–10. It is probably true that many American young people first learned about Pearl Harbor in this context, which shows that analogous historical situations can help to revive, preserve, and transmit the memory of similar past events.

132. For a discussion of this coup, see Gehrke (1985) 175–77; Cartledge (1987) 296–98; Buck (1994) 64–72.

declared common enemies by the allied cities" (Plut. *Pelop.* 6.4). In one respect, however, the situation was reversed. Whereas the Athenian refugees had been harbored in Thebes in 404, three hundred Theban exiles now found refuge in Athens.

> When they learned, however, that Ismenias was imprisoned in the Cadmea, then those who held the same views as Androcleidas and Ismenias retired to Athens, to the number of about three hundred. (Xen. *Hell.* 5.2.31)

Plutarch's account provides more details about the reception of the Theban refugees in Athens.

> Those around Leontidas [i.e., Leontiades],[133] learning that the fugitive Thebans were living at Athens, where they were not only in favor with the common people, but also honored by the elite, secretly plotted against them. (Plut. *Pelop.* 6.3)

It is evident from these passages that the presence of the three hundred Theban refugees in Athens was a matter of public debate. They stayed with the approval of the demos (τῷ τε πλήθει προσφιλεῖς ὄντας) and were honored by the elite (τιμὴν ἔχοντας ὑπὸ τῶν καλῶν καὶ ἀγαθῶν).

That these Thebans, supported by their Athenian friends, addressed the Athenian assembly, requesting formal recognition as exiles and political asylum, is proven by an inscribed stele found on the Acropolis (II^2 37 *addenda et corrigenda*, pp. 656–57 = *SEG* 32.47). Even though the inscription is badly damaged, some key terms allow its identification as a decree honoring the Boeotian exiles who had fled to Athens after the Spartan seizure of the Cadmea.[134]

The inscription contains a decree passed by the demos awarding certain honorands the status of *isoteleia* (line 5), "equality of obligations" with the citizens in terms of taxation and military service,[135] and granting them tax exemption (τὴν δὲ ἀτ|[έλειαν, lines 16–17). The decree is followed by a list of names, which Wilhelm mistook for Apollonians. Consequently, Wilhelm interpreted this inscription as an honorary decree for exiled Apollonians, which merely

133. For the difference in spelling, cf. Georgiadou (1997) 89.

134. Wilhelm discovered that fragments *a* and *c* were originally continuous. For his at times quite speculative reconstruction, see *IG* II^2 37 *addenda et corrigenda*, pp. 656–57.

135. Cf. Gehrke (1985) 176 note 75, who also interprets this inscription as an honorary decree for the Boeotian exiles after the seizure of the Cadmea.

followed the precedent of a decree for the Theban and Boeotian exiles, passed after the capture of the Cadmea (lines 16–20). Michael Walbank has argued convincingly that Wilhelm's interpretation and many of his reconstructions are untenable and that this decree is in fact one in favor of Boeotian exiles from 382, as the list of Boeotian names reveals.[136] That the Athenians passed a decree for Theban and other Boeotian exiles as a response to the illegal Spartan seizure of the Cadmea is evident from lines 19–20: Λακεδαιμό]νιοι τὴν Καδ[μ]||[είαν κατέλαβον.

Moreover, in Plutarch's *On the Sign of Socrates,* it is reported that the Theban refugees had the status of ἰδιόξενοι (Plut. *Mor.* 576a), "private friends in a foreign state,"[137] who are defined in relation to πρόξενοι by the third-century Alexandrian scholar Aristophanes of Byzantium as follows:

> Ἰδιόξενοι are those who, for a long time, sometimes even hereditarily from their fathers, preserve friendship [ὁμόνοιαν] with one another, even if they are separated from each other by their residence and their fatherlands, who are able to consort with each other in sacrifices and in other symbolic acts and to associate themselves with whom they want. (Ar. Byz. fr. 300P Slater)
>
> Πρόξενοι, on the other hand, are those who become patrons and advocates of entire *poleis* by a political decree, whom even those who do not know them personally inquire about and seek out.[138] (Ar. Byz. fr. 301P Slater)

This definition of ἰδιόξενοι brings out a crucial element for understanding the friendly reception of the Theban refugees in Athens. The Athenians were asked to repay their debt not to just any Thebans but to the very same people who had helped them twenty-two years earlier: Androcleidas and his followers were ἰδιόξενοι of Thrasybulus and his companions, people "who, for a long time, sometimes even hereditarily from their fathers, preserve friendship with one

136. Cf. *SEG* 32.47; Walbank (1982) 267–70, especially 268 note 19. Gehrke (1985) 176 note 75 follows some of Wilhelm's reconstructions (lines 16–20) and suggests, not unreasonably, that this decree might be an amendment of the original decree for the Theban exiles, e.g., an extension to newly arrived refugees from Boeotia.

137. Georgiadou (1997) 98 argues that this status also entailed an exemption from the tax on metics.

138. Herman (1987) 11 note 3 argues that there is no significant difference in usage between ἰδιόξενος and ξένος: "The prefix of *idioxenos* places perhaps a special emphasis on the private nature of the bond distinguishing one's own *xenoi* from the *xenoi* (or *proxenoi*) of the group to which one belonged."

another, even if they are separated from each other by their residence and their fatherlands."

That the personal ties forged in 404 between the exiled Athenian democrats and their Theban hosts endured over more than twenty years is evident from numerous sources. In the context of the events of 395, the Oxyrhynchus historian says explicitly that Ismenias, Antitheus, and Androcleidas were the leaders of the faction "who was accused of supporting the Athenians, arising from their support for the demos when it was in exile" (*Hell. Oxy.* 20. 1–2 Chambers); and after Ismenias was arrested in 382, Androcleidas is said to have headed the Theban exiles in Athens (Xen. *Hell.* 5.2.31; Plut. *Pelop.* 6.3).[139] Between 382 and 379, an unknown Athenian, who had been a ξένος in the house of the Theban Cephisodotus in 404/3, pleaded a case on behalf of Pherenicus, the son of his former host, who had fled from Thebes after the coup and now enjoyed the Athenian's hospitality in return (Lys. fr. 286 Carey). Moreover, a certain Boeotian Aristoxenos had been honored by an Athenian decree in 403/2 (*IG* II^2 2; *SEG* 32.38) as πρόξενος and εὐεργέτης and reappears on the aforementioned stele among the Boeotian refugees (*IG* II^2 37; *SEG* 32.47).[140] Similarly, among the Athenian democrats who had once received Theban support, leading figures such as Cephalus of Collytus and Thrasybulus of Collytus were still prominent and played a leading role in lobbying for support for their former Theban guest-friends.[141] According to the orator Dinarchus, it was Cephalus who proposed that the Athenians march out to aid the Thebans in their fight against the Spartan garrison after the successful countercoup in 379/8 (Din. 1.38).[142] Thrasybulus of Collytus is named by Aeschines as one of the pro-Theban Athenian politicians who were frequently sent as envoys to Thebes (Aeschin. 3.138).

139. Plut. *Pelop.* 6.3 mentions that Androcleidas was murdered by Leontiades' agents in Athens during his exile.

140. This identification is less than sure, though. Walbank (1982) identifies

[Ἀριστοξέ?]νωι Σίμωνος Βοιωτίωι
[Ἀθηναίων προξ]ένωι καὶ εὐεργέτηι (*IG* II^2 2.2–3)

and Ἀρισ[τόξ]ενος (*IG* II^2 37.28). He uses this identification, however, to date the proxeny inscription *IG* II^2 2 down to 382/1, which has been rightly rejected by Lewis (cf. *SEG* 32.38), who favors the date of 403/2. I suggest accepting Walbank's identification of the two honorands but keeping the traditional dating of both decrees. The historical context, as shown, renders it not unlikely that a Boeotian benefactor of the Athenian democrats in 404/3 would find himself a refugee in Athens in 382/1. For the dating of *IG* II^2 2 to 403/2, see also Raubitschek (1941) 287. Cartledge (1987) 291 prefers 398/7 BC.

141. For Cephalus and Thrasybulus of Collytus as members of the exiled Athenian democrats, see Din. 1.76; Dem. 24.134. Cf. Worthington (1992) 193–94; Strauss (1987) 103–4. For Thrasybulus' excellent relations with Thebes, see Schweigert (1939) 1–3.

142. For a detailed discussion of Athens' contribution to the liberation of Thebes, see the following section.

Aeschines' assertion is confirmed by epigraphic evidence. On the famous prospectus of the Second Athenian League from the spring of 377—one year after the successful countercoup—Thrasybulus is mentioned as one of three ambassadors sent to Thebes for further negotiations (*IG* II^2 43.72–77 = R&O 22.72–77). Lysias' client, Cephalus, and Thrasybulus thus did exactly what was expected of grateful guest-friends. For a ξένος was supposed to provide

> substantial assistance—in solving family affairs; in avenging personal grievances; in lending money; in offering shelter, refuge or asylum; in subverting governments; and overthrowing empires.[143]

The social institution of ξενία continued to exist throughout the classical period, underneath the superimposed polis ideology. Such personal ties between elite politicians from different *poleis* were therefore a crucial factor in political debates concerning the relations between their respective states.

Thus far, I have not provided any proof that the Theban support for the Athenian democrats in 404 was indeed brought up in Athenian public discourse in 382/1. I have merely emphasized the striking parallels between the situation in 404 and 382 and have shown that Theban refugees, supported by those Athenians who had once found a safe haven in Thebes themselves, managed to persuade the Athenian demos to grant them political asylum. In his *Life of Pelopidas,* however, Plutarch explicitly mentions the causal connection between the refuge granted to the Thebans in 382 and their previous aid to Thrasybulus of Steiria and his followers.

> There came also letters from the Lacedaemonians ordering the Athenians not to harbor or encourage the exiles but to expel them as men declared common enemies by the allies. The Athenians, however, in addition to their ancestral and inborn humanity, returning the favor to the Thebans, who had very much assisted in the return of the demos and had passed a decree that if any Athenians marched through Boeotia against the tyrants in Athens, no Boeotian should see or hear them, did no harm to the Thebans. (Plut. *Pelop.* 6.4–5)

Plutarch is not the only source that explicitly connects the Theban assistance against the Thirty and the Athenian aid against the Spartan-backed junta in Thebes. In the context of the overthrow of Leontiades' faction in 379/8, Diodorus reports that a Theban embassy requested military aid from the Athenians.

143. Herman (1987) 128.

> The Thebans, expecting a large army from Greece to come to the aid of the Lacedaemonians [under siege on the Cadmea], sent envoys to Athens to remind them that they too once aided in leading the demos of the Athenians back at the time when the Athenians had been enslaved by the Thirty Tyrants, and to request the Athenians to come in full force and assist them in reducing the Cadmea before the arrival of the Lacedaemonians. (Diod. 15.25.4)

Skeptics might object that the analogies drawn between the situation in Thebes in 404/3 and Athens in 382–379 are the creation of Plutarch and Diodorus, two historians fond of historical ironies, rather than accurate reflections of the arguments used in Athens in 382–379. Yet the aforementioned fragment of a court speech written by Lysias for an Athenian client on behalf of his Theban friend Pherenicus proves that Thebes' former benefactions were indeed talked about in Athenian public discourse during these years (Lys. fr. 286 Carey). Pherenicus is mentioned by Plutarch as one of Androcleidas' companions who found refuge in Athens after Leontiades' coup d'état and as one of the participants in the Theban countercoup in 379 (Plut. *Pelop.* 5.3, 8.1). When Androcleidas was assassinated in Athens, Lysias' Athenian client claimed Androcleidas' inheritance for Pherenicus in an Athenian court.[144] In this speech, delivered between 382 and 379, the unknown Athenian explicitly linked the events of 404 and 382: he and "any other Athenian who wanted" were received by Cephisodotus, Pherenicus' father, as ξένος into his house "when we were in exile,"[145] and Cephisodotus supported them privately and publicly until they returned home. It was this very experience, the Athenian claimed, that drove him to action in 382.

> Now when they experienced the same misfortune [ταῖς αὐταῖς τύχαις ἐχρήσαντο][146] and arrived as refugees in Athens, I—believing that I owed them the greatest gratitude [τὴν μεγίστην αὐτοῖς ὀφείλειν χάριν]—received them in such a friendly fashion that none of my visitors—unless any of them happened to know already—realized which of us was the owner of the house. (Lys. fr. 286.3 Carey)

---

144. For the legal ramifications of this trial, see Todd (2000) 352–56.

145. By using the unspecified pronoun *we* here, the speaker allows for members of the jury to be included in the number of exiles as well. For the distorted memory that the entire *demos* was in exile during the tyranny of the Thirty, see Wolpert (2002) 91–95; Forsdyke (2005) 262–67.

146. Todd's translation "When these men experienced their own misfortune" (Todd (2000) 355) is rather imprecise and misses the point that—in the speaker's eyes—both misfortunes (the takeover of the Thirty and the Spartan-backed junta) were indeed exactly the same.

Given this emphatic assertion of the bonds of guest-friendship (ξενία) and friendship (φιλία) that obliged the unknown Athenian to repay his debt to the son of his former Theban host by receiving him into his house in 382 and by pleading this case on his behalf, it is highly probable that this Athenian also lobbied for his Theban guest-friend in the Agora and in the Athenian assembly whenever the fate of the Theban refugees was under discussion.

To sum up, both the literary and the epigraphic evidence shows that the expulsion of the Thebans by the Spartan-backed junta became a political affair in Athens, where it was discussed in the council and the assembly. The arguments set forth by the Theban refugees and their Athenian supporters must have seemed convincing to the Athenians, since a decree was passed in their favor and their status as privileged exiles (*isoteleia* and *ateleia*) was recorded on a stele set up on the Acropolis. Moreover, the very analogy between the situations in Thebes in 382–379 and in Athens in 404/3 suggests—and our sources confirm—that the Theban exiles (and their Athenian supporters) drew heavily on the historical precedent of 404 in their efforts to win the support of the Athenian demos.[147] It is certainly possible that the Theban decree from 404 was even cited in the debates in 382–379, which would thereby become one of the occasions standing behind Dinarchus' assertion in 323 that this decree had been "quoted many times" before the Athenians (Din. 1.25).

Athenian Contribution to the Theban Countercoup, 379/8

The passage in Diodorus cited above (Diod. 15.25.4) opens up another problem closely related to our investigation. So far, I have focused my discussion on the Thebans' appeal for asylum in Athens, which was granted. But how far did the Athenian support for the exiled Thebans go? Did the Athenians merely provide a safe haven, or did they officially or privately lend aid to the exiles' successful coup against the pro-Spartan junta in 379? Our sources for this event differ to such a degree that the course of events leading to the expulsion of the Spartan garrison cannot be reconstructed with certainty.[148] This is not the place for a detailed historical reconstruction of the entire episode, but a few aspects related to Athenian social memory deserve our attention.

We know for sure that late in 379, a small group of Theban exiles traveled, in disguise, from Athens to Thebes and, with the help of a fellow conspirator with-

147. The fact that Dinarchus mentions the liberation of Thebes and the Theban aid for the Athenian exiles in 404/3 within one and the same speech (Din. 1.25 on 404/3 and Din. 1.38–39 on 379/8) can be seen as a further clue that this connection was indeed drawn.

148. For detailed historical discussion, cf. Cawkwell (1973); deVoto (1989); Buck (1992), (1994) 72–93; Stylianou (1998) 230–42.

in the Theban junta, managed to assassinate Leontiades and other key figures of the Theban government. The population of Thebes joined the conspirators and started to besiege the Spartan garrison on the Cadmea. Soon the garrison capitulated under terms and the Theban exiles changed the constitution and revived the Boeotian League. At some point in 378, probably after a Spartan raid against the Piraeus, the Athenians and Thebans concluded an alliance.[149]

There is much dissent concerning the degree of Athenian involvement in ousting the Theban junta and expelling the Spartan garrison. Diodorus, following Ephorus, his fourth-century source, reports that immediately after the assassination of the ruling pro-Spartan faction, the Thebans requested the Athenians to come in full force, and the latter voted to send at once an army of five thousand hoplites under the command of a certain Demophon. Owing to the scarcity of provisions and being hard pressed by the combined Athenian-Boeotian army, the besieged Spartan garrison was forced to surrender (Diod. 15.25–27). Dinarchus' allusion to this event seems consistent with Diodorus' version. In 323, the orator mentioned an official Athenian decree to send an army in support of the Thebans, proposed by Cephalus immediately after the Theban countercoup in 379.

> And others marched out when your ancestors were persuaded by the decree proposed by Cephalus . . . He proposed that the Athenians should march out and come to the aid of the exiles who had seized Thebes. And when your fathers went there, within a few days the commander of the Spartan garrison was expelled and the Thebans were set free. (Din. 1.39)

Xenophon's account, which is closer in time to the actual events, is more ambivalent concerning the Athenian support. He reports that immediately after the assassination of Leontiades,

> the returned exiles also sent horsemen to the troops of the Athenians who were on the borders under two generals. And the latter, knowing the purpose for which they had sent out the horsemen, came to their aid. (Xen. *Hell.* 5.4.9)

After the arrival of these troops, the Thebans and Athenians made an attack on the Theban acropolis (the Cadmea), which almost immediately caused the Spartan commander to ask for terms of surrender (Xen. *Hell.* 5.4.10–12). Xeno-

149. The sources are Xen. *Hell.* 5.4.1–19; Diod. 15.25–27; Plut. *Pelop.* 5–13; Plut. *Mor.* 596–98; Isoc. 14.29; Din. 1.38–39; Nep. *Pelop.* 2.1–4.1; Aristid. *Panath.* 282–84 Dindorf; *IG* II^2 43 = R&O 22.

phon, however, does not mention any official Athenian aid. On the contrary, he reports that the Athenians had second thoughts about going to war with Sparta, reflecting on Spartan might and the prospect of Attica becoming the battleground in this fight.

> As a result, the Athenians were so afraid that they brought to trial the two generals who had been privy to the uprising of Melon against Leontiades and his faction, put one of them to death, and, since the other did not remain to stand trial, exiled him. (Xen. *Hell.* 5.4.19)

According to Xenophon, the Athenians, persuaded by pro-Boeotian politicians (οἱ βοιωτιάζοντες), did decide "to give aid to the Boeotians with all zeal" (Xen. *Hell.* 5.4.34), but only after the Spartan authorities failed to punish Sphodrias, who had led a treacherous raid against the Piraeus in the spring of 378.[150]

The issue of Athenian involvement is hotly disputed among modern historians. Since the two accounts are irreconcilable, it becomes a matter of whose report is more trustworthy. This case provides an excellent example of scholarly prejudice toward our ancient sources. A majority of scholars lean toward Xenophon, since he is, after all, a historian and a contemporary of the events. The epitomator Diodorus and the orators Dinarchus and Aelius Aristides find less credibility; their claim that the Athenians passed a decree to send a major force for the siege of the Cadmea is easily dismissed as the result of confusion—a conflation of the unofficial Athenian help in December of 379 and the major campaign in the summer of 378 at the time of Agesilaus' invasion.[151]

Recently, Stylianou has made a strong case for Diodorus' (and Dinarchus') version, advancing two lines of argument.[152] First, he dismisses Xenophon's account on the basis of his anti-Theban prejudice and of certain inconsistencies in his story: Xenophon is silent about the official Athenian aid, decreed on Cephalus' motion, since he did not want to narrate Athenian actions that were responsible for Thebes' rise to hegemony.[153] His notorious silence about the

150. Plutarch, who mentions these events in his *Pelopidas* and *De genio Socratis,* seems to have used Xenophon but mainly follows Ephorus; cf. Stylianou (1998) 232.

151. Cf. Worthington (1992) 195: "Xenophon's account should be preferred, and it is likely, then, that both Dinarchus (at 1.39) and Diodorus have confused the *psephisma* of the Assembly after Sphodrias' attempt with the action of these so-called volunteers." Cf. Ryder (1965) 55.

152. Cf. Stylianou (1998) 230–36. He also provides an excellent summary of the scholarly debate and the key arguments employed.

153. Cf. Stylianou (1998) 233: "It is considered inconceivable that Xenophon could not have known of such a major expedition. However, it is not perhaps the case that Xenophon was not aware of the midwinter march to Thebes. It is simply that he chose to ignore an action which he would have ascribed to the influence of the βοιωτιάζοντες at Athens." Moreover, the suppression of Athens' significant contribution to the liberation of Thebes may also be due to Xenophon's moralizing objectives. Xenophon regards the Spartan seizure of the Cadmea as a sacrilege that was punished by the gods: the Spartans "were punished by the actions of these men, and these men alone,

constitution of the Second Athenian Confederacy can also be ascribed to this reason, and his dislike of Thebes is well known.[154] Second, Stylianou convincingly refutes the arguments brought to bear against Diodorus' account, such as the rejection of this official Athenian expedition on the shaky grounds that such an open act of hostility against Sparta at that time would be incredible.[155]

I should now like to provide further arguments in support of Stylianou's reconstruction. If we take into account the normative force of appeals to repay former benefaction and the characteristics of social memory that can explain why and how this episode was remembered in Athens, we have to reevaluate the reliability of our sources.[156] It will become clear that both Dinarchus' and Diodorus' accounts, while reflecting the patriotic exaggerations of the Athenian master narrative, still come closer to the historical situation in 379 than Xenophon, who deliberately suppressed distasteful information.

Both Dinarchus and Diodorus agree that before the successful completion of the coup, only private aid was rendered by Athenians, on their own initiative. Dinarchus says explicitly that influential Athenian politicians such as Cephalus, Thrason of Erchia, Eleus, and Phormisius, "lending help to the exiles who were returning to Thebes, at their own risk [βοηθήσαντες τοῖς εἰς Θήβας κατιοῦσι τῶν φυγάδων, τοῖς ἰδίοις κινδύνοις], liberated a neighboring city" (Din. 1.38). Voluntary Athenian aid can also be seen behind Diodorus' phrase "the exiles gathered together and, with Athenians supporting them [συνεπιλαβομένων Ἀθηναίων], returned by night to their native city" (Diod. 15.25.1). The omission of the article τῶν (in the genitive absolute συνεπιλαβομένων Ἀθηναίων) indicates that it was not official help, coming from *the* Athenians. Xenophon, too, reports unofficial Athenian aid at this stage of the operation. He stresses the conspiratorial aspect of the military aid provided by two Athenian generals whose troops "happened to be" at the Athenian-Boeotian border at the time of the Theban countercoup. These generals were privy to the plan of Melon, the exiles' leader, and led their troops into Thebes as soon as they were informed that the pro-Spartan junta had been toppled (Xen. *Hell.* 5.4.9, 19). It seems likely that these two generals conspired with other pro-Theban Athenian politicians, such as Cephalus, who provided aid to the Theban exiles on their own initiative. From our earlier discussion, it seems clear that it was the Athenian ξένοι of the Theban exiles who stood behind these actions; repaying the benefac-

whom they had wronged" (Xen. *Hell.* 5.4.1). Dwelling on the Athenian involvement would only undermine this point. For Xenophon's moralizing, see Pownall (2004) 65–112.

154. For the foundation of the Second Athenian League, see Cargill (1981) and Rhodes & Osborne (2003) 92–105, discussing the historical context of *IG* II^2 43 = R&O 22.

155. Cf. Stylianou (1998) 234.

156. That general characteristics of social memory can be used to identify specific historical distortions in our sources and thus aid in historical reconstructions is demonstrated by Forsdyke (2011) in the case of the popular traditions about Cleisthenes of Sicyon, found in Hdt. 5.67–68.

tions of 404/3, they had lobbied the demos to grant their friends asylum and now rendered them βοήθεια (βοηθήσαντες, Din. 1.38), as the norms of ξενία required.[157]

Both Dinarchus and Diodorus then report an official vote of the Athenian demos to send troops for the siege of the Cadmea (Din. 1.39; Diod. 15.25.4–27.4)—which Xenophon does not mention. Dismissing Diodorus' detailed description of the Athenian assembly meeting, Buck tries to reconcile at least Dinarchus with Xenophon's account, since the orator's audience did, after all, contain a few contemporaries of this event, who would have been in a position to check the veracity of his account. He asserts that Dinarchus' boastful claim "and others marched out when your ancestors were persuaded by the decree proposed by Cephalus, who was not swayed by the power of Sparta" (Din. 1.39) refers to a decree moved by Cephalus "authorizing troop movements near the frontier,"[158] which would explain the presence of Xenophon's two generals in the border region. This explanation seems improbable. Why should anybody—after more than fifty years—remember a decree as banal as the one suggested by Buck, authorizing the movement of troops within Athens' own territory? Dinarchus' diction suggests that the decree to which he refers was extraordinary and well known.

The motion to send Athenian troops for the liberation of the Spartan-held Cadmea was certainly more likely to be remembered, since it conformed to the Athenians' self-image and could easily be incorporated in their traditional memorial framework. Dinarchus' diction offers a clear hint concerning the source of this historical paradigm. Having mentioned the private efforts of some Athenian leaders (Din. 1.38), he continues,

> And others marched out when your ancestors were persuaded by the decree proposed by Cephalus, who was not swayed by the power of Sparta and did not take into account the military and political risks for the city. He proposed that the Athenians should march out and come to the aid of the exiles who had seized Thebes. And when your fathers went there, within a few days the commander of the Spartan garrison was expelled and the Thebans were set free, and your city did this in a manner worthy of your ancestors [διεπέπρακτο ἡ πόλις ἡ ὑμετέρα ἄξια τῶν προγόνων]. (Din. 1.39)

The last colon, "your city did this in a manner worthy of your ancestors," is a thought often found in the genre of the Athenian funeral orations, in which the

157. For the obligations of ξένοι, see Herman (1987) 129: "*Private services.* Here belong chiefly: (a) acts of opportune intervention (*boetheia*) . . ."

158. Buck (1992) 107.

heroic exploits of the ancestors are listed.[159] All of those feats have in common that they are symbolic and expressive of the timeless Athenian character. To perform a deed worthy of the ancestors means to be commemorated in the catalogue of manifestations of timeless Athenian ἀρετή, as those were propagated in the master narrative of the funeral orations. That Dinarchus is speaking in the tradition of the λόγοι ἐπιτάφιοι is evident from his immediately preceding praise of the deeds of the ancestors "who, at a time when many grave perils beset the city, faced danger in the interest of the people, in a manner worthy of their fatherland, of their own freedom and of their just reputation" (Din. 1.37). That Athens' support for the Theban exiles was capable of taking its place in the Athenian master narrative is furthermore indicated by the fact that Cephalus and his friends are mentioned in the same breath with Aristides and Themistocles, who laid the foundation for the Athenian empire (Din. 1.37).

Moreover, the qualities that Dinarchus ascribes to the Athenians' actions under Cephalus' leadership exemplify the well-known Athenian character. Undaunted by superior might (οὐ καταπλαγεὶς τὴν Λακεδαιμονίων δύναμιν) and selflessly, without any considerations of the dangers entailed (οὐδὲ λογισάμενος ὅτι τὸ κινδυνεύειν καὶ τὸ γράφειν ὑπὲρ τῆς πόλεως ἐπισφαλές ἐστιν), Cephalus convinced his fellow Athenians to march out and do what Athenians always do—oppose tyrants and free people from oppression (ἠλευθέρ<ω>ντο Θηβαῖοι, Din. 1.39)—just as his comrades Thrason of Erchia, Eleus, Phormisius, and others had lent

> help to the exiles, when the Spartans had garrisoned the Cadmea, so that they could return to Thebes, and at their own peril freed a neighboring city that had so long been enslaved [ἠλευθέρωσαν πόλιν ἀστυγείτονα καὶ πολὺν χρόνον δουλεύουσαν] (Din. 1.38).

Once again, the Athenians had proved themselves to be champions of Greek liberty, as they had on many occasions since Marathon.[160]

It must be admitted that this event is not mentioned in the two extant funeral orations written in the following decades,[161] but it is mentioned several times in other surviving speeches (twice in the surviving speeches of Aeschines and three times in Isocrates), showing that this episode had indeed become an integral part of the Athenians' shared image of the past.[162] Moreover, Aelius

159. For example, Hyperides said that Miltiades and Themistocles accomplished deeds worthy of the heroes before them (Hyp. *Epit.* 37). Demosthenes claims that the descendants of the various Athenian eponymous heroes were mindful to act in a manner worthy of their forefathers (Dem. 60.27–31).

160. Cf. "Funeral Orations" in chapter 1, 49–58.

161. The two extant funeral speeches postdating 379/8 are Dem. 60 and Hyp. *Epit.*

162. Cf. Aeschin. 2.164; Isoc. 14.28–29. Reciting a speech he delivered before Philip of Mace-

Aristides, an orator in the second century A.D., also exalted this episode in his encomium for the Athenians, most likely deriving his material from much earlier speeches of this genre.[163]

Not surprisingly, in the process of memorialization, the Athenian contribution to the ousting of the Theban-Spartan junta was greatly exaggerated. The role of the Theban conspirators and their fellow citizens in the events is hardly mentioned in Athenian public discourse. Aeschines, for instance, addressing his Athenian audience, boldly claimed, "You led the Theban refugees back into their fatherland" (κατηγάγετε φεύγοντας Θηβαίους εἰς τὴν πατρίδα, Aeschin. 2.164).

One problem still needs to be addressed, however: what are we to make of Xenophon's report of the trial of the two Athenian generals "who had been privy to the uprising of Melon against Leontiades and his faction" (Xen. *Hell.* 5.4.19)? This is one of the strongest arguments for Xenophon's version of merely unofficial Athenian aid. Buck, for instance, argues that the Athenians could not have punished the generals, if the Athenians had sent the troops with an official decree to besiege the Spartans in the Cadmea.[164] Yet Stylianou rightly asserts that the prosecution of the generals cannot be used as an argument against Diodorus' version: it seems that this trial must have occurred in a period of anxiety about potential Spartan repercussions, immediately after the expulsion of the Spartan garrison. There are two possible explanations for this trial. Either the Athenians punished the generals for purely political reasons (this had happened in Athenian history before) in an effort to reverse their current policy, even though the generals had acted in accordance with an assembly decree; or they had indeed acted outside the authority of the state by supporting their Theban friends in the early stages of the coup before the official decree was passed.[165] Considering the workings of social memory, it is not surprising that this unflattering short interlude of regret and anxiety, which led the Athenians to condemn these generals, began to fade in Athenian collective historical consciousness as soon as the expulsion of the Spartan-backed junta from Thebes turned out to be enduring and successful. From that moment forward, the whole episode could be remembered as an exemplary Athenian feat. Xeno-

---

don, Aeschines made another fleeting reference to this Athenian benefaction, which the ungrateful Thebans forgot; cf. Aeschin. 2.117: οὐ γὰρ ἂν δύναιο αὐτοὺς τηλικαῦτα εὐεργετῆσαι ἡλίκα Ἀθηναῖοι πρότερον, ὧν οὐ μέμνηνται. The brevity and vagueness of this allusion shows how well known this historical paradigm must have been to Aeschines' Athenian audience. That it is indeed a reference to the events of 379/8 is confirmed by Schol. Aeschin. 2.117 (257 Dilts). Isoc. 5.43 mentions the Athenian support of the restored Boeotian League soon after the restoration of the exiles.

163. Aristid. *Panath.* 283–84 Dindorf.

164. Cf. Buck (1994) 81–87; Worthington (1992) 195; Gehrke (1985) 179; Hack (1978) 58. Cawkwell (1973) prefers Diodorus' account.

165. Stylianou (1998) 236. For examples of political trials of Athenian generals, see Yunis (2000) 116 note 14.

phon, however, remembered and recorded the generals' punishment, whose actions had brought his Athenian homeland in conflict with his beloved Sparta.

This analysis has shown that when we are faced with irreconcilable versions in our sources, we should not automatically give the historian more credit. Sometimes it is the orator who gets it right, especially when the historian is as deeply prejudiced as Xenophon was against the Thebans. This case has demonstrated how crucial it is to consider the role of the audience. Speaking in front of a few hundred jurors, Dinarchus is more likely to reflect what his contemporaries knew about this incident in 379, even though we have to allow for exaggerations due to patriotic memorial practices. Xenophon was less subject to his audience's direct reaction and expected most of his upper-class readers to share his pro-Spartan sympathies. Accordingly, he had more latitude to present history as he saw it. To be fair, he did not disseminate any falsehoods, he merely chose to suppress certain events that did not seem meaningful to him.[166]

To sum up, in the years following the coup in Thebes in 382, the appeal of the Theban refugees in the Athenian assembly, their very presence in Athens, and the stele (granting them asylum) set up as a permanent reminder all brought the memory of Thebes' support for the Athenian democrats in 404 back to the forefront of Athenian historical consciousness. The roles of Cephalus, the two generals, and other Athenians sympathetic to the Thebans' plight shows that personal ties between elite politicians from different *poleis* (ἰδιόξενοι) were a crucial factor in interstate affairs. They functioned as preservers of the memory of cooperation between their respective states and were able to reintroduce fading memories into public discourse, once they gained new relevance.

The precedent of 404 was a crucial argument for granting the Theban refugees a safe haven and providing them resources for their countercoup of 379. The Athenian involvement in the ousting of the Spartan-Theban junta turned out to be such a success story that it became part of the Athenian master narrative. The memory of the restoration of the Theban exiles in 379/8 could thus indirectly serve as a further cue for the recollection of Thebes' aid for Thrasybulus in 404 and help to preserve this memory in Athenian historical consciousness.

Athens, Thebes, and Macedonia

We have found plenty of evidence that Thebes' aid for Thrasybulus played a significant role in Athenian public discourse during the reign of the Theban junta

166. Pownall (2004) 65–71 makes the case that Xenophon omitted historical events (e.g., the foundation of the Second Athenian League) if they were not suitable for moralizing paradigms, which constituted Xenophon's primary goal.

from 382 to 379/8 and, in turn, that these events refreshed Athenian memories of the events of 404/3. Yet fifty-five more years passed before Dinarchus mentioned this historical paradigm in his indictment of Demosthenes in 323. How important was this memory to the Athenians during these intervening years? Did it remain a much-evoked example of gracious Theban support, or was it, rather, suppressed in the light of renewed Athenian-Theban enmity? Indeed, the latter scenario is much more plausible. After a few years of Athenian-Boeotian cooperation against the Spartans during the Boeotian War (378–371), the Athenians became more and more frustrated with the Thebans thanks to Thebes' hegemonic politics in Boeotia, including its destruction of Plataea in 373.[167] Athenian annoyance with Thebes, apparent at the peace conference at Sparta in 371, turned into open enmity after the Theban victory over the Spartans at Leuctra. During the years of Theban hegemony (371–362), in the aftermath of the battle of Mantinea, and during the Third Sacred War (356–346), Athens was allied to Thebes' enemies. For more than thirty years, the Athenians cultivated their hatred of their northern neighbors, and the memory of Thebes' original sin, its collaboration with the barbarians during the Persian Wars, dominated Athenian public discourse again.[168]

In this particularly hostile atmosphere, the memory of Thebes' support for the Athenian democrats was likely to fade from Athenian collective consciousness if nothing happened to revive this memory in Athenian public discourse; after all, a whole generation of Athenians grew up hearing nothing positive about the Thebans.[169] The situation suddenly changed when King Philip's army stood at Elatea in 339 and threatened not only Athens but also Thebes, his own nominal ally. Although the extant sources do not contain any explicit remarks about the mutual Athenian-Theban aid in 404/3 and 379/8, I argue that several events between 339 and 323 revived the Athenian memory of these precedents of successful Athenian-Theban cooperation.

Demosthenes and the Athenian-Theban Alliance of 339/8

The first occasion for reintroducing the memory of mutual Athenian-Theban support into Athenian public discourse arose late in 339, when Philip II of Macedon bypassed Thermopylae and occupied the Phocian town of Elatea: the route to Boeotia and Attica was now open to his troops. Athens was in

167. Cf. Xen. *Hell.* 6.3.1. See "Plataean-Theban Antagonism" in chapter 2, 120–27.

168. For the orators' frequent allusions to Thebes' collaboration with the Persians during this particular period, see "Fourth-Century Allusions to Thebes' Medizing" in chapter 2, 101–3.

169. Hostile remarks about the Thebans and references to Athenian-Theban enmity abound in the speeches of the Attic orators during these years. Cf. Isoc. 5.248, 6.27, 8.17; Aeschin. 2.104, 3.116, 3.137–41; Dem. 18.18, 18.188, 18.202, 19.60. See also Buckler (1980) 275–77.

panic, and the assembly gathered for an emergency meeting (Dem. 18.169–73). Demosthenes advised his fellow Athenians to seek an alliance with Thebes, which had been Athens' foe for the last thirty years and a staunch ally of Philip throughout his ascendancy in the 340s. Yet, recently, Thebes' relationship with Philip had soured; some Thebans were discontented with Philip's settlement of affairs in central Greece after his victory against the Phocians and, earlier in 339, had expelled the Macedonian garrison from Nicaea, the fortress guarding Thermopylae (Philochorus *FGrHist* 328 F 56b). The Thebans, therefore, though formally still Philip's allies, could not be entirely sure of Philip's intentions.[170]

Confident that there was some chance of a rapprochement with Thebes, Demosthenes proposed to send an embassy to Thebes and to offer unconditional military aid (Dem. 18.177–78). The assembly adopted Demosthenes' motion and sent him on an embassy to Thebes (Dem. 18.179). After hearing the arguments of both Philip's ambassadors and the Athenian ambassadors, the Thebans decided to conclude an alliance with Athens (Dem. 18.211–15).

There are several clues to suggest that Demosthenes used the historical precedents of 404/3 and 379/8 both in Athens and in Thebes to promote an alliance against Philip. First, in the decisive assembly meeting in Athens, Demosthenes asked the Athenians to forget their negative experiences with the Thebans in the past (Dem. 18.176). This indicates that Demosthenes regarded the social memory of negative past experiences with the Thebans as a crucial political factor. Positive memories could possibly help to convince his audience. Even though he does not mention these positive past events in his account of this fateful assembly meeting in *On the Crown*, it is reasonable to assume that he or one of his supporters would have deployed these historical paradigms of successful Athenian-Theban cooperation. Moreover, even though the following decree inserted in the manuscript of *On the Crown* is utterly spurious, the list of past Athenian benefactions to Thebes suggests that such arguments from social memory played an important role in Greek interstate relations and could also be mentioned in official decrees (Dem. 18.186).[171] If the original decree did indeed contain an enumeration of past Athenian benefits, the restoration of the Theban exiles in 379/8 would most likely have been mentioned among them, since it was part of the Athenian master narrative and the most recent Athenian benefaction, which laid the foundation for Thebes' ascendancy in the 360s.

Second, in his defense of Ctesiphon in 330, although Demosthenes refrained

170. Cf. Sealey (1993) 194–98.

171. For the nature of these spurious documents, see Yunis (2001) 29–31. The spurious decree in Dem. 18.186 lists the restoration of the sons of Heracles, the asylum granted to Oedipus, "and many other notable acts of kindness . . . done to the Thebans." For the use of myths in Hellenistic decrees and their important role in inter*poleis* diplomacy, see Gehrke (2001).

from repeating the speech he made in the Theban assembly in 339/8 (Dem. 18.214), he did report the arguments used by Philip's ambassadors, who had spoken directly before the Athenians.

> They came forward and made their speech, full of praise of Philip and full of accusations of Athens, and recalled everything you had ever done in opposition to the Thebans. The main idea of the speech was that they were to show gratitude to Philip for the benefactions they had received from him and to punish you for the injuries they had suffered from you. (Dem. 18.213)

Again we see that arguments from social memory are used in diplomatic contexts to support requests for reciprocal favors—returning benefits and punishing past injuries. The Macedonian ambassadors ask the Thebans to choose whether they want to join Philip in his attack on Athens or simply grant him passage through Boeotia. In either case, they would gain many material benefits from continuing their alliance with Philip (Dem. 18.213). Unfortunately, Demosthenes' reply is not preserved. We do know, however, that the situation demanded that he counter the Macedonian ambassadors' arguments, for instance, by stressing Philip's evil and Athens' selfless intentions. The historical precedents of 404/3 and 379/8 would have served well as arguments for cooperation at the present time.

In the context of this episode, two further points can be made. The first concerns Thebes' decision to join the Athenians in fighting Philip. The historian Theopompus, a contemporary of the events, gave the following verdict about the effect of Demosthenes' speech on the Thebans in 339/8, preserved in Plutarch's *Life of Demosthenes.*

> What was to their own advantage [τὸ μὲν οὖν συμφέρον] did not escape the calculations of the Thebans. . . . But the power of the orator, as Theopompus writes, by stirring up their courage and inflaming their love of honor, cast a shadow over all other considerations, with the result that they threw aside fear, and calculation, and gratitude [toward Philip], being inspired [by his speech]. (Plut. *Dem.* 18.2 = Theopompus *FGrHist* 115 F 328)

Flower makes the case that Theopompus censured the Thebans for their irrational and foolish decision to go to war, swept away by Demosthenes' rhetoric.[172]

172. M. A. Flower (1994) 143–45. Shrimpton (1991) 175–76 views this fragment as evidence for Theopompus' approval of Demosthenes' policy of rapprochement with Thebes.

For our purpose, it is less important whether the Thebans were lauded or criticized for their decision by Theopompus. But his account proves that arguments based on a group's shared image of the past, evoking their ancestors' achievements and the values and beliefs of their community, carried great emotional weight and were therefore crucial factors in decision making. They can even lead to decisions against a community's rational self-interest, as Theopompus' comment suggests.[173] Modern historians too often ignore such "irrational" factors in their analysis of political decisions made by Greek *poleis*.[174]

Another aspect that deserves to be mentioned briefly is once more the role of personal ties in interstate relations. In his description of the situation in Thebes in 339, Demosthenes pointed out that there were two factions: one consisted of friends of Philip (οἱ μὲν ἑαυτοῦ φίλοι, Dem. 18.175); the other had sympathy for Athens (οἱ φρονοῦντες τὰ ὑμέτερα, Dem. 18.177). Emboldened by a show of force by their patrons, both factions would try to sway the majority of the Theban assembly. For that reason, Demosthenes wanted the Athenians to march their troops out to Eleusis.

Demosthenes denounced Philip's Theban supporters as those "whom he was able to win by fraud or corruption" (Dem. 18.175). This slander is probably not true, but it betrays that Demosthenes referred to Thebans who had a personal relationship with Philip. This is also confirmed by his use of the term φίλοι (Dem. 18.175). Such φίλοι were best suited to present the Macedonian king's point of view to their fellow citizens, since, through regular contacts and visits, they were probably most familiar with Philip's Macedonian homeland and its history.

Similarly, Demosthenes, as the πρόξενος, the official host and representative of Theban interests in Athens, was especially familiar with the Theban mindset and traditions.[175] This is evident, for instance, from an anecdote about Demosthenes' defense of the Thebans and Olynthians against a pro-Macedonian slanderer at Olympia in 324. Demosthenes came forward and "recounted with historical proofs all the benefits that the peoples of Thebes and Chalcidice had conferred upon Greece" (Plut. *Dem.* 9.1). Personal ties to citizens of other *poleis* were indeed an important mechanism by which to transmit and promote the social memories of other Greek communities to one's own fellow citizens.[176]

173. In his attack on Demosthenes, Aeschines denies that his rival's arguments made any difference, arguing that the Thebans made their decision solely driven by the crisis, fear, and the need of an alliance. Cf. Aeschin. 3.141. For the efficacy of Demosthenes' emotional appeals in Athens, see Montgomery (1983) 105–7.

174. Cf. Mosley (1971). Evaluating the fairness of the terms of the Athenian-Theban alliance, Mosley barely mentions the psychological aspect of these negotiations.

175. For Demosthenes' pro-Theban sympathies, see Trevett (1999).

176. For the role of πρόξενοι, see also Adcock & Mosley (1975) 160–64.

Thebans Exiled by Philip in 338

In the previous section, I have shown that arguments from social memory played a major role in the debates and negotiations surrounding the Athenian-Theban alliance in 339/8. Even though our extant sources do not contain any explicit references to the events of 404/3 and 382–378, I have argued that Demosthenes is likely to have used these historical paradigms of mutual Theban-Athenian benefactions, especially considering the lack of other outstanding examples of successful Athenian-Theban cooperation in historical times. After the battle of Chaeronea, events occurred that resembled the situation of Athens in 404/3 and of Thebes during 382–379 so closely that it is almost certain that these precedents were revived and intensely used in Athenian and Theban public discourse.

After his victory at Chaeronea in 338, Philip treated Athens relatively leniently but imposed severe terms on Thebes.[177] He executed some leading Thebans and drove others into exile (Justin 9.4.7). He recalled some Thebans who had been in exile and established from these a pro-Macedonian junta of three hundred men who immediately began to persecute their political opponents (Justin 9.4.8–9). He installed a Macedonian garrison on the Cadmea and restored the Boeotian towns of Orchomenus, Plataea, and Thespiae (Diod. 16.87.3; Paus. 9.1.8).[178]

The exact same measures had been taken by the Spartans and the pro-Spartan Theban junta in 382. Then as now, a small ruling clique, backed by a foreign power, had persecuted or exiled their political enemies. A foreign garrison was installed on the Cadmea, and other Boeotian towns were restored as base camps for the hegemonic power.[179] In Athens and in Thebes, these actions by themselves would have evoked the memory of the precedent of 382, at least among members of the oldest generations who had witnessed these events in their youth.

Yet the parallels do not stop here. Three years later, in 335, when the rumor spread that Alexander, the new Macedonian king, had been killed while on a campaign against the Illyrians, Thebes rose up in revolt.[180]

---

177. Cf. Sealey (1993) 198–201.

178. Furthermore, Philip exacted a ransom for Theban captives and corpses taken on the battlefield (Justin 9.4.6).

179. Cf. "Theban Exiles in Athens, 382–379" above, 254–60.

180. Already in 336, at the moment of Alexander's succession, the Thebans had shown signs of resistance. Yet Alexander was able to reaffirm his position through a speedy march into central Greece. Cf. Sealey (1993) 202.

> At his time [i.e., when Alexander was in Illyria] some of the exiles from Thebes slipped into Thebes by night—certain people from the city inviting them with a view to an uprising—seized Amyntas and Timolaus from among the force occupying the Cadmea, who had no suspicion of hostile movement outside the Cadmea), and killed them. Then, appearing in the assembly, they incited the Thebans to revolt against Alexander, promising freedom and <autonomy>, time-honored and noble slogans, and urging them to throw off—at long last—the burden of the Macedonian yoke.[181] (Arr. *Anab.* 1.7.1–2)

The Thebans resolved to resist Alexander, started to invest the Cadmea with trenches and stockades (Arr. *Anab.* 1.7.10), and sent embassies to Athens and other Greek *poleis* to ask for help (Diod. 17.8.3–5).

The similarities between this revolt and the ousting of the Spartan-backed junta in 379/8 are astonishing. It almost seems as though the Theban exiles in 335 used the account of the Theban countercoup as a script.[182] The refugees entered Thebes secretly at night; they coordinated their coup with conspirators inside Thebes; they first assassinated leading figures, then appealed to their fellow citizens in the assembly to join in the revolt, and finally besieged the foreign garrison in the Cadmea.[183]

When we remember that past experiences serve as an invaluable pool of information for future decision making, however, these similarities are less surprising.[184] Without doubt, the ousting of the pro-Spartan junta had become an integral part of the Theban master narrative of its past, since it laid the foundation of Thebes' hegemony in the 360s and was closely linked to the memory of its greatest statesmen, Epaminondas and Pelopidas.[185] There is every indication that the Theban exiles planned their coup based on the heroic precedent of 379/8.

Did Athens play any part in these events? Unfortunately, our sources do not tell us whence the Theban exiles set out and who might have supported them.

---

181. There must be a small lacuna in the manuscript between ἐλευθερίαν and the apposition παλαιὰ καὶ καλὰ ὀνόματα. Abicht's <καὶ αὐτονομίαν> is the most plausible emendation. Cf. Bosworth (1980) 74–75.

182. The other possibility—namely, that our source simply tried to cast the events of 335 into the narrative pattern of 379/8—seems highly unlikely. There are no explicit references in the text, and Ptolemy, Arrian's source for this passage (cf. Bosworth (1980) 79), cannot be suspected of using the Theban narrative of the coup in 379/8.

183. Emending Ἀμύνταν to Ἀνεμοίταν, some scholars have argued, perhaps rightly, that the victims were not Macedonian officers but the leading pro-Macedonian Thebans Anemoetas and Timolaus. For discussion, see Bosworth (1980) 74.

184. Cf. "Public Discourse and Decision Making" in the introduction, 30–36.

185. Cf. the long narrative in Plutarch's *Life of Pelopidas*.

Nevertheless, there are some clues to suggest that these Thebans indeed came from Athens. First, the Theban exiles must have found refuge somewhere, and Athens is the obvious first choice: it is the closest major city to Boeotia; it fought on Thebes' side against Philip; it preserved its independence after Chaeronea; its relationship to Macedonia remained ambivalent, to say the least;[186] and it had harbored Theban refugees before.[187]

Our sources report that the Thebans received from Demosthenes a free gift of weapons to arm those who lacked heavy armor (Plut. *Dem.* 23.1; Diod. 17.8.5). The narrative sequence in Plutarch indicates that Demosthenes supplied these weapons before the Thebans attacked the Macedonian garrison. I therefore suggest that Demosthenes secretly provided the Theban exiles with arms and resources *before* they attempted their coup, just as Ismenias in 404 and the pro-Theban Athenians around Cephalus had done in 379. Moreover, Diodorus reports that when the Thebans requested an alliance after their coup, "the Athenians, persuaded by Demosthenes, voted to support the Thebans, but failed to send out their forces, waiting to see how the war would go" (Diod. 17.8.6).[188]

Even though, since we cannot completely reconstruct the historical situation, many details remain obscure, we can still draw a few conclusions. Thebes' uprising against Alexander, initiated by Theban exiles, was modeled on the ousting of the pro-Spartan junta in 379/8. The exiles most likely set out from Athens and were secretly supported by Athenians sympathetic to their cause, such as Demosthenes. The basic similarity of the situations in 338–335 and 382–379, the presence of Theban exiles in Athens who were certainly lobbying for their cause,[189] and the Theban embassy who came to Athens to ask for an alliance after the coup were capable of reviving the memory of both historical precedents, Theban aid for Thrasybulus in 404/3 and Athenian support for the Theban exiles in 379/8.

Thebans Exiled by Alexander in 335

Philip's retribution against Thebes in 338 was not the last action that forced Thebans to seek asylum in Athens. Alexander brutally crushed the Theban revolt in

186. For Alexander's suspicion of Athens at the outbreak of the Theban revolt, see Arr. *Anab.* 1.7.4.

187. Athens would also provide a safe haven for the Thebans who escaped the annihilation of their city in 335, against Alexander's command. Cf. "Thebans Exiled by Alexander in 335" below.

188. Worthington (1992) 166 makes a strong case that the Athenians had not concluded a formal alliance and thus did not betray the Thebans.

189. Alexander, at least, considered the Athenians as guilty of the revolt as the Thebans themselves, demanded the extradition of the leading Athenian politicians, and only relented after the Athenians had sent a second embassy to him (Arr. *Anab.* 1.10.5–6). See the discussion below.

335. Over six thousand Thebans perished on the battlefield and in the ensuing massacre (Diod. 17.14.1). Arrian and Plutarch report that the Athenians, while celebrating their Great Mysteries, first learned the news from Thebans who had managed to escape the slaughter and fled straight to Athens (Arr. *Anab.* 1.10.2; Plut. *Alex.* 13.1). In panic, they abandoned the festival, began to move their possessions from the country into the city, and sent an embassy under Demades to placate Alexander (Arr. *Anab.* 1.10.3).

Meanwhile, Alexander convened a council of his Greek allies to decide the fate of Thebes. The verdict was brutal.[190]

> They finally voted to raze the city to the ground, to sell the captives, and that the Theban refugees should be liable to seizure [ἀγωγίμος ὑπάρχειν] from all Greece and that no Greek should harbor a Theban. (Diod. 17.14.3)

In his reply to the first Athenian embassy led by Demades, Alexander demanded the extradition of the Theban refugees, as ordered in the decree, and of ten Athenian political leaders who had opposed his interests, Demosthenes and Lycurgus the most prominent among them (Diod. 17.15.1; Arr. *Anab.* 1.10.4–5).[191] After a passionate debate in the assembly, the Athenians adopted Demades' motion to reject Alexander's request, promising, instead, "to punish them according to the laws, if they [i.e. the Athenian politicians] deserved punishment" (Diod. 17.15.1–4). They sent a second embassy under Demades to Alexander,

> instructing the ambassadors to make a plea to Alexander in favor of the Theban fugitives as well [καὶ περὶ τῶν Θηβαίων φυγάδων], that he allow the demos to provide a refuge for the Theban refugees [συγχωρῆσαι τῷ δήμῳ τοὺς πεφευγότας Θηβαίους ὑποδέχεσθαι]. (Diod. 17.15.4)

On this mission, Demades achieved all his objectives and prevailed on Alexander to grant all the requests of the Athenians (Diod. 17.15.5).

Even though the reaction to Alexander's demand to surrender the leading Athenian politicians dominates our sources (Diod. 17.15.1–3; Plut. *Dem.* 23.3–6), the fate of the Theban refugees was also an important issue in the debate, as this brief historical sketch shows. This is evident, too, from Justin; in his

190. For a discussion of the decision to raze Thebes to the ground, see "Alexander's Annihilation of Thebes" in chapter 5, 336–41.

191. For a discussion of the identity of the wanted Athenian politicians, cf. Bosworth (1980) 93–95.

account, Athens' decision to open its gates to the Theban refugees is responsible for Alexander's extradition order (Justin 11.4.9–11). Our sources indicate that their fate was publicly discussed in Athens on at least two occasions: first, when they arrived in Athens immediately from the battlefield amid the Great Mysteries and, second, in the assembly debate about the response to Alexander's extradition order.[192]

We find several clues to indicate that these Theban refugees and their Athenian friends fell back on the historical precedents of 404/3 and 382 in their desperate pleas for asylum. First, their basic state closely resembled the situation of the Athenian democrats in 404/3 and the Theban exiles in 382. Unlike in 339, when Philip expelled some of his opponents from Thebes, now (just as in 404/3 and 382) nobody in Greece was allowed to grant the fugitives asylum. Second, the wording of Alexander's decree itself—especially the juristic terminus technicus ἀγωγίμος, "liable to seizure" (Diod. 17.14.3)—could serve as a reminder of the very decree the Spartans once issued against the Athenian democrats;[193] as I have argued earlier, we can assume that this decree and the Theban counter-decrees were remembered in Thebes as manifestations of the Theban national character. It is very likely, therefore, that Dinarchus is referring to this situation of 335 with his remark in 323 that the Theban decree of 404 "had been read out often before [the Athenians]" (Din. 1.25). Finally, the wording of the Athenian plea to Alexander, as it is preserved in Diodorus, contains a further indication that the Theban help for the Athenian democrats in 404 was indeed explicitly mentioned in the debate in 335. The Athenians themselves always referred to that period as the time "when the demos was in exile." It might not be accidental, therefore, that the Athenians instructed their ambassadors to ask Alexander "to allow the demos to provide a refuge for the Theban refugees" (συγχωρῆσαι τῷ δήμῳ τοὺς πεφευγότας Θηβαίους ὑποδέχεσθαι, Diod. 17.15.4). The use of the term *demos* instead of the more common "the Athenians" might indeed have stemmed from discussion of the historical precedent of 404. That this sentence preserves the wording of the actual decree is also suggested by the repetition of the phrase "the Theban fugitives/refugees" instead of the use of a pronominal form.[194] Thus we can conclude that the fate of the Theban refugees in 335 was intensively discussed in Athenian public discourse, which almost

192. Plut. *Alex.* 13.1 mentions the kind treatment that the Theban refugees received in Athens in the context of the aborted Great Mysteries celebration.

193. For the wording of the Spartan decree, cf. Diod. 14.6.1; Plut. *Lys.* 27.2. See "The Situation in Thebes in 404/3" above, 217–19.

194. Diod. 17.15.4: ὁ μὲν οὖν δῆμος ἀποδεξάμενος τὴν ἐπίνοιαν τοῦ Δημάδου τό τε ψήφισμα ἐκύρωσε καὶ τὸν Δημάδην μεθ' ἑτέρων ἀπέστειλε πρεσβευτὴν πρὸς τὸν βασιλέα, δοὺς ἐντολὴν καὶ περὶ τῶν Θηβαίων φυγάδων ἀξιῶσαι τὸν Ἀλέξανδρον συγχωρῆσαι τῷ δήμῳ τοὺς πεφευγότας Θηβαίους ὑποδέχεσθαι.

certainly brought the memory of Thebes' help for the Athenian exiles in 404 back into the forefront of Athenian public discourse.

The Destruction of Thebes—a Case against Demosthenes

Throughout this chapter, I have tried to identify historical situations that could prompt the memory of Thebes' support for the Athenian democrats in 404/3. The last cue for this memory in the period under investigation was Demosthenes himself. In *On the Crown*, giving an account of his political career and justifying his role in opposing Philip, he called the Athenian alliance with Thebes his greatest political achievement and service to his city.[195] Naturally, his political opponents took up this theme of Demosthenes' special relationship with Thebes and used it against him in every way possible. Aeschines, for instance, called the Athenian-Theban alliance of 339/8, which had led to the defeat at Chaeronea, "most ill-fated" for Athens (Aeschin. 3.239); and after Thebes' destruction at the hands of Alexander in 335, Aeschines, Dinarchus, and others blamed Demosthenes for betraying this former Athenian ally. They trumped up the charge that Demosthenes had received three hundred talents of gold from the Persian king in order to foment an anti-Macedonian rebellion in Greece; yet, when Thebes revolted and was in dire need of money and allies, Demosthenes refused to pay the meager sum of ten talents demanded by the Arcadian leader as price for his support of the rebellion. As a result of this lack of assistance, the Theban uprising was brutally crushed by Alexander. Thus the responsibility for Thebes' destruction was placed squarely on Demosthenes' shoulders (Aeschin. 3.156, 239–40; Din. 1.18–24).[196]

One possible tactic in their attacks was to contrast Demosthenes, the self-proclaimed friend of Thebes, with other Athenian benefactors of Thebes in the past. In his indictment of Ctesiphon in 330, Aeschines challenged Demosthenes' claim that the Thebans concluded the alliance with Athens in 339 thanks to his diplomatic and rhetorical skill: nobody, Aeschines countered, had ever been able to persuade the Thebans to be friends of Athens, not even the closest Athenian friends and benefactors of the Thebans in the past:

> first, Thrasybulus of Collytus, a man trusted in Thebes as no other ever was; again, Thrason of Erchia, *proxenos* of the Thebans; Leodamas of Acharnae, a speaker no less able than Demosthenes but in my opinion, indeed more pleasing; Archedemus of Pelekes, a powerful speaker and

195. Cf. Dem. 18.169–87.

196. For a thorough discussion of this trumped-up charge against Demosthenes, see Worthington (1992) 164–68.

> one who has often run risks in his political life for the sake of the Thebans; Aristophon of Azenia, who for the longest time had been subject to the charge of favoring the Boeotians [τὴν τοῦ βοιωτιάζειν ὑπομείνας αἰτίαν]; Pyrrhandrus of Anaphlystus, who is still living. (Aeschin. 3.138–39)

Even though Aeschines does not mention in detail under which historical circumstances each of these politicians promoted pro-Theban policies in Athens, simply listing the names of these famous friends of Thebes was probably sufficient to evoke the memory of past Athenian-Theban collaborations. Thrasybulus of Collytus, for instance, was one of the leading Athenian democrats who had set out from Thebes to capture Phyle and topple the regime of the Thirty; his name was probably inscribed on the stele set up in honor of the heroes of Phyle due to Archinus' proposal (*SEG* 28.45).[197] During 382–379, he must have been among the Athenian supporters of the Theban fugitives who had found refuge in Athens after the Spartan seizure of the Cadmea, as his election as envoy to Thebes in 377 strongly suggests (*IG* II^2 43.72–77 = R&O 22.72–77). The mere mention of his name was therefore likely to prompt the memory of the events of 404/3 and 382–379 among Aeschines' audience.

Similarly, in the indictment of Demosthenes for his involvement in the Harpalus affair in 323, Dinarchus used positive historical paradigms in Athenian-Theban history to expose Demosthenes' treacherous dealings with Thebes, which led to its destruction.[198] In this context, he contrasted Demosthenes' corrupt leadership to the heroic leadership of Cephalus and other pro-Theban politicians who restored the Theban exiles in 379/8 (Din. 1.38–39), which I have already discussed at length.[199] In addition, he employed the social memory of Thebes' help for the Athenian democrats in 404 to juxtapose this gracious act with Demosthenes' alleged betrayal of Thebes in 335 (Din. 1.24–27). This historical allusion gave rise to the investigation presented in this chapter.

Having traced the transmission of this historical paradigm from its origin in 404/3 down to Dinarchus' indictment of Demosthenes in 323, I would like to return to Dinarchus' historical paradigm.

> And these men [i.e., the Thebans], as our elders say [ὡς οἱ πρεσβύτεροι λέγουσι]—when the democracy in our city had been dissolved [καταλελυμένης τῆς δημοκρατίας τῆς παρ' ἡμῖν] and Thrasybulus

197. For this honorary inscription, see the discussion in the section "Athenian Memorialization of the Men from Phyle" above, 237–39, as well as Raubitschek (1941) and Taylor (2002).

198. For the circumstances of this trial, see Worthington (1992) 41–78.

199. Cf. "Athenian Help for the Theban Democrats, 382–378" above, 253–67.

> was gathering together the exiles in Thebes for the seizure of Phyle [συνάγοντος ἐν Θήβαις Θρασυβούλου τοὺς φυγάδας ἐπὶ τὴν Φυλῆς κατάληψιν]—despite the strength of the Spartans and their prohibition to harbor or let depart any Athenian, nevertheless aided the demos in returning and passed the decree, so often read out before you [τὸ πολλάκις ἀνεγνωσμένον παρ' ὑμῖν ἐψηφίσαντο ψήφισμα], that they would ignore any Athenian bearing arms passing through their territory. (Din. 1.25)

At the beginning of this chapter, I called Dinarchus' historical allusion truly remarkable, since it is our earliest testimony for an event that happened eighty years before the orator's lifetime. In contrast to other scholars, I proposed to take Dinarchus' claims seriously and to investigate whether it is plausible that he and his audience had indeed heard about this event from the elders and a Theban decree read often in the Athenian assembly. In the course of this chapter, I have made the case that Phyle, which was commemorated as the beginning of Thrasybulus' triumphant return, could serve as a cue for the recollection of Theban support. Moreover, the recurrence of similar historical circumstances, the diplomatic practice of listing past benefactions (395, 382–379, 335), and the expectation of acts of reciprocity between guest-friends were capable of bringing an otherwise uncommemorated event back into public discourse, thus securing the transmission of a memory that would have been forgotten in an atmosphere of permanent enmity.

CHAPTER 5

Persistent Memories

The Proposed Eradication of Athens

In chapter 2, I analyzed historical references to Theban medizing in Athenian public discourse. I argued that in the process of memorialization, owing to the continuous Athenian-Theban enmity in the fifth century, Thebes' medism became an essential part of the Athenian memory of the Persian Wars. This heroic experience had tremendous consequences for the Athenians' view of themselves. The victory over the barbarian invaders (and their Greek allies) became a symbol of the Athenian character. From this point forward, the Athenians saw themselves as champions of Greek liberty. Their Theban archenemies, by contrast, came to epitomize the traitors of Greece. Through various forms of public commemoration, this shared heroic view of the Persian Wars was asserted and transmitted to younger generations.

This interdependence between social memory and ideology is typical and confirms the theories of sociologists who, following Durkheim's and Halbwachs' lead, emphasize the sociopolitical functions of a shared image of the past for the present generation:[1] it creates societal cohesion, legitimizes the status quo, and provides a model for future decision making. It is not surprising, therefore, that such often-commemorated events as the Persian Wars were frequently recalled in Athenian political discourse.

In chapter 3, I argued that the new Athenian self-image that was largely based on the Athenians' experience of the Persian Wars and the resultant hegemonic ideology was retrojected into the past. Consequently, Athenians extolled

1. See "Ideology and Social Memory" in the introduction, 13–19. Cf. Prager (2001).

the mythical exploits of their ancestors who—in accordance with the notion of unchanging national character—had always been champions of the Greeks and protectors of the weak, as seen, for instance, in the intervention on behalf of the fallen Argives. In chapter 4, I demonstrated that the recurrence of similar historical circumstances, the diplomatic practice of listing past benefactions, and the expectation of acts of reciprocity between guest-friends were capable of bringing an event that was otherwise uncommemorated back into public discourse, thus securing the transmission of a memory that would have been forgotten in an atmosphere of permanent enmity.

In chapter 5, I address a different and somewhat peculiar aspect of social memory, which does not seem to be primarily governed by present social needs. A mere proposal that was never carried out and was discussed only at a conference held far away from Athens is constantly mentioned in fourth-century Athenian public discourse and thus betrays a persistence in Athenian historical consciousness that demands an explanation. Before I set forth my own approach to this problem, a brief description of this proposal, its historical problems, and previous scholarly approaches seems useful.

The Debate about Athens' Fate in 405/4

After the Athenians lost their fleet in the battle of Aegospotami in 405 BC, their city was besieged by land and sea and finally starved into submission. During that time, Athens' fate was far from certain, as our sources indicate. Xenophon reports that the Spartans and their allies were discussing the terms of Athens' surrender at a conference in Sparta when

> the Corinthians and Thebans in particular but also many other Greeks spoke against making a treaty with the Athenians and proposed to destroy their city [ἐξαιρεῖν]. The Lacedaemonians, however, refused to enslave [ἀνδραποδιεῖν][2] a Greek city that had done great service in the greatest dangers that had befallen Greece. (Xen. *Hell.* 2.2.19–20)

2. For a comprehensive discussion of ἀνδραποδίζειν, see Gaca (2010), who demonstrates conclusively that this common practice of warfare was a premeditated "all-out assault on civilian inhabitants" (157), which involved severe collective violence in handling the nonfighting population and culminated in the selection of young women and self-mobile girls and boys for permanent removal from the conquered population. In light of these findings, rendering ἀνδραποδίζειν as "selling into slavery" or "enslaving" is indeed highly problematic, since it implies a "clean" mercantile transaction. Yet, with this in mind, I decided to stick to "enslaving" for the lack of a suitable alternative (Gaca's "andrapodizing" does not seem very useful).

Plutarch's account offers more details concerning this proposal. In his biography of the Spartan leader Lysander, he writes,[3]

> And some say that in very truth a proposal for the enslavement [ὑπὲρ ἀνδραποδισμοῦ] [of the Athenians] was made in the assembly of the allies, when the Theban Erianthus also proposed to raze the city to the ground [τὸ μὲν ἄστυ κατασκάψαι] and to abandon its territory as grazing land for sheep [τὴν δὲ χώραν ἀνεῖναι μηλόβοτον].[4] (Plut. *Lys.* 15.2)

There are numerous other references to this impending destruction of Athens in contemporary and later historians and especially in the Attic orators.[5] Even though all of these sources agree that Athens barely escaped annihilation, they vary greatly as to who actually made this proposal, who rejected it, why it was made, and why it was not carried out. Three main questions arise from these differing sources: First, what exactly happened? Second, why is this memory of a mere proposal so persistent in Athenian public discourse? Third, what are the reasons for the divergence concerning the proponents and opponents of this plan? The problems surrounding the proposed destruction of Athens have been addressed in a variety of different ways by modern historians. To illustrate my own line of attack more clearly, it seems useful to discuss briefly two previous approaches representing both ends of the spectrum: those of Charles Hamilton, a more traditional historian, and Anna Missiou, a scholar of ideology and discourse.

Using the long-standing historical-philological methods of source criticism, Hamilton sets out to complement and correct Xenophon's narrative of the events of 405/4 through information provided by other texts.[6] In so doing, he identifies biases (e.g., Xenophon's pro-Spartan and anti-Theban bias)[7] and resolves apparent contradictions (Polyaen. 1.45.5 and Paus. 3.8.6) by referring the actions in question to two different occasions, supposing a change of opin-

3. Hamilton (1997) 206–7 is convinced that Plutarch's testimony is derived from reliable sources, such as the fourth-century historians Ephorus and Theopompus, both of whom Plutarch himself mentions in Plut. *Lys.* 17.2.

4. Plutarch relates this detail in the context of Lysander's influence on regime change in Athens in 404, *after* the conclusion of peace. Lysander threatened to reopen the case of Athens' fate, since the Athenians had violated the terms of the peace. This leads Plutarch to mention that such a proposal had indeed been made before. The aorist προτεθῆναί clearly indicates an earlier occasion; cf. Lévy (1976) 23 note 1.

5. Cf. Xen. *Hell.* 2.2.3, 2.2.19, 3.5.8, 6.3.13, 6.5.35, 6.5.46; Andoc. 1.142, 3.21; Isoc. 18.29, 14.31, 8.78, 8.105, 7.6, 15.319; Dem. 19.65–66; Plut. *Lys.* 15.2–3; Paus. 3.8.6; Diod. 15.63.1; Justin 5.8.4; Polyaen. 1.45.5; Ael. *VH* 4.6.; Schol. Dem. 19.65 (165a, b Dilts).

6. Cf. Hamilton (1979) 25–98, (1997).

7. Hamilton (1997) 203.

ion on the part of the Spartan commanders Agis and Lysander.[8] His litmus test for the validity of particular information is that rational arguments and motives for the actors involved can be supplied. In his reconstruction, he relies heavily on Xenophon and later historical writers (Plutarch, Pausanias, Justin, Polyaenus), whose accounts he traces back to the fourth-century historians Ephorus, Theopompus, and the author of the *Hellenica Oxyrhynchia*. Hamilton, however, largely ignores the orators' versions and does not offer explanations for potential distortions in their accounts.

Missiou is more interested in studying the variant versions and in detecting the underlying ideological influences than in reconstructing the actual course of events. She claims that the only certain fact is that "Athens was not destroyed in 404, although somewhere, somebody proposed or thought of the devastation of Attica and the enslavement of the Athenians."[9] Presupposing a model of conscious manipulation and propaganda, she explores the specific historical circumstances in which these differing historical allusions were developed.

Both the philological-historical and the *ideologiekritische* approach have shortcomings.[10] Hamilton's analysis presupposes an oversimplified textual model of transmission, in which later writers use earlier historians, who are assumed to be the only reliable recorders of eyewitness accounts. Yet these historians were themselves subject to the general communicative conditions of the time and thus—like the orators—exposed to different sources (oral and written) for their accounts. Therefore, we should not automatically prefer the historians' version to that of the orators.[11] Moreover, Hamilton identifies biases in the historiographical accounts, but he does not explore the sociopolitical functions of the differing versions that the orators offer their audiences.

Missiou's *Ideologiekritik* is too pessimistic. She seems to assume that the memory of this proposal could be indefinitely manipulated and distorted to serve propagandistic ends. It is certainly true that present sociopolitical needs can shift the emphasis of a certain story and distort the memory of this incident, but to retreat to an agnostic position concerning its historicity seems unnecessary. Hamilton's reconstruction is certainly correct in its main outline, which holds that particularly the Thebans and Corinthians, but also many other allies, proposed the destruction of Athens and that, in the end, the Spartans opposed it. Many details in these historiographical reports can be verified by other

8. Hamilton (1997) 207–8.

9. Missiou (1992) 103.

10. For political propaganda and *Ideologiekritik*, see "Participant Evidence: The Attic Orators and Their Interpretation" in the introduction, 39–41.

11. Cf. "Athenian Contribution to the Theban Countercoup, 379/8" in chapter 4, 260–67, where I argue that Dinarchus' version should be preferred to Xenophon's.

sources and thus suggest the existence of a historical core in these accounts.[12] Furthermore, Missiou assumes that there were only two distinct ideological positions in Athens, a pro-Spartan oligarchic one and an anti-Spartan democratic one, and ascribes all extant allusions to one or the other of them. This is far too schematic: not all of the supposedly pro-Spartan references are designed to proclaim "the moral superiority of Sparta" or "as a direct plea for assistance to Sparta,"[13] as we will see. Moreover, neither Hamilton nor Missiou is able to explain the extraordinary persistence of this memory in Athenian historical consciousness.

Many of the peculiarities associated with this particular memory are less baffling when compared to similar cases in other cultures and time periods. I assert that viewing the evidence through the lens of social memory might explain the remarkable persistence of this memory as well as the reasons for some of its distortions. This, in turn, will help us to reconstruct the historical reality behind it. Surveying all fourth-century allusions to this proposal, I will first demonstrate that this event was very familiar to the Athenians and highly emotionally charged. I will then analyze the historical circumstances of the siege of Athens in 405/4 and argue that the impending threat of extermination (manifested in a brutal siege) constituted a traumatic experience that left a deep mark on Athenian historical consciousness, even though this event was never inscribed or otherwise officially commemorated. An examination of how this memory was "stored" and expressed will show that this proposal was remembered according to a paradigm, embodied in the alleged ritual destruction of Crisa, which consists of enslavement, city razing, and dedication of the land to Apollo as grazing land for sheep. I will then argue that this ritual polis destruction did not merely serve as a mnemonic concept into which the memory of this proposal was later cast but played a crucial role in the actual debate in 405/4. Moreover, this ritual concept can offer insights into why Athens was spared in the end, and it thus contributes to the solution of an old historical problem. Similar experiences, real and imagined, of other cities also contributed to the persistence of this graphic memory. The core of this memory—namely, that Athens was threatened by total annihilation—is deeply engraved in Athenian collective consciousness and cannot be challenged. The memory of the circumstances of this proposal, however, is less static and shows signs of distortion. We will see that as historical circumstances changed throughout the

12. The Theban representative at the conference is identified as Ἐριάνθος (Ziegler conjectures Ἐριάνθης) in Plut. *Lys.* 15.2 (= *FGrHist* 596 F 26) and as Εὔανθος in Schol. Dem. 19.65 (165a Dilts). Pausanias reports that Ἐριάνθης served as an officer in Lysander's fleet at Aegospotami and set up a dedication at Delphi (Paus. 10.9.9). Cf. M&L 95d.

13. Missiou (1992) 101.

fourth century, some details could be suppressed and others emphasized. This chapter ends with an analysis of Alexander's use of this memorial framework in his punishment of Thebes in 335.

Fourth-Century Allusions to the Proposed Destruction of Athens

Before I discuss the implications and circumstances of this proposal, a brief survey of fourth-century references to the proposed destruction of Athens seems useful. My objective is to let the passages themselves speak and demonstrate that this incident was notorious and highly emotionally charged in Athens throughout the fourth century. Furthermore, it will become clear that these allusions cannot simply be divided into pro-Spartan and anti-Spartan propaganda, as Missiou suggests; their purposes are more varied.

The earliest reference is a passage in the court speech *Against Callimachus,* written by Isocrates for a client around 402 BC. It reveals that the discussion of Athens' fate by the Spartans and their allies was well known to Athenians. To demonstrate the inviolability of oaths and treaties, Isocrates alludes to the events of 405/4: when the Athenians "had been conquered and fallen into the power of the enemies and many desired to destroy the city [διαφθεῖραι τὴν πόλιν]," the Spartans did not allow it, out of respect for the oaths and covenants in which the Athenians had taken refuge (Isoc. 18.29).[14]

In 399 BC, in his defense speech *On the Mysteries,* Andocides constructed an analogy to his own situation by referring to the impending destruction of Athens and to Sparta's intervention to save it:[15] just as the Spartans preserved the Athenians thanks to their ancestors' merits in the Persian Wars, the jury ought to acquit him thanks to the merits of *his* ancestors (Andoc. 1.142–43). It is worthwhile to cite his account of the event.

> For the benefit of the entire city, the achievements [ἀρεταί] of your own forefathers were held in the highest esteem. For after the ships had been destroyed, when many wanted to envelop our city with incurable disas-

14. It is not entirely clear from this passage which oaths and treaties Isocrates is referring to here. However, Pausanias similarly remarks about this proposal that it violated "the oaths that the Lacedaemonians as a state had sworn by the gods to the Athenians" (Paus. 3.8.6). These oaths have been identified as the oaths sworn by the Delphic Amphictyons to preserve one another from destruction. Cf. Hamilton (1997) 208; Zeilhofer (1959) 79–80; "Imagining the Unimaginable: The Eradication of Athens" below, 309–23.

15. MacDowell (1962) 204–5 does not follow the *communis opinio* and argues instead for dating this speech to the fall of 400 BC. The precise date is of no consequence for my argument, however.

> ter [ἀνηκέστοις συμφοραῖς], the Lacedaemonians, although then our enemies, decided to save our city because of the achievements of those men who had laid the foundations of freedom for all of Greece. (Andoc. 1.142).

In 395 BC, at the dawn of the Corinthian War, Theban ambassadors arrived in Athens to ask for an alliance against the Spartans. In Xenophon's account, they devote their very first argument to the Theban proposal made at the end of the Peloponnesian War.

> Athenians, as regards your complaints against us for having voted for harsh measures [χαλεπὰ] toward you at the conclusion of the war, your complaints are not right; for our polis did not vote for those measures, but only one man proposed them, who happened at that time to have a seat in the assembly of the allies. (Xen. *Hell.* 3.5.8)

Contrasting this incident to the refusal of the entire polis to join the Spartan campaign against the Athenian democrats in 403 BC, the ambassadors ask the Athenians to repay their debt now, and they proceed to list numerous advantages of a joint war against the Spartans. The fact that, according to Xenophon, the Thebans devote their very first argument to this and not to any other previous hostile incident between the two cities reveals the importance of Thebes' role in the proposal for Athenian collective consciousness: the Theban ambassadors—at least in Xenophon's view—regarded this particular memory as the biggest obstacle to an Athenian-Theban alliance.[16]

In 392/1, representatives of the warring parties met at a conference at Sparta to discuss terms for ending the Corinthian War. On his return to Athens, Andocides, one of the ambassadors, tried to convince the Athenians of the advantages of making peace with Sparta. Among other things, he reminded his listeners of the debate about Athens' fate in 405/4 BC.

> Now, Athenians, in which way is it possible for us to make peace? Finding what disposition toward us in the Lacedaemonians? If any of you

16. Missiou (1992) 106 considers the Theban authorship of this proposal a propagandistic invention of the Spartans and their oligarchic sympathizers in Athens at the time of the Corinthian War. Consequently, she argues that the Theban ambassadors would not have accepted the responsibility for this proposal, and she disregards Xenophon's report of this embassy as fictitious. By contrast, I consider the various testimonies of Erianthus' proposal at the conference at Sparta reliable and therefore regard the apologetic Theban remarks in Xenophon's account as entirely plausible. Cf. my discussion of the speech of the Theban ambassadors in "The Athenian-Theban Alliance in 395" in chapter 4, 245–53.

> is going to be upset, I beg his pardon; for I will be stating the facts. First, when we had lost the ships in the Hellespont and had become besieged, what proposal did they make about us, those, who are now our allies, who were then the allies of the Lacedaemonians [i.e., the Thebans and Corinthians]? Was it not to enslave our city [τὴν πόλιν ἡμῶν ἀνδραποδίζεσθαι] and to make our land desolate [τὴν χώραν ἐρημοῦν]? But who were the ones that prevented this from happening? Was it not the Lacedaemonians, dissuading their allies from the proposal and themselves not even undertaking to debate about such measures? (Andoc. 3.21)

It was clearly Andocides' objective to encourage the Athenians to show gratitude to the Spartans for saving them and to alienate the Athenians from their current allies, the Thebans and Corinthians. He sought to achieve this by stirring up his listeners' emotions. That he chose the graphic details of their proposal (τὴν πόλιν ἡμῶν ἀνδραποδίζεσθαι, τὴν χώραν ἐρημοῦν) for this purpose shows how powerful this memory was among the Athenians. The two rhetorical questions concerning the allies' proposal and the Spartans' refusal, introduced with the negation οὐ, indicate that he expected an affirmative answer, presupposing his audience's knowledge of this incident.[17]

In a similar manner, Plataean ambassadors in Isocrates' *Plataicus* (composed ca. 373) use this historical incident to stir up anti-Theban sentiments among the Athenians.[18]

> Who was consistently more hostile and more ill-minded toward you than they? In the Decelean War, were they not the cause of more mischief than the other invaders? When misfortune befell you, did not they alone of the allies vote that it be necessary both to enslave your city [τήν τε πόλιν ἐξανδραποδίσασθαι] and to abandon its territory as grazing land for sheep [τὴν χώραν ἀνεῖναι μηλόβοτον] as was the plain of Crisa [ὥσπερ τὸ Κρισαῖον πεδίον], so that if the Lacedaemonians had been of the same opinion as the Thebans, nothing would have prevented the

17. Andoc. 3.21: Πρῶτον μὲν γὰρ ἡνίκα ἀπωλέσαμεν τὰς ναῦς ἐν ῾Ελλησπόντῳ καὶ τειχήρεις ἐγενόμεθα, τίνα γνώμην ἔθεντο περὶ ἡμῶν οἱ νῦν μὲν ἡμέτεροι τότε δὲ Λακεδαιμονίων ὄντες σύμμαχοι; οὐ τὴν πόλιν ἡμῶν ἀνδραποδίζεσθαι καὶ τὴν χώραν ἐρημοῦν; οἱ δὲ διακωλύσαντες ταῦτα μὴ γενέσθαι τίνες ἦσαν; οὐ Λακεδαιμόνιοι, τοὺς μὲν συμμάχους ἀποτρέψαντες τῆς γνώμης, αὐτοὶ δ' οὐδ' ἐπιχειρήσαντες διαβουλεύσασθαι περὶ τοιούτων ἔργων. Cf. Smyth (1956) 598 § 2651. The authenticity of *De Pace* has sometimes been doubted, most recently by Harris (1995) 184 note 22 and (2000). But see the convincing counterargument to Harris by Grethlein (2010) 128–29 note 9.

18. For a discussion of the occasion of this speech, see "Plataean-Theban Antagonism" in chapter 2, 124.

> authors of the salvation of all Greeks from being themselves enslaved by the Greeks and from plunging into the greatest misfortunes? (Isoc. 14.31–32)

Just as in Andocides' passage, two particularly vivid details characterize the proposal: the plan to enslave the population and the plan to make the territory desolate, turning it into grazing land for sheep.[19] Again, rhetorical questions introduced by the negation οὐ indicate that the speaker presupposed his audience's familiarity with this incident.

Shortly thereafter, in 371 BC, at a conference in Sparta, the Athenian ambassador Callistratus declared that the Athenians were prepared to conclude peace, alluding to the Spartan intervention in 405/4 BC.

> And perhaps we also should like to show you what we rightly conceived toward you because you preserved us [ὧν ἕνεκα περιεσώσατε ἡμᾶς]. (Xen. *Hell.* 6.3.13)

The brevity of this remark shows that in Xenophon's view, Callistratus expected his Spartan audience to be familiar with this event, even though it happened thirty-four years earlier.

Xenophon reports that in 370/69 BC, one year after their catastrophic defeat at Leuctra, the Spartans and their allies sent an embassy to Athens to ask for help. They, too, used the memory of the threatened destruction of Athens to persuade the Athenians to save them from the Thebans. Evaluating their speech, Xenophon remarks that the

> strongest of the arguments [μέγιστον δὲ τῶν λεχθέντων] made by the Lacedaemonians seemed to be that at the time when they had conquered the Athenians, though the Thebans wanted to destroy Athens [ἀναστάτους ποιῆσαι τὰς 'Αθήνας], they prevented it. (Xen. *Hell.* 6.5.35)

Xenophon contrasts this argument from social memory to the Spartans' stress on Athens' legal obligation to help (Xen. *Hell.* 6.5.36). He calls the former the strongest (τὸ μέγιστον) argument and the latter merely the lengthiest (ὁ πλεῖστος λόγος) one. This shows that even though the Athenians resented being reminded of this incident by the Spartans (Xen *Hell.* 6.5.35), this memory was nevertheless very powerful.[20] This is further suggested by the fact that in

19. For the implications of these specific details, see "Semantic and Visual Conceptualizations: City Razing and Enslavement" below, 301–9.

20. Xen. *Hell.* 6.5.35: οἱ μέντοι 'Αθηναῖοι οὐ πάνυ ἐδέξαντο, ἀλλὰ θροῦς τις τοιοῦτος διῆλθεν

Xenophon's account, Procles of Philus, one of the Peloponnesian envoys, took up the Spartan argument in his speech.

> I also see the Thebans, who then did not succeed in persuading the Lacedaemonians to enslave you [ἐξανδραποδίσασθαι ὑμᾶς], now asking you to allow those who saved you to perish. (Xen. *Hell.* 6.5.46)

Four allusions in Isocrates' works illustrate that this proposal was familiar to Athenians even fifty years after it was made. The brevity of the remark that Athens was nearly enslaved is particularly noteworthy. Apparently, it was a sufficient cue for prompting the memory of the situation in 405/4. Isocrates mentioned it twice in *On the Peace* (ca. 355 BC) in order to demonstrate that Athens had become the object of bitter hatred thanks to abusing its allies.

> As a result, Athens came close to being enslaved [παρὰ μικρὸν ἐλθεῖν ἐξανδραποδισθῆναι], if we had not found the Lacedaemonians, who were at war with us from the beginning, more friendly than those who were formerly our allies. (Isoc. 8.78)

Later in the speech, Isocrates used the same event again to illustrate how hegemonic power was capable of corrupting a state.

> For we, having become hated by our allies and having gotten into the danger of enslavement [περὶ ἀνδραποδισμοῦ κινδυνεύσαντες], were saved by the Lacedaemonians. (Isoc. 8.105)

In the *Areopagiticus* (ca. 355/4 BC), he used this well-known event to illustrate the vicissitude in the history of states.

> After our city had been destroyed by the barbarians, we became, because we were anxious and gave attention to our affairs, the foremost of the Greeks; whereas when we believed that our power was invincible, we came close to being enslaved [παρὰ μικρὸν ἤλθομεν ἐξανδραποδισθῆναι]. (Isoc. 7.6)

ὡς νῦν ταῦτα λέγοιεν, ὅτε δὲ εὖ ἔπραττον, ἐπέκειντο ἡμῖν. Missiou (1992) 96–97 argues that this resentment shows that the oligarchic pro-Spartan version of the story was generally not accepted by the Athenian democrats. In my opinion, it simply shows the psychologically understandable reaction of an audience that does not want to be reminded of benefits bestowed on them by Sparta, their bitter enemy. For these diplomatic negotiations in 370/69, see also "Aiding Suppliants," 200–201.

In the *Antidosis* (354/3 BC), Isocrates attacked the Athenian demagogues, holding them responsible for Athens' fall.

> Having been plunged into war, we have seen that many of our citizens died, many became prisoners of the enemy, many were reduced to the last extremities of want; we have seen the democracy twice overthrown, the walls of our fatherland torn down, and, worst of all ([τὸ δὲ μέγιστον], the whole city in peril of enslavement [ὅλην τὴν πόλιν περὶ ἀνδραποδισμοῦ κινδυνεύσασαν] and our enemy encamped on the Acropolis. (Isoc. 15.319)

Thus Isocrates denoted the proposal to enslave Athens as a major disaster in the history of Athens in the fifth century and ranked it even higher than the oligarchic coups of 411 and 404 and the demolition of the Long Walls that marked Athens' defeat in the Peloponnesian War.

In 343 BC, prosecuting Aeschines in *On the False Embassy,* Demosthenes contrasted the destruction of the Phocians through Aeschines' agency to the Phocians' refusal to support the enslavement of Athens in 404.

> It's a terrible sight, Athenians, and a pitiful one. When we were traveling to Delphi recently, we couldn't avoid seeing it all—houses demolished [οἰκίας κατεσκαμμένας], town walls torn down [τείχη περιῃρημένα], a country deprived [χώραν ἔρημον] of those in their youth, a few poor women and children and pitiful old people; in short, nobody could find words to describe the distress that there is in that country now. And yet, that these men once voted against the Thebans [τὴν ἐναντίαν ποτὲ Θηβαίοις ψῆφον], when they made a proposal for our enslavement [περὶ ἡμῶν ὑπὲρ ἀνδραποδισμοῦ προτιθεῖσιν], I hear from you all [ὑμῶν ἔγωγ' ἀκούω πάντων]. (Dem. 19.64–65)

The phrase "I hear from you all" indicates that even sixty years after the end of the Peloponnesian War, the proposal to destroy Athens was still vividly remembered in Athenian collective consciousness.[21] This memory enabled Demosthenes to rouse his audience against Aeschines, by describing the sight of the shattered Phocian towns in terms evocative of the proposed destruction of Athens.

This brief survey of fourth-century allusions to the impending enslave-

21. Nouhaud (1982) 306, by contrast, regards "ὑμῶν ἔγωγ' ἀκούω πάντων" as an empty phrase. For discussion of this phrase, see "Participant Evidence: The Attic Orators and Their Interpretation" in the introduction to this present study, 41–43.

ment of Athens illustrates that this memory displays an amazing persistence in Athenian historical consciousness. In many cases, orators tend to point to their source—elders, a monument, an inscription, family members, and public commemorations—to corroborate their assertions, but, in this one, they take common knowledge for granted (a point reinforced by the brevity of some of the allusions). Moreover, some of the passages reveal that this particular memory was highly emotionally charged.

Traumatic Fear of Annihilation

This section will show that the monstrosity of this proposal (augmented by the loss of the fleet, the relentless siege, and the humiliating surrender) had a deep emotional impact on the Athenians and that this traumatic experience was responsible for the persistence of this memory in fourth-century Athenian public discourse, which cannot be explained by mere political instrumentalization, as Missiou suggested. As seen in the previous section, both the utilizations and the contexts in which this incident is mentioned are so variegated that present needs alone cannot sufficiently explain the frequency of this historical allusion.[22]

Some might question whether it is appropriate to call this case a "trauma" in the Freudian sense of a "[wound] too overwhelming to be fully absorbed and available to consciousness," which "lives on unconsciously—latently—but ultimately finds a voice in the present,"[23] as scholarship on the memory of the Holocaust particularly uses the word.[24] However, similar objections could be raised against the use of the term *trauma* to describe the effects of 9/11 on American consciousness or of the fall of the former communist regimes in Eastern Europe. Certainly traumata vary in degree. I use the term *traumatic experience* for highly emotional, negative events that leave a deep mark on the collective consciousness and thus lead to persisting memories. This phenomenon cannot be explained by theories of pure social constructivism, which view the past as being entirely at the disposal of the present; therefore, I consider the element of persistence, introduced by the neo-Freudian approach, a useful

22. Missiou (1992) 103 contends that "the pro-Spartan tradition . . . is behind the frequent references to the incident in the sources." I find this unconvincing, especially since many references are not made in a pro-Spartan context or lack any reference to the Spartan intervention (Dem. 19.65, Isoc. 15.319).

23. Cf. Prager (2001) 2225, paraphrasing Caruth (1996). For trauma and memory, see also LaCapra (1994).

24. For collective memory of the Holocaust, cf. Friedlander (1991), (1992), (1993); Novick (1999).

complement in memory studies.[25] Concerning the characteristics of *individual* memories, Schacter notes that "[p]ersisting memories are a major consequence of just about any type of traumatic experience."[26] Regarding the relationship between emotion and memory, he states,

> Everyday experience and laboratory studies reveal that emotionally charged incidents are better remembered than nonemotional events. The emotional boost begins at the moment that a memory is born, when attention and elaboration strongly influence whether an experience will be subsequently remembered or forgotten.[27]

I argue that the devastating defeat at Aegospotami and the murderous siege traumatized the Athenians *collectively;* their fear of annihilation was real and was responsible for the persistence of this memory throughout the fourth century.[28] Social psychologists have proven that extremely stressful events, such as wars, political disasters, an economic crisis, and periods of harsh repression, show an "affective impact on individuals and collectivities."[29] Social memories of such catastrophes persist, even if these events are not "publicly commemorated or preserved."[30] As will be shown, a number of these observations, including the absence of official commemoration, apply to the events of 405/4 BC.

Even though the link between emotional intensity and persistent memory is widely accepted on the personal level, critics doubt the existence of collective traumatic memory and especially its transferability to younger generations.[31] Addressing this problem, social psychologists have shown that the memory of political catastrophes is "a socially distributed memory."[32] This distribution is facilitated by the urge to "socially share" an emotional experience. Rimé and

25. See "Ideology and Social Memory" in the introduction, 18–19. Cf. Prager (2001).

26. Schacter (2001) 174.

27. Schacter (2001) 163.

28. The Athenians' nightmare did not end there. The humiliating surrender engendered further traumata: loss of the empire and the Long Walls, overthrow of the democracy, and the Spartan garrison and terror regime of the Thirty. In Athenian historical consciousness, the traumatic experiences of the defeat and the terror regime of the Thirty belonged closely together, as is evident from Isoc. 15.319 and Aeschin. 2.75–77. Wolpert (2002) 81–87, 120–21 argues convincingly that the trauma of the defeat and civil war was played out in Athenian memory in such a way that some of the more painful aspects of the recent events were not discussed in public, while defeat and civil war were collapsed so as to disconnect this painful period from Athenian past and future.

29. Paez, Basabe, & Gonzales (1997) 149.

30. Paez, Basabe, & Gonzales (1997) 150.

31. Prager (2001) 2226 admits that this is a problem of the neo-Freudian approach: "[T]hese concepts nonetheless seem inadequate analytic tools to provide a psychological justification for the survival of trauma long after its victims have disappeared. A more robust theory of the transmission of trauma across generations, or across eons, is necessary."

32. Paez, Basabe, & Gonzales (1997) 150.

Christophe argue that this general rule "that any emotion tends to be socially shared" also applies to persons who are exposed to the *narrative* of emotional experience, inducing them to relate the emotional story they heard to others (a process called "secondary social sharing").[33] The degree of distribution is correlated to the intensity of the emotional experience.

An extreme example of this phenomenon could be observed in the United States on September 11, 2001; immediately after learning of the terrorist attacks, people would spread the news and share their feelings even with strangers in the street. Xenophon vividly describes the same phenomenon in the context of the events of 405 BC. When news of the catastrophe of Aegospotami arrived in Athens, existential fear gripped the Athenians, and the news spread like wildfire. In a highly dramatic passage, which is rather unusual for his style, Xenophon writes,

> But in Athens, as the Paralus [i.e., the state trireme, used as dispatch boat] arrived at night, the disaster was reported, and a sound of wailing [οἰμωγὴ] ran from Piraeus through the Long Walls to the city, one man passing on the news to another [ὁ ἕτερος τῷ ἑτέρῳ παραγγέλλων]; and during that night no one slept, all mourning, not for the lost alone, but far more for their own selves, thinking that they would suffer the kind of things they had done to the Melians, colonists of the Lacedaemonians, after overcoming them by siege, and to the Histiaeans and Scionaeans and Toronaeans and Aeginetans and many other Greeks. (Xen. *Hell.* 2.2.3)

Xenophon's account raises three questions. First, what exactly did the Athenians fear so anxiously? Second, how long did this state of extraordinary terror last? And third, what gave rise to this fear? Instead of being explicit about the reason for this dread, Xenophon uses a paraphrasing comparison: the Athenians mourned for their own selves, "thinking that they would suffer the kind of things they had done to the Melians, colonists of the Lacedaemonians, after overcoming them by siege, and to the Histiaeans and Scionaeans and Toronaeans and Aeginetans and many other Greeks" (Xen. *Hell.* 2.2.3). We know from Thucydides that after forcing the Melians to surrender unconditionally in the winter of 415 BC, the Athenians put all the men of military age to death (οἱ δὲ ἀπέκτειναν Μηλίων ὅσους ἡβῶντας ἔλαβον) and enslaved the women and children (παῖδας δὲ καὶ γυναῖκας ἠνδραπόδισαν). The depopulated island

33. Cf. Rimé & Christophe (1997), especially 137.

was then given to Athenian colonists (Thuc. 5.116.3–4).[34] In 423 BC, the city of Scione on the Chalcidice revolted from Athens. On the motion of Cleon, a decree was passed in the Athenian assembly "to destroy Scione and to put its inhabitants to death" (Σκιωναίους ἐξελεῖν τε καὶ ἀποκτεῖναι, Thuc. 4.122.6). Scione was besieged and finally surrendered in 421 BC. Although the Peace of Nicias had already been concluded,[35] "the adult males were put to death, and the women and children were enslaved" (ἀπέκτειναν τοὺς ἡβῶντας, παῖδας δὲ καὶ γυναῖκας ἠνδραπόδισαν, Thuc. 5.32.1). The Athenian subject city of Torone on the Chalcidice was liberated by Brasidas in 423 BC and recaptured by Cleon a year later. The Athenians "enslaved the Toronaean women and children" (τῶν Τορωναίων γυναῖκας μὲν καὶ παῖδας ἠνδραπόδισαν) and sent the men as prisoners to Athens. Under the terms of the Peace of Nicias, they were exchanged, man for man, for Athenian prisoners of war (Thuc. 5.3.2–4). In 424 BC, an Athenian army attacked the city of Thyrea, which had been given to the expelled Aeginetans by the Spartans. The Athenians burned and looted the city and took back to Athens all the Aeginetans who were not killed in the fighting. There, they decided that all of them "who had been taken prisoner should be put to death, because of the inveterate hatred" (Αἰγινήτας δὲ ἀποκτεῖναι πάντας ὅσοι ἑάλωσαν διὰ τὴν προτέραν αἰεί ποτε ἔχθραν, Thuc. 4.57.2–4).

Judging from these passages, we can determine the reason for the panic that gripped the Athenians in 405, as described by Xenophon. The Athenians feared the extirpation of their entire community, encompassing the destruction of their city, the slaughter of the adult males, and the enslavement of women and children.[36] This fear was justified, particularly since all of the annihilated *poleis* mentioned by Xenophon had specifically been under the protection of Sparta and thus morally obliged the Spartans to take revenge.[37]

This state of terror lasted for more than five months (until the peace was concluded in March 404 BC), as becomes clear from Xenophon's account. After learning of the disaster of Aegospotami, the Athenians desperately prepared the city to endure a siege (Xen. *Hell.* 2.2.4). They restored to the disenfranchised their political rights, held out steadfastly, and—even though many were dying from starvation—refused to enter peace talks, since they did not see any chance

34. For a discussion of the treatment of captives in the Peloponnesian War, cf. Panagopoulos (1989), who analyzes the fate of the Melians (118–23), Scionaeans (103–5), Toronaeans (98–105), and Aeginetans (87–89).

35. Even though Scione and a few other cities were not protected by the Peace of Nicias (cf. Thuc. 5.18.8), it is remarkable that the Athenians carried out their decree mercilessly, two years after the decree was passed. Cf. Panagopoulos (1989) 104–5.

36. Cf. Lévy (1976) 22–23; Wolpert (2002) 9.

37. Melos was a Spartan colony, and the Scionaeans and Toronaeans had placed themselves under Brasidas' protection.

of averting the impending annihilation. When they ran out of provisions, they sent an embassy, offering submission on the condition that they be allowed to keep their walls for self-defense (Xen. *Hell.* 2.2.10–11). The Spartan refusal threw the Athenians into utter desperation (ἀθυμία ἐνέπεσε πᾶσιν), since "they believed that they would be enslaved" (ᾤοντο γὰρ ἀνδραποδισθήσεσθαι). Nobody dared to make any suggestion involving the destruction of the walls: someone who had done so had been thrown into prison, and a decree had been passed forbidding any such proposal (Xen. *Hell.* 2.2.14–15). In this situation, Theramenes offered to go to Lysander and find out whether the Lacedaemonians insisted on the destruction of the walls "in order to enslave the city" (ἐξανδραποδίσασθαι τὴν πόλιν βουλόμενοι) or merely to obtain a guarantee of good faith (Xen. *Hell.* 2.2.15).[38] After staying more than three months with Lysander, he returned to Athens and went on to Sparta as an ambassador endowed with the full power to conclude peace under any conditions (Xen. *Hell.* 2.2.16–19).[39] Xenophon's report illustrates vividly that the Athenians were tormented by the fear of enslavement for several months (from the loss of their fleet in September 405 to the peace conference at Sparta in March 404).

How can we explain this extraordinary fear of annihilation? There are several contributing factors. First, city destruction and enslavement were not beyond the Greek imagination but had happened in the past. Second, as Xenophon states in his moralizing comment, the Athenians were well aware of the brutal treatment they had meted out to other cities. Their guilty conscience nurtured their fear.[40] Third, I suggest that they had learned of concrete plans

38. Theramenes' role in the peace negotiations is highly controversial. While Xenophon's portrayal of Theramenes is mixed, Lysias' is thoroughly negative. According to Lys. 13.9, Theramenes had planned to betray Athens to the enemy from the outset, when he promised the Athenians to obtain a peace that would not require them to demolish their walls or hand over their ships and told them that such negotiations would require secrecy. This latter detail is also mentioned in the "Theramenes papyrus" (*P Mich.* 5982; cf. Merkelbach & Youtie (1968) and Engels (1993)). Diodorus and the Aristotelian *Athenaion Politeia* reflect an apologetic Theramenes tradition and omit his dubious role in the peace negotiations altogether. For a concise discussion of these events, see Wolpert (2002) 8–15.

39. In contrast to Xenophon, who reports that the Athenians appointed Theramenes twice as ambassador (first to go to Lysander and then to Sparta), Lysias mentions only one mission. Most historians believe that Lysias collapsed the two missions into one. Cf. Krentz (1982) 34–35; Wolpert (2002) 149 note 35.

40. In the passage discussed above (Xen. *Hell.* 2.2.3), Xenophon implicitly delivers a moral judgment by linking Athenian fear to the memory of the treatment of conquered cities by Athens. Later, however, he makes this moral judgment explicit. Explaining the desperation among the Athenians, he remarks, "and they thought that there was no salvation, save only to suffer what they had themselves done to the people of small states, not in retaliation, but in hubris and unjustly, for no other single reason than because they were in alliance with the Lacedaemonians" (Xen. *Hell.* 2.2.10). This comment clearly reflects Xenophon's critique of Athens' imperial hubris and betrays pro-Spartan sympathies. This bias, however, does not mean that Xenophon invented the entire scene. Cf. Panagopoulos (1989) 181 note 2; Hamilton (1997) 200 note 9.

of the Spartans and their allies concerning Athens' future. I argue that already after the decisive victory at Aegospotami, with the collapse of Athens' empire in sight, calls for revenge were voiced among the Spartan allies and were reported in Athens. The ever-escalating violence and brutality against conquered enemies throughout this war made the idea of eradicating the entire polis of Athens conceivable. There are several clues to indicate that plans and threats of annihilation were voiced long before the conference in Sparta, fueling anxiety in Athens.

First, in the wake of his triumph at Aegospotami, Lysander granted all Athenians he met safe conduct to Athens in order to swell the population of the city and thereby increase the scarcity of provisions and the panic (Xen. *Hell.* 2.2.2). Encountering Lysander's army, these Athenians certainly would have sensed the bitter hostility among the Spartan allies or even experienced vengeful threats concerning their city, which they would report in Athens. That hatred toward Athens had indeed reached a new level is evident from the treatment of the Athenian prisoners at Aegospotami: Lysander convened the allies to decide about their fate. Outraged about previous Athenian crimes, especially the recent execution of a Corinthian and an Andrian trireme crew, and about the Athenian decree to cut off the right hand of every man taken alive, the allies decided to kill all three thousand Athenian prisoners (Xen. *Hell.* 2.1.31–32; Plut. *Lys.* 13.1).[41] Reports of this decision certainly helped to spread panic in Athens. It is even possible that Lysander used threats of annihilation deliberately to intimidate the Athenians and break their resolve.

Second, on his way to Athens, Lysander restored the surviving Melians, Scionaeans, and Aeginetans to their native cities (Xen. *Hell.* 2.2.9; Plut. *Lys.* 14.3). Xenophon's remark that the Athenians feared to suffer what they had done to these peoples suggests that, in Athens, Lysander's ostentatious actions were understood as an unmistakable hint of what they could expect in turn.[42] A passage in Pausanias is the clearest indication that the extirpation of Athens was proposed and discussed among the Spartans and their allies long before the peace conference in Sparta.

> After the Athenian navy had been destroyed at Aegospotami, Lysander, the son of Aristocritus, and Agis violated the divine oaths [ὅρκους θεῶν

41. Paus. 9.32.9 even speaks of four thousand Athenians having been executed.

42. Cf. Hamilton (1997) 199–200. The fact that Xenophon mentions the Athenians' fearful thoughts concerning their cruel treatment of the Melians and Aeginetans immediately following the defeat at Aegospotami (Xen. *Hell.* 2.2.3), right before their restoration through Lysander (Xen. *Hell.* 2.2.9), hardly invalidates this argument; this chronological inversion can easily be explained by Xenophon's moralizing objective. Moreover, in Xen. *Hell.* 2.2.10, he explicitly links the Athenians' fear to their unjust treatment of such smaller *poleis*.

> ὑπερέβησαν] that the Lacedaemonians as a community had sworn to the Athenians, and on their own accord, without the approval of the Spartan community, they put forth to their allies the proposal to destroy Athens root and branch [ἐκκόψαι προρρίζους τὰς ᾽Αθήνας].[43] (Paus. 3.8.6)

Hamilton argues convincingly for the historicity of this incident, which he dates to the beginning of the siege, at a meeting of allied field commanders.[44] This statement cannot refer to the conference at Sparta in March 404, at which neither Agis nor Lysander was present in person, and according to Polyaenus, Lysander advised the Spartans to preserve Athens as a counterweight to Thebes (Polyaen. 1.45.5).[45] To reconcile these apparently conflicting statements, Hamilton proposes a change in Lysander's attitude toward Athens, due to Theramenes' persuasive plea for sparing that city.[46] I accept Hamilton's conclusion that at this meeting of the field commanders during the siege, Lysander, aware of his allies' bitter hatred toward the Athenians, supported their proposal to eradicate Athens "in order to retain possibly flagging support in those quarters" and at the same time to "strike dread in the hearts of the Athenians by calling for their destruction."[47] That some allies, especially the Thebans and Corinthians, favored the destruction of Athens already at this time (if not earlier)—and not just at the later conference in Sparta—is indicated by the outrage and hatred that led to the execution of the Athenian prisoners at Aegospotami. Moreover, the Theban Erianthus, who proposed the eradication of Athens at the conference in Sparta (Plut. *Lys.* 15.2), also was one of Lysander's navy commanders at Aegospotami (Paus. 10.9.9; M&L 95d). It is most likely that he was with Lysander throughout the siege, promoting extreme anti-Athenian policies from early on.

So far, I have tried to reconstruct the historical circumstances that gave rise to dread of annihilation in Athens between the battle of Aegospotami in September 405 and the peace conference in Sparta in March 404. It has become clear that the Athenians' horror was justified in light of both their own brutal

---

43. These ὅρκοι refer not to the peace treaty but to the oaths sworn by the Delphic Amphictyons to preserve one another from destruction. Cf. Hamilton (1997) 208; Zeilhofer (1959) 79–81; Lotze (1964) 45. I suggest that Isoc. 18.29 (cited in the preceding section, 285) is also alluding to the Amphictyonic oaths in the same context.

44. Cf. Hamilton (1979) 50–52; Hamilton (1997) 207–9, 211–18. Pausanias is known to have used fourth-century sources, such as Xenophon, Ephorus, and Theopompus. Moreover, details in Plutarch's *Lysander* show that other, more detailed accounts of the events surrounding this proposal existed in antiquity.

45. For arguments for the preservation of Athens, see "Why Was Athens Spared?" below, 319–23.

46. For a discussion of the problematic chronology of Theramenes' missions in 405/4, cf. Kagan (1987) 402; Wolpert (2002) 11–12.

47. Hamilton (1997) 212.

treatment of other *poleis* and concrete plans introduced and discussed among the Spartans and their vengeful allies in the course of the siege.[48] Thus, for the besieged Athenians, the threat of annihilation was real. Yet skeptics might question whether the relentless siege and the rumors of the impending annihilation actually constituted a traumatic experience able to produce persistent memories for generations to come, since, after all, the Athenians merely feared enslavement and utter destruction but were spared in the end. Moreover, although social psychologists have shown that emotional experiences are further distributed through "secondary social sharing," does this theory also apply to periods as long as half a century, stretching across generations?[49]

A case in contemporary German historical consciousness provides a striking parallel. At a secret conference in Quebec on September 15, 1944, U.S. president Franklin Roosevelt and British prime minister Winston Churchill agreed on a plan proposed by the U.S. Secretary of the Treasury, Henry Morgenthau Jr., outlining the treatment of postwar Germany. His *Program to Prevent Germany from Starting a World War III*[50] recommended splitting Germany into a northern and a southern state, making the economically important regions along the Rhine and Ruhr Rivers and the coast of the Baltic Sea into an international zone, demilitarizing and deindustrializing Germany, and turning it into an agrarian state. On September 21, the Morgenthau Plan was leaked to the public; shortly thereafter, it was abandoned due to its extremely negative reception and the opposition of other cabinet members.[51]

This is not the place to discuss Morgenthau's motives or the potential consequences of the implementation of this plan.[52] Its afterlife in German historical consciousness is what concerns us here.[53] The German people learned of this plan through Nazi media. Thanks to Goebbels' propaganda machinery, this proposal became a "jüdischer Mordplan" amounting to enslavement and geno-

48. Hamilton (1997) 211 argues that the proposal was made for the first time at a meeting of field commanders, when "Agis and Lysander, in anger and frustration, proposed to their allies that Athens be totally destroyed." Yet, considering the execution of the three thousand Athenian prisoners, the panic in Athens, and the ostentatious restoration of the survivors of Athenian crimes, I believe that plans and rumors to eradicate Athens were circulating as early as the victory at Aegospotami.

49. Cf. Rimé & Christophe (1997), especially 137.

50. This is the original title of this four-page memorandum. Cf. Morgenthau (1945) v–viii.

51. The Morgenthau Plan was opposed by British foreign minister Anthony Eden, U.S. secretary of state Cordell Hull, and U.S. secretary of war Henry Stimson, who called it "a crime against civilization." Cf. Benz (1990).

52. For Morgenthau's motives, see his own justification in Morgenthau (1945) and Greiner (1995).

53. In my discussion of the Morgenthau Plan in German social memory, I rely on Greiner (1995) 14–28.

cide through starvation: "Das industrialisierte Deutschland soll buchstäblich in einen riesigen Kartoffelacker verwandelt werden."[54] With the allied forces rapidly approaching German soil, Nazi propaganda tried to stiffen German resolve by spreading terror and fear of the invaders. The distorted picture of Germany as "Kartoffelacker" (potato field) and of Morgenthau's "extermination" plan was an important element in the German reception of this plan and probably inspired more desperate resistance by German forces against the Allied onslaught until the very end of the war.

More than forty-seven years later, in May 1992, seventeen students of a graduating class at a *Gymnasium* (high school) in Hamburg were asked to write down their associations with the name of Henry Morgenthau. The results included "Deutschland, ein Ackerland und Kornkammer für die USA" (fourteen times), "Amerikanischer Jude" (seven times), and "Jude, deshalb extrem und dem Rachegedanken anhängend" (twice).[55] The familiarity of this social memory makes it an effective historical paradigm in public discourse; criticizing the detrimental economic consequences of the Green Party's ecological policies, Hermann Rappe, a functionary of the Chemical Workers' Union, used the following analogy in an address to union members in 1985:

> Aus den ökologischen Forderungen der Grünen ergibt sich zwangsläufig eine Abschaffung unserer bisherigen Industriegesellschaft. Ein Vergleich mit dem vor rund 40 Jahren bekanntgewordenen "Morgenthau-Plan" drängt sich geradezu auf—also ein überdezentralisiertes, vorwiegend industriefeindliches, traditionslandwirtschaftliches, vom Weltmarkt weitgehend abgekoppeltes Land.[56]

In his analysis of the sources for this memory, Greiner found that for the first twenty-five years, the "Morgenthau-Legende" was for the most part transmitted orally, through stories and anecdotes told by parents and history teachers and through debates at the pub and in political parties and unions. In the

54. Goebbels in an address to factory workers on October 4, 1944, as quoted by Greiner (1995) 14–15. Goebbels calls this proposal "a Jewish plan for murder" and claims that "Germany, an industrialized country, is supposed to be turned, literally, into a huge potato field."

55. Greiner (1995) 16. "Germany, farmland and granary for the United States" (fourteen times), "American Jew" (seven times), and "Jew, therefore extreme and out for revenge" (twice).

56. Hermann Rappe, as cited in the *Frankfurter Rundschau* (February 2, 1985), quoted by Greiner (1995) 14. Rappe claims that "the ecological policies of the Green Party will necessarily lead to the abolition of our present industrial society. The Morgenthau Plan, which came to light about 40 years ago, comes to mind as an obvious analogy—a country, which is over-decentralized, predominantly anti-manufacturing, traditionally agricultural, and largely shut off from the global market."

1970s, this simplified memory of a vindictive American Jew Morgenthau who proposed to turn Germany into a potato field made its way into German schoolbooks and even determined Morgenthau's depiction in German historiography. This simplified memory is best illustrated by the choice of title for the German translation of John Morton Blum's book *From the Morgenthau Diaries: Years of War, 1941–1945*, which was changed into the catchphrase *Deutschland, ein Ackerland?* However, whereas mainstream German discourse merely betrays an "Echo nationalsozialistischer Propaganda,"[57] nationalistic German memory communities take Goebbels' version of Morgenthau's plan at face value and claim that it was indeed (at least partially) executed.[58]

The collective memories of the Morgenthau Plan and of the proposed eradication of Athens show many similarities but also some differences. First, just as in Athens, the Germans' fear of their impending destruction, incited and hammered in by Nazi propaganda and fueled by the awareness of their own heinous crimes, was real and constituted a traumatic experience, which contributed to the astonishing persistence of the Morgenthau Plan in German social memory across generations. Second, both in Athens and in Germany, the perceived threat was part of a series of more severe traumata, including war, atrocities, and utter defeat.[59] Third, memories of rather complex proposals were simplified into the visual and semantic conceptualizations of farmland in Germany and pasture for sheep in Athens, both easy to envision and remember.[60] There is, however, also a stark difference. As Greiner has shown, an important reason for the persistence of the collective memory of the Morgenthau Plan was that it fulfilled the psychological need of postwar Germans to exculpate their own commission of genocide by pointing to the "genocide" planned by others. The Morgenthau-Legend is thus an instance of "acting-out" and "transference" (in LaCapra's terms), instead of "working-through" the traumata of Nazi rule and genocide.[61] Even though the memory of the proposed destruction of Athens had the potential to fulfill a similar exculpatory function, it apparently was not used this way in Athenian public discourse.[62]

57. Greiner (1995) 22.

58. Cf. Keppler's (1971) revisionist discussion of the "Ausrottungsplan für Deutschland."

59. The extent of the crimes committed is, of course, not comparable.

60. For a discussion of the visual and semantic conceptualization of the Theban proposal, see the next section.

61. Cf. LaCapra (1994).

62. For the uses of this paradigm in Athenian public discourse, see "Contexts for the Recollection of the Theban Proposal" below, 326–41. Athenian orators did, however, point to the crimes of other states to extol the virtuous leadership exercised by the Athenians, a rhetorical strategy that might be viewed as an exculpatory reflex. Isocrates, for instance, chastises the Spartans for their destruction of Plataea in 427 BC (Isoc. 12.92–94).

Semantic and Visual Conceptualizations: City Razing and Enslavement

So far, I have emphasized the traumatic experience of the threatened annihilation to explain the persistence of this memory among the Athenians. Yet several aspects of this phenomenon need further attention. First, judging from our sources, it seems that this incident was well known beyond the boundaries of Attica. According to Xenophon, the Thebans refer to it in 395 (Xen. *Hell.* 3.5.8) and the Spartans in 370 (Xen. *Hell.* 6.5.35), and Arrian lists the Theban proposal as one of several Theban sins that led to Thebes' eradication by Alexander in 335 (Arr. *Anab.* 1.9.7).[63] Traumatic fear cannot account for the prominence of this event in the collective memory of non-Athenians.

Second, we have seen that Athenian memory of this near annihilation is highly emotionally charged, which explains its persistence. Yet in what form was this emotional memory "stored" and how was it expressed? All memories, whether personal or social, are visual and semantic conceptualizations, which become simplified as more people share in them.[64] It is therefore necessary to investigate the visual and semantic expression of this memory in order to clarify the reasons for its familiarity in Athens and beyond.

I argue that this memory's three components—selling the inhabitants into slavery (τήν πόλιν ἐξανδραποδίσασθαι), razing the city to the ground (τὸ ἄστυ κατασκάψαι), and dedicating the land to the god by abandoning it as grazing land for sheep (τὴν χώραν ἀνεῖναι μηλόβοτον)—constitute the well-known cultural concept of a ritual polis destruction, the first occurrence of which was said to be the annihilation of Crisa in the First Sacred War. It also played a role, as I will argue, in the proposed retribution for the medizing *poleis* in 480/79 and for Athens in 405/4.[65] I assert that each of these three components is a simple, yet vivid and highly emotionally charged, visual and semantic conceptualization, familiar to all Greeks. The actions constituting the planned punishment of Athens are thus easily understood and memorable for Greeks in the fifth and fourth centuries.

However, the existence of this concept of ritual destruction of a polis is hotly debated among modern historians.[66] Problems bedevil the historicity of

---

63. Cf. "Alexander's Annihilation of Thebes" below, 336–41.

64. For visual and semantic conceptualization and simplified memories, see Fentress & Wickham (1992) 32–36, 47–48. See also "Individual and Collective Memory" in the introduction to the present study, 8–13.

65. Cf. "Imagining the Unimaginable: The Eradication of Athens" below, 309–23.

66. Parke (1948), Bömer (1961) 24–44, Siewert (1972) 66–75, and Lehmann (1980) 245–46 argue for the existence of such a concept of ritual punishment. Bömer (1961) 29 speaks of a "rituel-

the First Sacred War, the meaning of δεκατεύειν in the context of the planned retribution for the medizing cities, and the authenticity of the Oath of Plataea, found as a fourth-century inscription.[67] In this section, I argue that—regardless of the historicity of the First Sacred War—such a concept indeed existed by the middle of the fourth century and served as the vivid visual and semantic conceptualization into which the memory of the Theban proposal could be cast.

This concept is most clearly expressed in Aeschines' speech *Against Ctesiphon* (330 BC), in which he relates in detail the destruction of Crisa/Cirrha by the Amphictyons in the First Sacred War (Aeschin. 3.107–13).[68] To corroborate his account, he tells the court secretary to read Apollo's oracle ordering the punishment of the Cirrhaeans, as well as the curse and the oaths sworn by the Amphictyons in response, which—he claims—all stand "recorded to this day" (Ταύτης τῆς ἀρᾶς καὶ τῶν ὅρκων καὶ τῆς μαντείας ἀναγεγραμμένων ἔτι καὶ νῦν, Aeschin. 3.113).[69] The original documents are not transmitted in the manuscripts of the speech. Yet Aeschines' paraphrase of the oracle and his account of its execution through the Amphictyons reveal the details of this ritual destruction of Crisa.

Aeschines opens his narrative with an ecphrasis marking the location to which this story is attached: "There is, fellow Athenians, the so-called plain of Cirrha and a harbor now called dedicated and accursed."[70] It is evident from this opening that the landmark of the Κιρραῖον πεδίον functions as one of

len Vernichtung einer Stadt und der unter religiösen Voraussetzungen erfolgten Versklavung ihrer Bevölkerung."

67. Robertson (1978) denies the historicity of the First Sacred War. Hall (2007) 276–81 is also extremely skeptical and emphasizes later elaborations meant to justify the present. J. K. Davies (1994) is more ambivalent. Lehmann (1980) emphasizes that it was an essential part of Greek historical consciousness long before the 340s. McInerney (1999) 165–72 views it as a local conflict that was later embellished. Howe (2003) examines the influence of Delphi's economic need of pasture for sacrificial victims as a potential motive for this war. For discussion of the historicity of the Plataean Oath, see Habicht (1961); Siewert (1972); Rhodes & Osborne (2003) 440–49.

68. Both names, Cirrha (Κίρρα) and Crisa (Κρῖσα), can be found in our sources. Robertson (1978) 41 has shown that they are interchangeable. From a linguistic point of view, the series Κρῖσα, Κῖρσα, Κίρρα is analogous to θράσος, θάρσος, θάρρος.

69. Parke (1948) 90–91 argues strongly in favor of the authenticity of these oaths, which he assumes to have been inscribed on a stele in Delphi: "But there is no reason to doubt that some record was preserved in Aeschines' day within the sanctuary, containing approximately the wording which he gives, and, though it might have been considerably after the First Sacred War that it was put in writing, the evidence which it supplies has every appearance to be authentic." He points to traces of the hexametrical oracle in Aeschines' paraphrase (e.g., πάντ' ἤματα, i.e., ἤματα πάντα) to support his argument, a point already noticed by Schol. Aeschin. 3.108 (238 (Dilts): πάντ' ἤματα] τοῦτο ἐκ τοῦ χρησμοῦ. συγκαταπέπλεκται δὲ τῷ μέτρῳ, διαλύσαντος τοῦ ῥήτορος τὸ μέτρον.)

70. Aeschin. 3.107: Ἔστι γάρ, ὦ ἄνδρες Ἀθηναῖοι, τὸ Κιρραῖον ὠνομασμένον πεδίον καὶ λιμὴν ὁ νῦν ἐξάγιστος καὶ ἐπάρατος ὠνομασμένος. In his 1875 edition, Weidner deleted ὠνομασμένον as a clumsy repetition. Yet I suggest accepting it as the original reading, since the Κιρραῖον πεδίον is indeed proverbial, as Isocrates' allusion (Isoc. 14.31) shows.

the carriers of this social memory.[71] According to Aeschines, the inhabitants of this area, the Cirrhaeans and Cragalidae, were most lawless tribes and had repeatedly committed sacrilege against the shrine at Delphi (εἰς τὸ ἱερὸν τὸ ἐν Δελφοῖς ἠσέβουν, Aeschin. 3.107). Exasperated by their conduct, the Amphictyons asked for an oracle from the god to tell them how they should punish these men. The Pythia prophesied to them

> to wage war against the Cirrhaeans and the Cragalidae day and night, and having destroyed their land and their city [τὴν χώραν αὐτῶν καὶ τὴν πόλιν ἐκπορθήσαντας] and enslaved them [αὐτοὺς ἀνδραποδισαμένους], to dedicate [ἀναθεῖναι] their land to the Pythian Apollo and Artemis and Leto and Athena Pronaia, that for the future it lie entirely uncultivated [ἐπὶ πάσῃ ἀεργίᾳ], that they must not work this land themselves nor permit another.[72] (Aeschin. 3.108)

On a motion of Solon, the Amphictyons decided to wage war against the accursed men "in accordance with the oracle of the god" (κατὰ τὴν μαντείαν τοῦ θεοῦ, Aeschin. 3. 108). Aeschines narrates in detail how Apollo's orders were executed.

> And having gathered a great force of the Amphictyons, they enslaved the people [ἐξηνδραποδίσαντο τοὺς ἀνθρώπους], razed their harbor and their city to the ground [τὸν λιμένα καὶ τὴν πόλιν αὐτῶν κατέσκαψαν], and dedicated their land in accordance with the oracle [τὴν χώραν καθιέρωσαν κατὰ τὴν μαντείαν]. And in addition, they swore a mighty oath, that they would not themselves cultivate the sacred land nor allow it to another [μήτ' αὐτοὶ τὴν ἱερὰν γῆν ἐργάσεσθαι μήτ' ἄλλῳ ἐπιτρέψειν],

71. For the role of topography in remembering the Camisard revolts, see Alcock (2002) 6; Fentress & Wickham (1992) 92–99. Cf. also the role of Phyle as topographical reminder of the Theban help for the Athenian democrats, as discussed in "Athenian Memorialization of the Men from Phyle" in chapter 4, 235–45. Moreover, the use of the epic technique of ecphrasis indicates the epic dimensions of this struggle. Even though Crisa must have been much smaller than Troy, making the war leading to Crisa's destruction a conflict on a much smaller scale, the fates of Troy and Crisa were remembered in similar terms in Greek social memory.

72. Aeschin. 3.108: καὶ αὐτοῖς ἀναιρεῖ ἡ Πυθία πολεμεῖν Κιρραίοις καὶ Κραγαλίδαις πάντ' ἤματα καὶ πάσας νύκτας, καὶ τὴν χώραν αὐτῶν καὶ τὴν πόλιν ἐκπορθήσαντας καὶ αὐτοὺς ἀνδραποδισαμένους ἀναθεῖναι τῷ Ἀπόλλωνι τῷ Πυθίῳ καὶ τῇ Ἀρτέμιδι καὶ Λητοῖ καὶ Ἀθηνᾷ Προναίᾳ ἐπὶ πάσῃ ἀεργίᾳ, [καὶ ταύτην τὴν χώραν μήτ' αὐτοὺς ἐργάζεσθαι μήτ' ἄλλον ἐᾶν]. The last colon has been identified as a gloss for the unusual phrase ἐπὶ πάσῃ ἀεργίᾳ and deleted by Papavasilios (cf. Dilts' 1997 edition ad locum). This seems very likely, especially since this explanation could easily have been inferred from the following paragraph (Aeschin. 3.109: καὶ ἐπὶ τούτοις ὅρκον ὤμοσαν ἰσχυρόν, μήτ' αὐτοὶ τὴν ἱερὰν γῆν ἐργάσεσθαι μήτ' ἄλλῳ ἐπιτρέψειν).

but that they would come to the help of the god and the sacred land with hand and foot and voice, and all their might. (Aeschin. 3.109)

Drawing on Apollo's order as well as on the account of its execution, we can identify three essential components of this ritual city destruction: (1) enslaving he inhabitants (αὐτοὺς ἀνδραποδισαμένους, ἐξηνδραποδίσαντο τοὺς ἀνθρώπους), (2) razing the city to the ground (τὴν χώραν αὐτῶν καὶ τὴν πόλιν ἐκπορθήσαντας, τὴν πόλιν αὐτῶν κατέσκαψαν),[73] and (3) dedicating the territory to the god (ἀναθεῖναι, τὴν χώραν καθιέρωσαν) as land withdrawn from agricultural use (ἐπὶ πάσῃ ἀεργίᾳ, μήτ' αὐτοὶ τὴν ἱερὰν γῆν ἐργάσεσθαι μήτ' ἄλλῳ ἐπιτρέψειν). Parke argues that Crisa's treatment constituted the historical precedent for the planned treatment of the medizing *poleis* in 480/79 and for the proposed eradication of Athens in 405/4.[74] For the moment, I will leave aside the problems of the First Sacred War and of "tithing" the medizers (δεκατεύσαι, Hdt. 7.132.2) and compare the proposed treatment of Athens—as it was *remembered* in fourth-century allusions—to Aeschines' description of Crisa's fate.

The near enslavement of Athens constitutes the core element of this memory, which was supplemented by other details. This is evident from the briefest allusions to this event in Isocrates' *Peace* (ὥστε παρὰ μικρὸν ἐλθεῖν ἐξανδραποδισθῆναι, Isoc. 8.78; περὶ ἀνδραποδισμοῦ κινδυνεύσαντες, Isoc. 8.105), his *Areopagiticus* (παρὰ μικρὸν ἤλθομεν ἐξανδραποδισθῆναι, Isoc. 7.6), and his *Antidosis* (ὅλην τὴν πόλιν περὶ ἀνδραποδισμοῦ κινδυνεύσασαν, Isoc. 15.319), as well as in Demosthenes' *On the False Embassy* (περὶ ἡμῶν ὑπὲρ ἀνδραποδισμοῦ προτιθεῖσιν, Dem. 19.65) and Procles' ambassador speech in 370/69, as reported by Xenophon (ἐξανδραποδίσασθαι ὑμᾶς, Xen. *Hell.* 6.5.46).[75] The near enslavement was certainly the defining characteristic of this event for the traumatized Athenians, as I have argued above. This finding neither supports nor contradicts my claim that fourth-century Greeks remembered this proposal in terms of the ritual destruction of a polis; enslavement of the population was indeed an essential component, but it does not suffice to prove the connection to this cultural concept.

There is no doubt, however, that Isocrates saw this concept of a ritual city destruction behind the punishment planned for Athens. In his *Plataicus,* he links the Theban proposal *explicitly* to the fate of Crisa.

---

73. Connor (1985) argues that the κατασκαφή of houses was a ritual punishment for crimes against the polis community, such as murder, treason, or tyranny. He suggests some connection to the κατασκαφή of the walls of Athens in 404. Later in this chapter, I will draw on his observations for illuminating the proposals against the medizers and against Athens.

74. Parke (1948). He is followed by Bömer (1961) 33–44.

75. Cf. "Fourth-Century Allusions to the Proposed Destruction of Athens" above, 285–91.

> When misfortune befell you, did not they [sc. the Thebans] alone of the allies vote that it be necessary both to enslave your city [τήν τε πόλιν ἐξανδραποδίσασθαι] and to abandon its territory as grazing land for sheep [τὴν χώραν ἀνεῖναι μηλόβοτον] as was the plain of Crisa [ὥσπερ τὸ Κρισαῖον πεδίον]. (Isoc. 14.31)

Besides the explicit reference to the Κρισαῖον πεδίον, this passage contains all three components of Crisa's ritual destruction. The enslavement of the entire polis (τήν πόλιν ἐξανδραποδίσασθαι) is mentioned explicitly. The phrase "to abandon its territory as grazing land for sheep" (τὴν χώραν ἀνεῖναι μηλόβοτον) does not occur in Aeschines' allusion to Crisa's punishment. Nevertheless, as I will show, it unmistakably signifies both the razing of the city to the ground and turning the territory into sacred land, withdrawn from agricultural use.

Although the physical destruction of the city of Athens is not mentioned explicitly, it has to be presupposed if the territory is to be turned into an uncultivated plain like τὸ Κρισαῖον πεδίον, since the city of Crisa was eradicated as well. Moreover, in the context of city destructions, the phrase τὴν χώραν ἀνεῖναι μηλόβοτον occurs together with the actions of "enslavement" and "city razing," as we will see.[76] This connection between κατασκαφή and μηλόβοτον ἀνεῖναι is well known throughout antiquity, as the explanation of μηλόβοτος in late antique lexicography shows. Photius and the *Lexica Segueriana* define it thus: μηλόβοτος πόλις ἐστὶ κατασκαφεῖσα καὶ ἀνεθεῖσα τοῖς μήλοις.[77] Turning a territory into grazing land for sheep thus presupposes the razing of the city.

Following Parke, I take the phrase τὴν χώραν ἀνεῖναι μηλόβοτον to signify the fate of the territory of Crisa. Parke argues that μηλόβοτος is a "ritual term, and one which was to become conventional in this connection without further reference to the Crisaean plain."[78] This connection becomes evident if one considers the characteristics of memory: memories are always semantic and, at the same time, visual conceptualizations.[79] In the case of the first two of Apollo's commands, ἀνδραποδισμός and κατασκαφή, visual images are easily available to complement the semantic components of these well-known concepts. The ἀνδραποδισμός is a well-established custom of war after conquering an enemy

76. Cf. Plut. *Lys.* 15.2; Schol. Dem. 19.65 (165a, b Dilts).

77. Photius *Lexicon* s.v. μηλόβοτος: ἡ κατασκαφεῖσα καὶ ἀνεθεῖσα τοῖς μήλοις· ἤτοι τοῖς κτήνεσιν, εἰς νομὴν διὰ τὴν ἐρημίαν; *Lexica Segueriana, Glossae rhetoricae* s.v. μηλόβοτος: μηλόβοτος πόλις ἐστὶ κατασκαφεῖσα καὶ ἀνεθεῖσα τοῖς μήλοις εἰς νομὴν διὰ τὴν ἐρημίαν.

78. Parke (1948) 100 cites as evidence a passage in Appian, in which Scipio curses the city of Carthage after its destruction: Σκιπίων αὐτήν, ὅτε κατέσκαπτεν, **ἐπηράσατο** ἐς ἀεὶ μηλόβοτον εἶναι (App. *B Civ.* 1.3.24).

79. See "Individual and Collective Memory" in the introduction, 8–13; Fentress & Wickham (1992) 32–36.

polis, familiar to the Greeks already from the epic depictions of the fall of Troy.[80] Visual images of slaves being led away in chains thus come easily to mind. This is also true for the razing of a city to the ground. Connor has shown that the κατασκαφή of the οἶκος was a common punishment for crimes against the polis community (e.g., sacrilege, murder, treason, and attempted tyranny) and was widely in use throughout the Greek world during the sixth and fifth centuries. It entailed burning down the house, destroying its hearth, and digging out its foundation. Given the familiarity of this concept of κατασκαφή of individual οἶκοι, to visualize the κατασκαφή of an entire polis was certainly not difficult.[81]

But how should one visualize Apollo's order "to dedicate the land to the god for total noncultivation" (ἐπὶ πάσῃ ἀεργίᾳ, Aeschin. 3.108)? Aeschines gave a paraphrase of this command, citing the oath sworn by the Amphictyons that they would "not themselves cultivate the sacred land nor allow it to another" (μήτ' αὐτοὶ τὴν ἱερὰν γῆν ἐργάσεσθαι μήτ' ἄλλῳ ἐπιτρέψειν, Aeschin. 3.109), but even these acts are hard to envision, since they are expressed through negations. The image of sheep grazing on abandoned land, however, is a memorable visual conceptualization of this divine prohibition of cultivating the land. Letting sheep graze on a piece of land that is set aside ἐπὶ πάσῃ ἀεργίᾳ (Aeschin. 3.108) does not transgress the order of withdrawing land from agricultural use, as modern readers might think, since plowing was—unlike grazing—seen as an intrusive use of the land. This becomes apparent when one considers Greek metaphors for plowing, such as "violating the earth."[82] Further, our sources confirm that the phrase χώρα μηλόβοτος indeed signifies untilled land, just as Aeschines says of Crisa: in Plutarch's *Pericles,* we find the hendiadys χώρα ἀργὴ καὶ μηλόβοτος (Plut. *Per.* 16.7),[83] and Demosthenes used the antithesis of sheep-grazing versus grain-bearing land in one of his speeches (Dem. fr. XIII 2 Sauppe & Baiter).[84]

---

80. See, for instance, the anticipated fate of Andromache in Hom. *Il.* 6.440–65. Cf. also, in the present chapter, the previous section, on Athenian treatment of conquered *poleis* during the Peloponnesian War, and "Plataea, Melos, and Troy as *Aide Mémoire*" below, 323–26. See Gaca (2010).

81. For this specific cultural concept of κατασκαφή of individual houses, see Connor (1985), especially 85. I will argue in the following section that this concept could indeed be transferred from individual οἶκοι to entire *poleis* for the same kind of offenses (sacrilege, murder, treason, and attempted tyranny).

82. Cf. Soph. *Ant.* 337–41 (trans. H. Lloyd-Jones): θεῶν τε τὰν ὑπερτάταν, Γᾶν ἄφθιτον, ἀκαμάταν ἀποτρύεται, ἰλλομένων ἀρότρων ἔτος εἰς ἔτος, ἱππείῳ γένει πολεύων (and he [i.e., man] **wears away** [my emphasis] the highest of the gods, Earth, immortal and unwearying, as his ploughs go back and forth from year to year, turning the soil with the aid of the breed of horses).

83. Plut. *Per.* 16.7: ἀπᾴδοντα μὲν οὖν ταῦτα τῆς Ἀναξαγόρου σοφίας, εἴγε καὶ τὴν οἰκίαν ἐκεῖνος ἐξέλιπε καὶ τὴν χώραν ἀνῆκεν ἀργὴν καὶ μηλόβοτον ὑπ' ἐνθουσιασμοῦ καὶ μεγαλοφροσύνης·

84. Dem. fr. XIII 2 Sauppe & Baiter: [ὁ Δημοσθένης] γράφει δὲ δεινὸν μηλόβοτον γενέσθαι τὴν Ἀττικήν, ἣ πρώτη τοῖς ἄλλοις ἐξήνεγκε τὸν ἥμερον καρπόν. The allusion to Attica as the first

This analysis has shown that Isocrates (Isoc. 14.31) described the proposed treatment of Athens in the same vivid terms in which the ritual city destruction of Crisa was remembered by Greeks in the fourth century. However, this is not a singular incident. Apart from Isocrates' explicit comparison to the fate of Crisa, there are several passages that demonstrate that other fourth-century Greeks as well remembered the punishment proposed for Athens in the form of a ritual city destruction. A passage in Plutarch's *Lysander,* most likely derived from the fourth-century historians Ephorus or Theopompus, reports the Theban proposal in detail.[85]

> And some say that in very truth a proposal for the enslavement [ὑπὲρ ἀνδραποδισμοῦ] [of the Athenians] was made in the assembly of the allies, when the Theban Erianthus also proposed to raze the city to the ground [τὸ μὲν ἄστυ κατασκάψαι] and to abandon its territory as grazing land for sheep [τὴν δὲ χώραν ἀνεῖναι μηλόβοτον]. (Plut. *Lys.* 15.2)

This passage lists all three components of a ritual city destruction, as described by Aeschines: enslavement, city razing, and dedication of the territory as land withdrawn from agricultural use. The ritual background is evident from the use of the terms κατασκάψαι and μηλόβοτον ἀνεῖναι, known from Crisa's punishment as described by Aeschines (3.108–9) and Isocrates (14.31). In a moralizing digression on the Spartan appeal for help in 370/69 BC, Diodorus—or, better, his fourth-century source Ephorus—used the same ritual language in referring to Athens' punishment as planned by the Spartans in 405/4.

> Hence the Lacedaemonians were compelled to have recourse to the aid of the Athenians, over whom they had, at an earlier time, set up thirty tyrants, whom they had prevented from rebuilding the walls of the city and against whom they had planned to utterly destroy their city [τὴν πόλιν ἄρδην ἀναιροῦντες] and to make Attica into grazing land for sheep [τὴν Ἀττικὴν ποιῆσαι μηλόβοτον].[86] (Diod. 15.63.1)

land to have bore τὸν ἥμερον καρπόν is certainly a reference to the Attic myth of Triptolemus, who received the gift of grain from Demeter and shared it graciously with all humankind. Cf. Isoc. 4.28–29.

85. For Ephorus and Theopompus as sources for Plutarch, see Plut. *Lys.* 17.2.; Smit (1939) 1–8; Hamilton (1997) 206–7.

86. Parke (1948) 100 argues convincingly that "for the simple rhetorical point, Diodorus, or rather his source, overlooks the question, which of the allies was in favour of the proposal in 404." Missiou (1992) 97–98 uses this passage as evidence for her claim that two distinct versions circulated in fourth-century Athens, a pro-Spartan version and an anti-Spartan one.

In two speeches from the 330s, which I have not yet cited as fourth-century references to the events of 405/4, Lycurgus uses the phrase μηλόβοτον τὴν Ἀττικὴν ἀνεῖναι as a metaphor for deserting Athens after the defeat of Chaeronea.[87] In *Against Leocrates,* he declares indignantly,

> . . . and this man who openly cast his vote [ὁ φανερᾷ τῇ ψήφῳ καταψηφισάμενος] to abandon Attica as grazing land for sheep [μηλόβοτον τὴν Ἀττικὴν <ἀν>εἶναι] is now resident in this very country among you. (Lycurg. 145)

The two phrases "casting the vote" and "abandoning Attica as grazing land for sheep" clearly allude to the Theban vote to annihilate Athens in the allies' council in 404 BC. Lycurgus' rhetoric certainly draws on the emotionally charged memory of this historical precedent. Moreover, it is obvious from this brief remark that Lycurgus expected his audience to be familiar with the concept of a ritual polis destruction entailing enslavement, city razing, and withdrawing the territory from agricultural use. Otherwise, the phrase μηλόβοτον τὴν Ἀττικὴν <ἀν>εἶναι would be a vague and rather weak rhetorical expression. From the *Suda,* a late antique encyclopedia, we know that Lycurgus had used this historical allusion before, in the trial of the deserter Autolycus. Moreover, with the paraphrase ὑπὸ πολεμίων ἐξερημωθεῖσα, the *Suda* confirms my argument that the phrase μηλόβοτον ἀνεῖναι presupposes a city destruction.

> *Suda* s.v. μηλόβοτος χώρα: land which, after having been made desolate by the enemy [ὑπὸ πολεμίων ἐξερημωθεῖσα], four-footed animals graze. This word is also used by Lycurgus in *Against Autolycus.* but he abandoned Attica as grazing land for sheep [ἀλλὰ καὶ μηλόβοτον τὴν Ἀττικὴν ἀνῆκε]. (Lycurg. fr. III 2 Conomis)

Judging from these passages in Lycurgus, it seems that by the middle of the fourth century, the brief phrase μηλόβοτον τὴν Ἀττικὴν ἀνεῖναι sufficed to evoke the memory of the proposed destruction of Athens in 404. With this in mind, we can—with some probability—identify the aforementioned fragment of Demosthenes as a similar allusion to the events of 405/4. He writes

> a terrible thing that Attica becomes grazing land for sheep [μηλόβοτον γενέσθαι τὴν Ἀττικὴν], the land which first disclosed the cultivated fruit to the others. (Dem. fr. XIII 2 Sauppe & Baiter)

87. Cf. Parke (1948) 112–13; Lévy (1976) 23 note 2. Both connect this phrase to the Theban proposal of 404 as well.

Besides these fourth-century references, there are several similar (undatable) allusions to the proposed eradication of Athens in the scholia to Demosthenes and in later authors, which confirm that viewing this near annihilation in terms of a ritual city destruction was indeed a widespread phenomenon, beginning in the fourth century.[88] At this point, I would like to draw a preliminary conclusion, summing up my minimal position. A review of several references to the events of 405/4 has shown that fourth-century Greeks remembered the proposed annihilation of Athens in exactly the same terms in which they believed the ritual city destruction of Crisa to have been executed by the Amphictyons. According to Aeschines' paraphrase of Apollo's command, this ritual destruction entailed (1) enslavement (ἀνδραποδισμός), (2) city razing (κατασκαφή), and (3) dedicating the land to the god by withdrawing it from agricultural use (ἀναθεῖναι τὴν χώραν ἐπὶ πάσῃ ἀεργίᾳ) (Aeschin. 3.108–9). Isocrates explicitly compared the planned treatment of Athens to the Κρισαῖον πεδίον, which he described as χώραν μηλόβοτον, a vivid visual conceptualization of the prohibition against cultivating the land (Isoc. 14.31). Plutarch—or, rather, Ephorus or Theopompus—described the Theban proposal by using the very terms known from the context of the ritual destruction of Crisa: ἀνδραποδισμός, κατασκαφή, and τὴν χώραν ἀνεῖναι μηλόβοτον (Plut. *Lys.* 15.2). The metaphorical use of the phrase μηλόβοτον τὴν Ἀττικὴν ἀνεῖναι by Lycurgus (Lycurg. 145; Lycurg. fr. III 2 Conomis) and Demosthenes (Dem. fr. XIII 2 Sauppe & Baiter) shows that the allusion to Crisa's fate in Isocrates' *Plataicus* is not exceptional. The fact that several fourth-century authors used the same visual and semantic conceptualizations as Aeschines shows indisputably that by the middle of the fourth century, Athenians envisioned the planned eradication of Athens in terms familiar from the alleged destruction of Crisa.

Imagining the Unimaginable: The Eradication of Athens

My minimal position is not affected by the problems surrounding the historicity of the First Sacred War or by the question of whether this concept of a ritual city-destruction indeed stood behind the Theban proposal. Yet we must confront the question whether this concept of Crisa's destruction is merely a fourth-century invention, which later served to evoke the memory of the proposed annihilation of Athens, or whether it was indeed an important factor in the actual debate in 405/4.

88. Cf. Schol. Dem. 19.65 (165a, b Dilts); Schol. Aristid. *Panath.* 274 Dindorf (iii.261 Dindorf); Schol. Aristid. *Leuc. A* 614 Dindorf (iii.346 Dindorf); *Suda* s.v. μηλόβοτος χώρα.

Crisa as Model for the Theban Proposal in 405/4

In this section, I will make the case that the alleged ritual destruction of Crisa stood behind the Theban proposal of 405/4. Several clues point to this conclusion. Our earliest references to the proposal, the implications of the punishment of κατασκαφή, and the precedent of 480/79 concerning the medizers all indicate that Crisa indeed served as the model for the punishment planned for Athens in 405/4.

Our earliest sources, Xenophon and Andocides, writing less than thirteen years after the event, describe the proposal essentially in the same terms as Isocrates in the *Plataicus* (Isoc. 14.31). Granted, they did not use the ritual terms κατασκαφή and τὴν χώραν ἀνεῖναι μηλόβοτον, nor did they explicitly link the proposal to the fate of Crisa. Nevertheless, they depict in effect the same action. In a passage probably written in the 390s,[89] Xenophon reports that

> the Corinthians and Thebans in particular but also many other Greeks spoke against making a treaty with the Athenians and proposed to destroy their city [ἐξαιρεῖν]. The Lacedaemonians, however, refused to enslave [ἀνδραποδιεῖν] a Greek city that had done great service in the greatest dangers that had befallen Greece. (Xen. *Hell.* 2.2.19–20)

Xenophon used the unspecific term ἐξαιρεῖν (to take out, to destroy), to signify the proposed destruction of Athens, but it becomes clear from the Spartan rebuttal that ἐξαιρεῖν includes the enslavement of the Athenians. Moreover, like κατασκάπτειν, the verb ἐξαιρεῖν can also be used to indicate the physical destruction of a city.

Andocides' description of the proposed treatment of Athens resembles the fate of Crisa even more closely than Xenophon's does. In 392/1, in *On the Peace with Sparta,* he claims that the Thebans and Corinthians wanted to enslave the polis (τὴν πόλιν ἡμῶν ἀνδραποδίζεσθαι) and to make the territory desolate (τὴν χώραν ἐρημοῦν, Andoc. 3.21). It is certainly not far-fetched to take the phrase τὴν χώραν ἐρημοῦν to signify the razing of the city to the ground and the abandonment of the territory as grazing land for sheep. This identification is also supported by the *Suda,* which uses the compound ἐξερημοῦν to define μηλόβοτος χώρα.[90]

89. Brownson (1918) viii–ix dates the first part of the *Hellenica* (1.1.1–2.3.10) to around the year 393 BC. Despite Gray's (1991) attempt to challenge the statistical evidence, the *communis opinio* still holds that the first part of the *Hellenica* (1.1.1–2.3.10), which seems to be a continuation of Thucydides' incomplete work, was written "significantly earlier than the rest of the *Hellenika*" (Krentz (1989) 5). Cf. Cawkwell (1979) 17–18; Tuplin (1993) 11; Dillery (1995) 13–14.

90. *Suda* s.v.: μηλόβοτος χώρα: ὑπὸ πολεμίων ἐξερημωθεῖσα, ἣν κατανέμεται τὰ τετράποδα.

In his account of the Spartan embassy to Athens in 370/69 BC, Xenophon uses the phrase ἀναστάτους ποιῆσαι τὰς Ἀθήνας to refer to the Theban proposal (Xen. *Hell.* 6.5.35). The term ἀναστάτους ποιῆσαι is frequently used in religious contexts (first and foremost in oaths) to denote a ritual city destruction and thus seems to be synonymous with such phrases as κατασκαφή, τὴν χώραν ἀνεῖναι μηλόβοτον, or δεκατεῦσαι. It appears, for instance, both in the founding oath sworn by the Amphictyons in Delphi (Aeschin. 2.115)[91] and in the Plataean Oath supposedly taken by the Greek alliance before the battle of Plataea in 479 (R&O 88; Lycurg. 81; Diod. 11.29.3).[92]

These early references in Andocides and Xenophon show that immediately after the event, the planned treatment of Athens was already viewed in terms of a ritual city destruction. Robertson's claim that the First Sacred War against Crisa was entirely invented by partisans of Philip—first and foremost Aeschines—to justify the Macedonian engagement in the Third Sacred War against the Phocians between 356 and 346 is therefore certainly wrong, as has already been noted by Lehmann.[93] The analogy inherent in the political alignment (an Amphictyonic alliance fighting against a Phocian polis) is clearly responsible for the increased use of Crisa's example in public discourse during that time, but Isocrates' *Plataicus,* written in 373, shows indisputably that the ritual destruction of Crisa was treated as a historical fact even before Philip's war against Phocis.[94] I contend that by the beginning of the fifth century, the Greeks believed in the historicity of a Sacred War that ended with the eradication of Crisa. If this war really took place, it was certainly not an epic struggle on the scale of the Trojan War, as embellished versions later described it.[95] Nevertheless, it held its place in Greek historical consciousness as the first, emblematic account of a ritual destruction of a Greek polis by a Greek alliance.[96]

91. Cf. Aeschin. 2.115: ἐὰν δέ τις ταῦτα παραβῇ, στρατεύσειν ἐπὶ τοῦτον καὶ τὰς πόλεις ἀναστήσειν, καὶ ἐάν τις ἢ συλᾷ τὰ τοῦ θεοῦ, ἢ συνειδῇ τι, ἢ βουλεύσῃ τι κατὰ τῶν ἱερῶν, τιμωρήσειν καὶ χειρὶ καὶ ποδὶ καὶ φωνῇ καὶ πάσῃ δυνάμει.

92. Cf. Bömer (1961) 24–44; cf. R&O 88.31–39: καὶ ν|ικήσας μαχόμενος τοὺς βαρβάρους δεκ|ατεύσω τὴν Θηβαίων πόλιν, καὶ οὐκ ἀνασ|τήσω Ἀθήνας οὐδὲ Σπάρτην οὐδὲ Πλαται|άς. Lycurg. 81: καὶ κρατήσας τῷ πολέμῳ τοὺς βαρβάρους, τῶν μὲν μαχεσαμένων ὑπὲρ τῆς Ἑλλάδος πόλεων οὐδεμίαν ἀνάστατον ποιήσω, τὰς δὲ τὰ τοῦ βαρβάρου προελομένας ἁπάσας δεκατεύσω. Diod. 11.29.3: καὶ κρατήσας τῷ πολέμῳ τῶν βαρβάρων οὐδεμίαν τῶν ἀγωνισαμένων πόλεων ἀνάστατον ποιήσω.

93. Robertson (1978) fails to mention Isocrates' reference to the plain of Crisa in Isoc. 14.31, which predates the Third Sacred War. Cf. Lehmann (1980).

94. See also J. K. Davies (1994) who dates the origin of the tradition of the First Sacred War at least to the end of the fifth century.

95. For these embellished versions, see Robertson (1978).

96. See also Bömer (1961) 33 note 1: "Es kommt auch hier . . . weniger darauf an, ob die Angaben tatsächlich in Einzelheiten historisch sind, als vielmehr darauf, daß die Griechen, die diese Dinge schrieben und hörten, diese Verhältnisse als einen Teil ihrer eigenen Vorzeit für möglich gehalten, d.h. geglaubt haben. Und daran dürfte kein Zweifel bestehen."

Based on the previously cited early references to the proposed destruction of Athens,[97] Lehmann proposes to understand these references to Crisa's fate not merely as authorial associations or comments but as integral element of the Theban (and Corinthian) proposal.[98] Apart from these early references, further arguments can be made in support of the thesis that Crisa indeed served as the model for the proposed punishment of Athens in 405/4. First, I will show that the punishment of κατασκαφή can be transferred from individual houses to entire *poleis*. Then, following Parke, Bömer, and Siewert, I will make the case that the same form of punishment had been planned for the medizing cities in 480/79.[99]

Connor has shown that the razing of an individual house, also called κατασκαφή, was a common punishment for the crimes of an individual against the community (e.g., sacrilege, murder, treason, or attempted tyranny) and was widely used throughout the Greek world during the sixth and fifth centuries.[100] It is certainly conceivable that this concept of punishing an individual οἶκος within the polis was extended to Athens, an individual polis within the Greek οἰκουμένη, especially since the crime with which Athens was charged, tyranny, features prominently among the offenses to be punished by κατασκαφή.[101] Three hints indicate that this concept was indeed transferred from an individual house to an entire polis.

First, even though Athens as a whole was not razed to the ground in the end, its walls were nevertheless subjected to the ritual of κατασκαφή.

> Lysander sailed into the Piraeus and the exiles returned; and they razed the walls to the ground [κατέσκαπτον] accompanied by flute girls, with great enthusiasm, considering that day to be the beginning of freedom for Greece [τῇ Ἑλλάδι ἄρχειν τῆς ἐλευθερίας]. (Xen. *Hell.* 2.2.23)
>
> After the Athenians had given in to all demands, Lysander sent for many flute girls from the city, and gathered all those who were already in the camp, and then razed the walls to the ground [κατέσκαπτε] and burned up the triremes, to the sound of the flute, while the allies crowned themselves with garlands and made merry together, counting that day as the beginning of their freedom [ἄρχουσαν τῆς ἐλευθερίας]. (Plut. *Lys.* 15.4)

97. Xen. *Hell.* 2.2.19–20; Andoc. 3.21; Xen. *Hell.* 6.5.35.
98. Lehmann (1980) 245.
99. Cf. Parke (1948); Bömer (1961) 22–44; Siewert (1972) 66–77.
100. Cf. Connor (1985) 83–89.
101. For Athens as tyrant city, see Raaflaub (1979).

According to Xenophon and Plutarch, the κατασκαφή of Athens' walls was executed in the form of an orgiastic freedom festival, celebrating the end of Athenian tyranny and the beginning of Greek liberty, much as the individual buildings of the tyrants in Syracuse were razed in 343/2 (Plut. *Tim.* 22.1–3).[102]

Second, the κατασκαφή of individual οἶκοι entailed burning down the house and destroying its hearth.[103] In the context of the debate concerning Athens' fate, the Spartans requested an oracle, and the Pythia warned them "not to destroy the common hearth of Hellas" (τὴν κοινὴν ἑστίαν τῆς Ἑλλάδος, Ael. *VH* 4.6; τὴν τῆς Ἑλλάδος ἑστίαν, Aristid. *Panath.* 319 Dindorf with Schol. [iii.341 Dindorf]). The metaphor of Athens as hearth of Hellas brings to mind the concept of κατασκαφή, since destroying the hearth was *the* essential element of ritually razing a house to the ground. We can infer from this oracular response that the plan or, at least, the possibility of razing Athens to the ground was already in the air at that time. This oracle therefore supports the suggested transference of the concept of κατασκαφή from an individual house to an entire polis.

Third, the analogy between individuals and entire cities can also be seen in a different but related context. After the battle of Cnidus in 394 BC, the Athenians erected honorary statues of Conon and Euagoras and placed them next to the image of Zeus Soter in front of the Stoa of Zeus Eleutherius (Isoc. 9.56–57; Paus. 1.3.2). The only other commemorative statues erected for individuals in this location were those of the tyrannicides Harmodius and Aristogeiton. Julia Shear argues convincingly that just as the tyrannicides had done at the end of the sixth century, Conon and Euagoras brought freedom to Athens by deposing a powerful tyrant; yet, in this case, it was not an individual tyrant but the city of Sparta that had held Athens and other Greeks in a despotic grip.[104]

Furthermore, there is strong evidence that the concept of Crisa's ritual destruction had served as the model for the planned punishment of Greek cities before, in the context of the Persian Wars. Herodotus reports that the members of the Greek alliance took an oath presumably in the fall of 481,

> which was this: if things go well for them, to "tithe" to the god in Delphi [δεκατεῦσαι τῷ ἐν Δελφοῖσι θεῷ] those of the Greeks who had given themselves to the Persian without compulsion. (Hdt. 7.132.2)

102. Cf. Connor (1985) 83, 97. Connor merely discusses the razing of the walls; he does not address the Theban proposal, which also entailed the enslavement of the population and the dedication of the territory to the god.

103. Cf. Connor (1985) 85–86. A prominent example is Eur. *Hec.* 21–26: ἐπεὶ δὲ Τροία θ' Ἕκτορός τ' ἀπόλλυται | ψυχὴ πατρώια θ' ἑστία κατεσκάφη | αὐτός τε βωμῶι πρὸς θεοδμήτωι πίτνει | σφαγεὶς Ἀχιλλέως παιδὸς ἐκ μιαιφόνου, | κτείνει με χρυσοῦ τὸν ταλαίπωρον χάριν | ξένος πατρῷιος.

104. Cf. Shear (2007) 106–8.

The connection of this oath to the punishment of Crisa hinges on the meaning of δεκατεῦσαι τῷ ἐν Δελφοῖσι θεῷ (to tithe to the god in Delphi). It clearly has a religious connotation, shown by the link to Apollo in Delphi and the synonym καθιεροῦν (to consecrate), cited by Didymus.[105] Yet what exactly does this "consecration" entail? According to some scholars, it merely means "to pay a tithe as a penalty to the god."[106] This view is untenable, however, for several reasons. First, in the context of the existential struggle the Greek allies faced in 480, a mere fine would hardly have been able to deter any Greek polis from cooperating with the Persians.[107] Second, after the battle of Mycale in August 479, at the conference of the allies in Samos, the Spartans proposed to remove the Ionians from Asia and resettle them in the territory of those who had medized (Hdt. 9.106.3). This resettlement presupposes that the medizers would lose their land. Thus δεκατεῦσαι in the aforementioned oath cannot denote a simple fine.[108]

That δεκατεῦσαι indeed denotes the destruction of a polis becomes clear from other testimonies of the punishment envisioned for the medizers. This oath against the collaborators is not only mentioned by Herodotus (7.132.2) but also cited in full by Lycurgus in *Against Leocrates* (81) and by Ephorus (preserved in Diodorus 11.3.3 and 11.29.3). Yet each of them ascribes it to a different stage of Xerxes' invasion. Herodotus mentions it in the early stages of Xerxes' invasion (Hdt. 7.132.2); Lycurgus places it right before the battle of Plataea, in 479; and Diodorus, splitting up the oath, mentions the planned punishment of the medizers, as does Herodotus, in the context of the meeting at the Isthmus in 481/80 (Diod. 11.3.3), while he mentions the other elements of the oath in connection with the battle of Plataea in 479 (Diod. 11.29.3). This oath also appears in a fourth-century inscription found on a stele in the Attic *deme* of Acharnae (R&O 88). The authenticity of this inscribed version of the so-called Oath of Plataea is extremely controversial.[109] For our purposes, it is sufficient to fall back on the bare minimum that is known: that at some point during Xerxes' invasion the Greek alliance did take an oath to subject the voluntary medizers

105. Cf. Harpocration s.v. δεκατεύειν: δεκατεῦσαι μέντοι, φησὶν [sc. Didymus], κυρίως ἐλέγετο τὸ καθιερῶσαι, ἐπειδήπερ ἔθος ἦν Ἑλληνικὸν τὰς δεκάτας τῶν περιγινομένων τοῖς θεοῖς καθιεροῦν.

106. Cf. Bömer's (1961) 34–35 discussion of such a fine: "'die Verzehntung', d.h. daß jeder Betroffene dem Gott den zehnten Teil seines eigenen Wertes (den er aufbrächte, *wenn* er als Sklave verkauft würde) und den Zehnten seines Besitzes schuldete. *Diese* 'Verzehntung' würde die Versklavung der Bewohner also *nicht* einschließen." Both Bömer (1961) 34–36 and Parke (1948) 83–95 reject this interpretation of δεκατεύειν as a simple fine and argue that it involves much harsher measures, such as city destruction and enslavement.

107. Cf. Siewert (1972) 68.

108. Cf. Parke (1948) 95; Bömer (1961) 36.

109. For a summary of the arguments and further literature, cf. Rhodes & Osborne (2003) 442–49.

to the ritual punishment of δεκατεῦσαι τῷ ἐν Δελφοῖσι θεῷ ("tithing" to the god in Delphi). Parke asserts that this punishment was modeled on the ritual destruction of Crisa and that δεκατεῦσαι (to tithe) means

> "to treat as a tithe," and therefore to regard as consecrated to the gods and set apart from secular use. So the city which is treated as a tithe has to be destroyed and left unoccupied and untilled. (The inhabitants were probably to be enslaved by the conquerors; though this is not usually made clear in our sources, which emphasise instead the destruction of the city itself.) It is to be expected that Apollo should be the typical god to receive such a consecration because he was particularly δεκατηφόρος.[110]

Tuplin raises two objections to Parke's hypothesis that Crisa served as model for the proposed punishment of the medizers in 480 and the Athenians in 405/4. First, the term δεκατεύειν is never used to describe the treatment of Crisa. Second, Parke cannot be right in his identification of δεκατεύειν as "'[to] treat like a tithe', i.e. (since tithes were dedicated) 'dedicate' (with no 10% limitation),"[111] since the term would be entirely divorced from its original meaning, which is connected to one-tenth.[112] Yet both of these objections can be dismissed. Parke never says explicitly that Crisa's case denotes a *wholesale* dedication. Moreover, Bömer, who accepts Parke's hypothesis, maintains the literal meaning of δεκατεύειν, defining it as "treatment as spoils of war, i.e., destruction of the city, enslavement, and handing over of one-tenth of people and property to Apollo."[113] Any wholesale city destruction, I argue, will produce slaves and spoils (i.e., movable property), in addition to the territory of the city itself. It is therefore likely either that the dedication of the land as χώρα μηλόβοτον was considered as one part (i.e., a "tithe") of the entire booty (including slaves and movable property) or that—in addition to the consecrated land—one-tenth of the spoils and slaves had to be dedicated to the god.[114] Tuplin's objection that

110. Parke (1948) 85. Similarly, Bömer (1961) 34; Siewert (1972) 66–69.

111. Tuplin (1993) 182.

112. Tuplin (1993) 183: "The Oath's possible Amphictyonic connections . . . do not alter the simple fact that a word patently associated with tenth parts ought not to be used precisely to express wholesale destruction/dedication. Metaphorical use of δεκατεύειν to mean 'destroy' derives not from Cirrha-style dedication of land but from tithing of spoil after an all-out assault on medizers, terminology adopted to mask political revenge with religious sanction."

113. Bömer (1961) 34. According to Bömer, δεκατεύειν denotes the "Behandlung als Kriegsbeute, d.h. ἀνάστασις [i.e., destruction of the city], Versklavung und Ablieferung des Zehnten von Menschen und Besitz an Apollon."

114. Both of these scenarios are compatible with Aeschines' account of the punishment of Crisa (Aeschin. 3.108–9).

there is no actual "tithing" in Parke's model of a ritual city destruction is thus insubstantial.[115]

Tuplin is right to point out that the Oath of Plataea does not list the specific elements of a ritual city destruction, which Parke first identified in Crisa's case, and that Aeschines' description of Crisa's punishment does not contain the term δεκατεύειν. Nevertheless, there are enough clues to support the claim that—in the context of 480—δεκατεῦσαι denotes a ritual polis destruction. First, in both cases, the god in Delphi is named as the beneficiary of this punishment. Second, the stark antithesis of tithing the medizers versus not destroying the patriotic cities (οὐκ ἀναστήσω, R&O 88.33–34; οὐδεμίαν ἀνάστατον ποιήσω, Lycurg. 81) indicates that δεκατεύειν entails the destruction of the city.[116]

Third, according to Xenophon, the phrase δεκατευθῆναι Θηβαίους (to have the Thebans tithed) was an old saying (τὸ πάλαι λεγόμενον) in fourth-century Athens (Xen. *Hell.* 6.3.20, 6.5.35). This saying is mentioned once in the immediate context of a reference to the Theban proposal of 405/4 (ἀναστάτους ποιῆσαι τὰς Ἀθήνας, Xen. *Hell.* 6.5.35).[117] From this juxtaposition, it is clear that the Athenians saw a direct link between the two proposals. As I have demonstrated earlier, the Theban proposal in 405/4 was modeled on Crisa's destruction, consisting of (1) enslavement (ἀνδραποδισμός), (2) city razing (κατασκαφή), and (3) dedicating the land to the god by withdrawing it from agricultural use (ἀναθεῖναι τὴν χώραν ἐπὶ πάσῃ ἀεργίᾳ, Aeschin. 3.108–9).[118] This link between the two events in Xenophon, therefore, implies that the planned tithing (δεκατεύειν) of the medizers entailed the same actions.

Fourth, a Latin reference shows that the planned punishment of the medizers involved the destruction of their city. In the context of Alexander's punishment of Thebes in 335, Justin reports that his Greek allies demanded the extreme penalty,

115. Tuplin (1993) seems to be unaware of Bömer's (1961) 24–44 study. Moreover, cf. the "misuse" today of the English word *decimate* ("to select by lot and kill every tenth man" and "to exact a tax of 10 percent") to indicate utter destruction.

116. Cf. Parke (1948) 84; R&O 88.31–39: καὶ ν|ικήσας μαχόμενος τοὺς βαρβάρους δεκ|ατεύσω τὴν Θηβαίων πόλιν, καὶ οὐκ ἀνασ|τήσω Ἀθήνας οὐδὲ Σπάρτην οὐδὲ Πλαται|ὰς οὐδὲ τῶν ἄλλων πόλεων τῶν συμμαχεσ|αμέμων οὐδεμίαν. Lycurg. 81: καὶ κρατήσας τῷ πολέμῳ τοὺς βαρβάρους, τῶν μὲν μαχεσαμένων ὑπὲρ τῆς Ἑλλάδος πόλεων οὐδεμίαν ἀνάστατον ποιήσω, τὰς δὲ τὰ τοῦ βαρβάρου προελομένας ἁπάσας δεκατεύσω. Diod. 11.29.3: καὶ κρατήσας τῷ πολέμῳ τῶν βαρβάρων οὐδεμίαν τῶν ἀγωνισαμένων πόλεων ἀνάστατον ποιήσω. Diodorus' version of the Oath of Plataea does not contain the tithing phrase. It is, however, mentioned in the context of the meeting of the Greek allies at the Isthmus at the beginning of Xerxes' invasion; see Diod. 11.3.3: οἱ δ' ἐν Ἰσθμῷ συνεδρεύοντες τῶν Ἑλλήνων ἐψηφίσαντο τοὺς μὲν ἐθελοντὶ τῶν Ἑλλήνων ἑλομένους τὰ Περσῶν δεκατεῦσαι τοῖς θεοῖς, ἐπὰν τῷ πολέμῳ κρατήσωσι.

117. This is reported in the context of the Spartan appeal for Athenian help in 370/69.

118. Cf. "Semantic and Visual Conceptualizations: City Razing and Enslavement" above, 301–9.

> reproaching the Thebans not only with their present, but also with their past support of the Persians against the freedom of Greece. [10.] For this reason, they said, Thebes was an abomination to all the peoples, which was obvious from the fact that they all had taken a solemn oath to raze Thebes to the ground once the Persians were defeated [*ut victis Persis Thebas diruerent*]. (Justin 11.3.9–10)

Justin's translation of the Greek term δεκατεῦσαι by *diruere* is remarkable. It shows that he (or, better, Pompeius Trogus, whose history he is epitomating) thought not of a fine (tithe) but of a city destruction. Moreover, the choice of the verb *diruere* brings us back to the beginning of our inquiry and to two further arguments, hitherto neglected in support of the identification of Crisa as the model for the proposed tithing of the medizing *poleis.*

The ritual aspect of the physical destruction of the city, the κατασκαφή has not been addressed by Parke, Bömer, and Siewert. It is noteworthy that Justin chose *diruere,* the Latin equivalent of κατασκάπτειν, to translate δεκατεύειν.[119] That confiscation of the property and "tithing to the god" (δεκατεύειν) regularly accompanied the κατασκαφή of individual houses has been pointed out by Connor, who remarks in a footnote that

> confiscation with tithe was probably the normal Attic practice as the fuller citations in T9 and T10 illustrate. The tithing should be compared with the tithing of cities such as that alluded to in the curse in the Plataean Oath.[120]

The analogy between the κατασκαφή of individual houses and entire *poleis* is apparent in the case of the medizers as well: treason is one of the crimes leading to κατασκαφή, and this is precisely the crime alleged against the collaborators, especially Thebes.[121]

The concept of κατασκαφή can also explain why Thebes and other medizing *poleis* were not enslaved and razed to the ground in 479. Parke has argued that this was only a "fantastic impossibility" proposed in the desperation of

119. *Diruere* is frequently used by Latin authors to signify the officially sanctioned razing to the ground of individual houses or captured cities; cf. *TLL* s.v. *diruo.* For the ritual destruction of individual houses, see Varro *Ling.* 5.147: "domus . . . quae ibi publice sit diruta"; Cic. *Cael.* 78: "meam domum diruit." For the memorial function of the destruction of Roman houses, see Roller (2010). For the destruction of captured cities, see Cic. *Inv.* 1.17: "utrum Carthago diruatur"; Cic. *Ad Q. Fr.* 1.1.25: "urbes dirutas ac paene desertas." Cf. Siewert (1972) 67.

120. Connor (1985) 88 note 28. The two passages explicitly mentioning tithing are Craterus *FGrHist* 342 F 17 (Connor's T9) and Craterus *FGrHist* 342 F 5 (Connor's T10).

121. This conclusion can be inferred from Connor (1985) 83. Connor himself does not discuss the reasons for tithing the medizers.

the struggle.[122] Connor's analysis of the ritual aspects of κατασκαφή provides a better explanation why the besieged Thebans were spared. Connor links the cultural practice of κατασκαφή to Greek ideas of pollution, brought about by such heinous crimes as tyranny or treason.

> Pollution, while invisible, is not abstract. It inheres in physical objects that come into contact with the guilty person, including the soil upon which he treads and the place in which he is buried.[123]

This attitude can explain the origin of razing a house to the ground and extirpating all its inhabitants. It is quite possible, I suggest, that the city of Thebes as a whole was spared because the Greeks under Pausanias' leadership considered a wholesale city destruction difficult and considered their oath as sufficiently fulfilled if they did away with the ringleaders who were first and foremost responsible for Thebes' treachery toward the Greeks. Eradicating the ringleaders (perhaps accompanied by the destruction of *their* houses) would remove all traces of this pollution, which was a principle objective of the ritual punishment of κατασκαφή. That many Greeks wanted to kill the children of the guilty Theban Attaginus as well is another indicator that ideas of pollution and the ritual extirpation of the entire οἶκος were indeed at play (Hdt. 9.88).[124] That the guilt of medizing was transferred from the entire community upon a few leaders, whose extradition was demanded, is evident in Herodotus' account (Hdt. 9.86) and is also supported by the Thebans' apology, given in Thucydides' Plataean debate: at the time of the Persian War, Thebes was ruled by a δυναστεία of few powerful leaders—they were to blame (Thuc. 3.62.3–4).

Finally, considering the characteristics of social memory, it makes sense that it was the Thebans who proposed the destruction of Athens at the end of the Peloponnesian War. Just as, for the Athenians, the traumatic fear of annihilation was at the heart of their memory of the events in 405/4, the Thebans vividly remembered the near destruction of their own city in 479, which had left a deep mark on *their* historical consciousness.

In sum, it is almost certain that the concept of a ritual city destruction stood behind the Theban proposal in 405/4. Our earliest references to the planned

---

122. Parke (1948) 96.

123. Connor (1985) 91.

124. Connor (1985) 94–95 regards Pausanias' refusal to hold the children responsible as evidence for a new, more human attitude toward guilt and the old belief of its infectiousness. Yet he also points out that "Athenian punishments for treason and conspiracy seem for a long time to have included the children or the genos in the penalties." A century later, this punishment of the Theban ringleaders was forgotten in Athens and the Athenians maintained that the Thebans had not yet been "tithed" for their medizing. Cf. Xen. *Hell.* 6.3.20, 6.5.35.

punishment of Athens by Andocides and Xenophon describe actions known from the fate of Crisa. The ritual punishment of κατασκαφή could be applied not only to individual οἶκοι within the polis but also to entire *poleis* within the Greek οἰκουμένη. The tithing (δεκατεύειν) of the οἶκος or the polis to the god was an essential element of this ritual punishment of κατασκαφή. The oath to tithe the medizers was therefore also modeled on the ritual destruction of Crisa. This threat of annihilation was preserved in Theban collective consciousness.

Why Was Athens Spared?

All these clues indicate that the ritual destruction of Crisa served as a model for the proposal to eradicate Athens in 405/4. This raises further questions: (1) Which arguments were made for destroying and for sparing Athens? (2) Why did the proponents of the annihilation of Athens invoke a ritual concept? (3) Why was Athens spared in the end? These questions once again touch on the underlying assumptions of this book, set forth in the introduction.[125]

Many modern historians adhere to the political theory of Realism, which regards the rational self-interest of states as the main, if not the only, factor in international politics. Consequently, many modern reconstructions of the events of 405/4 are based on these principles. Cartledge, for instance, cites two main reasons for Sparta's refusal to destroy Athens. First, Lysander wanted to extend Sparta's control into central Greece by installing a puppet regime of his personal clients in Athens. The second reason was "a matter of geopolitics":[126] Sparta wanted to preserve Athens as a counterweight to the emerging power of the Theban-led Boeotian League. Sparta "professed yet a third motive in public":[127] Athens' merits for Greece during the Persian Wars. Cartledge clearly considers this third motive as less real, as an argument that is merely used to conceal and cover up the true, underlying consideration of power and security. Similarly, Hamilton argues that Lysander changed his mind and, in the end, favored preserving Athens, since it would function as counterweight to Thebes, as a passage in the second-century AD author Polyaenus shows.[128]

> When the Lacedaemonians and their allies wanted to raze Athens to the ground [κατασκάπτειν], Lysander said that it was in no way beneficial [μηδαμῶς συμφέρειν]. For the city of the Thebans, being nearby,

125. Cf. "Public Discourse and Decision Making" in the introduction, 30–36.

126. Cartledge (1987) 275.

127. Cartledge (1987) 275, 280 (quote on 275).

128. Hamilton (1997) 215–17. For the course of events during the siege, see "Traumatic Fear of Annihilation" above, 291–300.

> would thus become stronger and bigger, but if they [i.e., the Spartans] controlled Athens through tyrants, they would check the Thebans from nearby and have them weaker in every regard. Seeming to give the best advice, Lysander persuaded them not to raze Athens to the ground [κατασκάψαι]. (Polyaen. 1.45.5)

According to Hamilton, Lysander (following this calculus of *Realpolitik*),

> hit upon the device of obtaining a Delphic oracle to justify this volte-face. Many, not only among the allies, but in Sparta as well, were determined to destroy Athens at this time; a religious injunction not to do this would have been a useful instrument in a propaganda campaign to spare Athens.[129]

The Pythia's order not to destroy the hearth of Hellas fulfilled this function.

There is no doubt that such rational calculations were important factors in the debate. However, I contend that other factors, such as Apollo's command or the memory of Athens' merits during the Persian Wars, were also important and not simply masks for *Realpolitik*, as Cartledge, Hamilton, and other historians believe.[130] After all, Athens' role in the Persian Wars features unequivocally as the main reason for sparing Athens in our contemporary sources.

> The Lacedaemonians, however, refused to enslave a Greek city that had done great service in the greatest dangers that had befallen Greece. (Xen. *Hell.* 2.2.20)
>
> The Lacedaemonians, although then our enemies, decided to save our city because of the achievements of those men who had laid the foundations of freedom for all of Greece [οἳ ὑπῆρξαν τῆς ἐλευθερίας ἁπάσῃ τῇ Ἑλλάδι].[131] (Andoc. 1.142)
>
> . . . so that if the Lacedaemonians had been of the same opinion as the Thebans, there would have been nothing to prevent the authors of the salvation of all Greeks from being themselves enslaved by the Greeks . . . (Isoc. 14.32)

129. Hamilton (1997) 216. For this oracle, see Parke & Wormell (1956) 2:74.

130. Cartledge (1987) 275–83 emphasizes the geopolitical factors in Sparta's decision to preserve Athens; he does, however, acknowledge the weight of Athens' merits among other members of the former anti-Persian alliance.

131. Andocides' emphasis of the beginnings of freedom (ὑπῆρξαν τῆς ἐλευθερίας) reminds his audience particularly of the Athenian victory at Marathon, the first solely Athenian victory over the Persians. The claim that the Athenians in this battle fought for the freedom of all of Greece (ἁπάσῃ τῇ Ἑλλάδι) was also well familiar from the Athenian funeral orations.

The victory over the Persian invaders had tremendous consequences for the Athenians. From that point forward, they saw themselves as champions of Greek liberty. This was also the ideological basis of the Delian League/Athenian empire. Considering the enormous cultural and political energy with which the Athenians promoted their interpretation of the Persian Wars among the Greeks, it should not surprise us if such an argument from social memory would also resonate—at least to some degree—with other Greeks.[132] It is, therefore, quite likely that, among other reasons, Athens was spared in the end particularly because of its service to the Greek cause.

The second problem pertains to the ritual aspect of this proposal. Why did the Thebans (and Corinthians) invoke the concept of a ritual city destruction, which involved withdrawing the land from agricultural use? Why did they not simply propose a secular destruction, familiar from the cases of Plataea, Melos, Torone, and many other Greek *poleis* during the Peloponnesian War? Again, I suggest a series of interlocking reasons. First, in the spirit of *Realpolitik,* the Thebans might have anticipated the Spartan objection to the Theban appropriation of Attica's resources. Withdrawing this vast territory from agricultural use by turning it into grazing land for sheep might have been regarded as a means to dispel Sparta's fear of an overbearing Thebes.[133] Second, as noted earlier, Thebes itself was once threatened by total annihilation. It makes sense that the Thebans, vividly remembering their own near destruction, wanted to visit this very punishment on their most hated enemy. The memory of this impending threat was kept alive in Thebes through the political alignment of the Peloponnesian War, since Thebes was fighting against Athens just as at Plataea in 479. Third, both attempted tyranny and sacrilege could be alleged against Athens, calling for the ritual punishment of a κατασκαφή.[134] The former charge was frequently brought by Athens' disillusioned allies,[135] the latter by the Thebans after the Athenian occupation of the sacred precinct of Delium in 424 (Thuc. 4.97).[136] Fourth, in the cases of Plataea, Melos, Torone, and other small *poleis,* their destruction simply did not matter as much; they were too small. But eradicating a city like Athens from the map was an abomination on another scale. The Thebans might have felt that they needed divine sanction for such an act.

This leads us to the third question: why was Athens spared in the end? I argue that, considerations of *Realpolitik* aside, Athens' annihilation would have deprived the Greeks of an integral element of their shared identity, thanks to

132. Cf. "Funeral Orations" in chapter 1, 49–58.
133. Cf. Lehmann (1980) 246.
134. Cf. "Crisa as Model for the Theban Proposal in 405/4" above, 310–19.
135. Cf. Raaflaub (1979).
136. Cf. Parke (1948) 104–5.

Athens' political and cultural importance. This interpretation is confirmed by our sources. The Delphic oracle called Athens "the hearth of Hellas" (Ael. *VH* 4.6), and the hearth was, after all, the most important element of any οἶκος. Zeilhofer links the Pythia's metaphor to Pericles' τῆς Ἑλλάδος παίδευσις (Thuc. 2.41.1), to Plato's τῆς Ἑλλάδος τὸ πρυτανεῖον τῆς σοφίας (Pl. *Prt.* 337d), and to Isocrates' ἄστυ τῆς Ἑλλάδος (Isoc. 15.299, 16.27), and he therefore takes the "hearth" to signify the cultural center of Hellas.[137] Athens' central importance for Greece is also expressed by the phrase with which the Phocians allegedly persuaded the Spartans to save Athens,

> advising them not to make Hellas one-eyed [μὴ ἑτερόφθαλμον τὴν Ἑλλάδα ποιῆσαι], implying that Hellas has two eyes, the polis of the Athenians and the polis of the Lacedaemonians.[138] (Schol. Dem. 19.65 [165a Dilts])

What the annihilation of Athens would have meant for the Greeks can be inferred from their reactions to the eradication of Thebes by Alexander in 335. This shock left a deep mark on Greek historical consciousness, as is evident from contemporary testimonies (Aeschin. 3.128, 133, 156–57; Din. 1.18–26, 74; Hyp. *Epit.* 17) and later ones ([Demad.] 16–17, 26, 28, 65).[139] Alexander brutally robbed Greece of the local setting of an essential part of its mythology. This can be seen, for instance, in the Thebans' plea to preserve their city, "which had given birth not only to men but to gods as well" (Justin 11.4.4).[140] Athens' case is similar:[141] its extermination would have deprived the Greeks of an integral element of their shared identity, especially thanks to their role in the Persian Wars, as is clear from the Spartan rebuttal (Xen. *Hell.* 2.2.20).

In the analysis of the situation in 405/4, we have seen that, apart from rational arguments pertaining to the self-interest of the victorious states, Athens' historical and cultural importance for Greece was an important factor in the political debate and at least partially responsible for its preservation. This case

137. Zeilhofer (1959) 79–80.

138. Cf. also Schol. Aristid. *Leuc. A* 614 Dindorf (iii.346 Dindorf). Cf. Justin 5.8.4: "Cum multi delendum Atheniensium nomen urbemque incendio consumendam censerent, negarunt se Spartani ex duobus Graeciae oculis alterum eruturos."

139. Cf. Worthington (1991a) 93; Worthington (1992) 21. For [Demades], I follow Burtt's 1954 edition.

140. Justin 11.4.4: "nec iam pro civibus se, qui tam pauci remanserint, orare, sed pro innoxio patriae solo et pro urbe, quae non viros tantum, verum et deos genuerit."

141. The fact that, in our sources, the phrase "to make Hellas one-eyed" could be applied to the threatened/actual destruction of Athens, Sparta, and Thebes alike confirms the centrality of these three cities for shared Greek identity. Cf. Arist. *Rh.* 1411a (Sparta in 370/69 BC); Aristid. *Leuc. A* 639 Dindorf with Schol. (iii.352 Dindorf) (Athens in 404 BC); [Demad.] 65 (Thebes 335 BC).

has shown that when reconstructing political decisions in the past, we should not deprive the ancient Greeks of their memories and beliefs by reducing them to emotionless cost-benefit analysts. People in the past and in the present base their decisions on a variety of factors, and not all of them are rational. For this reason, it is worthwhile to take arguments from social memory seriously; they are significant political factors and not just empty rhetorical phrases and disguise for *Realpolitik.*

Plataea, Melos, and Troy as *Aide Mémoire*

Thus far, I have used the concept of social memory to explain two aspects of the memory of the near destruction of Athens: its remarkable persistence and its visual and semantic conceptualization in terms of a ritual city destruction—a concept that played a significant role in the debate in 405/4. Another characteristic element of memory, whether personal or social, helps to illuminate the phenomenon at hand even further: similar experiences reinforce previous memories and excite vivid imagination and anticipation.[142]

One reason for the intense fear that seized the Athenians when they first learned of the catastrophe at Aegospotami is the fact that they knew very well what city destruction and enslavement meant.[143] For them, these terms were not elusive abstract concepts (as they are for us today) but tangible realities. Athens was utterly destroyed twice by the Persians, in 480 and 479, which, judging from Herodotus' account, was a terrible shock for the Athenians. When the few remaining defenders of the Acropolis realized that some Persians had managed to get inside the citadel,

> some threw themselves down from the wall and so perished, while others fled to the inner chamber of the temple. Those of the Persians who had climbed up, rushed, first, to the gates and, after opening them, massacred the suppliants. When all were slain, they plundered the temple and burnt the whole of the Acropolis. (Hdt. 8.53.2)

After the Persians had spent the winter in Thessaly, Mardonius reoccupied Athens in the spring of 479. Frustrated by the Athenians' refusal to surrender, Mardonius withdrew "after he burnt Athens and utterly overthrew and demolished whatever remained standing of the walls, the houses, and the temples" (Hdt.

142. For the role of mental frameworks for both the perception of reality and the shaping of memory, see "Ideology and Social Memory" in the introduction, 13–19.

143. Cf. "Traumatic Fear of Annihilation" above, 291–300.

9.13.2). Thucydides confirms the extent of Athens' destruction by the Persians: "Only isolated portions of the circumference had been left standing, and most houses were in ruins, though a few remained, in which the Persian grandees had taken up their quarters" (Thuc. 1.89.3).

Herodotus' vivid description, probably based on Athenian eyewitness accounts, shows what a deep mark the destruction of Athens had left on Athenian collective consciousness. Moreover, a provision in the Oath of Plataea, "Of the temples that have been burned and cast down I will rebuild none, but I will leave them to men hereafter as a monument of the impiety of the barbarians"[144] (Diod. 11.29.3)—whether genuine or not—proves that the destruction of temples was a traumatic experience for all Greeks and that it remained a relevant issue in public discourse and was not forgotten, as Alexander's reference to this event 150 years later confirms.[145] In Athens, moreover, the building fragments and columns of the demolished temples were inserted into the newly built wall of the Acropolis and thus functioned as enduring reminders of this disaster.[146]

During the Peloponnesian War, Athenian soldiers eradicated and enslaved numerous Greek *poleis* and probably talked about their experiences upon their return to Athens. Xenophon, for instance, immediately links Athens' likely fate after Aegospotami to its own treatment of the Melians, Histiaeans, Scionaeans, Toronaeans, and Aeginetans (Xen. *Hell.* 2.2.3), thus suggesting that these experiences were in everybody's mind at that time.[147] Reports by Plataean refugees of the extirpation of their entire community by the Spartans and Thebans in 427 also helped to make the abstract concepts of enslavement and city razing tangible and similarly reinforced Athenian social memory and imagination.[148] At the same time, Plataea's annihilation refreshed the Theban memory of their own near destruction in 480.[149]

The sack of cities and enslavement are well-established topics in Greek

---

144. Diod. 11.29.3: καὶ τῶν ἱερῶν τῶν ἐμπρησθέντων καὶ καταβληθέντων οὐδὲν ἀνοικοδομήσω, ἀλλ' ὑπόμνημα τοῖς ἐπιγινομένοις ἐάσω καὶ καταλείψω τῆς τῶν βαρβάρων ἀσεβείας. Cf. also Lycurg. 81: καὶ τῶν ἱερῶν τῶν ἐμπρησθέντων καὶ καταβληθέντων ὑπὸ τῶν βαρβάρων οὐδὲν ἀνοικοδομήσω παντάπασιν, ἀλλ' ὑπόμνημα τοῖς ἐπιγιγνομένοις ἐάσω καταλείπεσθαι τῆς τῶν βαρβάρων ἀσεβείας.

145. For a discussion of the historicity of this provision, see Rhodes & Osborne (2003) 446–47, who stress that this stipulation was so firmly part of the historical tradition that Plut. *Per.* 17 has a detailed account of Pericles organizing a conference to revise this decision. For arguments against its authenticity, see Siewert (1972) 102–6. For Alexander's justification of his war of revenge against Persia, see Cic. *Rep.* 3.15.

146. For photographs of this wall on the east and north with its column fragments as "war memorial," see Hurwit (2004) 71; Hopper (1971) 80.

147. For a discussion of these city destructions and the references in Thucydides, see "Traumatic Fear of Annihilation" above, 291–300.

148. See "Plataean-Theban Antagonism" in chapter 2, 120–27.

149. Cf. "Crisa as Model for the Theban Proposal in 405/4" above, 310–19.

poetry and are especially familiar from Homer's depiction of the fall of Troy. The famous passage where Hector anticipates Andromache's fate after the fall of Troy is certainly paradigmatic.

> For I know this thing well in my heart, and my mind knows it:
> there will come a day when sacred Ilion shall perish,
> and Priam, and the people of Priam of the strong ash spear.
> But it is not so much the pain to come of the Trojans
> that troubles me, not even of Priam the king nor Hekabe,
> not the thought of my brothers who in their numbers and valour
> shall drop in the dust under the hands of men who hate them,
> as troubles me the thought of you, when some bronze-armoured
> Achaian leads you off, taking away your day of liberty,
> in tears; and in Argos you must work at the loom of another,
> and carry water from the spring Messeis or Hypereia,
> all unwilling, but strong will be the necessity upon you;
> . . .
> But may I be dead and the piled earth hide me under before I
> hear you crying and know by this that they drag you captive.
> (Hom. *Il.* 6.447–65; trans. R. Lattimore)

Given the centrality of Homer's texts in Greek culture, especially in Athens, where his poems were annually recited at the Panathenaea, it is reasonable to assume that famous images like this one came to mind when the besieged Athenians were anticipating the sack of their own city in 405/4.

Moreover, city razing as a tragic theme was certainly a further stimulus for Athenian imagination. Soon after the failure of the Ionian revolt in 494, which the Athenians had supported with twenty ships, the tragedian Phrynichus produced *The Capture of Miletus.* Herodotus describes how much the display of the pitiful fate of the Milesians distressed the Athenians.

> Phrynichus having written a play entitled *The Capture of Miletus* and set it on the stage, the audience burst into tears; and they fined the author a thousand drachmas for reminding them of a calamity that was their very own [ἀναμνήσαντα οἰκήια κακὰ], and forbade forever the production of that play. (Hdt. 6.21.2)

This shows that the mere sight of other people's trauma had a traumatic effect on the Athenians, particularly thanks to the emotional bond they felt with their fellow Ionians.

It is certainly not incidental that city razings returned as a theme of tragedy during the brutal struggle of the Peloponnesian War. Both Euripides' *Hecuba*, probably performed in 424, and his *Trojan Women*, produced in the spring of 415, were set in the immediate aftermath of the sack of Troy and focused on the fate of the captives. Many scholars have read the *Trojan Women* as Euripides' critique of the Athenian annihilation of Melos a few months earlier. This view has recently been doubted on chronological grounds.[150] Yet even if Euripides did not conceive of this tragedy as an implicit critique of Athenian imperialism, this play certainly reminded the Athenians what the eradication of a polis meant for the defeated. We can thus conclude that the Athenians in 405/4 knew very well what fate awaited them if the Spartans and their allies did not change their plans. These vivid images doubtless contributed to the persistence of this memory in Athenian collective consciousness.

Contexts for the Recollection of the Theban Proposal

Thus far, I have focused on those elements that most references to the near destruction of Athens have in common: the high degree of emotionality, caused by traumatic fear of enslavement, and the memorable elements of a city destruction. In this section, however, I will explore the more dynamic aspects of this memory. It will become clear that with changing political circumstances, certain elements were suppressed or emphasized, perhaps even invented. The orators certainly had some leeway in how they presented the story, but they were constrained by the knowledge and attitudes of their audience, if they wanted to be persuasive. The core of this memory, that the destruction of Athens and the enslavement of its population had been proposed but was not carried out, could not be contested—it was too deeply rooted in Athenian historical consciousness. We can, however, observe changes in the course of the fourth century, especially concerning who were remembered as the proponents and the opponents of this plan.

Thebans Accused and Excused

The earliest speakers to refer to the event, Isocrates in 402 and Andocides in 399, simply mention that *many* desired to destroy Athens but that the Spartans decided to preserve it (Isoc. 18.29; Andoc. 1.142).[151] This most likely reflects the

150. Cf. Scodel (1979) 139; Erp Taalman Kip (1987).

151. Cf. "Fourth-Century Allusions to the Proposed Destruction of Athens" above, 285–91.

historical reality. Xenophon, for instance, confirms that, besides the Corinthians and Thebans,

> also many other Greeks [πολλοὶ δὲ καὶ ἄλλοι τῶν ῾Ελλήνων] spoke against making a treaty with the Athenians and proposed to destroy their city [ἐξαιρεῖν]. The Lacedaemonians, however, refused to enslave a Greek city that had done great service in the greatest dangers that had befallen Greece. (Xen. *Hell.* 2.2.19–20)

That the Spartans ultimately saved Athens is certainly true, since nobody could have saved Athens if the Spartans, Thebans, and Corinthians had agreed on this proposal. This does not preclude the possibility, however, that other Spartan allies also spoke out in favor of preserving the Athenians.[152] Missiou argues that since, from the outset, the exact circumstances of this debate were unknown to contemporaries, this story of Spartan benevolence in saving Athens was a mere propagandistic invention to bolster Sparta's reputation after the ousting of the Thirty.[153] Her skepticism in regard to our knowledge of the event seems excessive. If we believe our sources and accept that such a proposal was indeed made but then rejected, Sparta, as the hegemon, can—in the end—claim the credit for sparing Athens.

With regard to the proponents of this plan, we can be sure that Thebes was definitely one of them. Xenophon reports that Theban ambassadors, seeking an alliance with Athens in 395, acknowledged that one Theban had voted for the destruction of Athens at the conference in Sparta. They tried, however, to distance themselves and the Theban state from this one representative, "who happened at that time to have a seat in the assembly of the allies" (Xen. *Hell.* 3.5.8), by laying the blame on him alone and by emphasizing Thebes' support for the Athenian democrats in 404/3. Even if one considers this speech to be Xenophon's invention, it shows that Athenians in 395 would have expected a Theban embassy to begin with such an apology. That Thebes was one of the allies demanding Athens' destruction was regarded as historical fact in Athens.[154]

The next two references to the events of 405/4 date from the period of the Corinthian War (395–386) and show how certain elements could be emphasized in accordance with specific political circumstances. In 392/1, representatives of the warring parties met at a conference in Sparta to agree on terms by which to

152. Cf. "The Role of the Phocians" below, 231–36.

153. Missiou (1992) 104–6. For a critique of Missiou's approach, see "The Debate about Athens' Fate in 405/4" above, 281–85.

154. For a discussion of the historicity of this speech, see "The Athenian-Theban Alliance in 395" in chapter 4, 245–53.

conclude the Corinthian War. On his return to Athens, Andocides, one of the ambassadors, tried to persuade his fellow Athenians to make peace with Sparta, in part by reminding them of the events of 405/4. Andocides thereby singled out the current Athenian allies, Thebes and Corinth, and emphasized that they wanted "to enslave [the] city and to make the land desolate," whereas the Spartans, although enemies, prevented this from happening (Andoc. 3.21). Using this sharp antithesis, he sought to discredit Athens' allies in order to reconcile his fellow Athenians with the Spartans. At about the same time, Xenophon, whose pro-Spartan and anti-Theban bias is well known, composed his account of the events of 405/4.[155] In his case as well, the extraordinary volte-face leading to the Athenian-Theban-Corinthian alliance might have prompted him to single out the Thebans and Corinthians among the supporters of Athens' annihilation just nine years earlier (Xen. *Hell.* 2.2.19).

In 373, in his *Plataicus,* which purports to be a Plataean appeal to the Athenian assembly following the second destruction of their polis by the Thebans, Isocrates bent the historical facts for his rhetorical purpose. Even though he had written in 402 that "many desired to destroy the city" (Isoc. 18.29), he now claimed that "the Thebans alone of the allies" (μόνοι τῶν συμμάχων) voted that Athens "should be enslaved and its territory be abandoned as grazing land for sheep, as was the plain of Crisa" (Isoc. 14.31). Isocrates obviously thought that this hyperbolic invective was within the bounds of license granted to an orator by his audience. The anger against Thebes caused by the destruction of Athens' long-standing ally Plataea was probably at least partially responsible for the acceptance of Isocrates' distortion. The exaggeration "the Thebans alone of the allies" can be compared to the Athenians' hyperbolic claim that they fought alone of all the Greeks at Marathon, thereby ignoring Plataea's contribution. Such overstatements seem to be acceptable when they are in accordance with the demands of the occasion.[156] It is important to note, however, that Isocrates merely suppressed other proponents of the plan; he did not change the essence of this memory.

Sparta's Cry for Help

As seen in Isocrates' *Plataicus,* Thebes' destruction of Plataea in 373 marked a deterioration of Athenian relations with Thebes. This resulted in a change of

155. For the authenticity of Andoc. 3, see 287 note 17 above. For the likely time of composition of Xen. *Hell.* 1.1.1.–2.3.10, see 310 note 89 above.

156. See also President George W. Bush's portrayal of American achievements in World War II, as discussed in "Remembering the Plataeans" in chapter 2, 131–33.

Athenian sentiments vis-à-vis the Thebans.[157] We have seen that our earliest testimonies emphasized that *many* desired to destroy Athens in 405/4. Then, during the Corinthian War, it was stressed by Spartan sympathizers (Andocides and Xenophon) that it was the Corinthians and Thebans, the current Athenian allies, who had been most eager for the annihilation of Athens. After the battle of Leuctra, however, which initiated an era of Theban hegemony, the other proponents of Athens' destruction were forgotten, and the memory of this incident came to be focused exclusively on the Thebans.

After their catastrophic defeat at Leuctra in 371, the Spartans were, for the first time, threatened in their very existence by Epaminondas' invasion of their homeland. In this desperate situation, the Spartans and their remaining allies appealed for help in Athens in the winter of 370/69 (Xen. *Hell.* 6.5.33–49). According to Xenophon, the Spartan ambassadors recalled many acts of successful Athenian-Spartan cooperation in the past and stressed the fact that when the Thebans desired the destruction of Athens in 405/4, the Spartans prevented it (6.5.33–35). The Spartans' rhetorical strategy is clear. The event of 405/4 is analogous to the current situation: then as now, the Thebans desired the destruction of a major Greek city. When threatened in 405/4, Athens was saved by Sparta; now Sparta is threatened and can—according to the principle of reciprocity—expect to be saved by Athens. Comparing this argument from social memory to the Spartans' stress on Athens' legal obligation to help (resulting from the common peace concluded in Athens in 371),[158] Xenophon calls the former argument the strongest (τὸ μέγιστον) and the latter merely the lengthiest (ὁ πλεῖστος λόγος) (Xen. *Hell.* 6.5.35–36). This shows that even though the Athenians resented being reminded of Sparta's intervention in Athens' favor in 404 (in light of their predominately negative experiences with them during the last ninety years), this memory was nevertheless very powerful (Xen *Hell.* 6.5.35). The importance of the precedent of 404 is also suggested by the fact that, according to Xenophon, Procles of Philus, another Peloponnesian ambassador, took up the Spartan argument and asked the Athenians to reciprocate now by opposing the Thebans.

> I also see the Thebans, who then did not succeed in persuading the Lacedaemonians to enslave you [ἐξανδραποδίσασθαι ὑμᾶς], now asking

157. For the Athenians' anger at Thebes' destruction of Plataea and Thespiae, see Xen. *Hell.* 6.3.1, 6.3.5. See "Plataean-Theban Antagonism" in chapter 2 in the present study, 120–27.

158. For this peace conference held in Athens after the battle of Leuctra in 371, see Xen. *Hell.* 6.5.1–3; Cartledge (1987) 309; Buckler (2003) 300–301. For the speeches of the Peloponnesian ambassadors in 370/69, see also "Aiding Suppliants" in chapter 3, 198–201.

> you to allow those who saved you to perish [περιδεῖν ἀπολομένους τοὺς σώσαντας ὑμᾶς]. (Xen. *Hell.* 6.5.46)

In light of the political situation (Thebes being the dominant power in Greece), it is not surprising that the ambassadors focused on Thebes and did not mention Corinth or any other proponents of the plan in 405/4. Moreover, it is also likely that the memory of the Corinthians and other proponents of Athens' destruction had faded from Athenian collective consciousness by this time, thirty-five years after the event. It is a characteristic of social memory that details that are irrelevant for the present generation drop away and are forgotten. The renewed hostility between Athens and Thebes between 371 and 340 sufficed to attach the memory of this proposal solely to the Thebans. Indeed, after the Corinthian War (395–386), there are no more references to Corinth's role in the debate of 405/4.

From Xenophon's account of the events in 370/69, it is apparent that in particular historical circumstances and political alignments, certain past events can gain new relevance. They are employed as historical precedents and thus return to the forefront of public discourse. Yet the fateful moment of 405/4 was not the only historical parallel to be evoked by the Spartans in their time of crisis. The prospect of a new Athenian-Spartan alliance against Thebes recalled another equally important historical precedent: the heroic fight of the Greek alliance against the Persians and their Greek collaborators, most prominently the Thebans. Thus it is not surprising that Xenophon's Spartan ambassadors strongly emphasized the past blessings of the shared Athenian-Spartan leadership during the Persian Wars and ended their plea with an allusion to the oath sworn against the medizers in 480.

> But if you and we, men of Athens, agree, there is hope now that the Thebans will be "tithed" [δεκατευθῆναι Θηβαίους], as the old saying has it. (Xen. *Hell.* 6.5.35)

The new Athenian-Spartan alliance against Thebes brought the Persian Wars increasingly back into public discourse, as it gained new relevance as a paradigm for the present.[159] This trend continued in the 350s and 340s, when Thebes

159. Buckler (2003) 310 characterizes the new Athenian alignment with Sparta as a complete policy failure: "[This] policy was short-sighted, wasteful, and potentially dangerous, and from it Athens gained nothing but some regrets." This is a case in point, I would argue, for my assertion that political communities indeed very seldom base their foreign policy decisions on cost-benefit analyses. In explaining this blunder, we can either suppose a crass miscalculation on part of the Athenians or, what seems more probable to me, conclude that the Athenians were swayed by arguments from social memory and followed a policy that conformed to their own self-image but was ultimately not in their true self-interest.

was allied with Philip of Macedon, the new barbarian invader. In these years we can observe an increase in activities commemorating both the achievements of the Greek alliance and the treachery of the Thebans. It is known, for instance, that the Athenians rededicated shields at the newly built temple of Apollo in Delphi—the old one was destroyed by a fire in 373—with the inscription "The Athenians, from the Medes and Thebans, when they fought against the Greeks" (Aeschin. 3.116).[160] Moreover, the inscription of the Oath of Plataea found on a stele in Acharnae (R&O 88) has been dated to the middle of the fourth century and can be attributed to the same context.[161] Even Siewert, the staunchest defender of its historicity, admits that singling out the Thebans as medizers and naming Sparta, Athens, and Plataea explicitly as members of the Greek alliance (R&O 88.32–35) has to be interpreted as some form of adaptation to the current political situation, which he calls "Modernisierung."[162]

The Role of the Phocians

A new version of the events of 404, or at least a shift in emphasis, can be observed in Demosthenes' speech *On the False Embassy.* After describing the destruction of Phocis by Philip in 346, Demosthenes concludes,

> Nobody could find words to describe the distress that is there now. And yet, that these men once voted against the Thebans, when they made a proposal for our enslavement, I hear from you all [ὑμῶν ἔγωγ' ἀκούω πάντων].[163] (Dem. 19.65)

All previous allusions to the near eradication of Athens either name the Spartans as saviors or do not mention a savior at all. Now, all of a sudden, Demosthenes introduces the Phocians and even claims that he is talking about a historical fact that "he heard from them all" (ὑμῶν ἔγωγ' ἀκούω πάντων).[164] Nouhaud regards this as an *ad hoc* invention by Demosthenes and considers

160. Aeschin. 3.116: Ἀθηναῖοι ἀπὸ Μήδων καὶ Θηβαίων, ὅτε τἀναντία τοῖς Ἕλλησιν ἐμάχοντο.

161. Cf. Rhodes & Osborne (2003) 443; cf. also Habicht (1961); Kellogg (2008).

162. Cf. Siewert (1972) 71–75. See also "Monuments and Inscriptions" in chapter 1, 84–94.

163. Dem. 19.65: οὐδ' ἂν εἷς δύναιτ' ἐφικέσθαι τῷ λόγῳ τῶν ἐκεῖ κακῶν νῦν ὄντων. ἀλλὰ μὴν ὅτι τὴν ἐναντίαν ποτὲ Θηβαίοις ψῆφον ἔθενθ' οὗτοι περὶ ἡμῶν ὑπὲρ ἀνδραποδισμοῦ προτιθεῖσιν, ὑμῶν ἔγωγ' ἀκούω πάντων. Like Dilts (2005), I follow MacDowell (2000) 235–36, who conjectures προτιθεῖσιν, "when they [the Thebans] made a proposal," arguing that the "mss.' προτεθεῖσαν, 'when it was proposed', agreeing with ψῆφον, cannot be right, because ψῆφον here means the Phokians' vote *against* the proposal."

164. Demosthenes' "I hear from you all" can be taken either literally (i.e., members of the audience were indeed shouting out when he mentioned the plight of the Phocians) or, more likely, metaphorically (i.e., at the time of this disaster, Athenians recalled to one another the Phocians' heroic intervention on behalf of Athens in the past). Cf. MacDowell (2000) 236.

the remark ὑμῶν ἔγωγ' ἀκούω πάντων an empty rhetorical phrase.[165] I suggest that we should not dismiss Demosthenes' assertion *a priori* but should instead take it seriously and further investigate whether his claim is plausible. Two questions in particular need to be answered. First, is it possible or even likely that the Phocians had opposed the proposal in 404? Second, why should everybody in Athens know about it in 343, even though it is not mentioned in any earlier text?

If we consider the Phocians' disposition toward the Athenians at the time of the conference in 404, two arguments in particular can be advanced in support of the historicity of the Phocians' opposition to the proposed eradication of Athens. First, even though the Phocians fought against Athens during the Peloponnesian War, the Phocian-Athenian relations had been friendly for most of the fifth century. The Phocians fought alongside the Athenians and the other Greeks against the Persians until their towns were destroyed and they were forced into submission by Xerxes. During the Pentecontaetia, the Phocians became bitter enemies of Sparta, which intervened on behalf of the Dorians, the Phocians' hostile neighbors (Thuc. 1.107); this brought the Phocians closer to the Athenians' side. In 449, the Athenians supported the Phocians in their attempt to get control over Delphi and to push back Spartan influence in the Delphic Amphictyony (Thuc. 1.112).[166] This Athenian-Phocian cooperation during the Second Sacred War makes it seem plausible that the Phocians, in gratitude for these benefactions, spoke out against the proposed annihilation of their former brothers in arms.

Second, on the basis of their geopolitical position, it makes sense that the Phocians would have opposed the destruction of Athens. For if Athens were eradicated, the Thebans, the Phocians' powerful neighbors, would lose the southern rival that had kept them in check throughout the sixth and fifth centuries. This would have created a precarious situation for the Phocians, especially since they were usually bitter enemies of Thebes, as the outbreak of the Corinthian War would prove once more.[167] Even though there is no firm proof for the historicity of this event, this evaluation of the Phocians' situation in 404 makes it seem likely that they indeed rejected the proposal to eradicate Athens.

Yet why should every Athenian in 343 know about the Phocian vote in 405/4? This is, I argue, a result of the diplomatic activities during the Third Sacred War.

---

165. Cf. Nouhaud (1982) 306. For a discussion of this problem, see "Participant Evidence: The Attic Orators and Their Interpretation" in the introduction, 41–43.

166. Cf. Hornblower (1991) 168–69, 181–82. After their defeat at Coronea in 447/6, the Athenians lost control over central Greece, and the Phocians became part of the Spartan sphere of influence again. Cf. Thuc. 1.113; Rhodes (2010) 49, 57.

167. For the quarrel between the Phocians and the Thebans in 395, see Xen. *Hell.* 3.5.3; Cartledge (1987) 291–92.

After the Delphic Amphictyony, dominated by Thebes, had imposed a heavy fine on the Phocians, the latter launched a preemptive attack and seized the temple in Delphi in 356, which led to the outbreak of this war (Diod. 16.23–24).[168] Threatened by the Thebans and Thessalians under Philip's command, the Phocians sent out embassies to justify their actions and concluded formal alliances with Athens and Sparta (Diod. 16.27.3–5). This war continued for almost ten years and ended in 346 with the destruction of the Phocian towns, which Demosthenes deplored in the aforementioned passage.

I suggest that it was during the Third Sacred War that the version of the Phocian vote against the eradication of Athens in 405/4 emerged in Athenian public discourse. This version was the ideal historical precedent for Phocian ambassadors or sympathetic Athenians to use to garner Athenian support for the Phocians. There are two possible explanations for the emergence of this new version of the events of 404. Perhaps Athenian or Phocian politicians simply invented the detail of the Phocian intervention in 404 in order to manipulate the Athenian people into lending aid to Phocis. This has been suggested by Parke and is certainly conceivable.[169] Yet if we take the characteristics of social memory into account, it is equally plausible that if the Phocians actually did oppose the proposal, this fact remained obscure until it resurfaced in Athenian public discourse at the time of the Third Sacred War. As I have argued above, the Phocians were indeed likely to cast their vote against the proposal in 404. But since they were such a small polis, nobody really cared much about them, and due to their insignificance, this fact was soon forgotten among most of the participants in the debate—save among the Phocians themselves: for *their* community, this memory of a service rendered to the powerful Athens was meaningful and therefore preserved.

It is impossible to discern whether this version of the Phocian intervention was a pure invention or a genuine Phocian memory, but it seems evident that it was mentioned frequently in Athenian public discourse whenever the Athenian-Phocian alliance was debated in the 350s and 340s. At the outbreak of the Third Sacred War, when the Phocians were in desperate need of powerful allies against their many enemies, their leader Philomelus

> selected the best qualified of his friends for the embassies and sent some of them to Athens, some to Lacedaemon, and some to Thebes; and he likewise sent envoys to the other most distinguished cities in Greece. (Diod. 16.27.3)

168. Cawkwell (1978) 62–68.
169. Cf. Parke (1948) 102–3.

Diodorus treats these embassies summarily and reports only those arguments that pertained to all the Greeks, such as the justification of the Phocian seizure of Delphi, the promise to respect the sanctuary and to properly administer it, and an exhortation to support their cause (Diod. 16.27.3–4). Yet it is quite likely that the ambassadors who went to Athens also mentioned—in addition to their general points—past Phocian support for Athens and thus injected the story of their vote in 404 into Athenian public discourse, especially if one considers the diplomatic practice of enumerating past benefactions in order to gain favors in return. In *On the False Embassy,* delivered in 343, Demosthenes had the decree detailing the terms of the Athenian-Phocian alliance read out to the audience; it promised the Phocians φιλία, συμμαχία, and βοηθεία (Dem. 19.62).[170]

Moreover, thanks to an Athenian inscription (*IG* II^2 109 = *Syll.*^{3} 175), we know that just a few years earlier, in 363/2, a group of Delphians had been exiled by the Amphictyonic council and had found refuge in Athens. Their leader Astycrates received Athenian citizenship and tax exemption (*ateleia*), and his followers received *isoteleia,* "equality of burden."[171] Ethnically, the inhabitants of Delphi are Phocians; but politically, Delphi is independent and administered by the Amphictyonic council. Seibert makes the reasonable suggestion that these Delphians wanted to increase Phocian influence over the sanctuary against the prevailing Theban dominance in the Amphictyony. This is evident from the fact that as soon as the Phocians took over the temple by force in 356, these Delphian exiles were recalled.[172] It is possible that the Phocians' vote against the proposed annihilation of Athens was brought up as early as in 363/2, when the Athenian assembly debated about the exiles' fate. Moreover, we can be reasonably sure that these Delphian exiles and their Athenian supporters lobbied vigorously for the Phocians' case in Athens from 356 onward. Most likely, they would also have used this historical precedent whenever the Athenian-Phocian alliance was discussed in the assembly or the council.

We know from our sources that support for Phocis was a recurrent political issue in Athens during this decade. After a setback against Philip at the battle of the Crocus Field in 352, the Phocians again "summoned help from their allies" (Diod. 16.36.1), and the Athenians sent five thousand foot soldiers and four hundred horsemen under their general Nausicles, who successfully barred Philip from Thermopylae (Diod. 16.37.3, 16.38.2). In the winter of 347/6, ambassadors from Phocis arrived again in Athens, asking for support and inviting the

170. Unfortunately, the decree itself is not preserved in the manuscripts. It might well have contained a reference to Phocis' intervention for the Athenians in 404.

171. For the similar reception of Theban refugees in 382, see "Athenian Help for the Theban Democrats, 382–378" in chapter 4, 253–67.

172. Seibert (1979) 131–34 with note 1026. See also Buckler (2003) 398, 404; McInerney (1999) 205–6.

Athenians to occupy the forts that guarded the approach to Thermopylae. After a debate in the assembly, the Athenians passed a decree to accept the Phocian offer and send fifty triremes under Proxenus to guard the pass (Aeschin. 2.132–33).[173] On the return of the second Athenian embassy to Philip in the summer of 346, when it became clear that Philip was marching an army against Phocis, Phocian ambassadors were in Athens, and they "were concerned to know what these men [i.e. the Athenian envoys] would report and what [the Athenians] would decide" (Dem. 19.59). We can infer from Demosthenes' account that, for the last time, the Phocians lobbied their Athenian supporters to speak up for them in the assembly and to persuade the Athenians to oppose the impending destruction of their towns. The analogy of their present condition to the situation of the Athenians in 405/4 makes it seem very likely that they once more drew on the historical precedent of 404. Finally, after the devastation of their towns, many Phocians took refuge in Athens and, through their mere presence, could serve as a reminder of the Athenian failure to reciprocate the Phocians' benefaction of 404 (Dem. 5.19, 19.80).[174]

This review of the diplomatic interaction between Athens and Phocis during the Third Sacred War and its prelude shows that we can confidently believe Demosthenes' assertion that (by 343) everyone in Athens knew (ὑμῶν ἔγωγ' ἀκούω πάντων) the story "that the Phocians once voted against the Thebans, when they made a proposal for [Athens'] enslavement" (Dem. 19.65). This passage in Demosthenes is not the only reference to the Phocians' role in saving the Athenians in 405/4. We find three quite detailed explanations of this historical allusion in the scholia to Demosthenes (Schol. Dem. 19.65 [165a, b Dilts]) and in a scholion to Aelius Aristides (Schol. Aristid. *Leuc. A* 614 Dindorf [iii.346 Dindorf]). All of them mention both the Theban proposal to subject Athens to a ritual polis destruction and the Phocians' refusal to agree. The Phocian intervention is also mentioned in the *Suda* (s.v. μηλόβοτος χώρα) and in Plutarch's *Life of Lysander* (Plut. *Lys.* 15.3).[175] From these disparate references, it

173. It is irrelevant for my argument that—after a change of leadership in Phocis—these ambassadors were imprisoned and the Athenian troops turned away; what matters is the fact that the Athenians had a public debate and resolved to aid the Phocians. Cf. MacDowell (2000) 3.

174. Cf. MacDowell (2000) 13. The Athenian Hegesippus was one of the most vocal supporters of Phocis. He had proposed the Athenian-Phocian alliance in 356 (Aeschin. 3.118 with Schol. [265 Dilts]) and was the first to speak out against peace with Philip in 346 (Schol. Dem. 19.73 [173 Dilts]), perhaps by evoking the Phocians' intervention in 404.

175. Plut. *Lys.* 15.3 reports that a certain Phocian saved Athens incidentally, by reciting some verses of Euripides' *Electra* at a banquet after the Theban Erianthus had introduced the motion to eradicate Athens. Moved by compassion, the allies felt it to be a cruel deed to abolish and destroy a city that was so famous and produced such poets. It seems to me that, in this version, the historical core of the Phocian opposition to the plan has been embellished by a popular motif, which we find also in an anecdote about the Athenian captives of the Sicilian expedition (cf. Plut. *Nic.* 29.2–4; Satyr. *Vit. Eur.* 39.19.11–34).

is apparent that the memory of the Phocians' advocacy for preserving Athens in 405/4 was indeed well known by the 340s, as Demosthenes claims.

Alexander's Annihilation of Thebes

In the previous sections, I have shown how the memory of the near eradication of Athens was used in various diplomatic contexts, either to win the Athenians' support for their saviors (the Spartans and the Phocians) or to incite them against the proponents (the Corinthians and especially the Thebans). Yet the use of this historical precedent was not limited to an Athenian context; it also played a prominent role in the debate about Thebes' fate in 335. Unlike in 480/79 and 405/4, the concept of a ritual city destruction was indeed executed this time: in accordance with a decree passed by Alexander's Greek allies, the city of Thebes was wiped off the face of the earth. An analysis of the arguments used in this debate will reveal the extraordinary role of memories of events that happened 145, 92, and 69 years earlier.

In 335, Theban exiles secretly returned to their city and persuaded the Thebans to revolt against the Macedonians.[176] Alexander brutally crushed the revolt: more than six thousand Thebans perished on the battlefield and in the massacre accompanying the sack of the city. Diodorus reports that Alexander buried the Macedonian dead

> and then gathered together the representatives of the Greeks and put before the common council [τῷ κοινῷ συνεδρίῳ] the question what ought to be done with the city of the Thebans. (Diod. 17.14.1)

Pointing to the phrase τῷ κοινῷ συνεδρίῳ, some scholars have argued that Alexander entrusted Thebes' fate to the Council of the Corinthian League.[177] Yet this seems highly improbable, for there is no indication that there was enough time for delegates of the league to gather. Arrian, rather, describes an ad hoc convention of the "allies who took part in the action, to whom Alexander actually entrusted the question of Thebes" (Arr. *Anab* 1.9.9), and Justin speaks merely of deliberations *in concilio* (Justin 11.3.8); both descriptions are more apt of a meeting on the spot than of an official meeting of the league.[178] It is quite possible, however, that Alexander used the judgment of the Greek allies who participated in his campaign to pass judgment about Thebes on behalf of the league as a whole.[179]

176. Cf. "Thebans Exiled by Philip in 338" in chapter 4, 272–74.
177. See, for instance, Sealey (1993) 203; Rhodes (2010) 391.
178. Cf. Bosworth (1980) 89–90, (1988) 195–96; Lane Fox (2004) 87–88, 513.
179. Worthington (2010) 243.

It is worthwhile to review who these Greek allies of Alexander's were. The army that sacked Thebes consisted of Alexander's Macedonian, Thracian, and Thessalian troops and of Greek *poleis* from neighboring areas, traditionally hostile to Thebes; they were the only ones that had enough time to join Alexander before his rapid attack on Thebes. In his description of the sack of Thebes, Arrian mentions that

> the Phocians and Plataeans and the other Boeotians slaughtered the Thebans, even when they no longer put up any organized resistance, some in their houses by bursting into them, some who were fighting back, others when they were supplicating at the shrines—sparing neither women nor children. (Arr. *Anab.* 1.8.8)

Diodorus reports similarly that

> even Greeks—Thespians, Plataeans and Orchomenians, and some others hostile to the Thebans who had marched with the king—invaded the city along with him and now exhibited their own hatred amid the calamities of the unfortunate victims. (Diod. 17.13.5)

From this description, we can infer that Diodorus must have meant these longstanding enemies of Thebes when he reports that in the debate about the city's fate, "certain men who were hostile to the Thebans began to recommend that they should be visited with the direst penalties" (Diod. 17.14.2). Indeed, Justin says explicitly that it was the Phocians, Plataeans, Thespians, and Orchomenians who spoke out against the Thebans in this ad hoc council (Justin 11.3.8).

It is important to note that all of our sources regard the traditional charges against Thebes, now voiced once more by Alexander's Greek allies, as responsible for Thebes' ultimate punishment. The return of the exiles and the revolt against Alexander, which constituted a breach of the κοινὴ εἰρήνη, sworn by all members of the Corinthian League, seemed less important.[180] Two main charges can be discerned: (1) Theban medism and (2) the destruction of other Greek *poleis* by the Thebans. Diodorus, for instance, reports that Alexander's allies

> recommended that the Thebans should be visited with the direst penalties, and they pointed out that they had taken the side of the barbarians against the Greeks: for in the time of Xerxes, they were allied with the Persians and campaigned against Greece, and they alone of the Greeks

180. Cf. Bosworth (1988) 194–96. According to Justin 11.4.1–7, the Thebans similarly used arguments from social memory in their defense, noting, for instance, that Heracles, Alexander's ancestor, was born in Thebes.

> were honored as benefactors before the Persian kings, and for the ambassadors of the Thebans, thrones were set up in front of the kings. By relating many other things of that kind, they aroused the feelings of the councillors against the Thebans, and in the end, they voted to raze the city to the ground [ἐψηφίσαντο τὴν μὲν πόλιν κατασκάψαι] and to sell the captives. (Diod. 17.14.2–3)

Thebes' medism is also mentioned as the main charge in Justin's account (11.3.9–10) and in Arrian's (Arr. *Anab.* 1.9.7).[181] This is not surprising; we have seen in chapter 2 that the continuing Theban-Plataean conflict, prompting the antithesis of Plataean patriotism versus Theban medism, perpetuated the memory of Thebes' collaboration with the Persians in Athenian collective consciousness.[182] Certainly, these memories would be even more vivid among the Plataeans themselves. We have also seen that during the Theban hegemony and the rise of Philip II of Macedon (371–339), Spartans and Athenians drew heavily on the precedent of the Persian Wars, denouncing the Thebans as traitors of Greece.[183] The Thebans themselves sought to improve their relations with the Persian king during Epaminondas' and Pelopidas' ascendancy, as Xenophon's report of the Theban embassy to Susa in 367 shows (Xen. *Hell.* 7.1.34–35).[184] Finally, in 338, just three years earlier, Philip constituted the Corinthian League

> to make war on the Persians on the Greeks' behalf and to punish them for the sacrilege of the temples [λαβεῖν παρ' αὐτῶν δίκας ὑπὲρ τῆς εἰς τὰ ἱερὰ γενομένης παρανομίας], and this won for him the loyal support of the Greeks (Diod. 16.89.2).

Immediately after his accession in 336, Alexander followed in his father's footsteps and had the Corinthian League

---

181. Justin 11.3.9–10: "studia in Persas non praesentia tantum, verum et vetera adversus Graeciae libertatem increpantes, [10.] quam ob rem odium eos omnium populorum esse"; Arr. *Anab.* 1.9.7: (. . .) ὡς τῆς τε ἐν τῷ Μηδικῷ πολέμῳ προδοσίας τῶν Ἑλλήνων διὰ μακροῦ ταύτην δίκην ἐκτίσαντας Θηβαίους (. . .). In his account of the actual council (Arr. *Anab.* 1.9.9–10), Arrian does not explicitly report the charges brought against the Thebans. In the immediately preceding passage, however, he explains the tremendous effect Thebes' destruction had on the Greeks and attributes Thebes' fate to the vengeance of the gods for former Theban sins. Brunt (1976) 39 note 1 and Bosworth (1980) 88–89 argue convincingly that these sins are actually the accusations made in the council, which is evident from Justin's and Diodorus' accounts.

182. Cf. "Plataean Patriotism versus Theban Medism" in chapter 2, 119–42.

183. For the inscription of the Plataean Oath, the rededication of Athenian shields taken from the Persians and Thebans, and similar commemorative activities, cf. "Sparta's Cry for Help," 331.

184. Cawkwell (1978) 168 points to recent Theban contacts with Persia to explain the harsh treatment of Thebes by Philip after the battle of Chaeronea.

> pass a decree that he be στρατηγὸς αὐτοκράτωρ of Greece and that they themselves join in the expedition against the Persians seeking satisfaction for the offences which they had committed against the Greeks (Diod. 17.4.9).

The 145-year-old charge of medism was therefore a very serious one, when seen in the light of the declared reason for the upcoming war against Persia.[185]

The other main point in the accusation was Thebes' destruction of Greek cities in the past. The Thebans had annihilated Plataea twice, in 427 and again in 373, together with Thespiae; they had eradicated the city of Orchomenus in 364/3 and were instrumental in the razing of the Phocian towns, meted out as punishment by the Amphictyonic council at the end of the Third Sacred War.[186] These calamities, therefore, head the list of accusations against Thebes in Justin's account.

> When the eradication of the city was being discussed in council, the Phocians, the Plataeans, the Thespians, and the Orchomenians, Alexander's allies who now shared his victory, recalled the eradication of their own cities and the ruthlessness of the Thebans. (Justin 11.3.8)

Thebes' treacherous destruction of Plataea in 427 is also listed by Arrian as one of the reasons for Thebes' annihilation in 335 (Arr. *Anab.* 1.9.7). Remarkably, Arrian mentions, in addition, a city destruction that was not even executed but merely proposed by the Thebans in 404, namely, the planned eradication of Athens at the end of the Peloponnesian War. The Thebans were punished by the gods

> because they sought to annihilate the Athenians through their vote, when a motion was put before the allies of the Lacedaemonians about the enslavement of their polis [ὑπὲρ ἀνδραποδισμοῦ τῆς πόλεως γνώμη προὐτέθη]. (Arr. *Anab.* 1.9.7)

That the proposed eradication of Athens is mentioned in this context is less surprising when we consider that there is a direct link from Thebes' medizing, over the Theban proposal in 405/4, to the destruction of Thebes in 335: the concept of a ritual city destruction, well known from the example of Crisa.[187] Justin

185. Cf. Bosworth (1980) 89.

186. For Plataea, see "Plataean-Theban Antagonism" in chapter 2, 120–27. For the destruction of Orchomenus, see Diod. 15.79.3–6; Dem. 20.109; Buckler (1980) 182–84; Buck (1994) 36.

187. Cf. "Imagining the Unimaginable: The Eradication of Athens" above, 309–23.

makes this connection explicit by quoting the oath taken in 480/79 against the medizers.

> When the eradication of the city was being discussed in council, the Phocians, the Plataeans, the Thespians, and the Orchomenians . . . recalled the eradication of their own cities . . . , (9) reproaching the Thebans not only with their present, but also with their past support of the Persians against the freedom of Greece. (10.) For this reason, they said, the Thebans were an abomination to all the peoples, which was obvious from the fact that they all had taken a solemn oath to raze Thebes to the ground once the Persians were defeated [*ut victis Persis Thebas diruerent*]. (Justin 11.3.8–10)

If we consider the situation in 335 from the memorial perspective of fourth-century Greeks, the eradication of Thebes seems logical and well deserved. The Greek alliance of 480/79 had sworn to subject the voluntary medizers, first and foremost Thebes, to a ritual city destruction. Even though the Thebans evaded this fate, they themselves proposed the very same punishment for Athens in 405/4 and brutally annihilated smaller cities such as Plataea and Orchomenus. In the wake of the avenging campaign against Persia, ordered by the spiritual successors of the Hellenic League of 480 BC, the Thebans again collaborated with the Persian archenemies. What could have happened in 479, what was risked by subsequent Theban actions, was decided and executed now, namely,

> to raze the city to the ground [κατασκάψαι] and to apportion its land among the allies, save the land that was consecrated [ὅση μὴ ἱερὰ αὐτῆς], and to enslave [ἀνδραποδίσαι] the women and children and any Theban survivors, save for the priests and priestesses, and any guest-friends of Philip or Alexander, or *proxenoi* of Macedonians. (Arr. *Anab.* 1.9.9)

Parke claims that the "'tithing' of Thebes was never brought about. . . . [Its] destruction by Alexander was a completely secular act. . . . [The] time for ritual destruction was past."[188] Quite to the contrary: κατασκαφή and ἀνδραποδισμός, two constitutive elements of a ritual city destruction, are attested in Thebes' case. Arrian's remark that "Alexander saved the poet Pindar's house and any of his descendants" (Arr. *Anab.* 1.9.10) indicates that each οἶκος was subject to κατασκαφή and literally razed to the ground. That Alexander did not dedicate the entire territory to the god by withdrawing it from agricultural use does not make it "a completely secular act." This concept, modeled on the destruction of

188. Parke (1948) 112–13.

Crisa, is not a static category but, rather, serves as a model for the punishment of a Greek city by a Greek alliance. Moreover, in contrast to the medizing *poleis* in 479 and Athens in 404, Thebes really was razed to the ground. To withdraw the entire land of Thebes, which constitutes part of the fertile Boeotian plain, completely from agricultural use would have been economic nonsense. Furthermore, there are enough clues in our sources to indicate that religious aspects played a major role in the execution of this punishment. Arrian says that only that portion of the land that was not ἱερά was distributed among Alexander's allies (Arr. *Anab.* 1.9.9). It is possible that this χώρα ἱερά merely denotes the existing sanctuaries in Thebes, but it is equally possible that it includes additional land that was set aside for the gods. Finally, Arrian describes the destruction of Thebes as a visitation of the gods for previous sins, which also points to a ritual punishment (Arr. *Anab.* 1.9.6–8).

Few would deny that the eradication of Thebes constituted a brutal act of terrorism intended by Alexander to cow other Greek *poleis* into submission. Polybius and Diodorus unequivocally state that the destruction corresponded to Alexander's wishes (Polyb. 38.2.13; Diod. 17.9.4, 14.4), and Plutarch's assessment seems right to the point when he says that

> this was done, mainly because Alexander expected the Greeks would be terrified by so great a disaster and cower down in quiet, but apart from this, he also used the facade [καλλωπισαμένου] of gratifying his allies' complaints; for the Phocians and Plataeans had accused the Thebans. (Plut. *Alex.* 11.11)[189]

Lane Fox concludes that "Alexander shrewdly entrusted the fate of the city to the decision of these allied Greek assistants. . . . They voted for Thebes' utter destruction, as he knew they would."[190] The Plataeans, Thespians, Orchomenians, and Phocians had not forgotten what the Thebans had done to them in the past; the misfortunes they had suffered at their hands constituted an essential part of their common identity and of their shared image of the past. Although regrettable, it should not surprise us that they took brutal revenge when they finally had the chance. Paradoxically, Alexander of Macedon, masterfully appropriating the memorial framework of fourth-century Greeks, furnished the ultimate proof of his Greekness by annihilating one of the leading cities in the Greek world.

189. Worthington (2003) and (2010) 242–45 makes the case that Thebes' destruction was due to Thebans' harboring of Amyntas, the son of Perdiccas III and a potential rival of Alexander; this was surely a further factor in Alexander's decision.

190. Lane Fox (2004) 88.

Conclusion

Twenty years ago, the history of classical Athenian institutions was dependent on the study of inscriptions and space. We were able then to discover, largely under the inspiration of Mogens Hansen, how many Athenians attended the *ecclesia* and how the law courts worked in relationship to the assembly. Thanks to the detailed work of generations of archaeologists, we learned to walk the streets that the ancient Athenians had walked. But, for all of this splendid technical work, we still lacked a sense of what it was to be an Athenian. We had come to a much better understanding of the institutions that shaped the life of an Athenian, but we lacked the very different tools needed to understand the collective consciousness that bound these Athenians together within their institutions.

Although scholars of cultures less remote to us than those of the ancient world have used social memory successfully, historians of ancient Greece have as yet made too little use of the concept. By drawing on an often misunderstood type of evidence—the historical allusions in the surviving speeches of the Attic orators—we can begin to comprehend how ancient Greeks thought about and used their past. In this book, I have tried to develop the suggestive work of the ancient historians Rosalind Thomas and Josiah Ober, along with many other scholars who have looked at issues of social memory and political discourse, in order to examine how fifth- and fourth-century Athenians understood their lives in the context of their history, how knowledge of the past was constituted and transmitted, how individual speakers made use of the past and operated within the complex Athenian memorial framework, and to what extent these shared images of the past influenced the decision-making process in the assembly, the law courts, and other democratic institutions.

I have sought to break down what had increasingly become a distinction between Greek orators, as representatives (often unreliable) of an "oral tradition," and historians (particularly Thucydides and Xenophon), who were almost viewed as guardians of a Rankean truth. I argue that historians and orators alike operated within the same memorial framework but represent different approaches to the collective consciousness of the Athenians. An orator belonged to a variety of different memory communities and participated in different ways of transmitting social memory. The orator's historical allusions, therefore, constituted an integral part of the negotiation and manifestation of a shared image of the past. By contextualizing the orators' allusions within the complex net of remembrances and beliefs held by their audience, I try to assess the ideological and emotive power of these shared memories, which I regard as crucial factors in political decision making and not as merely empty rhetorical phrases or propagandistic cover-ups for *Realpolitik.*

In the introduction, I set forth my methodological framework by giving an account of the contemporary study of social memory and by looking at how we can best apply it to our evidence. In chapter 1, I show that there were constraints on what orators could and would say that were imposed by the general historical consciousness of their audience. For this purpose, I explore thematically the different carriers of social memory available to the orators and their listeners. Athenians learned about their past through polis-wide public commemorations and festivals, as well as in the process of socialization as members of smaller subgroups with their own memorial traditions, such as families, sympotic groups, *demes,* and tribes. Contact to "guest-friends" could provide insight into the memorial repertoire of other Greek communities. Landmarks, monuments, and inscriptions, forming the Athenian *cadre matériel,* functioned as material reminders of crucial events, while assembly and law courts provided the venue for the orators' refreshing and reshaping of the past.

In chapters 2–5, I test the views developed in the introduction and in chapter 1 against the evidence for Athens' relations with its northern neighbor Thebes. From early on, Athenian-Theban interactions were very complex, providing both cities with a broad spectrum of experiences ranging from friendly feelings to utter hostility. Whenever Athenian-Theban relations were under discussion, participants in the debate drew on earlier experiences to explain their analysis of the current situation and their proposed solution to others. Consequently, knowing the role of Thebes in Athenian social memory helps us to better comprehend some of the policy choices the Athenians made in the fifth and fourth centuries.

Historical references to Thebes cluster around four particular events (each discussed in a separate chapter of this book): Thebes' medizing in 480 (chap. 2), the mythical story of the burial of the fallen Argives (chap. 3), Thebes' help for the Athenian democrats in 403 (chap. 4), and the Theban proposal to eradicate Athens in 404 (chap. 5). Social memory is a complex phenomenon. Consequently, it is not surprising that in each of these four cases, different carriers and aspects of social memory come to the fore. In chapter 2, I expose Thebes' role as Athens' counterimage in the Athenian master narrative. Chapter 3 explores how the hegemonic Athenian self-image shaped the collective memory of Athens' relationship to Thebes in the mythical past. In chapter 4, I trace the transmission of a positive yet quite precarious memory through the fourth century, while I focus on the traumatic aspect of a mere proposal and the concept of a ritual city destruction in chapter 5.

In chapter 2, I look at charges of Theban assistance for the Persians, who were seen as the common enemies of Greek freedom. Thanks to their hostile predisposition and their immediate experience with the Thebans at the battle of Plataea, the Athenians perceived the Thebans as staunch medizers from the outset and transformed this memory from "remembered" to "commemorated" history by various means. The Greek victory over Xerxes and his Greek collaborators was memorialized both in the victorious cities and at Panhellenic sanctuaries, through the dedication of spoils and victory monuments, through the tombs and trophies on the battlefield, and through commemorative festivals for the gods and heroes who aided the Greeks in the defense of their homeland.

The analysis of the Athenians' memorialization of their experience of the Persian Wars shows that the Athenians perceived the Thebans as their own counterimage: while the patriotic Athenians fought as champions of the Greeks for Greek liberty, the treacherous Thebans became servile supporters of the Persian invaders. Since Thebes' treason was bound up with the master narrative of Athens' glorious achievements during the Persian Wars, it is unsurprising that the memory of Thebes' medizing became the dominant feature in Athenian discourse about Thebes. Continuing enmity and numerous military encounters with the Thebans in the decades following the Persian Wars provided the Athenians with suitable occasions for the recollection of their respective allegiances and thus perpetuated the simplified memory of Thebes' outright medizing. Herodotus' account and fourth-century oratory show that, in Athens, the memory of early anti-Persian actions by the Thebans (i.e., their participation at Tempe and Thermopylae) was distorted and obliterated during this process.

In the fourth century, Athenian orators used Thebes' medism in two particular contexts: in the conflict between Thebes and Athens' loyal ally, Plataea; and in the face of potential "barbarian" invasions, especially as the power of the Macedonian king Philip II increased in the third quarter of the century. The continuous Plataean-Theban antagonism helped to preserve the memory of Theban medizing in Athenian collective consciousness, for whenever this conflict was under discussion in Athens, it prompted the antithesis of Plataean patriotism versus Theban medism, as seen in Thucydides' Plataean debate, Isocrates' *Plataicus,* and Apollodorus' *Against Neaera.* This stark antithesis could also lead speakers to ignore the merits of other Boeotians (the Thespians and Haliartans) during the Persian Wars. Similarly, both the symbolic importance of the Athenian victory at Marathon and the persistent Plataean-Theban antagonism led to the suppression of the Plataeans' participation at Marathon—they are praised instead for their efforts against Xerxes' invasion. Yet as we can see in *Against Neaera,* Apollodorus was able to activate the latent memory of their contribution at Marathon by pointing his audience to an alternative carrier of this memory, the Marathon painting in the Stoa Poikile.

A second cue for the memory of Thebes' medizing in 480–479 was the prospect of further barbarian invasions from the north. With Athens under threat by a Macedonian-Theban alliance in 342, Demosthenes used the memory of the Persian Wars as expressed in the Athenian funeral orations in order to rally his fellow citizens against Philip. Inherited associations made Philip a greedy barbarian, the Athenians champions of Greek liberty, and the Thebans traitors by nature. Yet, when necessary, Greek orators ventured to challenge this dominant version of the past. In *On the Symmories,* Demosthenes tried to dispel Athenian fears of a looming Persian invasion by claiming that both the Persian King and the Thebans had indeed learned their lesson from history and would never attack again. Some clues indicate that Demosthenes' fellow Athenians could indeed know about Theban attempts to justify or obliterate their former collaboration with the Persians. Yet Demosthenes' elaborate argument betrays the difficulty in presenting the Thebans as born-again Greek patriots in contradiction to the Athenian master narrative.

In the eyes of fifth- and fourth-century Athenians, Thebes' crimes did not begin with its support for the Persians, however, but reached far back into the mythical past, when the Thebans refused to grant burial to the fallen Argives who had marched against Thebes. For this reason, I examine in chapter 3 the constitutive elements of this mythical story and explore the reasons why—out of the enormous pool of Greek myths—this particular collective memory came to be one of the four paradigmatic myths celebrated in the Athenian master narrative of the funeral orations. During the archaic period, the epic story of Adrastus' flight from the battlefield and the discovery of Bronze Age tombs in Eleusis led to the establishment of a heroön for the Seven (excavated by Mylonas) and gave rise to a local Eleusinian myth explaining their burial. Similarly, elsewhere in Attica (Eleutherae, Phyle, Colonus Hippius) and Boeotia (Harma, Thebes, Oropus), local communities tried to "write" themselves into the story of the Seven by connecting local landmarks or cults to the world of these epic heroes (see fig. 1). Not only are these local myths and cults important for understanding the origins and the further developments of this Athenian myth; they also give us a sense of how local and polis-wide memories mutually influenced and sustained each other during the classical period. Pindar's assertion that the Seven were buried in Thebes (*Nem.* 9.22–24; *Ol.* 6.15–17) constitutes a forceful counterclaim in the Athenian-Theban memory war over the true version of this myth.

Theseus' association with the Eleusinian tradition of the burial of the Seven probably dates to the last decade of the sixth century and is best understood in the context of his emergence as the Athenian version of the great Greek culture hero Heracles: Theseus rivals Heracles as πρῶτος εὑρητής of σπονδαί. He buries the Seven in Eleusis, which is seen as an integral part of Attica after Cleisthenes' tribal reform. Theseus' aid for Adrastus, a helpless suppliant, reflects the Athenians' historical experience with the Plataeans who (in 519 BC) sought protection against the overbearing Thebans. Adrastus' supplication played an important role in Athenian ideology and imagination. To properly assess the emotive power of this mythical paradigm, one has to look beyond the brief accounts of this myth in the Athenian funeral orations and consider other carriers of this collective memory. The ritual act of Adrastus' supplication was nowhere more palpable than on the tragic stage, as Euripides' *Suppliants* and a reconstruction of Aeschylus' *Eleusinians* show. Judging from the attested titles of other playwrights and considering the clues for fourth-century reproductions of Aeschylus' and Euripides' plays at the City Dionysia and at local festivals, it is clear that the tragic stage was a powerful carrier of this collective memory in fourth-century Athens. Consequently, evocations of this mythical paradigm would have had a special resonance with those Athenians who had watched their ancestors' exemplary attitude toward suppliants unfold on stage.

Visual representations of this myth likewise focused on the supplication scene. A black-figure *lekythos* (Athens N.M. 18606) features three pairs of (probably Argive) men sitting on three altars with suppliant branches in their hands. A cup by the Codrus Painter (Basel Antikenmuseum, Inv. BS 432) shows Theseus and a suppliant woman from Argos. The Spina volute krater by the Painter of Bologna 279 (Spina Ferrara T 579 = ARV^2 i.612), which was most likely modeled on Onasias' monumental panel painting in the temple of Athena Areia at Plataea, depicts both the struggle of the Seven before the gates of Thebes (fig. 2) and the subsequent supplication of Theseus by Adrastus, who is accompanied by the souls of his fallen comrades and their children (fig. 3).

The experience of the Persian Wars led to the promotion of four selected myths that were seen as mythical prefigurations of Athens' role as champion (*prostates*) of the Greeks. This position involved the defense of Greek liberty against not only barbarian invaders but also other Greeks. While the repulsion of the invading Amazons and Eumolpus' Thracian hordes served as mythical analogues for the fight against the Persians, Athens' role as protector against Greek oppressors is nowhere more manifest than in the myths of the Athenian aid for the Heraclidae and the burial of the fallen Argives. Although the basic outline of this latter myth most likely existed already at the end of the sixth century, it (like the others) was probably considerably reshaped under the influence of Athens' new hegemonic ideology. Judging from a synchronic survey of the extant funeral orations and other patriotic genres, this myth came to embody many aspects of the hegemonic Athenian self-image: Athens' exemplary attitude toward suppliants, its unique sense of justice and altruism, its defense of the Greek *nomos,* and its military power.

Many of these traits could be expressed by other Athenian myths as well. There is one reason why this particular collective memory became one of the four emblematic myths of the Athenian master narrative: it was the city of Thebes, the anti-Athens, which committed this outrage against the dead, by denying them the customary burial. Since defeating and punishing the Persians for their desecration of Greek temples was seen as a sacred obligation, Thebes' medism had a religious dimension as well: it was a transgression against the gods and the Greek *nomos.* The bellicose version of this myth, which was promoted in the funeral orations, was ideally suited to serve as a mythical analogue for the Athenian victory over the medizing Thebans in the battle of Plataea. In both cases, the Thebans committed an act of *hybris* and received their just punishment on the battlefield from the hands of the Athenians. There is further evidence for this particular connection: the temple of Athena Areia at Plataea, which was erected as a memorial of this very battle, featured a monumental painting of the Seven against Thebes and of Theseus' supplication by Adrastus and the Epigoni.

Even though the catalogue of deeds in the *epitaphios* was conventional, the authors of the funeral orations had some leeway to add, elaborate, downplay, or omit certain elements of this collective memory, depending on present attitudes and concerns. While this myth could convey all the aforementioned interrelated layers of meaning, there were various events during the Pentecontaetia and the Peloponnesian War that brought individual aspects of this myth into the forefront of Athenian public discourse. The parallels between the historical situation of 458 (an Athenian army, supported by Argos, faced the Thebans in Boeotia) and the story of the Athenian intervention for the fallen Argives were so obvious that this myth must have had a special resonance with Athenians at that time. Even though the bellicose version itself probably already existed, it is likely that the anti-Theban elements of this myth were particularly emphasized in the funeral orations following the Athenian-Theban clashes during the early 450s. The Argives who fell at Tanagra received the unusual honor of a monumental tomb in the *demosion sema* in Athens (M&L 35; Paus. 1.29.8) and might have received a share of the praise in that year's *epitaphios.*[1]

The issue of ensuring a proper burial (whether by force or persuasion) was certainly an essential part of this myth from early on. But this aspect of the myth received yet another boost after the Theban refusal to release the bodies of the Athenians who had fallen at Delium in 424. In his *Suppliants,* Euripides not only criticized the Thebans for their refusal to release the bodies of the Seven but increased the anti-Theban aspects of this myth in every possible way. He wrote this play "in a deliberately patriotic gesture."[2] By emphasizing the crime of the Thebans in the mythical past, he obscured any memory of Athens' recent sacrilege, and Theseus' glorious victory helped the Athenians to forget their recent defeat at Delium.

This bitter experience affected the treatment of this myth not only on the tragic stage but also in the visual arts. It was displayed on the Nike temple, alongside an assembly of the gods and goddesses of the Ephebic Oath, the Gigantomachy and Amazonomachy, the battle of Marathon, and the pursuit and capture of Eurystheus during the battle for the Heraclidae. The west frieze showed the Athenians and Thebans fighting over the bodies of the fallen Argives (fig. 4). After the experience of Delium, the anti-Theban aspects of this myth clearly took center stage. From this time on, Thebes' hubristic refusal to release the bodies of the Seven and its just punishment by the Athenians was literally etched in stone. This frieze served as a permanent reminder of Thebes' *hybris* and defeat for generations to come and thus reinforced the bellicose version of the funeral orations.

This exploration of the particular elements, formative influences, and different carriers of this collective memory allows us to assess the political use of this mythical paradigm in four particular historical instances. Despite its anachronisms, Herodotus' account of the quarrel between the Athenians and the Tegeans over the privilege to hold the left wing of the Greek army in the battle of Plataea allows us to infer how the Athenians of Herodotus' own time would have argued in a similar diplomatic situation (Hdt. 9.27.3). Herodotus' Athenians make excellent use of this mythical paradigm by adapting it perfectly to the situation at hand. It is the Athenians' objective to convince the Spartans that they are most deserving of this position of honor in the upcoming battle against the Persians and Greek medizers. Drawing on the bellicose version of

1. Walters (1980) 12 with note 29.
2. Collard (1975) 1:10 note 32.

the funeral orations and alluding to Thebes' Phoenician founder Cadmus, the Athenians drive home the point that they have defeated the barbarian-born Thebans once before and will do so again.

This myth was also used by people from other *poleis* who addressed the Athenian assembly. In 373, after the second destruction of their city, the Plataeans fled to Athens and supplicated the Athenians. In Isocrates' *Plataicus,* which purports to be this very speech, the Plataeans draw heavily on Athens' self-image as champion of the weak against unjust oppression and use Athens' intervention on behalf of the fallen Argives as a mythical precedent for their own situation. Naturally, Athens' exemplary attitude toward suppliants stands in the center of this analogy (Isoc. 14.53–54).

After the battle of Leuctra, Procles of Phlius made similar use of this mythical paradigm on behalf of the Spartans, who were in dire need of Athenian support against the Theban invaders (Xen. *Hell.* 6.5.45–46). Just like Isocrates' Plataeans, Procles first invoked, in general terms, Athens' self-image as a place of refuge for those wronged, and then he introduced the burial of the fallen Argives as a specific example. Coming to the aid of suppliants against the hubristic Thebans functioned as a *tertium comparationis* in this analogy.

Isocrates' *Panathenaicus,* an encomium on Athens, which was completed after a three-year-long illness in 339, also employs this myth but features a diplomatic resolution (Isoc. 12.168–72). In a highly unusual authorial comment, Isocrates acknowledged the discrepancy between this version and the earlier treatment of this myth in his *Panegyricus* and justified it with an oblique reference to his political σωφροσύνη, that is, his political tact and prudence. Revising this passage in 339, Isocrates deliberately wanted to spare Thebes' honor lest he should appear to be sabotaging the nascent Athenian-Theban rapprochement.

Previous scholars have exploited Isocrates' confession to bolster their case that the Attic orators manipulated the past without limitations according to the maxims "Each speech has its own truth" and "The end justifies the means."[3] I contend, however, that certain limits existed. Since it was the speaker's objective to persuade his listeners, he had to take their knowledge and attitudes into account. His version of the past had to be plausible and could not flatly contradict what his audience knew about a certain event. Consequently, this passage provides a unique insight into the challenges an orator faced when diverging from the predominant master narrative. I argue that Isocrates employed various techniques to make his version acceptable to his audience.

By mentioning the tragic poets at the Dionysia and by employing specific

3. Nouhaud (1982) 18–19.

cues that point toward alternative sources for this myth, Isocrates reminded his audience of less familiar pacifist versions of this story, which are less offensive to contemporary Thebans. Moreover, by using the lengthy phrase "those who were then in charge at Thebes" (οἱ κύριοι τότ' ὄντες Θηβῶν) instead of simply saying "the Thebans" (Isoc. 12.171), he gave up the notion of unchanging national characters and dissociated contemporary Thebans from their culpable ancestors. Isocrates was not alone in showing this kind of consideration for the Thebans in those days. In his funeral oration for the fallen at Chaeronea, Demosthenes exculpated the majority of Thebans by shifting the blame for this crime onto King Creon alone (Dem. 60.8). In all other respects, however, Isocrates presented this paradigm in the familiar vein of the funeral orations to make sure that it would resonate with his Athenian audience: not Theseus but the Athenian demos decides about Adrastus' request. The Athenians are concerned about the divine law and the νόμος Ἑλληνικός, and this example is set forth as proof of Athens' military ἀρετή.

This analysis of the use of this mythical paradigm by Herodotus' Athenians, Isocrates' Plataeans, Procles of Phlius, and Isocrates in his *Panathenaicus* shows that certain aspects of this myth could be emphasized, downplayed, or omitted depending on the speaker's rhetorical requirements in particular historical situations. Yet there were clearly limits to what an orator could and would say. Isocrates, like Demosthenes in *On the Symmorics*, had to acknowledge how difficult it was to go against long-standing anti-Theban stereotypes.

In chapter 4, I turn to a more positive memory of interaction between Athens and Thebes: Thebes' support for Athens in the time of the tyranny of the Thirty, the extreme antidemocratic group imposed on Athens at the end of the Peloponnesian War. Since Athenian-Theban relations were ordinarily hostile throughout the fifth and fourth centuries, this memory was much more precarious, and its transmission over three generations down to Dinarchus' time seems puzzling. The facts of the case were reasonably straightforward. Thebans, disillusioned by Sparta's hegemonic policies and persuaded by appeals to the altruistic Theban self-image, resolved to oppose Sparta's command and provide shelter to the Athenian democrats, who had fled Athens. Apart from official political asylum, Thrasybulus and his followers received private support from Ismenias and other Thebans, who provided arms and further resources for the seizure of Phyle. This marked the crucial first step in the overthrow of the Thirty.

In Thebes, this event was seen as a manifestation of the Theban character in the tradition of the Theban culture heroes Heracles and Dionysus. It thus became an integral part of the Theban master narrative and was memorialized in the form of colossal statues of Athena and Heracles, dedicated in gratitude by

Thrasybulus and his fellow exiles. The well-known cooperation of Heracles and Athena (cf. fig. 5) thus stood in for the recent Theban-Athenian collaboration. To overcome the painful memories of the civil war, the Athenians commemorated the reestablishment of democracy as a victory of the exiled demos over the Thirty.[4] Even though the Athenian master narrative by and large celebrated the return of the demos as an Athenian achievement, there were enough cues to prompt the memory of the Theban contribution. In Athenian social memory, the seizure of Phyle marked the beginning of Thrasybulus' triumphant struggle. Consequently, the Athenians memorialized the initial group of exiles who seized this fort on the Theban-Athenian border through an honorary inscription set up in the Metroon (fig. 6; *SEG* 28.45 = Raubitschek (1941) 289). The monumental inscription granting citizenship to the *xenoi* aiding the exiles in Phyle (*IG* II^2 10 = R&O 4) and the new citizens themselves, distributed among the ten Athenian tribes, helped to preserve the precarious memory of the democrats' foreign (e.g., Theban) supporters. These monumental inscriptions were read by the Athenians, and their wording was shown to circulate in public discourse, shaping the memory of these events. The expression ἀπὸ Φυλῆς φεύγοντα τὸν δῆμον κατάγειν, used as graphic shorthand for the restoration of the Athenian democracy, could prompt the memory of Thebes' contribution, since Phyle was located on the Athenian-Boeotian border and on the road leading from Thebes to Athens. Phyle's function as mnemonic aid is apparent in Dinarchus' allusion: he uses Thrasybulus' seizure of Phyle to link the Theban decree to the time when the Athenian democracy was dissolved (Din. 1.25).

Nevertheless, transmission of the memory of Theban help was by no means guaranteed, since, for the most part, Thebes played a negative role in Athenian social memory. The Thebans were remembered as prototypical medizers (see chap. 2) and played a negative role in Athens' mythical past (see chap. 3). Their proposal to eradicate Athens in 405/4 left a deep mark on Athenian collective consciousness (see chap. 5). Yet the diplomatic practice of listing former benefactions when lobbying for support periodically refreshed the memory of Thebes' aid to Thrasybulus in Athens. The Theban ambassadors were the first to utilize this incident in their request for an alliance in 395. Their use of this historical precedent and their emphasis on Athens' role as champion of Greek liberty show that arguments from social memory were indeed important factors in inter*poleis* politics.

The expulsion of Athens' sympathizers from Thebes by a narrow pro-Spartan faction in 382 was a public affair in Athens, as both literary and epigraphic evi-

4. The memories of the complicity of the oligarchic-minded men in the city and the passivity of large sections of the demos were thereby conveniently suppressed. Cf. Wolpert (2002).

dence shows. The Athenians granted asylum to these Theban refugees and set up a stele on the Acropolis to record their status as privileged exiles (*IG* II^2 37; *SEG* 32.47). Moreover, the very similarity between the situations in Thebes in 382–379 and in Athens in 404/3 suggests, as our historiographical sources confirm, that the Theban exiles and their Athenian supporters employed the historical precedent of 404. Remembering this past benefaction, the Athenians provided the Theban refugees with a safe haven and private and public resources for their countercoup in 379. This stands as an important example of how memory could be transformed into action. The official Athenian aid in toppling the pro-Spartan regime was so successful that it became an integral part of the Athenian master narrative. Orators often referred to it. Xenophon, however, chose to suppress this Athenian contribution to Thebes' eventual hegemony. The memory of the Athenian restoration of the Theban exiles in 379/8 could thus indirectly serve as a further cue for the recollection of Thebes' aid for Thrasybulus in 404.

After thirty years of hostility, Demosthenes most likely exploited both examples of successful Athenian-Theban cooperation in order to forge an Athenian-Theban alliance against Philip. After his victory at Chaeronea, Philip imposed harsh terms on Thebes that included the expulsion of all anti-Macedonian politicians. Theban exiles once again found refuge in Athens, where they set out to repeat the heroic feat of their fathers by ousting the foreign-backed junta. Yet their failed revolt against the new king Alexander led to Thebes' total destruction. Some Thebans, however, managed to escape the slaughter and beseeched the Athenians to grant them asylum. Despite Alexander's prohibition, the Athenians provided a safe haven for the refugees, just as the Thebans had for the Athenian democrats in 404 in defiance of Sparta's orders. We can therefore conclude with some confidence that Dinarchus' reference in 323 to the Theban decree of 404 was quite familiar to his Athenian listeners. They had learned of it, just as Dinarchus insisted, both from their elders and from frequent quotations of this decree by different generations of Theban exiles and their Athenian guest-friends.

Memory was, however, an uneven model for action: as we see in chapter 5, Thebes' call for the destruction of Athens in 405/4 (prior to the change of heart that led to support of the exiled democrats) remained a powerful force in the discourse—in this case offering a justification for the ruin of Thebes by Alexander in 335. In 405/4, at the end of the Peloponnesian War, the Thebans proposed that Athens be destroyed. Owing to its monstrosity, this proposal, though not carried out, was remarkably persistent in Athenian historical consciousness. A reconstruction of the events between the battle of Aegospotami in September 405 and the peace conference in Sparta in March 404 shows that the Athenians' fear of utter destruction was justified, both in light of their own brutal treatment of other *poleis* and because a specific plan to destroy Athens was introduced and discussed among the Spartans and their vengeful allies in the course of the siege. Thus, for the besieged Athenians, the threat of extinction was real; and such a threat is sufficient to leave a deep mark in a society's collective historical consciousness, as the Morgenthau Plan, a similar case in contemporary German memory, suggests.

Yet the way in which this experience was described deserves further attention. Fourth-century Greeks (not just the Athenians) remembered the proposed annihilation of Athens in terms of the alleged ritual city destruction of Crisa in the First Sacred War at the beginning of the sixth century. This ritual destruction by the Delphic Amphictyons involved (1) enslavement (ἀνδραποδισμός), (2) city razing (κατασκαφή), and (3) dedicating the land to the god by withdrawing it from agricultural use (ἀναθεῖναι τὴν χώραν ἐπὶ πάσῃ ἀεργίᾳ, Aeschin. 3.108–9). In 373, Isocrates explicitly compared the planned treatment of Athens to the Κρισαῖον πεδίον, which he described as χώραν μηλόβοτον, a vivid visual conceptualization of the prohibition of cultivating the land (Isoc. 14.31). The elements appear in accounts of and references to the Theban proposal—in Ephorus or Theopompus (preserved in Plut. *Lys.* 15.2), Lycurgus (145; fr. III 2 Conomis), and Demosthenes (fr. XIII 2 Sauppe & Baiter). Lycurgus' and Demosthenes' metaphorical use of the phrase μηλόβοτον τὴν Ἀττικὴν ἀνεῖναι proves that Isocrates' association of Athens' fate with that of Crisa was not an exception but was commonplace by the middle of the fourth century. It has been argued that the story of Crisa's destruction was propaganda invented by Philip's sympathizers during the Third Sacred War and was only later associated with the planned eradication of Athens.[5] Yet Isocrates' reference and the wording of the earliest testimonies of the Theban proposal in Andocides and Xenophon suggests that Crisa was seen as a model in the actual debate in 405/4 and really did stand behind the Theban proposal.

Whether or not Crisa's destruction actually occurred, fifth-century Greeks believed it had. It held its place in Greek historical consciousness as the first, emblematic account of a ritual destruction of a Greek polis by a Greek alliance. The well-attested ritual destruction (κατασκαφή) of individual houses for offenses like treason or attempted tyranny could easily be transferred onto entire Greek *poleis*. Thebes and the other medizing cities were guilty of the former, Athens of the latter. Moreover, the razing of individual houses often involved dedicating a tithe to the god (δεκατεῦσαι). This, too, suggests that Herodotus' "tithing of the medizers" denoted the ritual city destruction of the treasonous *poleis* in accordance with the model of Crisa.

It is a general characteristic of memory that similar experiences reinforce

5. Robertson (1978).

previous memories. The Thebans did not forget their own near annihilation in 479 since city destructions (e.g., that of Plataea) and the political alignments in the Peloponnesian War served as powerful reminders. City razings during this war (e.g., of Melos) and on the tragic stage similarly reinforced Athenian social memory and imagination.

In the end, Athens was spared for a series of interlocking reasons, some of which lay beyond considerations of *Realpolitik*. Arguments from social memory were an important factor in the debate. Although minor Greek cities had been destroyed and enslaved before, to eradicate a city like Athens or Thebes was an abomination on a greater scale. This is evident from the reactions to the annihilation of Thebes by Alexander, which deprived Greece of the local setting of an essential part of its mythology. This shock left a deep mark on Greek historical consciousness, as is evident from contemporary and later testimonies. Athens' case would have been similar. Athens was saved—at least in part—because of its contributions to Greece.

The core of the memory that Athens was once threatened with total annihilation was persistent and could not be challenged. Yet with changing political circumstances and under the pressure of the present, details of the event were distorted. Present needs could lead to shifting emphasis, simplification, and distortion, best seen in the memory of those who proposed and opposed this terrible plan. During the Corinthian War, the Spartans and their supporters emphasized Sparta's merits in saving Athens and denounced Thebes and Corinth as the chief advocates of Athens' destruction. In the years of Thebes' supremacy (371–362 BC), Corinth's role was soon forgotten, and Thebes' became the sole proponent of the plan. The Third Sacred War (356–346 BC), in turn, made the Phocians' memory of their opposition to the Theban proposal relevant and provided them a strong argument in their efforts to lobby for Athenian support.

In 335, it was the city of Thebes, not Athens, that was wiped off the face of the earth by Alexander, in accordance with a decree passed by Alexander's Greek allies. The charges launched against Thebes included its collaboration with the Persians, its destruction of Plataea, and its proposal to eradicate Athens—events that occurred 145, 92, and 69 years earlier. Thebes' belated punishment shows that Alexander of Macedon masterfully appropriated the memorial framework of fourth-century Greeks and thus furnished, paradoxically, the ultimate proof of his Greekness by annihilating one of the leading cities in the Greek world.

We have seen that the orator, as a political actor in the assembly and the law courts, played a crucial role in the formation of Athenian historical consciousness. Since each Athenian participated simultaneously in different memory communities and was exposed to various sources of knowledge of the past, the orator could choose the historical paradigm that best suited his argument. Naturally, not all of these historical examples were equally familiar to an orator's audience, nor did they all bear the same emotional and argumentative weight. An orator was more likely to sway public opinion if he simply alluded to the lessons provided by the Athenian master narrative, since he could be sure to strike an emotional chord with his audience. But sometimes his analysis required a less familiar historical parallel. In this case, the orator had to argue his case in more detail. Yet the assembly and the law courts were not only the arena where orators utilized the past for the case at hand; they were themselves central venues for the manifestation, contestation, and transmission of a shared image of the past. Changing political alignments and unexpected events played a crucial role in this process, since they often provided the occasion for the orator to bring latent memories back into public discourse, thereby reinforcing them and securing their transmission to younger generations.

Memory is a dynamic force. By its very nature, it is inconsistent. Athens could use the precarious memory of Phyle to forgive Theban sins or could revert to the memory of 480 or 404 to incite hatred against these very same people. What remains consistent—and important—is the use of the past to shape the future. For that to be possible, the past had to remain malleable, and that very malleability was ensured by the constant discourse of historical memory in Greek culture.

Bibliography

Adams, Abigail, & Adams, John. 1975. *The Book of Abigail and John: Selected Letters of the Adams Family, 1762–1784*. Ed. L. H. Butterfield, M. Friedlaender, & M.-J. Kline. Cambridge, MA.

Adams, C. D., ed. and trans. 1919. *The Speeches of Aeschines*. London.

Adcock, F., & Mosley, D. J. 1975. *Diplomacy in Ancient Greece*. London.

Aélion, Rachel. 1983. *Euripide: Héritier d'Eschyle*. 2 vols. Paris.

Alcock, Susan E. 2002. *Archaeologies of the Greek Past: Landscape, Monuments, and Memories*. Cambridge.

Allan, William, ed. and trans. 2001. *Euripides: The Children of Heracles*. Warminster.

Allen, Danielle. 2000. "Changing the Authoritative Voice: Lycurgus' *Against Leocrates*." *ClAnt* 19:5–33.

Allroggen, Dieter. 1972. *Griechische Geschichte im Urteil der attischen Redner des vierten Jahrhunderts v. Chr.* Freiburg im Breisgau.

Aloni, Antonio. 2001. "The Proem of Simonides' Plataea Elegy and the Circumstances of Its Performance." In Boedeker & Sider (2001) 86–105.

Anderson, Benedict. 1991. *Imagined Communities: Reflections on the Origins and Spread of Nationalism*. Rev. ed. London.

Anderson, Greg. 2003. *The Athenian Experiment: Building an Imagined Political Community in Ancient Attica, 508–490 B.C.* Ann Arbor.

Anderson, O. 1990. Review of Rosalind Thomas, *Oral Tradition and Written Record in Classical Athens*. *Gnomon* 62:673–77.

Appadurai, Arjun. 1981. "The Past as a Scarce Resource." *Man* 16:201–19.

Apter, D. E. 2001. "Political Discourse." In Smelser & Baltes (2001) 11644–49.

Assmann, Aleida. 2001. "History and Memory." In Smelser & Baltes (2001) 6822–29.

Assmann, Jan. 1992. *Das kulturelle Gedächtnis: Schrift, Erinnerung und politische Identität in frühen Hochkulturen*. Munich.

Assmann, Jan. 1995. "Collective Memory and Cultural Identity." *New German Critique* 65:125–33. Originally published in German in Assmann & Hölscher (1988) 9–19.

Assmann, Jan. 1997. *Moses the Egyptian: The Memory of Egypt in Western Monotheism*. Cambridge.

Assmann, Jan, & Hölscher, Tonio, eds. 1988. *Kultur und Gedächtnis*. Frankfurt am Main.

Azaryahu, Maoz. 1993. "From Remains to Relics: Authentic Monuments in the Israeli Landscape." *History and Memory* 5:82–103.

Bach, Wolfgang. 1977. *Geschichte als politisches Argument.* Stuttgart.

Baddeley, Alan D. 1976. *The Psychology of Memory.* New York.

Baddeley, Alan D. 1989. "The Psychology of Remembering and Forgetting." In Butler (1989) 33–60.

Badian, Ernst. 1995. "The Ghost of Empire: Reflections on Athenian Foreign Policy in the Fourth Century BC." In Walter Eder, ed., *Die athenische Demokratie im 4. Jahrhundert v. Chr.: Vollendung oder Verfall einer Verfassungsform?*, 79–106. Stuttgart.

Barber, G. L. 1935. *The Historian Ephorus.* Cambridge.

Barron, J. P. 1980. "Theseus, Bacchylides, and a Woolly Cloak." *BICS* 27:1–8.

Barron, J. P. 1988. "The Liberation of Greece." In *CAH*[2] IV:592–622.

Bartlett, F. C. 1932. *Remembering.* Cambridge.

Bartoletti, Vittorio, ed. 1959. *Hellenica Oxyrhynchia.* Leipzig.

Beazley, J. D. 1971. *Paralipomena.* Oxford.

Bender, B. 1992. "Theorizing Landscape, and the Prehistoric Landscapes of Stonehenge." *Man* 27:735–55.

Benz, Wolfgang. 1990. "Morgenthau-Plan." In Wolfgang Benz, ed., *Legenden, Lügen, Vorurteile: Ein Lexikon zur Zeitgeschichte,* 145–47. Munich.

Berger, Ernst. 1968. "Zur Deutung einer neuen Schale des Kodrosmalers." *AK* 11:125–36.

Bernabé, A., ed. 1987. *Poetarum Epicorum Graecorum Testimonia et Fragmenta.* Leipzig.

Bethe, Erich. 1891. *Thebanische Heldenlieder: Untersuchungen über die Epen des Thebanisch-Argivischen Sagenkreises.* Leipzig.

Blass, Friedrich. 1874. *Die attische Beredsamkeit.* Vol. 2, *Isokrates und Isaios.* Leipzig.

Bleckmann, Bruno. 2006. *Fiktion als Geschichte: Neue Studien zum Autor der Hellenika Oxyrhynchia und zur Historiographie des vierten vorchristlichen Jahrhunderts.* Göttingen.

Blight, David W. 2001. *Race and Reunion: The Civil War in American Memory.* Cambridge.

Blight, David W. 2002. *Beyond the Battlefield: Race, Memory, and the American Civil War.* Amherst, MA.

Boardman, John. 1975. "Herakles, Peisistratos, and Eleusis." *JHS* 95:1–12.

Boardman, John. 1982. "Herakles, Theseus, and Amazons." In D. Kurtz & B. Sparkes, eds., *The Eye of Greece: Studies in the Art of Greece,* 1–28. Cambridge.

Boardman, John. 1985. *Greek Sculpture: The Classical Period; A Handbook.* London.

Boedeker, Deborah. 1993. "Hero Cult and Politics in Herodotus: The Bones of Orestes." In C. Dougherty & L. Kurke, eds., *Cultural Poetics in Archaic Greece: Cult, Performance, Politics,* 164–77. New York.

Boedeker, Deborah. 1998. "Presenting the Past in Fifth-Century Athens." In Boedeker & Raaflaub (1998) 185–202.

Boedeker, Deborah. 2001. "Paths to Heroization at Plataea." In Boedeker & Sider (2001) 148–63.

Boedeker, Deborah, & Raaflaub, Kurt, eds. 1998. *Democracy, Empire, and the Arts in Fifth-Century Athens.* Cambridge, MA.

Boedeker, Deborah, & Sider, David, eds. 2001. *The New Simonides: Contexts of Praise and Desire.* Oxford.

Boehringer, David. 2001. *Heroenkulte in Griechenland von der geometrischen bis zur klassischen Zeit: Attika, Argolis, Messenien*. Berlin.

Bömer, Franz. 1961. *Untersuchungen über die Religion der Sklaven in Griechenland und Rom*. Part 3, *Die wichtigsten Kulte der griechischen Welt*. Wiesbaden.

Bommelaer, J.-F. 1991. *Guide de Delphes: Le site*. Paris.

Bosworth, A. B. 1980. *A Historical Commentary on Arrian's "History of Alexander."* Oxford.

Bosworth, A. B. 1988. *Conquest and Empire: The Reign of Alexander the Great*. Cambridge.

Bourdieu, P. 1991. *Language and Symbolic Power*. Trans. Raymond G. Adamson. Cambridge.

Bowie, Angus M. 1997. "Tragic Filters for History: Euripides' *Supplices* and Sophocles's *Philoctetes*." In C. B. R. Pelling, ed., *Greek Tragedy and the Historian*, 39–62. Oxford.

Bowie, Ewen L. 1986. "Early Greek Elegy, Symposium, and Public Festival." *JHS* 106:13–35.

Bowie, Ewen L. 1990 "*Miles Ludens*? The Problem of Martial Exhortation in Early Greek Elegy." In O. Murray (1990a) 221–29.

Braswell, Bruce Karl, ed. and trans. 1998. *A Commentary on Pindar Nemean Nine*. Berlin.

Bremmer, Jan, ed. 1987a. *Interpretations of Greek Mythology*. London.

Bremmer, Jan. 1987b. "What Is a Greek Myth." In Bremmer (1987a) 1–9.

Bremmer, Jan. 1990. "Adolescents, *Symposion*, and Pederasty." In O. Murray (1990a) 135–48.

Bremmer, Jan. 1997. "Myth as Propaganda: Athens and Sparta." *ZPE* 117:9–17.

Bremmer, Jan. 2006. "The Rise of the Hero Cult and the New Simonides." *ZPE* 158:15–26.

Brommer, Frank. 1982. *Theseus: Die Taten des griechischen Helden in der antiken Kunst und Literatur*. Darmstadt.

Brownson, C. L., ed. and trans. 1918. *Xenophon, "Hellenica" I–V*. London.

Bruce, I. A. F. 1963. "Athenian Foreign Policy in 395–396 B.C." *CJ* 58:289–95.

Bruce, I. A. F. 1967. *An Historical Commentary on the "Hellenica Oxyrhynchia."* Cambridge.

Bruit Zaidman, Louise, & Schmitt Pantel, Pauline. 1992. *Religion in the Ancient Greek City*. Trans. Paul Cartledge. Cambridge. Originally published in French in 1989.

Brundage, W. Fitzhugh. 2000. "Introduction: No Deed but Memory." In W. F. Brundage, ed., *Where These Memories Grow: History, Memory, and Southern Identity*, 1–28. Chapel Hill.

Brunt, P. A., ed. and trans. 1976. *Arrian: "History of Alexander" and "Indica" I*. Cambridge, MA.

Buchner, Edmund. 1958. *Der Panegyrikos des Isokrates: Eine historisch-philologische Untersuchung*. Wiesbaden.

Buck, Robert J. 1992. "The Athenians at Thebes in 379/8 B.C." *AHB* 6:103–9.

Buck, Robert J. 1979. *A History of Boeotia*. Edmonton.

Buck, Robert J. 1994. *Boiotia and the Boiotian League, 432–371 B.C.* Edmonton.

Buck, Robert J. 1998. *Thrasybulus and the Athenian Democracy: The Life of an Athenian Statesman*. Stuttgart.

Buckler, John. 1980. *The Theban Hegemony, 371–362 BC*. Cambridge, MA.

Buckler, John. 1982. "Xenophon's Speeches and the Theban Hegemony." *Athenaeum*, n.s., 60:180–204.

Buckler, John. 2003. *Aegean Greece in the Fourth Century BC.* Leiden.

Buckler, John, & Beck, Hans. 2008. *Central Greece and the Politics of Power in the Fourth Century BC.* Cambridge.

Burckhardt, L. A. 1996. *Bürger und Soldaten: Aspekte der politischen und miltärischen Rolle athenischer Bürger im Kriegswesen des 4. Jahrhunderts v. Chr.* Stuttgart.

Burke, P. 1989. "History as Social Memory." In Butler (1989) 97–113.

Burkert, Walter. 1985. *Greek Religion: Archaic and Classical.* Trans. J. Raffan. Oxford. Originally published in German in 1977.

Burn, A. R. 1962. *Persia and the Greeks: The Defense of the West, c. 546–478 B.C.* London.

Burtt, J. O., ed. and trans. 1954. *Minor Attic Orators.* Vol. 2. London.

Butler, T., ed. 1989. *Memory: History, Culture, and the Mind.* Oxford.

Calame, Claude. 1990. *Thésée et l'imaginaire athénien: Légende et culte en Grèce antique.* Lausanne.

Calhoun, C. 2001. "Public Sphere: Nineteenth- and Twentieth-Century History." In Smelser & Baltes (2001) 12594–99.

Calhoun, G. M. 1913. *Athenian Clubs in Politics and Litigation.* Austin.

Camp, John M. 1992. *The Athenian Agora: Excavations in the Heart of Classical Athens.* New York.

Carey, Christopher, ed. and trans. 1992. *Apollodoros, "Against Neaira": [Demosthenes] 59.* Warminster.

Carey, Christopher, ed. 2007. *Lysiae orationis cum fragmentis.* Oxford.

Cargill, J. 1981. *The Second Athenian League.* Berkeley.

Cartledge, Paul. 1987. *Agesilaos and the Crisis of Sparta.* London.

Caruth, C. 1996. *Unclaimed Experience: Trauma, Narrative and History.* Baltimore, MD.

Castriota, David. 1992. *Myth, Ethos, and Actuality: Official Art in Fifth-Century B.C. Athens.* Madison, WI.

Cawkwell, George L. 1973. "The Foundation of the Second Athenian Confederacy." *CQ* 67:47–60.

Cawkwell, George L. 1978. *Philip of Macedon.* London.

Cawkwell, George L., ed. 1979. *Xenophon: "A History of My Times."* Trans. Rex Warner. London 1979.

Chaffee, S. 2001. "Mass Communication: Empirical Research." In Smelser & Baltes (2001) 9321–28.

Chambers, Mortimer, ed. 1993. *Hellenica Oxyrhynchia.* Stuttgart.

Chantry, M., ed. 1994. *Scholia in Aristophanem.* Part 3, *Scholia in Thesmophoriazusas; Ranas; Ecclesiazusas et Plutum.* No. 4a, *Scholia. Vetera in Aristophanis Plutum.* Groningen.

Christ, Matthew R. 2001. "Conscription of Hoplites in Classical Athens." *CQ* 51:398–422.

Clairmont, Christoph W. 1983. *Patrios Nomos: Public Burial in Athens during the Fifth and Fourth Centuries B.C.: The Archaeological, Epigraphic-Literary, and Historical Evidence.* Part 1. Oxford.

Clark, Anna J. 2007. *Divine Qualities: Cult and Community in Republican Rome.* Oxford.

Clarke, Katherine. 2008. *Making Time for the Past: Local History and the Polis.* Oxford.

Cloché, P. 1918. "La politique thébaine de 404 à 396 av. J.-C." *REG* 31:315–43.

Coldstream, J. N. 1976. "Hero-Cults in the Age of Homer." *JHS* 96:8–17.

Coldstream, J. N. 1977. *Geometric Greece.* London.

Collard, Christopher, ed. 1975. *Euripides: "Supplices."* 2 vols. Groningen.

Connerton, Paul. 1989. *How Societies Remember.* Cambridge.
Connor, W. R. 1985. "The Razing of the House in Greek Society." *TAPA* 115:79–102.
Conomis, Nicos C., ed. 1970. *Lycurgi oratio in Leocratem. Cum ceterarum Lycurgi orationum fragmentis.* Leipzig.
Conomis, Nicos C., ed. 1975. *Dinarchi orationes cum fragmentis.* Leipzig.
Cook, Margaret. 1988. "Ancient Political Factions: Boiotia 404 to 395." *TAPA* 118:57–85.
Currie, Bruno. 2005. *Pindar and the Cult of Heroes.* Oxford.
Dalfen, Joachim. 1976. "Xenophon als Analytiker und Kritiker politischer Rede (Zu Hell. VI.3.4–17, VI.5.33–48)." *GB* 5:59–84.
Dasen, Veronique, & Späth, Thomas, eds. 2010. *Children, Memory, and Family Identity in Roman Culture.* Oxford.
Davidson, J. 2006. "Revolutions in Human Time: Age-Class in Athens and the Greekness of Greek Revolutions." In S. Goldhill & R. Osborne, eds., *Rethinking Revolutions through Ancient Greece,* 29–67. Cambridge.
Davies, John Kenyon. 1993. *Democracy and Classical Greece.* 2nd ed. Cambridge, MA.
Davies, John Kenyon. 1994. "The Tradition about the First Sacred War." In S. Hornblower, ed., *Greek Historiography,* 193–212. Oxford.
Davies, Malcolm, ed. 1988. *Epicorum Graecorum Fragmenta.* Göttigen.
Davies, Malcolm. 1989. *The Greek Epic Cycle.* Bristol.
Demand, Nancy H. 1982. *Thebes in the Fifth Century: Heracles Resurgent.* London.
de Romilly, Jacqueline. 1963. *Thucydides and Athenian Imperialism,* Trans. P. Thody. Oxford.
Deubner, Ludwig. 1932. *Attische Feste.* Berlin.
Develin, Bob. 1993. "The Battle of Oinoe Meets Ockham's Razor?" *ZPE* 99:235–40.
deVoto, J. 1989. "The Liberation of Thebes in 379/8 B.C." In R. Sutton, ed., *Daidalikon. Studies in Memory of R.V. Schoder S.J.,* 101–16. Wauconda, IL.
Dillery, John. 1995. *Xenophon and the History of His Times.* London.
Dilts, Mervin R., ed. 1983–86. *Scholia Demosthenica.* 2 vols. Stuttgart.
Dilts, Mervin R., ed. 1992. *Scholia in Aeschinem.* Stuttgart.
Dilts, Mervin R., ed. 1997. *Orationes Aeschinis.* Stuttgart.
Dilts, Mervin R., ed. 2005. *Demosthenis orationes.* Vol. 2. Oxford.
Dover, Kenneth J., ed. 1968. *Aristophanes: "Clouds."* Oxford.
Dower, John W. 2010. *Cultures of War: Pearl Harbor / Hiroshima / 9–11 / Iraq.* London.
Eber, Dena E., & Neil, Arthur G. 2001. "Memory, Constructed Reality, and Artistic Truth." In D. E. Eber & A. G. Neil, eds., *Memory and Representation: Constructed Truths and Competing Realities,* 3–18. Bowling Green, OH.
Echterhoff, Gerald. 2008. "Language and Memory: Social and Cognitive Processes." In Erll & Nünning (2008) 263–74.
Ellis, John R. 1976. *Philip II and Macedonian Imperialism.* London.
Ellis, John R. 1994. "Macedonian Hegemony Created." In *CAH*[2] VI:760–90.
Engels, J. 1993. "Der Michigan-Papyrus über Theramenes und die Ausbildung des 'Theramenes-Mythos.'" *ZPE* 99:125–55.
Erll, Astrid. 2008. "Cultural Memory Studies: An Introduction." In Erll & Nünning (2008) 1–18.
Erll, Astrid, & Nünning, Ansgar, eds. 2008. *Cultural Memory Studies: An International and Interdisciplinary Handbook.* Berlin.
Erp, Scott. 2003. *German Foreign Policy: Navigating a New Era.* London.

Erp Taalman Kip, A. M. van. 1987. "Euripides and Melos." *Mnemosyne* 40:414–19.
Étienne, R., & Piérart, M. 1975. "Un décret du Koinon des Hellènes à Platées en l'honneur de Glaucon, fils d'Étéoclès, d'Athènes." *BCH* 99:51–75.
Fabbro, Helena, ed. 1995. *Carmina Convivalia Attica.* Rome.
Farnell, L. 1921. *Greek Hero Cults and Ideas of Immortality.* Oxford.
Felten, F. 1984. *Griechische tektonische Friese archaischer und klassischer Zeit.* Waldsassen.
Fentress, James, & Wickham, Chris. 1992. *Social Memory.* Oxford.
Finley, Moses. 1982. *Authority and Legitimacy in the Classical City-State.* Copenhagen.
Finnegan, R. 1977. *Oral Poetry: Its Nature, Significance, and Social Content.* Cambridge.
Fisher, Nick. 2000. "Symposiasts, Fish-Eaters, and Flatterers: Social Mobility and Moral Concerns in Old Comedy." In D. Harvey & J. Wilkins, eds., *The Rivals of Aristophanes: Studies in Athenian Old Comedy,* 355–96. London.
Flower, Harriet I. 2006. *The Art of Forgetting: Disgrace and Oblivion in Roman Political Culture.* Chapel Hill.
Flower, Michael A. 1994. *Theopompus of Chios: History and Rhetoric in the Fourth Century B.C.* Oxford.
Flower, Michael A., 1998. "Simonides, Ephorus, and Herodotus on the Battle of Thermopylae." *CQ* 48:365–79.
Flower, Michael A. 2008. *The Seer in Ancient Greece.* Berkeley.
Flower, Michael A., & Marincola, John, eds. 2002. *Herodotus: "Histories," Book 9.* Cambridge.
Forsdyke, Sara. 1999. "From Aristocratic to Democratic Ideology and Back Again: The Thrasybulus Anecdote in Herodotus' *Histories* and Aristotle's *Politics.*" *CP* 94:361–72.
Forsdyke, Sara. 2001. "Athenian Democratic Ideology and Herodotus' *Histories.*" *AJP* 122:329–58.
Forsdyke, Sara. 2005. *Exile, Ostracism, and Democracy: The Politics of Expulsion in Ancient Greece.* Princeton.
Forsdyke, Sara. 2011. "Peer-Polity Interaction and Cultural Competition in Sixth Century Greece." In Nick Fisher & Hans van Wees, eds., *Competition in the Ancient World,* 147–74. Swansea.
Fortes, M., & Evans-Pritchard, E. E. 1940. "Introduction." In M. Fortes & E. E. Evans-Pritchard, eds., *African Political Systems,* 1–23. London.
Foxhall, Lin, Gehrke, Hans-Joachim, & Luraghi, Nino, eds. 2010. *Intentional History: Spinning Time in Ancient Greece.* Stuttgart.
Francis, E. D., & Vickers, M. 1985. "The Oenoe Painting in the Stoa Poikile, and Herodotus' Account of Marathon." *ABSA* 80:99–113.
Frazer, J. G., ed. and trans. 1965. *Pausanias's Description of Greece.* 6 vols. New York.
Friedlander, Saul. 1991. *When Memory Comes.* New York.
Friedlander, Saul. 1992. "Trauma, Transference, and 'Working Through' in Writing the History of the Shoah." *History and Memory* 4:39–59.
Friedlander, Saul 1993. *Memory, History, and the Extermination of the Jews of Europe.* Bloomington, IN.
Frost, F. J. 1961. "Some Documents in Plutarch's Lives." *C&M* 22:182–94.
Funkenstein, Amos. 1993. *Perceptions of Jewish History.* Los Angeles.
Gaca, Kathy L. 2010. "The Andrapodizing of War Captives in Greek Historical Memory." *TAPA* 140:117–61.
Gantz, Timothy. 1980. "The Aischylean Tetralogy: Attested and Conjectured Groups." *AJP* 101:133–64.

Gauer, Werner. 1968. *Weihgeschenke aus den Perserkriegen*. Tübingen.

Gawantka, Wilfried. 1975. *Isopolitie: Ein Beitrag zur Geschichte der zwischenstaatlichen Beziehungen in der griechischen Antike*. Munich.

Geertz, C. 1985. "Centers, Kings, and Charisma: Reflections on the Symbolics of Power." In S. Wilentz, ed., *Rites of Power: Symbolism, Ritual, and Politics Since the Middle Ages*, 13–38. Philadelphia.

Gehrke, Hans-Joachim. 1985. *Stasis: Untersuchungen zu den inneren Kriegen in den griechischen Staaten des 5. und 4. Jahrhunderts v. Chr.* Munich.

Gehrke, Hans-Joachim. 1994. "Mythos, Geschichte, Politik—antik und modern." *Saeculum* 45:239–64.

Gehrke, Hans-Joachim. 1997. "Ephebeia." In H. Cancik & H. Schneider, eds., *Der Neue Pauly: Enzyklopädie der Antike*, 3:1071–75. Stuttgart.

Gehrke, Hans-Joachim. 2001. "Mythos, History, and Collective Identity: Uses of the Past in Ancient Greece and Beyond." In Luraghi (2001) 286–313.

Gehrke, Hans-Joachim. 2003. "Marathon als Mythos: Von Helden und Barbaren." In G. Krumeich & S. Brandt, eds., *Schlachtenmythen. Ereignis—Erzählung—Erinnerung*, 19–32. Cologne.

Georgiadou, Aristoula. 1997. *Plutarch's "Pelopidas": A Historical and Philological Commentary*. Stuttgart.

Gerber, Douglas E., ed. 1997a. *A Companion to the Greek Lyric Poets*. Leiden.

Gerber, Douglas E. 1997b. "General Introduction." In Gerber (1997a) 1–10.

Gerber, Douglas E., ed. and trans. 1999. *Greek Elegiac Poetry: From the Seventh to the Fifth Centuries BC*. Cambridge, MA.

Goldhill, Simon. 1990. "The Great Dionysia and Civic Ideology." In Winkler & Zeitlin (1990) 97–129.

Goldhill, Simon. 2000. "Civic Ideology and the Problem of Difference: The Politics of Aeschylean Tragedy, Once Again." *JHS* 120:34–56.

Gombrich, E. H. 1972. *Art and Illusion: A Study in the Psychology of Pictorial Representation*. 4th ed. London.

Gomme, A. W. 1956. *A Historical Commentary on Thucydides*. Vol. 2, *Books II–III*. Oxford.

Goody, J., & Watt, I. 1963. "The Consequences of Literacy." *Comparative Studies in Society and History* 5:304–45.

Gotteland, Sophie. 2001. *Mythe et rhétorique: Les exemples mythiques dans le discours politique de l'Athènes classique*. Paris.

Gottesman, Alex. 2006. *A Branch on the Altar: Supplication and Symbolic Capital in Ancient Greece*. PhD diss., University of Chicago.

Gould, John. 1973. "HIKETEIA." *JHS* 93:74–103.

Gould, John. 2001. *Myth, Ritual Memory, and Exchange: Essays in Greek Literature and Culture*. Oxford.

Gowing, A. M. 2005. *Empire and Memory: The Representation of the Roman Republic in Imperial Culture*. Cambridge.

Graf, David Frank. 1979. *Medism: Greek Collaboration with Achaemenid Persia*. PhD diss., University of Michigan.

Gray, Vivienne. 1989. *The Character of Xenophon's "Hellenica."* London.

Gray, Vivienne. 1994a. "Images of Sparta: Writer and Audience in Isocrates' *Panathenaicus*." In Anton Powell & Stephen Hodkinson, eds., *The Shadow of Sparta*, 223–71. London.

Gray, Vivienne. 1994b. "Isocrates' Manipulation of Myth and the Image of Athens, *Panegyricus* 54ff., *Panathenaicus* 168 ff." In V. Gray, ed., *Nile, Ilissos, and Tiber: Essays in Honor of W. K. Lacey*, 83–104. Auckland.

Green, Peter. 1996. *The Greco-Persian Wars*. Berkeley.

Greiner, Bernd. 1995. *Die Morgenthau-Legende: Zur Geschichte eines umstrittenen Plans*. Hamburg.

Grethlein, Jonas. 2003. *Asyl und Athen: Die Konstruktion kollektiver Identität in der griechischen Tragödie*. Stuttgart.

Grethlein, Jonas. 2007. "The Hermeneutics and Poetics of Memory in Aeschylus's *Persae*." *Arethusa* 40:363–96.

Grethlein, Jonas. 2010. *The Greeks and Their Past: Poetry, Oratory, and History in the Fifth Century BCE*. Cambridge.

Grimaldi, William M. A. 1988. *Aristotle, "Rhetoric" II: A Commentary*. New York.

Haake, Matthias, & Jung, Michael, eds. 2011. *Griechische Heiligtümer als Erinnerungsorte: Von der Archaik bis in den Hellenismus*. Stuttgart.

Habicht, Christian. 1961. "Falsche Urkunden zur Geschichte Athens im Zeitalter der Perserkriege." *Hermes* 89:1–35.

Hack, H. M. 1978. *The Rise of Thebes. A Study of Theban Politics*. PhD diss., Yale University.

Hägg, R., ed. 1999. *Ancient Greek Hero Cult: Proceedings of the Fifth International Seminar on Ancient Greek Cult, 21–23 April 1995*. Stockholm.

Halbwachs, Maurice. 1925. *Les cadres sociaux de la mémoire*. Paris.

Halbwachs, Maurice. 1941. *La topographie légendaire des évangiles en terre sainte: Étude de mémoire collective*. Paris.

Halbwachs, Maurice. 1980. *The Collective Memory*. Trans. F. J. Ditter and V. Y. Ditter. New York. Originally published in French in 1950.

Hall, Jonathan M. 1999. "Beyond the Polis: The Multilocality of Heroes." In Hägg (1999) 49–59.

Hall, Jonathan M. 2007. *A History of the Archaic Greek World, ca. 1200–479 BCE*. Malden, MA.

Hamilakis, Y. 1998. "Eating the Dead: Mortuary Feasting and the Politics of Memory in the Aegean Bronze Age Societies." In K. Branigan, ed., *Cemetery and Society in the Aegean Bronze Age*, 115–32. Sheffield.

Hamilton, Charles D. 1979. *Sparta's Bitter Victories: Politics and Diplomacy in the Corinthian War*. Ithaca, NY.

Hamilton, Charles D. 1997. "Thucyides on the End of the Peloponnesian War." In Charles D. Hamilton & Peter Krentz, eds., *Polis and Polemos: Essays on Politics, War, and History in Ancient Greece, in Honor of Donald Kagan*, 193–229. Claremont.

Hammond, N. G. L. 1968. "The Campaign and the Battle of Marathon." *JHS* 88:13–57.

Hammond, N. G. L. 1988. "The Expedition of Xerxes." In *CAH*^{2} IV:518–91.

Hammond, N. G. L. 1992. "Plataea's Relations with Thebes, Sparta, and Athens." *JHS* 112:143–50.

Hammond, N. G. L., & Moon, Warren G. 1978. "Illustrations of Early Tragedy at Athens." *AJA* 82:371–83.

Hansen, Mogens Herman. 1991. *The Athenian Democracy in the Age of Demosthenes: Structure, Principles, and Ideology*. Trans. J. A. Crock. Oxford.

Hansen, Mogens Herman. 1993. "The Battle Exhortation in Ancient Historiography: Fact or Fiction?" *Historia* 42:161–80.

Hanson, V. D. 1989. *The Western Way of War: Infantry Battle in Classical Greece*. New York.

Harding, Phillip. 1987. "Rhetoric and Politics in Fourth-Century Athens." *Phoenix* 41:25–39.

Harding, Phillip. 1994. *Androtion and the Atthis: The Fragments Translated with Introduction and Commentary*. Oxford.

Harding, Phillip, ed. and trans. 2008. *The Story of Athens: The Fragments of the Local Chronicles of Attika*. London.

Harris, Edward Monroe. 1995. *Aeschines and Athenian Politics*. New York.

Harris, Edward Monroe. 2000. "The Authenticity of Andokides' *De Pace*: A Subversive Essay." In P. Flensted-Jensen, T. Heine Nielsen, & L. Rubinstein. eds., *Polis & Politics: Studies in Ancient Greek History*, 479–505. Copenhagen.

Harrison, E. B. 1972. "The South Frieze of the Nike Temple and the Marathon Painting in the Painted Stoa." *AJA* 76:353–78.

Harrison, E. B. 1997. "The Glories of the Athenians: Observations on the Program of the Frieze of the Temple of Athena Nike." In Diana Buitron-Oliver, ed., *The Interpretation of Architectural Sculpture in Greece and Rome*, 109–25. Washington, DC.

Harrison, S. 1995."Four Types of Symbolic Conflict." *Journal of the Royal Anthropological Institute, n.s.*, 1:255–72.

Hauvette, A. 1898. "Les 'Éleusiniens' d'Eschyle et l'institution du discours funèbre à Athènes." In *Mélanges Henri Weil*, 159–78. Paris.

Havelock, E. A. 1963. *Preface to Plato*. Oxford.

Head, B. V. 1881. *On the Chronological Sequence of the Coins of Boeotia*. London.

Henige, D. P. 1974. *The Chronology of Oral Tradition: Quest for a Chimera*. Oxford.

Hennig, Dieter. 1992. "Herodot 6, 108: Athen und Plataiai." *Chiron* 22:13–24.

Herman, Gabriel. 1987. *Ritualized Friendship and the Greek City*. Cambridge.

Herrman, Judson. 2008. "The Authenticity of the Demosthenic *Funeral Oration*." *AAntHung* 48:171–78.

Herter, Hans. 1939. "Theseus der Athener." *RhM* 88:244–86, 289–326.

Herter, Hans. 1973. "Theseus." *RE* Supp. 13:1045–1238.

Higbie, Carolyn. 1997. "The Bones of a Hero, the Ashes of a Politician: Athens, Salamis, and the Usable Past." *ClAnt* 16:278–307.

Hignett, Charles. 1963. *Xerxes' Invasion of Greece*. Oxford.

Hobsbawm, Eric J., & Ranger, Terence O., eds.. 1983. *The Invention of Tradition*. Cambridge.

Hölscher, Tonio. 1973. *Griechische Historienbilder des 5. und 4. Jahrhunderts v. Chr.* Würzburg.

Hölscher, Tonio. 1998. "Images and Political Identity: The Case of Athens." In Boedeker & Raaflaub (1998) 153–84.

Hopper, Robert John. 1971. *The Acropolis*. London.

Hornblower, Simon. 1991. *A Commentary on Thucydides*. Vol. 1, *Books I–III*. Oxford.

Hornblower, Simon. 1996. *A Commentary on Thucydides*. Vol. 2, *Books IV–V.24*. Oxford.

Horwitz, Tony. 1998. *Confederates in the Attic: Dispatches from the Unfinished Civil War*. New York.

How, W. W., & Wells, J. 1923. *A Commentary on Herodotus*. 2 vols. Rev. ed. Oxford.

Howe, Timothy Richard. 2003. "Pastoralism, the Delphic Amphiktyony, and the First Sacred War." *Historia* 52:129–46.

Hubbard, Thomas K. 1992. "Remaking Myth and Rewriting History: Cult Tradition in Pindar's Ninth Nemean." *HSCP* 94:77–111.

Hunt, Peter. 1998. *Slaves, Warfare, and Ideology in the Greek Historians*. Cambridge.

Hunt, Peter. 2010. *War, Peace, and Alliance in Demosthenes' Athens*. Cambridge.

Hurwit, Jeffrey M. 2004. *The Acropolis in the Age of Pericles*. Cambridge.

Hutchinson, G. O. 2001. *Greek Lyric Poetry: A Commentary on Selected Larger Pieces*. Oxford.

Huxley, George Leonard. 1969. *Greek Epic Poetry from Eumelos to Panyassis*. Cambridge, MA.

Huyssen, A. 1995. *Twilight Memories*. London.

Jackson, A. H. 1991. "Hoplites and the Gods: The Dedication of Captured Arms and Armour." In Victor Davis Hanson, ed., *Hoplites: The Classical Greek Battle Experience*, 228–49. London.

Jacoby, Felix. 1944. "*Patrios Nomos*: State Burial in Athens and the Public Cemetery in the Kerameikos." *JHS* 64:37–66.

Jacoby, Felix. 1949. *Atthis: The Local Chronicles of Ancient Athens*. Oxford.

Jaeger, Werner. 1938. *Demosthenes: The Origin and Growth of His Policy*. New York.

Jameson, M. H. 1960. "A Decree of Themistokles from Troizen." *Hesperia* 29:198–223.

Janko, Richard. 1992. *The "Iliad": A Commentary*. Vol. 4, *Books 13–16*. Cambridge.

Jebb, R. C. 1876. *The Attic Orators from Antiphon to Isaeos*. 2 vols. London.

Jeffery, H. L. 1965. "The *Battle of Oinoe* in the Stoa Poikile." *ABSA* 60:41–57.

Jeppesen, Kristian. 1968. *ΕΤΕΟΚΛΕΟΥΣ ΣΥΜΒΑΣΙΣ: Nochmals zur Deutung des Niobidenkraters, Louvre G 341*. Copenhagen.

Jones, C. P. 1999. *Kinship Diplomacy in the Ancient World*. Cambridge, MA.

Jones, Nicholas F. 1999. *The Associations of Classical Athens: The Response to Democracy*. Oxford.

Jost, Karl. 1935. *Das Beispiel und Vorbild der Vorfahren bei den attischen Rednern und Geschichtschreibern bis Demosthenes*. Basel.

Joutard, P. 1977. *La légende des Camisards*. Paris.

Joutard, P. 1983. *Ces voix qui nous viennent du passé*. Paris.

Jung, Michael. 2006. *Marathon und Plataiai: Zwei Perserschlachten als "lieux de mémoire" im antiken Griechenland*. Göttingen.

Kagan, Donald. 1987. *The Fall of the Athenian Empire*. Ithaca, NY.

Kammen, Michael. 1995. "Some Patterns and Meanings of Memory Distortion in American History." In Schacter (1995) 329–45.

Kapparis, Konstantinos A. 1995. "The Athenian Decree for the Naturalisation of the Plataians." *GRBS* 36:359–78.

Kapparis, Konstantinos A., ed. and trans. 1999. *Apollodoros, "Against Neaira" [D. 59]*. Berlin.

Karusu, S. 1972. "Choeur de tragédie sur un lécythe à figures noires." *RA* 195–204.

Kearns, Emily. 1989. *The Heroes of Attica*. London.

Kegley, Charles W., Jr., & Wittkopf, Eugene R. 2004. *World Politics: Trends and Transformations*. 9th ed. Belmont.

Kellogg, Danielle. 2005. *The Attic Deme of Acharnai: History and Identity*. PhD diss., University of Pennsylvania.

Kellogg, Danielle. 2008. "Οὐκ ἐλάττω παραδώσω τὴν πατρίδα: The Ephebic Oath and the Oath of Plataia in Fourth-Century Athens." *Mouseion*, 3rd ser., 8:355–76.

Kennedy, George, ed. and trans. 1991. *Aristotle, "On Rhetoric": A Theory of Civic Discourse*. Oxford.

Keppler, Kurt. 1971. *Tod über Deutschland: Der Morgenthauplan*. Tübingen.

Keramopoullos, A. D. 1917. "Θηβαικά." *Deltion* 3:1–503.

Kertzer, D. I. 2001. "Representation and Rituals of the State." In Smelser & Baltes (2001) 13174–80.

Kierdorf, Wilhelm. 1966. *Erlebnis und Darstellung der Perserkriege: Studien zu Simonides, Pindar, Aischylos und den Attischen Rednern*. Göttingen.

Kraay, Colin M. 1976. *Archaic and Classical Greek Coins*. London.

Krentz, Peter. 1980. "Foreigners against the Thirty: *IG* 2^2 10 Again." *Phoenix* 34:289–306.

Krentz, Peter. 1982. *The Thirty at Athens*. Ithaca, NY.

Krentz, Peter, ed. and trans. 1989. *Xenophon, Hellenika I–II.3.10*. Warminster.

Krentz, Peter, ed. and trans. 1995. *Xenophon, Hellenika II.3.11–IV.2*. Warminster.

Kron, Uta. 1976. *Die zehn attischen Phylenheroen: Geschichte, Mythos, Kult und Darstellungen*. Berlin.

Kron, Uta. 1999. "Patriotic Heroes." In Hägg (1999) 61–83.

Krummen, E. 1993. "Athens and Attica: Polis and Countryside in Greek Tragedy." In A. H. Sommerstein et al., eds., *Tragedy, Comedy, and the Polis*, 191–217. Bari.

LaCapra, Dominick. 1994. *Representing the Holocaust: History, Theory, Trauma*. Ithaca, NY.

Lamari, Anna. 2009. "Knowing a Story's End: Future Reflexive in the Tragic Narrative of the Argive Expedition against Thebes." In Jonas Grethlein & Antonios Rengakos, eds., *Narratology and Interpretation: The Content of Narrative Form in Ancient Literature*, 399–419. Berlin.

Lambert, S. D. 1993. *The Phratries of Attica*. Ann Arbor.

Lane Fox, Robin. 2004. *Alexander the Great*. New York.

Larsen, J. A. O. 1955. "The Boeotian Confederacy and Fifth Century Oligarchic Theory." *TAPA* 86:40–50.

Lawton, C. L. 1995. *Attic Document Reliefs: Art and Politics in Ancient Athens*. Oxford.

Lazenby, J. F. 1993. *The Defence of Greece*. Warminster.

Lefebvre, H. 1991. *The Production of Space*. Trans. D. Nicholson-Smith. Oxford. Originally published in French in 1974.

Lefkowitz, Mary R. 1985. "The Pindar Scholia." *AJP* 106:269–82.

Lehmann, G. A. 1980. "Der 'Erste Heilige Krieg'—eine Fiktion?" *Historia* 29:242–46.

Levine, R. M., & Sebe Bom Meihyb, J. C. 2001. "Oral History." In Smelser & Baltes (2001) 10891–97.

Lévy, Edmond. 1976. *Athènes devant la défaite de 404: Histoire d'une crise idéologique*. Paris.

Lewis, D. M. 1992. "The Archidamian War." In *CAH*^{2} V:370–432.

Loraux, Nicole. 1986. *The Invention of Athens: The Funeral Oration in the Classical City*. Trans. A. Sheridan. Cambridge. Originally published in French in 1981.

Loraux, Nicole. 2002. *The Divided City: On Memory and Forgetting in Ancient Athens*. New York. Originally published in French in 1997.

Lord, Albert Bates. 1960. *The Singer of Tales*. Cambridge, MA.

Lotze, D. 1964. *Lysander und der Peloponnesische Krieg*. Berlin.

Low, Polly. 2006. "Commemorating the Spartan War Dead." In A. Powell & S. Hodkinson, eds., *Sparta and War*, 85–109. Swansea.

Low, Polly. 2007. *Interstate Relations in Classical Greece: Morality and Power.* Cambridge.
Luraghi, Nino, ed. 2001. *The Historian's Craft in the Age of Herodotus.* Oxford.
Luraghi, Nino. 2008. *The Ancient Messenians: Constructions of Ethnicity and Memory.* Cambridge.
MacDowell, Douglas, ed. 1962. *Andokides: "On the Mysteries."* Oxford.
MacDowell, Douglas M., ed. and trans. 2000. *Demosthenes: "On the False Embassy" (Oration 19).* Oxford.
Macleod, Colin W. 1977. "Thucydides' Plataean Debate." *GRBS* 18:227–46.
Maehler, H., ed. 2004. *Bacchylides: A Selection.* Cambridge.
Manier, David, & Hirst, William. 2008. "A Cognitive Taxonomy of Collective Memories." In Erll & Nünning (2008) 253–62.
Marincola, John. 2007. "The Persian Wars in Fourth-Century Oratory and Historiography." In E. Bridges, E. Hall, & P. J. Rhodes, eds., *Cultural Responses to the Persian Wars: Antiquity to the Third Millennium,* 105–25. Oxford.
Markle, Minor M., III. 1976. "Support of Athenian Intellectuals for Philip: A Study of Isocrates' *Philippus* and Speusippus' *Letter to Philip.*" *JHS* 96:80–99.
Markovits, Andrei S., & Reich, Simon. 1997. *The German Predicament: Memory and Power in the New Europe.* Ithaca, NY.
Martin, Gunther. 2009. *Divine Talk: Religious Argumentation in Demosthenes.* Oxford.
Mastronarde, Donald J., ed. 1994. *Euripides: "Phoenissae."* Cambridge.
Mathieu, Georges, & Brémond, Émile, eds. and trans. 1961. *Isocrate: Discours.* Vol. 2. Paris.
Matthews, Victor J., ed. 1996. *Antimachus of Colophon: Text and Commentary.* Leiden.
McInerney, J. 1999. *The Folds of Parnassos: Land and Ethnicity in Ancient Phokis.* Austin.
McKechnie, P. R., & Kern, S. J., eds. and trans. 1988. *Hellenica Oxyrhynchia.* Warminster.
Meier, Christian. 1993. *Athen: Ein Neubeginn der Weltgeschichte.* Berlin.
Meiggs, Russell. 1972. *The Athenian Empire.* Oxford.
Meiggs, Russell, & Lewis, David. 1988. *A Selection of Greek Historical Inscriptions to the End of the Fifth Century B.C.* Rev. ed. Oxford.
Meister, Klaus. 1990. *Die griechische Geschichtsschreibung: Von den Anfängen bis zum Ende des Hellenismus.* Stuttgart.
Merkelbach, R., & Youtie, H. C. 1968. "Ein Michigan-Papyrus über Theramenes." *ZPE* 2:161–69.
Mette, Hans Joachim. 1963. *Der verlorene Aischylos.* Berlin.
Middleton, David, & Brown, Steven D. 2008. "Experience and Memory: Imaginary Futures in the Past." In Erll & Nünning (2008) 241–51.
Mikalson, Jon D. 1998. *Religion in Hellenistic Athens.* Berkeley.
Mills, Sophie. 1997. *Theseus, Tragedy, and the Athenian Empire.* Oxford.
Milns, R. D. 1995. "Historical Paradigms in Demosthenes' Public Speeches." *Electronic Antiquity* 2, no. 5.
Mirhady, David, & Too, Yun Lee, eds. and trans. 2000. *Isocrates I.* Austin.
Missiou, Anna. 1992. *The Subversive Oratory of Andokides: Politics, Ideology, and Decision-Making in Democratic Athens.* Cambridge.
Misztal, Barbara. 2003. *Theories of Social Remembering.* Maidenhead.
Mol, Hans. 1976. *Identity and the Sacred.* Oxford.
Montgomery, Hugo. 1983. *The Way to Chaeronea: Foreign Policy, Decision-Making and Political Influence in Demosthenes' Speeches.* Bergen.

Morgenthau, Henry, Jr. 1945. *Germany Is Our Problem*. New York.

Morgenthau, Hans J. 1948. *Politics among Nations: The Struggle for Power and Peace*. New York.

Morwood, James, ed. and trans. 2007. *Euripides: "Suppliant Women."* Oxford.

Mosley, D. J. 1971. "Athens' Alliance with Thebes 339 B.C." *Historia* 20:508–10.

Murray, Gilbert. 1946. *Greek Studies*. Oxford.

Murray, Oswyn. 1983a. "The Greek Symposion in History." In Emilio Gabba, ed., *Tria Corda: Scritti in onore di Arnaldo Momigliano*, 257–72. Como.

Murray, Oswyn. 1983b. "The Symposion as Social Institution." In Robin Hägg, ed., *The Greek Renaissance of the Eighth Century B.C.: Tradition and Innovation; Proceedings of the Second International Symposium at the Swedish Institute in Athens, 1–5 June, 1981*, 195–99. Stockholm.

Murray, Oswyn, ed. 1990a. *Sympotica: A Symposium on the Symposion*. Oxford.

Murray, Oswyn. 1990b. "Sympotic History." In O. Murray (1990a) 3–13.

Murray, Oswyn. 1990c. "The Affair of the Mysteries: Democracy and the Drinking Group." In O. Murray (1990a) 149–61.

Murray, Oswyn. 2001. "Herodotus and Oral History." In Luraghi (2001) 16–44. Originally published in 1987 in H. Sancisi-Weerdenburg and A. Kuhrt, eds., *Achaemenid History*. Vol. 2, *The Greek Sources*, 93–115. Leiden.

Murray, Oswyn, & Tecuşan, Manuela, eds. 1995. *In Vino Veritas*. London.

Mylonas, George. 1969. *Eleusis and the Eleusinian Mysteries*. Princeton.

Mylonas, George. 1975. Τὸ δυτικὸν νεκροταφεῖον τῆς Ἐλευσῖνος. Vol. 2. Athens.

Nagy, Gregory. 1996. *Homeric Questions*. Austin.

Naiden, F. S. 2006. *Ancient Supplication*. Oxford.

Natoli, Anthony Francis, ed. and trans. 2004a. *The Letter of Speusippus to Philip II*. Stuttgart.

Natoli, Anthony Francis. 2004b. Review of Peter Roth, *Der Panathenaikos des Isokrates: Übersetzung und Kommentar*. *BMCRev* 2004.10.32.

Neils, Jenifer, ed. 1996. *Worshipping Athena: Panathenaia and Parthenon*. Madison, WI.

Nolan, Mary. 2001. "The Politics of Memory in the Berlin Republic." *Radical Historical Review* 81:113–32.

Nora, Pierre. 1996. "General Introduction: Between Memory and History." In Pierre Nora, director, *Realms of Memory: Rethinking the French Past*. Vol. 1, *Conflicts and Divisions*, ed. L. D. Kritzman, trans. A. Goldhammer, 1–20. New York. Originally published in French in 1984.

Norlin, George, ed. and trans. 1928. *Isocrates*. Vol. 1. London.

Norlin, George, ed. and trans. 1929. *Isocrates*. Vol. 2. London.

Nouhaud, Michel. 1982. *L'utilisation de l'histoire par les orateurs attiques*. Paris.

Noussia-Fantuzzi, Maria. 2010. *Solon the Athenian, the Poetic Fragments*. Leiden.

Novick, Peter. 1999. *The Holocaust in American Life*. Boston.

Ober, Josiah. 1989. *Mass and Elite in Democratic Athens: Rhetoric, Ideology, and the Power of the People*. Princeton.

Ober, Josiah. 2001. "Thucydides Theôrêtikos/Thucydides Histôr: Realist Theory and the Challenge of History." In David R. McCann & Barry S. Strauss, eds., *War and Democracy: A Comparative Study of the Korean War and the Peloponnesian War*, 273–306. Armonk, NY.

Osborne, M. J. 1981. *Naturalization in Athens*. Vol. 1, *A Corpus of Athenian Decrees Granting Citizenship*. Brussels.

Osborne, M. J. 1982. *Naturalization in Athens. Vol. 2, Commentaries on the Decrees Granting Citizenship.* Brussels.

Osborne, Robin. 2004. "Competitive Festivals and the Polis: A Context for Dramatic Festivals at Athens." In P. J. Rhodes, ed., *Athenian Democracy,* 207–24. Edinburgh.

Paez, D.; Basabe, N.; & Gonzales, J. L. 1997. "Social Processes and Collective Memory: A Cross-Cultural Approach to Remembering Political Events." In Pennebaker, Paez, & Rimé (1997) 147–74.

Page, Denys L. 1934. *Actors' Interpolations in Greek Tragedy: Studied with Special Reference to Euripides' "Iphigeneia in Aulis."* Oxford.

Panagopoulos, Andreas. 1989. *Captives and Hostages in the Peloponnesian War.* Amsterdam.

Papillon, Terry L., ed. and trans. 2004. *Isocrates II.* Austin.

Pariente, A. 1992. "Le monument argien des 'Sept contre Thèbes.'" In M. Piérart, ed., *Polydipsion Argos,* 195–229. Paris.

Parke, E. W. 1948. "Consecration to Apollo: Δεκατεύειν τῷ ἐν Δελφοῖς θεῷ." *Hermathena* 72:82–114.

Parke, E. W. 1977. *Festivals of the Athenians.* London.

Parke, E. W., & Wormell, D. E. W. 1956. *The Delphic Oracle.* 2 vols. Oxford.

Parker, Robert. 1983. *Miasma: Pollution and Purification in Early Greek Religion.* Oxford.

Parker, Robert. 1987. "Myths of Early Athens." In Bremmer (1987a) 187–214.

Parker, Robert. 1996. *Athenian Religion: A History.* Oxford.

Parker, Robert. 2005. *Polytheism and Society at Athens.* Oxford.

Parry, Milman. 1971. *The Making of Homeric Verse: The Collected Papers of Milman Parry.* Ed. Adam Parry. Oxford.

Passerini, L. 1988. *Storia e soggettività: Le fonti orali, la memoria.* Florence.

Paulsen, Thomas. 1999. *Die Parapresbeia-Reden des Demosthenes und des Aischines: Kommentar und Interpretationen zu Demosthenes, or. XIX, und Aischines, or. II.* Trier.

Pavese, C. O. 1995. "Elegia di Simonide agli Spartiati per Platea." *ZPE* 107:1–26.

Pearson, L. 1941. "Historical Allusions in the Attic Orators." *CP* 36:209–29.

Pelling, Christopher. 2000. *Literary Texts and the Greek Historian.* London.

Pennebaker, James W.; Paez, Dario; & Rimé, Bernard, eds. 1997. *Collective Memory of Political Events: Social Psychological Perspectives.* Mahwah, NJ.

Perlman, S. 1958. "A Note on the Political Implications of Proxenia in the Fourth Century B.C." *CQ* 8:185–91.

Perlman, S. 1961. "The Historical Example, Its Use and Importance as Political Propaganda in the Attic Orators." *Scripta Hierosolymitana* 7:150–66.

Perlman, S. 1964a. "The Causes and the Outbreak of the Corinthian War." *CQ* 14:64–81.

Perlman, S. 1964b. "Quotations from Poetry in Attic Orators of the Fourth Century B.C." *AJP* 85:155–72.

Perlman, S. 1986. Review of Michel Nouhaud, *L'utilisation de l'histoire par les orateurs attiques. Gnomon* 58:359–60.

Persky, Richard K. 2009. *Kairos: A Cultural History of Time in the Greek Polis.* PhD diss., University of Michigan.

Pickard-Cambridge, Sir Arthur Wallace. 1988. *The Dramatic Festivals of Athens.* Oxford.

Pollitt, J. J. 1999. *Art and Experience in Classical Greece.* Rev. ed. Cambridge.

Potter, David S. 1999. *Literary Texts and the Roman Historian.* London.

Pownall, Frances. 2004. *Lessons from the Past: The Moral Use of History in Fourth-Century Prose.* Ann Arbor.

Pownall, Frances. 2008. "Critias' Commemoration of Athens." *Mouseion*, 3rd ser., 8:333–54.

Prager, J. 1998. *Presenting the Past: Psychoanalysis and the Sociology of Misremembering.* Cambridge, MA.

Prager, J. 2001. "Psychology of Collective Memory." In Smelser & Baltes (2001) 2223–27.

Pritchett, W. Kendrick. 1971–91. *The Greek State at War.* 5 vols. Berkeley.

Raaflaub, Kurt. 1979. "Polis Tyrannos: Zur Entstehung einer politischen Metapher." In G. Bowersock, W. Burkert, & M. Putnam, eds., *Arktouros*, 237–52. Berlin.

Raubitschek, A. E. 1941. "The Heroes of Phyle." *Hesperia* 10:284–95.

Rausch, M. 1999. *Isonomia in Athen: Veränderungen des öffentlichen Lebens vom Sturz der Tyrannis bis zur zweiten Perserabwehr.* Frankfurt.

Reinmuth, O. W. 1971. *The Ephebic Inscriptions of the Fourth Century B.C.* Leiden.

Rhodes, Peter John. 1981. *A Commentary on the Aristotelian "Athenaion Politeia."* Oxford.

Rhodes, Peter John. 1994. "In Defence of the Greek Historians." *G&R* 41:156–71.

Rhodes, Peter John. 2010. *A History of the Classical Greek World, 478–323 BC.* 2nd ed. Malden, MA.

Rhodes, Peter John, & Osborne, Robin, eds. and trans. 2003. *Greek Historical Inscriptions, 404–323 BC.* Oxford.

Rimé, B., & Christophe, V. 1997. "How Individual Emotional Episodes Feed Collective Memory." In Pennebaker, Paez, & Rimé, 131–46.

Robertson, Noel. 1978. "The Myth of the First Sacred War." *CQ* 28:38–73.

Robertson, Noel. 1984. Review of Michel Nouhaud, *L'utilisation de l'histoire par les orateurs attiques,* and Joseph W. Day, *The Glory of Athens: The Popular Tradition as Reflected in "The Panathenaicus" of Aelius Aristides. Phoenix* 38:381–85.

Roller, Matthew. 2010. "Demolished Houses, Monumentality, and Memory in Roman Culture." *ClAnt* 29:117–80.

Rosivach, Vincent J. 1987. "Autochthony and the Athenians." *CQ* 37:294–306.

Rösler, Wolfgang. 1980. *Dichter und Gruppe: Eine Untersuchung zu den Bedingungen und zur historischen Funktion früher griechischer Lyrik am Beispiel Alkaios.* Munich.

Rösler, Wolfgang. 1990. "*Mnemosyne* in the *Symposion.*" In O. Murray (1990a) 230–37.

Roth, Peter. 2003. *Der Panathenaikos des Isokrates: Übersetzung und Kommentar.* Munich.

Rowe, G. O. 1972. "A Problem of Quotation in Demosthenes' Embassy Speech." *TAPA* 103:441–49.

Rutherford, Ian. 2001. "The New Simonides: Toward a Commentary." In Boedeker & Sider (2001) 33–54.

Ryder, T. T. B. 1965. *Koine Eirene.* London.

Sage, Michael. 1996. *Warfare in Ancient Greece: A Sourcebook.* London.

Schachter, Albert. 1981–94. *Cults of Boiotia.* 4 vols. London.

Schacter, Daniel L., ed. 1995. *Memory Distortion: How Minds, Brains, and Societies Reconstruct the Past.* Cambridge.

Schacter, Daniel L. 2001. *The Seven Sins of Memory: How the Mind Forgets and Remembers.* Boston.

Schepens, G. 2001. "Who Wrote the *Hellenica Oxyrhynchia*? The Need for a Methodological Code." *Sileno* 27:201–24.

Schmitz-Kahlmann, Gisela. 1939. *Das Beispiel der Geschichte im politischen Denken des Isokrates.* Leipzig.

Schroeder, Otto. 1914. *De laudibus Athenarum a poetis tragicis et ab oratoribus epidictis excultis.* Göttingen.

Schudson, Michael. 1995. "Dynamics of Distortion in Collective Memory." In Schacter (1995) 346–64.

Schudson, Michael. 1997. "Lives, Laws, and Language: Commemorative versus Non-commemorative Forms of Effective Public Memory." *Communication Review* 2:3–17.

Schultz, Peter. 2009. "The North Frieze of the Temple of Athena Nike." In Olga Palagia, ed., *Art in Athens during the Peloponnesian War,* 128–67. Cambridge.

Schwartz, Barry. 1982. "The Social Context of Commemoration: A Study in Collective Memory." *Social Forces* 61:374–402.

Schwartz, Barry; Zerubavel, Yael; & Barnett, Bernice. 1986. "The Recovery of Masada: A Study in Collective Memory." *Sociological Quarterly* 27:147–64.

Schweigert, Eugene. 1939. "Greek Inscriptions (1–13)." *Hesperia* 8:1–47.

Scodel, Ruth. 1979. *The Trojan Trilogy of Euripides.* Göttingen.

Scodel, Ruth. 2002. *Listening to Homer: Tradition, Narrative, and Audience.* Ann Arbor.

Seager, Robin. 1967. "Thrasybulus, Conon, and Athenian Imperialism, 396–386 B.C." *JHS* 87:95–115.

Seager, Robin. 1994. "The King's Peace and the Second Athenian Confederacy." In *CAH*² VI:156–86.

Sealey, Raphael. 1993. *Demosthenes and His Time: A Study in Defeat.* New York.

Seibert, Jakob. 1979. *Die politischen Flüchtlinge und Verbannten in der griechischen Geschichte: Von den Anfängen bis zur Unterwerfung durch die Römer.* Darmstadt.

Shapiro, H. Alan. 1998. "Autochthony and the Visual Arts in 5th-Century Athens." In Boedeker & Raaflaub (1998) 127–51.

Shear, Julia L. 2001. *Polis and Panathenaia: The History and Development of Athena's Festival.* PhD diss. University of Pennsylvania.

Shear, Julia L. 2007. "Cultural Change, Space, and the Politics of Commemoration in Athens." In R. Osborne, ed., *Debating the Athenian Cultural Revolution: Art, Literature, Philosophy, and Politics, 430–380 B.C.,* 91–115. Cambridge.

Shear, Julia L. 2011. *Polis and Revolution: Responding to Oligarchy in Classical Athens.* Cambridge.

Sherman, D. J. 1999. *The Construction of Memory in Interwar France.* Chicago.

Shrimpton, Gordon S. 1991. *Theopompus the Historian.* Montreal.

Sickinger, James. 1999. *Public Records and Archives in Classical Athens.* Chapel Hill.

Sider, David. 2001. "Fragments 1–22 W²: Text, Apparatus Criticus, and Translation." In Boedeker & Sider (2001) 13–32.

Siewert, Peter. 1972. *Der Eid von Plataiai.* Munich.

Signes Codoñer, Juan. 1998. "El *Panatenaico* de Isócrates: 2 Tema y finalidad del discurso." *Emerita* 66:67–94.

Signes Codoñer, Juan. 2001. "El *Panatenaico* de Isócrates: 3 Las cartas a los Macedonios." *Emerita* 69:7–53.

Simon, Erika. 1963. "Polygnotan Painting and the Niobid Painter." *AJA* 67:43–62.

Simon, Erika. 1983. *Festivals of Attica: An Archaeological Commentary.* Madison, WI.

Slater, William J., ed. 1986. *Aristophanis Byzantii Fragmenta.* Berlin.

Smelser, N. J., & Baltes, P. B., eds. 2001. *International Encyclopedia of the Social and Behavioral Sciences.* 26 vols. Amsterdam.

Smit, J. 1939. *Plutarchus' Leven van Lysander.* Amsterdam.

Smyth, Herbert Weir. 1956. *Greek Grammar.* Rev. by Gordon M. Messing. Cambridge, MA.

Snodgrass, Anthony M. 1980. *Archaic Greece: The Age of Experiment.* London.

Stafford, Emma. 2000. *Worshipping Virtues: Personification and the Divine in Ancient Greece.* London.

Stein, A. 2001. "Realism/Neorealism." In Smelser & Baltes (2001) 12812–15.

Steinbock, Bernd. 2011. "A Lesson in Patriotism: Lycurgus' *Against Leocrates,* the Ideology of the Ephebeia, and Athenian Social Memory." *ClAnt* 30:279–317.

Steinbock, Bernd. Forthcoming. "Contesting the Lessons from the Past. Aeschines' Use of Social Memory." *TAPA* 143.

Stein-Hölkeskamp, Elke, & Hölkeskamp, Karl-Joachim, eds. 2006. *Erinnerungsorte der Antike: Die römische Welt.* Munich.

Stein-Hölkeskamp, Elke, & Hölkeskamp, Karl-Joachim, eds. 2010. *Die griechische Welt: Erinnerungsorte der Antike,* Munich.

Strasburger, Hermann. 1958. "Thukydides und die politische Selbstdarstellung der Athener." *Hermes* 86:17–40.

Strauss, Barry S. 1987. *Athens after the Peloponnesian War: Class, Faction, and Policy, 403–386 BC.* Ithaca, NY.

Stroud, R. 1971. "Greek Inscriptions: Theozotides and the Athenian Orphans." *Hesperia* 40:280–301.

Stupperich, Reinhard. 1977. *Staatsbegräbnis und Privatgrabmal im klassischen Athen.* Münster.

Stylianou, P. J. 1998. *A Historical Commentary on Diodorus Siculus, Book 15.* Oxford.

Sutton, D. E. 1998. *Memories Cast in Stone: The Relevance of the Past in Everyday Life.* Oxford.

Symeonoglou, Sarantis. 1985. *The Topography of Thebes.* Princeton.

Taylor, Martha C. 2002. "One Hundred Heroes of Phyle." *Hesperia* 71:377–97.

Thiele, Hans-Günter, ed. 1997. *Die Wehrmachtsausstellung: Dokumentation einer Kontroverse; Documentation der Fachtagung in Bremen am 26. Februar 1997 und der Bundestagsdebatten am 13. März und 24. April 1997.* Bremen.

Thomas, Eberhard. 1976. *Mythos und Geschichte: Untersuchungen zum historischen Gehalt griechischer Mythendarstellungen.* Cologne.

Thomas, Rosalind. 1989. *Oral Tradition and Written Record in Classical Athens.* Cambridge.

Thomas, Rosalind. 1992. *Literacy and Orality in Ancient Greece.* Cambridge.

Thompson, H. A., & Wycherley, R. E. 1972. *The Agora of Athens: The History, Shape, and Uses of an Ancient City Center.* Princeton.

Thompson, P. 1988. *The Voice of the Past: Oral History.* 2nd ed. London.

Tiverios, Michalis. 1981. "Sieben gegen Theben." *AM* 96:145–61.

Tod, Marcus N. 1933. "Greek Inscriptions." *G&R* 2:108–11.

Todd, Steven Charles, ed. and trans. 2000. *Lysias.* Austin.

Todd, Steven Charles. 2007. *A Commentary on Lysias, Speeches 1–11.* Oxford.

Toher, Mark. 1999. "On 'Thucydides' Blunder': 2.34.5." *Hermes* 127:497–501.

Travlos, J. 1971. *Pictorial Dictionary of Athens.* New York.

Trevett, Jeremy. 1990. "History in [Demosthenes] 59." *CQ* 40:407–20.

Trevett, Jeremy. 1992. *Apollodorus the Son of Pasion*. Oxford.
Trevett, Jeremy. 1999. "Demosthenes and Thebes." *Historia* 48:184–202.
Tritle, Lawrence. 2002. Review of Andrew Wolpert, *Remembering Defeat: Civil War and Civic Memory in Ancient Athens*. *BMCRev* 2002.12.13.
Tulving, E. 1983. *Elements of Episodic Memory*. Oxford.
Tuplin, Christopher. 1993. *The Failings of Empire: A Reading of Xenophon "Hellenica" 2.3.11–7.5.27*. Stuttgart.
Tyrrell, William Blake, & Brown, Frieda S. 1991. *Athenian Myths and Institutions: Words in Action*. Oxford.
Usher, Stephen. 1999. *Greek Oratory: Tradition and Originality*. Oxford.
Usher, Stephen. 2007. "Symbouleutic Oratory." In Worthington (2007) 220–35.
Vanderpool, Eugene. 1966. "A Monument to the Battle of Marathon." *Hesperia* 35:93–106.
Van Hook, LaRue. 1932. "On the Lacedaemonians Buried in the Kerameikos." *AJA* 36:290–92.
Van Hook, LaRue, ed. and trans. 1954. *Isocrates*. Vol. 3. Cambridge, MA.
Vansina, Jan. 1965. *Oral Tradition: A Study in Historical Methodology*. Trans. H. M. Wright. Chicago. Originally published in French in 1961.
Vansina, Jan. 1985. *Oral Tradition as History*. Madison, WI.
Vielberg, M. 1991. "Die religiösen Vorstellungen des Redners Lykurg." *RhM* 134:49–68.
Vince, J. H., ed. and trans. 1930. *Demosthenes*. Vol. 1. London.
von Arnim, Hans. 1917. "Das Testament des Isokrates: Gedanken über politische Sophistik." *Deutsche Revue* 42, no. 2:245–56; no. 3:28–41.
von Scala, Rudolf. 1892. *Isokrates und die Geschichtschreibung*. Leipzig.
von Wilamowitz-Moellendorff, Ulrich. 1899. *Griechische Tragoedien*. Vol. 1. Berlin.
von Wilamowitz-Moellendorff, Ulrich. 1914. *Aischylos: Interpretationen*. Berlin.
von Wilamowitz-Moellendorff, Ulrich. 1922. *Pindaros*. Berlin.
Walbank, M. B. 1982. "An Athenian Decree Re-considered: Honours for Aristoxenos and Another Boiotian." *EMC* 26:259–74.
Walker, Henry J. 1995. *Theseus and Athens*. Oxford.
Wallace, Robert W. 1989. *The Areopagos Council, to 307 B.C.* Baltimore.
Walter, Uwe. 2004. *Memoria und res publica: Zur Geschichtskultur im republikanischen Rom*. Frankfurt am Main.
Walters, K. R. 1978. "Diodorus 11.82–84 and the Second Battle of Tanagra." *AJAH* 3:188–91.
Walters, K. R. 1980. "Rhetoric as Ritual: The Semiotics of the Attic Funeral Oration." *Florilegium* 2:1–27.
Walters, K. R. 1981. "'We Fought Alone at Marathon': Historical Falsification in the Attic Funeral Oration." *RhM* 124:204–11.
Waltz, Kenneth N. 1959. *Man, the State, and War: A Theoretical Analysis*. New York.
Weil, Henri, ed. 1883. *Les Plaidoyers Politiques de Démosthène*. Paris.
Weißenberger, Michael. 1996. "Das persische Friedensangebot an Athen: Umdatierung und Umwertung eines historischen Faktums bei den Rednern des 4. Jhs." *Hermes* 124:418–24.
West, Martin L. 1974. *Studies in Greek Elegy and Iambus*. Berlin.
West, Martin L., ed. and trans. 2003. *Greek Epic Fragments: From the Seventh to the Fifth Centuries BC*. Cambridge, MA.

Whitehead, David 1984. "A Thousand New Citizens." *LCM* 9:8–10.

Whitehead, David. 1986. *The Demes of Attica, 508/7–ca. 250 B.C.: A Political and Social Study.* Princeton.

Whitehead, David. 2000. *Hyperides: The Forensic Speeches.* Oxford.

Willemsen, F. 1977. "Zu den Lakedämoniergräbern im Kerameikos." *AM* 92:117–57.

Wilson, Peter. 2000. *The Athenian Institution of the Khoregia: The Chorus, the City, and the Stage.* Cambridge.

Winkler, Heinrich August. 2004. "Aus der Geschichte lernen? Zum Verhältnis von Historie und Politik in Deutschland nach 1945." *Die Zeit* 14.

Winkler, John J., & Zeitlin, Froma I., eds. 1990. *Nothing to Do with Dionysos? Athenian Drama in Its Social Context.* Princeton.

Winter, J. 2001. "Public Commemoration." In Smelser & Baltes (2001) 12521–26.

Wischermann, Clemens. 2002. "Vorwort." In Clemens Wischermann, ed., *Vom kollektiven Gedächtnis zur Individualisierung der Erinnerung,* 7. Stuttgart.

Wolcott, James. 2004. "Color Me Khaki." *Vanity Fair* 529:228–35.

Wolpert, Andrew. 2002. *Remembering Defeat: Civil War and Civic Memory in Ancient Athens.* Baltimore.

Worthington, Ian. 1991a. "The Context of [Demades] *On the Twelve Years.*" *CQ* 41:90–95.

Worthington, Ian. 1991b. "Greek Oratory, Revision of Speeches, and the Problem of Historical Reliability." *C&M* 42:55–74.

Worthington, Ian. 1992. *A Historical Commentary on Dinarchus: Rhetoric and Conspiracy in Later Fourth-Century Athens.* Ann Arbor.

Worthington, Ian. 1994a. "History and Oratorical Exploitation." In Worthington (1994b) 109–29.

Worthington, Ian, ed. 1994b. *Persuasion: Greek Rhetoric in Action.* London.

Worthington, Ian. 2003. "Alexander's Destruction of Thebes." In W. Heckel & L. A. Tritle, eds., *Crossroads of History: The Age of Alexander the Great,* 65–86. Claremont.

Worthington, Ian, ed. 2007. *A Companion to Greek Rhetoric.* Malden, MA.

Worthington, Ian. 2010. "Intentional History: Alexander, Demosthenes, and Thebes." In Foxhall, Gehrke, & Luraghi (2010) 239–46.

Young, M. 1988. *The Metronomic Society: Natural Rhythms and Human Timetables.* London.

Yunis, Harvey. 2000. "Politics as Literature: Demosthenes and the Burden of the Athenian Past." *Arion* 8:97–118.

Yunis, Harvey, ed. 2001. *Demosthenes: "On the Crown."* Cambridge.

Yunis, Harvey, ed. 2003. *Written Texts and the Rise of Literate Culture in Ancient Greece.* Cambridge.

Zajonz, Sandra. 2002. *Isokrates' Enkomion auf Helena: Ein Kommentar.* Göttingen.

Zeilhofer, Gerhard. 1959. *Sparta, Delphoi und die Amphiktyonen im 5. Jahrhundert vor Christus.* Erlangen.

Zeitlin, Froma I. 1990. "Thebes: Theater of Self and Society in Athenian Drama." In Winkler & Zeitlin (1990) 130–67.

Zerubavel, E. 1996. "Social Memories: Steps to a Sociology of the Past." *Qualitative Sociology* 19:283–300.

Zerubavel, E. 1997. *Social Mindscapes: An Invitation to Cognitive Sociology.* Cambridge, MA.

Zerubavel, Y. 1995. *Recovered Roots: Collective Memory and the Making of Israeli National Tradition.* Chicago.
Zimmermann, Bernhard. 1998. *Die griechische Komödie.* Düsseldorf.
Zuntz, Günther. 1955. *The Political Plays of Euripides.* Manchester.

Index Locorum

LITERARY TEXTS

Achaeus (*TrGF* 20)
F 1 Snell, 181, 205
F 18 Snell, 181, 205
F 18a Snell, 181, 205
T 1 Snell, 181, 205
adespota elegiaca (adesp. el.)
fr. 1 West[2], 80
Aelian (Ael.)
Varia Historia (VH)
4.6, 282n5, 313, 322
Aeschines (Aeschin.)
1.61, 176n107
1.128, 62n67
1.151, 62n67
1.152, 62n67
2.15, 64n79
2.104, 268n169
2.105, 88n223
2.115, 311, 311n91
2.117, 266n162
2.132–33, 335
2.141, 153n171
2.143, 153n171
2.147–48, 218n17
2.164, 265n162, 266
2.172–76, 95
2.176, 236n78, 244n101
2.31, 27n120
2.31–33, 28
2.74, 88n223
2.74–78, 26n117, 75, 97
2.75–77, 209n240, 292n28
2.78, 74, 115n59
3.107, 302n70, 303
3.107–13, 302
3.108, 303, 303n72, 306
3.108–9, 309, 315n114, 316, 353
3.109, 303n72, 304, 306
3.113, 302
3.116, 88, 111, 152, 268n169, 331, 331n160
3.118, 335n174
3.128, 322
3.133, 322
3.137–41, 268n169
3.138, 257
3.138–39, 83n189, 278
3.141, 271n173
3.156, 277
3.156–57, 322
3.181, 236n79, 237
3.186, 23n98, 90
3.187, 92n248, 93n253, 236n77, 236n79, 239, 243
3.187–90, 237
3.190, 92n248, 236n79, 237n82, 239n86
3.191, 73n137, 236n78, 240, 244
3.208, 236n79
3.237, 34n157

Aeschines (Aeschin.) (*continued*)
3.239, 34n157, 277
3.239–40, 277
Aeschylus (Aesch.)
T 78 Radt, 177n111
Eleusinioi (Eleus.)
fr. 53a Radt, 178, 192n174
Eumenides (Eum.)
566–73, 180n128
1032–47, 180n128
Persae (Pers.)
807–8, 143n149
815–20, 110n38
816–22, 143n149
Septem contra Thebas (Sept.)
42, 206n226
Supplices (Supp.)
347–53, 180n127
418–37, 180n127
Alcaeus
fr. 75 Voigt, 77n162, 80n178
fr. 129 Voigt, 77n162, 80n178
fr. 311 Voigt, 79n176
fr. 348 Voigt, 77n162, 80n178
Andocides (Andoc.)
1.80, 236n79
1.106, 74
1.107, 53n28, 134
1.142, 282n5, 286, 320, 326
1.142–43, 285
3.3–8, 74
3.3–9, 95
3.21, 246n103, 287, 287n17, 310, 312n97, 328
3.29, 74
Anonymus, De Sparta (*FGrHist* 596)
F 26, 284n12
Antimachus of Colophon
Thebaid
fr. 31 Matthews, 163n37
Antiphanes (*PCG*)
fr. 85 Kassel–Austin, 79
Apollodorus (*TrGF* 64)
T 1 Snell, 181, 206n224
T 2 Snell, 181, 206n224
Apollodorus (Apollod.)
Bibliotheca (Bibl.)
3.77–79, 176
Appian (App.)
Bella civilia (B Civ.)
1.3.24, 305n78
Aristides, Aelius (Aristid.)
Leuctricus A (Leuc. A)
639 Dindorf, 322n141
Panathenaicus (Panath.)
172 Dindorf, 61n61
282–84 Dindorf, 261n149
283–84 Dindorf, 266n163
319 Dindorf, 313
Aristodemus (*FGrHist* 383)
F 3, 168
Aristophanes (Ar.)
Acharnenses (Ach.)
9–12, 63n75
178–85, 71
179–80, 53n26
204–36, 71
280–365, 71
665–75, 71
692–99, 53n26
980, 79n174
1093, 79n174
Ecclesiazusae (Eccl.)
304, 43
Equites (Eq.)
781–83, 53n26
1334, 53n26
Nubes (Nub.)
985, 53n26
1353–58, 79n177
Plutus (Plut.)
627–28, 67
1146, 60n57, 240
Ranae (Ran.)
866–69, 63n75
Vespae (Vesp.)
682–84, 53n26
711, 53n26
1225–26, 79n174
Aristophanes of Byzantium (Ar. Byz.)
fr. 300P Slater, 81n185, 256
fr. 301P Slater, 81n185, 256
Aristotle (Arist.)
Athenaion Politeia (Ath. Pol.)

15.4, 177n109
34–41.1, 216n8
35.4, 218n16
40.2, 240
42.3, 72
43.6, 176n100, 176n104
58.1, 68, 133
Rhetorica (Rh.)
1362a20, 35n162
1362b28, 35n162
1368a29–30
1393a26–b2
1396a12–14, 28
1408a32–36, 42
1411a, 94n256, 322n141
[Aristotle] [Arist.]
Rhetorica ad Alexandrum (Rh. Al.)
1425a10–16, 35n162
Armenidas (*FGrHist* 378)
F 6, 167
Arrian (Arr.)
Anabasis (Anab.)
1.7.1–2, 273
1.7.4, 274n186
1.7.10, 273
1.8.8, 337
1.9.6–8, 341
1.9.7, 301, 338, 338n181, 339
1.9.9, 336, 340, 341
1.9.9–10, 338n181
1.9.10, 340
1.10.2, 275
1.10.3, 275
1.10.4–5, 275
1.10.5–6, 274n189

Bacchylides (Bacchyl.)
17, 60
18, 60, 171
19.46–48, 197n193

Callinus
fr. 1 West², 78
fr. 6 West², 161n21
Cicero (Cic.)
Epistulae ad Quintum fratrem (Q Fr.)
1.1.25, 317n119
De inventione (Inv.)
1.17, 317n119
Pro Caelio (Cael.)
78, 317n119
De republica (Rep.)
3.15, 324n145
Cleidemus (*FGrHist* 323)
F 22, 73, 110
Craterus (*FGrHist* 342)
F 5, 317n120
F 17, 317n120
Critias
fr. 2 West² = DK 88 **B2**, 77n160
fr. 5 West² = DK 88 **B5**, 80

[Demades] [Demad.]
16–17, 322
26, 322
28, 322
65, 322, 322n141
Demon (*FGrHist* 327)
F 6, 67, 68
Demosthenes (Dem.)
5.9–10, 126
5.19, 335
6.6–12, 148
6.7, 143, 148
6.7–11, 58n50
6.7–12, 31n142, 69n119, 147, 148n162
6.9, 144
6.9–10, 144
6.10, 144
6.11, 96, 103, 144, 146, 147, 147n158
6.11–12, 101n2, 142
6.12, 147, 148
6.19, 147n161
14.1, 149
14.3, 149
14.3–5, 149
14.6, 150
14.7, 150
14.8, 149
14.14–28, 150
14.28–29, 150
14.29, 150
14.30, 151

Demosthenes (Dem.) (*continued*)
14.33, 151, 152
14.33–34, 46n212, 101n2, 142, 152, 208n235, 246n103
14.34, 153
14.41, 149
15.21, 98
15.21–23, 98
15.22, 218n17
15.35, 85
16.4, 125
16.25, 125
18.18, 268n169
18.50, 75n147
18.169–73, 269
18.169–87, 203, 277n195
18.175, 271
18.176, 269
18.177, 271
18.177–78, 269
18.179, 269
18.180, 64n78
18.186, 269, 269n171
18.188, 268n169
18.202, 86n210, 268n169
18.202–4, 144
18.208, 1, 29, 46, 85n202
18.211–15, 269
18.213, 270
18.214, 270
18.267, 62n67
19.12, 64n79
19.20–21, 126
19.42, 126
19.59, 335
19.60, 268n169
19.62, 334
19.64–65, 290
19.64–66, 42
19.65, 23n98, 41, 291n22, 304, 331, 331n163, 335
19.65–66, 246n103, 282n5
19.75, 34n157
19.80, 335
19.111–13, 97
19.112, 126
19.245, 62n67
19.247, 62n67
19.254–56, 79
19.261, 58n49
19.280, 236n79
19.303, 94
19.325, 126
20.52, 23n98, 75n147
20.73, 23n98
20.77, 23n98, 75n147
20.109, 151n169, 339n186
21.78, 23n98
21.170, 90
22.13, 88n223, 90
22.76, 88
23.65, 27n120
23.66, 61
23.70, 61
23.207, 88n223
24.129, 86, 110
24.134, 236n77, 257n141
24.135, 236n79
24.184, 88
60.1, 50n6, 146n157
60.4, 55n34, 58n48
60.8, 54n32, 56, 56n39, 157, 157n7, 173n89, 188, 189, 191, 206n225, 209, 209n238, 350
60.8–9, 27n120
60.10, 53, 131, 135n128
60.11, 53n24
60.27, 62
60.27–31, 73, 265n159
60.30, 209n238
fr. XIII 2 Sauppe & Baiter, 306, 306n84, 308, 309, 353
Demosthenes (Dem.)
Prooemia (Prooem.)
16, 144n150, 227n52
[Demosthenes] [Dem.]
7.46, 35n162
40.25, 74
59.75, 68
59.89, 122
59.94, 47, 89, 129, 138
59.94–104, 127
59.95, 101n2, 102, 118, 118n73, 127, 128n102, 137, 139, 246n103

59.95–96, 140
59.96–98, 108n22
59.98–99, 127
59.98–103, 95, 140n139
59.98–104, 127n100
59.103–4, 122
59.104, 93, 123
59.105, 93, 123

Dinarchus (Din.)
1.18–24, 277
1.18–26, 322
1.24–27, 278
1.25, 23n98, 46n212, 75n147, 97, 213, 213n4, 232, 244, 253, 260, 260n147, 276, 279, 351
1.37, 265
1.38, 264, 257, 263–65
1.38–39, 260n147, 261n149, 278
1.39, 261, 264, 265
1.74, 322
1.76, 257n141

Diodorus Siculus (Diod.)
4.16.4, 227n53
4.26.1, 227n53
4.39.1, 228n55
8.27.1–2, 78n169
11.3.3, 314, 316n116
11.4.7, 104n7, 118
11.29.3, 311, 311n92, 314, 316n116, 324, 324n144
11.33.3, 50n3
12.70.5, 69, 114n58
13.65, 80n179
13.97.6, 182
14.3–6, 216n8
14.6.1, 217, 218, 276n193
14.6.2, 218n17
14.6.2–3, 217
14.6.3, 217, 218n17, 219
14.17.3, 252n125
14.32.1, 225, 232, 243
14.32–33, 216n8
15.25–27, 261, 261n149
15.25.1, 263
15.25.4, 259, 260
15.25.4–27.4, 264
15.46.6, 123, 198, 198n197
15.63.1, 282n5, 307
15.79.3–6, 339n186
16.23–24, 333
16.27.3, 333
16.27.3–4, 334
16.27.3–5, 333
16.36.1, 334
16.37.3, 334
16.38.2, 334
16.87.3, 272
16.89.2, 338
17.4.9, 339
17.8.3–5, 273
17.8.5, 274
17.8.6, 274
17.9.4, 341
17.13.5, 337
17.14.1, 275, 336
17.14.2, 337
17.14.2–3, 338
17.14.3, 275, 276
17.14.4, 341
17.15.1, 275
17.15.1–3, 275
17.15.1–4, 275
17.15.2, 62n64, 73
17.15.4, 275, 276, 276n194
17.15.5, 275

Dionysius of Halicarnassus (Dion. Hal.)
Antiquitates Romanae (Ant. Rom.)
5.17.4, 50n3, 179n120
De Thucydide (Thuc.)
16, 229n58

Etymologicum Magnum (Etym. Magn.)
s.v. Ἱππία, 162, 163, 177
s.v. Ἐνηλύσια, 177n111

Euripides (Eur.)
Bacchae (Bacch.)
1–55, 226n47
1333–36, 197n193
Electra (El.)
1264–72, 61
Erechtheus (Erech.)
fr. 370.87–89 Kannicht, 62
Hecuba (Hec.)
1, 62n67

Euripides (Eur.) (*continued*)
- **21–26**, 313n103

Heraclidae (Heracl.)
- **114–19**, 169n65
- **843–63**, 194

Hercules furens (HF)
- **9–12**, 226n46
- **1001–8**, 235n70

Incertarum Fabularum
- **fr. 865** Kannicht, 62n67

Iphigenia Taurica (IT)
- **940–69**, 61
- **1469–72**, 61

Orestes (Or.)
- **1648–52**, 61, 61n61

Phoenissae (Phoen.)
- **131**, 168
- **145**, 168
- **159–60**, 168
- **638–39**, 197n193

Phoenix
- **fr. 812** Kannicht, 62n67
- **fr. 812.7–9** Kannicht, 62n67

Stheneboea
- **fr. 661.24–25** Kannicht, 62n67

Supplices (Supp.)
- **10**, 180
- **21–22**, 180
- **24–25**, 181
- **32–34**, 180
- **42**, 181
- **67**, 181
- **102–3**, 180
- **106–7**, 180
- **114**, 174n90, 181
- **168–75**, 181
- **184–89**, 189n161
- **229–31**, 181
- **256–62**, 181
- **271–85**, 181
- **293**, 174n90
- **311**, 181
- **328**, 188n155
- **346–48**, 188n154
- **346–55**, 181
- **349–57**, 174n90, 206n227
- **382–94**, 188n154
- **389–94**, 207
- **399**, 193
- **399–464**, 193
- **404–8**, 174n90
- **411**, 193
- **429–55**, 174n90
- **463–64**, 189, 192n177
- **467–71**, 193
- **511–12**, 189, 192n177
- **526**, 181
- **538**, 181
- **575**, 190, 192n177
- **598**, 206n226
- **631–33**, 189, 192n177
- **636**, 206n226
- **650–720**, 193
- **671**, 181
- **720–30**, 193
- **723–25**, 188n155
- **726–30**, 190, 192n177
- **743–44**, 190, 192n177
- **754–59**, 162n28, 163n32, 164n45
- **846–55**, 177n113, 180n125
- **857–917**, 179n120
- **1185–88**, 164, 172n81
- **1185–95**, 193n179
- **1200**, 163n32
- **1207**, 164
- **1211–12**, 164
- **1212**, 164n41
- **1213–26**, 193

Gorgias
- DK 82 **B5a**, 50n5
- DK 82 **B5b**, 50n5
- DK 82 **B6**, 50n5

Harpocration
- **s.v. ἀργυρόπους δίφρος**, 86n214
- **s.v. δεκατεύειν**, 314n105
- **s.v. χλῆδος**, 177n111

Hecataeus (*FGrHist* 1)
- **F 30**, 187n150

Hellenica Oxyrhynchia (Hell. Oxy.)
- **9.1** Chambers, 247
- **9.1–3** Chambers, 247
- **9.2** Chambers, 248

9.3 Chambers, 248
9–10 Chambers, 231
10.1–2 Chambers, 247
10.2 Chambers, 222
18.2 Chambers, 229n58
19 Chambers, 221n25
19.1 Chambers, 231n60
20.1 Chambers, 222, 231, 231n60
20.1–2 Chambers = **17(12).1–2** Bartoletti, 221, 257
20.2 Chambers, 223
20.3–5 Chambers, 221, 224
21.1 Chambers, 223
21.3–5 Chambers, 246
Hereas (*FGrHist* 486)
F 1, 170n69
Herodotus (Hdt.)
1.5, 26
3.122, 26
5.49–51, 175n97
5.67–68, 263n156
5.77, 106, 192
5.78, 106
5.81, 106
6.21.2, 325
6.100–101, 52n20
6.105, 68
6.108, 68, 106, 120, 173, 192
6.108.1, 128
6.108.2, 175
6.108.4, 175, 176n107
6.109, 107n16
6.110–17, 89
6.111.2, 129, 139
6.116, 134n126
6.117, 89n230
6.117.1, 85
6.118, 141
7.8, 143n149
7.10.β.1, 134n126
7.16, 143n149
7.132, 103, 112
7.132.1, 104n8, 105, 113
7.132.2, 304, 313, 314
7.148–52, 198n196
7.159, 28n128
7.161, 58, 58n48
7.161.3, 28n128
7.172.1, 104
7.189, 69
7.202, 140
7.205, 103, 116, 116n63, 117
7.222, 103, 116, 116n63, 140, 177
7.225.2, 85
7.228, 85, 118n74, 135n127
7.233, 103, 116, 116n63, 177
8.1.1, 140
8.34, 116n63
8.44, 140
8.50.2, 120, 128
8.53.2, 323
8.55, 66
8.64, 69
8.73, 198n196
8.109.3, 68
8.121, 69
8.136, 145
8.140–44, 145
8.142, 146
8.143, 68n106
8.143–44, 188n156, 189n164, 197
9.2, 116n63
9.13.2, 324
9.13–15, 107
9.16, 116n66
9.20–24, 110n39
9.20–25, 86
9.21.3, 86n213
9.26.1, 197n192
9.26–27, 28n128
9.26–28.1, 110n39
9.27, 28, 57, 134, 225n40
9.27.3, 157, 157n7, 159n11, 160, 173n86, 192, 196–97, 197n191, 209, 348
9.27.5, 130
9.28.1, 197n192
9.31.2, 116n63
9.32, 107
9.40, 116n63
9.41.4, 116n63
9.46–47, 110n39
9.67, 104, 106, 107, 116
9.67–69, 103

Herodotus (Hdt.) (*continued*)
9.73, 71, 71n126
9.81, 87, 108
9.85, 85, 108
9.86, 112, 197n193, 318
9.86.1, 116
9.87.2, 116n63
9.88, 318
9.106.3, 314
Hesiod (Hes.)
fr. 298 Merkelbach & West, 170n69
fr. 280 Merkelbach & West, 170n69
Scutum
182, 170n69
Hesychius
s.v. ἀπόσκημμα, 177n111
Homer (Hom.)
Iliad (Il.)
1.4–5, 167n57
1.265, 170n69
2.499, 162n29
2.553–54, 58n48
3.144, 170n69
4.376–98, 161n20
4.399–403, 161n20
5.801–8, 161n20
6.222–23, 161n20
6.440–65, 306n80
6.447–65, 325
14.113–21, 161n20
14.114, 165, 167n54
19.99, 226n46
23.346, 161
23.346–47, 161n20
Odyssey (Od..)
11.321–25, 170n69
11.326–27, 161n20
11.631, 170n69
15.247, 161n20
Homeric Hymn to Demeter (Hom. Hymn Dem.)
154, 56n41
Hyperides (Hyp.)
Against Athenogenes (Ath.)
31, 98
31–33, 98
33, 98, 98n275
Epitaphius (Epit.)
5, 58n48
7, 55n34
17, 322
37, 265n159

Ion (*TrGF* 19)
F 8a Snell, 181
F 9 Snell, 181
F 9a Snell, 181
T 1 Snell, 181
Isocrates (Isoc.)
1.34, 38n173
2.35, 38n173
4.9, 38n173
4.24, 58n48
4.28–29, 307n84
4.29–31, 67
4.30, 27n120
4.33–34, 228n54
4.52, 187
4.53, 188
4.54, 187, 189
4.54–55, 157
4.55, 188, 188n157
4.57, 189
4.58, 157, 157n7
4.66, 56
4.68, 27n120
4.68–70, 54n32, 56n39
4.86, 135
4.94–96, 144
5.30–31, 228
5.32, 226, 228
5.32–34, 34n157
5.33, 228
5.39–41, 34n157
5.42–45, 34n157
5.43, 266n162
5.114, 227
5.114–16, 227n52
5.148, 85
5.248, 268n169
6.24, 27n120
6.27, 268n169
6.42, 27n120
6.99–100, 42n201

7.6, 246n103, 282n5, 289, 304
8.17, 125, 268n169
8.78, 282n5, 289, 304
8.105, 282n5, 289, 304
8.115, 125
9.56–57, 313
10.31, 157, 157n7, 174
12.5, 202
12.17, 202
12.92–94, 300n62
12.93, 101n2, 102, 127, 128n102, 137, 139n138, 246n103
12.93–94, 122
12.151–98, 202
12.168, 158, 202, 203, 203n209, 205
12.168–69, 64, 182
12.168–70, 182n135
12.168–71, 202
12.168–72, 179n124, 196, 349
12.169, 206, 207n233
12.169–70, 207
12.170, 207, 207n232, 207n233, 208
12.170–71, 207
12.170–73, 158
12.171, 208, 350
12.172–73, 202, 204
12.173, 202, 203, 203n209
12.200, 203
12.268–70, 202
14.1, 34n160, 199, 253n130
14.3, 199n198
14.28–29, 265n162
14.29, 261n149
14.30, 101n2, 102, 124, 152, 246n103
14.31, 282n5, 302n70, 305, 307, 309, 310, 311n93, 328, 353
14.31–32, 246n103, 288
14.32, 320
14.52, 199
14.53, 157n7, 199
14.53–54, 199, 209, 349
14.53–55, 157, 173n89, 196
14.54–55, 199
14.57, 127, 128n102, 136, 253n130
14.58–59, 124
14.59, 54n30, 87, 109, 152
14.61, 101n2, 102, 124, 139n138
14.62, 102, 124
15.79, 35n162
15.299, 322
15.319, 246n103, 282n5, 290, 291n22, 292n28, 304
16.4, 23n98, 75n147
16.25–26, 74
16.27, 58, 322
18.29, 282n5, 285, 297n43, 326, 328

Justin
5.8.4, 282n5, 322n138
5.8–10, 216n8
5.9.4, 217, 218n17
5.9.8, 232, 243
9.4.6, 272n178
9.4.7, 272
9.4.8–9, 272
11.3.8, 336, 337, 339
11.3.8–10, 340
11.3.9–10, 317, 338, 338n181
11.4.1–7, 337n180
11.4.4, 322, 322n140
11.4.4–6, 226
11.4.9–11, 276

Lexica Segueriana
Glossae rhetoricae
s.v. μηλόβοτος, 305, 305n77
Lycurgus (Lycurg.)
41, 58
51, 90
62, 42n201
71, 144, 146
75, 42n201
76–78, 94
80–82, 94
81, 311, 311n92, 316, 316n116, 324n144
83, 27n120
93, 176n107
98–99, 62
98–101, 73
100, 62, 79n172
101, 62
105–6, 78n169
105–8, 78
106, 23n98

Lycurgus (Lycurg.) (*continued*)
- **107**, 79n172
- **145**, 308, 309
- **fr. III 2** Conomis, 308, 309
- **fr. X–XI 10** Conomis, 62n64, 73n133

Lysias (Lys.)
- **2.1**, 50n6, 146n157
- **2.4–6**, 54n32
- **2.5**, 55
- **2.5–6**, 55
- **2.7**, 188, 189, 190, 197n193, 206n225
- **2.7–10**, 157, 173n89
- **2.8**, 188
- **2.8–10**, 157n7
- **2.9**, 188, 188n157, 189, 191n170
- **2.10**, 160, 188, 188n159, 189, 209n238
- **2.11–16**, 228n54
- **2.17**, 55, 58n48, 187n152
- **2.18**, 55n34
- **2.20**, 52, 135n128, 141
- **2.20–26**, 131
- **2.20–47**, 54n30
- **2.21**, 52, 143n149
- **2.21–47**, 55n38
- **2.22**, 55, 187n153
- **2.23**, 135n128
- **2.25**, 54n30
- **2.26**, 54n30, 207n232
- **2.29**, 143n149
- **2.30–31**, 52
- **2.33**, 144
- **2.33–43**, 52
- **2.35**, 54n30
- **2.41**, 54n30
- **2.42**, 54n30
- **2.43**, 55n34
- **2.44**, 54n30
- **2.46**, 112, 141
- **2.46–47**, 52
- **2.47**, 54, 54n30, 186
- **2.49**, 56
- **2.50**, 56
- **2.52**, 56
- **2.53**, 57
- **2.57**, 54, 186, 187
- **2.61**, 91
- **2.62–63**, 91–92
- **2.63**, 242n96
- **2.66**, 85n202, 241
- **12.17**, 218n17
- **13.77**, 244
- **13.9**, 295n38
- **16.4**, 236n77
- **19.48**, 23n98
- **23.6**, 123
- **28.12**, 236n78, 244n101
- **31.8–9**, 236n77
- **fr. 128 Carey**, 92n248
- **fr. 129 Carey**, 92n248
- **fr. 286 Carey**, 29, 81, 218n17, 220, 257, 259
- **fr. 286.2 Carey**, 29, 223
- **fr. 286.3 Carey**, 29, 259

Mimnermus
- **fr. 9** West², 77
- **fr. 9.6** West², 78
- **fr. 10** West², 77
- **fr. 13** West², 77, 78n167
- **fr. 13a** West², 77, 78n167
- **fr. 14** West², 77
- **fr. 14.2** West², 77n163

Nepos (Nep.)
- *Epaminondas (Epam.)*
  - **6.1–3**, 61
- *Miltiades (Milt.)*
  - **4**, 94n256
- *Pelopidas (Pelop.)*
  - **2.1–4.1**, 261n149

Pausanias (Paus.)
- **1.3.2**, 313
- **1.10.4**, 162n30
- **1.15**, 88
- **1.15.3**, 88, 129
- **1.15.5**, 74n141
- **1.17.2**, 88
- **1.26.5–27.2**, 66
- **1.27.1**, 86, 110
- **1.29.3**, 92, 235n72, 237n80, 239
- **1.29.4**, 50n3
- **1.29.8**, 191, 348
- **1.30.4**, 162, 183n145

1.32.3, 85, 129
1.32.5, 84
1.34.2, 165n47
1.36.1, 84
1.38.8, 165n45
1.39.2, 90n235, 160, 168, 207n231
3.8.6, 282, 282n5, 285n14, 297
3.9.2, 247
4.15.3, 78n169
4.27.10, 126n98
5.10.4, 112n49
5.23, 108, 108n25
8.25.5–10, 163n37
8.25.8, 161
9.1.3, 140
9.1.4, 123
9.1.5–8, 123, 198
9.1.8, 126n98, 272
9.2.5, 85, 109n27
9.3.9, 73n135, 110n42
9.4.1, 111n44, 129
9.4.1–2, 111, 183
9.4.2, 183
9.8.3, 165
9.9.5, 161n21
9.11.2, 229, 235
9.11.4–6, 226
9.11.6, 231, 234, 245
9.12.3–4, 226
9.16.6–7, 226
9.16.7, 168
9.17.2, 168
9.18.1, 165
9.18.1–3, 165
9.18.3, 165
9.19.4, 162n29, 165n47
9.32.4, 128
9.32.9, 296n41
10.9.5–6, 87
10.9.7–10, 87
10.9.9, 284n12, 297
10.10.1–2, 87
10.10.3–4, 87
10.11.4, 171n76
10.11.5–6, 87
10.28.2, 170n69

Pherecydes (*FGrHist* 3)
F 84, 187n150
Philochorus (*FGrHist* 328)
F 27, 27n123
F 56b, 203, 269
F 109, 67
F 111, 67
F 112, 158, 164n45, 172, 207
F 113, 163, 172n80
F 177, 177
Philostratus (Philostr.)
Vitae sophistarum (VS)
1.16, 236n79
Photius
Lexicon
s.v. μηλόβοτος, 305, 305n77
Pindar (Pind.)
Nemean Odes (Nem.)
1.33–72, 226n46
2.16–17, 71
9.22, 166, 167
9.22–24, 166
Olympian Odes (Ol.)
6.15–17, 166
6.16, 166
Plato (Pl.)
Laches (Lach.)
179c–d, 115n59
Leges (Leg.)
629a, 78n169
Menexenus (Menex.)
234c–235c, 51
236d–249c, 50n5
237b, 58n48
237b–c, 55n34
237c, 67
238e–239a, 55n34
239b, 54n32, 56, 56n39, 157n7, 173n89, 186, 188, 191, 197n193, 206n225
240a, 52n20
240c, 52n20
244e, 251n124
245c–d, 55n34
Protagoras (Prt.)
337d, 322

Plato (Pl.) (*continued*)
- *Respublica (Resp.)*
  - **368a**, 80
  - **475d**, 64
- *Timaeus (Ti.)*
  - **21b**, 79

Pliny the Elder (Plin.)
- *Naturalis historia (NH)*
  - **35.49**, 234n68

Plutarch (Plut.)
- *Alcibiades (Alc.)*
  - **33.1**, 80
- *Alexander (Alex.)*
  - **11.11**, 341
  - **13.1**, 275, 276n192
- *Aristides (Arist.)*
  - **11.3–4**, 73n135, 110n42
  - **19.6**, 73, 110
  - **20**, 141n144
  - **20.3**, 111, 183
  - **21**, 109, 109n30
- *Cimon (Cim.)*
  - **8.5–7**, 67
- *Demosthenes (Dem.)*
  - **9.1**, 82, 271
  - **18.2**, 270
  - **23.1**, 274
  - **23.3–6**, 275
- *Lysander (Lys.)*
  - **13.1**, 296
  - **14.3**, 296
  - **15.2**, 282, 284n12, 297, 305n76, 307, 309, 353
  - **15.2–3**, 282n5
  - **15.3**, 335, 335n175
  - **15.4**, 312
  - **17**, 217n13
  - **17.2**, 282n3, 307n85
  - **20**, 217n13
  - **25**, 217n13
  - **27**, 224
  - **27.2**, 217, 219, 276n193
  - **27.3**, 213n4, 217, 219
  - **27.3–4**, 225, 227, 233
  - **27.4**, 232, 243, 245
  - **27.4–5**, 218n17
  - **30**, 217n13
- *Moralia (Mor.)*
  - **193c**, 61
  - **193d**, 61
  - **349e**, 68
  - **349e–f**, 110
  - **349f**, 69
  - **349f–350a**, 69
  - **576a**, 81, 256
  - **596–98**, 261n149
  - **628e**, 94n256
  - **628e–f**, 73n135, 110n42
  - **814a–c**, 39
  - **862a**, 68
  - **864e**, 103, 118
  - **867a**, 117n69
- *Nicias (Nic.)*
  - **29.2–4**, 335n175
- *Pelopidas (Pelop.)*
  - **5–13**, 261
  - **5.3**, 259
  - **6.3**, 255, 257, 257n139
  - **6.4**, 255
  - **6.4–5**, 258
  - **6.5**, 213n4, 217, 219
  - **8.1**, 259
- *Pericles (Per.)*
  - **16.7**, 306, 306n83
  - **17**, 324n145
  - **31.2**, 176n107
- *Themistocles (Them.)*
  - **10.5**, 98
- *Theseus (Thes.)*
  - **18.1**, 67
  - **20.1–2**, 170, 170n69
  - **24**, 171
  - **26.1**, 170n71
  - **26.1–27.2**, 56
  - **28.1**, 56
  - **29.3**, 172n82
  - **29.4**, 162n28, 207n230
  - **29.4–5**, 158, 160, 169, 172, 178, 205, 207
  - **36**, 178n114
  - **36.1–4**, 67
  - **36.4**, 67, 177n109
- *Timoleon (Tim.)*
  - **22.1–3**, 313

[Plutarch] [Plut.]
Vitae decem oratorum (X or.)
835f–836a, 241n90
Polyaenus (Polyaen.)
1.45.5, 224, 282, 282n5, 297, 320
Polybius (Polyb.)
38.2.13, 341

Satyrus (Satyr.)
Vita Euripidis (Vit. Eur.)
39.19.11–34, 335n175
Scholia (Schol.) on Aeschines
Aeschin. **2.117** (257 Dilts), 266n162
Aeschin. **3.108** (238 Dilts), 302n69
Aeschin. **3.118** (265 Dilts), 335n174
Scholia (Schol.) on Aristides, Aelius
Aristid. *Leuc. A* **614** Dindorf (iii.346 Dindorf), 309n88, 322n138, 335
Aristid. *Leuc. A* **639** Dindorf (iii.352 Dindorf), 322n141
Aristid. *Panath.* **274** Dindorf (iii.261 Dindorf), 309n88
Aristid. *Panath.* **319** Dindorf (iii.341 Dindorf), 313
Scholia (Schol.) on Demosthenes
Dem. **19.65** (165a Dilts), 284n12, 322
Dem. **19.65** (165a, b Dilts), 282n5, 305n76, 309n88, 335
Dem. **19.73** (173 Dilts), 335n174
Scholia (Schol.) on Euripides
Eur. *Phoen.* **159** Schwartz, 168
Scholia (Schol.) on Homer
Il. **14.114a** Erbse, 167n54
Il. **23.346a** Erbse, 161
Scholia (Schol.) on Pindar
Pind. *Ol.* **6.23a** Drachmann, 167, 167n57, 168n62
Pind. *Ol.* **6.23b** Drachmann, 166n50
Pind. *Ol.* **6.23d** Drachmann, 162n28, 166n51
Pind. *Ol.* **6.26** Drachmann, 167n54
Scholia (Schol.) on Sophocles
Soph. *OC* **712** de Marco, 162n31
Scholia vetera (Schol. vet.) on Aristophanes
Ar. *Plut.* **1146g** Chantry, 240n88
Ar. *Plut.* **1146h α** Chantry, 240n88
Ar. *Plut.* **1146h β** Chantry, 240nn88–89
scolia
PMG **893–96**, 79
Semonides
fr. 1 West[2], 79n176
Simonides
fr. 11 Sider = **11** West[2], 78n164, 109
fr. 13–17 Sider = **13–17** West[2], 110
Solon
fr. 4 West[2], 79, 79n170
fr. 4a West[2], 79n170
fr. 4c West[2], 79n170
fr. 5 West[2], 79n170
fr. 6 West[2], 79n170
fr. 9 West[2], 79n170
fr. 10 West[2], 79n170
fr. 11 West[2], 79n170
Sophocles (Soph.)
Antigone (Ant.)
141, 206n226
175–90, 62n67
337–41, 306n82
Oedipus Coloneus (OC)
53–65, 162n29
Oedipus Tyrannus (OT)
711–12, 209n237
Strabo (Strab.)
9.2.11, 162, 163, 165, 165n47, 236n76
Suda
s.v. μηλόβοτος χώρα, 308, 309n88, 310n90, 335

Thebaid
fr. 6a Davies, 161, 163
fr. 6c Davies, 161
fr. 7 Davies, 167n54
Theopompus (*FGrHist* 115)
F 328, 270
Theseid
fr. 2 Davies, 170n71
Thucydides (Thuc.)
1.9–12, 26n119
1.18.1, 134n126
1.20.3, 45n207
1.22, 121n84
1.23.6, 33

Thucydides (Thuc.) (*continued*)

1.73.2, 27n120
1.73.4, 134
1.89.3, 324
1.102.4, 191
1.105–6, 56
1.107, 114, 332
1.107–8, 191
1.108, 114
1.112, 332
1.113, 114, 332n166
1.132, 108n22
2.2–6, 114, 117, 120
2.6, 122
2.6.4, 122
2.13, 81
2.15, 26n119
2.15.1–2, 171
2.15.2, 67
2.20.4, 71
2.21.3, 71
2.22, 114
2.34, 51
2.34.1, 85n203
2.34.5, 85
2.35.2, 50n6
2.35–46, 50n5
2.36, 58n48
2.36.4, 50n7
2.41.1, 322
2.71, 34n155, 121n85, 253n130
2.71.2, 69, 109, 120
2.71–78, 95, 120
3.20–24, 95, 120
3.24, 122
3.24.2, 122
3.36, 34
3.52.5, 121n84
3.52–59, 120
3.52–68, 114, 120
3.53–59, 34n155, 135, 253n130
3.54, 140
3.54.1, 121
3.54.2–4, 121
3.54.3, 128n101, 128n102
3.54.5, 122n86
3.55.1, 122n86
3.56.4, 121
3.56.4–5, 121
3.57.2, 87, 108, 121
3.58.3–4, 109
3.58.4, 86n209, 121
3.58.5, 121
3.62, 118, 152, 208n237
3.62.3–4, 318
3.63–65, 135n130
3.64.5, 152, 208n237
3.68.5, 105n11
3.91, 114
4.57.2–4, 294
4.67.2, 123
4.89–101, 114
4.92, 114
4.92.7, 115n59
4.95, 119n78
4.95.3, 115
4.97, 321
4.97–99, 192n175
4.97–101, 192
4.122.6, 294
5.3.2–4, 294
5.17, 114
5.18.8, 294n35
5.22, 114
5.26, 114
5.32.1, 123, 294
5.116.3–4, 294
6.54.6, 176n103
6.83.2, 134n126
8.54, 76
8.60.1, 114
8.65, 76

Tyrtaeus

fr. 5 West^2, 78, 78n167
fr. 5.1–2 West^2, 78n165
fr. 6 West^2, 78
fr. 7 West^2, 78
fr. 10 West^2, 78
fr. 11 West^2, 78
fr. 12 West^2, 78

Varro

De lingua Latina (Ling.)
5.147, 317n119

Xenophanes
- **fr. B1** West[2], 75n151
- **fr. B1.19–20** West[2], 77
- **fr. B1.21–23** West[2], 77

Xenophon (Xen.)
- *Anabasis (An.)*
  - **3.2.11–14**, 37n171
  - **3.2.12**, 68
- *Hellenica (Hell.)*
  - **1.1.1–2.3.10**, 328n155
  - **2.1.31–32**, 296
  - **2.2.2**, 296
  - **2.2.3**, 282n5, 293, 295n40, 296n42, 324
  - **2.2.4**, 294
  - **2.2.9**, 296, 296n42
  - **2.2.10**, 295n40, 296n42
  - **2.2.10–11**, 295
  - **2.2.14–15**, 295
  - **2.2.15**, 295
  - **2.2.16–19**, 295
  - **2.2.19**, 220, 282n5, 328
  - **2.2.19–20**, 42, 224, 281, 310, 312n97, 327
  - **2.2.20**, 320, 322
  - **2.2.23**, 312
  - **2.3–4**, 216n8
  - **2.3.14**, 218n16
  - **2.3.38–40**, 218n16
  - **2.3.42**, 218n18
  - **2.4.1**, 216, 218n17, 218n18
  - **2.4.2**, 217, 239
  - **2.4.2–7**, 236
  - **2.4.11–42**, 91n240
  - **2.4.20–21**, 70
  - **2.4.25**, 240
  - **2.4.30**, 217, 224, 232
  - **2.4.33**, 91, 237n80, 247
  - **3.1.4**, 247
  - **3.2.25**, 247
  - **3.5.3**, 332n167
  - **3.5.3–7**, 246
  - **3.5.5**, 224
  - **3.5.8**, 246, 248, 250, 252, 282n5, 286, 301, 327
  - **3.5.8–15**, 33n153, 248
  - **3.5.9**, 248
  - **3.5.10**, 249, 251n121
  - **3.5.10–15**, 251
  - **3.5.11–12**, 249
  - **3.5.12**, 251n122
  - **3.5.13**, 251n121
  - **3.5.13–14**, 249
  - **3.5.14**, 249, 251n121
  - **3.5.15**, 249
  - **3.5.16**, 248, 252
  - **4.1.31–36**, 254
  - **5.2.25**, 254
  - **5.2.25–32**, 254
  - **5.2.31**, 153n172, 255, 257
  - **5.2.33–36**, 254
  - **5.4.1**, 254, 263n153
  - **5.4.1–19**, 261n149
  - **5.4.9**, 261, 263
  - **5.4.10**, 123
  - **5.4.10–12**, 261
  - **5.4.14**, 123
  - **5.4.19**, 262, 263, 266
  - **5.4.34**, 262
  - **5.4.48**, 123
  - **6.3.1**, 36, 83n191, 125, 128n103, 139n138, 200, 268n167, 329n157
  - **6.3.4–6**, 28, 83
  - **6.3.5**, 83, 125, 200, 329n157
  - **6.3.6**, 83
  - **6.3.13**, 34n160, 282n5, 288
  - **6.3.20**, 112, 125, 316, 318n124
  - **6.5.1–3**, 329n158
  - **6.5.33**, 34n160
  - **6.5.33–35**, 329
  - **6.5.33–48**, 200, 200n203
  - **6.5.33–49**, 329
  - **6.5.34**, 83n192
  - **6.5.35**, 112, 282n5, 288, 288n20, 301, 311, 312n97, 316, 318n124, 329, 330
  - **6.5.35–36**, 329
  - **6.5.36**, 288
  - **6.5.40**, 253n130
  - **6.5.44**, 253n130
  - **6.5.45**, 200
  - **6.5.45–46**, 209, 349
  - **6.5.46**, 201, 282n5, 289, 304, 330
  - **6.5.47**, 157, 157n7, 173n89, 196, 201n206
  - **6.5.48**, 201

Xenophon (Xen.) (*continued*)
7.1.34–35, 151, 153n170, 338
7.1.35, 151
7.1.38, 151
7.5.27, 125
Memorabilia (Mem.)
3.5.10, 174
Symposium (Symp.)
8.39, 82

INSCRIPTIONS

Inscriptiones Graecae (IG)
I³ **3**, 68
I³ **127**, 234
I³ **255.11**, 68
II² **1**, 234
II² **2** (*add.* p. 655), 243n97
II² **2**, 243n97, 257, 257n140
II² **2.2–3**, 257n140
II² **10**, 92n248, 122n88, 238, 239, 241, 243, 245, 351
II² **10.4**, 244
II² **14**, 247
II² **20.17**, 251n124
II² **37**, 82, 257, 352
II² **37** (*add.* pp. 656–57), 255n134
II² **37.5** (*add.* p. 656)
II² **37.16–17** (*add.* p. 656)
II² **37.16–20** (*add.* p. 656)
II² **37.19–20** (*add.* p. 656)
II² **37.28**, 257n140
II² **43**, 261n149, 263n154
II² **43.72–77**, 258, 278
II² **109**, 334
II² **1028.8**, 68
II² **4590**, 27n123
II² **11678**, 91
VII 2407, 235n71
VII 2408, 235n71

Meiggs & Lewis (M&L)
15, 106, 192
23, 94
27, 87, 108
35, 191, 348
36, 112n49
70, 74
94, 234n65
95d, 284n12, 297

Rhodes & Osborne (R&O)
2, 234n65
4, 238, 239, 241, 242, 243, 245, 351
4.4, 244
4.4–5, 241n93
6, 247
11.17, 251n124
22, 261, 261n149, 263n154, 278
22.72–77, 258
43, 235n71
88, 72, 94, 311, 314, 331
88.31–39, 311n92, 316n116
88.32–35, 331
88.33–34, 316

Supplementum Epigraphicum Graecum (SEG)
21.519, 72
28.45, 92n248, 237, 237n82, 237n84, 238, 239n86, 243, 245, 278, 351
28.45.1–2, 243n99
28.45.43–47, 237n82
28.45.73–76, 237n82
28.46, 92n248
32.38, 243n97, 257, 257n140
32.47, 82, 255, 256n136, 257
32.47.5, 255, 352
32.47.16–17, 255
32.47.16–20, 256
32.47.19–20, 256
Sylloge Inscriptionum Graecarum (Syll.³)
175, 334

PAPYRI

Michigan Papyri (P Mich.)
5982, 231n58, 295n38

Oxyrhynchus Papyri (P Oxy.)
1241 col. iii.12–28, 173n83

General Index

Acamas (son of Theseus), 28
Achaeus (playwright), 181, 205
Acharnae, 71, 94n257, 314, 331
Acharnians, 71–72
actors, professional, 64, 182
Adams, John, 15–16
Adrastus: aided by Theseus, 55, 160, 172, 174, 187; attacks Thebes, 64, 111, 155; escapes, 155, 160n16, 161–65, 165n45, 169, 206; in Greek art, 182–86, 190; Isocrates on, 201–9; Pindar on, 166–67; as suppliant, 54, 173–86, 189, 190, 198, 206; on tragic stage, 177–82, 190, 192, 205. *See also* burial of fallen Argives
Aegina, 56
Aeginetans, 56, 108, 293–96, 324
Aegospotami, battle of, 87, 281, 284n12, 285, 287, 292–98, 323–24, 352
Aeschines: on destruction of Crisa, 302–9, 311, 315n114, 316; use of Andocides, 95; use of family tradition, 75, 97
Aeschylus, as Eleusinian, 164, 180
Aethra, 170n69, 180–81, 188n155
a fortiori argument, 62, 199, 201
age-set, 70, 72, 80
Agesilaus (Spartan king), 125, 200n204, 247, 250, 262
Agis (Spartan king), 283, 296–97, 298n48
Aianteia, 69
aide-mémoire, 10n34, 126, 306, 323–26
Ajax of Salamis, 69
Alcamenes, 234
Alcibiades (the Elder), 80
Alcibiades (the Younger), 58, 74
Alcmene, 226
Alcock, Susan, 7n16, 19, 20, 28, 84
Alexander I of Macedon, 96, 144–46
Alexander the Great, 36, 82, 272–77, 324, 354; and Athens, 73, 275–77, 352; and council of Greek allies, 275, 336–41; destroys Thebes, 5n11, 45, 206, 212, 215, 226, 275, 277, 285, 301, 316, 322, 336–41, 352
alliance: Athenian-Plataean of 519 BC, 105, 105n11, 173, 174, 175, 175n95, 196n188, 346; Athenian-Argive of 460 BC, 179, 191; Athenian-Argive of 420 BC, 193n179; Athenian-Theban of 395 BC, 5, 36, 212, 214, 243–53, 286, 327, 351; Athenian-Theban of 378 BC, 261; Athenian-Spartan of 369 BC, 124, 200–201, 288–89; Athenian-Phocian of 356 BC, 43n203, 333–35; Athenian-Theban of 339/8 BC, 204, 214, 268–71, 271n174, 277, 352
allusion, historical, 2, 4, 5, 23, 30, 342; as analogue to present, 144–49, 153, 190,

allusion, historical (*continued*)
199, 200, 201, 209, 227n51, 233, 240, 260, 285, 299, 311, 330, 335, 347, 349; in battle harangues, 114–16, 119n78; to burial of fallen Argives, 156–58, 196–210, 348–50; corroborated by elders, 23, 23n98, 43, 75, 97, 212–14, 232, 244, 254, 278–79, 291, 352; corroborated through inscriptions, 93–94, 97, 291, 302; corroborated through monuments, 138; dependent on situation, 128, 131–35, 152n170, 174, 197, 199n198, 200, 209; familiarity of, 46–47, 89, 97, 137, 143, 207, 208; to Heracles, 226; to men from Phyle, 236–40, 243–44; to mythical past, 26–28, 44, 156–58, 196–210, 223–32; to proposed eradication of Athens, 248, 250, 285–91, 326–41, 354; to recent past, 23–25; resonance of, 2, 34n158, 43, 65, 74n140, 79, 83, 94, 95, 137, 144, 153, 165, 181, 191, 199, 200, 207, 229, 253, 321, 346, 347, 350; to Theban medizing, 101–3, 118–54, 224, 280, 337–39, 344–45; to Theban help for Thrasybulus, 212–16, 245–53, 253–60, 267–79, 351–52; to Theseus, 157, 173–74, 201–10
Amazonomachy. *See* Amazons, battle against
Amazons, battle against 27, 50, 54n32, 54–57, 88, 131, 174, 183, 186–87, 193, 194, 196, 211, 227, 347, 348
amnesty of 403 BC, 24, 91, 92, 215, 240
Amorges, 74
Amphiaraus, 160n16, 162, 163n35, 165–66, 167n54, 183
Amphictyons, 85, 126, 152, 285n14, 297n43, 302–3, 306, 309, 311, 315n112, 332–34, 339, 353
Amphipolis, 28
Amphissa, 152, 203
Amphitryon, 226, 229, 235
Amyntas (Macedonian officer), 273
Amyntas (son of Perdiccas III), 341n189
Anaxandrus, 117n69
Anbar, desserts of, 1
Anderson, Benedict, 7n17
Anderson, Greg, 5, 16nn63–64, 171
Andocides, 26; use of family tradition, 77–75; used by Aeschines, 95
andrapodizing, 281n2
Androcleidas, 220–21, 257, 257n139, 259
Andromache, 325
annihilation of Athens, proposed. *See* eradication of Athens, proposed
Antalcidas, Peace of. *See* King's Peace
Anthesteria, 63
Antigone, 168
Antiope (Amazon), 56, 170
Antiphanes, 79
Antitheus, 220, 257
Anytus, 218n18
Apaturia festival, 79
Aphidna, 71
Apollo, 67, 69, 209n237, 226, 284, 302–6, 309, 314–15, 320
Apollodorus (mythographer), on Adrastus, 176
Apollodorus (orator): Plataean paradigm, 93, 95, 126–27, 137–41; use of Thucydides, 95–96
Apollodorus (playwright), 181, 205, 206n224
Apollonians, 255
Arcadians, 61, 249
Archedemus of Pelekes, 277
archegetes, mythical, 56, 70n120, 83
Archelaus of Macedon, 224n35
Archidamian War, 71
Archidamus, 71, 81, 121n85
Archinus of Coele, 237, 240–41, 243, 245, 278
archive culture, modern, 22–23, 39
Areopagus, 61, 61n61, 180
Ares, 72
Arginusae, battle of, 182
Argives. *See* Argos; burial of fallen Argives
Argos, 34n157, 61, 147, 191, 222, 228, 249, 325, 346–47; and ashes of Seven, 164; and Attic Harma, 163; harboring Athenians, 217–18; heroön of Seven in, 161, 167; and Orestes, 61; and Philip, 143, 147; and Xerxes, 103, 198n196. *See also* burial of fallen Argives

Arion, 161, 163, 176
Aristagoras, 175n97
Aristides, 109, 265
Aristodemus (actor and ambassador), 64n79, 82n188
Aristodemus (Theban historian), 168
Aristogeiton, 79–80, 90, 313
Aristophanes (playwright), 60, 63, 72, 79, 240
Aristophanes of Boeotia, 103n3, 118
Aristophanes of Byzantium, 167n54, 256
Aristophon of Azenia, 278
Aristotle: *Rhetoric*, 28, 34n158, 35, 38n173, 41n194, 42
Aristoxenus (Boeotian), 257
Armenidas, 167–68
Artabanus, 134n126, 143n149
Artaxerxes III, 149–151
Artemis, 303; Agrotera, 68, 133; Munichia, 69
Artemisium, battle of, 1, 2, 46, 52, 52n22, 68, 69, 110, 121, 139, 140
Asclepiades, 167n54
Asias, 220–21
assembly, Athenian, 3–5, 20n86, 30, 37, 44, 48–50, 58, 59, 62–65, 69, 70, 73, 74, 82, 84, 89, 92, 96–99, 114, 123–26, 128n103, 133–37, 156, 172n80, 173–76, 181, 198–201, 204, 206n227, 246–53, 255, 260, 264, 267, 276, 269, 279, 328, 334–35, 342–43, 349, 354–55
Assmann, Aleida, 24–25, 24n105
Assmann, Jan, 8n22, 19, 24n105, 25n110, 28, 107n15
associations, religious, 70
Astycrates (Delphian), 334
asylum, for Delphians 334; for Thebans, 36, 81, 205, 255, 258, 260, 264, 267, 274, 276, 352; for Troezenians, 98
ateleia, 241n91, 260, 334
Athena: Areia, 72, 111, 129, 183, 190, 192n173, 194, 196n188, 346, 347; and Gigantomachy, 66; and Heracles, 171, 227–31, 234–35, 245, 350–51; Hippia, 162–63; at Marathon, 88; Nike, 193; Parthenos, 66n94, 88; Polias, 66, 86, 110; and Poseidon, 66–67; Pronaia, 303; and Seven against Thebes, 164, 183, 193, 193n179
Athènes imaginaire, 19
Athenian democrats, Theban help for. *See* Theban help for Thrasybulus
Athenian intervention. *See* burial of fallen Argives
Athenians: aiding suppliants, 105, 159, 173–86, 191–92, 198–200, 211, 287, 328, 346, 349; alone of the Greeks, 58, 136–37, 328; as champions of the Greeks, 1, 20, 27, 52–54, 58, 107, 130, 144, 154–55, 159, 186–89, 211, 225, 251, 265, 280–81, 321, 344–46, 349, 351; cooperate with Thebans, 4, 153, 206, 212, 227, 234, 267, 268–70, 272, 351–52; as defenders of the weak, 20, 54, 130, 187, 199, 210, 211, 225, 249, 251, 281, 349; dispute with Tegeans, 28n128, 57, 110n39, 130, 134, 156, 196, 348; eradicate Greek cities, 293–95, 323–24, 352–54; and the Greek *nomos*, 187–91, 197, 199, 207, 208, 347, 350; as hegemon, 20, 44, 53–56, 58, 61, 131, 134, 156, 159, 174, 186–89, 191, 199–200, 249, 280, 344, 347; and justice, 55, 58, 144, 148, 150, 151n169, 154, 187–89, 191, 199, 225, 249, 251, 347; military superiority of, 50, 51, 84, 187–89, 191, 196–98, 202, 203n212, 207, 225, 265, 350; and piety, 190–91, 228n55; as *prostates* of the Greeks, 52, 54, 186–89, 251, 346
Athenogenes, 98
Athens: besieged in 405/4 BC, 281, 284, 287, 291–98, 319n128, 325, 353; conference in 371 BC, 329; destroyed by Persians, 323–24; evacuation in 480 BC, 98, 137, 144–47, 189; as hearth of Hellas, 313, 320, 322, as oral society, 21, 39, 75, 94, 159n11, 213; surrender of, 42, 45, 215–16, 281, 290–91, 292n28; as tyrant city, 312, 313, 321, 353
Atrometus, 74
Attaginus (Theban), 104, 318
Atthidographer, 73, 95, 95n261, 97, 165n45, 173n84, 207, 207n230
Attic orators. *See* orators
Attica, map of, 6

Augeas, stables of, 229–30
Auschwitz, 22, 23n97, 26, 26n32, 116
autochthony, Athenian, 50, 55, 55n34, 58, 187n152
Autolycus, 308

Bartlett, F. C., 10n31, 10n34, 11n39
Boeotia, map of, 6
Boeotian League, 105–6, 114, 120, 125, 211, 220–23, 225, 247, 254, 261, 266n162, 319
Boeotians: against Athenians, 106, 114, 115, 192, 224n38; against Spartans, 246, 249, 268; aiding Thrasybulus, 236, 243, 245, 252; and Chalcidians, 106, 192; at Delium, 119n78, 192; during Persian Wars, 102, 104n8, 111n46, 118, 119, 125n94, 127, 135n127, 139, 140, 345; as exiles in Athens, 255–57; at Oenophyta, 114; Thebans as, 106n13
Bömer, Franz, 301n66, 304, 311n96, 312, 314n106, 315, 316n115, 317
Boreas, 68
boule, Boeotian federal, 221–22, 229; Theban, 223
bouleuterion, 243, 245
Bourdieu, Pierre, 31
Brasidas, 294, 294n37
Buck, Robert J., 33nn151–52, 223–24, 224n38, 264, 266
Buckler, John, 330n159
burial of fallen Argives, 5, 5n11, 43–44, 100, 111, 131, 281, 345–50; in art, 182–86, 190, 193–96, 346, 348; and Athenians as *prostates*, 186–89, 198–201; and battle of Plataea, 189–90, 196–98; by diplomatic means, 158, 159n11, 168–69, 173, 179, 182n135, 188, 191n172, 199, 202, 203n209, 203n212, 205, 207, 207n230, 208, 208n236, 209n238, 349–50; Eleusinian tradition of, 161–62, 164–65, 169, 173–74, 346; in Eleusis, 155, 157, 159–69, 172–74, 178–79, 186, 190, 197–98, 345–46; in Eleutherae, 160, 162–65, 167, 172, 345; in epic, 159, 160–69; in funeral oration, 156–57, 159–60, 164, 166, 173–75, 186–91, 196, 197n193, 201–2, 205–9; layers of meaning, 159, 190–91, 347; and local cults 156, 159–69; by means of battle, 157, 159n11, 173n83, 172, 178, 179, 188, 190–92, 196, 202, 203, 203n212, 207n230, 207n234, 209, 209n238, 347–48; as mythical analogue, 111, 190, 199, 200, 209, 225, 347; Theban refusal of, 155, 188, 189, 192, 194, 208, 345, 348; in Thebes, 165–69, 198, 346; and Theseus, 157, 169–74; in tragedy, 158, 159n11, 160, 164, 166, 169, 172–75, 177–82, 189, 191–93, 205–6, 346, 348; used by orators, 156–58, 196–210
Bush, George W., 1, 2, 131–33, 149n164, 328n156

Cadmea, 167, 168, 172, 178, 192n174, 199, 201, 235, 245, 255, 272–73; liberation of, 259, 261–66, 269, 278; Spartan seizure of, 29, 36, 45, 81, 82, 123, 205, 254–56, 278
Cadmeans, 157, 188, 191, 197, 197n193
Cadmus, 190, 197, 197n193, 209, 209n238, 226, 349
cadre matériel, 4, 19, 20, 44, 84, 109, 343
Callias, son of Hipponicus, 28, 82–83, 125
Callimachus (Athenian), 89
Callistratus (Athenian), 61, 288
Camarina, 134n126
Camisard revolts, 17, 55n37, 56n40, 303n71
carriers of Athenian social memory: cults, 48, 65–69, 156, 159–69; *demes*, 48, 71–72, 97, 239, 242, 343; dramatic festivals, 48, 58–65, 156, 174–82, 192–93, 240, 325; family, 73–75, 115n59; funeral oration, 48–58, 186–89, 264–66; guest-friendships, 48, 80–84, 97, 255–60, 271, 343; inscriptions, 48, 93–94, 97, 123, 237–45, 255–57, 302, 331, 343; literary sources, 49, 94–97, 127n100, 146; monuments and artifacts, 48, 84–93, 97, 156, 182–86, 237–45, 324, 343; mutual influence of, 26, 49, 61n61, 79, 89, 156, 164, 169, 172, 175, 183, 346; orators in assembly and law courts, 49, 96–99, 156, 343, 354–55; sympotic group, 48, 75–80, 97, 343; tribes, 72–73, 97, 239, 242, 343

Cartledge, Paul, 33nn151–52, 223–24, 250, 250n119, 253n129, 319–20
Centaurs, 77, 170
Cephalus, 81, 247–48, 257–58, 261–67, 274, 278
Cephisodotus (Theban), 29, 81, 220, 223, 257, 259
Ceramicus, 51, 90
Ceryneian Hind, 170n71
Chabrias, 69
Chaeron (Spartan), 91
Chaeronea, battle of, 1, 2, 46, 50n5, 58, 73, 98n273, 126n98, 157, 202, 203n211, 206, 209, 212, 212n3, 272, 274, 277, 308, 338n184, 350, 352; town of, 233
Chalcidians, 106, 192
Chalcidice, 82, 271, 294
character, national: Athenian, 2, 20, 27, 52, 60, 130, 147–49, 154, 186–87, 191, 201, 209, 225, 253, 265, 280–81; persistent, 54, 78n165, 117, 147–51, 154, 186, 209, 281, 350; Theban, 147–49, 154, 253, 276, 350; U.S., 2, 16
Charisteria, 68
charter myth, 7, 17. *See also* myth; social memory
chorus, dramatic, 63, 178–80, 189; Athenians as members of, 60, 64, 70, 72; secondary, 180
Christ, Matthew, 72n132
Churchill, Winston, 298
Cimon, 50n3, 67, 87n218, 88, 130, 177n109, 178
Cirrha. *See* Crisa
Cirrhaeans, 302–3
Cithaeron, Mount, 110, 162
citizenship, Athenian, 58, 71; for Delphian Astycrates, 334; for Plataeans, 93, 122, 126–27, 137, 140n139, 199n197; for Troezenians, 98; for *xenoi* from Phyle, 236–45, 351
city destruction, ritual, 45, 284, 295, 301–9, 335; of Athens (*see* eradication of Athens, proposed); of Crisa (*see* Crisa); and dedication of land, 284, 301, 304, 307, 313n102, 315, 315n112, 340–41; definition of, 301, 304, 309; and enslavement, 284, 295, 301, 304–10, 314n106, 315–16, 340, 353; by Greek alliance, 10n35, 45, 311, 341, 353; planned for Thebes in 479 BC, 112, 304, 313–19, 340, 353–54; of Thebes in 335 BC, 336–41; and treason, 304n73, 306, 312, 317–18, 353; and tyranny, 304n73, 306, 312–13, 318, 321, 353. *See also* tithing
civil war, Athenian, 215–16; memory of, 13n52, 24, 70, 91–92, 92n248, 216, 235n72, 237; Spartans and, 91–93, 215–16, 236, 242n96, 247; victory of the *demos*, 24, 92, 92n248, 216
Cleisthenes, reforms of, 16, 50n3, 71, 171, 174, 346
Cleisthenes of Sicyon, 263n156
Cleocritus, 70
Cleomenes, 175n97
Cleon, 34, 74, 294
club, upper-class, 70, 76n153, 76n158. See also *hetaeria*; symposium
Cnidus, battle of, 217n14, 313
Codrus Painter, 182, 346
Coeratadas, 220
Colonus (Hippius), 59, 60, 61, 162–63, 165, 172, 177, 206, 207n230, 345
comedy, 53, 59, 60, 72, 79, 240; chorus of, 64; reproduction of , 63. *See also* drama, Athenian
commemorated history, 5, 25–26, 28, 44, 89, 105, 144, 148, 149, 211, 344
commemoration, public, 4, 15, 24; Athenian, 30, 44, 49–58; of Persian Wars, 86, 109–10, 280; through performative media, 25
common peace, 329, 337
Connerton, Paul, 9n30, 25n112, 65n85, 86, 165
Connor, W. R., 304n73, 306, 312–13, 318–19
Conon, 247, 248n114, 251, 313
cooperation: Athenian-Spartan, 83, 200, 329; Athenian-Theban, 4, 153, 206, 212, 227, 234, 267, 268–70, 272, 278, 351–52
Core, 83, 180
Corinthian League, 336–38, 340
Corinthian War, 50n5, 123, 153, 157, 212

Corinthians, 42, 249; during Persian Wars, 108; propose eradication of Athens, 42, 281, 283, 287, 297, 310, 312, 321, 327–30, 336
Coronea, 114, 115n59, 225, 332n166
countercoup, Theban, 123, 205, 257–61, 263, 266–67, 273, 273n182, 352; Athenian contribution to, 261–67
coup d'état, in Thebes, 223n32, 254, 257, 259, 267
Cragalidae, 303
Cratippus, 217n14, 229, 229n58
Creon, 209, 226, 350
Cretan Bull, 170
Crisa, 10n35, 45, 284, 301–19, 328, 339, 341, 353
Critias, 77, 80, 215
Crocus Field, battle of, 334
Crommyonian Sow, 170
Cromwell, Oliver, 14
Ctesiphon, 269, 277, 302
cue for recollection, 11, 46, 48, 97, 115, 117, 118, 119, 128. 139, 141, 155, 206–7, 214, 245–46, 253, 267, 277, 279, 289, 345, 350–52
cults, religious, 27, 65–69, 110, 226; and collective identity, 66, 159, 160, 163, 225; and epic, 159–69; local, 156, 159–69; and mythology, 66, 159–69
cultural memory, 8, 8n22; and communicative memory, 19, 24n105, 25n110. *See also* Assmann, Jan; commemorated history; social memory
Cybernesia, 67

Daemachus of Plataea, 96n265
Danaids, 180, 189n162
Darius, 53, 55, 138, 143n149
Datis, 138
D-day landing. *See* Normandy, landing in
decarchy, 249–50
Decelean War, 114, 224, 287
decision making: factors in, 32–36, 152, 212, 223–24, 224n34, 249–50, 320; and ideology, 14, 224, 251; nature of, 7, 30–31; and public discourse, 30–36; and self-interest, 33–35, 36n166, 40, 200, 212, 249–50, 271, 319, 320, 322, 330n159; and social memory (*see under* social memory)
decree: of Cephalus, 261–67; of Demosthenes, 269; of Miltiades, 94; Theban, 213–14, 217, 219–21, 225, 227, 229, 231–33, 235, 236, 245, 252–54, 260, 276, 279, 351–52; of Themistocles, 94
dekateuein. *See* tithing
Delia, 69, 114n58
Delium, battle of, 69, 114, 119n78, 180n126, 192–93, 196, 321, 348; Persians at, 141
Delphi: Apollo temple in, 87, 108, 111, 303, 331; Athenian treasury in, 171; dedication of spoils in, 86–88, 108, 111–12, 171n76; oracle of, 302–3, 305, 309, 313, 320, 322; seized by Phocians, 333–34
Delphians, as exiles in Athens, 334
Delphinium, 67
Demades, 275
Demaenetus, 231, 247–51
deme, Athenian, 4, 46, 48, 63–64, 70–73, 80, 97, 123, 162, 239, 242n95, 314, 343; Acharnae, 71; Aphidna, 71; Decelea, 71; Melite, 27n123; Phyle, 237n82; Titacidae, 71n126
Demeter, 67, 83, 180, 307n84
democracy, Athenian: dissolution of, 46n212, 212, 215, 244, 278, 290, 292n28, 351; restoration of, 91, 92, 215–16, 234, 235, 238n85, 243, 244, 247; self-representation of, 20n86, 49, 59, 64
Demophon (Athenian general), 261
Demophon (son of Theseus), 169n65
demosion sema, 85, 86, 91, 191, 235n72, 237n80, 348
Demosthenes: as ambassador in Thebes, 203, 268–71; betrayal of Thebes, 212, 277–79; excuses Theban medizing, 142, 151–54; on Phocian intervention, 41–43, 331–36; on Theban medizers, 142–49; as Theban *proxenos*, 82, 153, 271; use of Herodotus, 96, 146
destruction of Athens, proposed. *See* eradication of Athens, proposed
didascalic records, 63

Dillery, John, 216n11, 310n89
Dinarchus, life of, 212n3
Diodorus Siculus, 45, 307n86, 314
Diodotus, 34
Dionysia, Great (or City), 59–60, 63, 64, 158, 182, 205, 207, 346, 349
Dionysia, Rural, 63, 64, 182
Dionysus, 225; theater of, 59, 182; and Thebes, 225–33, 245, 350
Dioscuri, 71, 83
diplomacy, 27–28, 28n129, 44; and social memory, 43n203, 44, 48, 58, 87, 129, 133, 134, 157, 165, 173n89, 175, 196–201, 207n230, 225–27, 234, 235, 246, 253, 269n171, 270, 279, 281, 289n20, 332–35, 336, 348, 351
Dirce, 168
diruere, 317, 340
distanciation, 17
distortion: of individual memory, 11; social memory and (*see under* social memory)
dithyramb, 59, 64, 169, 171, 197n193; and tribal identity, 60, 72. *See also* drama, Athenian
Dolopes, 105, 113
drama, Athenian, 30, 44, 58–65, 177–78, 180–82, 200, 206, 240; and the polis, 59; reproduction of, 63–64, 182, 206, 346. See also *Eleusinians*, by Aeschylus; *Suppliants*, by Euripides
dramatic festivals. *See* drama, Athenian

Echetlus, 88
Eden, Anthony, 298n51
Edict of Nantes, 17
Elatea, 83n189, 203, 268
elegy, historical/narrative, 77–79, 77n164; as martial exhortation, 78; at public festivals, 77n164; at the symposium, 77–79
Eleos, altar of, 176
Eleus, 263, 265
Eleusinian mysteries, 67, 70, 76n157, 83
Eleusinians, by Aeschylus, 59, 60n58, 158, 159n11, 160, 164, 166, 172–73, 175, 205–6, 346; chorus in, 178, 180n128; date of, 169, 177n113, 177–78, 178n114, 192; diplomatic resolution in, 179–80, 191n172, 205; outline of, 178–79; reproduction of, 182, 206; supplication in, 178, 206
Eleusis, 63n74, 216, 271; burial of fallen Argives in, 155, 157, 159–69; 172–74, 178–79, 186, 190, 197–98, 345–46; mysteries at, 67, 70
Eleutherae, 160, 162–65, 167, 172, 345
Eleutheria, 109, 109n33
Elis, 234, 247, 249
elite, Athenian, 4, 13, 30, 37n168, 94–96, 146, 223, 250, 255, 258, 267
Enyalius, 68
Epaminondas, 61, 273, 329, 338
ephebeia, 62, 66, 72, 72n132
ephebes, 64, 66, 68, 69, 194
Ephebic Oath, 72, 93, 94n257, 194, 348
Ephialtes, reforms of, 16
Ephorus, 39n181, 46, 104n7, 118, 182, 217–20, 225, 233n63, 261, 262n150, 282–83, 297n44, 307, 309, 314, 353
Epicrates, 247–48
Epigoni, 87, 161n20, 177, 180, 183, 188n157, 190, 193, 347
Epilycus, 74
episodic memory. *See under* memory, individual
epitaphios. *See* funeral oration
Epizelus, 89n230
eponymous heroes, 27n123, 71, 71n126; Athenian tribal, 16n64, 27, 72, 209n238, 265n159
eradication of Athens, proposed, 5, 5n11, 36, 41–45, 100, 281, 352–55; allusions to, 248, 250, 282, 284–91, 301, 304, 308, 311, 326–41, 354; anti-Spartan version of, 284–85, 307n86; Athenian fear of, 291–300, 352–53; and Corinthians, 42, 281, 283, 287, 297, 310, 312, 321, 327–30, 354; and Crisa, 287, 301–19, 328, 339, 341, 353; historical context of, 281–85, 293–98, 309–23; as persistent memory, 246, 281–82, 292, 298, 323, 352, 354 (*see also* traumatic experience); and Phocians, 41–43, 211, 290, 311, 322, 331–36, 337–42, 354; pro-Spartan version of, 284–85,

eradication of Athens (*continued*) 289n20, 291n22, 307; and Spartans, 201, 224, 285, 288–89, 307, 310, 320, 327–31, 353–54; and Thebans, 201, 220, 224, 246, 248, 281, 283, 287–89, 297, 305, 309–10, 312, 318, 321, 326–30, 335, 352–54; and tithing (*see* tithing); used by Alexander, 45, 285, 339–40, 352, 354. *See also* city destruction, ritual
Erechtheion, 66
Erechtheus, 55n34, 56, 59, 60n58, 62, 73, 79n172; daughters of, 62, 73
Eretria, 52n20, 138
Erianthus, 282, 286n16, 297, 307, 335n175
Erichthonius, 55n34
Erymanthian Boar, 170
Eteocles, 155, 165, 183n140
Euagoras, 251n124, 313
Euboea, 125, 138
Eumenides, 61, 180n128; cult of, 61n61
Eumolpus, 56n41; battle against, 50, 54, 54n32, 56, 62, 186, 211, 347
European Union (EU), 35
Eurymachus, 116–18
Eurymedon, 39
Eurystheus, 54, 187n150, 194, 201n206, 228, 348
exiles, Athenian democratic: in Argos, 98, 218; in Corinth, 218; dedication of statues by, 231, 234–35, 235n68, 240, 245, 350; in Megara, 216, 218; in Thebes, 29, 44, 81, 213, 218, 236, 239, 255, 267, 276, 350. *See also* Phyle, men from; Theban help for Thrasybulus
exodus from Egypt, 7

family tradition, 23n100, 39n187, 73–75; definition of, 73n138; and distortion, 74; and polis tradition, 74–75
Fentress, James, 3n5, 8n22, 9n30, 18, 19n79, 29n131
festivals, Athenian, 4, 16, 27, 30, 44, 47, 65–69; and collective identity, 66, 69; commemorating historical events, 68–69, 110, 133; dramatic, 58–65; and mythology, 66, 68; polis-wide, 58–69; reinterpretation of, 67, 68
Fischer, Joschka, 32
floating gap, 25n109, 27n122
foreign politics: Athenian, 33n151, 34nn157–58, 35, 170, 330n159; German, 4n9, 35, 36; Spartan, 215; Theban, 220–24
Forsdyke, Sara, 5, 20n86, 216n10, 218n18
Franco-Prussian War, 113
funeral, Athenian public, 16, 49–51, 64, 65, 69, 85n203, 86, 130, 133, 241; origin of, 50n3
funeral oration, Athenian, 19, 23, 49–58, 65, 78n165, 89, 91–92, 112, 116, 128–31, 133–35, 141, 143, 146–48, 156–57, 159–60, 164, 166, 173–75, 186–91, 196, 197n193, 201–2, 205–9, 225, 228, 251, 264–65, 320n131, 345–50; and Athenian self-image, 50–51, 144–49; catalogue of deeds, 50, 157, 191, 196n189, 265, 347; chauvinistic, 26n117, 51, 57, 188, 198, 207n231, 241; conventions of, 50; didactic function of, 51; distortions in, 51, 57, 57n44, 129; emotionally charged, 51; extant speeches, 50n5; orators' use of, 57–58, 144, 146–48, 264–67. *See also* master narrative, Athenian; polis tradition, official

garrison, Macedonian, 269; in Thebes, 272–74
garrison, Spartan: in Athens, 215, 292n28; in Thebes, 254, 257, 260–61, 264–66
Gedächtnis, kulturelles. *See* cultural memory
Geertz, Clifford, 31
Gehrke, Hans-Joachim, 8n22, 19–20, 28, 130–31
Gelon (of Syracuse), 28n128, 57
genos, 70, 318n124
Geraneia, 56
Giants, 77, 193
Gigantomachy, 66, 66n94, 348
Glaucon, 80
Goebbels, Joseph, 298, 299n54, 300
Gombrich, E. H., 10n32
graphe paranomon, 240

Gray, Vivienne, 201n207, 202n209, 216n11, 310n89
grazing land for sheep, 282, 284, 287–88, 301, 305–11, 315, 321, 328, 353. *See also* city destruction, ritual
Greek alliance, 104, 107, 109, 112, 116n66, 119, 120, 121n85, 311, 313, 314, 330, 331. *See also* Hellenic League
Green Party, German, 32, 139n137, 299
Greiner, Bernd, 298–300
Grethlein, Jonas, 77nn161–64, 78n166, 175n98, 181n133
guest-friendship, 4, 29, 44, 46, 48, 97, 200n204, 220–23, 224n38, 229, 236, 255–60, 263, 267, 279, 281, 340, 343, 352; definition of, 81–82, 256–57
Gyges (Lydian king), 77, 78n167

Hades, 170
Halbwachs, Maurice, 8–9, 18, 84, 109, 280
Haliartus, 119, 128, 247, 345
Hamilton, Charles D., 33nn151–53, 223–24, 249–50, 282–84, 297, 319–20
Hansen, Herman Mogens, 5, 342
Harma (Attic), 162–63, 163n32, 163n35, 165, 172, 172n80, 206, 207n230; and Argos, 163, 172n80
Harma (Boeotian), 162, 162n29, 163, 163n35, 165, 165n47, 345
Harmodius, 79–80, 90, 313
harmost, 249–50
Harpalus, 212n3, 278
Harrison, Evelyn, 89n229, 194
Hecale, 67
Hecalesia, 67
Hector, 325
Hegesippus, 335n175
Helen, 71, 157, 170, 170n69
Hellenic League, 340
Hellenica Oxyrhynchia, 46, 217n14, 221n23, 229n58, 248n112
Helot revolt, 44n205, 122n86
Heracleia, 68
Heracleia, at Marathon, 68
Heracles, 28, 34n157, 83, 88, 337n180; in art, 228–31; and Athena, 171, 227–31, 234–35, 245, 350–51; on coins, 225–26; festival of, 68; as Theban culture hero, 61n62, 224, 225–35, 245, 350–51; and Theseus, 169–74, 346; twelve labors of, 229–30, 234
Heraclidae, Athenian aid for, 28, 50, 54, 55, 57, 59, 131, 156, 169n65, 186–87, 194, 196–97, 201n206, 211, 225, 228, 269n171, 347, 348
hero cult, 90, 159, 160, 165; and group identity, 159
Herodotus: and Athenian sources, 115–17, 117n72; and attack on Plataea, 116, 117; and Marathon painting, 89; and Masistius, 86; mythical and historical period, 26; and oral traditions, 21, 86; on Thebans, 101, 115–17, 120n80, 344
heroes, local Attic, 27, 66
heroön of Seven: in Argos, 162n26, 164n43, 167; in Eleusis, 90n235, 160–62, 164, 169, 178n116, 198, 345
Hesperides, apples of, 229–30
hetaeria, 70, 76, 221–22, 231
Hippias, 176n103
Hippocrates, 119n78
Hippolyte (Amazon queen), 170
Histiaeans, 293, 324
historians, ancient Greek, 4, 7, 22, 36, 39, 45, 49, 97, 216
historians, of ancient Greece, 33, 36, 262, 271, 282, 301, 342
historical consciousness, collective, 2, 25n109, 31n141; Athenian 4, 7, 22, 24n103, 36, 48, 69, 88, 89, 92, 95, 96, 101, 113, 122, 123n91, 127, 128n103, 131, 133, 135, 137, 140, 146, 156, 189, 210, 232, 236, 242n96, 246, 253, 266–67, 281, 284, 291, 292n28, 302n67, 324, 326, 343, 352–54; in Europe, 35, 291; German, 54n54, 113n54, 298–300; Greek, 302n67, 303n71, 304, 307, 311, 322, 353–54; Jewish, 90n234; Phocian, 333; Plataean, 338; in southern France, 17, 56n40; Theban, 318–19, 321; U.S., 7, 13n51, 16–17, 131n114, 291. *See also* social memory
historical paradigm, *See* allusion, historical

historical reference. *See* allusion, historical
Hitler, Adolf, 17n70, 32n148
Hitler-Stalin Non-Aggression Treaty, 17n70
Holocaust, memory of, 18, 24n103, 25, 26n116, 32, 232n62, 291
hubris, of Persians, 52, 107, 143; of Thebans, 111, 189–96, 207
Hull, Cordell, 298n51
Hyacinthiae, 62, 73

Iatrocles, 82
identity, collective, 3, 7–8, 12, 19, 27, 31; Athenian, 46, 53, 251
Ideologiekritik, 41n193, 283
ideology: Athenian hegemonic, 19–21, 54–56, 148, 149, 174, 186–87, 191, 199, 280, 347; and decision making, 14, 30–31, 224; definition of, 13–14; derived from historical experience, 14, 19–20, 52, 54, 149, 186; and social memory, 13–19, 52, 54
image of the past, shared. *See* social memory
imagined community, 7n17, 16n63
imagined history, 8. *See also* social memory
innovation: by orators, 42, 150, 198n195, 331; by poets, 164, 172n81
inscriptions, 4, 44, 47, 84, 93–94, 97, 237–45, 255–57; authenticity of, 94; read by Athenians, 237–38, 243–44
intentional history, 8, 8n22, 19–20, 131. *See also* social memory
invasion: by Amazons, 27, 50, 54–56, 57, 88, 131, 156, 174, 186–87, 193, 196, 211, 347; by Eumolpus, 50, 54, 56, 62, 186, 211, 347; of Persia, 324n145, 338–40; potential barbarian, 101, 119, 142–55, 212, 344–45; by Xerxes, 52–53, 58, 100–108, 112, 116–19, 121, 124, 127, 134, 137–49, 152–53, 179, 186, 192, 196n189, 198, 314, 316n116, 345
invention of tradition, 16n65, 27, 31n140, 85n203, 167n57, 168, 171n79, 172, 309, 311, 327
Iocaste, 209n237
Ion (playwright), 181, 205
Ionian revolt, 52, 175n97, 325
Iphicrates, 201
Iraq, 1–2, 149n164
Ismenias, 220–23, 223n32, 225–33, 252, 254–55, 257, 274, 350
Isocrates: admits contradictory version, 158, 201–10, 349; as Athenian, 137, 229; *Panathenaicus*, 64, 127, 156, 158, 182, 201n207, 201–10, 349–50; *Panegyricus*, 50n5, 67, 134, 136, 144, 157–58, 187, 202–4, 349; and Philip II of Macedon, 203n211, 227–28; *Plataicus*, 124, 135–37, 198–200, 287–88, 328, 345, 349; spares Thebes' honor, 201–10, 349–50; speeches, 37n168, 124, 198, 201n207, 204; use of Heracles, 227–29
isoteleia, 82, 236, 240–43, 255, 260, 334
Isthmus, 86, 108, 164, 198; conference at, 314, 316n116
Ithome, 44n205, 122n86
Iwo Jima, 1–2

Janko, Richard, 161, 167n54
Jung, Michael, 19–20, 28, 130
junta (pro-Macedonian): in Thebes, 272
junta (pro-Spartan): in Athens (*see* Thirty Tyrants); in Thebes, 11, 45, 214, 254, 258–63, 266–67, 272–74, 352

Kalymnos, Rock War of, 26n114
Kandahar, 1
Kastéllia hills, 167–68
kataskaphe. *See* city destruction, ritual
Kearns, Emily, 27nn123–25, 62n65, 159
King's Peace, 123, 217n14, 254
Korea, 1, 2
Kulturstifter, Theseus as, 173

LaCapra, Dominick, 19n75, 291n23, 300
Lacedaemonians. *See* Spartans
Lacrates (Spartan), 91
Lampon (son of Olympiodorus), 86n213
Laodamas of Acharnae, 277
Laos, 209n237
law courts, Athenian, 3–5, 20n86, 30, 37,

44, 48–50, 58, 59, 62, 64, 65, 69, 70, 73, 74, 82, 96–99, 204, 259, 285, 342–43, 354–55
Lehmann, G. A., 301n66, 302m67, 311–12, 321n133
Lenaea, 63
Leocrates, 58, 62, 73, 78, 93–94, 146, 308, 314
Leon, 151
Leonidas, 85, 103, 104n7, 117–18, 118n74, 135n127, 139–40
Leontiades (the Elder), 117, 117n69
Leontiades (the Younger), 220–24, 229, 231, 232n61, 233, 257n139, 258–62, 266; and Phoebidas, 254
Leos, daughters of, 73
Leto, 303
Leuctra, battle of, 87, 111, 125, 157, 200, 211, 268, 288, 329, 349
lieux de mémoire, 19, 20, 20n84, 29, 84n197. *See also* social memory; *cadre matériel*
literacy: and orality, 21–23, 21n90
Locrians, 105, 113, 114, 246
Locris, 105, 113, 114, 246
Long Walls, 215, 290, 292n28, 293
Loraux, Nicole, 19–20, 28, 130–31, 133
Lysander, 91, 247; and Aegospotami, 87, 284n12; and the Thirty, 215, 224; and treatment of Athens, 282–83, 295–98, 312, 319–20
Lysias, opposes Thirty, 241n90, 241n93

Maastricht Treaty, 35
Malians, 105, 113
Mantinea, battle of, 69, 125, 211, 268
Marathon, battle of: 1, 2, 10, 28, 39, 56, 110, 127–42, 151, 154, 187n153, 265; and Athenian self-image, 18, 20, 27, 46, 52, 55, 186, 233, 237, 251, 345; in comedy, 53n26; commemoration of, 68–69, 110, 114n58, 129–30; dead of, 85, 85n203, 86n209; as epitome of Persian Wars, 53, 56n40, 131, 134; and hero Marathon, 88; on Nike temple, 194, 348; orators' use of, 57, 134–35, 156; painting of, 47, 88–89, 130, 137–39, 205n219, 345; Plataeans at, 47, 85, 88–89, 101, 106, 127–42, 328, 345; as solely Athenian victory, 52, 52n20, 53, 53n25, 128–31, 133–42, 186, 196, 320n131, 328; trophies and spoils of, 84–85, 87, 111n44, 133, 171n76
Marathon painting, 47, 88–89, 205n219, 345; and Plataeans, 129, 138–39
Marathonian Bull, 67, 170
marathonization, 18, 56, 56n40, 57n43, 59, 186–87, 188n159
Mardonius, 86, 110, 119, 139, 146, 189n164, 323
Masada, 90n234
Masistius, 86, 110, 110n39
master narrative, Athenian, 13n51, 16, 20, 20n86, 29, 30, 44, 46, 49, 54–60, 74–75, 92, 97, 107, 116–18, 129, 134, 138, 141, 143, 146–54, 157, 159, 186–90, 198, 202, 211–12, 227–28, 236, 251, 263–67, 269, 344–45, 347, 351–52, 355; challenging the, 26, 26n117, 32n149, 84, 149–54, 166, 204–10, 349; and local traditions, 95n261, 156, 164, 165n45, 186, 187n150, 204, 206, 207n230, 229, 345–46. *See also* polis tradition, official
medism. *See* medizing, Theban
medizing, Theban, 5, 5n11, 36, 43, 52, 100, 183n145, 189–90, 209n238, 246, 330, 344–45; excuses for, 118, 151–54, 318; historical allusions to, 101–3, 118–54, 224, 280, 337–39, 344–45; memorialization of, 87–88, 106–13, 211, 331; punishment of, 112, 116, 125, 189, 285, 301–2, 304, 304n73, 310, 312–19, 340, 353–54; religious dimension of, 189–90; used by Alexander, 337–39; used by Thebans, 151, 152n170, 338; versus Plataean patriotism, 119–42, 155, 338, 345
Megalopolis, 125
Megara, 80, 160, 216, 218
Megarians, 80n179, 108
Megarid, 56
Megistias, 85
Melanippus, 165
Melians, 293, 294n34, 296, 296n42, 324
Melite, 27n123
Melon, 262–63, 266

Melos, 294n37, 321, 323, 326, 354
memorial framework: Athenian, 3, 5, 7, 23, 28–30, 36, 48, 78, 84, 89, 94, 118n72, 143, 158, 172, 202n207, 264, 342–43; Greek, 107n19, 285, 341, 354; Theban, 82. *See also* social memory
memory, collective. *See* social memory
memory, "incorporated," 23n102, 25n112, 65, 86, 86n210, 109n32, 165
memory, individual: act of remembering, 11, 11n38; bodily, 9n30, 65, 69, 86n210; and collective memory, 8–13; and consistency bias, 11n41, 15n59, 116–17; cue for retrieval of, 11, 128, 141; declarative, 9n30; and emotion, 292; encoding of, 10, 11; episodic, 9n30, 25n110, 65; and hindsight bias, 11n39, 11n41, 15n59; long-term, 9n30, 10; perception and, 9n30, 10, 10n32, 14, 18, 24, 30, 105, 216nn10–11, 323n142; procedural, 9n30, 25n110; psychology of, 9, 12; semantic, 9n30, 10, 65; as semantic and visual conceptualization, 10, 10nn32–34, 17, 65, 300, 301–9, 323; sensory, 9n30, 10, 65n87; short-term, 9n30, 10; as simplification, 10, 10n32, 17; subsystems of, 9; textual model of, 11n43; and traumatic experience, 292
memory communities, 12–13, 83; Athenian 27, 30, 73, 83n193, 97, 163–65, 172; Boeotian, 165–68; German, 13n51, 29n134, 299–300; U.S., 13n50
memory politics, 15–16, 19, 172
memory studies: of the ancient world, 19; psychoanalytical approach, 18–19, 291–92; sociological approach, 18
memory war, 66, 87, 108n27, 168, 346
men of the city. *See* oligarchs, Athenian
Menestheus, 58n48
mental framework, 10, 16, 18, 24, 82, 105, 323n142; Athenian, 52, 101; as ideology 13–14, 106
Messenian War, First, 78
Messenians, 78, 143–44
metics, 212n3, 215, 218, 239–40, 241n90, 241n93, 256n137
Metroon, 93n253, 237, 243, 351
Milosevic, Slobodan, 32
Miltiades, 10, 27n122, 88–89, 94, 107n16, 236, 265n159
Mimnermus, 77–78
Minotaur, 170
Missiou, Anna, 282–85, 286n16, 289n20, 291, 307n86, 327
Misztal, Barbara, 3n5, 8n22, 12
Mnamias, 103, 118
mnemonic communities. *See* memory communities
monuments: of Athenian civil war, 92–93, 237–45, 247; as carrier of social memory, 4, 15, 16, 24, 30, 44, 47, 84–94, 233–34; and commemorative activity, 85–86, 109; definition of, 84; destruction of, 87; funeral, 85, 109; of Persian War, 86–90, 107–9, 324; symbolic meaning of, 90, 133
Morgenthau, Henry, 298–300
Morgenthau Plan, 298–300, 353; as historical paradigm, 299
Munichia, battle of, 70, 91, 92, 236, 240–42
Munichus, 27n123
mutilation of herms, 76n157
Mycale, battle of, 314
Mylonas, George, 160–61, 164, 345
Myronides, 56, 57n43, 115
myth: constellative, 7, 8, 17, 107, 189; as historical paradigm, 26–28, 44, 174n90, 186, 345; local, 27, 44, 65n82, 66, 68, 72, 95n261, 156, 159–69, 172, 172n80, 174, 179–80, 186, 187n150, 204, 206, 207n230, 229, 345–46; Panhellenic, 59, 172; polis-wide, 59, 65n82, 65–69, 162, 164, 165, 169, 172, 187n150, 190, 207n230, 346; as prefiguration, 44, 54, 186–87, 191–92, 346. *See also* allusion, historical; social memory
Mytilene, 80

Napoleon Bonaparte, 17
narrativization, 17, 52n19, 145–46, 236
NATO, 32, 209
Nausicles, 334
Nausithous, 67

Naxos, battle of, 69
Nazism, German, 24n104, 32, 133, 209, 298–300
Neaera, 126, 135, 137
Nemean lion, 229–30
neo-Durkheimians, 18
neo-Freudians, 18, 291–92, 292n31
Neoptolemus (actor and ambassador), 64
Nicaea, 203, 269
Nice temple: Amazonomachy, 193–94, 348; assembly of gods, 193–94, 348; battle of Marathon, 194, 348; capture of Eurystheus, 194, 348; recovery of fallen Argives, 193–96, 205, 348
Niceteria, 67
Niobids, 167–68
nomos, 187–91, 199, 207n233, 208, 347
Nora, Pierre, 19, 20n84, 84n194
Normandy, landing in, 1–2, 132–33
Nouhaud, Michel, 38n175, 40n188, 42nn197–98, 135–37, 142n146, 158, 331–32
numismatic evidence, 224–26

Oath of Plataea, 72, 93–94, 302, 311–17, 324, 331, 340
Obama, Barack, 1–2, 22, 23n97, 26, 26n116
Ober, Josiah, 5, 13–14, 30–31, 342
Odysseus, 111, 190n168
Oedipus, 59, 60, 61, 155, 162, 183n145, 206, 269n171
Oeneus, 209n238
Oenoe, battle of, 87, 88, 88n226
Oenophyta, 114, 115, 119n78, 191
oligarchic coup of 411 BC, 76, 290
oligarchs, Athenian, 24, 70, 90–91, 215–16, 218n18, 235n72, 248, 351n4
olive tree, sacred, 66
Olympia: dedications at, 87, 111n49; Demosthenes at, 82, 271; statue of Zeus, 86, 108; temple of Zeus, 229–30, 235
Olympiodorus (Athenian), 86n213
Olynthus, 254, 271
Onasias, 111, 183, 192n173, 194, 196n188, 346
Operation Iraqi Freedom, 149n164
oral history, 23, 24
oral tradition, 3, 19, 138, 216; Athenian, 86, 89n230; definition of 23; multipolarity of, 23, 179; study of, 21–23
orality. *See* oral tradition
orators: citation of poetry, 62, 78–79; constrained by audience, 41, 97, 101, 129, 141, 142, 154, 158, 204, 210, 214, 264, 267, 326, 343, 349; credibility of, 41, 94, 142, 143, 152, 214; and Greek historians, 4, 7, 22, 39, 45, 49, 95–96, 96n265, 137, 146, 216, 267, 283, 343; and inscriptions, 93–94, 237–38, 243–44, 302; leeway of, 4, 12, 96, 99, 101, 129, 158, 191, 204, 326, 328, 347; manipulation by, 4n10, 39–42, 75, 95n262, 99, 129, 140n139, 142, 145, 151n167, 158, 202n209, 204, 213, 283, 333, 349; and patriotic hyperbole, 129–33, 263, 267, 328; reference to own ancestors, 74–75, 291; refreshing the past, 11, 44, 45, 96, 117, 139, 146, 151, 254n131, 267–68, 324, 333–34, 343, 345, 351; scholarly approaches to, 30, 36–43, 136–37, 142, 158, 204, 213; social memory approach to, 43–47; speeches of, 4, 5, 7, 36–37, 37n168, 42, 124, 198, 201n207, 204; use of myth, 61–62, 111, 190, 199, 200, 209, 347; use of the past, 7, 26–28, 39, 40; and written sources, 25, 47, 94–96, 127n100, 146, 204
Orchomenus, 114, 272, 339, 339n186, 340
Orestes, 61
Oropus, 114, 165n47, 252n125, 345
Orpheus, 56n41
Oschophoria, 67–68

Pagondas, 114, 115n59
Painted Stoa. *See* Stoa Poikile
Painter of Bologna 279, 183–85, 346
paintings, monumental, 47, 88–89, 111, 183–85, 190, 192n173, 196n188, 205n219, 345–47
Paion, 79
Pan, 68
Panathenaic festival, 9n30, 66, 129, 130, 139, 201, 201n207, 202, 325
Panhellenic myths, 59, 172

Panhellenic sanctuaries, 66, 86–87, 107, 108, 111n49, 229, 344
Parke, E. W., 301n66, 302n69, 304–8, 312, 314n106, 315–18, 333, 340
Parthenon, 66n94, 66n95, 88, 89n233, 90
past, usable, 8. *See also* social memory
patriotism, religious, 66
Pausanias (Spartan general), 106, 108n22, 109–10, 120–21, 126–27, 318, 318n124
Pausanias (Spartan king), 90–92, 215, 217, 232, 242n96, 247, 252
Peace of Nicias, 114, 123, 294
Peace of Philocrates, 82n188, 126, 143, 203n211
Pearl Harbor, U.S. memory of, 132, 254n131
Peirithous, 162, 170, 183n145
Peisistratids, 14n56, 44n205, 170–71, 176n103, 216n10
Peisistratus, 79, 170n72, 177n109
Pelopidas, 273; at Susa, 151, 152n170, 338
Peloponnesian War, 24n103, 26n117, 33, 41, 59n54, 87, 95, 100, 101, 114–15, 120, 123, 191, 205, 211, 221, 249, 250, 254, 286, 290, 294n34, 306n80, 318, 321, 324, 326, 332, 339, 347, 350, 352, 354
Pentecontaetia, 74, 101, 113, 115, 191, 211, 332, 347
peplos, 66
Pericles, 50n5, 50n7, 71, 81, 90, 322, 324n145
Persian Wars: Athenian experience of, 16, 18, 44, 53, 56, 57, 142, 144, 155, 179n123, 186, 189–90; Athenian merits, 53–54, 134–35, 285–86, 319–20, 354; Athenian-Spartan cooperation in, 83, 200, 329; commemoration of, 68–69, 86–90, 107–12, 144, 147, 330–31; Plataean merits, 102, 121, 121n85, 122, 128n102, 135, 137, 139, 141, 174, 345; poems about, 110; Thespian merits, 125n94, 128n103, 345
Phaeax, 67
Phaedra, 56
Pherenicus, son of Cephisodotus, 29, 81, 220, 257, 259
Phidias, 129, 183
Philip of Macedon, 2, 28, 36, 82n188, 83n189, 94, 96, 102, 126, 203, 205, 211–12, 214, 227–28, 265n162, 268–74, 276, 277, 311, 331–36, 338, 340, 344, 345, 352, 353; and Xerxes, 142–49
Philippides, 68
Phliasians, 108
Phocians, 41–43, 125, 148n163, 211, 246–47, 269, 290, 311, 322, 331–36, 337–42, 354
Phocion, 62n64, 73
Phoebidas, 254
Phormisius, 263, 265
phratry, 70
Phrynichus: *Capture of Miletus*, 325; *Phoenissae*, 60
Phrynon, 82
Phyle, and Adrastus, 162, 172n80, 345; heroes of (*see* Phyle, men from); return from, 69, 214, 236, 239, 242–45; seizure of, 11, 29, 60n57, 72, 213, 215–16, 236, 240–41, 244–45, 252–53, 279, 303n71, 350–51, 355
Phyle, men from: 214, 235; allusions to, 236–40, 243–44; honorary decree for, 92n248, 93n253, 237–39, 243, 245, 278, 351. *See also* exiles, Athenian democratic
Phyle, *xenoi* from: citizenship decree for, 122n88, 238, 239, 241–45, 351; public funeral for, 240–41
Pindar, 340; defending Thebes, 166–69
Piraeus, 27n123, 63n74, 92, 217, 236, 240, 241, 247, 248, 252, 261, 262, 293, 312; democrats' return to, 91–92, 215, 241, 242
Plataea (battle of), 20, 28, 39, 57, 85–87, 103–4, 107–9, 145, 183, 196–98, 205; in Athenian memory 1, 2, 46, 52, 53, 57, 69, 73, 106, 110–15, 119, 189–91, 344, 347; commemorated at Plataea, 108–10, 121, 183–85, 192n173, 194, 196n188, 346
Plataea (town), 109, 272; destruction in 427 BC, 72, 93, 120–23, 300n62, 321, 324, 339, 354; destruction in 373 BC, 28, 36, 83, 102, 120, 123–25, 152, 157, 268, 328, 339; destruction of, 120; night assault on, 114–18, 120, 122, 126; Persian siege of, 95, 122

Plataeans, 52, 72; alone of the Boeotians, 102, 111n46, 125n94, 137; at Artemisium, 121, 139–41; and Athenian citizenship, 93, 122–23, 126; in Athenian social memory, 127–31, 133–41; during Persian Wars, 102, 118–19, 124–25, 136–42, 174; at Marathon, 47, 85, 88–89, 101, 106, 127–42, 328, 345; at Salamis, 139–41; as suppliants, 105, 173–77, 186, 191–92, 198–200, 287, 328, 346, 349; versus Thebans, 101, 114, 120–27, 141, 155, 175, 212, 287, 337–41, 344–45
Plutarch, 45; on Aeschylus' *Eleusinians*, 160, 172, 178, 205, 207n230; as Boeotian, 233
polis tradition, official, 16, 20n86, 23, 44, 46–47, 49, 69, 74–75, 92, 174, 186, 190. *See also* master narrative, Athenian
Polygnotus, 111, 183, 190n168
Polynices, 155, 156, 165, 166n51, 182, 183n140, 197, 206n225
Poseidon, 56, 66–67, 86, 108, 162–63, 163n37
Potter, David S., 37n169
Pownall, Frances, 77n160, 216n11, 263n153, 267n166
Praxiteles, 234, 234n68
Praxithea, 62
Priam, 325
private memory, 24–26, 29, 44, 89, 116–17. *See also* remembered history
Procles of Phlius, 156, 157, 196, 200–201, 209, 289, 304, 329, 349, 350
propaganda, 39–41, 51, 57n44, 251n124, 283, 285, 298–300, 320, 327, 353
proxenia, 80–84, 257n140, 277, 340; definition of, 82, 256
Proxenus, 335
public discourse: Athenian, 4, 13, 30; and decision making, 30–36; reintroduction of latent memories, 11, 44, 45, 96, 117, 139, 146, 151, 254n131, 268, 324, 334, 343, 345, 351; semiotic model of, 30–31
public memory. *See* commemorated history
public speakers, Athenian. *See* orators
Puritans, 14
Pyrrhandrus of Anaphlystus, 278
Pythia, 303, 313, 320, 322

Realism, 33, 224, 249, 250, 319. See also *Realpolitik*
Realpolitik, 4, 33–36, 212, 224, 320–23, 343, 354. *See also* Realism
reciprocity, 33, 34, 42, 43n203, 44, 80, 81, 98, 200, 227, 246–49, 252–53, 260, 263, 270, 279, 281, 286, 329, 334–35
remembered history, 5, 23–25, 27n122, 44, 74, 116–17; and local communities, 25; social aspects of, 24–25; three-generational, 25, 25n109. *See also* memory, individual
remembering, act of. *See under* memory, individual
rhetoric, classical, 38–39, 94–96, 146
Rhodians, 98
ritual house destruction, 304n73, 306, 312–13, 318–19, 340, 353
rituals, religious. *See* cults, religious
Robertson, Noel, 40n189, 302n67, 311, 353
Roosevelt, Franklin, 298

Sacred War, First, 301–4, 309, 311, 353
Sacred War, Second, 332
Sacred War, Third, 41, 43n203, 125, 211, 268, 311, 332–35, 339, 353, 354
Sacred War, Fourth, 203
Salamis, Ajax of, 69; battle of, 1–2, 28, 46, 52, 53, 53n25, 69, 75, 84, 90, 108, 110, 110n38, 139, 140, 145, 150, 154, 237, 251; island of, 69
Samians, 234, 234n65
Samos, 234, 314
Sardis, 52
satyr play, 60. *See also* drama, Athenian
Saussure, Ferdinand de, 12
Schacter, Daniel L., 9n30, 11n39, 11n41, 117n67, 292
Scione, 96n265, 123, 293, 294, 296, 324
Scodel, Ruth, 21n88, 326n150
Scyros, 178
Second Athenian Confederacy/League, 123, 258, 263, 263n154, 267n166; prospectus of, 258

Sedan, Day of, 113
self-image, 7, 11n42, 14, 17, 330n159; formation of Athenian, 5n11, 18, 100; Theban, 61n62, 69n118, 223–33, 350
self-interest. *See under* decision making
semantic memory. *See under* memory, individual
Semele, 226
sensory memory. *See under* memory, individual
Serpent Column, 86, 108, 121
Seven against Thebes, 87, 88n226, 111, 161, 167, 168n63, 177, 183, 190, 347. *See also* burial of fallen Argives
Seven Pyres, in Thebes, 166–68
Shear, Julia L., 13n52, 237n82, 313
Sicilian expedition, 75, 97, 335n175
Siewert, Peter, 301n66, 312, 314n107, 317, 324n145, 331
Siphnians, 108
Smyrna, 77, 78n165, 78n167
social memory: in analogous situations, 45, 124, 191, 200, 232, 246, 254, 254n131, 258, 260, 272, 277, 281, 311, 330, 335; bodily, 9n30, 65, 69, 86n210; carriers of, 4, 20, 48–99; and collective identity, 3, 7, 8, 19, 78, 148, 160, 322, 341; communicative aspect of, 8n24, 12, 19, 22, 28–29; competing, 13, 13n50; contestation of, 3, 13, 13n52, 22, 70, 143, 198, 205, 207n231, 355; as counterpart of history, 2; critics of, 8; and decision making, 3, 4, 8, 30–36, 98, 122, 133–34, 142, 200, 212, 223–32, 246, 248–53, 269–71, 320–23, 329, 330n159, 336, 343, 354; definition of, 7–8, 19, 28–29; in diplomatic contexts, 27–28, 28n129, 43n203, 44, 48, 58, 87, 129, 133, 134, 157, 165, 173n89, 175, 196–201, 207n230, 225–27, 234, 235, 246, 250–53, 269n171, 270, 279, 281, 289n20, 332–35, 336, 348, 351; and distortion, 4, 8, 15–19, 26, 40, 45–46, 101, 115–18, 144–45, 214, 216n10, 259n145, 263n156, 283–84, 299, 344, 354; emotive force of, 2, 4, 31, 34, 34n158, 35, 46–47, 51, 63, 65, 69, 86, 97, 114, 140, 148, 156, 165, 174, 183, 200, 201, 205, 250–51, 271, 284–85, 287, 291–93, 301, 308, 326, 343, 346, 355; formation of, 3, 15n61, 22, 48, 59, 65, 87, 105, 243, 354; and ideology, 13–19, 22, 31, 52, 54, 59, 106, 280; individual and collective dimensions of, 8–9, 12–13; malleability of, 18, 355; mutual influence of, 7, 26, 49, 61n61, 79, 89, 156, 164, 169, 172, 174, 346; as myth, 2, 8; negotiation of, 13, 13n52, 22, 24, 30, 36, 48, 59, 64, 70, 73, 97, 99, 343; paradigmatic function of, 16, 23, 27, 44, 46, 66, 72, 77n161, 131; and the present, 7–8, 15, 113, 146, 158, 191, 193n179, 280, 330; simplification of, 17, 52, 53, 103, 106, 118, 129, 130, 140, 145–46, 235, 300, 354; and secondary social sharing, 293; social relevance of, 12, 19, 26, 28–29, 118, 146, 267, 280, 330; and symbolic communication, 30–31, 133, 142, 149, 251; and topography, 9n25, 165, 244, 303n71; transmission of, 3, 21–22, 27, 48, 97–100, 113–15, 120, 165, 212, 214, 232, 278–81, 299–300, 343–44, 350–51, 355; and trauma (*see* traumatic experience); versus collective memory, 8–9, 8n24; as vision of future, 7–8, 273, 280. *See also* cultural memory; historical consciousness; memory, individual; memorial framework
Socrates, 51, 80, 82
Solon, 79, 303
Sparta: and Athenian diplomats in 432 BC, 134; conference in 404 BC, 42, 281, 288, 297, 327, 352; conference in 392/1 BC, 286, 327; invaded by Thebes, 200, 329; peace negotiations in 371 BC, 36, 124–25, 288; supremacy of, 254; and Thebes in 404/3 BC, 224; as tyrant city, 313
Spartans: and Argives, 198; and Athenian civil war, 90–93, 215–16, 236, 242n96, 247; cooperate with Athenians, 83, 200, 329; hostile toward Thebans, 246; and Plataeans, 102, 108
Sphacteria, 74n141
Sphodrias, 262, 262n151
Sphragithic Nymphs, 73, 110
Spina volute krater, 182–85, 190, 194, 346

spoils, dedication of, 69, 86, 107, 111, 113, 129, 183, 315, 344; in Athens, 86, 90; in Delphi, 86–88, 108, 111–12, 171n76; in Olympia, 86–87
stasis, in Thebes, 220–23, 231
stereotype, Athenian anti-Theban, 151, 151n169, 152, 208, 210, 212, 350
Stimson, Henry, 298n51
Stoa Poikile, 47, 74n141, 88, 129, 130–33, 138–39, 345
Stonehenge, 90n234
Stylianou, P. J., 260n148, 262–63, 266
Stymphalian birds, 229–30, 234
subgroups, 4, 24; Athenian, 28, 30, 46, 70–73, 76, 343. *See also* memory communities
Suppliants, by Euripides, 59, 158, 163n32, 164, 172, 174, 177, 189, 191–93, 206, 346, 348; anti-Theban, 192–93; date of, 180; reproduction of, 182; supplication in, 180–81, 200, 206
supplication, ritual: by Adrastus, 175–86; in art, 182–86; in Athenian Agora, 176; definition of, 175–76; in Homer, 175; by Plataeans, 105, 173–77, 186, 191–92, 198–200, 287, 328, 346, 349; in tragedy, 177–78, 180–82, 200, 206
Susa, 151, 152n170, 338
sycophants, 215
symbolic capital, 31, 87, 107, 175n98
symposium, 4, 48, 70, 75–80, 97, 343; definition of, 75; and group identity, 75–77, 80; and oligarchy, 76–77; and poetry at, 76; social memory, 76–80; socialization at; 79
sympotic group. *See* symposium
Synoecia, 67
synoecism of Attica, 26n119, 67, 171, 173

Tanagra, 111n49, 114, 162, 191, 348
Tegeans: dispute with Athenians, 28n128, 57, 110n39, 130, 134, 156, 196, 348; at Plataea, 52, 108, 112, 141; votive offering at Delphi, 87, 108
Telamon, 79
telescoping of events, 53, 57, 58, 134
Tempe, expedition to, 103–5, 116, 117n70, 118, 344
Tenians, 108
tertium comparationis, 137, 201, 227, 349
Theban help for Thrasybulus: commemorated in Athens, 235–45, 278, 351; corroborated by elders, 212, 232, 244, 254, 278–79, 291, 352; debated in Thebes, 223–33; evoked by Theban exiles, 5, 254–60, 272–77; historicity of, 215–23, 231–32; memorialized in Thebes, 232–35; mentioned in 395 BC, 245–53, 327; monument for, 231, 234–35, 235n68, 245, 350; as precarious memory, 36, 44–45, 232, 235, 243–46, 344, 350–52, 355; repaid by Athenians, 214, 246, 248, 252, 253–67, 272–79; and Theban decree, 213–14, 217, 219–21, 225, 227, 229, 231–33, 235, 245, 252–54, 260, 276, 279, 351–52; used against Demosthenes, 212, 215, 277–79; used by Demosthenes, 214, 268–71; in Xenophon, 217
Thebans: allied with Sparta, 114, 211; and Athenians in 479 BC, 105–6, 119, 179, 205; during Persian War, 101, 103–5, 116; excuse medizing, 118, 142, 151–54, 318; help Thrasybulus, 36, 43, 99, 100, 215–32, 243, 245, 253, 267, 274, 350, 352; in Herodotus, 115–18, 120n80; hubristic, 111, 159, 189–96, 207, 347–48; as medizers (*see* medizing); and Philip, 143–49, 268–74; propose eradication of Athens (*see* eradication of Athens, proposed); as refugees in Athens, 36, 45, 81, 153, 214, 254–60, 263–64, 272–77; refuse burial of Seven (*see* burial of fallen Argives); revolt against Alexander, 215, 272–77, 336–41; at Thermopylae, 103–4, 108, 116–18; as traitors, 102, 107, 111, 119, 142, 149, 155, 211–12, 235, 268, 280, 318, 331, 338, 345; versus Plataeans, 101, 114, 120–27, 141, 155, 175, 212, 287, 337–41, 344–45
Thebes: as Athens' counterimage, 61, 106–13, 189–90, 193, 211, 344, 347; countercoup in (*see* countercoup, Theban); coup d'état in 382 BC, 223n32, 254, 259;

Thebes (*continued*)
destruction of, 5n11, 45, 193, 215, 277–79, 301, 322, 336–41, 354; factions in, 104, 116, 118, 220, 221n24, 222, 231n59, 233, 254, 271; hegemony of, 114, 125, 211, 262, 268, 273, 329, 338, 352, 354; and Oedipus, 61; siege of, 112, 318; volte-face in 404 BC, 33n152, 220–23, 320
Themistocles, 68, 94, 236, 265, 265n159
Theopompus, on Demosthenes, 270–71; and *Hellenica Oxyrhynchia*, 217n14
Theramenes, 216, 218n18, 231n58, 295, 295nn38–39, 297, 297n46
Theramenes Papyrus, 231n58, 295n38
Thermopylae: battle of, 42n201, 85, 110, 139, 145, 251; and Philip, 143, 147, 268–69, 334–35; Plataeans at, 139–40; Thebans at, 103–5, 108, 116–18, 118n74, 140, 344
Thersander of Orchomenus, 116n66
Theseia, 67
Theseion, 67, 88, 177n109
Theseus: and Adrastus, 160, 172–83, 187, 190, 192, 206, 346–47, 350; adventures of, 60, 68, 165n45, 170n72; and Aethra, 170n69, 180–81, 188n155; and Amazons, 27, 187, 227; and Antiope, 56; in art, 171, 190, 195, 182–83, 185, 194, 346; as Athenian national hero, 169–72; as Attic culture hero, 159, 169–74, 179, 206; burial of fallen Argives, 157, 161, 165, 172–74, 181, 187, 346; and Cimon, 50n3, 178; and Crete, 67; cults of, 67–68, 170; cycle of deeds, 171, 173; and Decelus, 71; and Epigoni, 190, 346; in Greek epic, 169–71; and Hecale, 67; and Helen, 71, 170; and Heracles, 169–74, 170n71, 227n53, 346; as inventor of truce, 172–74, 178–79, 206, 207n230, 346; at Marathon, 88; and Marathonian Bull, 67; and Minotaur, 170; as national hero, 67; and Nausithous, 67; and Oedipus, 61; oratorical references to, 157, 173–74, 201–10; and Peisistratids, 170–71; and Perithous, 162, 170n69, 183n145; and Phaeax, 67; and Phaedra, 56; reign of, 26, 206; and synoecism, 26n119, 67, 171, 173; and Thebans, 178, 179n124, 188n155, 193–96, 207, 348; and Titacus, 71
Thespiae, 28, 36, 83, 119, 120, 125–26, 128, 272, 329n157, 339
Thessalians, 104, 333, 337
Thessaly, 103, 224, 323
Thibrachus (Spartan), 91
Thirty Tyrants, 11, 14n56, 215–20, 224–25, 227, 239, 307, 327; exile under, 29, 45, 74, 81, 98; memory of, 29, 38n179, 70, 236, 240, 248, 254, 259, 350–51; overthrow of, 24, 29, 45, 92, 214, 232–36, 240–46, 253, 258, 278; terror regime of, 238, 292n28
Thomas, Rosalind, 3, 19, 21–23, 28, 39, 48, 53, 94, 94n262, 130, 138, 213, 216, 342
Thrason of Erchia, 263, 265, 277
Thrasybulus of Collytus, 257, 277–78
Thrasybulus of Steiria: captures Phyle, 11, 29, 60n57, 72, 215–16, 233, 236, 237n82, 240–41, 244–45, 252–53, 279, 350–51; and Demaenetus, 248; as exile in Thebes, 46n212, 215, 217, 218n18, 229, 244; and foreign supporters, 72, 92n248, 215, 236, 239–44; grateful to Thebes, 231, 234, 245, 253; helped by Thebans, 44, 99, 214–15, 224, 243, 245, 253, 267, 274, 350, 352; and Ismenias, 223n32, 232; restores democracy, 92, 216, 234, 244; supports Thebans, 252–53, 256–58; tomb of, 92, 235n72, 237n80
Thrasyllus, 182
Thucydides: as Athenian, 128n102; as father of *Realism*, 33; and Herodotus, 45n207; Melian dialogue, 35; Mytilenaean debate, 33–34, Plataean debate, 34n155, 87, 108, 118, 120–22, 135, 152, 318, 345; speeches in, 37n170, 121–22
Thurii, 86n213
Thyrea, 294
Timagenidas (Theban), 104
Timagoras, 151
Timocrates, 222, 250
Timolaus, 273, 273n183
Titacidae, 71n126
Titans, 77

tithing, 112, 125, 302, 304, 311, 313–19, 330, 340, 353. *See also* city destruction, ritual
Tolmides, 114
tomb: of Argives, 191, 348; of Athenians, 1, 51, 85–86; Bronze Age, 90, 160–61, 167, 345; at Eleusis, 161–64, 169, 173, 180; at Eleutherae, 163–64; at Marathon, 130; at Plataea, 108–9, 113, 124, 344; of Spartans, 90–92, 237n80, 243n96; at Thebes, 165, 167–68; of Thrasybulus, 235n72, 237n80
topos, 38, 42–43, 92n245, 130, 134n126, 146, 157, 188n159, 213
Torone, 293, 294, 321, 324
tragedy: Athenian heroes in, 59; and Athenian ideology, 59–60; historical, 60, 325; orators' use of, 61–62, 158, 182, 205–10, 349; reproduction of, 63–64, 182, 206; written copies of, 63–64, 63n70. *See also* drama, Athenian
traumatic experience, 7, 14, 16, 18, 24n103, 25, 35, 106, 145, 291–92, 300, 324; Athenian, 24, 45, 53n25, 250, 284, 291–301, 318, 325, 326, 344, 352–53. *See also* eradication of Athens, proposed
tribe, Athenian, 4, 46, 48, 51, 60, 62, 70–73, 80, 97, 110, 123, 239, 242, 245, 343; Aiantis, 73, 110; Erechtheis, 62; Oeneis, 209n238; tribal identity, 60, 62, 72–73
Triptolemus (Athenian king), 28, 83, 307n84
Troezen, 94, 98, 171
Trojan War, 42, 57, 156, 194n187, 196, 311
trophy, 57, 84, 91–92, 194
Troy, 42n201, 88, 170n69, 303n71, 306, 323–26
Tuplin, Christopher, 216n11, 250n119, 315–16
Twelve Gods, 61n61; altar of, 175–76
Tydeus, 165, 167n54
Tyrtaeus, 77–79, as Athenian, 78

United States: civil rights movement, 13n51; Civil War memories, 13nn50–51; ideology of, 15, 16; Independence Day, 15–16; Revolutionary War, 7, 131n114; September 11, 254n131, 293; War of Independence, 16–17. *See also* World War II

Vansina, Jan, 21, 23
vaticinatio ex eventu, 182

Waigel, Theo, 29n134
Walters, K. R., 128–31
Wehrmacht, German, 29n134, 139n137
Wickham, Chris, 3n5, 8n22, 9n30, 18, 19n79, 29n131
Wolpert, Andrew, 19, 24, 28, 37n168, 292n28
World War I, 17
World War II: American memory of, 131–32, 149n164, 209, 328n156; Czech memory of, 133; German memory of, 24n104, 29n134, 32; German occupation of France, 17, 24n103; Russian memory of, 17n70

xenia. See guest-friendship.
Xenophon: on Aegospotami, 293; and Agesilaus, 200n204; anti-Theban, 216, 216n11, 218n15, 252, 262, 267, 282, 287, 328; as Athenian, 4, 37, 200n203, 252; as moralist, 216n11, 253, 262n153, 295n40; omissions in *Hellenica*, 216n11, 253; pro-Spartan, 216, 216n11, 218, 267, 282, 295n40, 328; speeches in *Hellenica*, 4, 30, 37, 200n203
Xerxes: hubris, 143; invasion of Greece: 52–53, 58, 100–108, 112, 116–19, 121, 124, 127, 134, 137–49, 152–53, 179, 186, 192, 196n189, 198, 314, 316n116, 345; peace offer, 144–47, 189; and Philip, 142–49; war council, 134n126

Zeitlin, Froma, 61, 193n178, 197n193, 212n1
Zenodotus, 167n54
Zethus, 168
Zeus, 86, 88, 108, 228, 229, 235; Eleutherius, 69, 109, 313; and Semele, 226; Soter, 313; Tropaeus, 68